ALBERTA
AND THE NORTHWEST TERRITORIES
HANDBOOK
INCLUDING BANFF, JASPER, AND THE CANADIAN ROCKIES

ALBERTA
AND THE NORTHWEST TERRITORIES
HANDBOOK

INCLUDING BANFF, JASPER, AND THE CANADIAN ROCKIES
SECOND EDITION

ANDREW HEMPSTEAD & NADINA PURDON

MOON
PUBLICATIONS INC.

ALBERTA AND THE NORTHWEST TERRITORIES HANDBOOK
SECOND EDITION

Published by
Moon Publications, Inc.
P.O. Box 3040
Chico, California 95927-3040, USA

Printed by
Colorcraft Ltd., Hong Kong

Please send all comments, corrections, additions, amendments, and critiques to:

**ALBERTA /NWT HANDBOOK
MOON PUBLICATIONS, INC.
P.O. BOX 3040
CHICO, CA 95927-3040, USA
e-mail: travel@moon.com**

Printing History
1st edition—June 1995
2nd edition—April 1997

ISBN: 1-56691-046-3
ISSN: 1079-9338

Editor: Michael Raymond Greer
Assisting Editors: Emily Kendrick, Matt Orendorff
Copy Editor: Deana Corbitt Shields
Production & Design: Dave Hurst, Carey Wilson
Cartographers: Robert Race, Brian Bardwell, Jason Sadler, Chris Folks, Mike Morgenfeld
Index: Deana Corbitt Shields

Front cover photo: Sunrise at Vermilion Lakes, Banff National Park, by Wolfgang Kaehler

All photos by Andrew Hempstead unless otherwise noted.

Distributed in the USA and Canada by Publishers Group West
Printed in Hong Kong

CONTENTS

ALBERTA 1

INTRODUCTION 3

The Land 4
Geology; Climate

Flora 8
The Mountains and Foothills; The Plains

Fauna 10
The Deer Family; Bears; Wild Dogs and Cats; Other Large Mammals;
Rodents and Other Small Mammals; Reptiles and Amphibians; Fish;
Birds

History 16
The Earliest Inhabitants; Exploration and the Fur Trade; Settlement;
Oil

Economy and Government 21
Economy; Government

The People 23

ON THE ROAD 25

Recreation 25
Parks; Outdoor Activities; Entertainment; Shopping; Festivals and
Events

Accommodations and Food 33
Food and Drink

Transportation 36
Getting There; Getting Around

Other Practicalities 39
Visas and Officialdom; Money; Health; Services, Communications,
and Measurements; Maps and Information

CALGARY 43

Introduction 43
History

Sights 45
Getting Oriented; Downtown; Museums; Historic Parks; Canada
Olympic Park; Other Parks

Recreation 55
Outdoor Activities; Spectator Sports; Arts and Entertainment;
Shopping; Festivals and Events

Calgary Stampede 60
Events; Other Entertainment; Practicalities

Accommodations 66
Hotels and Motels; Bed and Breakfasts; Backpacker
Accommodations; Campgrounds

Food 69
Downtown Dining; South of Downtown; North of Downtown

Transportation 73
Getting There; Getting Around

Services and Information 74
Services; Information

SOUTHERN ALBERTA 76

Calgary to Lethbridge 77
Nanton and Vicinity; Claresholm; Highway 23 South; Fort Macleod;
Head-Smashed-In Buffalo Jump

Lethbridge 85
Sights; Recreation; Entertainment; Accommodations; Food;
Transportation; Services and Information

East of Lethbridge 93
The Milk River; Writing-On-Stone Provincial Park; The Dry Belt;
Highway 3 East

Medicine Hat and Vicinity 99
Sights; Festivals and Events; Accommodations; Food and Drink;
Transportation; Services and Information; Cypress Hills Provincial
Park

Cardston 109
Sights; Practicalities; Vicinity of Cardston

Waterton Lakes National Park 113
The Land; History; Hiking; Scenic Drives; Other Recreation;
Accommodations; Food; Transportation; Services and Information

Crowsnest Pass and Vicinity 127
Pincher Creek and Vicinity; Bellevue; Hillcrest; Frank; Blairmore and
Vicinity; Coleman; West of Coleman

DINOSAUR VALLEY 141

Drumheller and Vicinity 142
Sights; Scenic Drives; Recreation; Accommodations; Food; Services
and Information; Highway 9 East; Highway 56 North

Calgary to Dinosaur Provincial Park 153
Strathmore; Bassano; Brooks

Dinosaur Provincial Park 155
Exploring the Park; Practicalities

WEST OF CALGARY 159

Ranchlands 159
Cochrane; Bragg Creek; Bragg Creek to Okotoks; Okotoks and
Vicinity; Highway 22 South; High River

Kananaskis Country 166
Ribbon Creek/Spray Lakes Area; Peter Lougheed Provincial Park;
Hiking in Peter Lougheed Provincial Park; East Kananaskis Country;
Highwood/Cataract Creek Area

Canmore 174
Sights and Recreation; Accommodations; Food; Services and
Information

BANFF NATIONAL PARK 180

Introduction 180
The Land; Flora; Fauna; History

Town of Banff 186
Sights and Drives; Bow Valley Parkway; Rainy Day Banff; Hiking;
Other Recreation; Wintertime; Festivals and Events;
Accommodations; Food; Nightlife; Shopping; Transportation;
Services; Information

Lake Louise 215
Sights and Recreation; Hiking; Wintertime; Accommodations; Food
and Drink; Transportation; Services and Information

Icefields Parkway/Banff 227
Sights; Hiking; Accommodations

JASPER NATIONAL PARK 234

Introduction 234
The Land; Flora; Fauna; History

Icefields Parkway/Jasper 239
Sights; Hikes along Icefields Parkway; Accommodations

Jasper Townsite 243
Sights and Drives; Hiking around Town; Hikes near Mount Edith
Cavell; Hiking in the Maligne Lake Area; Other Recreation;
Wintertime; Festivals and Events; Accommodations; Food and Drink;
Transportation; Services and Information

CENTRAL ALBERTA 262

West-central Alberta 263
Highway 22 North; Rocky Mountain House; Nordegg; West from
Nordegg; North from Rocky Mountain House

Calgary to Red Deer 272
Via Highway 2A; The Back Way; Red Deer

East of Highway 2: The Aspen Parkland 279
Highway 12 East; Wetaskiwin; Camrose; Highway 13 East; Highway
14 East

EDMONTON 285

Introduction 285
History

Sights 290
Downtown; Southside; Old Strathcona; West Edmonton; Vicinity of
Edmonton

Recreation 304
Wintertime; Spectator Sports; Arts and Entertainment; Shopping;
Festivals and Events

Accommodations 310
Hotels and Motels; Bed-and-Breakfast Inns; Hostels; Campgrounds

Food 313
Downtown; West End; Old Strathcona; Calgary Trail; Other Parts of
the City

Transportation 317
Getting There; Getting Around

Services and Information 319
Services; Information

NORTHERN ALBERTA 321

Lakeland 323
Elk Island National Park; East along the Yellowhead Highway;
Lloydminster; Highway 28 to Ashmont; Southeast to St. Paul and
Beyond; Northeast toward Cold Lake; Tri-Town Area; Lac La Biche;
Vicinity of Lac La Biche

Fort McMurray and Vicinity 335
Sights; Recreation and Events; Accommodations and Food;
Transportation; Services and Information; Fort Chipewyan

North-central Alberta 341
Edmonton to Athabasca; Athabasca and Vicinity; Athabasca to Slave
Lake; Slave Lake; To the Peace River; Highway 18 West; Swan Hills;
Whitecourt; Highway 43 West

West of Edmonton 355
From Edmonton to Edson; Hinton and Vicinity; Grande Cache

Grande Prairie and Vicinity 364
Sights; Recreation and Events; Accommodations and Food; Services
and Information; Vicinity of Grande Prairie

The Peace River Valley 369
Upper Peace Valley; Peace River; Mackenzie Highway

NORTHWEST TERRITORIES INCLUDING NUNAVUT 379

INTRODUCTION 381
The Land; Flora; Fauna; History; Government; Economy; People;
Recreation; Accommodations and Food; Getting There; Getting
Around; Information

NORTHWEST TERRITORIES 395

The Accessible North 395
60th Parallel to Hay River; Hay River; To Fort Smith; Fort Smith;
Wood Buffalo National Park; Hay River to Yellowknife

Yellowknife and Vicinity 410
Sights; Recreation; Accommodations; Food; Transportation; Services
and Information; Communities in the Vicinity of Yellowknife

Rivers of Myth, Mountains of Mystery 419
Fort Simpson; Liard Highway; Fort Liard; Nahanni National Park

Mackenzie River Valley 430
Norman Wells; Other Communities

Western Arctic 435
Dempster Highway; Inuvik; Aklavik; Tuktoyaktuk; Paulatuk; Banks
Island; Holman (Uluqsaqtuuq)

NUNAVUT 445

Arctic Coast 445
Cambridge Bay (Ikaluktutiak); Kugluktuk; Bathurst Inlet; Gjoa Haven
(Ursuqtuq); Taloyoak; Pelly Bay (Arviliqjuat)

Keewatin 451
Rankin Inlet (Kangiqtinq); Whale Cove (Tikirarjuaq); Arviat;
Chesterfield Inlet (Igluligaarjuk); Baker Lake (Qamanittuaq); Repulse
Bay (Naujat); Coral Harbour (Salliq)

Baffin and Beyond 457
Iqaluit; Kimmirut; Cape Dorset (Kingait); Belcher Islands; Hall Beach
(Sanirajak); Igloolik (Iglulik); Pangnirtung (Panniqtuuq); Auyuittuq
National Park; Broughton Island (Qikiqtarjuaq); Clyde River
(Kangiqlugaapik); Pond Inlet (Mittimatalik); Arctic Bay and Vicinity;
Resolute: Gateway to the High Arctic (Qausuittuq); Ellesmere Island

BOOKLIST 471

INDEX 475

MAPS

INTRODUCTION AND ON THE ROAD
Alberta 5
Alberta and California 4
Historical Boundaries of Alberta 18
Vegetation Zones 9

CALGARY
Calgary 46-47
Calgary City Center. 49

SOUTHERN ALBERTA
Cardston 109
Crowsnest Pass 132-133
Cypress Hills Provincial Park 107
Fort Macleod 82
Lethbridge. 86
Lethbridge, Downtown 88
Medicine Hat. 100
Medicine Hat, Downtown 101
Pincher Creek 129
Southern Alberta 78-79
Waterton Lakes National Park. . . . 114-115
Waterton Townsite 124

DINOSAUR VALLEY
Dinosaur Provincial Park Facility Area . . 155
Dinosaur Valley 142
Drumheller. 144
Drumheller, Vicinity of. 147

WEST OF CALGARY
Bragg Creek 162
Canmore. 174
Peter Lougheed Provincial Park 170
Ranchlands 161
West of Calgary 160

BANFF NATIONAL PARK
Banff National Park 181
Banff, Town of. 187
Banff, Vicinity of. 189
Icefields Parkway 228
Lake Louise 217

JASPER NATIONAL PARK
Columbia Icefield 240
Jasper National Park. 236-237

Jasper Townsite. 244
Jasper, Vicinity of 246

CENTRAL ALBERTA
Camrose. 282
Central Alberta 264-265
Red Deer. 275
Rocky Mountain House 266

EDMONTON
Edmonton. 286-287
Edmonton City Center 292-293
Old Strathcona 297
West Edmonton Mall 301

NORTHERN ALBERTA
Athabasca 344
Cold Lake and Vicinity 333
Elk Island National Park 325
Fort McMurray. 336
Grande Cache. 361
Grande Prairie 365
Grande Prairie/
    Upper Peace River Valley 368
Lakeland 324
Lloydminster. 327
Mackenzie Highway. 374
North-central Alberta 342
Northern Alberta. 322
Peace River 371
Slave Lake. 346
West of Edmonton 356

NORTHWEST TERRITORIES
Fort Simpson 421
Fort Smith 402
Hay River 398
Inuvik. 437
Nahanni National Park 425
Northwest Territories 396
NWT Road System 392
Wood Buffalo National Park 405
Yellowknife. 411

NUNAVUT
Iqaluit. 458
Nunavut 446

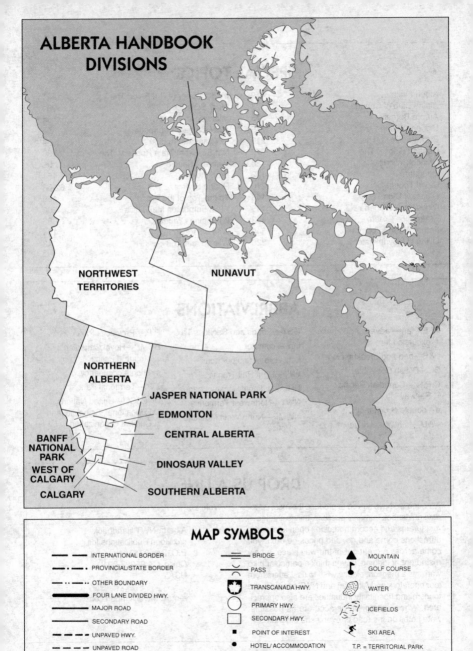

ALBERTA HANDBOOK DIVISIONS

NORTHWEST TERRITORIES

NUNAVUT

NORTHERN ALBERTA

JASPER NATIONAL PARK

EDMONTON

CENTRAL ALBERTA

BANFF NATIONAL PARK

DINOSAUR VALLEY

WEST OF CALGARY

CALGARY

SOUTHERN ALBERTA

MAP SYMBOLS

——— INTERNATIONAL BORDER

—··—··— PROVINCIAL/STATE BORDER

—···—···— OTHER BOUNDARY

▬▬▬ FOUR LANE DIVIDED HWY.

——— MAJOR ROAD

——— SECONDARY ROAD

— — — UNPAVED HWY.

— — — UNPAVED ROAD

—··—··— PATH/TRAIL

═══ BRIDGE

⌣ PASS

🍁 TRANSCANADA HWY.

◯ PRIMARY HWY.

▢ SECONDARY HWY.

■ POINT OF INTEREST

● HOTEL/ ACCOMMODATION

△ CAMPGROUND

▲ MOUNTAIN

⚑ GOLF COURSE

WATER

ICEFIELDS

SKI AREA

T.P. = TERRITORIAL PARK

P.P. = PROVINCIAL PARK

SPECIAL TOPICS

Albert Faille 419
Alpine Club of Canada, The 177
Aurora Borealis 375
Bighorn Sheep 249
Brewster Boys, The 213
Canada Goose, The 276
Chinook Winds 128
Cougars 172
David Thompson 270
Dinosaur Digs 143
Dinosaurs of Alberta 145
Eskimo Ice Cream 453
Father Albert Lacombe 349
Living in Lloydminster 328

Mad Trapper of Rat River, The 441
Mary Schäffer 251
Midnapore 54
1997 Calgary Stampede
    Ticket Information 64
Not-So-Great Train Robbery, The 138
Palliser Triangle 96
Pronghorn 151
Rodeo Events 62-63
To the Top of the World 469
West Edmonton Mall Trivia 300
Whooping Cranes 386
Wild Bill Peyto 194
Wildlife and You 13

ABBREVIATIONS

APEX fare—advance-purchase
    excursion fare
B&B—bed-and-breakfast inn
BC—British Columbia
C.P.R.—Canadian Pacific
    Railway
d—double occupancy
4WD—four-wheel drive

GST—Goods and Services Tax
km—kilometer
kph—kilometers per hour
LRT—Light Rail Transit
NHL—National Hockey League
NWT—Northwest Territories
NWMP—North West Mounted
    Police

P.P.—Provincial Park
RCMP—Royal Canadian
    Mounted Police
s—single occupancy
T.P.—Territorial Park
UNESCO—United Nations
    Educational, Scientific, and
    Cultural Organization

DROP US A LINE

Although we have strived to produce the most up-to-date guidebook humanly possible, things change—restaurants and accommodations open and close, attractions come and go, and prices go up. If you come across a great out-of-the-way place, a new restaurant or lodging, or you think a particular hike warrants a mention, please write to us. Letters from tour operators and Albertan and NWT people in the tourism and hospitality industries are also appreciated. When writing, be as accurate as possible; write notes on the road or even send brochures.

Write to:

Alberta-NWT Handbook
c/o Moon Publications Inc.
P.O. Box 3040
Chico, CA 95927-3040
USA

e-mail: travel@moon.com

ACKNOWLEDGMENTS

Whether they're pumping petrol, waiting tables, or whoopin' it up at the Stampede, Albertans are among the friendliest people you're likely to come across. So many of them have contributed to this update, most of them unknowingly (most of the research for the handbooks is done incognito), by telling of the town's highlights or pointing the way to favorite restaurants. Full marks for the information center volunteer who wasn't allowed to recommend any particular restaurant, then divulged, "But I can tell you where I always go for a meal." Of special assistance were Scott Mair of Kananaskis Country, Maureen McCrimmon of the Calgary Stampede, and Tony Bulman of Alberta Tourism Partnership.

North of the 60th parallel, a hearty thanks to Barb Dillon of Northwest Territories Tourism, Karen Siebold of Touch the Arctic Adventure Tours, and Darielle Talarico of Arctic Nature Tours. As always the Northwest Territories dredged up its own unique characters, who in their own special way make this handbook more complete. Most particularly Dennis, Broken-foot Brian, and the rest of the gang at Fort Smith, who don't really contribute anything to the book but whose hospitality over the years has been greatly appreciated and is, well, so typically Northern.

Back in my home base of Banff, thanks again to Wendy Lash for assistance with updating the mountain parks as well as for supplying a much-needed work space. Thanks also to Nancy DaDalt, who helps organize one of the world's great adventure film festivals, and Katherine Comino, who bakes a mean cottage pie, for providing accommodations.

ALBERTA

KAREN McKINLEY

INTRODUCTION

The prosperous province of Alberta is the heart of western Canada, sandwiched between the mountains of British Columbia to the west and the prairies of Saskatchewan to the east. Edmonton, Alberta's capital, and Calgary, to the south, are, respectively, Canada's fifth- and sixth-largest cities, between them holding over half the province's population. These boomtowns have been Canada's fastest-growing cities since WW II, centers for the staggering oil and gas reserves that have propelled Alberta to the forefront of world energy markets and technology. Edmonton is a modern, livable city boasting some of Canada's finest cultural facilities, as well as the world's largest shopping and amusement mall. Calgary, meanwhile, is home to the world-famous Calgary Stampede— a Western wingding of epic proportions—and the city received international attention as the host of the 1988 Winter Olympic Games. Its futuristic skyline rises from the prairie like the oil derricks that put the city on the map, and cattlemen in Caddies drive past gleaming skyscrapers on their way out to the ranch.

But for most visitors to Alberta, it's not the big cities or the fast bucks that are the draw, it's the great outdoors. The stunning mountain playgrounds of Banff, Jasper, and Waterton National Parks show off the Canadian Rockies at their best, with pristine glaciers, rushing rivers, and snowcapped peaks reflected in hundreds of high-country lakes. The parks, and much of the rest of the province, are home to an abundance of wildlife such as moose, elk, bighorn sheep, wolves, bears, and an amazing array of birds; some 340 species of birds migrate through or nest in Alberta. And ancient wildlife thrived here, too; one of the world's greatest concentrations of dinosaur bones continues to be unearthed in the Red Deer River Valley outside Drumheller. The "Dinosaur Valley," as it's called, attracts tourist tyros and professional paleontologists alike to learn more about earth's once-dominant former tenants.

Throughout the province, wide-open spaces, endless blue skies, and accessible wilderness beckon, and big-city culture awaits when you come down from the hills. So whether your interests lean toward high peaks or high tea, you're sure to find plenty to suit you in Alberta.

THE LAND

Alberta is the fourth-largest province in Canada. With an area of 661,185 square km, it's larger than all U.S. states except Alaska and Texas. The province lies between the 49th and 60th parallels, bordered on the south by Montana, USA, and on the north by Canada's Northwest Territories. To the west is British Columbia and to the east is Saskatchewan. Along its roughly rectangular outline, the only natural border is the Continental Divide in the southwest. Here, from the International Boundary to Jasper, the lofty peaks of the **Rocky Mountains** rise to heights of over 3,000 meters. Alberta's Rockies are only one small but exquisitely beautiful link in this mountain chain that forms the backbone of North America, extending from the jungles of central Mexico to the Arctic. Running parallel to the mountains along their eastern edge is a series of long, rolling ridges known as the **foothills.** This region was once a coal-mining center, and today holds abundant recreational opportunities. Finally, east of the foothills and across the rest of Alberta are **plains,** which cover almost three-quarters of the province. The plains provide practically all of Alberta's arable soil and natural resources. The term "plains" is very broad. Alberta's plains encompass three distinct vegetation zones: prairies, parklands, and boreal forests (see "Flora," below).

GEOLOGY

The rocks of Alberta range in age from ancient to almost "brand-new," in geologic time. The 70-million-year-old Rocky Mountains, Alberta's most distinctive natural feature, are relatively young compared to the world's other major mountain ranges. By contrast, the Precambrian rock of the Canadian Shield, exposed in the province's northeast corner and underlying parts of the rest, was the progenitor of North America. It was the first land on the continent to remain permanently above sea level, and is among the oldest rock on earth, formed over 2.5 billion years ago.

Around 700 million years ago, in the Precambrian era, forces beneath the earth caused uplift, pushing the coastline of the Pacific Ocean —which then covered most of the province— westward. The ocean advanced, then receded, several times over the next half billion years. Each time the ocean flooded eastward it deposited layers of sediment on its bed, layers that built up with each successive inundation. This sediment is now a layer of sedimentary rock covering most of Alberta, up to seven km deep in the southwest.

Alberta's Oil
Oil pools are created when oil globules—converted from decayed organic matter by the forces of heat and pressure beneath the earth's surface—are trapped in porous rock capped by nonporous rock. During the Middle Devonian period, 375 million years ago, with the Pacific Ocean once again covering Alberta, coral reefs formed. Over time, this coral would be transformed into the porous rock that would hold the

ALBERTA AND CALIFORNIA

0   100 mi

0   100 km

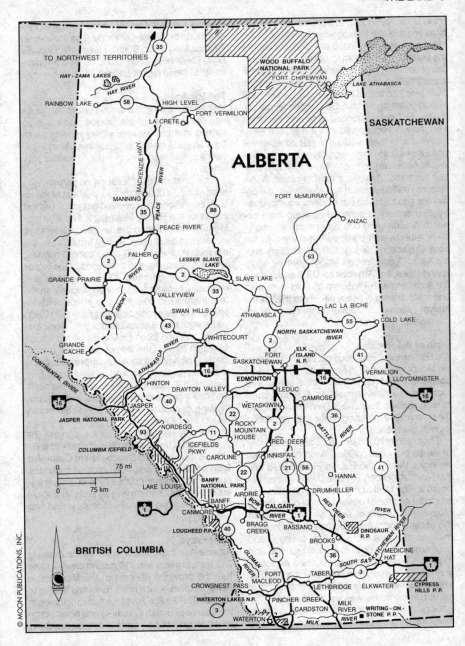

pools of oil. Also during this period, as well as in later years of the Paleozoic era, trillions of microscopic organisms in the sea died and sank to the bottom of the ocean, creating mass quantities of decaying organic matter in and around the coral. This organic matter would be transformed over time into the oil itself. Finally, around 300 million years ago, in the Carboniferous period, the Pacific Ocean extended as far as the foothills and many rivers flowed into it from the east, carrying with them sediment that covered the porous reefs in nonporous layers. All the elements necessary to eventually create and contain reserves of oil were then in place. A few hundred million years of "cooking" later, the primordial goo that fuels our modern, internal-combustion society is pumped nonstop from beneath Alberta. And one other huge source of oil in Alberta isn't pumped but *mined.* In the early Cretaceous period, 130 million years ago, the Arctic Ocean flooded Alberta from the north, laying down the **Athabasca Oil Sands** along the Arctic seaway. These sands hold more than one trillion barrels of heavy oil—more than all the known reserves of conventional crude oil on the planet.

Birth of the Rockies

Also during the Cretaceous period, the Mackenzie Mountains began to rise, cutting off the Arctic seaway and forming an inland sea where marinelife such as ammonites, fish, and large marine reptiles flourished. Dinosaurs roamed the coastal areas, feeding on the lush vegetation as well as on each other.

Then, some 70 million years ago, two plates of the earth's crust collided. According to plate tectonics theory, the Pacific Plate butted into the North American Plate and was forced beneath it. The land at this subduction zone was crumpled and thrust upward, creating the Rocky Mountains. Layers of sediment laid down on the ocean floor over the course of hundreds of millions of years were folded, twisted, and squeezed; great slabs of rock broke away, and in places older strata were pushed on top of younger. By the beginning of the Tertiary period, around 65 million years ago, the present form of mountain contours was established and the geological framework of Alberta was in place. Then the forces of erosion went to work. The

plains of the Late Tertiary period were at a higher altitude than those of today. The flat-topped Caribou Mountains, Buffalo Head Hills, Cypress Hills, Clear Hills, and Porcupine Hills are remnants of those higher plains.

The Ice Ages

No one knows why, but around one million years ago the world's climate cooled and ice caps formed in Arctic regions, slowly moving south over North America and Eurasia. These advances, followed by retreats, occurred four times.

The final major glaciation began moving southward 35,000 years ago. A sheet of ice up to 2,000 meters deep covered all but the highest peaks of the Rocky Mountains and Cypress Hills. The ice scoured the terrain, destroying all vegetation as it crept slowly forward. In the mountains, these rivers of ice carved hollows, known as **cirques,** into the slopes of the higher peaks. They rounded off lower peaks and reamed out valleys from their preglacier V shape to a trademark, postglacial U shape. The retreat of this ice sheet, beginning around 12,000 years ago, was just as destructive. Rock and debris that had been picked up by the ice on its march forward melted out during the retreat, creating high ridges known as **moraines.** Many of these moraines blocked natural drainages, resulting in thousands of lakes across the north. And meltwater drained into rivers and streams, incising deep channels into the sedimentary rock of the plains.

The only remnants of this ice age are the scattered icefields along the Continental Divide—including the 325-square-km **Columbia Icefield.** But wind and water erosion continues, uncovering dinosaur bones hidden among layers of sediment and carving an eerie landscape of badlands along the sides of many prairie river valleys.

Waterways

Alberta has three major watersheds draining 245 named rivers and 315 named creeks. Over half the province drains into the **Mackenzie River System,** which flows north into the Arctic Ocean. The **Peace River**—which originates in the interior of British Columbia and flows northeast through Alberta—and the **Athabasca River**

The face of Banff's Temple Mountain reveals horizontal layers of sedimentary rock.

—whose initial source is the Columbia Icefield—are the province's two major tributaries in this system. They eventually meet to form the Slave River, which flows into the Mackenzie at Great Slave Lake in the Northwest Territories.

Central Alberta is drained mainly by the **Saskatchewan River System,** the major source of water for Alberta's farmers. This river system, which eventually flows into Hudson Bay, has three main tributaries: the **North Saskatchewan River,** originating from the Columbia Icefield; the **Red Deer River,** originating in the heart of Banff National Park and flowing through "Dinosaur Valley" on its way east; and the **South Saskatchewan River.** The latter is fed in large part by the **Bow River,** flowing down from Banff, and the **Oldman River,** which cascades out of the Rockies south of Kananaskis Country.

A small area in the south of the province is drained by the **Milk River,** which flows southeast into the Mississippi River System, ending up in the Gulf of Mexico.

The amount of water flowing in any one of Alberta's rivers is dependent on that particular river's source. Rivers originating from melt-out of the winter snowpack reach peak flow in midsummer and often run dry by late summer. Those that originate from glaciers run light in spring and also reach a peak in midsummer, but continue a light flow until winter. Those that rise in the foothills and higher areas of the plains have highly variable flows, dependent entirely on precipitation.

CLIMATE

Alberta spans 11 degrees of latitude, and its varied topography includes elevations ranging from 170 to over 3,700 meters. As a result, the climate of the province varies widely from place to place. In addition, the Rocky Mountains create some of Alberta's unique climatic characteristics. As prevailing, moisture-laden westerlies blow in from British Columbia, the cold heights of the Rockies wring them dry. This makes for clear, sunny skies in southern Alberta; Calgary gets up to 350 hours of sunshine in June alone—good news, unless you're a farmer. In winter, the dry winds blasting down the eastern slopes of the Rockies can raise temperatures on the prairies by up to 40° C in 24 hours. Called **chinooks,** these desiccating blows are a phenomenon unique to Alberta.

Another interesting phenomenon occurring in southern Alberta's Rocky Mountain regions is the **temperature inversion,** in which a layer of warm air sits on top of a cold air mass. During these inversions, high- and low-country roles are reversed; prairie residents can be shivering and bundling up, while their mountain fellows are sunning themselves in shirtsleeves.

The Seasons

On the whole, Alberta features cold winters and short, hot summers. May to mid-September is ideal for touring, camping out, and seeing the sights; a month either side and the weather is cooler, but still pleasant; and the rest of the year the skiing is fantastic.

January is usually the coldest month, when Calgary's mean average temperature is -13° C and Fort McMurray's is -20° C. In winter, extended spells of -30° C are not uncommon anywhere in the province and occasionally temperatures drop below -40° C. Severe cold weather is often accompanied by sunshine; the cold is a dry cold, unlike the damp cold experienced in coastal regions. Cold temperatures and snow can continue until mid-March.

Although March, April, and May are officially the months of spring, snow often falls in April, many lakes may remain frozen until May, and snow cover on higher mountain hiking trails remains until June. Late snowfalls, though not welcomed by golfers in Calgary, provide important moisture for crops.

The official months of summer are June, July, and August, with July being the hottest month and providing the most uniform temperatures throughout the province. On hot days, the temperature will hit 30° C (usually every second summer day in the south) and very occasionally climb above 40° C. Again, because of the dryness of the air, these high temperatures are more bearable here than in coastal regions experiencing the same temperatures.

The frost-free growing season is over by late September, when the air begins to have a distinct chill. October brings the highest temperature variations of the year, with the thermometer hitting 30° C but also dipping as low as -20° C. Mild weather can continue until early December, but generally the first snow falls in October and by mid-November winter has set in.

FLORA

Alberta can be divided into two major geographical areas: the mountain-and-foothill region along its southwestern border, and the plains covering the rest of the province. Within each of these two main areas are distinct vegetation zones, the boundaries of which are determined by factors such as precipitation, latitude, and altitude.

THE MOUNTAINS AND FOOTHILLS

In southwest Alberta, west of Hwy. 2 between the U.S. border and Edmonton, the land climbs through foothills to the high peaks of the Rockies. Along the way it gains over 2,000 meters of elevation and passes through the montane, subalpine, and alpine vegetation zones. Although Banff and Jasper National Parks are the obvious places to view these mountain biomes, the changes in vegetation are more abrupt and just as spectacular in less-visited Waterton Lakes National Park.

Montane
The foothills, along with most major valleys

below an elevation of about 1,500 meters, are primarily cloaked in montane forest. **Aspen, balsam poplar,** and **white spruce** thrive here, and **lodgepole pine** dominates areas affected by fire. On dry, south-facing slopes, **Douglas fir** is the climax species. Where sunlight penetrates the forest, such as along riverbanks, flowers like **lady's slipper, Indian paintbrush,** and **saxifrage** are common. Large tracts of **fescue grassland** are common at lower elevations.

The montane forest holds the greatest diversity of life of any vegetation zone in the province, and is prime winter habitat for larger mammals. But much of this habitat has been given over to agriculture and development.

Subalpine
Subalpine forests occur where temperatures are lower and precipitation higher than the montane. Generally, this is 1,500-2,200 meters above sea level. The climax species in this zone are **Engelmann spruce** and **subalpine fir,** although extensive forests of **lodgepole pine** occur in areas that have been scorched by fire in the last 100 years. At higher elevations, stands of **larch** are seen. Larches are conifers, but unlike other evergreens, their needles turn a burnt-

VEGETATION ZONES

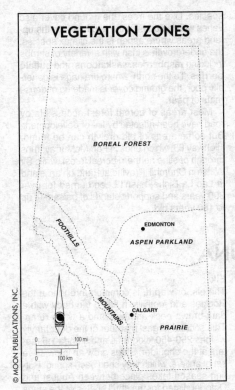

BOREAL FOREST

FOOTHILLS

EDMONTON

ASPEN PARKLAND

MOUNTAINS

CALGARY

PRAIRIE

0   100 mi

0   100 km

© MOON PUBLICATIONS, INC.

orange color each fall, producing a magnificent display for photographers.

Alpine

The alpine zone extends from the treeline to mountain summits. Vegetation at these high altitudes occurs only where soil has been deposited. Large areas of alpine meadows burst with color for a short period each summer as **lupines, mountain avens, alpine forget-me-nots, moss campion,** and a variety of **heathers** bloom.

THE PLAINS

Like the mountain-and-foothill region, Alberta's plains also are made up of three different vegetation zones. Across Hwy. 2, east of the mountains and foothills, southeast Alberta is domi-

nated by the prairie—a vast, dry region of grasslands. Just north of the prairie is the aspen parkland, a belt of forest that runs across central Alberta to the foothills and covers approximately 10% of the province. Finally, Alberta's largest ecological zone by far, covering over half of the province, is the boreal forest. It is located north of the aspen parkland and extends into the Northwest Territories to the treeline, where the tundra begins.

Prairie

Prairie is the warmest and driest ecological zone, with an annual precipitation under 750 millimeters. This harsh climate can support trees only where water flows, so for the most part, the prairie is open grassland—flat or lightly undulating. Irrigation has made agriculture possible across much of the south, and the patches of native grasses such as **rough fescue** and **grama** are rapidly disappearing. Among the cultivated pastureland and seemingly desolate plains, flowers punctuate the otherwise ochre-colored landscape. Alberta's floral emblem, the **prickly wild rose,** grows here, as do **pincushion cactus, buckbrush** (or yellow rose), and **sagebrush.** In river valleys, **aspen, willow,** and **cottonwood** grow along the banks.

The stands of large cottonwoods in Dinosaur Provincial Park were part of the reason this park was designated a UNESCO World Heritage Site. (The park is a good example of prairie habitat.) The Cypress Hills, which rise above the driest part of the province, contain vegetation not generally associated with the prairies, including **spruce, aspen,** a variety of **berries,** and the **calypso orchid.**

Aspen Parkland

This is a transition zone between the prairie grassland to the south and the boreal forest to the north. As the name suggests, **aspen** is the climax species, but much of this zone has been given over to agriculture—its forests burned and its soil tilled. Scattered stands of aspen, interspersed with **willow, balsam poplar,** and **white spruce,** still occur, while areas cleared by early settlers now contain **fescue grass.** Flowering plants such as **prairie crocus, snowberry, prickly wild rose,** and **lily-of-the-valley** decorate the shores of the many lakes and marshy areas found in this biome. Elk Island National Park, best known for its mammal populations, is an ideal example of this unique habitat.

Boreal Forest

Only a few species of trees are able to adapt to the harsh northern climate characteristic of this zone. The area is almost totally covered in forest, with only scattered areas of prairielike vegetation occurring in the very driest areas. In the southern part of the boreal forest the predominant species are **aspen** and **balsam poplar.** Farther north, conifers such as **white spruce, lodgepole pine,** and **balsam fir** are more common, with **jack pine** growing on dry ridges, and **tamarack** is also present. The entire forest is interspersed with lakes, bogs, and sloughs where **black spruce** and **larch** are the dominant species. Like the trees, the ground cover also varies with latitude. To the south, and in the upland areas where aspen is the climax species, the undergrowth is lush with a variety of shrubs including **raspberries, saskatoons,** and **buffalo berries.** To the north, where drainage is generally poor, the ground cover is made up of dense mats of **peat.**

Most areas of boreal forest accessible by road have been affected by fire or development. But some areas of old growth can be found. Highway 63, which ends in Fort McMurray, runs through pristine northern boreal forest, while Sir Winston Churchill Provincial Park, on an island in Lac La Biche, hasn't been burned for over 300 years and supports stands of balsam fir up to 150 years old.

FAUNA

For 10,000 years, hundreds of thousands of bison roamed Alberta's plains, and wolves and grizzly bears inhabited all parts of the province. But this all changed with the coming of white men. Trappers and traders first devastated beaver and mink populations, then killed off all the bison, wolves, and grizzlies on the prairies.

Today, due to the foresight of early conservationists, mammal populations have stabilized and Alberta's wilderness once again provides some of North America's best opportunities for viewing wildlife.

THE DEER FAMILY

Deer

Alberta's **mule deer** and **white-tailed deer** are similar in size and appearance. Their color varies with the season but is generally light brown in summer, turning dirty-gray in winter. Both species are considerably smaller than elk. The mule deer has a white rump, a white tail with a dark tip, and large mule-like ears. It inhabits open forests bordering prairie. The white-tailed deer's tail is dark—on top. But when the animal runs, it holds its tail erect, revealing an all-white underside. Whitetails frequent thickets along the rivers and lakes of the foothills and aspen parkland.

Elk

The elk, or **wapiti,** is common throughout the Rockies and foothills. It has a tan body with a dark-brown neck and legs and a white rump. This second-largest member of the deer family weighs 250-450 kilograms and stands 1.5 meters at the shoulder. Stags grow an impressive set of antlers, which they shed each spring. Rutting season takes place between August and October; listen for the shrill bugles of the stags serenading the females. During the rut, randy males will challenge anything with their antlers and can be dangerous. In spring, females protecting their young can be equally dangerous.

Moose

The giant of the deer family is the moose, an awkward-looking mammal that appears to have been designed by a cartoonist. It has the largest antlers of any animal in the world, stands up to 1.8 meters at the shoulder, and weighs in excess of 450 kilograms. Its body is dark brown, and it has a prominent nose, long spindly legs, small eyes, big ears, and an odd flap of skin called a "bell" dangling beneath its chin. Apart from all that, it's good-looking. Each spring the bull begins to grow palm-shaped antlers which by August will be fully grown. Moose are solitary animals preferring marshy areas and weedy lakes.

They forage in and around ponds on willows, aspen, birch, grasses, and all aquatic vegetation. Although they may appear docile, moose will attack humans if they feel threatened.

Caribou
Small populations of caribou inhabit the forest and alpine regions of northern and west-central Alberta. Diminishing habitat and declining numbers have led to their placement on Alberta's Threatened Wildlife List. These woodland caribou are smaller than elk and have a dark-brown coat with creamy patches on the neck and rump. Both sexes grow antlers—those of the females are shorter and have fewer points. On average males weigh 180 kilograms, females 115 kilograms.

BEARS

Alberta's two species of bears—black bears and grizzlies—can be differentiated by size and shape. Grizzlies are larger than black bears and have a flatter, dish-shaped face and a distinctive hump of muscle behind their neck. Color is not a reliable way to tell them apart. Black bears are not always black. They can be brown or cinnamon, causing them to be confused with the brown-colored grizzly.

Black Bears
If you spot a bear feeding beside the road, chances are it's a black bear. These mammals are widespread throughout all forested areas of the province (except Cypress Hills Provincial

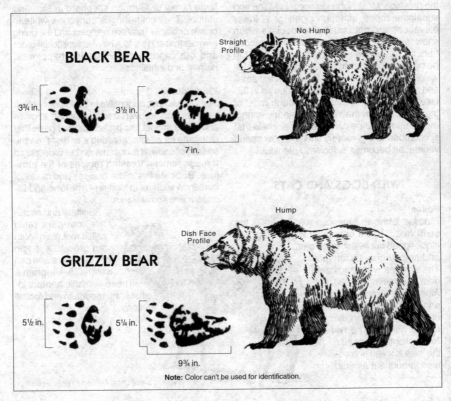

BLACK BEAR

No Hump

Straight Profile

3¾ in.　3½ in.

7 in.

GRIZZLY BEAR

Hump

Dish Face Profile

5½ in.　5¼ in.

9¾ in.

Note: Color can't be used for identification.

Park). Their weight varies considerably, but males average 150 kilograms and females 100 kilograms. Their diet is omnivorous, consisting primarily of grasses and berries but supplemented by small mammals. In winter, they can sleep for up to a month at a time before changing position.

Grizzly Bears

Most of Alberta's grizzlies are spread through the Rockies—in Banff and Jasper National Parks, Kananaskis Country, and Alberta's four designated wilderness areas. A small population inhabiting the Swan Hills is distinct from those found in the mountains and is probably related more closely to the grizzlies that once roamed the prairies.

Grizzlies are widespread, but not abundant in the province. Most sightings occur in alpine and subalpine zones, although sightings at lower elevations are not unusual, especially when snow falls early or late. The bears' color ranges from light brown to almost black, with dark tan being the most common. On average, males weigh 200-250 kilograms. The bears eat small and medium-sized mammals, and berries in fall. Like black bears, they sleep through most of the winter. When they emerge in early spring, the bears scavenge carcasses of animals that succumbed to the winter, until the new spring vegetation becomes sufficiently plentiful.

WILD DOGS AND CATS

Foxes

Smallest of North American wild canids is the **swift fox.** It has a gray body with a long, black-tipped bushy tail, large ears, and smoky-gray facial spots. The species was eradicated from the prairies by 1928, but Alberta is currently considering a program to reintroduce the animals to their former habitat. The **red fox** is slightly larger than the swift fox and is common throughout Alberta.

Coyotes

The resilient coyote has successfully survived human attempts to eradicate him from the prairies; today his eerie concerts of yips and howls can be heard across much of Alberta. A mottled mix of brown and gray, with lighter-colored legs and belly, the coyote is a skillful and crafty hunter preying mainly on rodents. Both foxes and coyotes have the remarkable ability to hear the movement of small mammals under the snow, allowing them to hunt these animals without actually seeing them.

Wolves

Now inhabiting only the mountains and boreal forests, the wolf was once the target of a relentless campaign to exterminate the species. Wolves are larger than coyotes, resembling a large husky or German shepherd in size and stature. Their color ranges from snow-white to brown or black. They are complex and intriguing animals that adhere to a hierarchical social order and are capable of expressing happiness, humor, and loneliness.

Wild Cats

The elusive **lynx** is identifiable by its pointy black ear tufts and an oversized "tabby cat" appearance. The animal has broad, padded paws that distribute its weight, allowing it to "float" on the surface of snow. It is uncommon but widespread through remote, forested regions of the province. **Bobcats** live in the coulees and caves of badlands such as in Writing-On-Stone and Dinosaur Provincial Parks.

Solitary and secretive, **cougars** (also called mountain lions) can grow to a length of 1.5 meters and can weigh 75 kilograms. These versatile hunters inhabit the mountain and foothill regions.

BOB RACE

Wolves were once hunted to near extinction.

bighorn sheep

OTHER LARGE MAMMALS

Mountain Goats
The remarkable rock-climbing ability of these nimble-footed creatures allows them to live on rocky ledges or near-vertical slopes, safe from predators. They also frequent the alpine meadows and open forests of the Rockies, where they congregate around natural licks of salt. The goats stand one meter at the shoulder and weigh 80-130 kilograms. Both sexes possess black horns and a peculiar beard, or rather, goatee.

Bighorn Sheep
Bighorn sheep are found on grassy mountain slopes throughout the mountains. The males have impressive horns that curve backwards up to 360 degrees. The color of their coat varies with the season; in summer it is brownish-gray (with a cream-colored belly and rump), turning grayer in winter.

Pronghorn
Found roaming the prairie grasslands of southeastern Alberta, the pronghorn, often called pronghorn antelope, is one of the fastest animals in the New World, capable of sustained speeds up to 80 kph. Other remarkable attributes also ensure its survival, including incredible hearing and eyesight, and the ability to go without water for long periods.

Bison
Conservative estimates put the population of bison at around 60 million before the coming of Europeans. Within Alberta, these shaggy beasts are found in Elk Island and Wood Buffalo National Parks and in a number of privately owned herds throughout the province. Two subspecies of bison inhabit Alberta, but for the

---

WILDLIFE AND YOU

Alberta's abundance of wildlife is one of its biggest drawcards. To help preserve this unique resource, obey fishing and hunting regulations and use common sense.

- **Do not feed the animals.** Many animals may seem tame, but feeding them endangers yourself, the animal, and other visitors, as animals become aggressive when looking for handouts.

- **Store food safely.** When camping keep food in your vehicle or out of reach of animals. Just leaving it in a cooler isn't good enough.

- **Keep your distance.** Although it's tempting to get close to animals for a better look or photograph, it disturbs the animal and, in many cases, can be dangerous.

- **Drive carefully.** The most common cause of premature death for larger mammals is being hit by cars.

most part they have interbred. **Wood bison** are darker in color, larger (an average bull weighs 840 kilograms), and have long, straight hair covering the forehead. **Plains bison** are smaller, have shorter legs, a larger head, and frizzy hair. In summer they grow a distinctive cape of woolly hair that covers their front legs, head, and shoulders.

RODENTS AND OTHER SMALL MAMMALS

Squirrels

Several species of squirrels are common in Alberta. The **golden-mantled ground squirrel,** found in rocky outcrops of subalpine and alpine regions, has black stripes along its sides and looks like an oversized chipmunk. The **Columbian ground squirrel** has reddish legs, face, and underside, and a flecked, grayish back. The bushy-tailed **red squirrel,** bold chatterbox of the forest, leaves telltale shelled cones at the base of conifers. The lightly colored **Richardson's ground squirrel,** which chirps and flicks its thin tail when it senses danger, is found across much of Alberta; on the prairie, it is often misidentified as a "gopher." Another species, the nocturnal **northern flying fox,** glides through the montane forests of mountain valleys but is rarely seen.

Other Rodents

One of the animal kingdom's most industrious mammals is the **beaver.** Tipping the scales at around 20 kilograms, it has a flat, rudderlike tail and webbed back feet that enable it to swim at speeds up to 10 kph. Beavers build their dam walls and lodges of twigs, branches, sticks of felled trees, and mud. They eat the bark and smaller twigs of deciduous plants and store branches underwater, near the lodge, as a winter food supply. **Muskrats** also inhabit Alberta's waterways and wetlands. They are agile swimmers, able to stay submerged for up to 12 minutes.

Closely related to muskrats are **voles,** often mistaken for mice. They inhabit the prairies and lower elevations of forested areas. **Kangaroo rats** live on the shortgrass prairie within the Palliser Triangle. They propel themselves with leaps of up to two meters. The furry **shrew** has a sharp-pointed snout and is closely related to the mole. It must eat almost constantly as it is susceptible to starvation within only a few hours of its last meal. One variety, the **pygmy shrew,** is North America's smallest mammal.

High in the mountains, **hoary marmots** are often seen sunning themselves in rocky areas at or above the treeline. When danger approaches, these large rodents emit a shrill whistle to warn their colony. **Porcupines** are common and widespread throughout all forested areas of the province.

Hares and Pikas

Hares and pikas are technically lagomorphs, distinguished from rodents by a double set of incisors in the upper jaw. Alberta's **varying hares** are commonly referred to as snowshoe hares because their thickly furred, wide-set hind feet mimic snowshoes. Unlike rabbits, which maintain a brown coat year-round, snowshoe hares turn white in winter, providing camouflage in the snowy climes they inhabit. One of their Albertan cousins, the **white-tailed prairie hare,** has been clocked at speeds of 60 kph. Finally, the small, gray pika, or **rock rabbit,** lives among the rubble and boulders of scree slopes above the treeline.

Weasels

The weasel family is composed of several species of small, carnivorous mammals, many of which can be found in Alberta. The **badger,** a large member of the weasel family, inhabits the grasslands. It is endowed with large claws and strong forelegs, making it an impressive digger. The **wolverine** is the largest of the weasels, inhabiting northern forests and subalpine and lower alpine regions. It is powerful, cunning, and cautious. Males weigh around 15 kilograms. **Fishers,** carnivores weighing up to five kilograms, also frequent subalpine and lower alpine regions; **marten** prey on birds, squirrels, mice, and voles.

Two other related species can be found around Alberta's waterways. **River otters** have round heads, short, thick necks, webbed feet, and long facial whiskers. These playful characters are active both day and night, and prey on both beaver and muskrat. **Mink,** at home in or out of water, are smaller than otters and feed on muskrats, mice, voles, and fish.

REPTILES AND AMPHIBIANS

Two species of snakes, the **wandering garter snake** and the **red-sided garter snake** (North America's northernmost reptile), are found as far north as the boreal forest. The other six species of snakes in the province, of which the **plains garter snake** is the most common, are restricted to the southern grasslands. **Rattlesnakes** are rarely encountered; their range is restricted to the badlands.

Three species of **frogs** and one species of **salamander** are present in Alberta.

FISH

Alberta's waters hold eight species of trout; **rainbow, cutthroat,** and **brook trout** are the predominant species in southern Alberta and the mountain regions, while **lake trout,** which grow to 20 kilograms, are common in the north. The **bull trout,** often confused with the brook trout but lacking black markings on the dorsal fin, is a unique species whose slow growth makes it prone to overfishing. Other fish inhabiting Alberta's waters include **arctic grayling,** two species of **whitefish, sturgeon** (largest of the freshwater fish), **burbot, northern pike,** and **walleye.**

BIRDS

Birdwatching is popular in Alberta, thanks to the 340 species of birds recorded in the province and the millions of migratory birds that pass through each year. All it takes is a pair of binoculars, a good book detailing species, and patience.

Shorebirds and Waterfowl
Alberta is home to 40 species of shorebirds, among them **plovers, sandpipers, dowitchers, turnstones, gulls, terns,** and **herons.** Widespread waterfowl species include **loons, grebes, ducks, geese,** and the threatened **trumpeter swan.**

Raptors
Bald eagles soar over the northern half of the province, the foothills, and mountains. **Golden eagles** inhabit open and sparsely vegetated areas of grasslands and mountains. Both species are migratory. **Ospreys** are uncommon; look for them around mountain and parkland lakes. The territory of the **prairie falcon** extends from the prairies to the foothills. The threatened **ferruginous hawk,** largest hawk in North America, also inhabits the prairies. The rare **peregrine falcon** has been clocked at speeds of up to 290 kph when diving for prey.

Alberta's provincial bird, the **great horned owl,** is identified by its prominent "horns," which are actually tufts of feathers. Owls have acute hearing, and binocular vision gives them excellent depth perception.

Others
Birdwatchers will be enthralled with the diversity of eastern and western bird species in Alberta. Widespread are **magpies, sparrows, starlings, grouse, ravens,** and **crows. Blackbirds, finches, thrushes, hummingbirds, woodpeckers, flycatchers,** and 28 species of **warblers** are common in forested areas. The popular campground visitor, the cheeky **gray jay,** is similar in appearance to that of the curious **Clark's nutcracker.**

BOB RACE

bald eagle

HISTORY

THE EARLIEST INHABITANTS

The first *Homo sapiens* probably arrived in North America some 15,000 years ago—migrating from northeastern Asia across a land bridge spanning Bering Strait. At the time, most of what is now western Canada was covered by an ice cap, so these first immigrants headed south along the coast and into the lower, ice-free latitudes of North America (to what is now the United States). Other waves of similar migrations followed, and eventually these ancestors of today's American Indians fanned out across North and South America.

Thousands of years later, the receding polar ice cap began to uncover the land north of the 49th parallel. Indian hunters probably first ventured into the area around 11,000 years ago, in pursuit of large mammals at the edge of the melting ice mass. The population gradually spread north, and the people who ended up in what would become Alberta formed several different tribes, each with a unique language and lifestyle. The Assiniboine, a breakaway of the more southerly Sioux, lived on the prairies; Cree territory extended into Alberta from Hudson Bay; Chipewyan, Beaver, and Slavey lived in the north; Stoney lived in the southwest; Sarcee migrated across southern Alberta; and the Blackfoot tribe, made up of Blackfoot, Piegan, and Blood bands, lived on the prairies and was the most powerful and feared of all.

The Indians of the prairies relied on buffalo *(Bison bison)* for almost all their needs. They ate buffalo meat, both fresh and dried into pemmican; made clothing, blankets, and tepee covers from the hides; and fashioned the bones into knives and other tools. One of their most successful ways of killing buffalo was by stampeding a whole herd over a cliff, at places known today as "buffalo jumps." The best example of such a site is Head-Smashed-In Buffalo Jump, northwest of Fort Macleod.

EXPLORATION AND THE FUR TRADE

In 1670 the British government granted the Hudson's Bay Company the right to govern Rupert's Land, a vast area of western Canada that included all of present-day Manitoba, Saskatchewan, Alberta, and Northwest Territories. The land was rich in fur-bearing mammals, which both the British and the French sought to exploit for profit. The Hudson's Bay Company first built forts around Hudson Bay and encouraged Indians to bring furs to the posts. But soon, French fur traders based in Montreal began traveling west to secure furs, forcing their British rivals to do the same.

In June 1754, Anthony Henday embarked on a journey up the North Saskatchewan River from York Factory on Hudson Bay, becoming the first white man to enter what is now Alberta on 11 September 1754. He returned to the east the following spring, bringing canoes loaded with furs and providing reports of snowcapped peaks.

In 1787 traders from Montreal formed the North West Company, whose men were known as Norwesters. A year later, Norwester Peter Pond built Fort Chipewyan on Lake Athabasca. It was the first fur-trading post in what is now Alberta. The Hudson's Bay Company built *its* first post in present-day Alberta—Buckingham House—right beside the North West Company's Fort George on the North Saskatchewan River. This practice of moving in right next to the competition—engaged in by both companies—produced a rivalry between the two that continued unabated until they merged in 1821.

Trading posts were scattered over the entire west. Most were of solid log construction and were located beside rivers, the main routes for transportation. Furs were the only reason white man came west for over a century. Traders lived by their own rules and were opposed to settlement, which would have changed their lifestyle. But change was in the wind. In 1857 the British government sent Capt. John Palliser west to Rupert's Land to determine whether the land was fit for agriculture. The Palliser Report, which he prepared upon his return to England, was unfavorable to an area in what is now southern Alberta (an area known as "Palliser Triangle"; see the special topic in the Southern Alberta chapter), but it encouraged settlement to the north.

The Dominion of Canada

By 1867, some of the eastern provinces were tiring of British rule, and a movement was abuzz to push for Canadian independence. The British government, wary of losing Canada as it had lost the U.S., passed legislation establishing the Dominion of Canada. It created a central government with certain powers and delegated other powers to the provinces.

At that time, the North-West Territories, as Rupert's Land had become known, was a foreign land to those in eastern Canada: life was primitive with no laws, and no post had more than a couple of dozen residents. But in an effort to solidify the Dominion, the government bought the North-West Territories back from the Hudson's Bay Company in 1869, even as beaver stock was being depleted and the whiskey trade was having disastrous effects on the native population.

Native animals, such as this moose, were used for more than meat and clothing.

End of an Era

For centuries the buffalo population of the prairies had remained relatively constant. The Indians slaughtered many, but not enough to make a significant impact on total numbers. As beaver populations dwindled, however, traders turned to buffalo hides. Within 10 years, the once-prolific herds had been practically eradicated. Without their traditional food source, the Indians of the plains were weakened and left susceptible to European-borne diseases such as smallpox and scarlet fever. The whiskey trade also took its toll on native populations. Living conditions among the Indians were pitiful and frequent uprisings were taking place.

On 6 June 1874, a band of North West Mounted Police left Toronto under the command of Col. James F. Macleod. Their task was to curb the whiskey trade and restore peace on the western prairies. They built a post on the Oldman River, and within a year, three other posts had been established in what is now southern Alberta.

Facing starvation, many Indian chiefs had no choice but to sign treaties, relegating the tribes to reservations. Chief of all chiefs, Crowfoot, of the powerful Blackfoot Confederacy, signed the first major treaty on 22 September 1877, followed by the chiefs of the Piegans, Stoneys, Sarcees, and Bloods. Their self-sufficiency taken away, the tribes were forced to accept what they were given.

HISTORICAL BOUNDARIES OF ALBERTA

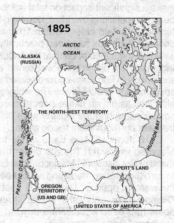

SETTLEMENT

An essential ingredient to the success of settling the west was the construction of a rail line across the continent, replacing canoe and cart routes. This idea was met with scorn by those in the east, who saw it as unnecessary and uneconomical. In 1879 a line reached Winnipeg. After much debate over a route through the Rocky Mountains, the Canadian Pacific Railway line reached Fort Calgary and what is now Banff in 1883. Workers pushed on across the mountains, and on 7 November 1885, the final spike was laid, linking the fledgling province of British Columbia to the rest of the country. A northern route, through Edmonton and Jasper, was completed by the Grand Trunk Railway in 1914.

With two expensive rail lines in place, the government set about putting them to use by settling the land and encouraging tourists to visit the thriving resort towns of Banff and Jasper. The prairies were surveyed and homesteads were offered at $10 per quarter section (160 acres). People from diverse ethnic backgrounds flooded the western prairies, tending to settle in communities of their own people. Life was hard for the early settlers; those in the south found the land dry, while those in the north had to clear land.

The first to take advantage of the extensive grasslands that had once supported millions of bison was Sen. Matthew Cochrane, who in 1881 secured a grazing lease on 100,000 acres west of Calgary. This was the first of many ranches in the foothills, and many herds of cattle were driven to their new homes by American cowboys.

Entering The Confederation

British Columbia had gained provincial status in 1871, four years after the Dominion of Canada was established. But the North-West Territories remained under federal control. It had been divided into districts, of which Alberta—named after Princess Louise Caroline Alberta, the fourth daughter of Queen Victoria—was one. On 1 September 1905, Alberta and Saskatchewan were admitted as provinces of the Canadian Confederation, and Edmonton was named Alberta's capital.

For the years preceding WW I, the new province of Alberta led the way in Canadian agricultural export. But strict controls on wheat prices left many farmers in debt. After the war, the Canadian Wheat Board, later to become the Alberta Wheat Pool, was established to give farmers a fairer price and an incentive to stay on the land. The early 1930s were a time of terrible drought and worldwide depression, both of which hit especially hard in a province dependent almost entirely on agriculture. But again, for the second time in 30 years, war bolstered the economy and agricultural production increased. For 50 years agriculture was Alberta's primary industry and the main attraction for settlers, but this was to change dramatically.

OIL

Arguably the most important date in Canada's industrial history was 13 February 1947. Until that date, small discoveries of oil and gas beneath Alberta had been made, and the modest reserves under Turner Valley constituted the British Empire's largest oil field. But when Leduc Oil Well No. 1 belched black rings of smoke on that cold February morning, Alberta had hit the jackpot. A new economy for Alberta and all of Canada had begun.

American capitalists poured billions of dollars into Alberta as every valley, hill, and flat was surveyed. Seismic cut lines (lines cut through the forests by seismologists charting new oil fields) across northern Alberta are testimony to this frantic period. Early in 1948 a major field at Redwater was tapped and farmers' fields throughout the province were soon littered with beam pumps bobbing up and down. Calgary became the financial and administrative headquarters of the industry, while Edmonton—in the center of a large proportion of the fields—became the technological, service, and supply center.

By 1954 the eight major fields had been proven to contain eight billion barrels of recoverable crude oil; the Leduc-Woodbend field alone had 1,278 wells, and Pembina had 1,700. But nothing came close to the staggering resources of the Athabasca Oil Sands in northern Alberta, where one trillion barrels of oil lay—

WHYTE MUSEUM OF THE CANADIAN ROCKIES

Turner Valley became a hive of activity when oil was discovered there in 1914.

more than all the proven reserves of conventional oil on earth. By 1967 Alberta was producing 67% of Canada's crude oil and 87% of its natural gas.

Each of the major fields needed services, and towns such as Drayton Valley, Swan Hills, High Level, and Rainbow Lake sprang up in otherwise unsettled areas. In less than a decade, the province's population doubled to over one million.

The 1970s

In the early '70s, despite abundant resources and frenzied activity in Alberta, the eastern Canadian provinces were importing oil from overseas—taking advantage of low prices obtained, most notably, from the oil-exporting countries of the Middle East. But then the Arab oil ministers got smart, banding together to form the Organization of Petroleum Exporting Countries (OPEC). OPEC began demanding $6 a barrel—up from under $2—and the price of oil quadrupled within three months. Suddenly, cheap, foreign oil was a thing of the past, and Alberta—after decades of feeling snubbed by the eastern provinces—held a trump card. With enormous reserves of oil, and constitutional control over all of it, Alberta braced itself for the coming boom. The value of the province's petroleum resources tripled almost overnight; within another four years it quadrupled again.

A change in government roughly coinciding with the oil boom also contributed to Alberta's success. For 36 years the agricultural-based Social Credit party had controlled Alberta. But in 1971, the Conservative Party—led by Peter Lougheed—came to power. Lougheed was an uncompromising leader who cared little what the powers in eastern provinces thought of his policies. Described by many as an Albertan sheik, he tripled oil-royalty rates for the province, requiring Alberta's producers to pay the province 65 cents out of every dollar earned from the oil. The federal government refused to allow the oil companies to deduct those royalties on their federal income-tax returns, and many major oil companies pulled out of Alberta. But not for long. Alberta had the goods, and with incentives from the government, the companies returned. It was only a slight hiccup in Lougheed's vision of a new and powerful west.

Revenues were flowing into the provincial coffers at $6,000 per minute, more millionaires were created than at any other time in Canadian history, and Calgary and Edmonton became two of North America's greatest boomtowns and the center of world oil technology. Calgary became the fastest-growing city in the country — a city of dreams, where no expense was spared and to where the power and wealth of eastern provinces moved.

After the Boom

Things have slowed down in Alberta today. The late 1970s to the mid-'90s have been a quiet time. World oil prices steadied in the late '70s, and international oil companies spent money elsewhere. But the boom's impact on the province has been positive and the feeling of a western frontier made good still prevails. The Heritage Savings and Trust Fund—a legacy of Lougheed's days—amassed fortunes in oil royalties to be spent on facilities for the people of Alberta. Kananaskis Country was the most grandiose creation of the fund, while other facilities—interpretive centers, urban park systems, and museums—preserve the province's natural and human history.

Self-made millionaires, who often came from humble beginnings, poured their enormous wealth back into the province that had made them rich. The philanthropies of oilman Eric Harvie—including the Glenbow Foundation, Banff Centre for the Arts, and Calgary Zoo—totaled at least $100 million.

The 1978 Commonwealth Games and 1988 Winter Olympic Games provided boosts to Alberta's economy, but petroleum has remained the province's number-one money earner. With staggering resources still in the ground and a relatively young and well-educated population, the future remains bright.

ECONOMY AND GOVERNMENT

ECONOMY

Alberta's economy has always been closely tied to the land—based first on the fur trade, then agriculture, now on abundant reserves of oil and gas. The province's location away from main trade routes has hindered economic diversity and fostered a boom-or-bust dependence on the land's resources. Without these resources, Alberta's industrial and commercial sectors would collapse. The Alberta Department of Energy promotes effective management of the province's mineral resources and collects royalties for the government. The Energy Resources Conservation Board administers the Conservation Act and regulates the production rate of wells.

Oil

Alberta lies above a vast basin of porous rock containing abundant deposits of oil, natural gas, and coal. The oil in Alberta occurs in three forms: crude oil, heavy oil, and oil sands. Conventional crude oil is recovered through normal drilling methods. More than 5,000 pools have been discovered, but half the oil production comes from just 25 of them. Most of this oil is refined for use as gasoline in cars, diesel for trucks, and heating fuel for homes. Heavy oil is more difficult to extract and its uses limited. But in the future,

as technology improves, recovering Alberta's estimated 300 million barrels of this oil will become viable. Oil sands consist of a tarlike mixture of sand and bitumen that is mined, then refined into synthetic crude for use in fuel products. The Athabasca Oil Sands, near Fort McMurray, are the world's largest such deposit, and Alberta is the world's largest producer of synthetic crude. As conventional crude diminishes, Alberta's heavy oil and oil sands will play

Beam pumps, also called donkey pumps, dot the Albertan landscape.

BRIAN BARDWELL

an increasingly important role in meeting world energy demands.

Natural Gas

Natural gas was first discovered near Medicine Hat in 1883, but it wasn't until 1900 that it was seen as a viable source of energy. The province has always had more gas than it can use (currently proven reserves stand at two trillion cubic feet), and 70% of it is exported, via pipelines to other provinces and the United States. Gas is mostly used for home heating but is also a source material for the petrochemical industry.

Coal

Large deposits of coal were mined early on in Crowsnest Pass, Drumheller, and the foothills, and by the 1920s coal mining had developed into a major industry. Coal was first used to heat homes and provide fuel for steam locomotives, but oil took over those duties in the early 1950s. The industry was revived in 1962 when a coal-fired electric power plant opened at Wabamun, west of Edmonton. This market has since broadened and today Alberta supplies 44% of Canada's coal, of which 70% is used for power production.

Minerals

Industrial, nonmetallic minerals such as limestone, shale, and salt are mined for consumption within Alberta. Sulphur, extracted as a coproduct of natural gas, is exported to the large agricultural markets of the United States, Europe, and Africa, for use in fertilizer. Metallic minerals such as copper, silver, and gold have all been mined at some stage, but compared to other areas of Canada, the province has been poorly explored.

Agriculture

Although oil and gas form the backbone of Alberta's economy, farms and ranches still dominate the landscape. Over 20 million hectares are used for agriculture, over half of them cultivated—a back-breaking job that was started when the first homesteaders moved west. Alberta produces about 20% of Canada's total agricultural output, directly employing 50,000 people in the process. The largest portion of the province's $4 billion annual farm income comes from cattle ($1.2 billion). Alberta has four

million head of beef cattle—just under half of Canada's total—as well as 140,000 dairy cows. The largest crop is wheat, used mainly for bread and pasta. Barley, used for livestock feed and making beer, accounts for over $500 million. The other major crops are canola (recognizable by the bright yellow fields), oats, rye, and flax. The largest areas of vegetable production are east of Lethbridge, where the corn and sugar beet industries thrive.

Forestry

Although 60% of Alberta is forested, the forestry industry makes up only one-tenth of one percent of the province's gross domestic product; current annual harvest is five million cubic meters. The main reason for such a small yield is the slow regrowth rate of the northern forests. The province has 300 sawmills, primarily producing dressed lumber.

Tourism

Tourism is the second-most important industry to the economy, lagging only slightly behind the petroleum industry in revenues but employing twice as many people. The government's Alberta Tourism agency markets the province worldwide as a tourist destination. The government has helped in other ways too, investing millions of dollars of royalties from the oil-and-gas industry into improved facilities, interpretive centers, and the development of Kananaskis Country.

GOVERNMENT

Canada is part of the British Commonwealth, but the monarchy and the elected government of Great Britain have no control over Canada's political affairs. The British monarchy is represented in Canada by a governor general. The country's constitution is based on five important acts of British Parliament, the most recent being the Canada Act of 1982. That act gave Canada the power to amend its constitution, provided for recognition of the nation's multicultural heritage, and most importantly for Alberta, strengthened provincial ownership of natural resources.

The Canadian government operates through three main agencies: the Parliament (made up of the Senate and House of Commons), which makes the laws; the Executive (Cabinet), which applies the laws; and the Judiciary, which interprets the laws. Elections are held every five years, and the leader of whichever political party is voted into power by Canadian citizens becomes the head of government, known as the prime minister. The prime minister then chooses a cabinet of ministers from members of his or her party. Each of the ministers is responsible for the administration of a department.

In Alberta, like the other nine provinces, the monarchy is represented by a lieutenant governor. Like the governor general, the position is mainly ceremonial. The members of the Alberta Legislature are elected on a party system for a maximum of five years. Alberta's three main political parties are the Progressive Conservative, New Democratic, and Liberal parties. The leader of the party in power is known as a premier. With so much control over the province's natural resources and, in turn, Alberta's future, many premiers have enjoyed a particularly high profile. One, Peter Lougheed, initiated the Heritage Savings and Trust Fund, which collected billions of dollars in oil royalties for the people of Alberta.

THE PEOPLE

For thousands of years before the arrival of Europeans to Alberta, several distinct indigenous peoples had lived off the land's abundant natural resources. But with the coming of the white man, the native groups were overrun and reduced in numbers, today making up only about two and a half percent of Alberta's population. The Europeans came in droves—first drawn by game and arable land, later by the oil-and-gas boom. People of many diverse cultures moved west, forming a melting pot of traditions. A census as early as 1921 noted 30 different languages in the province, above and beyond the many distinct languages of the natives. Today Alberta's population, 2,700,000, is the fourth largest among the Canadian provinces and slightly less than 10% of the country's total.

Natives

As natives signed treaties, giving up traditional lands, their lifestyles changed forever. They were no longer free, they no longer hunted or fought,

a Stoney family, photographed by Mary Schäffer in 1907

WHYTE MUSEUM OF THE CANADIAN ROCKIES

their medicine men could do nothing to stop the spread of the white man's diseases, and slowly they lost their pride. Today, 64,000 "status" Indians live in Alberta, approximately 60% of them on reservations. Alberta has 93 Indian reserves covering 6,598 square km. The largest is a Blood reserve near Fort Macleod covering 136,760 hectares. Other major reserves include the Stoney reserve at Morley, Sarcee reserve near Calgary, Blackfoot reserve at Gleichen, and the Piegan reserve at Brocket. The reservations are administered by Indian and Northern Affairs Canada. Most of the 41 bands are governed by a chief, elected for two years. Only three, all in the northern half of the province, are governed by a chief elected for life.

Many reserves generate revenue from natural resources, and some bands have become wealthy owning factories, housing developments, and, in the case of the Sarcee near Bragg Creek, a golf course. A biweekly magazine focuses on native issues in the province. For subscription information, write to *Windspeaker*, 15001 112th Ave., Edmonton, AB T5M 2V6; or call (403) 455-2700.

Nonnatives

In the last 100 years, Alberta has seen a great influx of people from around the world. The Dominion census of 1881 recorded only 18,072 nonnatives in the province; Calgary had a population of only 75. The French, predominantly fur traders and missionaries, were the first permanent settlers and today make up the fourth-largest ethnic group in the province. The first Asians to settle in the province were Chinese who came seeking gold in the 1860s and later settled, took up trades, and opened businesses.

One of the largest migrant influxes occurred between 1901 and 1906, when the Canadian government was selling tracts of land to homesteaders for $10. During this time the population increased from 73,000 to 185,400; in another five years it doubled again. A large percentage of settlers during this period were British, and it is this group that today makes up Alberta's largest ethnic group. Germans also migrated to Alberta for a variety of reasons and today make up the province's second-largest ethnic group. Many were lured by cheap land. Others, such as Hutterites, were persecuted in their homeland for refusing to do military service. Hutterites have become the most successful of all ethnic groups at working the land. They live a self-sufficient lifestyle in tight-knit communities throughout southern and central Alberta. Ukrainians make up the third-largest ethnic group. They were also attracted by the province's agricultural potential, and today over 130,000 residents of Ukrainian descent live mostly in Edmonton and to the east.

The oil-and-gas boom brought a population explosion similar to that of 1901-06, but this time, with one exception, the immigrants came from eastern provinces rather than from other countries. The exception was a wave of Americans, whose oil business acumen and technological know-how were vital to the burgeoning industry.

In the lead-up to the 1 January 1997 transfer of Hong Kong to the People's Republic of China, Canada saw a significant influx of immigrants from Hong Kong. Although Vancouver and Toronto have the largest Chinese communities in the country, those of both Edmonton and Calgary grew during this period. Calgary has a thriving pan-Asian population of about 50,000-60,000, and the pride of the city's Chinese community is well evidenced by such facilities as the Chinese Cultural Centre.

KAREN McKINLEY

ON THE ROAD
RECREATION

PARKS

Alberta has five national parks, 62 provincial parks, four wilderness areas, a wilderness park, a forest reserve covering much of the foothills, over 200 ecological reserves and natural areas, and one historic park. Combined, they encompass all the province's most spectacular natural features, are home to a large proportion of Alberta's mammals, provide safe nesting areas for millions of birds, and protect areas that would otherwise be given over to agriculture or other resource-based industry.

Banff National Park is the jewel of the Canadian national parks system, although **Waterton Lakes,** to the south, and **Jasper,** to the north, are equally beautiful mountain parks. The others are **Elk Island National Park,** where mammal densities are similar to the Serengeti Plains, and **Wood Buffalo National Park,** second-largest national park in the world,

accessible by road only through the Northwest Territories. A Great Western Pass, valid for all 11 Alberta and British Columbia national parks, is $35 per person to a maximum of $70 per vehicle.

Provincial parks, widespread throughout Alberta, provide ample opportunities to explore the province's varied natural habitat. All the parks provide day-use facilities or campgrounds. Those not to miss are: **Writing-On-Stone Provincial Park,** so named for the abundant native rock art; **Dinosaur Provincial Park,** a UNESCO World Heritage Site with one of the world's highest concentrations of dinosaur bones; and **Cypress Hills Provincial Park,** a forested oasis that rises from the prairies.

Wilderness areas are located high in Alberta's Rockies. None has road access and all are in remote locations, perfect for wilderness trips for those with backcountry experience. From south to north they are **Ghost River, Siffleur, White Goat,** and **Willmore.**

OUTDOOR ACTIVITIES

The great outdoors is one of Alberta's prime attractions, and a diverse array of activities is available to those who seek them out. The mountains are center of most activity. Raft and canoe tours operate on many mountain rivers, and the vast wilderness provides virtually limitless opportunities for camping, photography, and wildlife viewing. The national parks are a mecca for hikers and climbers in summer, downhill and cross-country skiers in winter. Fishing is good in almost all lakes and rivers in the province, while golfers can enjoy over 220 courses. A comprehensive listing of all outfitters and tour operators is available from Alberta Tourism Partnership, P.O. Box 2400, Edmonton, AB T5J 2Z4, tel. (403) 427-4321 or (800) 661-8888.

Hiking
It's no wonder that hiking is the most popular outdoor activity in Alberta—it's free, anyone can participate, and the mountains offer some of the world's most spectacular scenery. **Banff National Park** holds the greatest variety of trails in the province. Here you can find anything from short interpretive trails with little elevation gain to strenuous slogs up high alpine passes. Trailheads for most of the best hikes are accessible by public transportation or on foot from the town of Banff. Those farther north begin at higher elevations, from which access to the high country is less painful. The trails in **Jasper National Park** are oriented more toward the experienced backpacker, offering plentiful routes for long backcountry trips. Other areas popular for hiking are **Kananaskis Country,** where crowds are minimal; **Waterton Lakes National Park,** where many trails lead to beautiful subalpine lakes; and the province's four wilderness areas, remote mountain regions accessible only on foot.

Some out-of-the-ordinary companies based at the helipad in Canmore offer **heli-hiking** packages. The day starts with a helicopter ride into the alpine, where short, guided hikes are offered and a picnic lunch is served. For details contact **Alpine Helicopters,** tel. (403) 678-4802, or **Assiniboine Heli Tours,** tel. (403) 678-5459. Another option is hiking into backcountry lodges. The **Alpine Club of Canada,** P.O. Box 2040,

Canmore, AB T0L 0M0, tel. (403) 678-3200, maintains a series of huts, each generally a full-day hike from the nearest road. And Banff National Park has a number of privately owned backcountry lodges—great bases for day-hiking—where on-site hosts provide hot meals; rates start at $95 per person per day including meals. Hikers must register at park information centers for all overnight hikes in national parks.

Topographic maps aren't required for the hikes detailed in this book, but they provide an interesting way to identify natural features. For extended hiking in the backcountry they are vital. Several series of maps, in different scales, cover the entire province. You can purchase them from park information centers, some bookstores, and specialty map shops in Calgary and Edmonton.

Cycling
Alberta is perfect for both road biking and mountain biking. On-road cyclists will appreciate the wide shoulders on all main highways, while those on mountain bikes will enjoy the many designated trails in the mountain national parks. One of the most challenging and scenic on-road routes is the **Icefields Parkway** between Lake Louise and Jasper, which has a number of well-placed hostels along its length.

Most large bookstores stock copies of cycling publications. Also, the **Alberta Bicycle Association** represents all touring clubs in the province and can provide further information. Write to 11759 Groat Rd., Edmonton, AB T5M 3K6, or call (403) 453-8518.

Tour operators include **Rocky Mountain Cycle Tours,** P.O. Box 1978, Canmore, AB T0L 0M0, tel. (403) 678-6770 or (800) 661-2453, which offers guided trips through the Rockies; and **Canusa Cycle Tours,** P.O. Box 45, Okotoks, AB T0L 1T0, tel. (403) 560-8959 or (800) 938-7986, whose three-day tour along the Icefields Parkway costs $270, including campground fees, all meals, and use of a back-up van.

Horseback Riding
Horses are a traditional means of transportation in the Canadian West; many of the main hiking trails began as horse trails. Within national parks, horse travel is restricted to certain areas. And horse-packing guide companies are

also limited; many of them have been operating since before the parks were established. Outside the parks, riding is available at many ranches and outfitting operations in the foothills and at **Grande Cache.** Major operators include **Brewster Mountain Pack Trains,** P.O. Box 964, Banff, AB T0L 0C0, tel. (403) 762-5454 or (800) 691-5085; **Holiday on Horseback,** P.O. Box 2280, Banff, AB T0L 0C0, tel. (403) 762-4551; **Skyline Trail Rides,** P.O. Box 207, Jasper, AB T0E 1E0, tel. (403) 852-4215; and **Wild Rose Outfitting,** P.O. Box 113, Peers, AB T0E 1W0, tel. (403) 693-2296. For a full list, see the back of *Alberta Accommodation and Visitors' Guide,* available at information centers throughout the province or by calling (800) 661-8888.

Rafting, Kayaking, and Canoeing

Canoeing, like horseback riding, has long been a form of transportation in the province, going back to the days of the voyageurs. Qualified guides operate on major whitewater rivers such as the **Maligne River** in Jasper National Park, offering the biggest thrills, and the **Kicking Horse River,** on the British Columbia side of the Rockies. Guides also operate on larger, quieter rivers such as **Milk River,** through Writing-On-Stone Provincial Park; **Red Deer River,** through the foothills or badlands; **Athabasca River,** in Jasper National Park; and **Bow River,** in Banff National Park. Extended trips are possible along the Peace and Athabasca Rivers in the northern part of the province, but any wilder-

ness trips should be attempted only by those with experience.

Canoeing provides an unparalleled opportunity for viewing wildlife around lakes that would otherwise be inaccessible. Most provincial parks with lake systems offer canoe rentals. The book *Canoeing Alberta,* by Lone Pine Publishing (currently out of print but most libraries have a copy), is the best source of information on all canoe routes.

Rocky Mountain Paddling Centre, P.O. Box 34140, Calgary, AB T3C 2W2, tel. (403) 651-4849, offers more than a dozen different courses in all aspects of canoeing and kayaking year-round. In Calgary, their office is in Totem Outdoor Outfitters at 341 10th Ave. SW, tel. (403) 266-1527.

Fishing

Fishing is productive in almost all Alberta's lakes, rivers, and streams, and the fly-fishing on the Bow and Crowsnest Rivers is world renowned. Many lakes are stocked annually with a variety of trout. Although fishing is good throughout the province, northern Alberta is the destination of most dedicated anglers.

Fishing licenses are required for all fishing in the province. Licenses are available at Natural Resource Service offices (Mon.-Fri. only) and many sporting and hardware stores. An annual license for Alberta residents ages 16-64 is $18; for nonresidents it is $36, or $24 for a five-day license. A sturgeon license is an extra $5. The *Al-*

WILD WATER ADVENTURES

Whitewater rafting is an exciting way to enjoy mountain scenery.

berta Guide to Sportfishing, which outlines all the open seasons and bag limits, and has a handy identification chart, is available from outlets selling licenses, or by writing to Natural Resource Services, Alberta Environmental Protection, Main Floor, North Tower, Petroleum Plaza, 9945 108th St., Edmonton, AB T5K 2G6.

Fishing in national parks requires a separate license, available from park offices and some sport shops; $6 for a seven-day license, $13 for an annual license.

Climbing and Mountaineering

The Canadian Rockies are a mecca for those experienced in mountain sports. The main centers of activity are Kananaskis Country and Banff and Jasper National Parks. **Canmore** is the self-proclaimed capital, with many skilled mountaineers in town offering instruction and guiding services. Experienced climbers should gather as much information as possible before attempting any unfamiliar routes; quiz locals, hang out at climbing stores, and contact park information centers. For further information contact Parks Canada, Information Services, Room 552, 220 4th Ave. SE, Calgary, AB T2G 4X3.

For the inexperienced, the Rockies are the perfect place to learn to climb. Climbing schools are located in Canmore, Banff, and Jasper. Each offers personalized instruction, courses, and mountain guiding for all levels of ability. **Canadian School of Mountaineering,** P.O. Box 723, Canmore, AB T0L 0M0, tel. (403) 678-4134, offers mountaineering, rock-climbing, and ice-climbing courses as well as guided summit attempts on nearby peaks. **Ascent** is a group of highly qualified guides offering basic climbing courses through summer and guided ascents of peaks through the Rockies. Write Ascent, P.O. Box 1624, Canmore, AB T0L 0M0, tel. (403) 678-2815.

Golfing

With beautiful scenery, long sunny days, over 220 courses, and a golfing season that extends from April to October, Alberta is a golfer's hole-in-one. Getting a game can be difficult on city courses, especially on weekends. Rates range from $5 a round on the smaller municipal courses to $90 in the national parks. Outside of Edmonton and Calgary most courses are public

or semiprivate, and getting a game, with advance reservations, isn't a problem.

The best courses are: **Banff Springs Golf Course,** tel. (403) 762-6801, a 27-hole championship course strung out along the Bow River and rated one of the world's most scenic; **Jasper Park Lodge Golf Course,** tel. (403) 852-6090, a challenging par-73 course surrounded by spectacular mountain scenery; **Kananaskis Country Golf Course,** tel. (403) 591-7272, a 36-hole, Robert Trent Jones–designed course built in the 1980s at a cost of $1 million per hole; and **Wolf Creek Golf Resort,** tel. (403) 783-6050, an oasis on the prairies between Calgary and Edmonton.

Scuba Diving

Being landlocked, Alberta is not renowned for scuba diving. A few interesting opportunities do exist, however, and rentals are available in Lethbridge, Calgary, and Edmonton. The old townsite of **Minnewanka Landing,** in Banff National Park, has been flooded, and although a relatively deep dive, the site is interesting. **Patricia Lake,** in Jasper National Park, has a sunken WW II barge, and due to the high altitude and clear water, visibility is exceptional. Another sunken boat is located at the bottom of Emerald Bay in Waterton National Park. Nearby are some wagons that fell through ice many winters ago. For a list of dive shops and sites contact Alberta Underwater Council, 11759 Groat Rd., Edmonton, AB T5M 3K6, tel. (403) 453-8566.

Downhill Skiing

Six world-class ski areas are perched among the high peaks of Alberta's Rockies. The largest, and also Canada's largest, is **Lake Louise,** overlooking the lake of the same name in Banff National Park. The area boasts 1,500 hectares of skiing on four distinct faces, with wide-open bowls and runs for all abilities. Banff's other two resorts are **Sunshine Village,** sitting on the Continental Divide and accessible only by gondola, and **Banff Mt. Norquay,** a resort with heart-pounding runs overlooking the town of Banff. Just outside Banff in Kananaskis Country is **Nakiska at Mt. Allan,** a resort developed especially for the downhill events of the 1988 Winter Olympic Games. Nearby **Fortress Mountain** is in a spectacular location and has runs for

The skiing is legendary in the Canadian Rockies.

all abilities. **Marmot Basin,** in Jasper National Park, has minimal crowds with a maximum variety of terrain.

Nearly 50 other ski hills are scattered through the province, most with less than a 200-meter vertical drop. One area unique for its proximity to the city center is the **Edmonton Ski Club** hill in the North Saskatchewan River Valley, overlooking downtown Edmonton. **Canada Olympic Park,** within Calgary city limits, was built for the 1988 Winter Olympic Games and maintains some of the world's finest ski-jumping facilities. Most major resorts begin opening in early December and close in May or, in the case of Sunshine Village, early June.

Other Winter Activities
Many hiking trails provide ideal routes for **cross-country skiing,** and many are groomed for that purpose. The largest concentration of groomed trails is in Kananaskis Country. Other areas are Banff, Jasper, and Waterton National Parks, the urban parks of Calgary and Edmonton, and the many provincial parks scattered through the province. Anywhere you can cross-country ski you can **snowshoe,** a traditional from of winter transportation that is making a comeback. **Ice fishing** for whitefish and burbot is good in all major rivers and those lakes large enough not to freeze to the bottom. **Sleigh rides** are offered in Banff, Lake Louise, and Jasper.

Winter travel brings its own set of potential hazards such as hypothermia, avalanches, frost-bite, and sunburn. Necessary precautions should be taken. All park information centers can provide information on hazards and advise on current weather conditions.

ENTERTAINMENT

Museums
The best way to gain insight into Alberta's natural and human history is to visit one of its many museums. Not all are the crowded, stuffy kind, and many of the best are outside the cities. The **Royal Tyrrell Museum of Palaeontology,** located in the dinosaur-rich badlands of the Red Deer River Valley, is the largest paleontological museum in the world. Inside you'll find over 50 full-size dinosaurs on display. If you only visit one museum in Alberta, make it this one. Other major museums include the **Provincial Museum of Alberta** in Edmonton; **Glenbow Museum** in Calgary; **Remington-Alberta Carriage Centre** at Cardston, which houses over 200 carriages, buggies, and wagons; and the **Reynolds-Alberta Museum** on the outskirts of Wetaskiwin, which catalogs the history of machinery in western Canada.

Performing Arts
For a province that prides itself on a Western heritage, Alberta has a surprising number of cultural diversions. Edmonton alone has a dozen professional theater companies, equal to any

Calgarian Wilf Carter, better known as "Montana Slim," was a country-music superstar in the 1930s.

WHYTE MUSEUM OF THE CANADIAN ROCKIES

North American city of comparable size. Both Edmonton and Calgary have ballet troupes, an orchestra, and opera.

Country Music

For most of this century, singers and songwriters have found inspiration in the ranching lifestyle and mountain scenery of Alberta. In the 1930s, **Wilf Carter,** a cowboy by trade, began singing on Calgary radio. Within three years he had become a star in the United States as "Montana Slim," the yodeling cowboy. More recently **k.d. lang,** of Consort, has become a country superstar with Grammy-winning albums pushing the boundaries of country music toward pop. **George Fox** and **Ian Tyson,** who both have ranches west of Calgary, also have made their mark on Canadian country music. Most recently, **Terri Clark,** from Medicine Hat, and **Paul Brant,** of Calgary, have hit the big time south of the border. Large outdoor concerts that run over a number of days are popular venues for country music in Alberta. The biggest of these are the **Big Valley Jamboree** at Camrose and the **Bud Country Jamboree** at Lethbridge.

Nightlife

Although most cities have dance clubs and rock 'n' roll discos, it's in the Western bars that Alberta's heritage lives on. Bars like **Ranchman's,** which has a chuck wagon hanging from the roof, **Cowboy's,** and **Rockin' Horse Saloon** in Calgary; **Cook County Saloon** and **Mustang Saloon** in Edmonton; and **Wild Bill's Legendary Saloon** in Banff keep the Western image alive.

Spectator Sports

The **ice hockey** season may be only seven months long, but to fans of the Edmonton Oilers and Calgary Flames—Alberta's National Hockey League (NHL) teams—it's a year-round obsession. The best seats are taken by die-hard season-ticket holders, but for $15-60 you can usually score tickets through Ticketmaster a few days in advance. Both cities also have professional Canadian Football League (CFL) teams and AAA Pacific Coast League baseball teams.

SHOPPING

Arts and Crafts

The arts and crafts of Canada's indigenous people are available throughout the province. Jewelry, beaded moccasins, baskets, and leatherwork such as headdresses are favorite souvenirs. The stylistic art of the native people is also popular, but prints of the most recognizable works run into thousands of dollars. Two of the best outlets are the **Indian Trading Post** in Banff and **Northern Images** in West Edmonton Mall.

Western Wear

You don't have to be able to ride a horse to dress like a cowboy—just ask the thousands of city folk who dress the part for the Calgary Exhibition and Stampede. Major department stores are the best places to find the basic Western accessories, while specialty shops are the places to go for gear that the real cowboys wear. Most of the latter sell handmade jewelry, authentic Stetsons, belt buckles big enough to fry an egg on, and hundreds of pairs of boots in every style imaginable.

FESTIVALS AND EVENTS

Spring

The year's first major event for cowboys is the **Rodeo Royal,** held at Calgary's Saddledome in March, followed the next weekend by the **Spring Outdoor Rodeo** in Medicine Hat and in April the **Silver Buckle Rodeo** in Red Deer. The annual spring migration of birds through the province is celebrated during the Tofield **Snow Goose Festival** through April. Calgary hosts an **International Children's Festival** in May, with a wide variety of events for the younger generation. Alberta's ski resorts usually have snow on the ground until late spring, and many ski resorts hold major events at season's end. Sunshine

Village hosts **Dummy Downhill** the first Saturday in May ends the season with its **Slush Cup.**

Summer

Summer is the biggest event season in Alberta. Edmonton hosts a major festival just about every weekend, and there's almost always something going on in the rest of the province.

The **Alberta Cowboy Poetry Gathering** comes to Pincher Creek in June . . . hear cowpokes read poems by the light of the, uh, stars? Stars of another type come to perform at the **Calgary International Jazz Festival,** in late June. The festival draws famous jazz musicians from around the world.

Canada Day, 1 July, is a national holiday celebrated in many towns with various events, often including a rodeo (Ponoka hosts the largest of the weekend's rodeos). Vegreville celebrates its multicultural past on this weekend with the **Ukrainian Folk Festival.**

The best-known of Alberta's events is the **Calgary Stampede,** the world's richest rodeo with 10 days of action and a winner-take-all format. This Western extravaganza is a not-to-be-missed event that takes place in early July. Equestrian events of a very different kind take place throughout summer just down the road from Stampede Park at **Spruce Meadows,** one of the world's finest international riding centers. The first event on the calendar, in early June, is the **National,** a showjumping competition attracting thousands of enthusiasts.

What's a parade without a local show band?

In early July, the **Edmonton International Street Performers Festival** offers over 1,000 free performances at outdoor venues throughout the city, while Lethbridge's **Whoop-Up Days** celebrates that city's past.

Late July brings **Edmonton's Klondike Days,** a celebration centered around the city's tenuous connection to the Yukon goldfields; the **Edmonton Heritage Festival,** a celebration of days gone by; and the big **Medicine Hat Exhibition and Stampede,** held annually since 1887. Calgary hosts a **Folk Music Festival** in July, and the month ends on a high note with the **Red Deer International Air Show** on the last weekend, featuring performances by some of the world's best stunt pilots. Meanwhile, the air over Grande Prairie is also alive with color when one of many **hot air balloon championships** takes place.

The **Edmonton Folk Music Festival** picks and strums its way into town in early August; the city's **Fringe Theatre Event** in mid-August is centered around Old Strathcona, with performances of alternative theater from throughout North America. Calgary's cultural festivals are low-profile affairs compared to those in Edmonton, but the city does offer the **International Native Arts Festival** in August.

Fall

Just when all the summer festivals are winding down, the action at Spruce Meadows equestrian center, outside Calgary, is heating up. **Spruce Meadows Masters** is the world's richest showjumping event and the finale to a packed season. Also in Calgary is a large **antique show** in September. In late fall, the mountain ski resorts begin opening and Banff hosts **Winterstart,** a six-week period of cheap deals and events held throughout the town. The first weekend of November is the **Banff Festival of Mountain Films,** a gathering of the world's greatest adventure-film makers.

Winter

Most Albertan towns and cities have **winter carnivals** featuring weird and wonderful events that only people affected by the long winter could dream up. The largest ones, each lasting two weeks, are in Calgary, Banff, Jasper, and Edmonton; all are in January. The one in Canmore, in late January, is held in conjunction with the **Alberta Sled Dog Championship. First Night** is an alcohol-free celebration of the New Year that takes place in downtown Calgary, Edmonton, and Banff.

Ankylosaurus

BOB RACE

ACCOMMODATIONS AND FOOD

Hotels and Motels

Hotels and motels of some sort exist in just about every Albertan town. They range from substandard road motels advertising "Color TV" to sublime resorts high in the Rocky Mountains. The only time you'll have a problem finding a room is in Calgary during Stampede Week and in the national parks in July and August. In both cases plan ahead or be prepared to camp. Accommodation prices in Banff and Jasper National Parks are slashed by as much as 70% outside summer. In cities always ask for the best rate available and check local tourist literature for discount coupons. Rates are usually lower on weekends. All rates quoted in this handbook are for the cheapest category of rooms during the most expensive time period (summer). To all rates quoted you must add the seven percent Goods and Services Tax (GST) and five percent provincial room tax. The former is refundable to nonresidents of the province (keep receipts).

In many towns, you'll find older-style hotels where bathrooms are shared, the phone is in the lobby, and check-in is at the bar. Rooms are generally sparsely furnished, and what furniture there is dates to the 1960s. Expect to pay from $18 s, $25 d for shared bathroom, and a few bucks more for a private bathroom. ·

Park-at-your-door, single-story road motels are located in all towns and on the outskirts of all major cities. In most cases rooms are fine, but check before paying, just to make sure. Most have a few rooms with kitchenettes, but these fill fast. In the smaller towns expect to pay $25-40 s, $30-50 d.

Most major towns and all cities have larger hotels, each of which typically has a restaurant, cafe, lounge, and pool. At these establishments expect to pay from $50 s, $55 d for a basic room. Downtown hotels in Calgary and Edmonton begin at $70. A good deal can be suites or executive suites, with kitchenettes and one or two bedrooms for little more money than a regular room.

Finding inexpensive lodging in the mountain national parks is difficult in summer. By late afternoon the only rooms left will be in the more expensive categories and by nightfall all of these

will go. Hotel rooms in Banff begin around $100; those in Jasper and Waterton are a little less. For a list of all hotels and motels in the province, pick up a copy of *Alberta Accommodation and Visitors' Guide,* available from tourist information centers or by calling (800) 661-8888. This guide is also on CD-Rom, available through the **Alberta Hotel Association,** Centre 401, 5421 Calgary Trail, Edmonton, AB T6H 5G8, tel. (403) 436-6112 or 436-5404.

Bed and Breakfasts

The bed and breakfast phenomenon is well-entrenched in Alberta. Hosts are generally well-informed local people and rooms are cozy. The establishments are often moneymaking ventures so don't expect the bargains of European bed and breakfasts. The best way to find out about individual lodging is from local tourist information centers or listings in the back of the *Alberta Accommodation and Visitors' Guide.* Major bed and breakfast associations are: **Alberta's Gem B&B Reservation Agency,** 11216 48th Ave., Edmonton, AB T6H 0C7, tel. (403) 434-6098, which has listings throughout the province; **B&B Association of Calgary,** 6016 Thornburn Dr. NW, Calgary, AB T2K 3P7, tel. (403) 531-0065, listing homes in Calgary and surrounding areas; **Canada West Accommodations,** P.O. Box 86607, North Vancouver, BC V7L 4L2, tel. (604) 929-1424, offering accommodations in Calgary, Edmonton, and the Rockies; and **Edmonton B&B,** 13824 110A Ave., Edmonton, AB T5M 2M9, tel. (403) 455-2297, which books homes in that city.

Backcountry Huts and Lodges

Scattered through the backcountry of Banff and Jasper National Parks are huts maintained by the Alpine Club of Canada. The huts are rustic—typically bunk beds, a woodstove, wooden dining table, and an outhouse. Reservations should be made in advance by contacting the Alpine Club of Canada, P.O. Box 2040, Canmore, AB T0L 0M0, tel. (403) 678-3200. Banff National Park has two privately operated backcountry lodges, **Shadow Lake Lodge,** northwest of Banff, and **Skoki Lodge,** east of Lake Louise

Banff Springs Hotel

(see the Banff National Park chapter for more information). Both require some degree of effort to reach—either by hiking or on horseback in summer, or by cross-country skiing in winter. The lodges are typically eight to 15 km from the nearest road. Rates begin at $95 per person including three meals. Neither has television, but both have running water and a congenial atmosphere.

Backpacker Lodges
Hostelling International–Alberta operates 16 hostels in the province. They are located in Calgary, Edmonton, the town of Banff, at Lake Louise, all along the Icefields Parkway (which runs through Banff and Jasper National Parks), in the town of Jasper, in Kananaskis Country, and in the towns of Coleman, Drumheller, and Nordegg. All are accessible by road, and all but the Nordegg hostel are accessible by public transportation. During busy periods males and females have separate dormitories. A sheet or sleeping bag is required although these can usually be rented. All are equipped with a kitchen and lounge room, and some have laundries. Those in Banff and Lake Louise are world-class, with hundreds of beds as well as libraries and cafes. The five rustic hostels along the Icefields Parkway are evenly spaced, perfect for a bike trip along one of the world's great mountain highways. Rates for members are $9-17 per night, nonmembers $14-21. Whenever you can, make reservations in advance, especially in summer. The easiest way to do this is through Hostelling

International's **International Booking Network** (I.B.N.) or by contacting the individual hostel. Staying in hostels is an especially good bargain for skiers; packages including accommodation and a day pass at a local ski resort start at $43.

If you plan to travel extensively using hostels, join Hostelling International before you leave home. In the U.S. write to American International Hostels, Inc., 133 1st St. NW, Suite 800, Washington, DC 20005. In Canada contact Hostelling International–Canada, 333 River Rd., Vanier City, ON K1L 8B9, tel. (800) 668-4487. Membership in Canada is $26.75 for one year or $37 for two years.

Hostel Shops sell memberships and reasonably priced camping gear. They also provide general travel information, and can book air, bus, and train trips for you. You'll find the shops in Edmonton at 10926 88th Ave., tel. (403) 432-3089, and in Calgary at 1414 Kensington Rd. NW, tel. (403) 283-5551.

The **YMCA** and **YWCA** are other inexpensive lodging alternatives, often with prime locations. Calgary has a YWCA for women only; Banff has a YWCA open to both sexes, with some family rooms; Edmonton has one of each. Rates begin at $15 per night with reasonable weekly rates available.

Campgrounds
Spending some money on a reliable tent and sleeping bag quickly pays off wherever you are traveling, but especially so in many parts of Al-

berta. Calgary has a half dozen campgrounds spread around its outskirts, Edmonton has one near downtown, and most towns have a **municipal campground**. These range in price from free to $16 depending on facilities and location. Often those in smaller towns are a bargain—it's not uncommon to pay less than $10 for a site with hookups and hot showers. Except in major cities, reservations aren't necessary—just roll up and pay the campground host or use the honor box. Most **provincial parks** have a campground; prices are $7-15 depending on facilities available. Some have hookups, showers, boat rentals, and occasionally laundry facilities. Throughout the foothills are **Forest Service campgrounds,** which have pit toilets, picnic tables, and a supply of firewood. Most are accessed along the Forestry Trunk Road. Each of Alberta's **national parks** has excellent campgrounds. At least one campground in each park has hot showers and full hookups. Prices are $7-19. All national park campgrounds operate on a first-come, first-served basis and often fill by midday in July and August. Banff, Jasper, and Waterton have winter camping but with limited facilities. Backcountry camping in all national parks is $6 per person per night. Before heading out you must register at the respective park information center. Most campgrounds in the backcountry have pit toilets, and some have bear bins for secure food storage. Fires are discouraged so bring a stove.

FOOD AND DRINK

The best way to eat cheap is with a campstove. Those made by Coleman are the most reliable.

Most urban campgrounds discourage open fires, and many provincial and national parks charge $3-5 for firewood. The two largest supermarkets, Safeway and I.G.A., generally have the least expensive groceries, but prices are still higher than in the United States. In most I.G.A. stores you'll find an excellent bakery.

Although Alberta isn't renowned for its culinary delights, the staple of the province—Alberta beef—is delicious and is served in most restaurants. For a three-course meal in a family-style restaurant, including a steak dish, expect to pay $20-25 per person—double that in the better eateries. Edmonton, Calgary, and Banff have an astonishing array of ethnic restaurants with the last, a town of 7,000, having over 100 restaurants. Inexpensive options are Husky restaurants, located in gas stations of the same name along all major routes. Their portions are generous, prices are good, and they're open 24 hours. Calgary and Edmonton also have a number of excellent buffets where an all-you-can eat Chinese or Western meal is $5-7 for lunch and $8-11 for dinner.

Drink

Calgary and Edmonton each have specialty brewers who brew boutique beers for sale in the immediate area. Alberta's largest homegrown brewery is **Big Rock** in Calgary. The Banff Springs Hotel has a beer bottled for itself, available only in Banff. The province's only winery is west of Edmonton.

The minimum age for alcohol consumption in Alberta is 18. From the United States, visitors may bring 1.1 liters of liquor or wine or 24 cans or bottles of beer into Canada free of duty.

TRANSPORTATION

GETTING THERE

Air

Calgary and Edmonton have international airports served by major airlines from throughout the world. Many flights from the south are routed through Calgary before continuing to Edmonton, giving you a choice of final destinations for little or no price difference. **Canadian,** based at Calgary International Airport, is one of the world's largest airlines, serving five continents. It offers direct flights to Calgary from all major Canadian cities, as well as from Seattle, Los Angeles, San Francisco, Reno, Las Vegas, Phoenix, Chicago, Boston, Washington, Dallas/Fort Worth, New York, Atlanta, and St. Louis. From Europe, Canadian flights from London are direct while those from Paris, Frankfurt, and Rome are routed through Toronto. From Australia and the South Pacific, Canadian operates in alliance with Qantas and Air New Zealand, which fly passengers to Honolulu where they change to Canadian. Asian cities, served in conjunction with Malaysian, include Bangkok, Kuala Lumpur, Hong Kong, Taipei, Nagoya, Beijing, and Tokyo. Canadian's flights originating in the South American cities of Santiago, Buenos Aires, Sao Paulo, and Rio de Janeiro are routed through Toronto. For further information on Canadian's routes and schedules call (800) 665-1177 in Canada, (800) 426-7000 in the U.S., and (081) 577-7722 in Great Britain.

Air Canada also offers flights from all major Canadian cities as well as nonstop service from Los Angeles and San Francisco. The only Air Canada nonstop international flights to Alberta originate in London. All other European flights are routed through Toronto, and those from Asia and the South Pacific through Vancouver. For information on Air Canada flights, call (800) 332-1080, (800) 776-3000 in the U.S., or (081) 759-2331 in London.

U.S. carriers offering service to Calgary are: **American Airlines,** tel. (800) 443-7300; **Delta Air Lines,** tel. (800) 221-1212; and **United Airlines,** tel. (800) 241-6522. Edmonton is served by American, Delta, and **Northwest Airlines,** tel. (800) 225-2525. Other international carriers serving the province include **Air New Zealand, Alitalia, Japan Airlines, KLM,** and **Qantas.**

Cutting Flight Costs

Ticket structuring for international air travel is so complex that often even travel agents have problems coming to grips with it. The first step when planning your trip to Alberta is to contact the airlines that fly there and ask for the best price they have for the time of year you wish to travel. Then shop around the travel agencies—you should be able to save 30-50% of the price you were quoted by the airline. Check the Sunday travel section of most newspapers for an idea of current discount prices. Many cheaper tickets have strict restrictions regarding changes of flight dates, lengths of stay, and cancellations. A general rule is: the cheaper the ticket, the more restrictions in place. Apart from airline promotional fares, consolidators—bucket shops as they are commonly called—consistently offer the lowest airfares. Once prevalent only in Asian cities such as Singapore and Bangkok and in the popular European travel hubs, this form of travel agent is now common throughout the world. They buy blocks of seats on scheduled flights that airlines decide they wouldn't normally be able to sell, then either sell them directly to the public or to other travel agents. Within Canada, **Travel Cuts,** with offices in all major cities, consistently offers the lowest airfares available. Within the U.S., one of the largest consolidators is **Unitravel,** tel. (800) 325-2222. In London, **Trailfinders,** 194 Kensington High St., London W8 7RG, tel. (071) 938-3232, always has good deals to Canada and other North American destinations.

Rail

VIA Rail provides transcontinental rail service from coast to coast. This form of transportation, which opened up the West to settlers and the Rocky Mountains to tourists, began to fade with the advent of efficient air services. Scheduled services to Calgary ended in 1991; the remaining transcontinental route passes through Edmonton and Jasper. The **Canadian,** as this train is known, operates three days a week in either direction and provides four classes of travel: **Coach, Manor** or **Chateau Sleeping-car,** and **Silver and Blue.** Silver and Blue class is the most luxurious, providing extra amenities and use of a dome car reserved exclusively for passengers in this class. Discounts of 25% (40% if booked seven days in advance) apply to travel Oct.-June (applicable to all classes). Those over 60 and under 25 receive a 10% discount which can be combined with other seasonal fares. Check for advance purchase restrictions on all discount tickets.

The **Canrailpass** allows unlimited travel anywhere on the VIA Rail system for 13 days within any given 30-day period. During high season (15 May-15 Sept.) the pass is $535, $365 the rest of the year. Extra days are $42 and $27 respectively. Even if you plan limited train travel, the pass is an excellent deal—but remember, if you travel on a service that, say, departs at 10 p.m. and arrives at 2 a.m., it counts as two days of travel); the regular Toronto-Edmonton one-way fare alone is $375.57. For VIA Rail information and reservations in western Canada call (800) 561-8630; for other Canadian locations contact your local VIA Rail Station. In the U.S. call (800) 561-3949 or contact any travel agent. Other general sales agents are Walshes World, 92 Pitt St., Sydney, Australia, tel. (02) 9232-7499 or (1800) 22-7122; Walshes World, 2nd Floor, Dingwall Building, 87 Queen St., Auckland, New Zealand, tel. (09) 379-3708; Canada Reise Dienst, Rathausplatz 2, 22926 Ahrensburg/Hamburg, Germany, tel. (04) 102-51167; Long-Haul Leisurail, P.O. Box 113, Peterborough, Cambridgeshire PE1 1LE, England, tel. (0733) 33-5599.

Rocky Mountaineer Railtours operates a summer-only luxurious rail trip through the spectacular interior mountain ranges of British Columbia. Travel is during daylight hours only so you don't miss anything. Options from Vancouver are to Banff ($565 per person one-way), Calgary ($625), or a more northerly route from Vancouver through the spectacular Monashee Mountains to Jasper ($565). Rates include overnight accommodations in Kamloops, BC, two breakfasts, two lunches, and light snacks. During value season (late May and late September) fares are reduced $100. For further information and reservations call (800) 665-7245.

Bus
Greyhound serves areas throughout Canada and the United States. From Vancouver, the main routes are along the TransCanada Hwy. to Banff and Calgary and a more northern route through to Jasper and Edmonton. From the east, buses depart Toronto daily for Calgary and Edmonton along two different routes. If you're traveling to Alberta from the U.S., get yourself to Great Falls, Montana, from where regular services continue north to the Coutts/Sweetgrass port of entry. There you change to a Canadian Greyhound bus. Calgary buses depart from the port of entry daily at 12:10 p.m.

Travel by Greyhound is simple—just roll up at the depot and buy a ticket. No reservations are necessary. Greyhound bus depots in all major Albertan cities are near inexpensive accommodations and other public transportation. Always check for any promotional fares that might be available at the time of your travel. Regular-fare tickets are valid for one year and allow unlimited stopovers between paid destinations.

The **Greyhound Canada Pass** is valid on all Greyhound routes in Canada. It is sold in periods of seven days ($212), 15 days ($277), 30 days ($373.43), and 60 days ($480.43). It must be purchased seven days in advance and is nonrefundable. You can buy the pass at any bus depot. For more information call (403) 265-9111 or, in Canada only (800) 661-8747. In the U.S. the pass can be bought from most travel agents. Outside of North America it is sold as the **International Canada Pass** with a similar pricing structure except that there is a low season with a 25% discount that runs mid-September to mid-June. In England purchase the pass at Greyhound World Travel, Sussex House, London Rd., East Grinstead, West Sussex RH19 1LD, tel. (0342) 31-7317.

GETTING AROUND

Air
Canadian Regional, tel. (800) 665-1177, and **Air B.C.,** tel. (800) 332-1080, are air carriers with scheduled flights to all cities and many larg-

er towns within the province. Newcomers to the marketplace are **WestJet,** with services between Calgary and Edmonton and various British Columbia destinations, and **Greyhound,** linking the prairie provinces and Toronto to Alberta. From Calgary, Canadian Regional serves Lethbridge, Medicine Hat, Edmonton, Grande Prairie, and many BC towns. From Edmonton it serves Grande Prairie, Peace River, High Level, Rainbow Lake, Fort McMurray, and northern BC towns. These flights out of Edmonton depart from the municipal airport, so allow time for a trip across the city if you're coming in from the U.S. or other international destinations. Domestic flights are generally expensive but discounts apply if tickets are purchased in advance or in conjunction with a long-haul flight.

Traditionally, airlines in Alberta rarely offered promotional fares, but in the summer of 1996, with the two new airlines competing for business, airfares were slashed to as low as $29 for travel between Calgary and Edmonton. Outside this or any future airfare war, by buying a roundtrip ticket seven to 14 days in advance and staying over a Saturday night, discounts of up to 50% apply.

Departure tax on all domestic flights is seven percent of the ticket price plus a Canadian International Transportation Tax of $6 to a maximum of $55. Add to this the GST and you have the actual price you'll be paying. For example, after adding taxes to the one-way Calgary-Edmonton fare of $136, you'll pay $162.12.

Rail
The only scheduled rail service within the province is between Jasper and Edmonton. This thrice-weekly service is part of the transcontinental route. For further information on VIA Rail services, see "Getting There," above, or call (800) 561-8630 in Canada only.

Bus
Greyhound bus routes radiate from Calgary and Edmonton to points throughout the province. Service is regular, fast, and efficient. The only downside is that in larger centers, bus depots are often in seedy parts of town. Many depots have cafeterias, some have lockers, but none of them remain open all night. For schedules and fares call (403) 265-9111 or in Canada only

(800) 661-8747. **Red Arrow,** tel. (403) 424-3339 or (800) 232-1958, operates a more luxurious service that connects Calgary and Edmonton four times daily, continuing once daily to the oil sands city of Fort McMurray.

Brewster provides coach service between Calgary and Banff and Jasper National Parks. Brewster's advantage over Greyhound is that its service departs from Calgary International Airport and major Calgary hotels. One-way fare to Banff is $30, to Lake Louise $35, and to Jasper $56. You can book a trip at their booking desk on the arrivals level of Calgary International Airport, or call (403) 762-6700.

Car and RV Rental
All major car rental agencies have outlets at Calgary and Edmonton International Airports; to ensure a vehicle is available for you, book in advance. Generally vehicles can be booked through parent companies in the United States. Rates start at $55 a day for a small economy car, $65 for a midsize car, and $75 for a full-size car. Most major agencies now offer unlimited mileage, but check to make sure. Cheaper cars are available from agencies such as **Rent-A-Wreck,** but each kilometer driven over 100 km each day will cost 15-30 cents. In all cases insurance is from $12 per day and is compulsory. Rates are often lower outside summer. Charges apply if you need to drop off the car at an agency other than the rental location. All agencies provide free pick-up and drop-off at major city hotels. Major rental agencies include: **Avis,** tel. (800) 879-2847; **Budget,** tel. (800) 268-8900; **Discount Car Rentals,** tel. (403) 299-1222; **Dollar,** tel. (800) 263-6552; **Economy,** tel. (403) 291-1640; **Hertz,** tel. (800) 263-0600; **Thrifty,** tel. (800) 367-2277; and **Tilden,** tel. (800) 387-4747.

Camper-vans, recreational vehicles, and travel trailers are a great way to get around the province without having to worry about accommodations each night. The downside is cost. The smallest vans, capable of sleeping two people, start at $80 per day with 100 free kilometers. The major agencies, based near Calgary and Edmonton International Airports, are: **Canada Campers,** tel. (403) 250-3209; **Cruise Canada,** tel. (403) 291-4963 or (800) 327-7799 or, in the U.S., (800) 327-7778; **Everett's,** tel. (403)

291-0077; and **Go Vacations,** tel. (403) 291-6450 or (800) 387-3998.

Driving in Alberta

Driving is the most practical and popular way to travel to and around Alberta. Driver's licenses from all countries are valid in the province for up to three months. An **International Driving Permit,** available in your home country, is valid in Alberta for one year. You should also carry car registration papers or rental contracts. Proof of insurance must be carried and you must wear seat belts. If coming from the U.S., check that your American insurance covers travel in Canada. All highway signs in Alberta give distances in **kilometers** and speeds in **kilometers per hour** (kph). The speed limit on major highways is 100 kph (62 mph). U.S. motorists are advised to obtain a Canadian Non-resident Inter-provincial Motor Vehicle Liability Insurance Card, available through U.S. insurance companies, which is accepted as evidence of financial responsibility in Canada. Members of the American Automobile Association are entitled to services provided by the Canadian Automobile Association, including travel information.

Buying a car is relatively straightforward in Alberta. Proof of insurance in your home country will lower the standard liability insurance of $1,600 per year. Automobiles are cheaper in the U.S. but insurance is higher, and unless you can convince customs that you won't be selling the car in Canada, you'll be up for hefty import charges.

Tours

For those with limited time, an organized tour is the best way of seeing the province. **Brewster,** P.O. Box 1140, Banff, AB T0L 0C0, tel. (403) 762-6767 or (800) 661-1152, offers tours to various parts of the province, as well as car rental and accommodation packages, overnight packages in Calgary and Edmonton, Calgary Stampede packages, golfing adventures, and roundtrips to Alberta from Vancouver, British Columbia.

OTHER PRACTICALITIES

VISAS AND OFFICIALDOM

Entry for U.S. Citizens

Citizens and permanent residents of the United States do not require a passport for entry to Canada. Although photo driver's licenses are acceptable forms of identification for entry, it is advisable to carry extra identification such as a birth certificate, passport, or alien card (the latter essential for U.S. resident aliens to re-enter the United States).

Other Foreign Visitors

Visitors from countries other than the U.S. require a valid passport and, in some cases, a visa for entry to Canada. Presently, citizens of the British Commonwealth and Western Europe do not require a visa, but check with the Canadian embassy in your home country. The standard entry permit is valid for six months; proof of onward tickets and/or sufficient funds is required in order to obtain the permit. Extensions are possible from the Employment and Immigration Canada offices in Calgary and Edmonton ($60 per person).

Employment and Study

Anyone wishing to work or study in Canada must obtain authorization *before* entering Canada. Authorization to work will only be granted if there are no qualified Canadians available for the work in question. Applications for work and study are available from all Canadian embassies and must be submitted with a nonrefundable processing fee.

The Canadian government has a reciprocal agreement with Australia for a limited number of **holiday work visas** to be issued each year. Australian citizens under the age of 26 are eligible; contact your nearest Canadian embassy or consulate for more information.

Entry by Private Aircraft

For a list of Canadian airports with customs clearance facilities, request the *Canada Flight Supplement* from Canada Map Office, 130 Bentley Ave., Ottawa, ON K1A 0E9, tel. (613) 952-

where the rules are made—the legislature building in Edmonton

7000. This office also has aeronautical charts; $15 each. The publication *Air Tourist Information–Canada* (TP771E) lists all Alberta's airports and has other necessary information for visiting pilots; it's available from Transport Canada, AAN DHD, Ottawa, ON K1A 0N8, tel. (613) 991-9970.

Taxes
Canada levies a seven percent **Goods and Services Tax** (GST) on most goods and services sold in Canada. Non-Canadians can obtain a refund of the tax they pay on their accommodations (except campgrounds) and on most goods that they take out of Canada within 60 days of purchase. To make a claim, keep all receipts, grab a **GST Rebate Form** (available at most gift shops and airports), and mail it to Revenue Canada, Customs, Excise, and Taxation, Visitor Rebate Program, Ottawa, ON K1A 1J5, Canada. For more information call (800) 668-4748 or, outside Canada, call (613) 991-3346.

Rebates cannot be claimed on groceries, restaurant meals, flightseeing trips, gas, alcohol, tobacco, or antiques.

Provincial Sales Tax applies in all provinces except Alberta and ranges five to 12% on most goods purchased in shops or restaurants. Although Alberta doesn't have this tax, it does have a five percent **Room Tax.**

Note: All accommodations prices quoted in this guide do not include tax.

Firearms
Handguns, automatic guns, and sawed-off rifles and shotguns are not allowed entry into Canada. Visitors must declare all firearms at the border, and those that are restricted will be held by customs for the duration of your stay. Those not declared will be seized and charges may be laid. It is also illegal to be in possession of a firearm in a national park unless it is dismantled *and* carried in an enclosed case. Up to 5,000 rounds of ammunition may be imported but should be declared on entry. For further information on firearm regulations call Canadian Customs Service at (613) 954-7129 or (800) 461-9999.

MONEY

As in the United States, Canadian currency is based on dollars and cents. Coins come in denominations of one, five, 10, and 25 cents, and one and two dollars. The one-dollar coin is the 11-sided gold-colored "loonie," named for the bird featured on it. The unique two-dollar coin, introduced in 1996, is silver with a gold-colored insert. The most common notes are $5, $10, $20, and $50. A $100 bill does exist but is uncommon. Each note features a different bird. Until recently they depicted various Canadian scenes, including the town of Bluesky, north of Grande Prairie (on the $2 note, before a coin replaced it), and Moraine Lake, in Banff National Park (on the $20 note).

All prices quoted in this book are in Canadian dollars. The exchange rate varies. For most of the '80s and early '90s it was around C$1.20 to US$1, but by 1996 the Canadian dollar had lost value against its American counterpart. The rate is currently in the neighborhood of C$1.40 to

US$1. American dollars are accepted at many tourist areas, but the exchange rate will be more favorable at banks. Traveler's checks are the safest way to carry money, but often a fee is charged to cash them if they're in a currency other than Canadian dollars. All major credit cards are honored at Canadian banks, gas stations, and most commercial establishments.

Tips are not usually added to a bill, and in general 15% of the total amount is given. Tips are most often given to waiters, waitresses, taxi drivers, doormen, bellhops, and bar staff.

Costs

The cost of living is lower in Alberta than in other provinces, but higher than in the United States. By planning ahead, having a tent or joining Hostelling International, and being prepared to cook your own meals, it is possible to get by on well under $50 per person per day. Gasoline is sold in liters (3.78 liters equals one U.S. gallon) and is generally 50-65 cents a liter for regular unleaded. North of Edmonton the price is higher, up to 75 cents a liter.

HEALTH

Compared to other parts of the world, Canada is a relatively safe place to visit. Vaccinations are required only if coming from a endemic area. That said, wherever you are traveling, carry a medical kit that includes bandages, insect repellent, sunscreen, antiseptic, antibiotics, and water-purification tablets. Good first-aid kits are available through most camping shops.

Taking out a travel-insurance policy is a sensible precaution, as hospital and medical charges start at around $1,000 a day. Copies of prescriptions should be brought to Canada for any medicines already prescribed.

Giardia

Giardiasis, also known as beaver fever, is a real concern for those heading into the backcountry. It's caused by an intestinal parasite, *Giardia lamblia,* that lives in lakes, rivers, and streams. Once ingested, its effects, although not instantaneous, can be dramatic; severe diarrhea, cramps, and nausea are the most common. Preventive measures should always be taken,

and include boiling all water for at least 10 minutes, treating all water with iodine, or filtering all water using a filter with a small enough pore size to block the *Giardia* cysts.

Winter Travel

Travel through the province during winter months should not be undertaken lightly. Before setting out in a vehicle, check antifreeze levels, and always carry a spare tire and blankets or sleeping bags. **Frostbite** is a potential hazard, especially when cold temperatures are combined with high winds (a combination known as **windchill**). Most often it leaves a numbing, bruised sensation, and the skin turns white. Exposed areas of skin, especially the nose and ears, are most susceptible.

Hypothermia occurs when the body fails to produce heat as fast as it loses it. It can strike at any time of the year but is more common during cooler months. Cold weather, combined with hunger, fatigue, and dampness, creates a recipe for disaster. Symptoms are not always apparent to the victim. The early signs are numbness, shivering, slurring of words, dizzy spells, and, in extreme cases, violent behavior, unconsciousness, and even death. The best way to dress for the cold is in layers, including a waterproof outer layer. Most importantly, wear headgear. The best treatment is to get the patient out of the cold, replace wet clothing with dry, slowly give hot liquids and sugary foods, and place the victim in a sleeping bag. Warming too quickly can lead to heart attacks.

SERVICES, COMMUNICATIONS, AND MEASUREMENTS

All **mail** posted in Canada must have Canadian postage stamps attached. First-class letters and postcards are 45 cents to destinations within Canada, 49 cents to the U.S., and 90 cents to all other destinations. If you would like mail sent to you while traveling, have it addressed to yourself, c/o General Delivery, Main Post Office, in the city or town you request, Alberta, Canada. The post office will hold all general delivery mail for 15 days before returning it to the sender.

The telephone **area code** for Alberta and most of the Northwest Territories is **403**. All phone numbers in this book (except in the Kee-watin and Baffin regions of the NWT which are **819**), unless otherwise noted, must be dialed with this prefix, including long-distance calls made within the province. The country code for Canada is 1, the same as the United States. Public phones accept five-, 10-, and 25-cent coins. Local calls are 25 cents, and most long-distance calls cost at least $2.50 for the first minute from public phones. Phonecards, available from drug and grocery stores, provide considerable savings for those using public phones.

Electrical voltage is 120 volts, the same as the United States. Alberta is on the **metric system** (see the "Metric System" chart at the back of this book), although many people talk in miles and supermarket prices are advertised in ounces and pounds.

Alberta is in the **mountain time zone,** one hour later than Pacific time, two hours earlier than eastern time.

Shops are generally open Mon.-Fri. 9 a.m.-5 p.m., Saturday 9 a.m.-noon, and are closed on Sunday. Major shopping centers and those in resort towns are often open till 9 p.m. and all weekend. **Banks** are open Mon.-Fri. 9:30 a.m.-3:30 p.m., and till 4:30 or 5 p.m. on Friday.

MAPS AND INFORMATION

Maps

The best source of maps are the specialist map shops; in Calgary contact **Map Town,** 640 6th Ave. SW, tel. (403) 266-2241, and in Edmonton **Map Town,** 10815 100th Ave., tel. (403) 429-2600. By request they can send out a catalog of maps designed specifically for hiking (topographical maps), camping (road/access maps), fishing (hydrographic charts of over 100 lakes), and canoeing (river details such as gradients). They can also supply **Alberta Wall Maps, Canada Wall Maps, Thematic Maps, Historic Maps,** and **Aerial Photography.** These maps

are also available over the counter at some sport and camping stores.

Information

The best source of tourist information—up-to-date information on all accommodations, attractions, and events—is **Alberta Tourism Partnership,** P.O. Box 2400, Edmonton, AB T5J 2Z4, tel. (403) 427-4321 or, from within North America, (800) 661-8888. It also produces two excellent publications, *Alberta Accommodation and Visitors' Guide* and *Alberta Campground Guide* and a road map. All major routes into the province have a **Travel Alberta Information Centre,** generally open in summer only with all the same information (except you must pay for the road maps). Each town has a **Tourist Information Centre,** each with its own hours, and usually open June-August. When these are closed head to the chamber of commerce (year-round, Mon.-Fri. only) for information.

Canada House, Trafalgar Square, London SWI 5BJ, has a large tourism section with current information and well-informed staff. **Alberta House,** 1 Mount St., London, tel. (071) 491-3430, has limited tourism information, but a small library and business section is open to the public.

U.Wanna.What

U.Wanna.What is a unique service on the Internet that provides web surfers with a wealth of information on Alberta's two largest cities, Calgary and Edmonton. The web site covers all aspects of entertainment and recreation, such as attractions, sporting events, concerts, movies, and hundreds of accommodations and restaurants. The restaurant listings are particularly comprehensive, with cuisine, price range, and business hours listed. As well, the site features daily weather information, transportation routings, even where the police have set up their latest photo-radar speed traps. Access the site at http://www.UWannaWhat.com.

KAREN McKINLEY

CALGARY
INTRODUCTION

Calgary's nickname, Cowtown, is cherished by the city's 600,000 residents, who prefer that romantic vision of their beloved home to the city's more modern identity as a world energy and financial center. The city's rapid growth, from a NWMP post to a large and vibrant metropolis in little over 100 years, can be credited largely to the effects of resource development, particularly oil and natural gas.

Once run by gentlemen who had made their fortunes in ranching, Calgary is still an important cattle market. But the oil-and-gas bonanzas of the 1940s, '50s, and '70s changed everything. The resources discovered throughout western Canada brought enormous wealth and growth to the city, turning it into the headquarters for a burgeoning energy industry. Ignored by the eastern provinces, the city grew (at one time by 60 people a day) into a western dynamo, in constant conflict with the country's capital, Ottawa.

With the city's rapid growth came all the problems plaguing major cities around the world,

with one major exception—the distinct lack of manufacturing and industrial sites has meant little pollution.

Today the city is home to 20,000 Americans, many of them big oilmen with Texas twangs. Downtown is a massive cluster of modern steel-and-glass skyscrapers, a legacy of an explosion of wealth in the '70s. And in this futuristic mirage on the prairie are banks, insurance companies, investment companies, and the head offices of hundreds of oil companies. But not forgetting its roots, each July the city sets aside all the material success it's achieved as a boomtown to put on the greatest outdoor show on earth—the Calgary Stampede, a Western extravaganza second to none.

HISTORY

As well as being one of Canada's largest cities, Calgary is also one of the youngest; at 120 years old it has a heritage rather than a history. Native Blackfoot moved through the area around 2,000 years ago, but had no particular interest in the direct vicinity of what is now Calgary. Around 300 years ago Sarcee and Stoney natives moved down from the north and there was continual warring between tribes. White settlers first arrived in the late 1700s. David Thompson wintered in the area, then the Palliser Expedition passed by on its way west to the Rockies. But it wasn't until the late 1860s that any real activity started. Buffalo had disappeared from the American plains, and as hunters moved north so did the whiskey traders, bringing with them all the problems associated with this illegal trade.

Fort Calgary

The North West Mounted Police established a post at Fort Macleod soon after they came west to quell the whiskey trade. In 1875, a second fort was established on a terrace at the confluence of the Bow and Elbow Rivers. It was named Fort Calgary after the Scottish birthplace of Inspector J.F. Macleod, who took over command of the fort in 1876. It is an apt name for a city that straddles the clear Bow River—*calgary* is Gaelic for "clear, running water," a fact of which Macleod was probably well aware.

The Coming of the Railway

For many years the Canadian Pacific Railway had planned to build a northern route across the continent through Edmonton and Yellow-head Pass. But eventually the powers in the east changed their minds and decided on a southern route through Kicking Horse Pass. This meant that the line passed right through Fort Calgary. In 1883 a station was built on an alluvial plain between the Bow and Elbow Rivers. A townsite was laid out around it, settlers streamed in for free land, and nine years after the railway arrived Calgary acquired city status—something that had taken its northern rival, Edmonton, over 100 years to obtain.

In 1886 a major fire destroyed most of the town's buildings. City planners decreed that all new structures were to be built of sandstone, which gave the fledgling town a more permanent look. The many sandstone buildings still standing today—the Palliser Hotel, Hudson's Bay Company store, and the courthouse, for example—are a legacy of this early bylaw.

Ranching

An open grazing policy, initiated by the Dominion Government, encouraged ranchers in the United States to drive their cattle from overgrazed lands to the fertile plains around Calgary. Slowly a ranching industry and local beef market developed. The first large ranch was west of Calgary, and soon many NWMP retirees, English aristocrats, and wealthy American citizens had invested in nearby land. Calgary's first millionaire was Pat Burns, who developed a meat-packing empire that still thrives today. Linked to international markets by rail and sea,

Sandstone buildings gave Calgary a permanent look, even in its earliest years.

PROVINCIAL ARCHIVES OF ALBERTA

Calgary's fortunes continued to rise with those of the ranching industry, receiving only a minor setback in 1905 when Edmonton was declared the provincial capital. During the first 10 years of this century the city's population increased 1000% and rail lines were built in all directions, radiating from the city like enormous spokes. Immigration slowed and the economy spiraled downward as the effects of WW I were felt.

Oil

The discovery of oil at Turner Valley in Calgary's backyard in 1914 signaled the start of an industry that was the making of modern Calgary. The opening of an oil refinery in 1923 and further major discoveries nearby transformed a medium-sized cowtown into a world leader in the petroleum and natural-gas industries. At its peak, the city was the headquarters of over 400 related companies. Calgary became Canada's fastest growing city, doubling its population between 1950 and 1975. During the worldwide energy crisis of the '70s, oil prices soared. Although most of the oil was extracted from farther afield, the city boomed as a world energy and financial center. Construction in the city center during this period was never ending, as many corporations from around the world moved their headquarters to Alberta. During this period Calgary had Canada's highest per capita disposable income and was home to more Americans than any other Canadian city. Much of the wealth obtained from oil and gas was channeled back into the city. Not just for office towers but for sporting facilities, cultural centers, and parks for citizens and visitors alike to enjoy. Calgary today also has tremendous civic support. Many of the city's self-made millionaires bequeath their money to the city, and the residents have always been willing to volunteer their time at events such as the Winter Olympic Games and the Calgary Exhibition and Stampede. This makes the city a great place to live and an enjoyable destination for the millions of tourists who visit each year.

1988 Winter Olympic Games

During the early '80s the province was hit by a prolonged downturn in the oil market. But good fortune prevailed when the International Olympic Committee announced that Calgary had been awarded the 1988 Winter Olympic Games. Life was injected into the economically ravaged city, construction started anew, and the high-spirited Calgarians were smiling once again.

The games are remembered for many things: the lack of snow, a bobsled team from Jamaica, the antics of English plumber/ski-jumper "Eddie the eagle," and most of all for their acclaimed success.

SIGHTS

GETTING ORIENTED

The TransCanada Hwy. (Hwy. 1) passes through the city north of downtown and is known as **16th Ave. N** within the city limits. Highway 2, Alberta's major north-south highway, becomes **Deerfoot Trail** as it passes through the city. Many major arteries are known as **trails,** named for their historical significance, not, as some suggest, for their condition. The main route south from downtown is **Macleod Trail,** a 10-km strip of malls, motels, restaurants, and retail stores. If you enter Calgary from the west and are heading south, a handy bypass to take is **Sarcee Trail,** then **Glenmore Trail,** which joins Hwy. 2 south of the city. **Crowchild Trail** starts downtown and heads northwest past the university to Cochrane.

The street numbering system is divided into four quadrants. At first it can be more confusing than the well-meaning city planner intended, but after initial disorientation, the system soon proves its usefulness. Basically the four quadrants are geographically named—northwest, northeast, southwest, and southeast. Each street address has a corresponding abbreviation tacked onto it (NW, NE, SW, and SE). The north-south division is the Bow River. The east-west division is at Macleod Trail, and north of the downtown at **Centre Street.** Streets run north to south and avenues from east to west. Both streets and avenues are numbered progressively from the quadrant divisions (e.g., an ad-

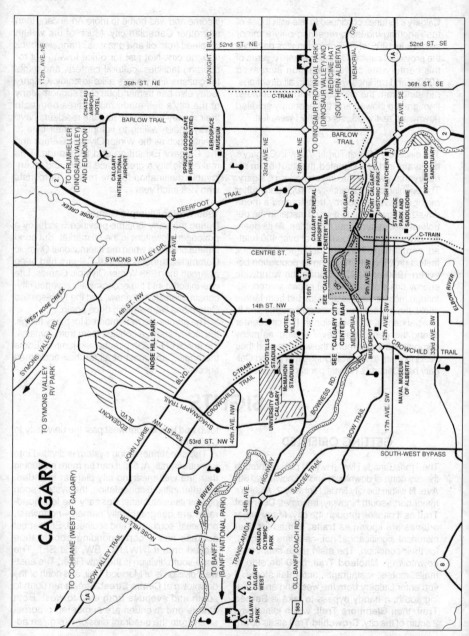

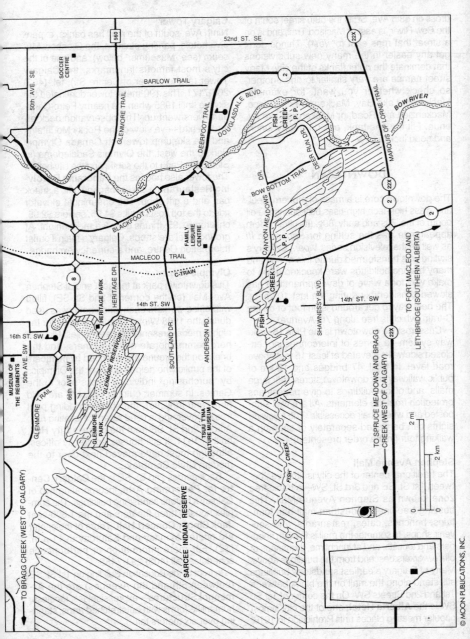

© MOON PUBLICATIONS, INC.

dress on 58th Ave. SE is the 58th street south of the Bow River, is east of Macleod Trail, and is on a street that runs east to west). Things don't get any easier in the many new subdivisions that dominate the outer flanks of the city. Many street names are *very* similar to one another, so check whether you want, for example, Mackenzie Lake Bay, Mackenzie Lake Place, Mackenzie Lake Road, or Mackenzie Lake Avenue. Fill the gas tank, pack a hearty lunch, and good luck!

DOWNTOWN

The downtown core is a mass of modern steel-and-glass high-tech high-rises built during the oil boom of the '70s and early '80s. (Its ultramodern appearance was the setting for *Superman III* as well as the television series *Viper*.) Calgary's skyline was transformed during this period and many historic buildings were knocked down to make way for a wave of development that has slowed considerably during the last 10 years. The best way to get around is on foot or on the C-train (which is free along 7th Avenue).

Crisscrossing downtown is the Plus 15 walkway system—a series of interconnecting, enclosed sidewalks elevated at least 15 feet above road level. In total, 47 bridges and 12 km of public walkway link downtown stores, four large malls, and office buildings to give pedestrians protection from the elements. All are well signposted and wheelchair accessible. The following sights can be visited separately or seen on a walking tour (in the order presented).

Stephen Avenue Mall

The traditional center of the city is 8th Ave., between 1st St. SE and 3rd St. SW—a traffic-free zone known as Stephen Avenue Mall. This bustling tree-lined pedestrian mall has fountains, benches, cafes, restaurants, and souvenir shops. In summer the mall is full with shoppers and tourists, and at lunchtime, thousands of office workers descend from the buildings above. Many of Calgary's earliest sandstone buildings still stand along the mall on the block between 1st and 2nd Streets SW. On the corner of 1st St. SW is the **Alberta Hotel,** one of the city's most popular meeting places until Prohibition in 1916.

Calgary Tower

Ninth Ave. south of the mall has banks, expensive hotels, parking stations, the Glenbow Museum (see "Museums," below), and one of the city's most famous landmarks, the Calgary Tower (at the corner of Centre St.), tel. (403) 266-7171. This 190-meter tower dominated the skyline until 1985 when the nearby Petro-Canada towers went up. The observation deck affords a birds-eye view of the Rocky Mountains and the ski-jump towers at Canada Olympic Park to the west, the Olympic Saddledome (in Stampede Park) to the south, and the city below. The tower also houses the **Panorama Revolving Restaurant,** a casual bar and grill, a snack bar, and a gift shop. The one-minute elevator ride to the top costs adults $4.95, seniors $2.95, children $1.95. It runs daily 8 a.m.-midnight. At ground level are shops, Calgary's main Tourist Information Centre, and a currency exchange.

Olympic Plaza

This downtown park at the east end of Stephen Ave. Mall (on the corner of 2nd St. SE), filled with office workers each lunch hour, was used during the 1988 Winter Olympic Games for the nightly medal-presentation ceremonies. Plaques here commemorate medal winners, and the bricks on the ground are inscribed by members of the public who helped sponsor the Olympics by "purchasing" individual bricks prior to the Games. In summer, outdoor concerts are held here, and in winter, the shallow wading pool freezes over and is used as an ice-skating rink. Across 2nd St. SE from the plaza is **City Hall,** built in 1911. It still houses some city offices, although most have moved next door to the modern **Civic Complex.**

Back across 2nd St. SE is the **Calgary Centre for Performing Arts,** incorporating two of Calgary's historic sandstone buildings. The complex houses three theaters and the 1,800-seat **Jack Singer Concert Hall.** Tours of the center are offered Monday and Saturday at 11 a.m. ($2). For more information or performance schedules call (403) 294-7455.

In front of the Education Building on 1st St. SE (between 5th and 6th Avenues) are the **Armengol Structures**—expressionless, raceless, humanlike forms with outstretched arms, standing over six meters tall.

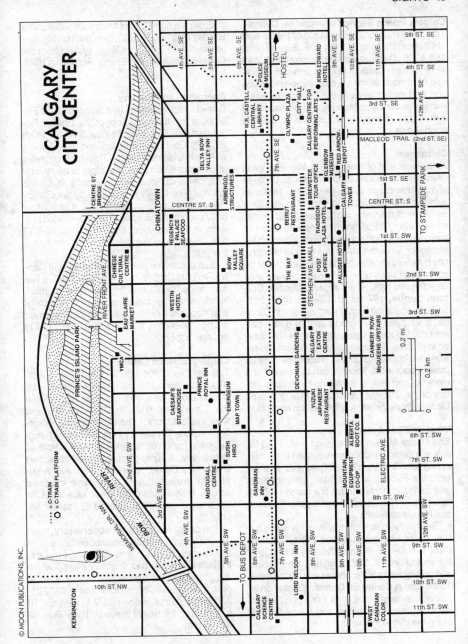

CALGARY CITY CENTER

© MOON PUBLICATIONS, INC.

Calgary Police Service Interpretive Centre

This small museum lies a couple of blocks east of Olympic Plaza at 316 7th Ave. SE, tel. (403) 268-4566. Displays include memorabilia from all of western Canada's police services, mock-ups of famous crime scenes, a modern police car, and descriptions of the policing process. Admission $2. Open Monday and Wednesday 9 a.m.-4 p.m., Saturday 11 a.m.-4 p.m., Sunday noon-4 p.m.

Chinatown

At the east end of town on 3rd Ave. is a small Chinatown of around 2,000 residents. Chinese immigrants came to Calgary in the 1880s to work on the railroads and stayed to establish exotic food markets, restaurants, and import stores here. Chinatown has seen its share of prejudice—from marauding whites gaining revenge for an outbreak of smallpox to bungling city bureaucrats who demanded the streets be narrow and signs be in Chinese to give the area an authentic look. The **Calgary Chinese Cultural Centre,** 197 1st St. SW, tel. (403) 262-5071, is one of the largest such centers in Canada. It's topped by a grand central dome patterned in the same style as the Temple of Heaven in Beijing. The centerpiece of its intricate tile work is a glistening golden dragon hanging 20 meters above the floor. Within the center is a museum and gallery displaying the cultural history of the Chinese; open daily 11 a.m.-5 p.m. Other facilities include a gift store and restaurant.

West on First Avenue

Eau Claire Market at the north end of 3rd St. SW is a colorful indoor market filled with stalls selling fresh fruit from British Columbia, seafood from the Pacific, Alberta beef, bakery items, and exotic imports. Under the same roof are specialty shops, an IMAX and regular theaters, and nine restaurants.

The northern limit of downtown is along the Bow River, where picturesque **Prince's Island Park** is linked to the mainland by a bridge at the end of 3rd St. SW. Jogging paths, tables, and grassy areas are scattered among the trees. To the east is **Centre St. Bridge,** guarded on either side by large stone lions. For a good view of the city, cross the bridge and follow the trail along the cliff to the west.

From the north end of town walk south along Barclay Mall (3rd St. SW), then west on 5th Ave. (or take the Plus 15 walkway system from the Canterra Tower) to the Energy Resources Building.

Energeum and Vicinity

One of Calgary's many free attractions, the Energeum, on the main floor of the Energy Resources Building, 640 5th Ave. SW, tel. (403) 297-4293, outlines the history and development of Alberta's largest industry. Through interpretive and hands-on displays, the story of oil, natural gas, oil sands, coal, and electricity in Alberta unfolds. The facility is operated by the Energy Resources Conservation Board, a regulatory body overseeing virtually all energy-related projects in the province. Open 10:30 a.m.-4:30 p.m., Sun.-Fri. in summer, Mon.-Fri. the rest of the year.

Just across the road is the **McDougall Centre,** 455 6th St. SW, tel. (403) 297-8687, a Renaissance Revival building that is the southern headquarters for the government of Alberta. It was declared a historic site in 1982. The center is open weekdays 8:15 a.m.-4:30 p.m.; call to arrange a tour.

Calgary Science Centre

This complex at 701 11th St. SW, tel. (403) 221-3700, is a little farther out (you could either walk the five blocks west from 6th St. or jump aboard the C-train that runs along 7th Ave. SW and walk the last block). The center's main attractions include **Discovery Hall,** featuring changing, often hands-on, science exhibits; **Circle of Discovery,** a photographic display area; and **Discovery Dome,** where dynamic audiovisuals are projected onto a massive concave screen. Visitors can enjoy these attractions for the admission charge of adult $8, senior $6, child $6.

The center also offers an **observatory,** open on clear nights, with the telescopes focused on the moon, planets, and clusters of stars. **Pleiades Theatre** has "mystery plays," which are presented throughout the year. For show details and ticket information call (403) 221-3700. The center is open daily in summer 10 a.m.-8 p.m.; the rest of the year, Tues.-Sun. 10 a.m.-5 p.m.

Devonian Gardens

The C-train will whisk you from the Calgary Science Centre back into the heart of the city to Devonian Gardens. A glass-enclosed elevator rises to the fourth floor of Toronto Dominion Square, 8th Ave. and 3rd St. SW, where a one-hectare indoor garden features 16,000 subtropical plants and 4,000 local plants—138 species in all. Within the gardens are waterfalls, fountains, pools, and bridges. Lunchtime entertainers and art exhibits can often be enjoyed in this serene environment. Admission is free, and it's open year-round, daily 9 a.m.-9 p.m.

MUSEUMS

Glenbow Museum

This excellent museum, 130 9th Ave. SE (another entrance is on Stephen Ave. Mall), tel. (403) 268-4100, chronicles the entire history of western Canada through three floors of informative exhibits and well-displayed artifacts. The second-floor galleries display the museum's permanent collections of contemporary and Inuit art, as well as special exhibitions from national and international collections. The third floor presents historical displays on each aspect of the Canadian West. The stories and traditions of the native Indian peoples unfold through displays of clothing, jewelry, ceremonial objects, and art and crafts, while other displays chronicle the fur trade; the early pioneers; the NWMP; the ranching, oil, and agriculture industries; and the impact of the railway. On the fourth floor is a large collection of military paraphernalia, mineralogy displays (including a meteorite), and exhibits on the Warrior in Society and West Africa. The museum is open daily 9:30 a.m.-5:30 p.m.; adult $5, senior $3.50. The library and archives are open Mon.-Fri. 10 a.m.-5 p.m., Saturday 1-5 p.m.

Aerospace Museum

This museum, beside McKnight Blvd. at 4629 McCall Way NE, tel. (403) 250-3752, traces the history of aviation in Canada through a large collection of aircraft scattered around the grounds, as well as engines, uniforms, and old photographs dating back to the flight of one of Calgary's first airplanes, *West Wind,* in 1913.

The engine collection is one of the largest in North America. The museum also features an extensive library and archives, and a gift shop. It's open daily 10 a.m.-5 p.m.; adult $5, senior $3. Take the Whitehorn C-train to Whitehorn and then bus no. 57.

Nickle Arts Museum

This museum on the University of Calgary campus, off 32nd Ave. NW at 434 Collegiate Blvd., tel. (403) 220-7234, has a collection of coins from the Ancient World. Throughout the year more than 20 exhibitions of contemporary and historical art are displayed in one of three galleries. Hours are Tues.-Fri. 10 a.m.-5 p.m., Sat.-Sun. 1-5 p.m.; admission $2, free on Tuesday. From downtown take the Brentwood C-train to the university or bus no. 9 Varsity Acres.

Naval Museum of Alberta

Canada's second-largest naval museum is located here in Calgary, over 1,000 km from the ocean. It honors those who served for Canada, many of whom were from the prairie provinces. The Royal Canadian Navy grew from humble beginnings in 1910 to become the Allies' third-largest navy in 1945. On display are three fighter aircraft that flew from the decks of aircraft carriers, as well as uniforms, models, flags, and photographs. The museum is open Tues.-Fri. 2-5 p.m., Sat.-Sun. 10 a.m.-6 p.m.; admission is free. It's located beside HMCS *Tecumseh* at 1820 24th St. SW; tel. (403) 242-0002. Take bus no. 2 (Killarney) from the corner of 7th Ave. and 8th St. SW.

Museum of the Regiments

Opened by Queen Elizabeth in 1990, this is the largest military museum in western Canada. It highlights four regiments—Lord Strathcona's Horse Regiment, Princess Patricia's Canadian Light Infantry, the King's Own Calgary Regiment, and the Calgary Highlanders—with realistic life-size figures, uniforms, badges, medals, photographs, and an audiovisual show. The museum is open daily (except Wednesday) 10 a.m.-4 p.m.; admission by donation. It's located on the Canadian Forces Base at 4520 Crowchild Trail SW, tel. (403) 240-7057. Take bus no. 13 (Mount Royal) from the Bay to 50th Ave. and walk north for five blocks.

Tsuu T'ina Culture Museum

Commemorating the history of the Sarcee peoples, this small museum features a model tepee and two headdresses dating to the late '30s. Many displays were donated by the Provincial Museum in Edmonton. The museum is open Mon.-Fri. 8 a.m.-4 p.m.; admission by donation. It's located on the eastern flanks of the Sarcee Reserve at 3700 Anderson Rd. SW, tel. (403) 238-2677. The closest public transportation is the Anderson C-train station.

HISTORIC PARKS

Fort Calgary Historic Park

In 1875, with the onset of a harsh winter, the newly arrived North West Mounted Police built Fort Calgary at the confluence of the Bow and Elbow Rivers in less than six weeks. Since the park was spared the fate of becoming an industrial wasteland in the early 1970s, much work has taken place on the 15-hectare site, including the construction of an excellent interpretive center. Recently, park officials launched an ambitious program to construct an exact replica of the original fort. In the meantime, all the activity happens in the interpretive center, which re-creates the earliest days of Canada's famous "Mounties"—the legacy of natives, hardy pioneers, and the wild frontier they tamed. Slide presentations about the NWMP are shown every 30 minutes. It's free to wander around the grounds, but to really appreciate the hardships of Calgary's earliest European settlers, visit the interpretive center and partially completed fort; it's worth the $3 admission. The grounds, at 750 9th Ave SE, are open year-round. To get there, either walk along the river from downtown or hop aboard bus no. 1 (Forest Lawn) or no. 14 (East Calgary) from 7th Avenue. The interpretive center, tel. (403) 290-1875, is open daily 9 a.m.-5 p.m.

Across the Elbow River from the interpretive center stands **Hunt House,** thought to be the

Irish-born Sam Livingston was Calgary's first official settler.

PROVINCIAL ARCHIVES OF ALBERTA

oldest structure on its original site in Calgary. The house was built in 1876 for a Hudson's Bay Company employee. On the same side of the Elbow River as Hunt House is the larger **Deane House** with sweeping river views. Built in 1906 for a commanding officer of the NWMP, this is one of the oldest restored homes in the city. In the past it has been used as a stationmaster's house, boardinghouse, and artists co-op. Since being restored in 1983, it has operated as a teahouse. The menu features light lunches—mainly salads, sandwiches, and traditional English desserts. Those with a hearty appetite should try the Captain's Tea Plate ($15.95 for two). The Deane House, tel. (403) 269-7747, is open daily 11 a.m.-2 p.m.; call for reservations.

Heritage Park

This 26-hectare park is located on a peninsula jutting into Glenbow Reservoir southwest of downtown. Over 100 buildings and exhibits help recreate a turn-of-the-century pioneer village. Many of the buildings have been moved to the park from their original locations. Highlights include a Hudson's Bay Company fort, two-story outhouse, working blacksmith's shop, 1896 church, tepee, and an old schoolhouse with original desks. A boardwalk links stores crammed with antiques, while horse-drawn buggies carry passengers along the streets. You can also ride in authentic passenger cars pulled by a steam locomotive or enjoy a cruise in a paddlewheeler on the reservoir. A traditional bakery sells cakes and pastries, and full meals are served in the Wainwright Hotel (including an excellent Sunday brunch served 10 a.m.-2 p.m. in winter). Park admission only is $10; admission with all rides is $16. Seniors and children pay $6 for general admission; $12 with the rides. It's open mid-May to mid-October, daily 10 a.m.-5 p.m., till 6 p.m. on weekends. The park is located at 1900 Heritage Dr. SW, tel. (403) 259-1990. To get there by bus take no. 53 south from downtown or take the Anderson C-train to Heritage Station and transfer to bus no. 20 (Northmount).

CANADA OLYMPIC PARK

On the western outskirts of the city, beside the TransCanada Hwy., is 95-hectare Canada Olympic Park, developed for the '88 Winter Olympic Games. Ski jumping, luge, bobsled, freestyle skiing, and disabled events were held here. Now the park offers activities year-round, including tours of the facilities, luge rides, summer ski jumping, and sport training camps. In winter the beginner/intermediate ski slopes are filled with Calgarians who are able to ski as early as November with the help of a complex snowmaking system. Many ski jumping, bobsled, and luge events of national and international standard are held throughout winter.

Olympic Hall of Fame

This is North America's largest museum devoted to the Olympic Games. Three floors catalog the entire history of the Winter Olympic Games through over 1,500 exhibits, interactive video displays, costumes and memorabilia, an athletes timeline, a bobsled and ski-jump simulator, and highlights from the last two Winter Olympic Games held at Albertville (France) and Lillehammer (Norway). The museum is open daily 10 a.m.-5 p.m.; admission adult $3.75, senior $3.

Ski Jumping, Luge, and Bobsled Facilities

Visible from throughout the city are the 70- and 90-meter ski jump towers, synonymous with the Winter Olympic Games. These two jumps are still used for national and international competitions and training. A glass-enclosed elevator rises to the observation level. The jump complex has three additional jumps of 15, 30, and 50 meters—used for junior competitions and training. All but the 90-meter jump have plastic-surfaced landing strips and are used during summer.

At the western end of the park are the luge and bobsled tracks. A complex refrigeration system keeps the tracks usable even on relatively hot days (up to 28° C). Summer luge rides are $12 per person.

Practicalities

A "Grand Olympic Tour" package that includes admission to the Hall of Fame, a trip to the observation deck of the 90-meter-ski-jump tower, a short bus ride to the luge and bobsled tracks, and a movie showing highlights from the '88 Winter Olympic Games is adult $9, senior $7.50, child $5. Admission to the tower only is adult $3.75, senior $3, child $2.75.

On the main level of the day lodge is a gift shop selling Olympic souvenirs, books, and clothing. The former start-house for the luge is now the **Naturbahn Teahouse,** open in summer Mon.-Fri. 10 a.m.-5 p.m. and year-round for Sunday brunch, 11 a.m.-4 p.m.; reservations required, call (403) 247-5465. For general information on the park call (403) 247-5452. A **Tourist Information Centre** is located on the main level of the day lodge; open summer only, daily 9 a.m.-5 p.m.

OTHER PARKS

The Calgary Zoo

The Calgary Zoo, Botanical Gardens, and Prehistoric Park, to use its full name, is one of Canada's finest zoos. It was established in 1920 near the heart of downtown on St. Georges Island and has become noted for its realistic simulation of animal habitat. Unique viewing areas have been designed to allow visitors the best look at the zoo's 1,000-plus animals. For example, underwater observation points provide a look at swimming polar bears and seals, and a darkened room allows visitors to watch nocturnal animals during their active periods (lights are turned on at night, reversing night and day). Other highlights include a section on Australian animals, exotic mammals, greenhouses filled with tropical birds, and a Canadian Wilds display featuring animals of the aspen parkland. In the Prehistoric Park section, the world of dinosaurs is brought to life with 27 full-size replicas set amid plantlife and rock formations supposedly similar to those found in Alberta in prehistoric times, but looking more like badlands. The zoo also has a fast-food restaurant and a number of picnic areas dotting the grounds. Admission is $7.50 for adults, $5.50 for seniors, and $3.75 for youths under 15. It's open in summer, daily 9 a.m.-6 p.m., the rest of the year 9 a.m.-4 p.m. The Prehistoric Park section is only open June-Sept. and is free with general grounds admission. The zoo is located at 1300 Zoo Rd. NE. The main parking lot is off Memorial Dr. just west of the Deerfoot Trail. For more information call (403) 232-9300 or 232-9372 (recorded message). From downtown take the Whitehorn C-train northeast.

Stampede Park

Best known for hosting the Calgary Exhibition and Stampede, these grounds south of downtown are used for a multitude of activities and events year-round. In the center of the park is the saddle-shaped **Olympic Saddledome,** which has the world's largest cable-suspended roof and is one of Calgary's most impressive structures. It was used for the ice-hockey and figure-skating events during the '88 Winter Olympic Games and is home to the Calgary Flames of the National Hockey League. "The Dome" is constantly in use for concerts, trade shows, and entertainment events. One-hour tours of the Saddledome are given on weekdays (nonevent days). Groups are preferred, but if you're interested, and don't have a family of 10, ring ahead and try anyway; tel. (403) 261-0400. The **Grain Academy** on the Plus 15 level of the **Roundup Centre,** tel. (403) 263-4594, is a museum cataloging the history of agriculture in the province through working models and hands-on displays. It's open April-Sept. Mon.-Fri. 10 a.m.-4 p.m., Saturday noon-4 p.m. Admission is free. The Big Four Building and Agriculture Building also host trade shows and exhibitions, and thoroughbred and harness racing takes place on the grounds year-round. Stampede Park is located at 17th Ave. and 2nd St. SE. Take the C-train from downtown to Victoria Park/Stampede or Stampede/Erlton.

Sam Livingston Fish Hatchery

Pearce Estate Park, a pleasant spot for a picnic, is home to this hatchery. The facility produces around 3.5 million trout a year, used to stock rivers and streams throughout the province. A self-guided tour (grab a brochure at the main office) leads through the hatchery, from the incubation room to holding tanks and an area containing various displays. In summer the hatchery is open Mon.-Fri. 10 a.m.-4 p.m.,

Sat.-Sun. 1-5 p.m.; the rest of the year weekdays only. To reach the park and hatchery, tel. (403) 269-6688, take 17th Ave. east from the city and turn north onto 17th St. SE.

Inglewood Bird Sanctuary

Over 260 species of birds have been noted in this 32-hectare park on the bank of the Bow River, east of downtown. The land was originally owned by a member of the NWMP and was established as a park in 1929. Walking trails are open year-round, an interpretive center in summer only. Take 9th Ave. SE to Sanctuary Rd. and follow the signs to a parking area on the south bank of the river. On weekdays bus no. 14 East turns off 9th Ave. at 17th St. SE, only a short walk from the park.

Fish Creek Provincial Park

At the southern edge of the city, this 1,170-hectare park is one of the largest urban parks in North America. Many prehistoric sites have been discovered on its grounds, including campsites and buffalo jumps. In more recent times the Calgary–Fort Benton Trail passed through the park. The site—much of which was once owned by Patrick Burns, the meat magnate—was officially declared a park in 1975. Three geographical regions meet in the area, giving the park a diversity of habitat. Stands of aspen and spruce predominate, while a mixed-grass prairie,

---

MIDNAPORE

The last rest stop for early travelers along the Macleod Trail, linking Fort Macleod to Fort Calgary, was just south of Fish Creek. A trading post and crude cabins constituted the town. The post office opened and was manned by a postmaster with dubious reading skills. One of the first parcels he received was addressed to Midnapore, India, and had been misdirected through him. Fear of losing his job kept him from asking too many questions, and as the community had no official name he directed that all mail to this post be addressed to Midnapore. The name stuck and that's how a suburb of Calgary came to have the same name as an Indian city on the opposite side of the world.

balsam, poplar, and willow can be found along the floodplains at the east end of the park. The ground is colorfully carpeted with 364 recorded species of wildflowers, and wildlife is abundant. Mule deer and ground squirrels are common, and white-tailed deer, coyotes, beavers, and the occasional moose are also present. An interpretive trail begins south of Bow Valley Ranch and leads through a grove of balsam and poplar to a shallow, conglomerate cave. An information display is located on the west side of Macleod Trail overlooking the site of Alberta's first woolen mill. To get to the main information center turn east on Canyon Meadows Dr., then south on Bow River Bottom Trail. For more information call (403) 297-5293.

RECREATION

OUTDOOR ACTIVITIES

Walking and Biking
A good way to get a feel for the city is by walking or biking along the 210 km of paved trails within city limits. The trail system is concentrated along the Bow River as it winds through the city; other options are limited. Along the riverbank the trail passes through numerous parks and older neighborhoods to various sights such as Fort Calgary and Inglewood Bird Sanctuary. From Fort Calgary a trail passes under 9th Ave. SE and follows the Elbow River, crossing it a number of times before ending at Glenmore Reservoir and Heritage Park. Ask at tourist information centers for a map detailing all trails. Bicycle rentals are available from **The Bike Shop,** 1321 1st St. SW, tel. (403) 264-0735.

Swimming
Calgary Parks & Recreation operates nine outdoor pools (open June-early Sept.) and 12 indoor pools (open year-round). Facilities at each vary. Admission at indoor pools includes the use of the sauna, jacuzzi, and exercise room. Admission to all pools is $4. For general information and pool locations call (403) 268-3888 or 268-2300 (recorded message).

The **YMCA,** 101 3rd St. SW, tel. (403) 269-6701, is a modern fitness center beside Eau Claire Market at the north end of downtown. All facilities are first class, including an Olympic-size pool, weight room, exercise room, jogging track, squash courts, a jacuzzi, and sauna. It's open Mon.-Fri. 6 a.m.-10 p.m., Sat.-Sun. 7:30 a.m.-6:30 p.m.; admission is $6.50 ($9 Mon.-Fri. 11 a.m.-1:30 p.m. and daily 4-6:30 p.m.).

Golfing
Over 20 public, semiprivate, and private golf courses are located within the city limits. Many courses begin opening in April for a season that extends for up to seven months. The courses operated by Calgary Parks & Recreation are all public. Those with 18 holes include **Maple Ridge,** 1240 Maple Glade Dr. SE, tel. (403) 974-1825; **McCall Lake,** 1600 32nd Ave. NE, tel. (403) 291-3596; and **Shaganappi Point,** 1200 26th St. SW, tel. (403) 974-1810. Each has a pro shop with club rentals. Green fees are $22.50 during the week and $25 on the weekend. **Fox Hollow Golf Club,** at the corner of Deerfoot Trail and 32nd Ave. SE, tel. (403) 277-4653, is an inexpensive public course with an indoor full-flight driving range open year-round.

Ballooning
All summer, balloons can be seen floating peacefully over the city. Various companies offer flights, but be prepared to pay (usually $150). One of the most professional is **Aero Dynamics,** 3413 8th St. SE, tel. (403) 287-9393. Launch sites vary depending on the wind direction, the basic aim being to float over the downtown area. After making a reservation you will be contacted an hour before launch time and asked to meet at the Aero Dynamics office, from where you'll be ferried to the launch site and back. Flights generally last 90 minutes and the cost includes all transportation, a champagne reception on landing, and a framed picture of your flight.

Calaway Park
This is western Canada's largest outdoor amusement park, and it has many rides, including a double-loop roller coaster. Other at-

ballooning over Calgary

ALBERTA TOURISM

tractions include an enormous maze, golf driving range, a zoo for the kids, live entertainment in the "Alphatheatre," and many restaurants and eateries. Admission to the park is $8, or $17.50 with unlimited rides. For children under seven and seniors admission with unlimited rides is only $12. The park is 10 km west of the city limits on Springbank Rd., tel. (403) 240-3822. It's open in summer daily 10 a.m.-8 p.m.; in May, June, and September, Friday 5-10 p.m. and weekends 10 a.m.-8 p.m.

Leisure Centers

The large **Family Leisure Centre,** 11150 Bonaventure Dr. SE, tel. (403) 278-7542, is an excellent facility offering a giant indoor water slide, wave pool, swimming pools, steam room and sauna, weight room, skating rink, lounge, and restaurant. It's open daily 9 a.m.-9 p.m. but there are only waves during certain sessions; admission is $5.50 ($7 4-7 p.m.). Similar facilities are **Village Square Leisure Centre,** 2623 56th St. NE, tel. (403) 280-9714, and **Southland Leisure Centre,** just off Macleod Trail at 2000 Southland Dr. SW, tel. (403) 251-3505.

Kart Gardens International has one kart track where you can reach speeds of 80 kph, and another slower, twisting one for first-time drivers. The park also has kiddy karts, mini-golf, and a snack bar. It's located off Macleod Trail at 5202 1st St. SW, tel. (403) 253-8301. Open in summer only from 11 a.m. to dusk.

Winter Activities

When Calgarians talk about going downhill skiing for the day they are usually referring to the five world-class resorts in the Rockies, an hour and a half drive to the west. The city's only downhill facilities are at **Canada Olympic Park,** tel. (403) 286-2632. Although the park has world-class luge, bobsled, and ski-jumping facilities, snow-making capabilities, two triple chairs, and a T-bar, its vertical rise is only 150 meters. On the plus side, however, are the extensive lodge facilities, excellent teaching staff, ski rentals, and night skiing till 10 p.m. on weeknights. Lift tickets cost $18 per day or $15 for four hours.

SPECTATOR SPORTS

Ice Hockey

Calgary's favorite sports team is the **Calgary Flames,** the city's franchise in the National Hockey League. The Olympic Saddledome in Stampede Park fills with 20,000 ice-hockey fans who follow every game with a passion; the atmosphere at a Flames' home game is electric. The season runs from October to April, and games are usually held in the early evening. The Flames are among the most competitive of NHL Canadian franchises. They last won the Stanley Cup in 1989. Tickets aren't cheap, starting around $15 for nosebleed seats. For general information call (403) 777-2177; for tickets call (403) 777-0000.

Baseball

The **Calgary Cannons** are a farm team for the National League Pittsburgh Pirates and play in the AAA Pacific Coast League during the regular baseball season (April to October). Tickets start at $6; seats closest to the home plate cost $9. The team plays at Foothills Stadium on Crowchild Trail, across from the Banff Trail C-train station. For home-game dates and ticket information call (403) 284-1111.

Football

The **Stampeders** are Calgary's franchise in the Canadian Football League, an organization similar to the U.S. NFL, with slight modifications. The team's popularity fluctuates with its performance, but it usually does well enough to have a chance come finals time in November when the best teams compete for the Grey Cup. Later in the season, weather can be a deciding factor in both the games' results and attendance. At kick-off in the Stampeders' final game of 1993 the temperature was -20° C and -33 with the windchill, but still over 20,000 Calgarians braved the weather to attend. The season runs from July to November. Home games are played at **McMahon Stadium** at the University of Calgary, 1817 Crowchild Trail NW. Take the C-train to Banff Trail Station. For more information, call (403) 289-0258.

Soccer

Soccer is gaining popularity in North America, and Calgary is home to the only facility on the continent specially designed for playing soccer indoors. The **Calgary Soccer Centre** features four indoor fields (plus outdoor fields); games are played each evening and on weekends but the building is always open (free admission). The complex is located off Glenmore Trail and 52nd St. SE (7000 48th St. SE, tel. 403-279-8453).

Motor Racing

Race City Speedway has three world-class tracks and is the premier motorsport facility in western Canada. It hosts national stock-car, motorcycle, and drag-racing events. Prices vary according to event but generally run $8-17. The speedway is located at 68th St. SE and 114th Avenue. For upcoming events call (403) 264-6515 or 236-7223 (recorded message).

ARTS AND ENTERTAINMENT

Art Galleries

It may put a dent in Calgary's cowtown image, but the city does have a remarkable number of galleries displaying and selling work by Albertan and Canadian artisans. Unfortunately they are not concentrated in any one area and most require some effort to find. **Creative Picture Gallery,** 106A 10th St. NW, tel. (403) 270-8353, features western Canadian artists who specialize in the land and its people. **Cotton & Willow,** 313A 19th St. NW, tel. (403) 283-8946, is similar but also makes bent-willow furniture.

Theater

Calgary's Western image belies a cultural diversity that goes further than being able to get a few foreign beers at the local dance hall. In fact, the city has 10 professional theater companies, an opera, orchestra, and a ballet troupe. The main season for performances is Sept.-May. For details on exact dates and prices contact the companies directly or pick up a copy of *City Scope* (free), available throughout the city.

Alberta Theatre Projects, tel. (403) 294-7475, is a well-established company based in the Calgary Centre for Performing Arts at 205 8th Ave. SE, beside the Glenbow Museum. Usual performances are of contemporary material. **Theatre Calgary,** tel. (403) 294-7440, is also based in Calgary Centre, but performs in the city's other world-class facility, the Max Bell Theatre at 220 9th Avenue. **Loose Moose Theatre Company,** 2003 McKnight Blvd. NE, tel. (403) 291-5682, offers lighthearted live entertainment on Friday and Saturday nights; tickets begin at $4. **Lunchbox Theatre,** located on the second floor of Bow Valley Square, 205 5th Ave. SW, tel. (403) 265-4292, usually features comedy productions Mon.-Sat. at noon. Tickets are $7. For experimental productions head to **One Yellow Rabbit,** 205 8th Ave. SW, tel. (403) 264-8131. **Storybook Theatre,** 2140 9th Ave., tel. (403) 291-2247, specializes in children's productions.

Music and Dance

Calgary Opera, tel. (403) 262-7286, performs at the Jubilee Auditorium at 1415 14th Ave. NW,

October through April. Tickets begin at $12. The Jack Singer Concert Hall at the Calgary Centre for Performing Arts is home to the **Calgary Philharmonic Orchestra,** tel. (403) 571-0270, one of Canada's top orchestras. **Alberta Ballet** performs at locations throughout the city; for dates and ticketing details call (403) 245-4222.

Cinemas
Most major shopping malls—including Eau Claire Market, closest to downtown—have a **Cineplex Odeon Cinema.** For information call the 24-hour film line, tel. (403) 289-7799. Also in Eau Claire Market is an **IMAX Theatre,** tel. (403) 974-4629, with a screen five and a half stories tall. Tickets are $7.25, or $10.50 for a double feature. **Uptown Stage & Screen,** 612 8th Ave. SW, tel. (403) 265-0120, is a newly restored downtown theater featuring alternative, art, and foreign films.

Casinos
Calgary has a few low-key Alberta-style casinos that have little glitz and low maximum bets. Downtown is **Tower Casino,** 501 Tower Centre, 131 9th Ave. SW, tel. (403) 262-5655, with a complimentary shuttle from major downtown hotels. Farther out is **Cash Casino Place,** 4040 Blackfoot Trail SE, tel. (403) 287-1635. Both are open noon-midnight.

Bars and Nightclubs
With a nickname like "Cowtown," it's not surprising that Calgary's hottest nightspots play country music. Along Macleod Trail are three favorites. **Ranchman's,** 9615 Macleod Trail SW, tel. (403) 253-1100, is *the* place to check out first, especially during Stampede Week. Some of country's hottest stars have played this famous honky-tonk. Food is served at a bar out front all day, then at 7 p.m. the large dance hall opens. The hall is a museum of rodeo memorabilia and photographs with a chuck wagon hanging from the ceiling. Most nights feature live performances and on Sunday mornings a church service is held. Toward the city is **Rockin' Horse Saloon,** 7400 Macleod Trail SE, tel. (403) 255-4646, another popular country spot. In the same part of town as Stampede Park lies **Dusty's Saloon,** 1088 Olympic Way, tel. (403) 263-5343, a legendary country music

venue featuring Calgary's largest dance floor, live music, and free two-step lessons Tuesday and Wednesday nights.

Eleventh Ave. SW, known locally as Electric Avenue, holds a number of dance clubs, but the glitz and glamor of this colorful strip has diminished in recent years as it's rife with serious crime. Most clubs on Electric Ave. are between 5th and 6th Streets. Each plays Top 40 or dance music till the early hours. Cover charges run $5-12 depending on the night. If you desire live music, head to the **Backstreet Bar** in the Smuggler's Inn, 6920 Macleod Trail, tel. (403) 252-3394 (nightly except Sunday) or **Buckingham's,** 805 9th St. SW, tel. (403) 233-7550.

Jazz, Blues, and Comedy
The **Classic Jazz Guild of Calgary** performs throughout the year at the Jack Singer Concert Hall. Call Ticketmaster at (403) 299-8888 for details. One of the most popular jazz clubs in town is **Kao's Cafe,** 718 17th Ave. SW, tel. (403) 228-9997, with live performances Wed.-Sunday. Another jazz club is **Panchos,** 1220 Kensington Rd. NW, tel. (403) 270-7278.

The best place to listen to blues is the **King Edward Hotel,** 438 9th Ave. SE, tel. (403) 262-1680, with live performances most nights and jazz jams on Saturday and Sunday.

Yuk Yuk's Komedy Kabaret is in the Blackfoot Inn, 5940 Blackfoot Trail SE, tel. (403) 258-2028. Shows run Wed.-Sun. nights and tickets are $7-12.

Jester's, 10th Ave. SE, tel. (403) 269-6669, gives comedians the stage Wednesday and Thursday at 8 p.m. and on Friday and Saturday at 8:30 p.m.

SHOPPING

Plazas and Malls
The largest shopping center downtown is **Calgary Eaton Centre,** on Stephen Ave. Mall at 4th St. SW. This is linked to other plazas by the Plus 15 Walkway System, which provides shelter from the elements. Other downtown shopping complexes are **Eau Claire Market,** at the entrance to Prince's Island Park, where the emphasis is on fresh foods and trendy boutiques; **TD Square,** at 7th Ave. and 2nd St. SW; and

The Bay, part of Alberta's history with its link to the Hudson's Bay Company. **Uptown 17** is a strip of over 400 retail shops, restaurants, and galleries along 17th Ave. SW. **Kensington,** across the Bow River from downtown, is an eclectic mix of specialty shops.

Camping Gear and Western Wear

Mountain Equipment Co-op, 830 10th Ave. SW, tel. (403) 269-2420, is Calgary's largest camping store. This massive outlet boasts an extensive range of high-quality clothing, climbing and mountaineering equipment (including a climbing wall), tents, sleeping bags, kayaks and canoes, books and maps, and other accessories. The store is a co-operative owned by its members, similiar to the American R.E.I. stores, except that to purchase anything you must be a member (a once-only $5 charge). To order a copy of their mail order catalog call (800) 663-2667. Just down the road, a similar supply of equipment is offered at **Totem Outdoor Outfitters,** 341 10th Ave. SW, tel. (403) 264-6363.

Smaller, yet with a good variety of equipment, is the **Hostel Shop,** 1414 Kensington Rd. NW, tel. (403) 283-8311, operated by Hostelling International.

Alberta Boot Co., 614 10th Ave. SW, tel. (403) 263-4623, within walking distance of downtown, is Alberta's only Western boot manufacturer. This outlet shop has thousands of pairs for sale in all shapes and sizes, all made from leather. **Western Outfitters,** 128 8th Ave. SE, tel. (403) 266-3656, across from the Convention Centre, has an extensive range of boots and Western wear. You'll find **Lammle's Western Wear** outlets in all the major malls including the Eaton Centre.

FESTIVALS AND EVENTS

Spring

Calgary's rodeo season kicks off with **Rodeo Royal** at the Saddledome on the last weekend of March. **Calgary International Children's Festival** is the third week of May. Events include theater, puppetry, and performances by musicians from around the world. It's held in Jack Singer Concert Hall and Olympic Plaza; call (403) 294-7414 for details.

Summer

Few cities in the world are associated as closely with an event as Calgary is with the **Calgary Stampede.** For details of the "Greatest Outdoor Show on Earth," held each summer, see below. **Calgary International Jazz Festival** features various jazz and blues artists at clubs and concert halls throughout the city, the last week of June. For locations call (403) 233-2628. **Canada Day** (1 July) is celebrated in Prince's Island Park and Heritage Park. **Calgary Airshow,** the second weekend of July, is a small event held at the Springbank Airport west of the city. **Calgary Folk Music Festival,** the last week of July, is an indoor and outdoor extravaganza of Canadian and international performers; tel. (403) 233-0904. The third week of August is the **International Native Arts Festival,** with performances by native dancers and musicians. Tepees are erected along Stephen Avenue Mall and workshops are held at locations throughout the city all week; tel. (403) 233-0022.

Fall

In October **hockey** and **downhill skiing** fever hits the city as the **Calgary Flames** start their season and the first snow flies. A good place for kids on Halloween is Calgary Zoo, where **"Howl"oween** celebrations take place.

Winter

Calgary has joined other major Canadian cities by celebrating New Year's Eve with a **First Night** festival. Although severely curtailed by the weather, Calgarians enjoy the winter with the opening of the theatre, ballet, and opera seasons. National and international ski-jumping, luge, and bob-sledding events are held at **Canada Olympic Park** Nov.-March. The 11-day **Calgary Winter Festival** takes place in early February at locations throughout the city; call (403) 268-2688 for details.

Spruce Meadows

This equestrian mecca, one of the world's greatest, is an oasis among the sprawling ranches that surround the city. An endless line of white paddock fencing surrounds the 120-hectare village that has an international-events ring the size of a football field, six warm-up rings, and a three-story tournament center. The name

Spruce Meadows is marked on the calendars of all the world's best riders. Each year the site hosts 15 televised events with over $23 million in prize money. The three biggest tournaments are the **National,** during the first week of June; the **North American,** held early July the same week as the Stampede, and the **Spruce Meadows Masters,** the first week of September. The Masters is the world's richest show-jumping

tournament; one of its events—the du Maurier International—has the largest purse of any single event anywhere. Up to 25,000 enthusiasts gather at the Masters each day. Entry is $5-6, making it an affordable day out. For information on Spruce Meadows write to R.R. No. 9, Calgary, AB T2J 5G5; tel. (403) 254-3200. To get there take Macleod Trail south to Hwy. 22X and turn right toward the mountains.

CALGARY STAMPEDE

Every July, the city's perennial rough-and-ready cowtown image is thrust to the forefront when a fever known as Stampede hits town. For 10 days, Calgarians let their hair down—business leaders don Stetsons, bankers wear boots, half the town walks round in too-tight denim outfits, and the rate of serious crime drops. Nine months later maternity hospitals report a rise in business. For most Calgarians it is known simply as The Week (always capitalized). The stampede is many things to many people but is certainly not for the cynic. It is a celebration of the city's past—of endless sunny days when life was broncos, bulls, and steers, of cowboys riding through the streets, and saloons on every corner. But it is not just about the past. It's the cowtown image Calgarians cherish and the frontier image that visitors expect. On downtown streets everyone is your neighbor. Flapjacks and bacon are served free of charge around the city, normally staid citizens shout "Ya-HOO!" for no particular reason, Indians ride up and down the streets on horseback, and there's drinking and dancing till dawn every night.

The celebration epicenter is **Stampede Park,** immediately south of the city center, where over 100,000 people converge each day. The nucleus of the Stampede, the park hosts the world's richest outdoor rodeo and the just-as-spectacular chuck wagon races, where professional cowboys from all over the planet compete in a winner-take-all $50,000 showdown. But Stampede Park offers a lot more than a show of cowboy skills. The gigantic midway takes at least a day to get around: a staggering number of attractions, displays, and free entertainment cost only the price of gate admission; some of

the biggest stars in country music perform; and a glittering grandstand show, complete with fireworks, ends each day's shenanigans.

History
Earlier this century Guy Weadick, an American cowpoke, got the idea that people would pay to see traditional cowboy skills combined with vaudeville showmanship. With the backing of four Calgarian businessmen who contributed $25,000 each, Weadick put on an inaugural show billed as the "The Last and Best Great West Frontier Days." The name was a reference to the fact that many people thought the cattle industry in Alberta was near its end, and that wheat would soon be king. On 2 September 1912 the show kicked off with a parade of cowboys and over 2,000 Indians in traditional dress. Its popularity proved so immense that the competition was extended two days. Canada's governor general, the Duke of Connaught, opened the show, and enjoyed himself so much that he stayed for the duration. An estimated 60,000 people lined the streets for the parade, and 40,000 attended each day of rodeo events. Amazing, considering that barely more than 65,000 people lived in Calgary at the time. The prize money for the rodeo was an incredible $20,000. The highlight of the event was on the final day when Tom Three Persons, a little-known Blood Indian rider from southern Alberta, rode the legendary bronc "Cyclone" for eight seconds to collect the world-championship saddle and $1,000.

The following year Weadick took the show to Winnipeg, then WW I intervened and it was not until 1919 that the Calgary show was revived with Weadick at the helm. In the era of popular Hollywood Westerns, Weadick convinced movie-makers down south the event was worthy of screening. In 1925 *Calgary Stampede* was released, putting the city on the map. As it turned out the inaugural show wasn't the first and last, but the beginning of an annual extravaganza that is billed, and rightly so, as "The Greatest Outdoor Show on Earth."

EVENTS

Stampede Parade
Although Stampede Park opens on Thursday evening for **Sneek-a-peek** (an event that alone attracts around 40,000 eager patrons), Stampede Week officially begins Friday morning with a spectacular parade through the streets of downtown Calgary. The approximately 150 entries include close to 4,000 people and 700 horses and takes two hours to pass any one point. It features an amazing array of floats, each cheered by 250,000 people who line the streets up to 10 deep. The loudest Ya-HOOs are usually reserved for Alberta's oldest residents, Stampede royalty, and members of the Calgary's professional sports teams, but, hey, this is the Stampede, so even politicians and street sweepers elicit enthusiastic cheers.

The parade proceeds west along 6th Ave. from 2nd St. SE, then south on 10th St. SW, and east on 9th Avenue. Starting time is 9 a.m. but crowds start gathering at six and you'll be lucky to get a front-row spot much after seven.

Rodeo
The pinnacle of any cowboy's career is walking away with the $50,000 winner-take-all on the last day of competition in the Calgary Stampede. For the first eight days, heats are held each afternoon from 1:30 p.m., with finals held the last Saturday and Sunday. Although Stampede Week is about a lot more than the rodeo, this is the event everyone loves to watch. Cowboys compete in bronc riding, bareback riding, bull riding, calf roping, and steer wrestling, while cowgirls compete in barrel racing. Wild cow milking, a wild horse race, bull fighting, and nonstop chatter from hilarious rodeo clowns all keep the action going between the more traditional rodeo events.

Chuck Wagon Races
The **Rangeland Derby** chuck wagon races feature nine heats each evening starting at 8 p.m. At the end of the week, the top four drivers from the preliminary rounds compete in a winner-take-all, $50,000 dash-for-the-cash final. Chuck wagon racing is an exciting sport any time, but here at the Stampede the pressure is intense as drivers push themselves to stay in the running. The grandstand in the infield makes steering the chuck wagons difficult through an initial figure eight, heightening the action before they burst onto the track for what is known as the Half Mile of Hell to the finish line. The first team across the finish line does not always win the race; drivers must avoid 34 penalties, ranging from one to 10 seconds added to the overall time.

Rope Square
During the Stampede, downtown's Olympic Plaza is known as Rope Square. Every morning 8:30-10:30, free pancake breakfasts are served from the back of chuck wagons. For the rest of the morning, the square is the scene for a variety of entertainment, which might include country-music bands, native dance groups, marching bands, or mock gunfights. West along Stephen Avenue Mall, square dancing takes place each morning at 10 a.m. Also at 10, horse-drawn carriages leave the Palliser Hotel for an hour-long tour through town. Get there early to ensure seats.

OTHER ENTERTAINMENT

The cavernous **Roundup Centre** holds a variety of commercial exhibits and demonstrations (plenty of free samples), an International Photo Salon with prints submitted from around the world, Kitchen Theatre showcasing Calgary's culinary scene, and a Western Art Auction. At the front of the Roundup Centre is **Stampede Corral,** where you might find dog shows, the Calgary Stampede Show Band, or a talent show for seniors. **Stampede Square** is an outdoor entertainment venue where modern rides such as a reverse bungee are set up. Also here are free phones to call anywhere in Canada, a petting zoo, and other activities for the kids. A **mid-**

RODEO EVENTS

For those watching for the first time, a rodeo can look like organized confusion. Although staying on the animals isn't as easy as professional cowboys make it look, learning the rules is, and it will make the events more enjoyable. The rodeo is made up of six basic events of which three are judged on points and three are timed. Other team contests are included by the organizers to liven things up even more.

Bareback Riding

In this event the rider doesn't use a saddle or reins. He is cinched to a handhold and leather pad attached to the horse's back. The idea is to stay on the wildly bucking horse for eight seconds. As the cowboy leaves the chute he must keep both spurs above the horse's shoulders until the horse's front hooves hit the ground. Riders are judged on style and rhythm, achieved by spurring effectively and remaining in control. The cowboy is disqualified if he doesn't last eight seconds, if he loses a stirrup, or if he touches the animal with his hand. Scores above 80 (out of 100) are usually good enough to win.

Saddle Bronc Riding

This event differs from bareback riding in that the horse is saddled and the rider, rather than being cinched to the animal, hangs onto a rein attached to the halter. Again, both spurs must be above the horse's shoulders after the first jump. Riders are judged by spurring action and are disqualified for falling before eight seconds have elapsed.

Bull Riding

Traditionally the last event in a rodeo, bull riding is considered to be the most exciting eight seconds in sport. The cowboy must hang onto an 1,800-pound Brahma bull for the required eight seconds with as much control as possible. No spurring is required (for obvious reasons), although if he gets the chance it will earn the cowboy extra points. Disqualification occurs if the cowboy's loose hand touches either himself or the animal, or if he doesn't last the eight seconds, which more often than not is the case. Like bareback riding, the cowboy has one hand cinched to the animal in a handhold of braided rope. Riders are tied so tightly to the animal that if they are bucked off on the side away from their riding hand they often become "hung up" and are dragged around like a rag doll until rescued by a rodeo clown.

Calf Roping

This timed event has its roots in the Old West, when calves had to be roped and tied down to receive medical treatment. The calf is released from a chute, closely followed by a mounted cowboy. The cowboy must lasso the calf, dismount, race to

saddle bronc riding

the animal, and tie a "pigging string" around any three of its legs. He then throws his hands in the air to signal the end of his run. After remounting his horse the cowboy rides forward, slackening the rope. He's disqualified if the calf's legs don't remain tied for six seconds. The fastest time wins.

Steer Wrestling

This timed event is for the big boys. The steer jumps out of the chute, closely followed by a mounted cowboy who rides alongside, jumps off his horse at full speed, and slides onto the steer's back attempting to get hold of its horns. The cowboy slows down by digging his feet into the ground, using a twisting motion to throw the steer to the ground. The fastest time wins.

Barrel Racing

This is the only rodeo event for women. Riders must guide their horse around three barrels, set in a cloverleaf pattern, before making a hat-flying dash to the finish line. The fastest time wins, and there's a five-second penalty for knocking down a barrel.

Wild Cow Milking

Although not an official rodeo event, participants in the wild cow milking are greeted with just as much hootin' and hollerin' as those in the main events. At the Stampede, 20 two-man teams race into a herd of wild cows aiming to collect a few squirts of milk in a container and race with it to the judges' table.

Wild Horse Race

In this fun event, three-man teams select a horse from among a herd in the ring. Their aim is to saddle it and have one team member ride it across the finish line.

Mutton Busting

Mutton busting is for all the little cowboys and cowgirls. Youngsters jump aboard a sheep for a wild and woolly ride across the ring.

---

way extends along the western edge of the park with the **Safeway Skyride** overhead.

The agricultural displays are in the center of Stampede Park. **Centennial Fair** is an outdoor stage with events for children such as duck races and magicians. In the **Agricultural Building** livestock is displayed, while next door in the **John Deere Show Ring,** the World Blacksmith's Competition and horse shows take place.

At the far end of Stampede Park, across the Elbow River, is the **Indian Village.** Here, members of the five nations who signed Treaty Seven 100 years ago—the Blackfoot, Blood, Piegan, Sarcee, and Stoney—set up camp for the duration of the Stampede. Each tepee has its own colorful design; tours are available. Behind the village is a stage where native dance competitions are held.

Once you've paid gate admission, all entertainment (except the rodeo and chuck wagon races) is free. Well-known Canadian performers appear at the outdoor **Coca-Cola Stage** between 11 a.m. and midnight. **Nashville North** is an indoor venue with a bar, live country acts, and a dance floor; open till 2 a.m.

PRACTICALITIES

Food

No chance of anyone starving to death here. Within the grounds are three restaurants, two food courts, and an endless stream of fast-food stands. The **Saddledome Restaurant** holds an all-you-can-eat buffet. The selection isn't huge, but at $6.95 (less than a burger, fries, and a drink from a stand) it's the best deal on the grounds. Open daily 11 a.m.-9 p.m.; expect a wait after 4 p.m. **O`Reillys Pub,** upstairs in the Roundup Centre, serves typical pub grub throughout the day.

Transportation

Parking around the grounds is limited; most people use public transport. The **C-train** runs at least every 10 minutes from 7th Ave. downtown to the Victoria Park/Stampede C-train station ($1.50 one-way). Many hotels and campgrounds run shuttle services to the park during Stampede Week; get details before making reservations as each service is different. Generally they leave pick-up points at 11 a.m. and 6 p.m., and

1997 CALGARY STAMPEDE TICKET INFORMATION

SECTION CODE	RODEO (1:30 P.M.)		EVENING SHOW (8 P.M.)	
	4-11 JULY	12-13 JULY	4-11 JULY	12-13 JULY
A	$26	$29	$33	$36
C	$18	$21	$22	$25
D	$25	$28	$33	$36
E	$18.50	$21.50	$26	$29
F	$33	$36	$40	$43
G	$23.50	$26.50	$35	$38
J	$21	$24	$28	$31
K	$17	$20	$21	$24
W	$17	$17	$17	$17

Sections A and C:	Grandstand Main Level
Sections D and E:	Clubhouse Seats
Sections F and G:	Clubhouse Restaurant (in pairs only)
Sections J and K:	Balcony
Section W:	Wheelchair Accessible (one companion only; limited wheelchair seating in section D)

Tickets purchased in advance include the gate price. For information, write to P.O. Box 1860, Station M, Calgary, AB T2P 2L8; or call (403) 261-0101 or (800) 661-1260 anywhere in North America. You can also visit the Stampede home page at http://www.calgary-stampede.ab.ca.

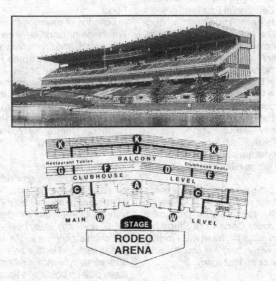

return at 6 p.m. and midnight. A 7 a.m. shuttle to the city center for the parade on the opening Friday is usually offered also; expect to pay $10 roundtrip per person. A taxi from downtown to Stampede Park runs around $5. If you decide to drive, parking close to the grounds is possible but the roads can be chaotic. Many local residents turn their gardens into parking lots—most stand out on the road waving at you like the month's rent depends on the $5-10 parking fee. The official parking lots nearby charge around $7 per day, rising to $9-10 in the afternoon, depending on how busy they are.

Tickets

Advance tickets for the afternoon rodeos and evening chuck wagon races/grandstand shows go on sale a year ahead of time. These are the good seats, and are sold out by the time the event rolls around. The grandstand is divided into sections, each with a different price tag. The best views are from "A" section, closest to the infield yet high enough not to miss all the action. These sell out first. To either side are the "B" and "C" sections, also with good views. Above the main level is the Clubhouse level, divided into another four sections, all enclosed by glass and air-conditioned. These seats might not have the atmosphere of the lower or higher levels, but they are protected from the elements and patrons have access to a bar, full-service restaurant, and lounge area. At the top of the grandstand is the Balcony level, divided into two sections. Both are great for the chuck wagon races (you can see the wagons around the full circuit). Ticket prices for the first eight days of rodeo competition range $17-33 ($26 for section A). The evening chuck wagon races/grandstand shows run $17-40 ($33 for section A). Tickets to both the rodeos and chuck wagon races/grandstand shows include admission to Stampede Park (normally $8). Tickets for the final two days of competition are an extra $3.

If you didn't purchase your tickets in advance, you'll need to pay the **general admission** of $8 at the gate. Once inside the park, you can purchase tickets for the afternoon's rodeo or the chuck wagon race/grandstand show from the booths behind the grandstand. Tickets are $8 to either event, and you'll only have access to either an area of the infield with poor views, or seats well away from the action.

Information

An Events Schedule and map are handed out at all park gates, and the *Calgary Sun* newspaper publishes a pull-out each day during the Stampede with results of the previous day's competition and upcoming events throughout town. Thousands of volunteers (dressed in red and white) contribute to the Stampede's success. They can answer most questions or at least direct you to one of many **Howdy Folk Chuckwagons** for more information. The **Bank of Montreal** operates daily 11 a.m.-5 p.m. at the Agricultural Building, or use one of many automated banking machines located throughout the park.

In 1997, the Calgary Stampede will be held 4-13 July; in 1998 it's 3-12 July. For more information write to P.O. Box 1860, Station M, Calgary, AB T2P 2L8; or call (403) 261-0101 or (800) 661-1260 anywhere in North America. You can also visit the Stampede home page at http://www.calgary-stampede.ab.ca.

ACCOMMODATIONS

Accommodations in Calgary vary from campgrounds, hostels, and budget motels to a broad selection of high-quality hotels catering to top-end travelers and business conventions. Many of the older, cheaper downtown hotels have been demolished in recent years to make way for office buildings. Every middle- to top-end hotel in the city was renovated for the '88 Winter Olympic Games. Most of the downtown hotels offer drastically reduced rates on weekends—Friday and Saturday nights might be half the regular room rate. During Stampede Week prices are higher than the rest of the year and many accommodations are booked up months in advance.

HOTELS AND MOTELS

Downtown Hotels

The gracious **Palliser Hotel** was built in 1914 by the C.P.R. and is still a part of that company chain (which includes the Banff Springs Hotel and Chateau Lake Louise). The rooms may seem small by modern standards, and it lacks certain recreational facilities, but the elegance and character of this Calgary favorite are priceless. When the queen of England visits Calgary this is where she stays. Each of the 336 rooms has been restored. The cavernous lobby has original marble columns and staircases, a magnificent chandelier, and solid-brass doors that open onto busy 9th Avenue. As you'd expect, staying in this Calgary landmark isn't cheap, but it's a luxurious way to enjoy the city. Located at 133 9th Ave. SE, tel. (403) 262-1234 or (800) 441-1414; rates start at $180 s or d.

Least expensive of the hotels right downtown is **Prince Royal Inn,** 618 5th Ave. SW, tel. (403) 263-0520 or (800) 661-1592, where each of the 300 rooms has kitchen facilities; $90 s, $100 d. A few blocks west, and close to C-train stations, you'll find the **Sandman Inn,** 888 7th Ave. SW, tel. (403) 237-8626 or (800) 726-3626, and **Lord Nelson Inn,** 1020 8th Ave. SW, tel. (403) 269-8262 or (800) 661-6017. Of the two, Lord Nelson is less expensive, with rooms under $70, but those at the Sandman are larger, and it offers more facilities.

In the heart of the shopping district, the **Westin Hotel,** 320 4th Ave. SW, tel. (403) 266-1611 or (800) 228-3000, has a wide range of facilities and over 500 rooms. Rates are $139 s, $159 d. In the same part of the city is the **Delta Bow Valley Inn,** 209 4th Ave. SE, tel. (403) 266-1980 or (800) 268-1133, featuring 300 luxurious rooms with all the amenities; $150 s, $165 d. Across from the Calgary Tower and on the same block as the Glenbow Museum is the **Radisson Plaza Hotel,** 110 9th Ave. SE, tel. (403) 266-7331 or (800) 333-3333, one of Calgary's newest and largest downtown hotels. It offers elegantly decorated rooms and a large indoor pool with a waterfall. Rates are $159 s, $169 d.

Across the railway tracks from downtown, the **Quality Hotel Westward,** 119 12th Ave. SW, tel. (403) 266-4611 or (800) 221-2222, features recently renovated rooms each with a private balcony. Parking is free, and one floor is reserved for women only. Rates start at $85 s or d.

Motel Village

Motel Village is Calgary's main concentration of moderately priced motels. The village is not an official designation, just a dozen motels bunched together at the intersection of 16th Ave. NW and Crowchild Trail, an $8 cab ride from downtown and directly opposite McMahon Stadium.

One of the best values in the village, the **Comfort Inn,** 2363 Banff Trail NW, tel. (403) 289-2581, features an indoor pool and complimentary breakfast; $49 s, $59 d. Banff Trail spurs north off 16th Avenue. Along this stretch of road, within a few blocks of 16th Ave., you'll find a few other choices. **Holiday Inn Express,** 2227 Banff Trail NW, tel. (403) 289-6600, where rooms are $62 s or d, is a good option. Only slightly more expensive is the **Econo Lodge,** 2231 Banff Trail NW, tel. (403) 289-1921; $63 s, $73 d. The nearby **Quality Inn,** 2359 Banff Trail NW, tel. (403) 289-1973 or (800) 661-4667, has an indoor pool, fitness center, and restaurant. Rates here are $64 s, $79 d.

Best Western Village Park Inn, 1804 Crow-child Trail NW, tel. (403) 289-0241 or (800) 528-1234, features large rooms and an indoor atrium containing a lounge with adjoining restaurant. Rates are $94 s, $104 d. Next door is **Super 8 Motel,** 1904 Crowchild Trail NW, tel. (403) 289-9211 or (800) 800-8000; $68 s, $78 d. East of the village towers the imposing **Highlander Hotel,** 1818 16th Ave. NW, tel. (403) 289-1961 or (800) 661-9564, an older-style place offering all the usual eating and entertainment facilities along with an airport shuttle. Rates are $73 s, $79 d.

Northeast (Airport)

Of the many hotels close to Calgary International Airport, **Chateau Airport Hotel**—a stone's throw from the arrivals level of the main terminal—is the closest. It's another C.P.R. hotel, and although not as grand as others in the chain (many of the rooms are small) it's modern and very handy for late arrivals or early departures. For advance reservations call (403) 291-2600 or (800) 828-7447. Rates are $135-150.

Most of the dozen other motels in the northeast corner of the city have shuttles to the airport and can be contacted directly by courtesy phone from the airport. Of the bunch clustered around the intersection of 16th Ave. and 19th St. NE., least expensive is the **Pointe Inn,** 1808 19th St. NE, tel. (403) 291-4681 or (800) 661-8164. It offers basic rooms and a restaurant for $45 s, $53 d. **Best Western Airport,** 1947 18th Ave. NE, tel. (403) 250-5015 or (800) 528-1234, is of a similar standard and also has a restaurant; $56 s, $64 d. But the pick of the crop is **Crossroads Hotel,** 2120 16th Ave. NE, tel. (403) 291-4666 or (800) 661-8157, which supplies air-conditioning and an indoor pool; $84 s, $94 d. Closer to the airport is **Best Western Port-o-call Inn,** 1935 McKnight Blvd. NE, tel. (403) 291-4600 or (800) 661-1161, a full facility hostelry where rooms are $101 s or d.

South on Macleod Trail

The following accommodations are lined up along Macleod Trail, the main route out of the city to the south. Those in the southwest sector of the city lie on the west side of Macleod Trail and those in the Southeast sector to the east of it.

The **Elbow River Inn,** 1919 Macleod Trail SE, tel. (403) 269-6771 or (800) 661-1463, is close to downtown and directly opposite Stampede Park, but don't even dream of staying here during Stampede Week unless you make reservations a year in advance. Within the motel is a restaurant, pub, and casino. Rates are $49 s, $59 d rising to $79 s, $89 d during the Stampede. The next motel, to the south, is **Stampeder Inn,** 3828 Macleod Trail SW, tel. (403) 243-5531, an older-style place with all facilities; $63 s, $69 d. A few blocks farther south, with a C-train station on its back doorstep, stands **Holiday Inn,** 4206 Macleod Trail SW, tel. (403) 287-2700 or (800) 661-1889. Facilities here include a large indoor pool, restaurant, and lounge. Rooms cost $69 s, $74 d. Well-priced and only slightly farther from the city is the **Econo Lodge South,** 5307 Macleod Trail SE, tel. (403) 258-1064 or (800) 268-6128; $42 s, $48 d.

The following accommodations lie south of Glenmore Trail, mingled with a strip of shopping malls and fast-food restaurants. The first of these is **Calgary South TraveLodge,** 7012 Macleod Trail SW, tel. (403) 253-1111 or (800) 578-7878; $74 s, $79 d. Nearby, and better value, is **Flamingo Motor Hotel,** 7505 Macleod Trail SE, tel. (403) 252-4401, with a large indoor pool and comfortable rooms decorated in pastels; from $48 s, $56 d. The 10-story **Carriage House Inn,** 9030 Macleod Trail SW, tel. (403) 253-1101 or (800) 661-9566, offers a wide range of facilities including a restaurant and English-style pub, but the rooms are pretty basic for $100 s or d. **TraveLodge Calgary Macleod Trail** is at 9206 Macleod Trail SW, tel. (403) 253-7070 or (800) 578-7878. Guests enjoy an indoor pool and restaurant, and rooms are reasonably priced at $72 s, $82 d. It's also right across the road from the famous Ranchman's saloon. The 261-room **Best Western Hospitality Inn,** 135 Southland Dr. SE, tel. (403) 278-5050 or (800) 528-1234, features an array of facilities including an indoor pool, two restaurants, lounge, pub, and nightclub; $90 s, $95 d. Southernmost of the motels on Macleod Trail is **Stetson Village Inn,** 10002 Macleod Trail SW, tel. (403) 271-3210, an older-style place tucked between shopping malls; $57 s, $61 d.

West of Downtown

Known as 16th Ave. N within city limits, a string of reasonably priced motels line the Trans-Canada Hwy. heading west from the city toward the mountain parks. Usually not the best value, these accommodations offer the best location for visiting Canada Olympic Park or for day trips to the mountains. Closest to the city lies **Budget Host Motor Inn,** 4420 16th Ave. NW, tel. (403) 288-7115 or (800) 661-3772. The rooms are fairly standard, but the rates are right at $49 s, $54 d. Complimentary coffee is served in the lobby. Across the road is the **Travellers Inn,** 4611 16th Ave. NW, tel. (403) 247-1388, nothing special, but reasonably priced at $49 s, $55 d. On the same side of the road and similarly priced are the **Olympia Motel,** 5020 16th Ave. NW, tel. (403) 288-4461, and **Red Carpet Inn,** 4635 16th Ave. NW, tel. (403) 247-9239. Directly opposite Canada Olympic Park is **Bow Ridge Motel,** 8220 Bow Ridge Crescent NW, tel. (403) 288-4441. Rooms are small but comfortable and there's an outdoor pool; $50 s, $60 d. Like other motels in the chain, the **Econo Lodge,** west of Canada Olympic Park, tel. (403) 288-4436, provides decent quality rooms for a good price; $49 s, $59 d. A little farther out is **Westwind Inn,** tel. (403) 286-0333 or (800) 665-0856; $65 s, $75 d.

BED AND BREAKFASTS

Tourist information centers in Calgary keep a list of places offering bed-and-breakfast accommodations and will make a booking for you. The **Bed & Breakfast Association of Calgary** represents 40 homes offering rooms to visitors. Prices are $30-80 s, $40-120 d. For information write to 6016 Thornburn Drive NW, Calgary T2K 3P7; tel. (403) 531-0065. One of the nicest is **Inglewood B&B,** 1006 8th Ave. SE, tel. (403) 262-6570, named for the historic neighborhood in which it lies. Its location is excellent—close to the river and Stampede Park as well as a 10-minute stroll from downtown. The four rooms, each with private facilities, range $55-85 s, $65-95 d depending on the room configuration. Rates include a cooked breakfast.

BACKPACKER ACCOMMODATIONS

Calgary International Hostel

At 520 7th Ave. SE, tel. (403) 269-8239, this large hostel is ideally located only two blocks east of City Hall and Stephen Ave. Mall. It has 110 beds, many in eight-bed dormitories, some in private rooms. Other facilities include a fully equipped kitchen, laundry, large common room, outdoor barbecue, game room, snack bar, lockers, and an information service. From the airport, shuttle buses stop two blocks away at the Delta Bow Valley Inn. A cab from the airport will run around $20. Rates are $14 for members and $19 for nonmembers. This place becomes crowded during summer so book ahead.

CAMPGROUNDS

No camping is available within the Calgary city limits, although campgrounds can be found along all major routes into the city. Shuttle buses run to and from campgrounds into Stampede Park during the Calgary Exhibition and Stampede. Reservations are necessary for this week.

West

K.O.A. Calgary West, tel. (403) 288-0411 or (800) 291-5797, is located on a hill a short way west of Canada Olympic Park. The modern facilities include showers, a laundry, outdoor pool, and game room. Unserviced sites are $18, hookups $19-30. **Calaway Park,** tel. (403) 249-7372, Canada's largest amusement park, is 10 km farther west along the TransCanada Highway. It offers a large open camping area. Trees are scarce but on clear days the view of the Rockies is spectacular and prairie falcons often hover overhead. The toilets, showers, and laundry are in a trailer, but are of reasonable standard. The large overflow area is unserviced but is only needed during Stampede Week. Tent sites are $15, hookups $21.

North

Northwest of the city is **Symons Valley R.V. Park,** tel. (403) 274-4574, which has showers, laundry, and a restaurant. Unserviced sites are

BOB RACE

$10, hookups $17-19. To get there take 14th St. NW north past Nose Hill Park to Symons Valley Rd., continue northwest along W. Nose Creek to the campground at 144th Ave. NW. Also north of the city, but farther out, is **Whispering Spruce Campground,** tel. (403) 226-0097, in the small town of Balzac. The campground has showers and a small grocery store. Tent sites are $14, unserviced sites $16, hookups $18-20.

East

Mountain View Farm Campground, three km east of city limits on the TransCanada Hwy., tel. (403) 293-6640, doesn't have a view of the mountains, but does have a small petting farm, mini-golf, and hay rides. The sites are very close together. Facilities include showers, a grocery store, and laundry. Tent sites are $14, hookups $18-20.

South

South of Calgary on the Bow River is **Nature's Hideaway Campground,** tel. (403) 938-8185. Although farther out than all of the above, it is located in a densely wooded floodplain. Birds are abundant, and deer and coyotes are often seen. Many guests stay here for the entire summer, and the facilities are a little run-down. There are showers, a grocery store, a dance hall (music on weekends), and a beach with swimming; unserviced sites $14, hookups $16-20. To get there head south on Hwy. 2, then take Hwy. 552 east for 12 km, then north for one km, then east for two more. It's open year-round.

FOOD

Calgary may lack the cultural trappings that Alberta's capital, Edmonton, boasts, but it gives that city a run for its money in the restaurant department. All the major high-rise buildings downtown have plazas with inexpensive food courts, coffeehouses, and cappuccino bars—the perfect places for people-watching. South of downtown, along 17th Ave. and 4th St., a once quieter part of the city has been transformed into a focal point for Calgary's restaurant scene with cuisine to suit all tastes. Familiar North American fast-food restaurants line Macleod Trail south of the city center.

DOWNTOWN DINING

Eau Claire Market

At the entrance to Prince's Island Park, this expansive indoor market has a large food court as well as a number of restaurants. In the food court you'll find a great seafood outlet, a bakery, and some Asian-food places. **Cajun Charlies,** tel. (403) 233-8101, opposite the food court, is a striking orange-and-black eatery serving Louisiana Bayou dishes. Outside the market's western entrance is **Joey Tomato's Kitchen,** tel. (403) 263-6336, a trendy bistro-style restaurant serving moderately priced Italian food. Near the same entrance you'll find **1886 Cafe,** tel. (403) 269-9255, named for the year it was built. This restaurant oozes an authentic Old Calgary ambience. Breakfast attracts the most interesting group of diners but the place is busy all day. Portions are generous, coffee refills are free, and when you've finished your meal ask to see the museum downstairs. It's open daily 7 a.m.-3 p.m.

Japanese

Yuzuki Japanese Restaurant, 510 9th Ave. SW, tel. (403) 261-7701, is a good downtown eatery where the most expensive lunch item is the assorted sushi for $12. Excellent value considering it comes with 10 of those little rice packages and a bowl of miso soup. Less expensive items start at $6 and are priced only slightly higher at dinner.

More upscale is **Sushi Hiro,** 727 5th Ave. SW, tel. (403) 233-0605. Sushi choices change regularly but generally include red salmon, yellowtail, sea urchin, and salmon roe. If you sit at the oak-and-green-marble sushi counter you'll be able to ask the chef what's best. Closed Sunday.

Chinese

Chinatown, along 2nd and 3rd Avenues east of Centre St., naturally has the best assortment of Chinese restaurants. **Hang Fung Restaurant,** 119 3rd Ave. SE, tel. (403) 269-4646, tucked behind a Chinese grocery store, serves one-plate meals for under $7. The barbecue pork is delicious and only $4.50. Just as inexpensive is **Golden Inn Restaurant,** 107 2nd Ave. SE, tel. (403) 269-2211, popular with the local Chinese, as well as with professionals, and shift-workers appreciate its long hours (open till 4 a.m.). The menu features mostly Cantonese-style deep-fried food. With more atmosphere is **Silver Dragon,** 106 3rd Ave. SE, tel. (403) 264-5326, a large restaurant with subdued lighting and a relaxed and comfortable setting. For a Chinese buffet, head to **Regency Palace Seafood Restaurant,** 328 Centre St., SE, tel. (403) 777-2288, a cavernous restaurant seating around 600 people. Open for lunch Mon.-Fri. and daily for dinner.

Lebanese

The **Beirut Restaurant,** 112 8th Ave. SW, tel. (403) 264-8859, makes up for what it lacks in ambience with hearty portions of traditional middle-eastern dishes such as hummus ($4.75). Also inexpensive are the falafel-pita sandwiches and chicken-breast sandwiches (both under $6).

Seafood

The city's best seafood is available at **Cannery Row** and directly upstairs at the aptly named **McQueens Upstairs,** 317 10th Ave. SW, tel. (403) 269-4722. Cannery Row is a casual affair, with an open kitchen, oyster bar, and the ambience of a San Francisco seafood restaurant. Typical fish dishes available are salmon, halibut, swordfish, and marlin. A good choice of southern-style entrees is also offered. The menu at McQueens Upstairs is more varied and slightly more expensive (dinner entrees $14-23). Both restaurants are open daily for lunch (except Sunday) and dinner and are busy during office lunch hours.

Upscale

For the best steaks in the city that produces the best beef in Canada, head to **Caesar's Steakhouse,** 512 4th Ave. SW, tel. (403) 264-1222. The dimly lit, elegant restaurant is decorated in a Roman-style setting. The chef is enclosed in a glass bubble, allowing diners to watch him at work. Although the menu is varied it's the juicy prime cuts that Caesar's is famous for. Entrees are $10-35. Open Mon.-Fri. noon-2 p.m. and daily 4:30 p.m.-midnight.

The **Owl's Nest,** 320 4th Ave. SW, tel. (403) 266-1611, in the Westin Hotel is an upscale restaurant with elegant surroundings where ladies are presented with a rose and gentlemen with a cigar. Many entrees are low-cholesterol; others, such as turtle soup, quail, and beluga caviar certainly aren't. Entrees are $15-30, lunch is slightly less expensive. Open Mon.-Fri. for lunch and dinner and on Saturday for dinner only. In the Delta Bow Valley Hotel is **The Conservatory,** 209 4th Ave. SE, tel. (403) 298-5088, a fine-dining restaurant with a French chef. Enjoy a pre-dinner drink in **The Lobby Lounge.** Other high-end restaurants in town include the **Rimrock Restaurant,** 133 9th Ave.

SW, tel. (403) 262-1234, in the historic Palliser Hotel, and **Trader's,** 110 9th Ave. SE, tel. (403) 266-7331, in the Radisson Plaza Hotel (where waiters wear white gloves and diners are entertained by a pianist). At the top of the Calgary Tower is **Panorama Restaurant,** 101 9th Ave. SW, tel. (403) 266-7171, a revolving restaurant that takes one hour for a full rotation. As far as revolving restaurants go the food is excellent; the menu features mainly local game. It's open daily 7:30 a.m.-midnight.

Kensington

Across the Bow River from downtown lies the trendy suburb of Kensington, home to a number of coffeehouses and restaurants. One of the nicest is **Higher Ground,** 1126 Kensington Rd. NW, tel. (403) 270-3780, a specialty coffee shop with a few windowfront tables. **Diva,** 1154 Kensington Crescent NW, tel. (403) 270-3739, is another stylish place in the same area. The casual two-story **Stromboli Ristorante,** 1147 Kensington Crescent NW, tel. (403) 283-1166, featuring a few tables on private balconies, serves gourmet pizza and pastas (most under $12). **Charly Chan's,** 1140 Kensington Rd. NW, tel. (403) 283-6165, is a yuppie Chinese restaurant. You won't see many Chinese eating here, but the Peking-style dishes are well prepared and popular with Calgarians. Kensington's busiest intersection offers another bunch of eateries, namely **Tandoori Hut,** 201 10th St. NW, tel. (403) 270-4012, serving a small lunch buffet for $6.95 and, at the same address, **Osteria de Medici,** tel. (403) 283-5553, a stylish Italian restaurant with main meals starting at $7.95 for lunch and $9.95 for dinner.

SOUTH OF DOWNTOWN

Breakfast

Usually I try to avoid restaurants named after their owners, but **Nellies,** 738 17th Ave. SW, tel. (403) 228-3667, was a pleasant surprise. It's a small low-key place with fast and friendly service and, most importantly, great food. Breakfasts claim the spotlight; a pile of bacon and eggs with all the trimmings is just $7 and there are plenty of other lighter choices. It's open daily for breakfast and lunch.

Italian

Few restaurants in the city are as popular as **Chianti,** 1438 17th Ave. SW, tel. (403) 229-1600. Over 20 well-prepared pasta dishes are featured on the menu; all the pasta is made daily on the premises. Among many specialties are the Veal Chianti and Frutti Di Mare. Pasta entrees are all under $10 and no dish is over $13. The restaurant is dark and noisy in typical Italian style. The owner often sings with an accordionist on weekends. It's open daily till midnight.

French

For many years **La Chaumiere,** one of North America's premier French restaurants, occupied an unpretentious building down by Stampede Park, but in 1996 it moved to a location more befitting its prestige at 139 17th Ave. SW, tel. (403) 228-5690. Dishes such as duck in brandy, flaming duck, and escargot are authentically prepared, and the formal service is meticulous. Reservations are required for dinner. It's open for lunch Mon.-Fri. noon-2:30 p.m., and for dinner Mon.-Sat. from 5:30 p.m. Less expensive is **Entre Nous,** 2206 4th St. SW, tel. (403) 228-5525, where a three-course lunch is under $20 per person. The tin ceiling and glass-topped tables are a legacy of the way this restaurant began—as a French bistro. **Jo Jo Bistro Parisien,** 917 17th Ave., tel. (403) 245-2382, is a small, cozy eatery decorated simply with definitive French influence. Lunch items are mostly under $10 while dinners range $14-18. The service is excellent. Open Mon.-Fri. 11:30 a.m.-2 p.m. and 5:30-10:30 p.m. and on Saturday for dinner only 5:30-11 p.m.

Moroccan

When you enter **Sultan's Tent,** 909 17th Ave. SW, tel. (403) 244-2333, a server appears with a silver kettle and basin filled with orange-blossom-scented water to wash your hands. It's all part of Moroccan custom and part of the fun. The restaurant features swinging lanterns, hassocks, piped-in Arabic music, and most importantly, delicious Moroccan delicacies. Try Guelli's Sultan Feast ($22.75), a six-course dinner.

Other Ethnic Restaurants

Restaurant Indonesia, 1604 14th St. SW, tel. (403) 244-0645, is a busy, inexpensive eatery at the west end of 17th Avenue. Indonesian food is very similar to Chinese, although the sauces prepared here are usually richer. Entrees are $5-9. On 4th St. SW between 17th and 25th Avenues are a number of ethnic restaurants. **Rajdoot,** 2424 4th St. SW, tel. (403) 245-0181, has an excellent lunchtime buffet ($9.95) with around 25 different Indian dishes, each rated mild, medium, or hot. The turnover of food is fast, ensuring that items stay fresh and hot. The Sunday brunch buffet ($10.95) has even more choices. Toward the city a couple of blocks is **Pita's Cafe,** 2308 4th St. SW, tel. (403) 228-3667, featuring build-your-own falafels and doniers for $2.50-6.

Another good place for budget-minded travelers with exotic tastes is **Cafe Med,** 2202 4th St. SW, tel. (403) 245-0352. This restaurant has a pastel-pink interior with large windows and a relaxed atmosphere. The cuisine is Lebanese, many dishes are vegetarian. The Platter Sampler ($13.90) is a good chance to taste everything. It's open Mon.-Sat. 11 a.m.-11 p.m., Sunday 4-11 p.m. Next door is **Andrea's Taverna,** 2210 4th St. SW, tel. (403) 244-1771, a traditional blue-and-white-decorated Greek restaurant with a belly dancer on Friday night. Entrees are $8-12; finish with Greek coffee and baklava. It's open Mon.-Fri. 11 a.m.-midnight; weekends for dinner only.

Macleod Trail South

This commercial strip from 36th Ave. to Anderson Rd. is crammed with all the familiar fast-food restaurants found everywhere in North America. Aside from these a few family restaurants along this stretch are worth searching for. **Cactus Club Cafe,** 7010 Macleod Trail SE, tel. (403) 255-1088, has a yuppie Western atmosphere. The interior is absolutely crammed with cow-related artifacts, although the only thing that's authentic are the peanut shells on the floor. **Billy MacIntyre's,** 7104 Macleod Trail SE, tel. (403) 252-2260, features Alberta beef at reasonable prices. All entrees include an extensive salad bar that, unlike most restaurants, is tucked out of sight of other diners. For those with cash to

splash try the High Roller Special that comes with a bottle of Jack Daniels. Farther south is **Fuddruckers,** 9823 Macleod Trail SW, tel. (403) 255-2269, a burger joint with an in-house bakery, butcher, and build-your-own burger bar.

NORTH OF DOWNTOWN

Italian

Mamma's, 320 16th Ave. NW, tel. (403) 276-9744, is the most popular Italian eatery on the northside and has been around for decades. Start with the antipasto buffet, then try one of the many veal dishes, and finish with one of their spectacular desserts, all for under $20 per person. Closed Sunday.

Nick's Steakhouse

Whether it's professional sportsmen, their managers, or their fans, chances are if they're from Calgary they've eaten at Nick's. Its prime location directly opposite McMahon Stadium, good food, and large-screen TV all contribute to the restaurant's success. Lunch specials are $6.95, dinner specials $10.95, and charbroiled steaks begin at $12. Open daily till one or two in the morning. No reservations taken. Nick's is at 2430 Crowchild Trail NW, tel. (403) 282-9278.

Dining with a Difference

Named after the mothballed flying machine of the late Howard Hughes, **Spruce Goose Cafe,** Shell Aerocentre, 1441 Aviation Blvd. NE, tel. (403) 295-4140, is adjacent McCall Field, the southern end of Calgary International Airport. The Spruce Goose attracts a wide range of patrons, from grease-stained airplane mechanics to private-plane pilots, and they all come for one reason: great food in a relaxed atmosphere. The building's east wall is all window, great for watching the outdoor action. Breakfast costs around $5 (the Flying Start, at $4.75, is a particularly good value), lunch and dinner dishes start at $6. Open Mon.-Thurs. 7 a.m.-2:30 p.m., Friday 7 a.m.-8 p.m., Saturday 10 a.m.-8 p.m., Sunday 10 a.m.-2 p.m.

TRANSPORTATION

GETTING THERE

Air

Calgary International Airport (YYC), Canada's fourth busiest, is located within the city limits northeast of downtown. It is served by over a dozen scheduled airlines and used by 4.5 million passengers each year. **Arrivals** is on the lower level where passengers are greeted by Welcome Hosts—dressed in traditional Western attire, they answer visitor questions about the airport, transportation, and the city. Among the baggage carousels is an information booth shaped like a chuck wagon (open daily 7 a.m.-10 p.m.). Also on the arrivals level are hotel courtesy phones and rental-car agencies. **Chateau Airport,** connected by a skywalk, is the only hotel at the airport. A cab to the city center runs around $25, or you can catch the **Airporter** bus, tel. (403) 531-3909, to major downtown hotels for $8.50 one-way, $15 roundtrip. A couple of times daily **Brewster,** tel. (403) 762-6767 or (800) 661-1152, offers transfers between the airport and Banff ($30 one-way), Lake Louise ($35), and, in summer only, Jasper ($56).

Scheduled airlines using Calgary International Airport include: **Air B.C.,** tel. (403) 265-9555; **Air Canada,** tel. (403) 265-9555 or (800) 332-1080; **American Airlines,** tel. (800) 433-7300; **Canada 3000,** tel. (403) 266-8095; **Canadian,** tel. (403) 235-1161 or (800) 665-1177; **Canadian Regional,** tel. (800) 665-1177; **Delta,** tel. (800) 221-1212; **Horizon,** tel. (800) 547-9308; **K.L.M.,** tel. (403) 236-2600 or (800) 361-1887; **Northwest Airlines,** tel. (800) 225-2525; **NWT Air,** tel. (403) 265-9555 or (800) 661-0789; **United Airlines,** tel. (800) 241-6522; and **West-Jet,** tel. (403) 266-8086.

Bus

The **Greyhound Bus Depot** is at 850 16th St. SW, tel. (403) 265-9111 or (800) 661-8747. Two blocks away from the depot is the C-train stop ($1.50 into town), or cross the overhead pedestrian bridge at the terminal's southern entrance and catch a transit bus. To walk the entire distance to town would take 20 minutes. A cab from the bus depot to downtown runs $6, to Calgary International Hostel $7. The depot is cavernous. It has a restaurant, Royal Bank cash machine, information boards, and lockers large enough for backpacks ($2).

Buses connect Calgary daily with Edmonton (three and a half hours, $33.17 one-way), Banff (two hours, $16.85 one-way), Vancouver (15 hours, $98.44 one-way), and all other points within the province. No reservations are taken. Just turn up, buy your ticket, and hop aboard. If you buy your ticket seven days in advance, discounts apply. If you plan to travel extensively by bus, the Canada Travel Pass is a good deal.

Red Arrow is a more luxurious bus service that shuttles passengers between downtown Calgary and downtown Edmonton with some services continuing to Fort McMurray in northern Alberta. To Edmonton it's $33 one-way. The Calgary office and pick-up point is downtown at 205 9th Ave., tel. (403) 531-0350 or (800) 232-1958.

GETTING AROUND

Bus

You can get just about everywhere in town by using the Calgary Transit System, which combines three light-rail lines with extensive bus routes. Buses are $1.50 one-way to all destinations—deposit the exact change in the box beside the driver and request a transfer (valid for 90 minutes) if you'll be changing buses. A day pass, valid for unlimited bus and rail travel, is $4.50. The best place for information and schedules is the **Calgary Transit Customer Service Centre** at 240 7th Ave. SW (opposite the Bay department store). Open Mon.-Fri. 8:30 a.m.-5 p.m. An information line is available seven days; call (403) 262-1000.

C-Train

C-train, the light-rail transit system, has three lines that converge downtown on 7th Avenue. The **Anderson C-train** parallels Macleod Trail south to Anderson Rd., **Whitehorn C-train** heads out of the city northeast, and **Brentwood C-train** heads northwest past the university. The system is operated by Calgary Transit, so fares are the same as buses, $1.50 one-way or $4.50 for a day pass. Transfers in the same direction are free, as is travel on the downtown route along 7th Avenue. For route information call (403) 276-7801. Route maps and ticket-vending machines are located at all C-train stations.

Passengers with Disabilities

Bus no. 31 around downtown is wheelchair accessible, as are five other routes through the city. The Brentwood line (northwest) is the only fully accessible route on the C-train system. For information on all wheelchair-accessible services call (403) 262-1000. **Calgary Handi-bus** provides wheelchair accessible transportation throughout the city. A book of eight tickets is $12, but visitors receive free service for a limited length of time. For more information call (403) 276-8028. A small number of manual wheelchairs are available for loan from the **Red Cross Society,** tel. (403) 541-4400.

Taxi

Flag charge for a cab in Calgary is $2.25, and it's $1.30 for every kilometer. Taxi companies include: **Associated Cabs,** tel. (403) 299-1111; **Calgary Cab Co.,** tel. (403) 777-2222; **Checker Cabs,** tel. (403) 299-9999; **Metro Cabs,** tel. (403) 250-1800; and **Yellow Cab,** tel. (403) 974-1111.

Car Rental

If you've just arrived in Calgary, call around and compare rates. Lesser-known agencies are often cheaper, and all rates fluctuate with the season and demand. Many larger agencies have higher rates for unlimited mileage and built-in drop-off charges to nearby centers. (Drop-off charges to Banff are usually $50 extra, and to Edmonton $80 extra.) All agencies provide free pick-up and drop-off at major Calgary hotels and have outlets at Calgary International Airport. Rental agencies include **Avis,** tel. (403) 291-1475 or (800) 879-2847; **Budget,** tel. (403) 226-1550 or (800) 268-8900; **Discount Car Rentals,** tel. (403) 299-1222 or (800) 263-2355; **Dollar,** tel. (403) 269-3777 or (800) 800-4000; **Economy Car Rentals,** tel. (403) 291-1640; **Enterprise,** tel. (403) 299-1249 or (800) 387-4747; **Hertz,** tel. (403) 221-1300 or (800) 263-0600; **Stampede Rent-a-car,** tel. (403) 287-1423; **Thrifty,** tel. (403) 262-4400 or (800) 367-2277; and **Tilden,** tel. (403) 263-6386.

Tours

Brewster, tel. (403) 221-8242, runs a Calgary City Sights tour lasting four hours. Included on the itinerary are downtown, various historic buildings, Canada Olympic Park, and Fort Calgary. The tour costs $35. Pick-ups are at most major hotels. Brewster also runs tours departing Calgary daily to Banff (nine hours, $65), Lake Louise (nine hours, $68), and the Columbia Icefield (15 hours, $84; Snocoach an additional $21.50). Find their downtown office on Stephen Avenue Mall at the corner of Centre St. and 8th Avenue.

SERVICES AND INFORMATION

SERVICES

The downtown **post office** is located at 207 9th Ave. SW. **Currencies International** occupies 304 8th Ave. SW, tel. (403) 290-0330, as well as 131 9th Ave. SW, tel. (403) 264-8009. **American Express Travel Service,** 421 7th Ave. SW, tel. (403) 261-5982, offers all the same currency services with the advantages of also being a travel agency. Most major banks carry U.S. currency and can handle basic foreign-exchange transactions.

West Canadian Color, 1231 10th Ave. SW, tel. (403) 244-2711, is the most efficient and reliable photo lab in town. Turnaround time on print film is an hour; on E6 slide film five hours. Drop any film off before closing time and it will be ready first thing the following day. It's open Mon.-Sat. 7 a.m.-5:30 p.m., Saturday 8 a.m.-4 p.m.

For further travel arrangements, **Travel Cuts,** 1414 Kensington Rd. NW, tel. (403) 531-2070, is the best place to start looking for inexpensive tickets.

Handy self-service laundromats are: **Avenue Towers,** 333 17th Ave. SW; **Heritage Hill Coin**

Laundry, 8228 Heritage Hill Rd. SE at the corner of Macleod Trail and Heritage Dr.; and **The Great Canadian Cleaners,** 4949 Barlow Trail SE.

Emergency Services

For medical emergencies call 911 or contact one of the following hospitals: **Calgary General Hospital,** 841 Centre Ave. NE, tel. (403) 268-9111; **Foothills Hospital,** 1403 29th Ave. NW, tel. (403) 670-1110; **Holy Cross Hospital,** 2210 2nd St. SW, tel. (403) 541-2000; **Rockyview General Hospital,** 7007 14th St. SW, tel. (403) 541-3000; or **Alberta Children's Hospital,** 1820 Richmond Rd. SW, tel. (403) 229-7211. For the **RCMP** call (403) 230-6483.

INFORMATION

Libraries

The Calgary Public Library Board's 16 branch libraries are scattered throughout the city. The largest is **W.R. Castell Central Library** located at 616 Macleod Trail SE, tel. (403) 260-2600. Four floors of books, magazines, and newspapers from around the world (including the all-important *Sydney Morning Herald*) are enough to keep most people busy on a rainy afternoon. Other main branches are **Nose Hill Library** at 1530 Northmount Dr. NW, **Village Square Library** at 2623 56th St. NE, and **Fish Creek Area Library** at 11161 Bonaventure Dr. SE. Hours at each are generally Mon.-Thurs. 10 a.m.-9 p.m., Fri.-Sat. 10 a.m.-5 p.m. (and on Sunday in winter only).

Bookstores

Downtown, **The Book Company** in Bankers Hall, 315 8th Ave. SW, tel. (403) 237-8344, is a good place to find books on western Canada as well as general travel writing and nonfiction works. Another good bookshop is **Sandpiper Books,** 720 11th Ave. SW, tel. (800) 267-4737. Sandpiper also runs an outlet in Eau Claire Market. Both are open daily. The suburb of Kensington, immediately northwest of downtown, has a variety of new and used bookstores, including **Pages,** 1135 Kensington Rd. NW, tel. (403) 283-6655, which sells new titles. Another concentration of secondhand and collector bookstores is 16th Ave. NE between 6th and 9th Streets.

For topographic, city, and wall maps, as well as travel guides, **Map Town,** 640 6th Ave. SW, tel. (403) 266-2241, should have what you're looking for.

Information Centers

Within the city limits are four visitor service centers operated by the Calgary Convention and Visitors Bureau. One is on the main floor of the **Calgary Tower Centre** at the corner of Centre St. and 9th Ave. SW. This small center is open year-round, daily 8:30 a.m.-5 p.m. On the arrivals level at **Calgary International Airport** is another, open year-round, daily 7 a.m.-10 p.m. Seasonal locations are at **Canada Olympic Park** and on the westbound side of the TransCanada Hwy. between 58th and 62nd St. NE. Both are open June-Aug., daily 9 a.m.-5 p.m. For more information on Calgary call (403) 263-8510 or (800) 661-1678 (toll-free anywhere in North America).

On the Internet

For the latest news about Calgary's recreation and entertainment, along with a full listing of sights, accommodations, restaurants, and transportation, surf the Internet to **U.Wanna.What** at http://www.UWannaWhat.com. The site is updated regularly, with many listings, such as weather forecasts, updated daily.

KAREN McKINLEY

SOUTHERN ALBERTA

Southern Alberta is bordered to the east by Saskatchewan, to the south by Montana, USA, and to the west by British Columbia. The Alberta/British Columbia border is along the Continental Divide, where the Rocky Mountains rise dramatically from the prairies and are visible from up to 200 km away. From high in these mountains the Oldman, Crowsnest, Waterton, St. Mary, and Belly Rivers flow east through the rolling foothills and across the shortgrass prairies into the South Saskatchewan River, which eventually drains into Hudson Bay. Among southern Alberta's rivers, only the Milk River is not part of this system; from its headwaters in northern Montana, the river flows north and east across southern Alberta before re-entering the U.S. west of Wild Horse. From there it joins the Missouri/Mississippi River System, eventually draining into the Gulf of Mexico. All these rivers have carved deep gorges into the prairies, providing havens for many species of wildlife including pronghorn, deer, foxes, coyotes, and bobcats.

For many people, a trip to southern Alberta starts in Calgary from where they take Hwy. 2 south through Claresholm and Fort Macleod to

Alberta's third-largest city, Lethbridge, a farming and ranching center 216 km southeast of Calgary. Lethbridge offers a host of interesting things to see including Fort Whoop-Up, a reconstruction of a notorious post where whiskey was traded with the Indians for buffalo hides, guns, and horses.

East of Lethbridge, in an area declared "unsuitable for agriculture" by early explorer John Palliser, the city of Medicine Hat has grown up on top of vast reserves of natural gas. Traveling south from Medicine Hat, the Cypress Hills soon come into view, rising 500 meters above the prairies. The tree-covered plateau provides a refuge for many species of mammals, and mountain plants flourish here, far from the Rockies.

Southern Alberta reveals plentiful evidence of its history and prehistory. Thousands of years of wind and water erosion have uncovered the world's best-preserved dinosaur eggs near Milk River and have carved mysterious-looking sandstone hoodoos farther downstream at Writing-On-Stone Provincial Park—named for the abundant rock carvings and paintings created there by ancient artists. And Head-Smashed-In Buffalo

Jump, west of Fort Macleod, was used for at least 5,700 years by native peoples to drive massive herds of buffalo to their deaths.

The breathtaking mountainscapes of Waterton Lakes National Park are comparable to those of Banff and Jasper National Parks, Waterton's two northern neighbors. The route to the park is scenic as the transition from prairie to mountain peaks is abrupt. Most activities in the park center around a series of deep lakes, but the park also offers some of the best wildlife-viewing opportunities in the province. One of the highlights of a visit to Waterton is an international cruise across the border to Goat Haunt, Montana.

The Municipality of Crowsnest Pass comprises several small communities that extend from the ranching center of Pincher Creek west to the British Columbia border. They were established to serve the pass's coal-mining industry, but after a series of disasters—some mining related, some not—the mines closed. Today the towns are only shadows of their former selves, and the entire corridor has been declared an ecomuseum. Here you can walk through the foundations of once-thriving communities, tour an underground mine, or climb infamous Turtle Mountain.

For more information on southwestern Alberta, write to Chinook Country Tourist Association, 2805 Scenic Dr., Lethbridge, AB T1K 5B7; tel. (403) 329-6777 or (800) 661-1222. For information on the Medicine Hat region including Cypress Hills write to Southeastern Travel Association, P.O. Box 605, Medicine Hat, AB T1A 7G5; tel. (403) 527-6422 or (800) 481-2822.

CALGARY TO LETHBRIDGE

The trip between Alberta's largest and third-largest cities takes about two hours each way, with many worthwhile detours in between, including the ranching country southwest of Calgary (see "Ranchlands" in the West of Calgary chapter), the Porcupine Hills west of Claresholm, historic Fort Macleod, and Head-Smashed-In Buffalo Jump, one of North America's best-preserved such sites.

NANTON AND VICINITY

In this town of 1,600, 70 km south of Calgary, Nanton Spring Water Company bottles some of Canada's finest drinking water and distributes it throughout the world. The town, a stop along busy Hwy. 2, is also a supply center for nearby ranches.

Sights
The **Nanton Lancaster Society Air Museum,** tel. (403) 646-2270, features one of the few Lancaster bombers still in existence. The Lancaster is a Canadian-built, four-engined, heavy bomber that played a major role in WW II air offensives on Nazi Germany. On the guided tour you can sit in the plane's cockpit and look through the sight of the machine gun. A replica of another classic—a Vickers Viking biplane—sits outside. Other displays focus on Canada's role in WW II. The museum, on Hwy. 2 southbound, is open mid-May to October daily 9 a.m.-5 p.m., the rest of the year weekends only 10 a.m.-4 p.m.

A turn-of-the-century schoolhouse on the corner of Hwy. 2 northbound and 18th Ave. now holds the town's **Tourist Information Centre.**

We have passed through a country, dry, desolate, and barren, a very Sahara. It was the northern portion of the Great American Desert: but now we have fortunately come into a country that shows even in this late season, evidence of great fertility. We are just near the base of the Rocky Mountains; their snow-capped summits rise up to our left in jagged, rough peaks; the sun sinks behind them every night in one blaze of glory, making the most gorgeous sunsets that I have ever seen.

—R.B. Nevitt, 11 October 1874

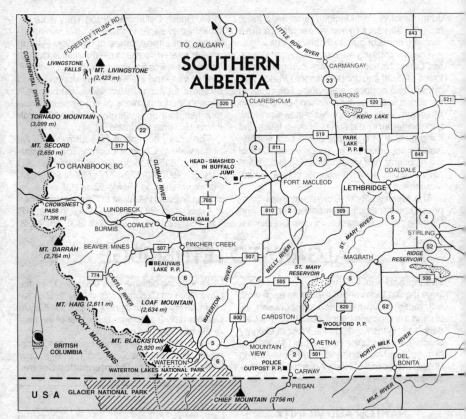

Events

Every Friday during July and August at the Rodeo Grounds, the **Nanton Nite Rodeo** attracts local amateurs keen to test their skills. **Roundup Days,** the town's midsummer festival, held the last weekend of July, features a rodeo, beerfest, and road rally. Some of Canada's best musicians gather for the **Shady Grove Bluegrass and Old Tyme Music Festival.** It takes place the third weekend of August at Broadway Farm, 13 km east of Nanton; for more information call (403) 646-2076.

Accommodations and Food

Nanton's two motels, the **Ranchland Inn Motel,** tel. (403) 646-2933, and **Double "D" Motel,** tel. (403) 646-2170, are both on Hwy. 2 northbound.

Expect to pay $40 s, $45 d. **Nanton Campground** is east of town on 18th St., adjoining the golf course. Scattered among a grove of trees, the sites here have picnic tables, a kitchen shelter, and pit toilets; $8 per night. Originally a blacksmith's shop constructed at the turn of the century, **Subs 'n Such** is the best place for lunch or a light snack. The forge sat in the corner near the chimney and imprints of hot horseshoes still mar the wooden floor. Coffee and teas cost $1.50, salads and sandwiches start at $3; leave room for the delicious desserts.

Willow Creek Provincial Park

South of Nanton, along the eastern edge of the Porcupine Hills and 14 km west of the traffic roar on Hwy. 2, tree-lined Willow Creek flows

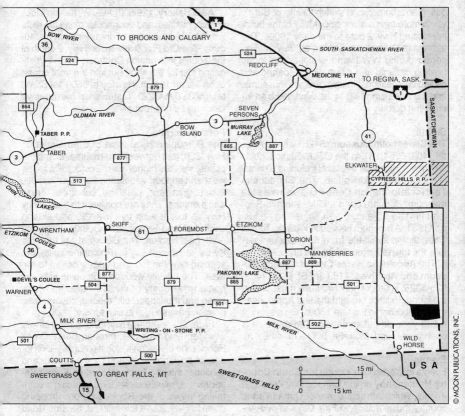

through quiet Willow Creek Provincial Park. Generations of native tribes hunted and camped in the area; just outside the park you can find a buffalo jump and tepee rings well hidden in the grass. Visitors today swim in the creek and camp here. Up on the benchland is a campground with limited services; $9 per night. To reach the park, head west from Stavely.

Farther downstream on Willow Creek lies another historical site. **The Leavings** was a stopover on the Macleod Trail, aptly named to remind travelers they were leaving the last supply of water before Calgary. Later used as a North West Mounted Police post, the site was abandoned when the railway was laid farther to the east. Many of the sandstone foundations remain, as well as some log cabins and a sandstone

barn with tree-trunk floorboards. By road the site is seven km west of Hwy. 2 near Pultenay.

CLARESHOLM

When the Calgary and Edmonton Railway Line extended south in 1891, a new town emerged at its southern terminus. As boomtown storefronts sprang up along the rail line and large landholdings were bought nearby, the town quickly gained a reputation as the hub of a leading grain-producing area. The town has prospered ever since. Clare Amundsen, the town's namesake, was one of its earliest settlers.

Most people stop at Claresholm, 100 km south of Calgary, just long enough to fill up with gas, grab a burger, and stretch their legs. But it's worth more than a quick stop. Many of the buildings facing Hwy. 2 date to the early 1900s. The airbase at Claresholm was an aircrew training center during WW II and is still active today hosting national and international soaring and gliding competitions. In town are two museums, and the Porcupine Hills to the west make an interesting detour.

Sights
The **Claresholm Museum,** 5126 Railway Ave., tel. (403) 625-3131, in the C.P.R. Station, holds an array of historical displays, including a dental clinic and rail ticket office. The Claresholm **Tourist Information Centre** is also inside the museum. Both are open mid-May to mid-September daily 10 a.m.-6 p.m.; museum admission is $1. A brochure entitled *A Walking Tour of Claresholm,* available from the museum, details the town's historic buildings and sites.

The **Appaloosa Horse Club of Canada Museum and Archives,** 4189 3rd St. E, tel. (403) 625-3326, is one of only two such museums in the world. Indians brought the first Appaloosas over the border in the late 1800s. On display is a 200-year-old Indian saddle. The museum is open year-round, Mon.-Fri. 8:30 a.m.-4:30 p.m.

Events
Events in Claresholm include the **South Country Hootenanny** on the Canada Day Weekend in July, which attracts some of Canada's top country music acts, and **Fair Days** in mid-August. In addition, there's always something going on at the **Claresholm Agriplex.**

Accommodations and Food
Motels and fast-food restaurants line Hwy. 2. Nicest of the accommodations is **Bluebird Motel,** tel. (403) 625-3395 or (800) 661-4891, at the north end of town. Most rooms have refrigerators and all have coffeemakers; $46 s, $54 d. Two other motels to the south are slightly less expensive.

Centennial Campground, 4th St. W, north off Hwy. 520, tel. (403) 625-3830, is in a residential area close to the golf course. It offers powered sites, showers, and kitchen shelters; tents $8, RVs and trailers $9-11.

A&B Bakery, 129 50th Ave. W, has delicious breads, pastries, and doughnuts. Along the highway you'll find a string of greasy-spoon restaurants. The **Old Fox Drive-In,** on Hwy. 2 south of the Tourist Information Centre, is worth investigating just for the effort put into the front doors; open 7 a.m.-10 p.m. **Hawley's,** 5009 1st St. W, tel. (403) 625-3222, features an inexpensive lunch and dinner buffet.

Porcupine Hills
The Porcupine Hills, west of Claresholm on Hwy. 520, rest between the mountains and the plains, yet rise higher than the foothills to the west and support vegetation from four climatic zones: grassland, parkland, subalpine forest, and montane. They are bordered to the east by Hwy. 2, to the west by Hwy. 22, and extend south to Head-Smashed-In Buffalo Jump and north past Nanton. The Blackfoot call the area Ky-es-kaghp-ogh-suy-is (Porcupine Tails), describing how the forested ridges looked to natives. The heavily wooded Porcupine Hills are home to a variety of wildlife including white-tailed and mule deer, elk, moose, coyote, lynx, beaver, pheasant, and wild turkey.

From Claresholm Hwy. 520 climbs slowly west for 32 km, passes through Burke Creek Ranch (one of Alberta's oldest ranches—look for classic buildings scattered by the creek), and continues into the **Rocky Mountain Forest Reserve.** It eventually crests a hill affording breathtaking views of the Rockies before dropping down to Hwy. 22. At this hillcrest, **Skyline Road** branches off to the south into the Porcupine Hills, where rewarding trails and sweeping views await explorers. Roads through this area can take you all the way to Cowley.

HIGHWAY 23 SOUTH

An eastern alternative to four-lane Hwy. 2 between Calgary and Lethbridge is Hwy. 23. From High River it runs east past Frank Lake; after 35 km it turns south, skirting the western edge of the prairies. Along the way you'll pass the wheat-farming towns of Vulcan, Champion, Carmangay, and Barons. Highway 23 dead-ends at Hwy. 3, 17 km west of Lethbridge.

Brant

After passing Frank Lake, Hwy. 23 east intersects with Hwy. 804, which detours south to Brant. The town was named for the Brant geese that rest in the area on their migration to and from the north. In 1915, Brant was a prosperous town of 125. But the Great Depression brought grain prices down, forcing farmers to make do with existing machinery. As a result, the dealerships, banks, and other businesses began to close, and many of the children of the '40s and '50s moved away. As the old-timers died and no one moved in to replace them, the town's population dwindled. The railway cut back services, the general store closed, and today only empty buildings and a grain elevator remain.

Vulcan

Halfway between Calgary and Lethbridge on Hwy. 23 lies Vulcan (pop. 1,400), named for the Greek god who lived on Mt. Olympus—the townsite sits on a not-so-Olympian rise above the surrounding prairie. Vulcan is also known as the "Wheat Capital of Canada" and has 12 grain elevators capable of holding over two million bushels of grain.

Little Bow Provincial Park

On the banks of Travers Reservoir east of Champion is Little Bow Provincial Park, an extremely popular place for fishing, swimming, and boating, especially on summer weekends. Heavy irrigation creates the park's green lawns and lush vegetation—a welcome sight after driving through parched and scorched prairies. Some of the province's largest pike live in the reservoir, a feature that attracts anglers year-round. The large campground has a beach, kitchen shelter, showers, firewood, and a concession in the day-use area; $11 per night.

On the access road to the park, 1.5 km from Hwy. 23, a stone cairn marks the site of Cleverville, a once-busy town forced to move when bypassed by the Canadian Pacific Railway. The new town was named Champion and today serves as a center for nearby wheat farms. The **Champion Inn**, tel. (403) 897-3055, offers basic but clean rooms with shared bathrooms for $16 s or d, $22 with private bathroom. Downstairs is a restaurant (open daily 7 a.m.-10 p.m.) and a bar.

Tepee Rings in a Field

In an unimposing grassy field between Hwy. 23 and Little Bow River just north of Carmangay are nine circles of stone, mute testimony to the prehistoric people who roamed the plains of North America. Known as tepee rings, the stones were used to hold down the edges of natives' conical, bison-hide-covered tents. The lack of other artifacts, such as tools and bones, leads archaeologists to believe that this particular site was used for only a short time. A well-worn path leads from the parking lot to a ring that has been partially disturbed; better rings lay to the left of the path.

FORT MACLEOD

Southern Alberta's oldest permanent settlement is Fort Macleod, 44 km west of Lethbridge and just east of the junction of Hwys. 2 and 3. In 1873, the West was in turmoil. Relations between American whiskey traders and natives had reached an all-time low, and intertribal Indian wars were resulting in murder and massacre. That's when politicians in eastern Canada decided to do something about it. A paramilitary mounted police force, led by Colonel James F. Macleod, was sent west with orders to close down Fort Whoop-Up, a notorious whiskey-trading post located where the city of Lethbridge now stands. After finding it empty they decided to push on farther west and build their own fort. The site chosen was an island in the Oldman River, one km east of the present town of Fort Macleod. These early Mounties constructed the fort for the same reason as the whiskey traders—to prevent attacks by natives. But while the whiskey traders were encouraging natives to visit and trade their precious pelts, the police force was trying to drive the traders out of the region. These first troops of the North West Mounted Police eventually put an end to the illicit whiskey trade. And with the help of Metis scout Jerry Potts—who ironically didn't mind a drop of the hard stuff himself—they managed to restore peace between the warring tribes. The original fort had continual flooding problems. It was relocated to higher ground in the 1880s, and the town of Fort Macleod gradually grew up around it.

Historic Downtown

In 1906, a fire destroyed most of the wooden buildings on Main Street, so a bylaw was passed requiring any new structures to be built of brick or stone. The legacy of this bylaw remains in the 30 buildings of historical significance forming the downtown core (which has been declared a historic district). Many of the buildings function as they did during the town's boom years; the **Queens Hotel** has rooms, the **Empress Theatre** is the oldest operating theater in the province, and Main Street comes alive with parades and dances during the summer months. Throughout summer, guided walking tours of town leave regularly from the Fort Museum. Or you can get the walking-tour brochure and do it at your own pace.

Fort Museum

The original fort on the Oldman River would have looked much like the Fort Museum does today, a crude structure aproximately 40 meters wide and 50 meters long lined with buildings facing a central courtyard. The museum details the history of the North West Mounted Police and the early days of settlement in southern Alberta. Inside are various buildings reflecting as-

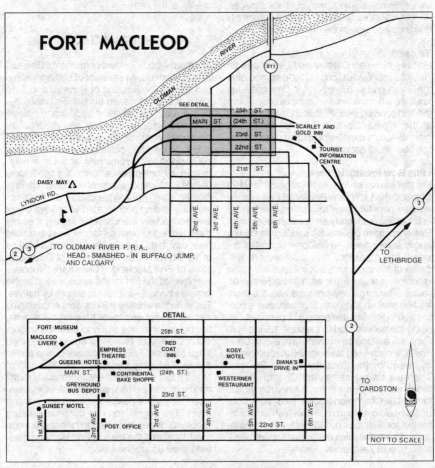

FORT MACLEOD

pects of frontier life including a chapel, blacksmith shop, NWMP building, law office, tepee, and the Centennial Building, which is devoted to the history of the plains Indian tribes. Two corner blockhouses with panoramic views of the Oldman River were used as lookouts. In the arena during summer, riders dress in period costume and perform the **Mounted Police Musical Ride**—a spectacular display of precision riding—four times daily at 10 a.m., 11:30 a.m., 2 p.m., and 3:30 p.m. The museum is at 219 25th St. (westbound), tel. (403) 553-4703. It's open July-Aug. daily 9 a.m.-8:30 p.m.; May, June, and September daily 9 a.m.-5 p.m.; and the rest of the year weekdays 9:30 a.m.-4 p.m. Admission is $4, which includes the Musical Ride.

Macleod Livery

Beside the museum is Macleod Livery, tel. (403) 553-4868, a reconstruction of pioneer buildings, with farm animals running around and a shaded picnic area. A small admission fee is charged. Horse-drawn carriage rides through town are $6.10 per person, and rides down to the old fort site are $6.85 per person. The carriages used are beautifully restored and worth a look even if you don't plan on a tour.

Entertainment

The stage of the venerable 1912 **Empress Theatre** at 235 24th St. has been graced by acts from as far away as New York and Australia. Through its long history it has hosted vaudeville shows, opera and theater performances, political rallies, and film screenings—changing uses with the changing times. The theater has been renovated and returned to its former glory, and it once again provides a venue for live shows and musical theater. Through the months of summer three different productions are performed by the Great West Summer Theatre. For schedule and ticket information call (403) 553-4404. Most shows are under $10. If nothing's happening at the Empress, check out the loud and boisterous **Midnight Lounge** in the Westerner Restaurant. It's open till 2 a.m. nightly, with a DJ on Saturday nights.

Accommodations

Motel rooms fill up fast every afternoon in summer, so book ahead or check in early. Rates fluctuate with the season; expect to pay 20-30% less outside of summer. The least expensive rooms in town (with good reason) are at the **Queens Hotel**, 207 24th St., tel. (403) 553-4343, $20 s, $25 d. The strip of motels along the east end of 24th St. is the best place to start looking. At **Kosy Motel**, 433 24th St., tel. (403) 553-3115, rates include a hot breakfast at the restaurant next door; $45 s, 55 d. One step up is the **Red Coat Inn**, 359 24th St., tel. (403) 553-4434, offering an indoor pool; $42 s, 46 d. At the west entrance to town is the **Sunset Motel**, 104 Hwy. 3 W, tel. (403) 553-4448, where each room has a fridge, and coffee and toast are available at reception in the morning; $46 s, $52 d.

Daisy May Campground is beside Alberta's oldest golf course and within walking distance of the museum and downtown. It provides showers, a heated pool, laundry, and game room. Tent sites cost $11, sites with hookups $14-16; tel. (403) 553-2455. North of the junction of Hwys. 2 and 3 toward Calgary is **Oldman River Provincial Recreation Area** with primitive campsites going for $7 a night.

Food

The restaurant scene in Fort Macleod is not particularly exciting. The **Silver Grill** and **Rex Cafe** (lunch specials $4) on 24th St. have been restored and offer some nostalgic value. A better choice is the **Continental Bake Shoppe**, 220 24th St., tel. (403) 553-4124. It offers tasty cooked breakfasts from $4.25 and similarly priced sandwiches and bagels daily until 5 p.m. The **Westerner Restaurant**, 404 Main St., tel. (403) 553-4066, has big breakfasts for $4-6; the omelettes are excellent. Lunch and dinner items range $5.50-10 and all include soup or salad. It's open Mon.-Sat. 6 a.m.-2 a.m., Sunday 6 a.m.-10 p.m. The **Scarlet and Gold Inn** at the east end of town, 2323 7th Ave., tel. (403) 553-3337, has a busy coffee shop and a dining room. Breakfast starts at 6 a.m., then it's salads, sandwiches, and hamburgers the rest of the day. The dining room opens at 4:30 p.m. for dinner and the choices are many: steaks (from $10.50), seafood (from $10), prime rib (from $12), and house specials (from $10). For low-priced fast food try **Diana's Drive In**, at the corner of 24th St. and 6th Ave., tel. (403) 553-

4227, where you can get a burger, fries, and shake for under $6.

Services and Information
Greyhound, 2302 2nd Ave., tel. (403) 553-3383, leaves five times daily for Calgary ($21.60) and twice daily for Lethbridge ($8.13). **Laundrette Kome Kleen** is behind the Sunset Motel and open daily 8 a.m.-10 p.m. The **library,** 264 34th St., tel. (403) 553-3880, is open Mon.-Sat. 1-5 p.m. The museum gift shop has a large selection of local history and Canadiana books. The **Tourist Information Centre** is at the east end of town on 24th St., tel. (403) 553-4955; open mid-May to August daily 9 a.m.-8 p.m.

HEAD-SMASHED-IN BUFFALO JUMP

Archaeologists have discovered dozens of buffalo jumps across the North American plains. The largest, oldest, and best preserved is Head-Smashed-In, located along a weathered sandstone cliff in the Porcupine Hills 19 km northwest of Fort Macleod. At the base is a vast graveyard with thousands of years worth of bones from butchered bison piled 10 meters high. The jump represents an exceptionally sophisticated and ingenious hunting technique used by plains Indians at least 5,700 years ago—possibly up to 10,000 years ago—to cunningly outwit thousands of bison, once the largest mammal on the plains.

At the time white settlers arrived on the prairies, over 60 million American bison (also known as buffalo) roamed the plains. The Indians of the plains depended almost entirely on these prehistoric-looking beasts for their survival. They ate the meat fresh or dried it for pemmican; made tepees, clothing, and moccasins from the hides; and fashioned tools and decorations from the horns. The Indians used several means to kill the bison, but by far the most successful method was to drive entire herds over a cliff face. The topography of this region was ideal for such a jump. To the west is a large basin of approximately 40 square km where bison grazed. They were herded from the basin east along carefully constructed stone cairns (known as drive lines) that led to a precipice where the stampeding bison, with no chance of stopping, plunged to their deaths below. Nearby was a campsite where they butchered and processed the meat.

The site has been well preserved. Although a small section of the hill has been excavated, most of it appears today the same as it has for thousands of years. The relative height of the cliff, however, drastically decreased with the build-up of bones. Along with the bones are countless numbers of artifacts such as stone points, knives, and scrapers used to skin the fallen beasts. Metal arrowheads found in the top layer of bones indicate that the jump was used up until the coming of whites in the late 1700s. In recognizing the site's cultural and historical importance, UNESCO declared the jump a World Heritage Site in 1981.

How the Jump Got Its Name
The name Head-Smashed-In has no connection to the condition of the bison's heads after tumbling over the cliff. It came from a Blackfoot legend: about 150 years ago a young hunter want-

Allow at least two hours in the interpretive center.

ed to watch the buffalo as they were driven over the steep cliff. He stood under a ledge watching as the stampeding beasts fell in front of him, but the hunt was better than usual and as the animals piled up he became wedged between the animals and the cliff. Later his people found him, his skull crushed under the weight of the buffalo—hence the name, Head-Smashed-In.

Interpretive Centre

As you approach the jump site along Spring Point Rd., the Head-Smashed-In Interpretive Centre doesn't become visible until you've parked your car and actually arrived at the entrance. The center—disguised in the natural topography of the landscape—is set into a cliff, part of which had to be blasted away to build it. A series of ramps and elevators marks the beginning of your tour as you rise to the roof from where a trail leads along the cliff-top to the jump site. It isn't hard to imagine the sounds and spectacle of thousands of bison stampeding over the rise to the north and tumbling to their deaths below. To the east is the **Calderwood Buffalo Jump,** which can be seen farther along the cliff face.

Back inside you walk down floor by floor passing displays and films explaining in an interesting and informative way the traditional way of life that existed on the prairies for nearly 10,000 years, as well as the sudden changes that took place when the first white men arrived. The lowest level describes the archaeological methods used to excavate the site and how the ancient cultures of the various plains Indians are unraveled from the evidence found. A 10-minute movie, *In Search of the Buffalo,* cataloging the hunt, is shown every half hour on Level Four.

Outside the center is another trail that leads along the base of the cliff for a different perspective. Here a large aluminum building covers a recent dig site; the ground is littered with shattered bones. The center also has a gift shop and cafe selling, of all things, buffalo burgers. The year's largest event is the **Annual Pow Wow** in mid-July, when a large tepee village is constructed on the grounds and native dance competitions, food tastings, and activities for all ages are presented. Each Saturday afternoon in July and August, a noted authority on a subject relevant to the jump presents a short show on his or her field of expertise.

The center is open in summer daily 9 a.m.-8 p.m., the rest of the year Tues.-Sun. 9 a.m.-5 p.m. Admission is adult $6.50, senior $5.50, child $3; half-price on Tuesday from October through April. For more information, contact the center at P.O. Box 1977, Fort Macleod, AB T0L 0Z0, tel. (403) 553-2731.

LETHBRIDGE

An urban oasis on the prairies, this city of rich ethnic origins has come a long way since the 1860s when Fort Whoop-Up, the most notorious whiskey-trading fort in the West, was the main reason folks came to town. Today, Lethbridge is an important commercial center serving the surrounding ranch and farm country. With a population of 64,000, it is Alberta's third-largest city, and on any given day the downtown streets are busy with a colorful array of ranchers, cowboys, Hutterites, Indians, and suited professionals. The city is also a transportation hub, with Hwys. 3, 4, and 5 converging here. Calgary is 215 km to the north, Medicine Hat 168 km to the east, Waterton Lakes National Park 130 km to the west, and the International Boundary 105 km to the south.

In the last 20 years, Lethbridge has blossomed in a controlled way. Many of the city's sites of historical importance have been preserved, or in the case of Fort Whoop-Up, reconstructed. The Sir Alexander Galt Museum is one of the best museums in the province, and the Nikka Yuko Japanese Garden is symbolic of the culture from which many of the city's residents descended.

History

Lethbridge has always been a transportation and trade crossroads. Until the first half of the 19th century it was the territory of various tribes of the powerful Blackfoot Indians. The tribes sheltered from the extreme winters at a site in the Oldman River Valley known to them as Sikooh-kotoks or "Black Rocks" because of an exposed coal seam on the east bank of the river at that spot. The first white traders to the area ar-

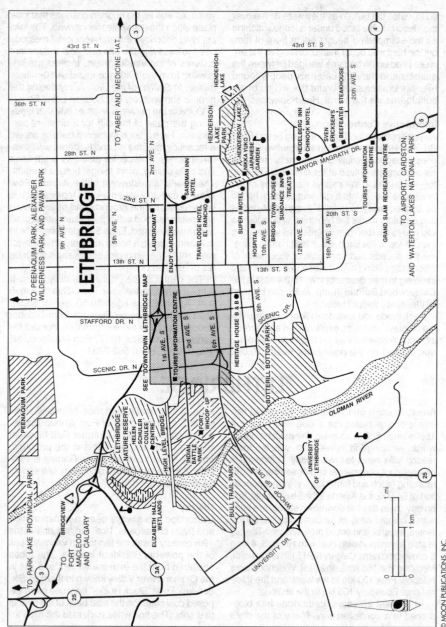

LETHBRIDGE

© MOON PUBLICATIONS, INC.

rived in the 1850s. Soon after came the whiskey traders who had been forced north by the U.S. Army. Fort Whoop-Up, built on the east bank of the Oldman River, became the most notorious of some 50 whiskey posts in southern Alberta.

The arrival of whiskey on the plains coincided with a smallpox epidemic and the dislocation of Cree, who had been forced by the arrival of European settlers into the territory of the Blackfoot, their traditional enemies. These factors all combined to create a setting for the last great intertribal Indian battle to be fought in North America.

At dawn on 25 October 1870, a party of around 800 Cree warriors attacked a band of Blood Blackfoot camping on the west bank of the Oldman River. Unknown to the Cree, a large party of Piegan Blackfoot was camped nearby. Alerted by scouts, the Piegan crossed the river and joined the fray, forcing the Cree back into what is now known as Indian Battle Park. Over 300 Cree and around 50 Blackfoot were killed.

By 1880, the whiskey forts had been closed down by the North West Mounted Police and the last of the plains Indians had been resettled in reservations.

Nicholas Sheran, an Irish-American adventurer, was the first to realize the potential of the coal-bearing seams along the Oldman River. He established the first mine on the river, named Coalbanks. It was only a small operation, but it was large enough to attract the attention of English entrepreneur Elliot Galt. With the help of his father—Sir Alexander Galt—Elliot financed a large-scale drift mine in the east bank of the river, where the Coalbanks Interpretive Site now sits. By 1884, the hamlet of Coalbanks had sprung up around the mine entrance and a sawmill was established. At first the Galts used sternwheel river steamers to transport the coal to Medicine Hat. But on many occasions, the current was so strong that the steamers required as much coal for the return trip as they were capable of hauling on the way out. So after two years, a narrow-gauge railway was constructed to haul the coal. This shifted the community's focus away from the river's edge and up onto the prairie, where the town that took root came to be named Lethbridge. William Lethbridge was an Englishman who never set foot in Alberta, but being a friend of Galt, and a major financier in the Galt's coal mine, the town was named for him.

In 1909 the High Level Bridge—at that time the highest and longest structure of its type in the world—was constructed over the river valley, completing a more permanent link to Fort Macleod and Calgary. The last of the mines closed in 1942 and by 1960 the first of what is now a string of urban parks along the valley was established.

SIGHTS

Downtown

With Lethbridge continuing to sprawl, particularly on the west side of the river, downtown businesses are trying their hardest to convince shoppers and visitors that "Downtown L.A." really does have something to offer. Almost all sites downtown are within walking distance of each other. **Lethbridge Centre** is a modern shopping mall; **Galt Gardens** is a pleasant spot for people-watching; a small **Chinatown** is located along 2nd Ave. S; and many historic buildings still stand. On market days, the many Hutterites who come to town are easy to recognize—the men wear black pants and those that are married have beards, the women wear colorful purple and red dresses and bonnets. The **Southern Alberta Art Gallery,** 601 3rd Ave. S in Galt Gardens, tel. (403) 327-8770, has contemporary and historical exhibitions that change throughout the year. It's open Tues.-Sat. 10 a.m.-5 p.m., Sunday 1-5 p.m.; admission by donation.

Sir Alexander Galt Museum

This excellent history-and-art museum is in a former hospital, named for Sir Alexander Galt, who helped finance the coal-mining operation that was fundamental in the establishment of the city. It was renovated in 1985 at a cost of $2.85 million and is now considered one of the best small-city museums in the country. The first gallery provides a view across the valley— in effect a panorama of the city's past. From this vantage point you can see the site of the last major intertribal battle in North America, old coal mines, Fort Whoop-Up, and the High Level Bridge. Other galleries contain exhibits explaining the history of the coal mines, the introduction of irrigation, the area's immigrants, and the city since WW II. Two additional galleries have rotating art exhibits of local interest. The museum is at the west end of 5th Ave. S off Scenic Drive. It's open July-Aug. Mon.-Thurs. 9 a.m.-8 p.m., Friday 9 a.m.-4 p.m., Sat.-Sun. 1-8 p.m.; the rest of the year Mon.-Fri. 10 a.m.-4 p.m., Sat.-Sun. 1-4 p.m. Admission is free. For more information call (403) 320-3898.

Fort Whoop-Up

This impressively palisaded structure in Indian Battle Park is a replica of the most notorious whiskey-trading post in the West. After the U.S. Army put a stop to the illicit trade in Montana, these traders of sorts simply began moving north into what is now Alberta. In December 1869, John J. Healy and Alfred B. Hamilton came north from Fort Benton, Montana, and established a fort on the Oldman River which soon became the whiskey-trading headquarters for southern Al-

berta. The story goes that its name was coined by someone who had returned to Fort Benton and when asked how things were going at Hamilton's Fort replied, "oh, they're still whoopin' it up." Trading was simple. Indians pushed buffalo hides through a small opening in the fort wall. In return they were handed a tin cup of whiskey, which was often watered down. The success of the trade led to the formation of the North West Mounted Police, who rode west with orders to close down all whiskey-trading forts and end the lawless industry. The Mounties were preceded by word of their approach and the fort was empty by the time they arrived. A cairn marks the fort's original location.

A reconstruction of the fort, complete with costumed staff, relives the days when firewater was traded for hides and horses. The fort looks much as it would have in 1869. A cannon used to de-

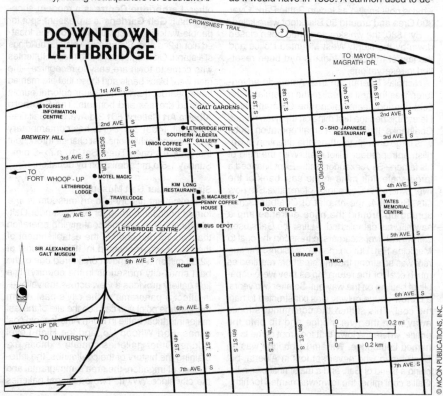

fend the fort is on display, an audiovisual presentation is shown, and the Whoop-Up flag—now the official flag of Lethbridge—flies high above. To get there from the city center turn west onto 3rd Ave. S and follow it down into the coulee. It's open mid-May to early September, Mon.-Sat. 10 a.m.-6 p.m., Sunday noon-8 p.m.; admission by donation. For more information call (403) 329-0444.

Fort Whoop-Up's flag is now the official flag of Lethbridge.

park, the **Coalbanks Interpretive Site** is located at the site of the original mine entrance between Fort Whoop-Up and the Helen Schuler Coulee Centre. Coalbanks, founded in 1874, was the original settlement in the valley. Indian Battle Park extends from the Oldman River to behind the buildings up on Scenic Drive. Many viewpoints can be found along the top of the coulee, accessible by timber steps leading up from the floodplain.

Botterill Bottom Park, adjacent to Indian Battle Park, houses underground utility lines and cannot be developed. Across the Oldman River is **Bull Trail Park,** an undeveloped area that extends south to the university. To the north is **Elizabeth Hall Wetlands,** a 15-hectare reserve of floodplain habitat that encompasses an oxbow pond. North of the Lethbridge Nature Reserve is **Peenaquim Park,** 97 hectares of floodplain that was formerly a stockyard. Access to **Alexander Wilderness Park** is from Stafford Dr. N. This road descends into a coulee and three short trails radiate out along the floodplain to viewpoints of the Oldman River. The northernmost river-valley park is **Pavan Park.** The entrance road winds down a narrow coulee to a day-use area by the Oldman River. Here a reclaimed gravel pit is stocked with trout, short walks lead along the floodplain, and a picnic area has firewood and fire rings.

Lethbridge Nature Reserve and Helen Schuler Coulee Centre

Lethbridge is unique in that it's built on the prairie benchlands and not beside the river that flows so close to town. The largely undisturbed Oldman River Valley has been developed into reserves and parks. One of these, the Lethbridge Nature Reserve, is an 82-hectare area of floodplain and coulees. It's home to Alberta's provincial bird—the great horned owl—porcupines, white-tailed deer, and prairie rattlesnakes. It's also home to the Helen Schuler Coulee Centre, which offers interpretive displays focusing on the entire urban park system. The center is the best place to start exploration of the valley. From here three short trails lead through the reserve. To get there from downtown, head west on 3rd Ave. S, take a right just before Fort Whoop-Up, and pass under the High Level Bridge. It's open June-Aug., Sun.-Thurs. 10 a.m.-8 p.m., Fri.-Sat. 10 a.m.-6 p.m.; the rest of the year, Tues.-Sun. 1-4 p.m. For more information call (403) 320-3064.

Other Valley Parks

The most historically important urban park in Lethbridge is 102-hectare **Indian Battle Park.** It is named after the last great battle fought between Cree and Blackfoot, which took place on the west side of the river in 1870. Within the park, near Fort Whoop-Up, is a "medicine stone" that the Blackfoot believed had sacred significance—for many years they left offerings around it. Also in the

High Level Bridge

High Level Bridge spans 1.6 km and towers 100 meters above the Oldman River Valley—the longest and highest trestle-construction bridge in the world. It was built by the C.P.R. for $1.3 million in 1909, replacing 22 wooden bridges and drastically reducing the length of line between Lethbridge and Fort Macleod. Over 12,000 tons of steel were used in its construction, as well as 17,000 cubic yards of concrete, and 7,600 gallons of paint. Of the many views of the bridge available along the valley, none is better than standing directly underneath (walk down from the Tourist Information Centre on Brewery Hill).

Nikka Yuko Japanese Garden
This garden was established in 1967 by the City of Lethbridge and its Japanese residents as a monument "to the contribution made to Canadian culture by Canadians of Japanese origin." It has been designed as a place to relax and contemplate, with no bright flowers, only green shrubs and gardens of rock and sand. The buildings and bridges were built in Japan under the supervision of a renowned Japanese architect. The main pavilion is of traditional design, housing a *tokonoma* or tea ceremony room. Japanese women in traditional dress lead visitors through the gardens and explain the philosophy behind different aspects of the design. The best view of the garden is from the bell tower whose gentle "gong" signifies good things happening in both countries simultaneously. Open mid-May to early October, daily 9 a.m.-5 p.m., till 8 p.m. during summer; admission $3. The gardens are located in Henderson Lake Park on Mayor Magrath Dr., tel. (403) 328-3511.

RECREATION

Activities in **Henderson Lake Park** on Mayor Magrath Dr. center around a 20-hectare lake that attracts residents year-round. The park features an outdoor swimming pool, tennis courts, demonstration gardens, boat rentals on the lake, and an 18-hole golf course. A paved trail for hikers and cyclists encircles the lake. Another popular recreation spot is **Park Lake Provincial Park,** 17 km north of Lethbridge on Hwy. 25. This once-arid prairie region has been transformed by irrigation. In summer, the lake is a good spot for swimming, windsurfing, fishing, and boating (boat rentals available). Camping is $11 per night; a concession sells fast food.

Golfers can choose among five area golf courses. **Henderson Lake Golf Club,** tel. (403) 329-6767, is within walking distance of the lake's campground ($26); **Bridge Valley Golf Course,** tel. (403) 381-6363, is a par-three course on the west side of the High Level Bridge ($11); and **Paradise Canyon,** tel. (403) 381-7500, near the University, is Alberta's newest championship course and was constructed on a reclaimed floodplain along the Oldman River ($34). The other two courses are private.

Across from the library is the **YMCA,** 515 Stafford Dr. S, tel. (403) 327-9622, which has a pool, weight room, and health club available for $3 per session. Ask about the "first visit is free" program. The $5.3-million **Max Bell Regional Aquatic Centre** in the University of Lethbridge, tel. (403) 329-2583, is also open to the public; $3 for a swim. **Grand Slam Canada Recreation Centre,** on the corner of Mayor Magrath and Scenic Drives, tel. (403) 320-5800, has automated batting cages, go-carts, and mini-golf. It's open in summer daily 10 a.m.-6 p.m., shorter hours the rest of the year.

Anderson Aquatics, 314 11th St. S., tel. (403) 328-5040, is one of Alberta's few scuba-diving shops. Diving trips and lessons run throughout summer. The shop also rents equipment and fills tanks for those heading to Waterton Lakes National Park.

ENTERTAINMENT

A Little Bit of Culture
The Sterndale Bennett Theatre in the Yates Memorial Centre at 110 4th Ave. S is home to **New West Theatre Society,** an amateur company whose popular summer performances sell out most nights. Productions are generally a combination of comedy, song, and dance appealing to everybody. For ticket information call (403) 381-9378. The **Lethbridge Symphony Orchestra** has its office in Yates Centre but performs at locations throughout the city; call (403) 328-6808 for dates and prices. The **Performing Arts Centre** at the University of Lethbridge attracts national and international acts to its three theaters. For upcoming events call (403) 329-2656. The four **movie theaters** in town charge $6-7 and Tuesday is half-price night. One is in the Lethbridge Centre downtown, another on the corner of 8th St. and 4th Ave. S.

A Little Less Culture
The **Cactus Club** in the Parkside Inn at 1009 Mayor Magrath Dr. S whoops it up with live country music on Friday and Saturday nights; cover charge $2.

Another country music venue is **Bridge Country Night Club** at 1713 2nd Ave., tel. (403) 380-2826. If country music isn't your style, head to **Goose Loonies** at 202 5th St. S for Top 40, or have a beer with the boys next door in the **Lethbridge Hotel.**

Festivals and Events

For a city of its size, Lethbridge offers surprisingly few festivals. The year's biggest event, **Whoop-Up Days,** is held at Fort Whoop-Up and at other locations in the city throughout the first week of July. The celebration features pancake breakfasts, a parade, midway, casino, trade show, and grandstand events such as a rodeo. Nightly concerts and cabarets end each day's excitement. For more information call (403) 328-4491.

The **Bud Country Jamboree** is one of the largest gatherings of country-music superstars.

ACCOMMODATIONS

Downtown

Of the four downtown accommodations, **Motel Magic,** 100 3rd Ave. S, tel. (403) 327-6000 or (800) 661-8085, has the best-value rooms. Rates include a continental breakfast, coffee, and use of an exercise room; $49 s, $53 d. Nearby is the **TraveLodge Lethbridge,** 207 4th Ave. S, tel. (403) 327-2104 or (800) 578-7878, which has large rooms; $54 s, $56 d. **Lethbridge Lodge,** 320 Scenic Dr. S, tel. (403) 328-1123 or (800) 661-1232, has the most modern facilities. Many rooms have views of the Oldman River Valley, the others of an enclosed tropical atrium. Amenities include a cafe, restaurant, cocktail lounge, and an indoor pool with a whirlpool; rooms from $78 s or d. At the other end of the scale is the **Lethbridge Hotel,** 202 5th St. S, tel. (403) 327-3151, where rooms with shared bathrooms are $26-31 s or d.

Mayor Magrath Drive

About a dozen motels of varying standards but similar prices line Mayor Magrath Dr. S (Hwy. 5). Many have restaurants, but those that don't are within walking distance of others that do. Also nearby is Nikka Yuko Japanese Garden and Henderson Lake Park. From north to south the best are: **Sandman Inn Hotel,** 421 Mayor Magrath Dr. S, tel. (403) 328-1111 or (800) 663-6900, with an indoor pool and a 24-hour restaurant, $67 s, $75 d; **TraveLodge Hotel El Rancho,** 526 Mayor Magrath Dr. S, tel. (403) 327-5701, with rooms much nicer than the exterior suggests, $54 s, 62 d; **Super 8,** 2210 7th Ave., tel. (403) 329-0100 or (800) 800-8000, featuring large rooms, a heated pool, and a laundry, $56 s, $58 d; **Bridge Town House,** 1026 Mayor Magrath Dr. S, tel. (403) 327-4576, which has large rooms, $44 s, $48 d; **Sundance Inn,** 1030 Mayor Magrath Dr. S, tel. (403) 328-6636 or (800) 561-9815, with rooms as good as anywhere along the strip but only $48 s or d; **Heidelberg Inn,** 1303 Mayor Magrath Dr. S, tel. (403) 329-0555 or (800) 528-1234, a Best Western with a pool and restaurant, $61 s, $63 d; and **Chinook Motel,** next door to the Heidelberg Inn, $34 s, $38 d. Check into Chinook at the Heidelberg.

Heritage House B&B

Heritage House B&B, 1115 8th Ave. S, tel. (403) 328-9011, is an excellent alternative to the motels. The 1937 home is considered one of the finest examples of International–Art Deco design in the province. Its rooms are spacious and tastefully decorated, a hearty breakfast is served downstairs in the dining room, and town is only a short walk along the tree-lined streets of Lethbridge's most sought-after suburb. The bathroom is shared, but for $40 s, $50 d, that is of little consequence.

Campgrounds

Henderson Lake Campground is located on 7th Ave. S. in Henderson Lake Park, tel. (403) 328-5452. It has full hookups, showers, a laundry, groceries, firewood, and fire rings. The serviced section is little more than a paved parking lot, but tenters and those with small vans will enjoy the privacy afforded by trees at the back of the campground. Unserviced sites cost $13, those with hookups are $16-21. Open year-round. **Bridgeview Campground,** on the west bank of the Oldman River at 910 4th Ave. S, tel. (403) 381-2357, has similar facilities to Henderson Lake Campground (as well as a heated pool), but the nearby highway can be noisy. Unserviced sites here go for $11, while hookups are

$17-25. Another alternative is **Park Lake Provincial Park,** 17 km northwest of town on Hwy. 25, which offers camping (no showers) for $11-13 per night.

FOOD

Downtown

Anton's, in the Lethbridge Lodge, tel. (403) 328-1123, is the only true fine-dining restaurant in town, serving dinner daily from 5 p.m. The menu is extensive and the dishes well prepared. Appetizers start at $4, entrees from $14. Also in the lodge is the **Garden Cafe,** open daily 6:30 a.m.-11:30 p.m. and always busy with guests and locals alike. Moderately priced meals are served amid much greenery. The dessert cabinet is strategically placed so that even the most health-conscious diner can't help but be tempted by it.

Good, inexpensive Vietnamese food is dished up at **Kim Long Restaurant,** 329 5th St. S, tel. (403) 380-3866, open daily 10 a.m.-10 p.m., till midnight on Friday and Saturday. Most dishes are under $8. If the menu looks Greek to you, ask to see the family photo album with color photographs of each dish.

Lethbridge has some fine coffee shops—pick of the bunch is **The Penny Coffee House,** 331 5th St. S, tel. (403) 320-5282, where coffee is $1.25, refills are free, and a nice, thick, healthy, sandwich with soup is $6. It's open Mon.-Fri. 7:30 a.m.-10 p.m., Saturday 7:30 a.m.-5:30 p.m., Sunday 10-5 p.m. Another downtown choice is the **Union Coffee House,** at 222 5th St., tel. (403) 328-4677.

Third Avenue South

The popular Chinese buffet at **Enjoy Gardens,** 1903 3rd Ave. S, tel. (403) 328-8770, features lunch (daily 11 a.m.-2:30 p.m.) for $5.25 and dinner (5-8:30 p.m.) for $7.95. Nearby, **Travaglia's,** 1520 3rd Ave., S, tel. (403) 328-4818, offers dishes from all regions of Italy. **O-Sho Japanese Restaurant,** 1219 3rd Ave. S, tel. (403) 327-8382, serves authentic Japanese cuisine; you can sit at standard tables or dine in traditional style on mats in partitioned lounges. Lunch is $4-6, dinner $6.70-10. It's open for lunch Mon.-Fri. 11:30 a.m.-2:30 p.m. and for dinner Mon.-Fri. 4:30-10 p.m., Saturday 4-10:30 p.m.

Mayor Magrath Drive

As well as having the bulk of Lethbridge's accommodations, this road has many fast-food and family restaurants. **Treats Eatery,** 1104 Mayor Magrath Dr. S, tel. (403) 380-4880, is a Western-style family-dining restaurant. It has an enormous gold-rimmed wagon wheel hanging from the ceiling—ask to sit away from it if you like. The menu is straightforward, basically burgers and beef, but is well-priced. Hours are Mon.-Sat. 11 a.m.-10 p.m., Sunday 4-10 p.m. The **Beefeater Steakhouse,** 1917 Mayor Magrath Dr. S, tel. (403) 320-6211, is a traditional English restaurant offering traditional Albertan dishes; the prime rib of beef is especially good. Lunch is $7-12, and dinner specials start at $13. It's open Mon.-Sat. 11 a.m.-midnight, Sunday 11 a.m.-9 p.m. Farther up the road is the impressive **Sven Ericksen's Family Restaurant,** 1715 Mayor Magrath Dr. S, tel. (403) 328-7756. The menu here is heavy on the seafood—odd for a place so far from the ocean. But enough beef and chicken dishes are offered for fishophobes to get by. It's open Mon.-Fri. 11 a.m.-10 p.m., Sat.-Sun. 11 a.m.-11 p.m.

TRANSPORTATION

Lethbridge Airport is eight km south of town on Hwy. 5. It is served by **Canadian Regional,** tel. (403) 327-3000 or (800) 665-1177, and **Air B.C.,** tel. (800) 332-1080, an Air Canada connector. Both fly to Calgary four to seven times daily ($84 one-way, $105 roundtrip if bought seven days in advance) with connections to Edmonton and other national and international destinations. Some motels and car rental companies have courtesy phones at the airport. A cab to downtown is around $18.

The **Greyhound** bus depot is at 411 5th St. S, tel. (403) 327-1551 or (800) 661-8747. Buses leave twice daily for Fort Macleod ($8.13), four times daily for Calgary ($29.10) with connections to Edmonton ($59.17), twice daily to Medicine Hat ($21.67) and to the United States border at Coutts ($14.39), where connections to Great Falls and Helena (Montana) can be made. The depot is open daily 7:30 a.m.-7:30 p.m. and has a small cafe and lockers that are large enough for backpacks ($1).

L.A. Transit city buses run daily with limited service on Sunday. The main routes radiate from Lethbridge Centre on 4th Ave. S out to the university, Henderson Lake Park, and along Mayor Magrath Drive. The adult fare is $1.20. Call (403) 320-3885 for schedules and information. The various car rental agency numbers are: **Rent-A-Wreck,** tel. (403) 328-9484 ($31.95 per day with 100 free km); **Avis,** tel. (403) 382-4880; **Budget,** tel. (403) 328-6555; **Enterprise,** tel. (403) 328-3517; and **Tilden,** tel. (403) 380-3070. For a taxi call **Fifth Avenue Cabs,** tel. (403) 381-1111; **Lethbridge Cabs,** tel. (403) 327-4005; or **Royal Taxi,** tel. (403) 328-5333.

SERVICES AND INFORMATION

The **post office** is in a historic stone building at 704 4th Ave. S. Make a day of it at **Family Coin Laundry,** 128 Mayor Magrath Dr. N, one block north of the highway, where there's a lounge, TV, and free coffee; open daily 8 a.m.-9 p.m. **Lethbridge Regional Hospital** is at 9th Ave. and 18th St. S, tel. (403) 382-6111. For the **RCMP** call (403) 329-5010.

Lethbridge Public Library, 810 5th Ave. S, tel. (403) 380-7310, is an excellent facility with a wide range of literature; open Mon.-Fri. 9:30 a.m.-9 p.m., Saturday 9:30 a.m.-5:30 p.m., and Sunday 1:30-5 p.m. The best bookstore in town is **B. Macabee's Booksellers** at 333 5th St. S, tel. (403) 329-0771. It has a large selection of local history and Canadiana books. After browsing, why don't you let the smell from the Penny Coffee House lure you next door. The *Lethbridge Herald* is a daily (except Sunday) newspaper available throughout town.

Lethbridge's main **Tourist Information Centre** is at 2805 Scenic Dr. (at the corner of Hwys. 4 and 5). It's open in summer daily 9 a.m.-8 p.m., the rest of the year Mon.-Sat. 9 a.m.-5 p.m., tel. (403) 320-1222 or (800) 661-1222 from western Canada and the northwestern United States. A second office near downtown is on Hwy. 3 W (1st Ave. S from the east) at Brewery Hill, beside the former site of the Lethbridge Brewery (a site known as **Brewery Gardens** for the thousands of vividly colored flowers that bloom there each summer). This small center is open in summer daily 9 a.m.-8 p.m., the rest of the year Tues.-Sat. 9 a.m.-5 p.m.; tel. (403) 320-1223.

EAST OF LETHBRIDGE

THE MILK RIVER

The Milk River is unique among western Canada's river systems. All the others eventually drain east into Hudson's Bay, but the Milk River flows south to the Missouri River, eventually draining into the Gulf of Mexico. The area itself is historically unique for western Canada in that it has come under the jurisdiction of eight different governments and countries. During the 1700s, France claimed all the lands of the Mississippi, so a small part of Alberta was under French rule. Later, the same area was part of the Spanish empire, and it's also at one time or another fallen under the rule of the Hudson's Bay Company, the British, and the Americans. It finally became part of the province of Alberta in 1905. A flag display and a historical cairn on the north bank of the river explain this complicated piece of Albertan history.

The town of Milk River (pop. 920) sits on the northern bank of its namesake, 90 km southeast of Lethbridge and 40 km north of the Montana border.

Devil's Coulee

On 14 May 1987, an amateur paleontologist was exploring the coulees near her family's ranch outside of Milk River when she discovered some fossilized egg shells. The find sent waves of excitement around the scientific world and the site became known as **Devil's Coulee Dinosaur Egg Site,** one of the most exciting fossil discoveries ever made. What she had discovered were clutches of eggs that had been laid by hadrosaurs around 75 million years ago. Each prehistoric egg was about 20 centimeters long and contained the perfectly formed embryonic bones of unborn dinosaurs. No find in the world has taught scientists more about this part of the dinosaur's life cycle. The site has recently been opened to the public, but access is only on a guided tour. Tours leave from the village of Warner twice daily throughout summer. Tour cost is $10 per person and advance reservations are required; tel. (403) 329-8875. The Royal Tyrrell Museum of Palaeontology in Drumheller, which manages the site, offers weeklong Field Experience trips to the site. Days are spent involved in the actual excavation and cataloging of specimens. The field camp is basic, with portable toilets and shower facilities; you must supply your own tent, but this is a small price to pay for the thrill of involvement in working at this important site. The cost, which includes all meals, is $800 in June and July and $700 in August. For further information write Field Experience, Royal Tyrrell Museum, P.O. Box 7500, Drumheller, AB T0J 0Y0; tel. (403) 823-7707.

Water Sports on the Milk River
The Milk River is popular with canoeists of all levels of expertise, although no rapids exceed class I. What the river lacks in rapids it more than makes up for in scenic beauty and rich history. The first section from Del Bonita to Milk River passes through shortgrass prairie, and the shallow river valley allows panoramic views of the landscape. This long section (103 km) passes through mainly private property and has a few fence wires that cross the river. Past the town of Milk River, the river valley becomes deeper and enters the badlands of Writing-On-Stone Provincial Park (69 km from Milk River).

Milk River Raft Tours, P.O. Box 396, Milk River, Alberta T0K 1M0, tel. (403) 647-3586, offers a selection of trips down the river in inflatable rafts. The trips last from two to four hours and can be enjoyed by everyone. Tours run throughout summer, leaving from various staging areas downstream of the town of Milk River. Costs range $10-25. Call ahead for more information and reservations. **Roger's Outdoor Adventures,** 922 9th St. S, Lethbridge, AB T1J 2M2, tel. (403) 329-1374, offers longer canoe trips lasting one to four days. Each trip has a different theme such as wildlife (two days, $130), history and geology (two days, $130), and painting and drawing (four days, $250).

Practicalities
The **Southgate Inn,** at the north end of town, tel. (403) 647-3733, has basic rooms ($40 s, $44 d),

as does **Milk River Inn** downtown, tel. (403) 647-2257. **Milk River Campground** in town is nothing more than a dusty parking lot with firewood and power; $5 per night. South toward Montana, 20 km along Hwy. 4, **Gold Springs Park** is much nicer and $2 extra. A cafe/restaurant in the Milk River Inn is open till 10 p.m., and across the road is the **Delicia Bakery,** which lives up to its name. Highway 4 is the main route into Alberta from the United States. The Coutts/Sweetgrass border crossing is open 24 hours a day year-round. A **Travel Alberta Information Centre** south of Milk River greets travelers crossing the border. It provides copious information and an interpretive center highlighting aspects of tourism within the province. The center, tel. (403) 647-3938, is open mid-May to mid-June 9 a.m.-6 p.m. and through summer 8 a.m.-7 p.m.

WRITING-ON-STONE PROVINCIAL PARK

This park 43 km east of the town of Milk River on Hwy. 501 has everything: a warm river for swimming, great canoeing, intriguing rock formations, abundant wildlife, and the largest concentrations of petroglyphs (rock carvings) and pictographs (rock paintings) found in North America. The native rock art lies hidden on sandstone cliffs along the banks of the Milk River, which has cut a deep valley into the rolling shortgrass prairie. The soft sandstone and shale cliffs here are capped with harder, iron-rich sediments. Years of wind and water erosion have carved out the softer, lower rock, leaving mushroom-shaped pinnacles and columns called **hoodoos.** A number of plant and animal species here are found nowhere else in Alberta. Look for pronghorn on the grassland, bobcats and mule deer in the coulees, yellow-bellied marmots sunning themselves on sandstone outcrops. Don't look *too* hard for rattlesnakes, usually found in shady spots among the cliffs.

The Meaning of It All
Writing-On-Stone was a place of great spiritual importance to generations of plains Indian tribes, a place for contact with the supernatural. They attempted to interpret previous carvings and paintings, added their own artwork to the rock,

and left gifts of tobacco and beads as a way of communicating with the spirits of the dead. Much of the cliff art remains visible today, providing clues to the region's early inhabitants.

Artifacts excavated from below the cliffs suggest the area had been inhabited for at least 3,000 years, but any rock art of that age would have been destroyed by erosion long ago. Dating the remaining petroglyphs and pictographs is difficult. They aren't covered in the layers of sediment usually used to date sites, nor can radiocarbon dating be applied—it requires wood or bone to test. The only way of dating the rock art is to estimate its age based on recognizable artistic styles or the depiction of certain historic events (such as the arrival of the white man). Of the carvings visible today, the earliest are thought to be the work of the Shoshoni, done around 700 years ago. Their work is characterized by warriors on foot carrying ornately decorated shields, while isolated images of elk, bears, and rattlesnakes appear as simple stylized outlines. During the 1730s, the Shoshoni were driven into the mountains by Blackfoot Indians, who had acquired horses and guns before other plains Indians. The valley's strange rock formations led the Blackfoot to believe that the area was a magical place—a place to be respected and feared—and that existing carvings were created by the spirits. The Blackfoot added their own artistry to the rocks, and many of the Blackfoot carvings are panels that tell a story. A striking change of lifestyle was documented on the rock faces, corresponding to the arrival of

guns and horses to the plains Indian tribes. Mounted warriors armed with rifles dominate later artworks, the most famous being a battle scene containing over 250 characters.

Into the Twentieth Century
A North West Mounted Police post was established at Writing-On-Stone in 1889 to stop the whiskey trade and curb fighting among Indian tribes. The Mounties passed time by using the petroglyphs for target practice and carving their names into a cliff that has become known as Signature Rock. The original NWMP post buildings were washed away by floodwaters, replaced, then destroyed by fire in 1918. In 1957 the area was officially designated a provincial park. Access to much of the park is restricted to prevent further damage to the carvings. A reconstructed NWMP post sits within this area at the mouth of **Police Coulee.** The best way to get a feel for the park and its history is by participating in the interpretive program; details are posted on notice boards throughout the park. The **Hoodoo Interpretive Trail** is a two-km (one-way) hike along the cliffs, with numbered posts that correspond to a trail brochure available from the information center. Along the way are some examples of petroglyphs and pictographs (including the famous battle scene) that have been ravaged by time and vandals.

Accommodations and Information
The nearest motel rooms are in Milk River, but the park has an excellent campground nestled

hoodoos above the campground

below the hoodoos in a stand of cottonwood trees; $11 per night. For more information on the park write to Writing-On-Stone Provincial Park, P.O. Box 297, Milk River, AB T0K 1M0; tel. (403) 647-2364.

THE DRY BELT

Not a tree in sight—just rolling shortgrass prairie, occasionally dissected by dried-up streams and eroded gullies. This is the sight that first greeted settlers to the area, and even with the help of complex irrigation systems the land looks similar today. The far southeastern corner of Alberta has never been heavily populated, but not for a lack of trying. Before it was linked to the outside world by rail, settlers entered the area. Small villages emerged, but as was often the case, the Canadian Pacific Railway decided to bypass many of these and create its own towns. Population bases moved and towns slipped into oblivion. Highway 61 passes through this dry, unforgiving part of the province, past the towns of Wrentham and Skiff with their boarded-up buildings and grim futures to the town of Foremost and on through other small communities whose future hangs in the balance. The highway finally peters out at Manyberries. A gravel road (Hwy. 889) heads northeast from Manyberries to Hwy. 41 just south of Cypress Hills Provincial Park.

Foremost

In 1915, the Canadian Pacific Railway built a line east from Stirling through to Saskatchewan with great hopes of the area becoming heavily settled. But they hadn't counted on years of heavy drought, dust storms, and outbreaks of influenza that severely affected the populations of towns in the area. One of the few surviving towns was Foremost, whose population of 500 has remained relatively stable through trying times. Irrigation has played a major role in Foremost's longevity. The interpretive center at **Forty Mile Coulee Reservoir,** 23 km north of town, explains the importance of irrigation to these farming communities. Nearby is a viewpoint and day-use area. On the west side of town a small campground has tent sites for $5.50, hookups $8-11.

PALLISER TRIANGLE

On 4 July 1857, Capt. John Palliser set out west from Winnipeg on an assignment from the British government to make a comprehensive assessment of the agricultural potential, mineral reserves, soil quality, and timber resources of the prairies. Under his command were 20 men, two wagons, six Red River carts and 29 horses. For three long years the expedition traveled the length and breadth of the prairies, before eventually submitting their findings in 1862. Palliser's report favored a band of territory stretching from Manitoba to the Peace River in northern Alberta. On the other hand, to the south he reported a vast land of shortgrass prairie that he called "an extension of the Great American Desert." He considered it unfit for agriculture: "[The land] is desert or semi-desert in character . . . [and] can never be expected to become occupied by settlers." This region—extending along the U.S. border and as far north as Red Deer—soon became known as the Palliser Triangle. Although the report wasn't favorable to the southern part of the province, it changed people's perception of the west. His report led to the settlement of southern Alberta, although it didn't happen overnight. Eventually the C.P.R. rail line was built across the prairies, and irrigation opened up arid parts of the land previously thought unsuitable for settlement.

Etzikom

The C.P.R. built towns approximately every 16 km along its lines, its strategy being that farmers would have access to a grain elevator within a day's haul of their farm, yet the towns would be far enough apart to survive independently. Between Foremost and Etzikom, the town of Nemiskam hasn't survived. The once busy streets are quiet. The residents that remain head to the larger centers of Foremost and Medicine Hat to go shopping and do their business. The fate of Etzikom is similar. Once a thriving center with many businesses and two hotels, the streets are now quiet, and fewer than 100 people live in town. Travel 16 km east or west of Etzikom to see what the town's future holds. **Etzikom Museum,** tel. (403) 666-3737, relives the past—the railway, influenza, droughts, and the tenacity of its people. An outdoor display includes a large collection of windmills. The museum is open during summer Tues.-Sat. 10 a.m.-6 p.m., Sunday 1-6 p.m.

Continuing East

The farmland east of Etzikom is particularly poor. The railway town of **Pakowki** slipped into oblivion long ago, its early residents preferring to do business in **Orion,** the next town to the east. Orion was once a thriving prairie town, but a terrible drought throughout much of the 1920s forced most farmers into bankruptcy. Those that survived were moved by the government to other parts of the province. A few residents still hang on, forever optimistic. And why not? The elevators still take in grain. To the south of Orion on Hwy. 887 are the **Manyberries Sandhills,** a prairie phenomena well worth the detour—especially in the berry-picking season. From Orion Hwy. 887 heads north to Seven Persons and Medicine Hat. Highway 61 jogs south and east from Orion to the small town of **Manyberries,** from where Hwy. 889 heads northeast to Cypress Hills Provincial Park or south then east to Saskatchewan; either way it's gravel.

HIGHWAY 3 EAST

The first town east of Lethbridge on Hwy. 3 is Coaldale. The area was first settled in 1889 by Mennonites, and when the C.P.R. built a rail line between Lethbridge and Medicine Hat in 1926 they encouraged more Mennonite families to farm in the region. With their long agricultural traditions and doctrines of simple living, Mennonites were always welcome additions to prairie communities such as Coaldale. Today this rural community and its Mennonite population continue to prosper, mostly due to their proximity to Lethbridge.

The main reason to leave the highway here is to visit the **Alberta Birds of Prey Centre,** north of Hwy. 3 at 20th St., then left on 16th Ave., tel. (403) 345-4262. The aim of the center is to ensure the survival of birds of prey such as hawks, falcons, eagles, and the great horned owl, Alberta's provincial bird. Many of the birds are brought to the center injured or as young chicks. They are nurtured at the center until they are strong enough to be released back into the wild.

The interpretive building features the works of various wildlife artists and has displays cataloging human fascination with birds of prey through thousands of years. The center is open April-Oct., daily 10 a.m.-5 p.m. Admission is $5.

Taber

Taber, 51 km east of Lethbridge, is most famous for its deliciously sweet corn. It's also a base for the food-processing industry and a service center for the oil-and-gas industry. The original settlement began around Water Tank No. 77 (the site was 77 miles from Medicine Hat) along the C.P.R. rail line. In 1901, the area was opened up to homesteaders, attracting settlers from eastern Canada and the United States, many of whom were Mormons. The name Taber was taken from Tabernacle, reflecting the religious influence of the Mormons. Local Blackfoot called the settlement "itah soyop," which translates to "where we eat from." Apparently they mistook the name Taber for table.

Taber corn, as it is called, can be bought throughout western Canada and is the cornerstone of the town's economy. August is the best time to look for corn vendors along the road. Or find corn along with other fresh, local produce each Thursday at the farmer's market in the Taber Agriplex. On the last weekend of August, when the corn has ripened, the town's **Cornfest** celebration takes place, with a pancake breakfast, a midway, hot-air-balloon flights, a classic-car show, and of course, plenty of corn to taste.

On the eastern outskirts of town is the **Taber Sugar Beet Factory,** which processes in excess of 500,000 tons of sugar beets annually. During peak periods, enormous piles of beets sit beside the highway waiting to be processed into icing sugar, granulated sugar, and various powdered sugars. The factory does not offer tours, and judging by the smell *outside* the factory this is a good thing. One plant that does offer tours is **Lucerne Foods,** 5115 57th St., tel. (403) 223-3566, which bottles fruit juices and cans vegetables at its Taber plant. Tours are available weekdays 9 a.m.-3 p.m.

Taber Motel, tel. (403) 223-4411, has the least expensive rooms in town. They are clean, but don't expect much; $37 s, $43 d. The much nicer and larger **Heritage Inn,** tel. (403) 223-4424, offers a restaurant, cafe, and lounge;

rooms start at $50 s, $58 d. **Taber Provincial Park,** on a floodplain above the Oldman River two km west and three km north of town, is a welcome relief from the surrounding prairie. Campsites are near a stand of large cottonwood trees. The unserviced sites are $13; call (403) 223-7929 for bookings.

Bow Island

Vast reserves of natural gas in the area around Bow Island were first tapped in 1909 by a discovery well named "Old Glory," which soon developed into Alberta's first commercial gas field. The reserve of gas declined by the '20s and Bow Island's role in the industry changed—it became the first major gas-storage field in Canada. Today its storage reservoirs help meet southern Alberta's peak winter demand. Agriculture now plays an important role in the town's economy, as evidenced by large grain elevators and an **Alfalfa Dehydrating and Cubing Plant** two km west of town (for tours call 403-545-2293). On the east side of town are two inexpensive motels and an information booth which is open in summer daily 9 a.m.-6 p.m. On the west side of town is a campground.

Red Rock Coulee

South of Seven Persons, the last community on Hwy. 3 before Medicine Hat, is a small area of badlands on a gentle rise in the surrounding plains. The bedrock here is relatively close to the surface, and wind and water erosion have cut through the topsoil to expose it. In some places, the erosion has extended into the bedrock itself, revealing varicolored strata laid down millions of years ago. This strange landscape is dotted with small hoodoos and red boulder-shaped concretions measuring up to 2.5 meters across. These concretions formed under the surface of a prehistoric sea, when sand, calcite, and iron oxide collected on a nucleus of shells, bones, and corals. They became part of the bedrock as layers of sediment were laid down. But as erosion took its course, the surrounding bedrock disappeared and the concretions emerged. The formations here are believed to be the largest of their type in the world. To get there follow Hwy. 887 south from Seven Persons for 23 km. Where the road curves sharply to the east (left) continue uphill straight ahead on an unsealed road. You can't miss it.

Petroglyphs record early human history in the region.

MEDICINE HAT AND VICINITY

The prosperous industrial city of Medicine Hat (pop. 45,000) is in the southeastern corner of the province, 168 km east of Lethbridge and 40 km west of the Saskatchewan border. The city straddles the South Saskatchewan River and is above some of western Canada's most extensive natural-gas fields. The gas was discovered by accident in 1883, by a C.P.R. crew drilling for water. At first nobody was particularly excited, except for the workers who got to heat their isolated homes. But eventually the word got out about the size of the reserves beneath the town, leading English writer Rudyard Kipling to describe Medicine Hat as "a city with all hell for a basement."

It wasn't long before industries developed around the gas fields; oil-and-gas extraction operations, petrochemical plants, mills, farms, and fertilizer factories today generate $1.5 billion annually. New housing estates, shopping centers, and an award-winning city hall are testimony to the success of these local industries. As an added bonus, a river that flows beneath the the city gives Medicine Hat an unlimited supply of water for its industries.

One other area resource is no longer exploited today but has left its mark on the face of the city. Nearby clay deposits led to a large pottery and brick industry that thrived from late last century until WW II. Many turn-of-the-century brick buildings have been restored and can be seen in the downtown core (where gas lamps still burn 24 hours a day).

Also of note is the **Saamis Archeological Site,** within city limits, regarded as one of the most extensive and richest finds from the late prehistoric time period of native history. And an hour south of the city is **Cypress Hills Provincial Park,** an upland plateau that survived the last ice age. This densely forested plateau that rises abruptly from the surrounding prairie is home to many species of mammals and provides a variety of recreational opportunities. (See "Cypress Hills Provincial Park," below.)

The Name Medicine Hat

For centuries before white settlers had come to the area, the Cree and Blackfoot had battled each other over their right to claim this land as their own. Many tales recording these battles describe how the name Medicine Hat evolved. One of the most popular tells the story of the Cree chief who led his people to the cliffs above the South Saskatchewan River. Here, the Great Serpent told him that he must sacrifice his wife to the river in exchange for a *saamis* or medicine hat. This would give him magical powers and allow him to defeat the Blackfoot when they attacked later that night. Another story tells of how the Blackfoot were forced into the waters of the South Saskatchewan River by the Cree, who then fired an arrow into the heart of the Blackfoot medicine man. As he slowly sank below the water's surface, his hat was swept away into the hands of the Cree. The Blackfoot saw this as a terrible omen and retreated.

SIGHTS

Downtown

Many turn-of-the-century buildings located in the downtown area are still in active use, including private homes, churches, and businesses. The availability of local clay led to thriving brick-manufacturing plants here during the late 1800s; many original buildings still stand in mute testimony to the quality of the bricks. Near City Hall on 1st St. SE are three fine examples of this brickwork. The 1919 **Provincial Courthouse** has been restored. It features an elaborately carved entrance, an interior marble-walled stairway, and a leaded-glass archway. Across the road is the 1887 **Ewart-Duggan Home.** This is the oldest brick residence still standing in Alberta and is topped by its original cedar shingles. On the corner of 4th Ave. is the **Kerr-Wallace Home,** the first of many early prestigious homes along 1st St. toward the TransCanada Hwy. (Hwy. 1).

Among other historical landmarks are the 1913 **St. Patrick's Church** (across the river from downtown on 2nd St.), said to be one of the finest examples of Gothic Revival architecture in North America; the **C.P.R. Station** (east of

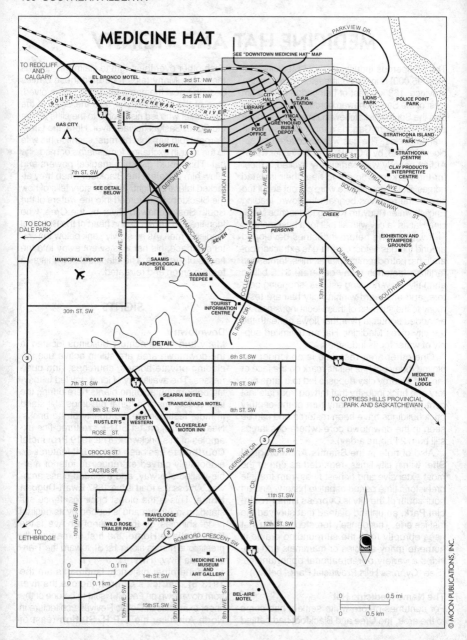

MEDICINE HAT

TO REDCLIFF AND CALGARY

EL BRONCO MOTEL

PARKVIEW DR.

SEE "DOWNTOWN MEDICINE HAT" MAP

3rd ST. NW

2nd ST. NW

SOUTH   SASKATCHEWAN   RIVER

CITY HALL

LIBRARY

C.P.R. STATION

LIONS PARK

POLICE POINT PARK

11th AVE. SW

GAS CITY

1st ST. SW

YMCA

POST OFFICE

GREYHOUND BUS DEPOT

STRATHCONA ISLAND PARK

BRIDGE ST

STRATHCONA CENTRE

HOSPITAL

5th ST. SE

CLAY PRODUCTS INTERPRETIVE CENTRE

7th ST. SW

GERSHAW DR.

4th AVE. SE

KINGSWAY AVE.

INDUSTRIAL AVE.

SOUTH   RAILWAY   ST.

SEE DETAIL BELOW

DIVISION AVE.

HUTCHINSON AVE.

CREEK

TO ECHO DALE PARK

TRANSCANADA HWY.

SEVEN

PERSONS

EXHIBITION AND STAMPEDE GROUNDS

MUNICIPAL AIRPORT

SAAMIS ARCHEOLOGICAL SITE

COLLEGE AVE.

DUNMORE RD.

SOUTHVIEW DR.

30th ST. SW

SAAMIS TEEPEE

TOURIST INFORMATION CENTRE

S. RIDGE DR.

13th AVE SE

DETAIL

6th ST. SW

MEDICINE HAT LODGE

7th ST. SW

7th ST. SW

TO CYPRESS HILLS PROVINCIAL PARK AND SASKATCHEWAN

CALLAGHAN INN

SEARRA MOTEL

TRANSCANADA MOTEL

8th ST. SW

RUSTLER'S

BEST WESTERN

CLOVERLEAF MOTOR INN

8th ST. SW

ROSE ST.

CROCUS ST.

8th ST. SW

GERSHAW DR.

CACTUS ST.

11th ST. SW

10th AVE. SW

WILD ROSE TRAILER PARK

TRAVELODGE MOTOR INN

12th ST. SW

BULIVANT CR.

TO LETHBRIDGE

BOMFORD CRESCENT SW

0   0.1 mi

0   0.1 km

14th ST. SW

MEDICINE HAT MUSEUM AND ART GALLERY

15th ST. SW

10th AVE. SW

9th AVE. SW

8th AVE. SW

BEL-AIRE MOTEL

0   0.5 mi

0   0.5 km

© MOON PUBLICATIONS, INC.

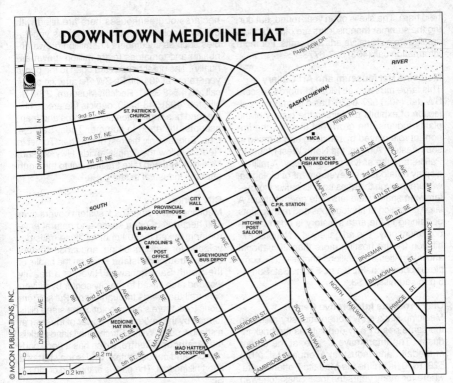

DOWNTOWN MEDICINE HAT

downtown), built shortly after the railway came to town in 1883; and the 1905 **Canadian Bank of Commerce** (corner 6th Ave. and 2nd St.), a classic example of early bank architecture. These buildings and others are listed in the *Historic Walking Tour* brochure available from the Tourist Information Centre.

Another notable piece of architecture from a much later era is the **Medicine Hat City Hall,** which won the Canadian Architectural Award in 1986. Located on the banks of the South Saskatchewan River, it's open to the public on weekdays and contains many fine pieces of art.

Because of the abundance of natural gas in the area, city officials in the early days found it cheaper to leave the city's gas lamps on 24 hours a day rather than pay someone to turn them on and off. Over 200 copper replicas of the early gaslight fixtures were imported from England and now line the streets, burning 24

hours a day in the historical section of downtown.

Saamis Teepee

Standing over 20 stories high beside the TransCanada Hwy., with a base diameter of 50 meters and made entirely of steel, this is one sight that you don't need directions to find. The Saamis Teepee was originally erected at the 1988 Calgary Winter Olympics to commemorate the cultural roles played by natives in the history of North America and has since been moved to its present site. It overlooks Seven Persons Creek Coulee, an archaeological site which was used in late prehistoric times as a native camp where buffalo were dried and processed. A self-guided interpretive trail, beginning at the tepee, leads to a bluff and into the valley where the camp was located. Native American ceremonial events are sometimes held here. The site is open year-round, but during the summer months tours are offered and a small store sells native arts and crafts. For more information call (403) 527-6773.

Medicine Hat Museum and Art Gallery

This large museum at 1302 Bomford Crescent SW, tel. (403) 527-6626, has a permanent collection of exhibits explaining the history of the plains Indians, the growth of the city, the important role played by ranching and farming in southeastern Alberta, the North West Mounted Police, and the arrival of the railway. A military display catalogs the development of biological warfare through the ages from its earliest form—throwing snake-filled jars onto enemy ships! A large collection of photographs and manuscripts pertaining to the area's history is open by appointment only. The art gallery is a National Exhibition Centre hosting more than 20 national and international exhibitions annually. The complex is open Mon.-Fri. 9 a.m.-5 p.m., Sat.-Sun. 1-5 p.m.; admission $3.

Clay Products Interpretive Centre

Medicine Hat's early pottery industry relied on the same nearby clay deposits as the brick industry. The Interpretive Centre, at the corner of Medalta and Industrial Avenues, tel. (403) 529-1070, is on the old Medalta Potteries site, where for many years the local Saskatchewan clay was mass-produced into high-quality china. For most of the middle period of this century Medalta was a household name in Canada. The china was popular in homes and was used exclusively by C.P.R.-owned hotels. During WW II, German prisoners of war worked in the factory making plates that were sent to allied soldiers fighting in Europe. Since closing in 1954, fire, wind, and rain have taken their toll on the building, which has been declared a National Historical Site. The center displays the history of the clay and pottery industries in Medicine Hat, has some fine examples of the now highly prized Medalta pieces, and is the start of a walking tour of the area. It's open mid May-Oct. daily 10 a.m.-6 p.m.

Redcliff

This small suburb of Medicine Hat bills itself as "Greenhouse Capital of the Prairies": over 10 hectares of greenhouses here are filled with brilliantly colored flowers and various vegetables such as cucumbers (12 million grown annually) and tomatoes (eight million grown annually). The greenhouses are open to the public year-round at 404 4th St. SW. To arrange a tour call (403) 548-3931. **Redcliff Museum,** 2 3rd St. NE, tel. (403) 548-6260, depicts the area's history and has some interesting photos and manuscripts. It's open in summer Tues.-Sat. 2-4 p.m., Sunday only the rest of the year. To get to Redcliff follow the TransCanada Hwy. west of Medicine Hat and take the first exit to the north after the industrial estate.

City Parks

Medicine Hat's urban park system covers over 400 hectares of open space and natural environment linked by 50 km of multiuse trails developed for walking, biking, and cross-country skiing. **Strathcona Island Park,** on the banks of the South Saskatchewan River, is a heavily wooded area linked to the city center by a riverside trail that leads through **Lions Park.** From Lions Park there's a viewpoint of the steep cliffs formed by the undercutting power of the river at a shallow point. Within Strathcona Island Park is the **Strathcona Centre,** which has a pool, paddleboat and canoe rentals, and is the start of a short hiking trail. The park is at the end of 5th St. SE.

On the north side of the river, opposite Strathcona Island Park is **Police Point Park** (turn off Parkview Dr. just past the golf club), which has many kilometers of trails that wind through stands of giant cottonwood trees and provide plentiful wildlife-spotting opportunities. White-tailed deer, foxes, and beavers are commonly seen. The **interpretive center,** tel. (403) 529-6225, outlines the area's natural and human history through exhibits and films; open in summer daily 1-9 p.m., the rest of the year weekends only 9 a.m.-5 p.m.

West of the airport on Holsam Rd. is **Echo Dale Park,** where the locals head on hot weekends to sunbake on the sandy beach and swim, fish, and boat in the human-made lake. Within the park is **Echo Dale Farm,** where you'll find farm animals, a two-story log house currently being restored, and an interpretive center that's open in summer daily 9 a.m.-9 p.m.

FESTIVALS AND EVENTS

Medicine Hat holds one of the year's earliest rodeos, the **Spring Outdoor Rodeo.** The first weekend of June is the **Spectrum Festival,** a celebration of Medicine Hat's claim as the sunniest city in Canada. Kids' activities and street performers are plentiful, and tons of sand are dumped in a parking lot, transforming it into a beach for a volleyball tournament and beer garden. A mountain-bike race is held through the nearby river valley. A free pancake breakfast in Lions Park kicks off **Canada Day** (1 July) celebrations, which end with a spectacular fireworks display in the evening—watch it from Athletic Park or the Golf and Country Club off Parkview Drive. The **Medicine Hat Exhibition and Stampede,** held on the last weekend of July, has been an annual event since 1887. It has grown to become Alberta's second-richest rodeo (behind the Calgary Exhibition and Stampede), guaranteeing three days of knuckle-clenching, bronc-riding, foot-stompin' fun. Various events are held throughout the city the preceding week, culminating Thurs.-Sat. with the rodeo and chuck wagon races. The stampede also features many exhibitors displaying their wares, as well as a midway, free entertainment, and pig and duck races. Each night, top U.S. country-music stars strut their stuff. For more information, call the stampede office at (403) 527-1234. Throughout summer various other events are held at the Exhibition and Stampede Grounds, including tractor pulls, sporting events, concerts, horse races, and smash-up derbies. For dates and prices, call the Tourist Information Centre at (403) 527-6422.

ACCOMMODATIONS

Hotels and Motels
The **Medicine Hat Inn,** 530 4th St. SE, tel. (403) 526-1313, is the only accommodation downtown. Although small, it is relatively modern, has a restaurant, and is within walking distance of most sights. Rooms are $65 s or d.

With only a couple of exceptions, all other motels are clumped along the TransCanada Hwy. around Gershaw Dr., separated only by fast-food restaurants and gas stations. They range from poor to excellent (as far as road motels go). Those on the downtown side of the highway are the least expensive, including the **TransCanada Motel,** 780 8th St. SW, tel. (403) 526-5981, probably Alberta's cheapest motel at $18 s, $24 d (as good a reason as any to check the room out before handing over your cash). Other options on this side of the highway are: **El Bronco Motel,** 1177 1st St. SW, tel. (403) 526-5800, $30-35 s or d; **Searra Motel,** 767 7th St. SW, tel. (403) 526-3355, with divey rooms for $28 s, $32 d, but free coffee; and **Cloverleaf Motor Inn,** 773 8th St. SW, tel. (403) 526-5955, with a laundry, $35 s, $40 d.

Good value across the highway is **Callaghan Inn,** 954 7th St. SW, tel. (403) 527-8844, with an indoor pool and restaurant; $46 s, $49 d. Larger, and with rooms of a similar standard is **Best Western Inn,** 722 Redcliff Dr. SW, tel. (403) 527-3700, with a pool and exercise room; $55 s, $65 d. South of these two is the **TraveLodge Motor Inn,** 1100 Redcliff Dr. SW, tel. (403) 527-2275 or (800) 578-7878. It has a large indoor water slide complex, indoor pool, restaurant, and lounge. Standard rate for rooms is $75-85, but ask about off-season and weekend rates. A cheapie on this side of the highway is the **Bel-Aire Motel,** 633 14th St. SW, tel. (403) 527-4421, the best value of all Medicine Hat's bottom end accommodations; $24 s, $28 d.

Medicine Hat Lodge, 1051 Ross Glen Dr. SE, tel. (403) 529-2222, is away from those listed above and is overpriced; $75 s or d.

Campgrounds
Gas City Campground, tel. (403) 526-0644, is on the edge of town, has nearly 100 sites, and is far enough away from the highway to be relatively quiet. From the back of the park a trail heads to the river and into town. At night this is a good spot to view the illumination of Medicine Hat's industrial core. It's open early May to late September; tent sites are $11, hookups $15-19. Good hot showers, laundry facilites, groceries, and full hookups make this the place to try first. To get there, turn off the highway at 7th St. SW and follow the signs down 11th Avenue. Another option, **Wild Rose Trailer Park,** 28 Camp Dr., tel. (403) 526-2248, is in the same general area and has a large population of trail-

ers. Unserviced sites go for $8, hookups $13-15. It's open year-round. Finally, west of town in Redcliff, a municipal campground offers showers and electrical hookups for $7 per night.

FOOD AND DRINK

Downtown
Cafe Mundo, 579 3rd St. SE, tel. (403) 528-2808, is the best of many downtown coffee shops. It's located in Gaslight Plaza, in a pleasant atmosphere away from busy downtown streets. Food is limited to bagels heaped with healthy fillings (from $2.50), but the coffee is good.

Lunchtime at bright and airy **Caroline's,** 101 4th Ave. SE, tel. (403) 529-5300, is always busy; soups, salads, sandwiches, and daily specials begin at $4. The service is fast and efficient for those who don't want to dawdle. Thursday at Caroline's is Beer and Bones night when Brontosaurus Ribs are 25 cents each.

Moby Dick's Fish and Chips, 140 Maple Ave. SE, tel. (403) 526-1807, has a delightful variety of English dishes. Fish in batter is $2.10 per piece, fries $1.25. Also on the menu are other seafood specialties (from $9), traditional pub grub (from $2.50), and nine different meat pies (from $6). English draught beers are around $6 a pint. You can eat in the restaurant, the pub next door, or get it to go. Hours are Mon.-Sat. 11 a.m.-9 p.m., Sunday 3-8 p.m. **Season's Restaurant** in the Medicine Hat Inn, 530 4th St. SE, tel. (403) 526-1313, is a typical hotel restaurant and is always busy. Dinner specials are $13, menu items $9-18, and all dishes include a helping from a small salad bar. It's open daily 6 a.m.-10 p.m.

Rustler's
Rustler's, 901 8th St. SW, tel. (403) 526-8004, within walking distance of the strip motels along the TransCanada Hwy., is one of the town's oldest eating establishments. Located in a historic house (see the menu for its amusing history), a real Wild West atmosphere prevails. Set out under the glass top of one table is a poker game complete with gun and bloodstained playing cards. The place is popular all day but breakfast is especially crowded. Large portions of eggs, bacon, and hash browns begin at $4, omelettes at $4.95. For the rest of the day, it's

southwestern-style cooking from $4.25, salads from $4, and pasta, steak, and chicken dishes from $8. It's open daily 6 a.m.-10 p.m. Coffee is 50 cents and refills are free.

Other Restaurants
Close to Rustler's are two excellent, inexpensive restaurants. **O'Rileys Restaurant and Bar** in the Callaghan Inn on 7th St. SW, tel. (403) 527-8844, is a dimly lit, nostalgic place with gold-rimmed furniture and old posters on the walls. Monday is Mexican night (dishes from $7), Wednesday is pasta night (dishes from $6), and Friday and Saturday are rib nights (dishes from $12). Expect a wait on weekends. It's open daily 6 a.m.-11 p.m. Across the motel parking lot and beside the Best Western is **Black Angus Restaurant,** 925 7th St. SW, tel. (403) 529-0777, a family-style steakhouse specializing in Alberta beef. To the east along Dunmore Rd. is a smattering of chain restaurants including A&W, Bonanza (ask for the all-you-can-eat ice cream for $1.50), Earl's, and Moxie's.

Drinking and Dancing
Captain's Cabin Pub, 140 Maple Ave. SE, tel. (403) 529-6629, has English and Scottish draught beers on tap and is decked out in the style of a traditional British pub. On S. Railway St., **Hitchin' Post Saloon,** tel. (403) 526-0300, often has local bands playing. Just around the corner is **Gas Light Pub,** which has pool tables. **O'Rileys** in the Callaghan Inn on 7th St. SW, tel. (403) 527-8844, is popular with the local population of British soldiers. On Mug Mondays all glass mugs, vases, and jars will be filled with beer for $1. And Tuesday night is Yuk Yuk's Komedy Kabaret, admission $5. **Concerts** are often held at the Exhibition and Stampede Grounds—look for big-name country-music stars during Stampede Week at the end of July; call (403) 527-1234 for details.

TRANSPORTATION

Medicine Hat Municipal Airport is five km west of downtown on Hwy. 3 toward Lethbridge. Within the airport is a small cafe and courtesy phones for Avis, Budget, and Tilden rental cars. **Canadian Regional,** tel. (403) 526-6633 or (800)

665-1177, flies five times daily between here and Calgary, $96 one-way or $108 roundtrip if purchased seven days in advance. No city bus serves the airport. Cabs meet all flights; expect to pay around $6 to get downtown.

The **Greyhound** bus depot is at 557 2nd St. SE, tel. (403) 527-4418, in a convenient downtown location. The ticket office is open 5 a.m.-11 p.m. Inside the terminal are coin lockers and a popular cafe. Buses run twice daily to and from Calgary with a change in Fort Macleod. The fare to Lethbridge is $21.67, to Calgary $38.15. Buses also go east to Regina and Winnipeg four times daily. **Medicine Hat Transit** buses run from the terminal downtown throughout the suburbs. One-way fare anywhere on the route is $1.25; a day pass is $4.50. The following car rental agencies have outlets in town: **Avis,** tel. (403) 527-3310 or (800) 879-2847; **Budget,** tel. (403) 527-7368 or (800) 268-8900; **Enterprise,** tel. (403) 526-8064 or (800) 325-8007; **Rent-A-Wreck,** tel. (403) 526-5400; and **Tilden,** tel. (403) 527-5665 or (800) 387-4747.

SERVICES AND INFORMATION

The **post office** is at 403 2nd St. SE. The spotless **Crestwood Coin Laundry** at 1753 Dunmore Rd. SE is open Mon.-Sat. 9 a.m.-9 p.m., Sunday 10 a.m.-9 p.m., and has a TV and free coffee. The **YMCA,** 150 Ash Ave. SE, tel. (403) 527-4426, has a pool, weight room, and squash courts; $2.50 for a swim, $5 for use of all facilities, first visit free. The large **Medicine Hat Public Library,** 414 1st St. SE, tel. (403) 527-5551, overlooks the river and has a free paperback exchange. It's open Mon.-Thurs. 10 a.m.-9 p.m., Fri.-Sat. 10 a.m.-5:30 p.m., Sunday 1-5:30 p.m. **Mad Hatter Bookstore,** 399 Aberdeen St. SE, tel. (403) 526-8563, has thousands of secondhand books. **Medicine Hat Regional Hospital** is at 666 5th St. SW, tel. (403) 529-8000.

The **Tourist Information Centre** is at 8 Gehring Rd. SE, tel. (403) 527-6422 or (800) 481-2822. To get there take the Southridge Dr. exit from the TransCanada Hwy. just east of the big tepee. It's open in summer daily 8 a.m.-9 p.m., the rest of the year daily 9 a.m.-5 p.m. The Medicine Hat Museum also has a small information booth.

CYPRESS HILLS PROVINCIAL PARK

Covering an area of 200 square km, Cypress Hills is the second-largest provincial park in Alberta. It occupies only a small section of an upland plateau that extends well into Saskatchewan. The hills rise as much as 500 meters above the surrounding grasslands, and at their highest elevation (1,466 meters, the same as Banff townsite) they are the highest point between the Canadian Rockies and Labrador. A forested oasis in the middle of the prairies, the park is thickly covered in lodgepole pine with stands of white spruce, poplar and aspen. The French word for lodgepole pine is *cyprès,* which led to the hills being named Les Montagnes de Cyprès and in turn Cypress Hills, when in fact cypress trees have never grown in the park. Fall and spring are particularly pleasant times of year to visit the park—crowds are nonexistent and wildlife is more visible—but bring a jacket.

The park is 70 km southeast of Medicine Hat along Hwy. 41. It offers good hiking, fishing, or just plain relaxing and is very popular as a place to escape the high summer temperatures of the prairies. The only commercial facilities within the park are in the townsite of **Elkwater,** which sits in a natural amphitheater overlooking **Elkwater Lake.** The facilities are limited (no bank, one restaurant, one motel, one gas station) so come prepared.

The Land

The hills are capped with a conglomerate composed of rounded pebbles carried east from the Rockies by a broad stream around 40 million years ago. When the massive sheets of ice moved slowly southward during the ice age, they thinned and split at the 1,400-meter level of the plateau. The top 100 meters remained unglaciated, forming a nunatak (an island of land surrounded by ice) of approximately 150 square km. When the climate warmed and the sheet of ice slowly receded, its meltwaters rushed around and through the hills, slashing into the plateau and forming the narrow canyons and coulees that are visible today.

Flora

The park supports over 400 recorded plant species in four ecological zones: prairie, parkland, foothills, and boreal forest. The best way to view the flora of the park is on foot; many trails pass through two or three zones in the space of a couple of kilometers. Sixteen species of orchids are found in the park—some are very common, while others such as the sparrow's egg lady's slipper are exceedingly rare. The book *A Guide to the Orchids of Cypress Hills* by Robert M. Fisher will tell you all you want to know. The Visitor Centre has a copy of the book you can look at.

Fauna

The unique environment of the hills provides a favorable habitat for 37 species of mammals, 400 species of birds, and a few turtles. Big game was at one time common throughout the hills, but in 1926 the last remaining large mammal—a wolf—was shot. Soon thereafter, elk were reintroduced to the park and now number over 200. Moose, never before present in the park, were introduced in the 1950s and now number about 60. Other large mammals present in the park are mule deer, white-tailed deer, coyotes, and beavers.

Many bird species here are more typically found in the Rocky Mountain foothills, 250 km to the west. About 90 species are transient, coming to the hills only to nest. Other species spend the entire year in the park. This is the only spot in the province with recordings of the common poorwill, which is rarely seen but occasionally heard. Wild turkeys were introduced in the '30s and their descendants can be heard warbling in certain parts of the park. Elkwater Lake and Spruce Coulee Reservoir are good spots for water-bird watching. Cormorants and trumpeter swans are common. A bird checklist is available at the Visitor Centre.

Cultural History

To the native bands of Cree, Blackfoot, and Assiniboine, the area was known as "Thunder Breeding Hills," a mysterious place that was home to plains grizzly bears, cougars, wolves, and kit foxes—all long since extinct in the area.

orchid

These people followed the wandering herds of bison and had little need to visit the hills except to pick berries and collect various plants for medicinal and ceremonial uses. Little evidence of this early culture remains, although one archaeological site dating from 5000 B.C. has been studied. After the Cypress Hills Massacre, when 20 innocent Assiniboine were killed, the North West Mounted Police sent nearly 300 men to Fort Walsh (on the Saskatchewan side of the hills). The fort is now a National Historical Site.

Exploring the Park

Various roads link the townsite of Elkwater to lakes and viewpoints within the park. Due to glacial sediment called loess, the paved roads at higher elevations are terribly potholed. Unpaved roads are even worse and can become impassable after heavy rain. To access the center of the park, take Reesor Lake Rd. east from Hwy. 41, passing a herd of cattle and a viewpoint with spectacular vistas of the transition from grassland to boreal forest. The road then descends steeply to **Reesor Lake**, which has a campground, picnic area, a short hiking trail to a viewpoint, and excellent fishing for rainbow trout.

Bull Trail Rd. off Reesor Lake Rd. leads to **Spruce Coulee** and a reservoir stocked with eastern brook and rainbow trout. Unmarked gravel roads crisscross the park and head into Saskatchewan. Hiking within the park is limited. Most of the trails are easy to moderate, following the shores of Elkwater Lake (wheelchair accessible) and climbing out of the townsite into open fields and mixed forests. **Spruce Coulee Trail** (eight km) is the longest hike. It starts behind the rodeo grounds and leads through woodland and past a number of beaver ponds before ending at Spruce Coulee.

At the marina, **Elkwater Boat & Bike Rentals,** tel. (403) 893-3877, rents mountain bikes ($5 per hour, $25 a day), canoes ($8 per hour, $40 a day), motorboats ($12 per hour), and jet skis ($45 per hour). The **Elkwater Complex** opposite the marina holds a restaurant to avoid, a grocery store, a post office, and a laun-

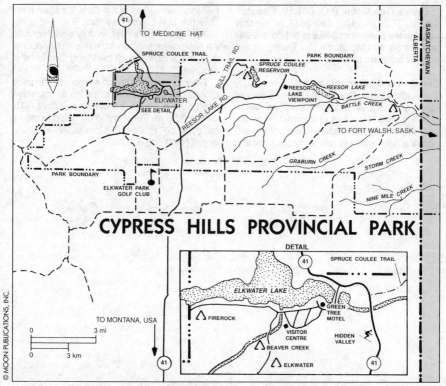

dromat. The town has a gas station but no bank. **Elkwater Park Golf Club,** tel. (403) 893-2167, offers a nine-hole course at $12 per round.

Wintertime

Although summer is the park's busiest time of year, many people are attracted by the range of winter activities possible. **Hidden Valley,** tel. (403) 893-3961, is a large ski hill (by prairie standards) with a vertical drop of 176 meters and two lifts and two rope tows that access a limited number of beginner and intermediate runs. Lift tickets are $21. The hill is three km south of Elkwater and is closed on Monday. Equipment rentals are available at the hill or from **Lauder Cycles and Ski,** 702 Kingsway Ave. SE, tel. (403) 526-2328, in Medicine Hat.

The park also offers 25 km of cross-country ski trails for all levels of expertise, ice fishing in the lakes, toboggan hills, and winter camping for the brave.

Campgrounds and Lodging

Within the park are over 500 campsites in 12 campgrounds. Closest to Elkwater are **Beaver Creek Campground** ($17) with full hookups and **Elkwater Campground** ($13) with unserviced sites. Both have showers. **Firerock Campground** ($13) on Elkwater Lake is particularly nice. It is linked to town by the Shoreline Trail. **Reesor Lake Campground** ($11, no showers or hookups) at the eastern end of the park is much quieter—listen for bugling elk in the fall. An eight-km hike from the rodeo grounds follows an abandoned road to **Spruce Coulee,** where you'll find 10 sites ($7) and good fishing in the reservoir. Reservations for campsites are taken; phone (403) 893-3777.

Green Tree Motel, P.O. Box 19, Elkwater, AB T0J 1C0, tel. (403) 893-3811, is the only motel in the park; from $40 s or d, kitchenettes an extra $5, and log cabins $55. During winter, ski packages are offered.

Services and Information
The large **Visitor Centre** overlooks Elkwater Lake, a short walk from the townsite campgrounds, and offers lots of information on the park and its history. Audiovisual programs explain the natural history and archaeological and historical resources of the park. It's open mid-May through Labor Day daily 9 a.m.-5 p.m. (until 9 p.m. Thurs.-Sat. in July and August). An interpretive program operates nightly during July and August; ask at the Visitor Centre for a program.

For information in the off season, try the park office along the first road to the left as you enter town from the east. It's open weekdays 8:15 a.m.-4:30 p.m. For more information, write to the office at P.O. Box 12, Elkwater, AB T0J 1C0; or call (403) 893-3777.

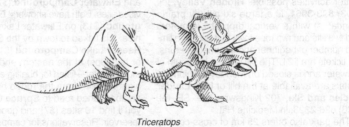

Triceratops

BOB RACE

CARDSTON

Cardston is a town of 3,500 at the base of the foothills 76 km southwest of Lethbridge and 35 km north of the United States border. Its rich heritage and many museums make it an interesting stop in itself, as well as a good base for exploring Waterton Lakes National Park (a half-hour drive to the west). The town was founded in 1887 by Charles Ora Card of the Church of Jesus Christ of Latter-day Saints (better known as the Mormon Church) after leading 11 families north from Utah in covered wagons. Card chose

a spot to settle on Lee Creek and soon established a townsite, including a main street over 30 meters wide, resembling those in Salt Lake City. These settlers developed Alberta's first irrigation system, which has grown to become the lifeblood of southern Alberta's economic base.

Cardston was the birthplace of Fay Wray, a leading lady during the golden years of Hollywood. She appeared in 80 movies but is best known for her role as the leading-ape's love object in the 1933 classic *King Kong*.

© MOON PUBLICATIONS, INC.

SIGHTS

Remington-Alberta Carriage Centre

This world-class museum focusing on the era of horse-drawn transportation opened in 1993. It is one of North America's largest collections of carriages, buggies, and wagons—over 200 at last count. The main exhibit galleries tell the story of the horse-and-buggy era through a life-sized turn-of-the-century townscape. You can transport yourself through time by watching blacksmiths at work in the carriage factory, listening to deals being made at the carriage dealer, or wandering over to the racetrack, where the rich liked to be seen on their elegant carriages. A program of equestrian events featuring Clydesdales and quarter horses takes place daily in the demonstration arena, and rides are offered on restored and replica carriages. The center also has a theater, cafeteria, gift shop, and information booth. It's located at 623 Main St., tel. (403) 653-5139; open 15 May to Labour Day 9 a.m.-8 p.m., the rest of the year 9 a.m.-5 p.m. Admission is adult $6.50, senior $5.50, child $3, half-price on Tuesday from October through April.

Alberta Temple

While living in simple log cabins, the early Mormon pioneers started planning the construction of the first Mormon temple built outside of the United States. The grand marble and granite structure was completed in 1923 and has become the town's centerpiece. Only members of the Mormon faith in good standing may enter the temple itself. To be in good standing, a Mormon must neither smoke, nor drink coffee or tea, and must pay 10% of his or her net annual income to the church. A visitor center open to the public shows films and pictures depicting the interior of the temple and its history. The landscaped gardens make for a pleasant stroll. The center is open May-Sept. 9 a.m.-9 p.m. You can see the temple from almost anywhere in town. It's located at 348 3rd St. W; tel. (403) 653-1696.

C.O. Card Home

When Charles Ora Card first arrived in 1887 he built a small log cabin on what would become Cardston's main drag. Today his humble home stands in its original location at 337 Main Street. It was the center of the community for many years. Town meetings were held inside, and travelers rested there until a hotel was built in 1894. The building is now a Provincial Historic Site, open June-Aug. Mon.-Sat. 10 a.m.-5 p.m.; admission by donation.

Courthouse Museum

This impressive courthouse, on 3rd Ave. just off Main St., tel. (403) 653-4322, was built in 1907 from locally quarried sandstone and was used longer than any other courthouse in the province before being refurnished as a museum. Exhibits

Alberta Temple

include a pioneer home, artifacts from early settlers, and a geology display. In the basement are the original jail cells with graffiti-covered walls. The museum is open June-Aug. Mon.-Sat. 10 a.m.-5 p.m.; admission by donation.

PRACTICALITIES

Accommodations

Plenty of choices here—two motels, many bed and breakfasts, and camping downtown or in one of the nearby provincial parks. Both motels have basic but clean rooms. They are two blocks up the hill from the Remington-Alberta Carriage Centre at the corner of Main St. and 8th Avenue: **Trail's End Motel,** tel. (403) 653-4481, $40 s, $45 d; and **Flamingo Motel,** tel. (403) 653-3952, which has a coin laundry and pool, $45 s, $50 d.

In the last few years a number of private residences have converted spare rooms to accommodate paying guests. One of the best is the **Historic Granite Inn,** 140 2nd Ave. W, tel. (403) 653-3157, which was built in 1918 and has been kept in the family ever since. The small single room is $35, a larger room runs $45 s or d, and the rose room, which has a small private sitting area, is $50 s or d. The bathroom is shared, and a hot breakfast is served in the communal dining room. Also right in town is **Temple Sunset View,** 221 3rd St., tel. (403) 653-3539, with rooms going for $25 s, $35 d. South of town in a rural setting are **Country Manor,** 901 Homeseeker's Ave., tel. (403) 653-4608, and **Lamb's Gate B&B,** 1010 Homeseeker's Ave., tel. (403) 653-3647. Both have rooms with shared or private bath starting at $35 s, $45 d, including a hot breakfast.

Within walking distance of the Remington-Alberta Carriage Centre is **Lee Creek Campground,** an excellent facility open May-Oct. with full hookups and showers. Tent sites are $8, hookups $15. It's at the end of 7th Ave. W, off Main Street. Another option is **Buffalo View Campground,** at the Agridome along 9th Ave., which has no services except pit toilets; $5 per night. Farther out you'll find camping at **Woolford Provincial Park,** 16 km to the east ($7); **Police Outpost Provincial Park,** 33 km south of town ($13); and at **Payne Lake,** 24 km southwest toward Waterton ($9).

Food

The **Cobblestone Manor Restaurant,** 173 7th Ave. W, tel. (403) 653-1519, is a unique place to indulge in some fine food. The original log structure was built in 1889, two years after the first Mormons arrived. In 1913 the house was bought by a Belgian immigrant who added more rooms, using cobblestones as building blocks. The interior wall panels and ceilings are inlaid with thousands of pieces of hardwood, and the stained glass bookshelves, Tiffany lights, and antique furniture give you the feeling of dining in an English manor. And the food isn't too bad either. Light lunches start at $8, dinner entrees of steak, seafood, and chicken, all served with baked potato, fresh vegetables, and delicious homemade bread start at $12. The restaurant is open daily for lunch 11 a.m.-2 p.m. and for dinner 5-9 p.m. It's located on a quiet residential street, across the road from Lee Creek Campground.

The only other dining choices in Cardston are along Main Street. Pick of the bunch is **Mings Garden,** 226 Main St., tel. (403) 653-1682. A buffet is offered, but stick to the menu. The dishes are surprisingly good, mostly under $10, and freshly prepared. Other choices include a couple of pizza places and **Humpty's Family Restaurant,** which is the place to go for breakfast.

Entertainment and Events

The **Carriage House Theatre,** 353 Main St., tel. (403) 653-1000, has a summer program of live theater productions including musicals, comedy, and special events with a local theme. The performances are held July-Aug. Tues.-Sat. nights at 7:30.

On the third weekend of September is the **Combined Driving Event** held in conjunction with the Remington-Alberta Carriage Centre. The meet consists of three events: carriage dressage, an obstacle course, and a marathon. With the exception of the marathon, all the excitement takes place at the Carriage Centre.

Services and Information

The **post office** is on 2nd Avenue. Laundromats are located at 165 Main St. and 77 3rd Ave. W. **Cardston Hospital** is at 144 2nd St. W, tel. (403) 653-4411. The **Tourist Information Centre** is beside Lee Creek at 490 Main St., tel. (403) 653-3787. It's open mid-May to August daily 8 a.m.-9 p.m., or try the information booth at the Remington-Alberta Carriage Centre, which is open year-round, tel. (403) 653-1993.

VICINITY OF CARDSTON

Woolford Provincial Park

Original surveys of the area show this park as an island in the St. Mary River. A stand of large cottonwood trees here provides a pleasant shaded area surrounded by prairie. A North West Mounted Police post was established in 1883 one km northwest of the park to patrol the Canada/U.S. border but was short-lived, closing in 1908. Annual flooding after spring break-up is a continuing problem; the main river channel changes and chunks of the island break off. To reach the park, travel three km northeast of Cardston on Hwy 3, then southeast for 13 km along a gravel road. The campground is small and facilities are limited to cook shelters, firewood, and pit toilets. Sites are $7 a night.

From the beginning of the park access road, Hwy. 5 runs northeast to Magrath and Lethbridge. **Magrath** has a "Buffalo Slope" grain elevator, the latest concept adopted by the Alberta Wheat Pool; open for tours Mon.-Fri. 8 a.m.-5 p.m., tel. (403) 758-3231.

South from Cardston

South of Cardston is the Old Mormon Trail that settlers from Utah used on their way north. The town of **Aetna,** just off Hwy. 2, was once a thriving Mormon community with a cheese factory, school, and store. A worthwhile stop in Aetna is **Jensen's Trading Post,** a general store with an interesting collection of antiques. This is the beginning of the true prairie, and if you're heading east from here, it's hard not to keep glancing in the rear-view mirror for glimpses of the Rocky Mountains you're leaving behind. From Aetna, Hwy. 501 skirts the International Boundary, passing the ruins of a community once known as Whiskey Gap. It crosses Hwy. 62 north of the Del Bonita port of entry (open 1 June to 15 September 9 a.m.-9 p.m., the rest of the year 9 a.m.-6 p.m.) and continues east to Milk River through arid grassland not suitable for cultivation (see "Milk River" under "East of Lethbridge" earlier in this chapter). Along much of the way the **Sweetgrass Hills** in Montana are visible rising high above the prairies south of Writing-On-Stone Provincial Park.

Beyond the turnoff to Aetna, Hwy. 2 continues to the International Boundary. **Police Outpost Provincial Park,** on a small lake beside the International Boundary, is accessible along a 23-km gravel road 10 km south of Cardston. The police outpost that gave the park its name was set up in 1891 to control smuggling, but the remote location led to its closure before the turn of the century. From the park, spectacular **Chief Mountain** can be seen to the southwest. Most of the park is grassland interspersed with isolated stands of aspen and marshy areas. The park's campground has pit toilets and cook shelters; sites are $11. The highway crosses into Montana at the Carway/Piegan port of entry (open daily 7 a.m.-11 p.m.).

WATERTON LAKES NATIONAL PARK

Everybody traveling to this rugged 526-square-km park does so by choice. It's not on the way to anywhere else or on a major highway but is tucked away in the extreme southwestern corner of Alberta. The park is bounded to the north and east by the rolling prairies covering southern Alberta; to the south by the U.S. border and Glacier National Park in Montana; and to the west by the Continental Divide, which forms the Alberta/British Columbia border. The natural mountain splendor, a chain of deep glacial lakes, large and diverse populations of wildlife, an unbelievable variety of day hikes, and a changing face each season make this park a gem that shouldn't be missed.

The route to Waterton is almost as scenic as the park itself. From whichever direction you arrive, the transition from prairie to mountains is abrupt, almost devoid of the foothills that characterize other areas along the eastern slopes of the Canadian Rockies. From the park gate, two roads penetrate the mountains to the west. One ends at a large glaciated lake, the other at a spectacular canyon. All visitors to the park are required to stop at the gate and buy a permit. Park entry for one day is $4 per person, to a maximum of $8 per vehicle; an annual permit for Waterton is $28 per person to a maximum of $50, and a Great Western Pass, valid for all Alberta and British Columbia national parks, is $35 per person to a maximum of $70.

THE LAND

Geology

Major upheavals under the earth's surface around 85 million years ago forced huge plates of rock upward and began folding them over each other. One major sheet known as the Lewis Overthrust forms the backbone of Waterton's topography as we see it today. It slid up and over much younger bedrock along a 300-km length extending north to the Bow Valley. Around 45 million years ago this powerful uplift ceased and the forces of erosion took over. About 1.9 million years ago, glaciers from the sheet of ice

that once covered most of Alberta crept through the mountains. As these thick sheets of ice advanced and retreated with climatic changes, they gouged out valleys such as the classically U-shaped **Waterton Valley.** The three Waterton Lakes are depressions left at the base of the steep-sided mountains after the ice had completely retreated 11,000 years ago. The deepest is 150 meters. **Cameron Lake,** at the end of the Akamina Parkway, was formed when a moraine—the pile of rock that accumulates at the foot of a retreating glacier—dammed Cameron Creek. From the lake, Cameron Creek flows through a glaciated valley before dropping into the much deeper Waterton Valley at **Cameron Falls,** behind the town of Waterton. The town itself sits on an alluvial fan composed of silt and gravel picked up by mountain streams and deposited in Upper Waterton Lake.

Climate plays an active role in the park's natural landscape. This corner of the province tends to receive more rain, snow, and wind—much more wind—than other parts of Alberta. These factors, combined with the park's varied topography, create an environment where some 900 species of plants have been recorded, more than half the known species in Alberta. Wind is the most powerful presence in the park. Prevailing winds from the south and west bring Pacific weather over the divide, creating a climate similar to that experienced farther west. These warm fronts endow the region with **chinooks,** dry winds that can raise temperatures in the park by up to 40° C in 24 hours. One of the nicest aspects of the park is that it can be enjoyed in all seasons. Summer for the sunny windless days, fall for the wildlife viewing, winter for the solitude, and spring for the long days of sunlight as the park seems to be waking up from its winter slumber. Be aware, however, that many of the park's best sights and hiking trails lie at high elevations; some areas may be snowed in until mid-June.

Flora

Botanists have recorded 1,200 species of plants growing within the park's several different veg-

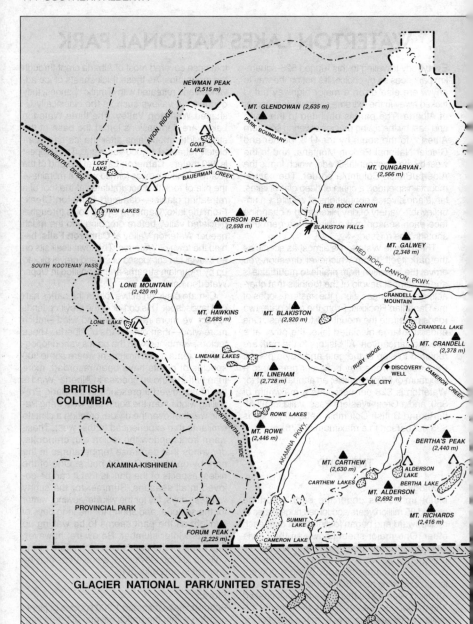

NEWMAN PEAK
(2,515 m)

MT. GLENDOWAN (2,635 m)

AVION RIDGE

PARK BOUNDARY

CONTINENTAL DIVIDE

GOAT
LAKE

LOST
LAKE

BAUERMAN CREEK

MT. DUNGARVAN.
(2,566 m)

TWIN LAKES

RED ROCK CANYON

ANDERSON PEAK
(2,698 m)

BLAKISTON FALLS

SOUTH KOOTENAY PASS

MT. GALWEY
(2,348 m)

RED ROCK CANYON PKWY.

LONE MOUNTAIN
(2,420 m)

CRANDELL
Mountain

MT. HAWKINS
(2,685 m)

MT. BLAKISTON
(2,920 m)

CRANDELL LAKE

LONE LAKE

MT. CRANDELL
(2,378 m)

LINEHAM LAKES

RUBY RIDGE

DISCOVERY
WELL

MT. LINEHAM
(2,728 m)

OIL CITY

CAMERON CREEK

BRITISH
COLUMBIA

CONTINENTAL DIVIDE

ROWE LAKES

AKAMINA PKWY.

MT. ROWE
(2,446 m)

BERTHA'S PEAK
(2,440 m)

AKAMINA-KISHINENA

MT. CARTHEW
(2,630 m)

ALDERSON
LAKE

CARTHEW LAKES

BERTHA LAKE

MT. ALDERSON
(2,692 m)

PROVINCIAL PARK

MT. RICHARDS
(2,416 m)

SUMMIT
LAKE

FORUM PEAK
(2,225 m)

CAMERON LAKE

GLACIER NATIONAL PARK/UNITED STATES

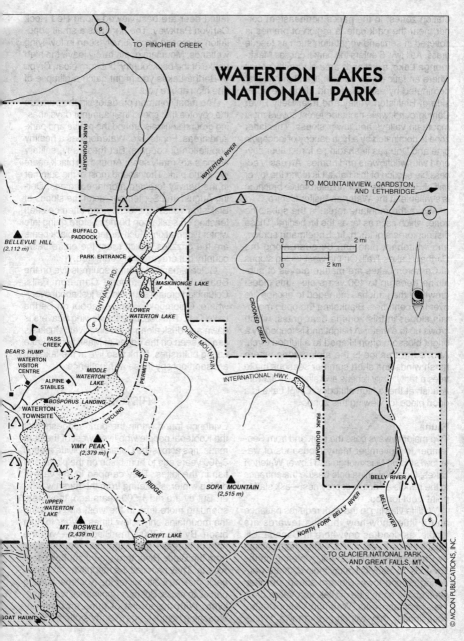

WATERTON LAKES NATIONAL PARK

TO PINCHER CREEK

TO MOUNTAINVIEW, CARDSTON, AND LETHBRIDGE

WATERTON RIVER

PARK BOUNDARY

BUFFALO PADDOCK

BELLEVUE HILL (2,112 m)

PARK ENTRANCE

MASKINONGE LAKE

LOWER WATERTON LAKE

CROOKED CREEK

CHIEF MOUNTAIN

PASS CREEK

BEAR'S HUMP

WATERTON VISITOR CENTRE

ALPINE STABLES

MIDDLE WATERTON LAKE

INTERNATIONAL HWY.

PARK BOUNDARY

BELLY RIVER

BOSPORUS LANDING

WATERTON TOWNSITE

CYCLING PERMITTED

VIMY PEAK (2,379 m)

VIMY RIDGE

SOFA MOUNTAIN (2,515 m)

NORTH FORK BELLY RIVER

BELLY RIVER

UPPER WATERTON LAKE

MT. BOSWELL (2,439 m)

CRYPT LAKE

TO GLACIER NATIONAL PARK AND GREAT FALLS, MT

GOAT HAUNT

0   2 mi
0   2 km

© MOON PUBLICATIONS, INC.

etation zones. In the park's northeastern corner, near the park gate, a region of prairies is covered in semiarid vegetation such as fescue grass. As Hwy. 5 enters the park it passes **Maskinonge Lake,** a wetlands area of marshy ponds where aquatic plants flourish. Parkland habitat dominated by aspen is found along the north side of Blakiston Valley and near Belly River Campground, while montane forest covers most mountain valleys and lower slopes. This latter zone is dominated by a high canopy of lodgepole pine and Douglas fir shading a forest floor covered with wildflowers and berries. An easily accessible section of this habitat is along the lower half of Bertha Lake Trail; an interpretive brochure is available at the Waterton Visitor Centre.

Above the montane forest is the subalpine zone, which rises as far as the timberline. These distinct forests of larch, fir, Engelmann spruce, and whitebark pine can be seen along the Carthew Lakes Trail. On the west-facing slopes of Cameron Lakes are mature groves of subalpine trees up to 400 years old—this oldest growth in the park has managed to escape fire over the centuries. Blanketing the open mountain slopes in this zone is bear grass, which grows up to a meter in height and is topped by a bright blossom often likened to a lighted torch. Above the treeline is the alpine zone where harsh winds and short summer seasons make trees a rarity. Only lichens and alpine wildflowers flourish at these high altitudes. Crypt Lake is a good place for viewing this zone.

Fauna

Two major flyways pass the park and from September to November many thousands of waterfowl stop on Maskinonge and Lower Waterton Lakes. On a powerline pole beside the entrance to the park is an active osprey nest—ask staff to point it out for you.

Wildlife viewing in the park requires patience and a little know-how, but the rewards are ample, as good as anywhere in Canada. Elk inhabit the park year-round. A large herd gathers by Entrance Road in late fall, wintering on the lowlands. By early fall many mule deer are wandering around town. Bighorn sheep are often seen on the north side of Blakiston Valley or on the slopes above the Waterton Visitor Centre; occasionally they will end up in town. White-

tailed deer are best viewed along Red Rock Canyon Parkway. The park has a small population of moose occasionally seen in low-lying wetlands. Mountain goats rarely leave the high peaks of the backcountry, but from Goat, Crypt, or Bertha Lakes you might catch a glimpse of one high above you.

The most common predators in the park are the coyotes that spend their summer days chasing ground squirrels around the prairie and parkland areas. For its size, Waterton has a healthy population of cougars. But these shy, solitary animals are rarely seen. Around 50 black bears live in the park. They spend most of the summer in the heavily forested montane regions. During August and September, scan the slopes of Blakiston Valley where they can often be seen feasting on saskatoon berries before going into winter hibernation. Much larger than black bears are the grizzlies, which roam the entire backcountry but are rarely encountered.

Golden-mantled ground squirrels live on the Bear's Hump and around Cameron Falls. Columbian ground squirrels are just about everywhere. Chipmunks scamper about on Bertha Lake Trail. The best time for viewing beavers is dawn and dusk along the Belly River. Muskrats can be seen on the edges of Maskinonge Lake eating bulrushes. Mink also live in the lake but are seen only by those with patience.

HISTORY

Evidence found within the park suggests that the Kootenai people who lived west of the park made trips across the Continental Divide around 8,400 years ago to hunt bison on the plains and fish in the lakes. They camped in the valleys during winter, sheltering from the harsh weather. But by around 1,500 years ago, they were spending more time in the west and crossing the mountains only a few times a year to hunt bison. By the 1700s, the Blackfoot—with the help of horses—had expanded their territory from the Battle River throughout southwestern Alberta. They patrolled the mountains on horseback, making it difficult for the Kootenai hunting parties to cross. But their dominance was short-lived. With the arrival of guns and the encroaching homesteads of early settlers, Blackfoot tribes retreated to the east, leaving the Waterton Lakes Valley uninhabited.

"Kootenai" Brown

John George Brown was born in England in the 1840s and reputedly educated at Oxford University. He joined the army and went to India, later continuing to San Francisco. Then, like thousands of others, he headed for the Cariboo goldfields of British Columbia, quickly spending any of the gold he found. After a while he moved on, heading east into Waterton Valley, where his party was attacked by Blackfoot Indians. He was shot in the back with an arrow and pulled it out himself. For a time he worked with the U.S. Army as a Pony Express rider. One day he was captured by Chief Sitting Bull, stripped, and tied to a stake until his fate could be decided, but he managed to escape during the night with his scalp intact. Brown acquired his nickname through his close association with the Kootenai people, hunting buffalo and wolves with them until they had all but disappeared. Even though Brown had been toughened by the times he was a conservationist at heart. After marrying in 1869 he built a cabin by the Waterton Lakes and became the valley's first permanent resident. Soon he started promoting the beauty of the area to the people of Fort Macleod. One of his friends, local rancher F.W. Godsal, began lobbying the federal government to establish a reserve. In 1895 an area was set aside as a Forest Reserve, with Brown as its first warden. In 1911 the area was declared a national park and Brown, age 71, was appointed its superintendent. He continued to push for an expansion of park boundaries until his final retirement at age 75. He died a few years later. His grave along the main access road to the townsite is a fitting resting place for one of Alberta's most celebrated mountain men.

Oil City

It was Kootenai Brown who first noticed beads of oil floating on Cameron Creek. He and a business partner siphoned it from the water's surface, bottled it, and sold it in Fort Macleod and Cardston. This created much interest among the oil starved entrepreneurs of Alberta, who formed the Rocky Mountain Development Co. to do some exploratory drilling. At this stage the park was still a Forest Reserve; the trees were protected, but prospecting and mining were still allowed. A rough road was constructed through the Cameron Creek Valley, and in September 1901 the company struck oil at a depth of 311 meters. It was the first producing oil well in western Canada and only the second in the country. In the resulting euphoria, a townsite named Oil City was cleared and surveyed, a bunkhouse and dining hall were constructed, and the foundations for a hotel were laid. The boom was short-lived. Drilling rigs kept breaking down and the flow of oil soon slowed to a trickle. A monument along the Akamina Parkway stands at the site of the well, and a little farther up the road at a roadside marker a trail leads through thick undergrowth to the townsite. All that remains are the ill-fated hotel foundations and some depressions in the ground.

Waterton-Glacier International Peace Park

Shortly after Montana's Glacier National Park was created in 1910, the Canadian government set aside an area of land in the Waterton Valley as Waterton Lakes Dominion Park (later to be renamed a national park). Many people followed the footsteps of Kootenai Brown and a small town named Waterton Lakes grew up on the Cameron Creek Delta. The town had no rail link, so unlike Banff and Jasper—its famous mountain neighbors to the north—it didn't draw large crowds of tourists. Nevertheless, it soon became a popular summer retreat with a hotel, restaurant, and dance hall. The Great Northern Railway decided to operate a bus service from its Montana rail line to Jasper, with a stop at Waterton Lakes. This led to the construction of the **Prince of Wales Hotel.** Boat cruises from the hotel across the International Boundary were soon the park's most popular activity. This brought the two parks closer together, and in 1932, after much lobbying from Rotary International members on both sides of the border, the Canadian and U.S. governments agreed to establish Waterton-Glacier International Peace Park, the first of its kind in the world. The parks are administered separately but cooperate in preserving this pristine mountain wilderness. Peace Park celebrations take place each year, and the **Peace Park Pavilion** by the lake is dedicated to this unique bond. In 1979,

UNESCO declared the park an **International Biosphere Reserve,** only the second such reserve in Canada.

HIKING

Although the park is relatively small, its trail system is extensive; 183 km of well-maintained trails lead to alpine lakes and lofty summits affording spectacular views. One of the most appealing aspects of hiking in Waterton is that with higher trailheads than other parks in the Canadian Rockies, the treeline is reached quickly. Most of the lakes can be reached in a few hours. Once you've finished hiking the trails in Waterton, you can cross the border and start on the 1,200 kilometers of trails in Glacier National Park.

The eight hikes detailed below comprise only a small cross-section of Waterton's extensive trail system. As most of the hikes climb to alpine lakes or viewpoints, the ratings that are given reflect the elevation gain. Anyone of reasonable fitness could complete them in the time allotted. Strong hikers will need less time, and if you stop for lunch it will take you a little longer. Remember, all distances and times are one-way—allow yourself time at the objective and time to return to the trailhead. Topographic maps (one map covers the entire park) are available at various outlets in town. If you are planning to stay overnight in the backcountry you must obtain a permit ($6 per person per night) from Waterton Visitor Centre or the administration office.

Don't underestimate the forces of nature. Weather can change dramatically anywhere in the park and at any time. That clear sunny sky that looked so inviting during breakfast can turn into a driving snowstorm within hours. Ill-prepared hikers get lost in the park each year. Read the updated weather reports that are posted at all information centers before setting out, go prepared for all climatic conditions (always carry food, a sweater, and matches), and take plenty of water—open slopes can get very hot on sunny days.

Bear's Hump
- Length: 1.2 km (40 minutes) one-way
- Elevation gain: 215 meters
- Rating: moderate

This is one of the most popular short hikes in the park, and although steep, it affords panoramic views of the Waterton Valley. The trailhead is at the Waterton Visitor Centre, opposite the Prince of Wales Hotel. The trail consists of switchbacks up the northern flanks of the Bear's Hump, finishing at a rocky ledge high above town. From this vantage point the sweeping view extends across the prairies and down Upper Waterton Lake to the northern reaches of Glacier National Park.

Bertha Lake Trail
- Length: 5.8 km (2 hours) one-way
- Elevation gain: 460 meters
- Rating: moderate

Bertha Lake is a popular destination with dayhikers and campers alike. The trail begins at the end of Evergreen Ave. near the far corner of Townsite Campground. For the first 1.5 km little elevation gain is made as the trail coincides with the Lakeshore Trail. Then the trail branches right and climbs steadily through a forest of lodgepole pine and Douglas fir along a well-maintained section to **Lower Bertha Falls.** Signs along this first, easier section correspond with the *Bertha Falls Self-Guiding Nature Trail* brochure available from the Visitor Centre. From here the trail passes **Upper Bertha Falls** and begins switchbacking steeply through a subalpine forest to its maximum elevation on a ridge above the hanging valley in which Bertha Lake lies. A trail encircles the lake. The backcountry campground on the lake's edge is one of the park's busiest.

Waterton Lakeshore Trail
- Length: 13 km (4 hours) one-way
- Elevation gain: minimal
- Rating: easy/moderate

This trail follows the heavily forested western shores of Upper Waterton Lake across the International Boundary to **Goat Haunt, Montana,** linking up with over 1,200 km of trails in Glacier National Park. Many hikers take the **Inter-Nation Shoreline Cruise Co.** boat one-way ($9; tel. 403-859-2362) and hike the other. The boat dock at Boundary Bay, six km from town, is a good place for lunch. Hikers heading south and planning to camp in Glacier National Park must register at the Goat Haunt ranger station.

Crypt Lake Trail
- Length: 8.7 km (3-4 hours) one-way
- Elevation gain: 680 meters
- Rating: moderate/difficult

This is one of the most spectacular day hikes in Canada. Access to the trailhead on the eastern side of Upper Waterton Lake is by boat. The trail switchbacks for 2.5 km past a series of waterfalls and continues steeply up to a small green lake before reaching a campground. The final ascent to Crypt Lake from the campground causes the most problems, especially for those who suffer from claustrophobia. A ladder on the cliff face leads into a natural tunnel that you must crawl through on your hands and knees. The next part of the trail is along a narrow precipice with a cable for support. The lake at the end of the trail, nestled in a hanging valley, is no disappointment. Its dark green waters are rarely free of floating ice, and the steep walls of the cirque rise over 500 meters above the lake on three sides. The International Boundary is at the southern end of the lake. A good way to avoid the crowds on this trail is to camp at the dock and set out before the first boat arrives in the morning. The **Crypt Lake Shuttle** leaves the marina regularly for Crypt landing; $9 roundtrip. Reservations are necessary in summer; call (403) 859-2362.

Crandell Lake
- Length: 2.4 km (40 minutes) one-way
- Elevation gain: 120 meters
- Rating: easy

This easy hike to a subalpine lake from the Red Rock Canyon Parkway is popular with campers staying at Crandell Mountain Campground. The trailhead can be reached from within the campground or by noncampers along the Canyon Church Camp access road. The lake can also be accessed from a trailhead seven km west of town along the Akamina Parkway. This trail is shorter (0.8 km) and follows a wagon road that was cut through the valley to Oil City.

Goat Lake Trail
- Length: 6.7 km (2 hours) one-way
- Elevation gain: 500 meters
- Rating: moderate

The first hour of walking from the trailhead at Red Rock Canyon follows the Snowshoe Trail along **Bauerman Creek** before branching to the right and climbing switchbacks through a mixed forest. The steep gradient evens out as the trail enters the Goat Lake cirque. The lake is a welcome sight after the uphill slog, its emerald-green waters reflecting the towering headwalls that surround it. Look for the lake's namesake on the open scree slopes to the west of the lake.

Carthew-Alderson Trail
- Length: 20 km (6-7 hours) one-way
- Elevation gain: 650 meters
- Rating: moderate/difficult

This hike linking Cameron Lake to Waterton townsite can be completed in one long strenuous day or done with an overnight stop at Alderson Lake, 13 km from Cameron Lake. It leads through most of the climatic zones of the park and offers some of the best scenery to be had on any one hike. Most hikers begin at Cameron Lake. Transportation to the trailhead can be arranged through the **Park Transport Company** in the Tamarack Mall ($6 one-way; tel. 403-859-2378), which operates a hiker shuttle service to this and other trailheads in the park. From Cameron Lake the trail climbs four km to **Summit Lake,** a worthy destination in itself. The trail then forks to the left and climbs steeply to Carthew Ridge. After rising above the treeline and crossing a scree slope the trail reaches its highest elevation of 2,310 meters at **Carthew Summit.** The views from here are spectacular, even more so if you scramble up to one of Mt. Carthew's lower peaks. To the north is a hint of prairie, to the southeast the magnificent bowl-shaped cirque around Cameron Lake, to the south, directly below are the Carthew Lakes, and on the horizon are glaciated peaks in Montana. From this summit, the trail descends steeply to the Carthew Lakes, reenters the subalpine forest, and emerges at **Alderson Lake,** nestled under the headwalls of Mt. Alderson. The trail then descends through the Carthew Creek Valley and finishes at Cameron Falls in the townsite.

Vimy Peak
- Length: 12 km (5 hours) one-way
- Elevation gain: 825 meters
- Rating: moderate

Vimy Peak overlooks the townsite from across Upper Waterton Lake. It was once part of a ridge that extended across the Waterton Valley and was worn down by the relentless forces of glacial action. The trailhead is along the Chief Mountain International Hwy., a half km from the Hwy. 5 junction. The first six km is along the eastern bank of Lower Waterton Lake through forest and grassland. The trail then continues along the lake to Bosporus Landing opposite the town or climbs steeply to Vimy Peak (2,379 meters). The Vimy Peak trail actually ends at a basin short of the summit, which is still a painfully steep 40-minute scramble away.

SCENIC DRIVES

Akamina Parkway

This 16-km drive starts in the townsite and switchbacks up into the Cameron Creek Valley, ending at Cameron Lake. The viewpoint one km from the junction of the park road is on a tight curve so park off the road. It looks out over the townsite and the **Bear's Hump,** which was originally part of a high ridge that extended across the lake to Vimy Peak until glacial action wore it down. This section of the road is also a good place to view bighorn sheep. From here to Cameron Lake are a number of picnic areas and stops of interest including the site of Alberta's first producing oil well, and a little farther along the road, the site of **Oil City,** the town that never was. **Cameron Lake,** at the end of the road, is a subalpine lake in a large cirque carved around 11,000 years ago by a receding glacier. Mount Custer at the southern end of the lake is in Montana. Waterton has no glaciers, but Herbst Glacier on Mt. Custer can be seen from here. To the west (right) of Custer is **Forum Peak** (2,225 meters), whose summit has a cairn marking the boundaries of Alberta, Montana, and British Columbia. Canoes ($8-10 per hour), rowboats ($8 per hour), and paddleboats ($8-10 per hour) can be rented at the lake or you can hike one of the many nearby trails. See "Hiking," above, for details. Grizzlies frequent the avalanche slope at the southwestern end of the lake so hike with someone you can outrun.

Red Rock Canyon Parkway

The best roadside wildlife viewing within the park is along this 13-km road which starts near the golf course and finishes at **Red Rock Canyon.** The transition between rolling prairies and mountains takes place abruptly as you travel up the Blakiston Valley. Black bears and very occasionally grizzly bears can be seen feeding on saskatoon berries along the open slopes to the north. **Mount Blakiston** (2,920 meters), the park's highest summit, is visible from a viewpoint three km along the road. The road passes interpretive signs, picnic areas, and Crandell Mountain Campground. Red Rock Canyon, at the end of the road, is a water-carved gorge. The bedrock, known as argillite, has a high concentration of iron that oxidizes and turns red when exposed to air—it is literally going rusty. A short interpretive trail leads along the canyon.

prairies to peaks along the Red Rock Canyon Parkway

Chief Mountain International Highway

This 25-km highway borders the eastern boundaries of the park and joins it to Glacier National Park in Montana. It starts east of the park gate at **Maskinonge Lake** and climbs for seven km to a viewpoint where many jagged peaks and the entire Waterton Valley can be seen. The next stop, three km farther south, has views of Chief Mountain, which has been separated from the main mountain range by erosion. The road then passes more spectacular viewpoints, Belly River Campground, and Chief Mountain. Hours of operation at the port of entry are 1 June to 22 September 7 a.m.-10 p.m. When the post is closed you must use the Carway/Piegan port of entry. It's on Alberta Hwy. 2 south of Cardston or Montana Hwy. 89 north of St. Mary (depending on your direction of travel). From the border it's 50 km to St. Mary and the spectacular Going-to-the-Sun highway through Glacier National Park. For more information on Glacier Park write to Park Superintendent, Glacier National Park, West Glacier, MT 59936, USA

OTHER RECREATION

On the Water

Winds of up to 70 kph attract hard-core windsurfers throughout summer and into fall. The winds are predominantly south to north, providing fast runs across Upper Waterton Lake from the beach at Cameron Bay. The lake is deep, keeping the water temperature low and making a wetsuit necessary. Read the warning signs at the beach before heading out. Fishing in the lakes is above average with most anglers chasing brook and rainbow trout, pike, and whitefish. A National Park fishing license is required and can be obtained from the Waterton Visitor Centre or any of the administration offices. The license costs $4 for one day, $6 for seven days, or $13 for an annual permit.

On any given summer day, scuba divers can be seen slipping into the frigid waters of Emerald Bay. A steamer was scuttled in the bay in 1918. It had been used to haul logs and as a tearoom but now sits on the lake's floor, attracting divers who find it a novelty to explore a sunken ship so far from the ocean. No equipment rental is available in the park. The closest is at **Anderson**

Waterton Lakes is one of Alberta's premier scuba diving locations.

Aquatics in Lethbridge at 314 11th St. S, tel. (403) 328-5040, where you can also get your tanks filled. Full gear rental from Anderson is $50 per day, $75 for the weekend, including air fills. Members of the National Association of Underwater Instructors (NAUI) run certification courses and field trips to Waterton Lakes throughout the summer. Stop in on your way through for a rundown on all the dives, or ask at the Waterton Visitor Centre.

Cruising to Goat Haunt, Montana

From the marina in downtown Waterton townsite **Waterton Inter-Nation Shoreline Cruise Co.** runs scheduled cruises across the International Boundary to Goat Haunt, Montana, at the southern end of Upper Waterton Lake. The 45-minute trip along the lakeshore passes spectacular mountain scenery and usually wildlife. A half-hour stopover is made at Goat Haunt, which is located in a remote part of Glacier National Park and consists of little more than a dock, a peace-park pavilion, and a ranger station. You can return on the same boat or go hiking and return later in the day. If you are planning an overnight hike from here you are required to register at the ranger station. Another popular option is to take an early boat trip and walk back to town on the **Waterton Lakeshore Trail,** which takes about four hours. Boats leave the Waterton marina five times daily during summer. Fewer trips are made during May and September. The cruises operate until the end of September, but after the U.S. ranger station closes for the season in midmonth, the boats pass by Goat Haunt without stopping. Tickets cost $17 roundtrip, $10 one-way, and you'll need to book ahead in summer; tel. (403) 859-2362. The same company operates a regular shuttle service to the Crypt Lake trailhead for $9 roundtrip.

On Dry Land

The rolling fairways and spectacular mountain backdrop of **Waterton Lakes Golf Course** can distract even the keenest golfer's attention. The 18-hole course, designed by Stanley Thompson, is located four km north of the townsite on the main access road and is open June to early October. Its facilities include a rental shop, clubhouse, and restaurant serving sandwiches and snacks. A round of golf costs $28 during the day, dropping to $14 after 5 p.m. (which may have something to do with the healthy local bear population). Club rentals are $7.50 and an electric cart is an additional $22 per round. For tee times call (403) 859-2383.

Just off the main park access road is **Alpine Stables,** tel. (403) 859-2462, which offers hourlong trail rides (starting on the hour) for $15. Two-hour wildlife rides leave at 10 a.m., 1 p.m., and 5 p.m. and cost $28. If you find Emerald Bay a little cold for swimming, try the outdoor heated swimming pool on Cameron Falls Dr. ($2.50 per day). Across the road are four tennis courts. The courts are free, but you'll need your own racket.

When the Sun Goes Down

Interpretive programs are held nightly during the summer in Crandell Campground and at the **Interpretive Theatre** opposite Cameron Falls. Programs begin at 8:30 p.m. Ask at the Waterton Visitor Centre or call (403) 859-2445

for details. Being the biggest bar in town, the **Thirsty Bear Saloon** in the Bayshore Inn gets crowded. It pours happy hour daily 3-6 p.m., and a band plays three or four nights a week. It's open 11 a.m.-2 a.m. Much smaller and much quieter is **Levi's Pub** on Windflower Ave., tel. (403) 859-2020; open 11 a.m.-2 a.m. In the Prince of Wales Hotel, the **Windsor Lounge** has live entertainment most nights, and the **Rams Head Lounge** in the Kilmorey Lodge has a fireplace and an outside deck with views of the lake. **Waterton Lakes Opera House,** 309 Windflower Ave., tel. (403) 859-2466, shows movies daily at 7:30 and 9:30 p.m. In July and August, live shows featuring songs from movies are performed at the Bayshore Inn Convention Centre; tickets are $5-10, available from the inn.

Wintertime

Winter is a quiet time in the park. Traffic on the roads is light, a few trails are maintained for cross-country skiing, and the snowcapped peaks and abundant big game provide plenty of photographic opportunities. The main access road is plowed regularly and the Akamina Parkway is cleared to allow access to ski trails. Skiing in the park is usually possible from December to March, but conditions can change dramatically. Arctic fronts scream down from the north, and chinook winds from the west can raise temperatures by up to 20° C in an hour. Ski trails are set on weekends and the ski-touring opportunities are endless. Trails in the backcountry are not marked. Groups should carry avalanche beacons, be capable of self rescue, and register with the warden before setting out. Ice climbing, snowshoeing, and backcountry winter camping are also popular. Winter camping is possible at Pass Creek where there is a kitchen shelter, woodstove, and pit toilets. The **Kilmorey Lodge** stays open year-round and offers all-inclusive winter packages. Gas may or may not be available in winter. Obtain trail information and weather forecasts at the park administration office on Mount View Rd., open weekdays 8 a.m.-4 p.m., tel. (403) 859-2262, or call the Warden's Office at (403) 859-2224. For information regarding backcountry skiing conditions and avalanche danger contact the **Canadian Avalanche Association,** tel. (800) 667-1105.

ACCOMMODATIONS

Hotels and Motels

Waterton has a limited number of seasonal accommodations. They start opening in May and will be full every night during July and August. By mid-October many are closed. They are all within the townsite so walking to the marina and shops isn't a problem.

The **Kilmorey Lodge,** P.O. Box 100, Waterton Park, AB T0K 2M0, tel. (403) 859-2334, is a historic inn on the shores of Emerald Bay. From the lobby a narrow stairway leads up to rooms tucked under the eaves, many of which have spectacular lake views. Each is furnished with antiques and the beds have down comforters to ensure a good night's sleep. Downstairs is one of the town's finest restaurants, along with a lounge and gazebo for enjoying a quiet drink on those warm summer nights. The lodge is the only accommodation that stays open year-round. Rooms during summer start at $78 s or d, with more comfortable larger rooms from $90. Some rooms have lake views, but book in advance for these. Inexpensive packages are offered during the off season.

Across the road from the Kilmorey Lodge is **Crandell Mountain Lodge,** P.O. Box 114, Waterton Park, AB T0K 2M0, tel. (403) 859-2288, a country-style inn with beautifully furnished rooms of a high standard. Rooms are $94-103 s or d in the height of summer with reduced rates (from $69) from May to mid-June and in September.

Waterton's most well-known landmark is the **Prince of Wales Hotel,** General Delivery, Waterton Park, AB T0K 2M0, tel. (403) 859-2231, a seven-story gabled structure built in 1927 on a hill overlooking Upper Waterton Lake. It was another grand mountain resort financed by the railway, except, unlike those in Banff and Jasper, it had no rail link. It was built as part of a chain of first-class hotels in Glacier National Park. Early guests were transported to the hotel by bus from the Great Northern Railway in Montana. After extensive restoration inside and out, the hotel has been returned to its former splendor (look for it in the movie *Excess Baggage,* starring Harry Connick Jr. and Alicia Silverstone). Guests from the U.S. travel to the park in vintage touring buses. Rooms with a view start at $160 s, $170 d, but some are pretty small. Lakeside rooms, with the best views, are $187 s, $197 d. The hotel is open May to late September. Its off-season mailing address is Mail Station 0928, Phoenix, AZ 85077-0928, USA; tel. (602) 207-6000.

Other accommodations in the park are: **Northland Lodge,** General Delivery, Waterton Park, AB T0K 2M0, tel. (403) 859-2353, a converted house with guest lounge, $55-85 s or d; **Stanley Hotel,** Waterton Ave., Waterton Park, AB T0K 2M0, tel. (403) 859-2345, usually full and with shared bathrooms, $50 s or d; **El Cortez Motel,** P.O. Box 67, Waterton Park, AB T0K 2M0, tel. (403) 859-2366, with some kitchenettes, $60 s or d; **Aspen Village Inn,** P.O.

Prince of Wales Hotel

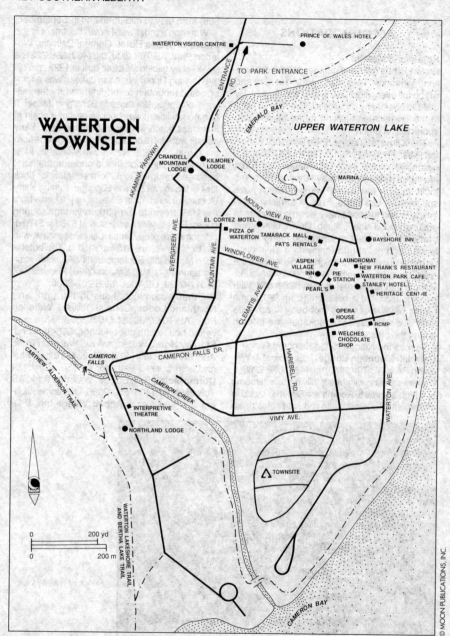

WATERTON
TOWNSITE

PRINCE OF WALES HOTEL

WATERTON VISITOR CENTRE

TO PARK ENTRANCE

ENTRANCE RD.

EMERALD BAY

UPPER WATERTON LAKE

AKAMINA PARKWAY

CRANDELL
MOUNTAIN
LODGE

KILMOREY
LODGE

MARINA

MOUNT VIEW RD.

EL CORTEZ MOTEL

EVERGREEN AVE.

PIZZA OF
WATERTON

TAMARACK MALL

PAT'S RENTALS

BAYSHORE INN

FOUNTAIN AVE.

WINDFLOWER AVE.

ASPEN
VILLAGE
INN

CLEMATIS AVE.

PIE
STATION

PEARL'S

LAUNDROMAT
NEW FRANK'S RESTAURANT
WATERTON PARK CAFE
STANLEY HOTEL
HERITAGE CENTRE

OPERA
HOUSE

RCMP

WELCHES
CHOCOLATE
SHOP

CARTHEW-ALDERSON TRAIL

CAMERON
FALLS

CAMERON FALLS DR.

CAMERON CREEK

HAREBELL RD.

WATERTON AVE.

INTERPRETIVE
THEATRE

NORTHLAND LODGE

VIMY AVE.

TOWNSITE

WATERTON LAKESHORE TRAIL
AND BERTHA LAKE TRAIL

0   200 yd
0   200 m

CAMERON BAY

© MOON PUBLICATIONS, INC.

Box 100, Waterton Park, AB T0K 2M0, tel. (403) 859-2255, $86 s, $93 d; **Bayshore Inn,** P.O. Box 38, Waterton Park, AB T0K 2M0, tel. (403) 859-2211, waterfront location, private balconies, hot tub, and restaurant, $99 s or d for a basic room, $109 lake view.

Campgrounds
Townsite Campground, tel. (403) 859-2224, is in a prime location on the lake within walking distance of many trailheads, restaurants, and shops. Many of its over 200 sites have power, water, and sewer hookups. The campground also has showers and kitchen shelters. Sites are available on a first-come, first-served basis and fill up by midafternoon most summer days. Open mid-May to mid-October; unserviced sites $17, full hookups $21. **Crandell Mountain Campground** is located 10 km from the townsite on Red Rock Canyon Parkway. It has 129 unserviced sites, flush toilets, and kitchen shelters. It's open mid-May to August, sites $13. **Belly River Campground** is 29 km from the townsite on Chief Mountain International Hwy. and is the smallest and most primitive of the park's three developed campgrounds. It has pit toilets and kitchen shelters; sites are $10 per night. All the campgrounds supply firewood but charge $3 per site to burn it.

Waterton also has 13 backcountry campgrounds. Each has pit toilets, a cook shelter, and a water supply. Open fires are discouraged, and prohibited during periods of high fire danger; check with a warden. If you are planning to camp in the backcountry you must obtain a permit from Waterton Visitor Centre or the administration office. Permits are $6 per person per night. Half of all sites can be reserved in advance ($10 per booking). Call (403) 859-2445 for reservations. If your planned itinerary takes you over the border, ask at the information center about border-crossing regulations.

Outside of the park, two private campgrounds take up the nightly overflow. **Waterton Homestead Campground,** tel. (403) 859-2247, has full hookups, showers, laundry, and a heated pool. It is three km north of the park gate on Hwy 6. Tent sites are $10, trailers and RVs $13-17. On Hwy. 5, five km east of the park gate, **Waterton Riverside Campground,** tel. (403) 653-2888, has powered sites, showers, and a barbecue on Saturday nights. Tent sites are $10, powered sites $13. Both these campgrounds close by the middle of September.

FOOD

Restaurants range from pizza and fast food to elegant dining. If you plan on cooking your own food, stock up before you get to the park. Groceries are available at the **Rocky Mountain Food Mart** on Windflower Ave. (open 8 a.m.-10 p.m.) and in the Tamarack Mall on Mount View Road. For great pizza try **Pizza of Waterton,** 103 Fountain Ave., tel. (403) 859-2660, where they pile the dough with all kinds of meats, fresh vegetables, and a special savory sauce. It's open 4:30-10 p.m. For inexpensive breakfasts, homemade soups, delicious salads, and breads covered in homemade preserves head to **Pearl's,** 305 Windflower Ave., tel. (403) 859-2284, where the indoor/outdoor tables are always busy. Next door is the **Pie Station,** a city-style deli serving meat and fruit pies. **New Frank's Restaurant,** 106 Waterton Ave., tel. (403) 859-2240, serves inexpensive Chinese food (from $7) and western food (from $9.50) and lays out a simple six-course buffet every night in summer ($10). **Gazebo Cafe on the Bay** in the Kilmorey Lodge serves light snacks and simple meals; seating is on an outdoor deck on the waterfront. It's open daily 10 a.m.-10 p.m. **Waterton Park Cafe,** on Waterton Ave., tel. (403) 859-2393, serves basic hamburgers starting at $4. It has a liquor license and fills up with the seasonal worker crowd after 10 p.m. Its hours are noon-2 a.m.

One Step Up
The **Kootenai Brown Dining Room** in the Bayshore Inn, tel. (403) 859-2211, overlooks Upper Waterton Lake and the mountains. Mule deer often feed within sight of diners. The food is excellent, especially the trout and beef dishes which start at $13. The view is free. It's also open for breakfast and lunch. Hours are daily 7 a.m.-10 p.m. One of the most popular restaurants in town is in the Kilmorey Lodge. The **Lamp Post Dining Room,** tel. (403) 859-2334, has all the charm of the Prince of Wales Hotel but with a more casual atmosphere and low

prices to match. The mouthwatering menu has appetizers starting at $3, entrees ranging $10-18, and you should leave room to finish with a delicious piece of homemade pie. It's open 7:30 a.m.-10 p.m. The **Garden Court Dining Room** is a formal restaurant in the Prince of Wales Hotel with views of the lake through large windows. Its high ceiling and Old World elegance create a first-class ambience that is overshadowed only by the quality of the food. Prices are similar to any big-city restaurant of the same standard—expect to pay around $90 for two with a bottle of wine. If you are going to splurge, do it here. A large breakfast buffet every morning (6:30-10 a.m.) is worth trying if you won't be coming for dinner. It's open for lunch noon-2 p.m., dinner 5:30-9:30 p.m. Reservations are required; tel. (403) 859-2231.

TRANSPORTATION

Getting There
The nearest commercial airport is at Lethbridge, 140 km away. Cars can be rented at the airport. The closest **Greyhound** buses come to the park is Pincher Creek, 50 km away. From the depot there, at 1015 Hewetson St., **Shuttleton Services,** tel. (403) 627-2157, departs three times daily for the park, loading and unloading passengers at Welches Chocolate Shop on the corner of Windflower Ave. and Cameron Falls Drive. The fare is $15 one-way, $25 roundtrip. A cab to Waterton will cost around $45. Call **Crystal Taxi** at (403) 627-4262.

Getting Around
The **Park Transport Company** operates hiker shuttle services to various trailheads within the park. Cameron Lake, the starting point for the Carthew-Alderson Trail, which ends back in town is a popular drop-off point; $6 one-way. You could take one of these shuttles, and return on the bus later in the day if driving the steep mountain roads doesn't appeal to you. The company also runs two-hour tours ($20 per person) through the park and a taxi service around town. Its office is in Tamarack Mall on Mount View Rd., tel. (403) 859-2378.

The **Crypt Lake Shuttle** leaves the marina regularly for Crypt landing; $9 roundtrip. Reser-

vations are necessary in summer; call (403) 859-2362.**Pat's Rentals** is on Mount View Rd., tel. (403) 859-2266. Pat rents mountain bikes ($6 per hour, $30 per day) and motorized scooters ($15 per hour, $64 per day).

SERVICES AND INFORMATION

Shopping and Services
The proliferation of tourist-oriented gift shops along Waterton Ave. is worth browsing through when the weather isn't cooperating. In the **Tamarack Mall** on Mount View Rd. you'll find a sports store selling camping gear and fishing tackle, a good bookshop, an outdoor-clothing store, and a Royal Bank cash machine. The **post office** is beside the fire station on Fountain Avenue. The **Itussiststukiopi Coin-Op Launderette** at 301 Windflower Ave. is open daily 8 a.m.-10 p.m. The closest **hospitals** are in Cardston, tel. (403) 653-4411, and Pincher Creek, tel. (403) 627-3333. The park's 24-hour emergency number is (403) 859-2636. For the **RCMP** call (403) 859-2244.

Maps and Information
Topographical maps of the park (one map covers the entire area) are available from the Waterton Visitor Centre, administration office, and Heritage Centre for $9.50. For an in-depth look at the natural and human history of the park, pick up a copy of *A Guide to Waterton Lakes National Park* by Heather Pringle at bookshops in town. A free brochure entitled *Catalogue of Publications* lists every book ever written about the park as well as many titles pertaining to western Canada in general. It's available from the Waterton Natural History Association in the Heritage Centre, P.O. Box 145, Waterton Park, AB T0K 2M0.

On the main access road opposite the Prince of Wales Hotel is the **Waterton Visitor Centre,** tel. (403) 859-2445, which provides general information on the park, sells fishing licenses, and issues backcountry permits. Open June-Aug. 8 a.m.-9 p.m., May and early September 9 a.m.-5 p.m., closed the rest of the year. The park's administration office on Mount View Rd. offers the same services as the Visitor Centre and is open year-round, weekdays 8 a.m.-4 p.m.; tel. (403) 859-2224. The **Heritage Centre,** 117 Waterton Ave., tel. (403) 859-2267, is another good source of information and has a good selection of books and an art gallery. It's open May-Oct. 10 a.m.-5 p.m., longer hours in summer. For more information on the park write to Superintendent, Waterton Lakes National Park, Waterton Park, AB T0K 2M0.

CROWSNEST PASS AND VICINITY

The Municipality of Crowsnest Pass is located along Hwy. 3 between Pincher Creek and the Continental Divide in the southwestern corner of the province. The municipality encompasses a handful of once-bustling coal-mining communities, including Bellevue, Hillcrest, Frank, Blairmore, and Coleman. Many topographic features in the area are named "Crowsnest," including a river, a mountain, and the actual pass (1,396 meters) on the Continental Divide. From Pincher Creek it is 62 km to the pass. Continuing west from there, the highway (known as the Crowsnest Highway, of course) descends into British Columbia to the coal-mining and logging towns of Sparwood and Fernie, then on to the major population center of Cranbrook. The area is worth exploring for its natural beauty and recreation opportunities alone; the Crowsnest River reputedly offers some of Canada's best trout fishing. But a trip wouldn't be complete without visiting the historic towns and mines along the route. The Mu-

nicipality of Crowsnest Pass is Alberta's only ecomuseum and was declared a Historic District in 1988, meaning that entire communities are preserved for future generations to explore.

History
The tumultuous history of the pass is one of strikes, disasters, and, in more recent times, unemployment, as one by one the coal mines have closed. Coal had been reported on the eastern slopes as early as 1845, but it wasn't until the Canadian Pacific Railway opened its southern line through the pass in 1898 that the eastern slopes attracted mining companies. Mines were opened and townsites laid out, attracting workers to the area. Many of them were immigrants who brought expectations of high wages and a secure future. But the area's entire economy revolved around just one industry— coal mining. Unfortunately for the miners, the coal here turned out to be of poor quality and lo-

PROVINCIAL ARCHIVES OF ALBERTA

Hillcrest was devastated by a mine explosion that claimed 189 lives in 1914.

CHINOOK WINDS

On many days in the dead of winter, a distinctive arch of clouds forms in the sky over the southwestern corner of the province as a wind peculiar to Alberta swoops down over the mountains. The warm wind raises temperatures by up to 20° C in an hour and up to 40° C in a 24-hour period. The wind's impact on the environment is profound, its effect on the snowpack legendary. One story tells of a backcountry skier who spent the better part of a day traversing to the summit of a snow-clad peak on the front range of the Rockies. As he rested and contemplated skiing down, he realized that the slope had become completely bare!

Chinooks (a native word meaning "snow eater") originate over the Pacific Ocean as warm, moist air which is pushed eastward by prevailing westerlies. As the air crosses British Columbia's rugged interior and climbs the western side of the Rockies, it releases moisture and picks up heat. The warm, dry air then descends the eastern slopes of the Rockies and blows across the prairies. The "chinook arch" is formed as the clear air pushes the cloud cover westward. The phenomenon is most common in southern Alberta but occurs to a lesser degree as far north as the Peace River Valley. Pincher Creek experiences around 35 chinooks each winter.

PACIFIC OCEAN / ROCKY MOUNTAINS / PRAIRIES

cated in seams at steep angles, making extraction difficult. In addition, most of the mining companies were foreign owned and severely undercapitalized, leading to serious problems. The C.P.R. was the mining companies' largest customer, but as the coal was inferior to that from the British Columbia mines, the price paid was considerably less. The first mine closed in 1915 and one by one the others have followed suit. Today many of the local miners work in British Columbia, commuting over the Continental Divide each day. To the residents of this job-starved valley, the tourism industry is something new, but it's catching on quickly. At present only Blairmore and Coleman have tourist services, but this will certainly change.

PINCHER CREEK AND VICINITY

This medium-sized town of 3,800 is surrounded by some of the country's best cattle land. It is reputed to be the windiest spot in Alberta. The bitter winters are tempered by chinook winds that will raise temperatures by up to 20° C in an hour. The town is located in a shallow valley in the southwest corner of the province, 211 km south of Calgary and 70 km north of the International Boundary. The town has many historic buildings, makes a good base for exploring the Castle River Valley and historic Crowsnest Pass, and is known as the gateway to Waterton Lakes National Park.

The North West Mounted Police established a horse farm at what is now known as Pincher Creek in 1876. They found that oats and hay, the horses' main source of sustenance, grew much better here in the foothills than at their newly built post at Fort Macleod. The story goes that a member of the detachment found a pair of pincers near the river—lost many years earlier by prospectors from Montana—and the name stuck. Word of this fertile agricultural land quickly spread and soon the entire area was settled. As was so often the case for towns across the west, the C.P.R. bypassed Pincher Creek and built a siding to the north called Pincher Station. Most towns either moved to the railway or struggled for a few years and died. But not Pincher Creek; it stayed put and has thrived ever since.

Sights

The **Pincher Creek Museum,** tel. (403) 627-3684, is located in **Kootenai Brown Historic Park** on James Avenue. It houses many displays associated with early pioneers of the region. Within the park are numerous historic buildings including the cabin of Kootenai Brown, a turn-of-the-century folk hero (see "History" under "Waterton Lakes National Park," above). The cabin was moved from its original site on Waterton Lakes in 1969. It's open May, June, and September daily 9 a.m.-5 p.m., July and August daily 9 a.m.-7 p.m., the rest of the year Tues.-Fri. 1-4 p.m. Admission is $2. Overlooking Pincher Creek's main street is **Lebel Mansion,** 696 Kettles St., tel. (403) 627-5272, a dignified brick house that has been restored by the Allied Arts Council. Inside is a small art gallery and cultural center open weekdays 1-5 p.m.

The **Oldman Dam** north of Pincher Creek is the latest attempt to irrigate regions of southern Alberta not normally able to produce crops. The reservoir, located just below the confluence of the Crowsnest, Castle, and Oldman Rivers, is becoming a popular recreation spot for windsurfing, boating, and fishing. Just below the dam wall is a specially built kayaking course. The road to the dam (Hwy. 785) also leads to two museums. **Heritage Acres,** tel. (403) 627-5212, a museum run by the Oldman River Antique Equipment and Threshing Club, is nine km along Hwy. 785. It includes a schoolhouse, Doukhobor barn, and Crystal Village—a collection of buildings made entirely from glass telephone insulators (200,000 of them). It's open May-Sept. daily 8 a.m.-6 p.m.; admission $1. A further eight km along the road is **Three Rivers' Rock and Fossil Museum,** tel. (403) 627-2206, a large private collection of shells, minerals, rocks, and oddities of nature. It's open May to mid-October 10 a.m.-5 p.m.; closed Monday.

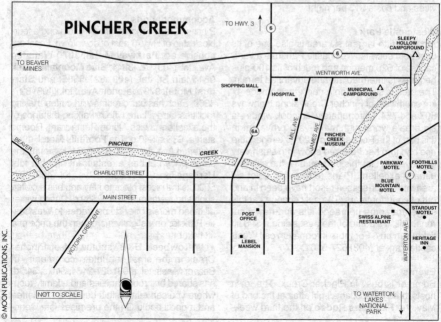

PINCHER CREEK

TO HWY. 3   6

SLEEPY HOLLOW CAMPGROUND

← TO BEAVER MINES

WENTWORTH AVE.

6

SHOPPING MALL

HOSPITAL

MUNICIPAL CAMPGROUND

BEAVER DR.

PINCHER

6A

MILL AVE.

JAMES AVE.

PINCHER CREEK MUSEUM

CREEK

CHARLOTTE STREET

PARKWAY MOTEL

FOOTHILLS MOTEL

6

BLUE MOUNTAIN MOTEL

MAIN STREET

STARDUST MOTEL

POST OFFICE

SWISS ALPINE RESTAURANT

WATERTON AVE.

HERITAGE INN

VICTORIA CRESCENT

LEBEL MANSION

NOT TO SCALE

TO WATERTON LAKES NATIONAL PARK

© MOON PUBLICATIONS, INC.

The Pincher Creek **Hutterite Colony** is one of the few in Alberta that actively invites outsiders to tour the grounds and view the residents' intriguing lifestyle. It is located between Pincher Creek and Cowley. Turn south off Hwy. 3 at the airport sign, then turn south again at the first junction. Follow this road to a "T" intersection, then turn right. The colony comes into view after 1.5 km. Before visiting you are requested to phone ahead, tel. (403) 627-4021.

Beauvais Lake Provincial Park

Located deep in the foothills 24 km southwest of Pincher Creek, Beauvais Lake Provincial Park is a wilderness area with a rich history of early settlement. Foundations of buildings are all that remain of the first homesteaders' efforts to survive in what was then a remote location. The park's most famous settler was James Whitford, one of General Custer's scouts at the famous Battle of Little Bighorn. He is buried at Scott's Point. A reservoir in the southeast corner of the park supplies water to Pincher Creek. The reservoir is also good for boating and fishing for trout. The campground has limited services and costs $13 per night.

Westcastle Park

Alberta's fifth-largest ski area is also one of its best-kept secrets. Westcastle Park has a vertical rise of 520 meters, and much of its 100-plus hectares is intermediate and advanced terrain. The area is situated on a north-facing ridge 47 km southwest of Pincher Creek along highways 507 and 774. Unfortunately, chinook winds—a ski area's worst nightmare—are prevalent in this part of the Rockies, and a 20° C temperature rise can turn hard-packed snow into slush very quickly. Don't let this put you off—the skiing is usually excellent. Plans to turn this quiet ski area into a four-season resort have been in and out of court for years. The only changes at this stage are some upgraded lifts and newly cut runs. Still, it's some of the best skiing a $28 lift ticket can buy. For more information call Westcastle Park at (403) 627-5101.

Events

Summer is busy in Pincher Creek. The town hosts three rodeos: an all-girl affair at the end of May, the **Ranchers Rodeo** on the third week-end of June, and the **Pincher Creek Fair and Rodeo** the third week of August. The Ranchers Rodeo is part of a larger celebration—the **Alberta Cowboy Poetry Gathering and Western Art Show.** The gathering isn't a festival or competition—just a group of cowboys who come together each year to entertain each other. Poems are recited on Friday and Saturday—those known by heart are greeted with the most appreciation. On Saturday night a huge barbecue takes place with more beef than you could poke a brand at. This gets everyone in the mood to kick up their heels at the dance. Demonstrations and sales of traditional Western arts and crafts take place throughout the weekend. For ticketing information call (403) 627-5855.

Other annual events in Pincher Creek include the **Parade of Power and Annual Show** (including working demonstrations of farm equipment) put on by the Oldman River Antique Equipment and Threshing Club on the third weekend in July. The following weekend, celebrations on the Piegan reservation in nearby Brocket include traditional dancing, a rodeo, and native-food tasting.

Accommodations

Pincher Creek's motels are spread along a four-block strip of Hwy. 6 east of downtown. Least expensive are **Parkway Motel,** 1070 Waterton Ave., tel. (403) 627-3344; **Blue Mountain Motel,** 981 Main St., tel. (403) 627-5335; and **Stardust Motel,** 979 Waterton Ave., tel. (403) 627-4366. Each has basic rooms with coffee-making facilities, and all are within walking distance of the excellent Swiss Alpine Restaurant. Rooms start at $36 s, $40 d. The **Foothills Motel,** 1049 Waterton Ave., tel. (403) 627-3341, is around the same price but has a restaurant and hot tub. **Heritage Inn,** 919 Waterton Ave., tel. (403) 627-5000, is the nicest place to stay and has a coffee shop and restaurant; $54 s, $59 d. During winter all these motels offer ski packages to Westcastle Park for only slightly more than the price of a lift ticket.

Willowback B&B, southwest of Pincher Creek in the small mountain community of Beaver Mines, tel. (403) 627-2434, $40 s, $45 d, has shared bathroom facilities and a family room where you can relax with a cup of tea or coffee and a good book. On the premises is a wood-carving studio and gallery. Only a few minutes' walk away is the local general store, which sells excellent ice cream.

Pincher Creek Municipal Campground is in a residential area on Wentworth Ave. just off Hwy. 6. It has no services but is central to town. A short path leads to Kootenai Brown Historic Park. The fee is $6 per night. On the northeast side of town on Hwy. 6 is **Sleepy Hollow Campground,** tel. (403) 627-2033, with lots of permanent trailers, full hookups, and showers. Unserviced sites are $11, serviced $13-15. Along Hwy. 3 eight km west of town is **Castle River Provincial Recreation Area** ($7), and to the southwest toward Beaver Mines is **Beauvais Lake Provincial Park** ($13). Both have pit toilets, kitchen shelters, and firewood.

Food and Drink

The **Swiss Alpine Restaurant,** 988 Main St. at Waterton Ave., tel. (403) 627-5079, is a good place for a meal, whether it's a casual lunch or an intimate dinner in a homey atmosphere. The lounge has lots of stuffed animals and a Western-style atmosphere, and the dining area has good food, including Alberta beef and lamb, delicious salads, and traditional Swiss dishes such as fondue. Most entrees are over $10 but portions are generous. It's open 11 a.m.-10 p.m. for food, but the lounge stays open till the wee hours. **Seasons Eatery** in the Heritage Inn, tel. (403) 627-5000, is slightly cheaper but lacks the atmosphere of the Swiss Alpine. It's open for breakfast, lunch, and dinner. A good place for a light snack is the **Country Bakery** at 967 Main St., tel. (403) 627-2532. You'll find a few Chinese restaurants along Main Street.

Also on Main St., the **King Edward Hotel** has live country music on most nights, **Leo's Marco Polo Club** has exotic dancing on weekends, and **Ezzie's** in the Heritage Inn on Waterton Ave. is where the under-20 crowd hangs out.

Services and Information

The **Greyhound** bus depot is at 1015 Hewetson Ave., tel. (403) 627-2716. The fare between Calgary and Pincher Creek is $30.82 one-way. In summer buses are met by **Shuttleton Services,** tel. (403) 627-2157, which transports passengers onto Waterton Lakes National Park;

$15 one-way, $25 roundtrip. For a cab call **Crystal Taxi** at (403) 627-4262.

The **post office** is at 998 East Avenue. **Pincher Coin Wash** is on Main St. opposite the theater; open daily 8 a.m.-9 p.m. **Pincher Creek Municipal Hospital** is at 1222 Mill Ave., tel. (403) 627-3333. The Tourist Information Centre, an imposing two-story building on the river that is the town's namesake, is open daily 9 a.m.-5 p.m. in summer and weekdays only the rest of the year; 1041 Hewitson St., tel. (403) 627-5199.

To Leitch Collieries

If you had an old 1894 Department of the Interior map of this area, you'd find **Massacre Butte** on it, just west of Pincher Creek. A small group of Dutch immigrants making their way to Fort Edmonton was attacked by Indians there. The only survivor was a young girl who was scalped. Many years later a local businessman, George Gill, was visiting the nearby Piegan Indian Reserve when he saw a white-haired scalp hanging in the home of an old Indian. Remembering the story of the massacre and the fate of the young girl he asked for the scalp, and for some years it hung in a Pincher Creek liquor store.

Southwest of Lundbreck is **Lundbreck Falls** (signposted from Hwy. 3) where the Crowsnest River plunges 12 meters into the canyon below. The campground at the falls has pit toilets, kitchen shelters, and firewood; $9 per night. From Lundbreck the highway passes the junction of Hwy. 22, which heads north to Kananaskis Country and Calgary. The next community west on Hwy. 3 is **Burmis,** well known for the **Burmis Tree,** a photogenic limber pine beside the highway on the west side of town.

At the turn of the century, **Leitch Collieries** was the largest mining and coking operation in Crowsnest Pass, and the only one Canadian owned. In 1915 it became the first to cease production. Now it's a series of picturesque ruins with one of the most informative interpretive exhibits in the area. The collieries opened in 1907, mining a steep coal seam south of the ruins. The No. 2 Mine, beside the highway, commenced operation in 1909. To house workers, a town named Passburg was built east of the mine. Today this site is the most accessible of the the area's "ghost towns," although nothing

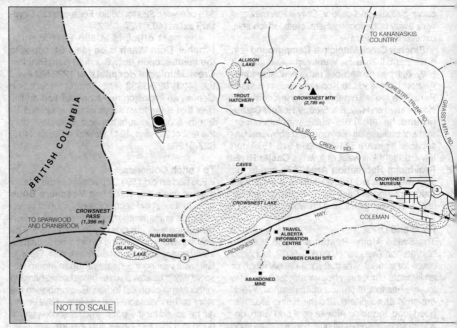

TO KANANASKIS
COUNTRY

ALLISON
LAKE

TROUT
HATCHERY

CROWSNEST MTN
(2,785 m)

BRITISH COLUMBIA

FORESTRY TRUNK RD.

GRASSY MTN. RD.

ALLISON CREEK RD.

CAVES

CROWSNEST
MUSEUM

CROWSNEST
PASS
(1,396 m)

CROWSNEST LAKE

HWY.

COLEMAN

TO SPARWOOD
AND CRANBROOK

RUM RUNNERS
ROOST

ISLAND
LAKE

3

CROWSNEST

TRAVEL
ALBERTA
INFORMATION
CENTRE

BOMBER CRASH SITE

ABANDONED
MINE

NOT TO SCALE

more than a few depressions remains; most buildings were moved after the mine closed. The early development of the site included a sandstone manager's residence, a powerhouse used to supply electricity to Passburg, a row of 101 coke ovens, and a huge tipple. A boardwalk through the mine ruins leads to "listening posts" (where recorded information is played) and interpretive signs. The site is open year-round, with guided tours running daily 9 a.m.-5 p.m. in summer. For more information on the site, write to Crowsnest Pass Ecomuseum Trust, P.O. Box 1440, Blairmore, AB T0K 0E0, or call (403) 564-4700.

BELLEVUE

A French company, West Canadian Collieries, had been prospecting in the pass since 1898 and had bought up 20,000 acres of land. Fortunately, the most impressive coal seams it found were right beside the main C.P.R. line. This became the site of the **Bellevue Mine.** At 8 p.m. on 9 December 1910, an explosion rocked the mine and destroyed the ventilation fan. Thirty men died as a result. Most survived the initial blast but died after inhaling "afterdamp," a term used to describe the carbon dioxide and carbon monoxide left after fire has burned the oxygen from the air. The mine reopened soon after the tragedy and at one time employed 500 men. But the gradual decline in the demand for coal led to the mine's closure in 1962.

The original town of Bellevue was built in 1905, before the mine disaster. The townsite centered around two streets: Front St. (now 213th St.) and Main St. (now 212th St.). The earliest single-story, wood-framed buildings had false facades to make them appear taller and more important than they really were. In 1917, fire destroyed many of the town's buildings, but these were soon replaced by more permanent structures, many of which still stand today. For detailed information on the buildings, purchase *Crowsnest Pass Historical Driving Tour: Bellevue and Hillcrest* ($2.25), available from information centers and museums along the pass

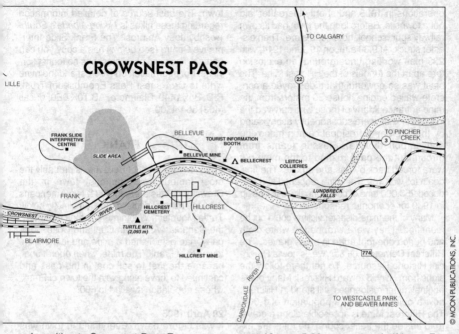

CROWSNEST PASS

TO CALGARY

LILLE

TO PINCHER CREEK

FRANK SLIDE INTERPRETIVE CENTRE

SLIDE AREA

BELLEVUE

TOURIST INFORMATION BOOTH

BELLEVUE MINE

BELLECREST

LEITCH COLLIERIES

FRANK

LUNDBRECK FALLS

CROWSNEST

RIVER

HILLCREST CEMETERY

HILLCREST

BLAIRMORE

TURTLE MTN. (2,093 m)

HILLCREST MINE

CARBONDALE RIVER RD.

774

TO WESTCASTLE PARK AND BEAVER MINES

© MOON PUBLICATIONS, INC.

or by writing to Crowsnest Pass Ecomuseum Trust, P.O. Box 1440, Blairmore, AB T0K 0E0. On Hwy. 3 beside Bellecrest Campground is the **Wayside Chapel,** which seats eight people. Recorded sermons are held throughout summer and the doors are always open. On the last weekend in June the town celebrates Bellecrest Days with a parade, pancake breakfasts, mud-bog race, and a Jell-O–eating contest.

Bellevue Mine Tour

The Crowsnest Pass Ecomuseum Trust opened the former Bellevue Mine for underground tours in 1991. It is the only mine on the pass open to the public. The tour is as realistic as possible without actually making you shovel dirt. The mine is cold, dark, and damp. Before entering you are given a hard hat and a lamp, which you can attach to your hat or carry by hand. The guides carry blankets for those who get cold— average temperature in the mine is 7° C. The tour costs $5; buy tickets from Jeanies Gifts on 213th Street. Tours run from mid-May to Au-

gust 10 a.m.-5:30 p.m., every half hour. For more information call (403) 564-4700.

Practicalities

The **Bellevue Inn,** 2414 213th St., tel. (403) 564-4676, was built in 1921 to house business clients from the mine. Today it still operates as a bar and hotel, with renovated rooms for $35 s, $45 d. The **Bellecrest Campground** on Hwy. 3 at the west end of town has limited services but is free. Bellevue has only one restaurant and it's Chinese, with a limited western menu. It's located at 2438 213th St., tel. (403) 564-4801, and open Tues.-Sun. 11 a.m.-9 p.m. A **tourist information booth** beside the campground on Hwy. 3 is open during summer.

HILLCREST

Named after Charles Plummer Hill, one of the pass's earliest prospectors, Hillcrest is best remembered for Canada's worst mine disaster. The Hillcrest Coal and Coke Company began operations in 1905 and shortly thereafter laid out a townsite. Before long the town had its own railway spur, school, hotel, and store. Then disaster struck. At 9:30 a.m. on 19 June 1914, with 235 men working underground, an explosion tore apart the tunnels of the Hillcrest Mine. The blast was so powerful that it destroyed a concrete-walled engine house 30 meters from the mine entrance. Many of those who survived the initial explosion were subsequently asphyxiated by the afterdamp (residual carbon monoxide and carbon dioxide). Rescue teams from throughout the pass rushed to the mine but were forced back by gas and smoke. The final death toll was 189. The mine reopened and produced 250,000 tons of coal annually until closing in 1939 for economic reasons.

Many of the mine-disaster victims could not be identified. They were wrapped in white cloth and buried one foot apart in mass graves. The **Hillcrest Cemetery** off 8th Ave. is now a Provincial Historic Resource. To get there follow the signs from Hwy. 3 toward Hillcrest. Many of the original miner residences still stand in Hillcrest, now a quiet town with a population of 1,000. The **Hillcrest Mine** is accessible along a gravel road beside the trailer court. The ruins are extensive—look for the sealed mine entrance at the rear of the ruins, half hidden by trees.

To the south of Hillcrest is some good hiking and camping along the Carbondale River Rd. (also known as Adanac Rd.), which spurs south from the Hillcrest access road east of the

town. The best source of detailed information regarding these hikes is *Hiking Alberta's Southwest* by Joey Ambrosi. The Frank Slide Interpretive Centre (see below) has a copy you can peruse. The town of Hillcrest has no tourist services. For information on Hillcrest and the mine write to Crowsnest Pass Ecomuseum Trust, P.O. Box 1440, Blairmore, AB T0K 0E0, or call (403) 564-4700.

FRANK

Frank, two km west of Bellevue, is probably the most famous (or infamous) town in the Crowsnest Pass area. In 1901, two Americans acquired mineral rights to the area directly below Turtle Mountain. Within months their company, the Canadian-American Coal and Coke Company, had established a mine and laid out the townsite of Frank. The mine, when operational, became the first to sell coal in the pass and continued to thrive along with the town of Frank, whose population swelled to 600.

29 April 1903
It was before dawn. Everything in town was quiet and the night shift was hard at work deep inside Turtle Mountain. Then, without warning, a gigantic chunk of the north face of the mountain sheared off, thundering into the valley below and burying part of Frank. It was the world's most destructive rock slide, burying 68 of the

Turtle Mountain before the slide

PROVINCIAL ARCHIVES OF ALBERTA

town's residents. Amazingly, none of the working coal miners were killed. After being trapped for 14 hours they dug themselves out. In times of tragedy there are usually heroes, and the hero of the Frank Slide was Sid Choquette. After realizing that the rail line had been covered he scrambled over the still-moving mass of boulders and flagged down the morning express, stopping it before it reached the slide. As a token of appreciation, the C.P.R. gave Choquette $25 and a letter of commendation. Within three weeks the tracks were dug out and the railway reopened. A week later the mine reopened. Most of Frank was intact, but fear of another slide led to the relocation of all the buildings across the railway line to a safer location. The mine closed in 1917.

It is impossible to calculate the amount of rock that fell from the mountain. It has been estimated at 82 million tons by some, 30 million cubic meters by others. Looking at the north face of Turtle Mountain will give you a visual idea of the slide. But it isn't until you actually drive through the slide area, or view the fan of limestone boulders that spread over three km from the base of the mountain and over two km to the east and west that the full extent becomes apparent. Scientists to this day puzzle over what caused the slide and the vast spread. Most believe that a number of factors contributed to the initial slide, and the weakening of the mountain by mining operations was only a small part of it. As to the spread of rock, one theory put forward by scientists is "air lubrication": as the huge mass of rock slid downward it compressed and trapped air on which it rode across the valley. Today Turtle Mountain is monitored daily with some of the world's most advanced seismographic equipment but has shown no sign of moving since.

Sights

The original townsite of Frank is now an industrial park. To get to it cross the rail line at 150th St. (just west of the turnoff for the interpretive center). Take the first left and look for a rusty fire hydrant to the right. This is all that remains of the ill-fated town. This hydrant once stood on Dominion Ave., Frank's main street. Directly behind it was the grand Imperial Hotel, now just a depression in the ground with a tree growing in it. This road then continues across Gold Creek and into the slide area. A memorial was erected here by Delbert Ennis, whose entire family survived the slide—and they lived on the south side of Gold Creek! This was the main route through the area before the slide and has since been cleared. It eventually joins up with the Hillcrest access road. The mine entrance is partially visible on the northern edge of the slide area, just above Frank Lake. For those with a sense of adventure it is possible to climb Turtle Mountain (2,093 meters). The trailhead is in East Blairmore on Pipeline Road. The trek to the summit is actually easier than it looks as the trail follows the mountain's northwest ridge. Only the last 20 meters along an exposed section are tricky. Allow two to three hours each way.

The **Frank Slide Interpretive Centre,** on a slight rise at the northern edge of the slide area, is an excellent place to learn more about the history of the valley, its settlers, and its tragedies. The audiovisual presentation *In the Mountain's Shadow* is a particularly moving account of the terrible working and social conditions in the valley. A 1.5-km self-guided trail leads down into the slide. Better still, scramble up the slope behind the parking lot and walk along the ridge for a view of the entire slide area. Admission to the center is $4. It's open mid-May through August 9 a.m.-8 p.m., the rest of the year 10 a.m.-4 p.m. For more information call (403) 562-7388. In the Frank Community Hall at the west end of Frank is **Crowsnest Pass Art Gallery,** tel. (403) 562-2218, which displays local and traveling exhibitions; open Tues.-Sat. 1-5 p.m., extended hours in summer. No tourist services are available in Frank, but who wants to camp under Turtle Mountain anyway?

BLAIRMORE AND VICINITY

With a population of 1,800, Blairmore is the largest of the Crowsnest Pass communities. The town was originally known as Tenth Siding before being renamed in honor of the Federal Minister of Railways, A.G. Blair. The town had only a small mine itself, but when the Frank Mine opened in 1901, Blairmore thrived. It became a main center for the surrounding mines and a supply point for the other towns. Real-estate brokers, insurance agents, doctors, and barristers all made their homes here, and in 1907, West Canadian Collieries—who owned the Lille and Bellevue mines—relocated their offices to Blairmore. A brickyard opened and many of the wooden-front buildings along the main street were replaced by impressive brick structures.

Still, it was coal mining that dictated the town's economy, and by the 1920s tensions between the workers and the mining companies had increased to the breaking point; in 1925, hundreds of miners protested on the streets of Blairmore. When the depression of 1929 set in, the companies cut wages, leading to further strikes. Communist labor leaders rallied local miners, and in February 1932 an election swept union representatives into power. The workers' town council had been elected with overwhelming support by their fellow miners. In an early act of rebellion they renamed Blairmore's main street to Tim Buck Boulevard, honoring the leader of the Communist Party of Canada.

Sights
Many of Blairmore's original buildings still stand, including the brick structures on Main St. (20th Ave.). The three-story **Cosmopolitan Hotel** is the most impressive. It was built in 1912. The bar was always full of thirsty workers whom the manager obligingly served, even after hours (leading to the hotel's liquor license being revoked many times). Opposite the hotel is a **gazebo** that was a rallying point for miners during the '20s. For detailed information on all Blairmore's early buildings purchase a copy of *Crowsnest Pass Historical Driving Tour: Blairmore,* available at information centers and museums throughout the pass.

Recreation and Events
Crowsnest Pass Golf and Country Club in Blairmore is the only golf course in the pass. Green fees are $15 for nine holes, $20 for 18. **Pass Powder Keg Ski Hill** features some runs ending right in town, but the main day lodge is accessed along a steep road spurring off 27th Street. The hill has a vertical rise of 400 meters and some surprisingly steep runs. Open for night skiing daily except Monday and all day on weekends; tel. (403) 562-8334.

The annual **Rum Runner Days** on the second weekend of July is a rip-roaring celebration of the town's seedy past. It kicks off with a pancake breakfast and parade on Saturday, followed by a barbecue and music in Bandstand Park. The weekend culminates at Leitch Collieries on Sunday with a picnic.

Accommodations
Two historic hotels on 20th Ave.—the **Cosmopolitan Hotel,** 13001 20th Ave., tel. (403) 562-7321, and **Greenhill Hotel,** 12326 20th Ave., tel. (403) 562-2232—have rooms starting at $35 s, $38 d. Ask to see them first. Some have shared bathrooms, others have TVs, all are noisy on Saturday night. At the west end of town is **Highwood Motel,** 11373 20th Ave., tel. (403) 562-8888, which has a popular restaurant and pub on the premises; $40 s, $43 d. The nicest hotel is **Cedar Riverside Inn,** 11217 21st Ave., tel. (403) 562-8851, also at the west end of town and only two blocks from Hwy. 3. It has a sauna, jacuzzi, coin laundry, and restaurant. Rooms start at $45 s, $50 d. Rather than paying $40 for a basic, boring motel room consider **Nestle Inn B&B,** 12313 21st Ave., tel. (403) 562-2474. The former mine-manager's residence was built in 1915 and still retains its historic charm. The rooms are cozy and the coffeepot is always on in the large guest parlor. Rates are $40 s, $55 d, which includes a good hot breakfast. **Lost Lemon Campground,** tel. (403) 562-2932, is across the railway tracks at the west end of town. It has showers, a swimming pool, and a laundry, and is right beside the Crowsnest River; tent sites are $12, hookups $14-18.

Food and Drink
Blairmore has a string of restaurants on 20th Ave., none being particularly special. The **London Arms Pub,** tel. (403) 562-8888, in the Highwood Inn, provides glimpses of mountain scenery from the window tables. For breakfast expect to pay $5, lunch $7, and dinner $8 and up. It's open Mon.-Sat. 6 a.m.-10:30 p.m., Sunday 7:30 a.m.-9 p.m. The restaurant in the **Cedar Riverside Inn,** tel. (403) 562-8851, is open daily 6 a.m.-10 p.m. and has a buffet each Sunday from 4 p.m. Opposite the Greenhill Hotel is **Yummy Inn,** tel. (403) 562-7357, for eat-in or take-out Chinese and a buffet for Tuesday lunch and Thursday dinner. The **Nestle Inn Tea Room,** 12313 21st Ave., tel. (403) 562-2474,

serves light snacks and lunches in a historic building; open Mon.-Sat. 11 a.m.-4 p.m.

The bar in the Cosmopolitan Hotel is always busy, as is the Greenhill Hotel, which has live country music on Friday and Saturday nights. Don't ask for an umbrella in your drink at either of these places. The Cedar Riverside Inn has a lounge, as does the Highwood Motel.

Transportation, Services and Information
Greyhound buses head to Pincher Creek ($8.19) and on to Calgary ($30.82) twice daily. They also go west into British Columbia. The depot is at 2022 129th St., tel. (403) 562-8551. The **post office** is at 12537 20th Avenue. The only medical services on the pass are at **Crowsnest Pass Hospital,** at 2001 107th St., tel. (403) 562-2831. A good source of information on the area is the **Crowsnest Pass Ecomuseum Trust,** housed in the old **Blairmore Courthouse** on 20th Avenue. Their mailing address is P.O. Box 1440, Blairmore, AB T0K 0E0; tel. (403) 564-4700.

In the Vicinity
The foundations of **Lille,** once a thriving community north of Hwy. 3, can only be accessed on foot. The hike is short but the rewards are ample. The Lille mines and townsite were run by West Canadian Collieries, the same company that owned the Bellevue Mine. Its isolation from the pass and poor quality of coal forced the mines to close in 1913. The town's population of 400 moved out and everything that could be salvaged was moved to Bellevue.

Two possible routes can be taken to Lille—the shortest is from Blairmore, the other follows Gold Creek up a valley from east of Frank. To access the shorter trail, turn north just east of the Blairmore Golf Course on Grassy Mountain Rd. and follow it for eight km to an intersection. The road to the right leads to Lille, but from here you're on foot; it's a three-km (one-hour) hike along an old railway grade to the abandoned townsite in a grassy meadow.

Most of the building materials have been salvaged through the years, leaving only foundations. To the right of your path, you'll pass an impressive row of 50 coke ovens and the foundations of a once-grand hotel. Scattered through the meadow on the left-hand side of the trail lie the ruins of the miners' cottages, schools, and even a couple of rusty fire hydrants. A 4WD drive track leads east (left) through the meadow to two of the mines, which require some bushwhacking to find. On the south (right) side of this road are the foundations of the bakery, butcher shop, general store, and hospital.

COLEMAN

Westernmost of the Crowsnest Pass communities is Coleman, 15 km from the British Columbia border. The colliery in Coleman closed in December 1983, the last in the pass to do so. Many of the town's miners joined the ranks of the unemployed, some found work in the BC mines, while others packed up their belongings and left the pass completely. The effect on the town has been devastating. A walk down Coleman's 17th Avenue is like what walking down the main street of Bellevue, Frank, Passburg, and Lille must have looked like after their respective mines had closed. Most of the buildings are boarded up, all are dilapidated. Many businesses have relocated to the highway hoping to catch passing trade. Those that remain are breathing their last gasp of air.

History
Shortly after the land on which Coleman sat had been purchased by the International Coal and Coke Company, the town expanded rapidly. By 1904 it had two hotels, two churches, and a number of stores along Main Street. In 1918 the coal market collapsed and the mine closed. Still, the folks in Coleman were confident of the town's future and in due course concrete sidewalks were constructed. During the time leading up to WW II the mine opened, but with a scaled-down operation. The '50s was a time of amalgamation among the coal-mining companies in the pass, enabling the Coleman Colliery to remain open until 1983. Across the railway tracks at the west end of 17th Ave. are the remains of the coke ovens, the most complete in the pass. Many of the buildings that remain are of historical significance. For information pick up a copy of *Crowsnest Pass Historical Driving Tour: Coleman* ($2.25), available from the Crowsnest Museum or by writing to Crowsnest Pass Ecomu-

THE NOT-SO-GREAT TRAIN ROBBERY

It was August 1920, and the Lethbridge-Cranbrook train had just pulled out of Coleman toward the Crowsnest Pass, loaded with passengers. Suddenly, under orders from three gun-wielding bandits, the train jerked to a halt. The trio, later identified as Aulcoff, Akroff, and Bassoff, had heard that successful local businessman Emilio Picariello—known to everyone as Emperor Pic—would be aboard carrying $10,000. The robbers' luck was short-lived from the start. They missed the wad of cash, fleeing with only $400 and several watches. After a night of drinkin' and dancin' in Coleman and evidently in no hurry, Akroff and Bassoff were spotted reading their "wanted" poster outside the Bellevue Cafe. The RCMP was alerted and confronted the pair. In the violent shoot-out that followed, Akroff and two policemen were killed. Bassoff was wounded and limped off in the direction of Frank Slide. On the run for several days, he was tracked to a Pincher Creek train yard where he sat passive and composed, eating lunch. Arrested and charged, he was hanged on 22 December 1920. Three and a half years later Aulcoff was apprehended in Montana, extradited, and sentenced, but he died in prison before the death sentence could be carried out. Today the only reminder of this lawless episode is a plaque at the Frank Slide Interpretive Centre memorializing the slain officers (although bullet holes were visible in booths at the Bellevue Cafe for many years after the incident).

seum Trust at P.O. Box 1440, Blairmore, AB T0K 0E0.

Museum
Located in the old Coleman High School building is the **Crowsnest Museum,** 7701 18th Ave., tel. (403) 563-5434. The museum takes a full hour to view as it has two floors crammed with exhibits and artifacts from throughout the region. The schoolyard has displays of farming, mining, and fire-fighting equipment. It's open daily in summer 10 a.m.-noon and 1-4 p.m., closed weekends the rest of the year. Across the street is the *Coleman Journal* building. The

Coleman Journal was a Pulitzer Prize-winning weekly newspaper that was published until 1970. After extensive restoration, the Crowsnest Pass Ecomuseum Trust has opened the building to the public. Interpretive panels explain the slow process involved in early newspaper publishing. It's open daily in summer 10 a.m.-noon and 1-4 p.m.

Bomber Crash Site
From Coleman you can hike to the remains of a Royal Canadian Air Force Dakota that clipped the top of Andy Good Peak and crashed into the valley below in 1946. All seven airmen aboard lost their lives. The crash is on the south side of the Crowsnest River, nine km from town. Cross the railway lines at 81st St., then cross the river at 83rd St. and turn right (west) onto 13th Avenue. Because this road becomes gravel and fairly rough, it is recommended only for 4WDs. At the wooden bridge four km from town the road deteriorates and it's five km farther to the crash site (a two-and-a-half-hour hike from town). Keep right at all intersections. All that remains of the plane is the tail section, wing section, and the landing gear.

The Forestry Trunk Road
The Forestry Trunk Rd., also known as Hwy. 940 or Kananaskis Rd., is a well-graded gravel road that parallels the Rocky Mountains for over 1,000 km. The southernmost section starts in Coleman and heads north through the **Livingstone Range** to the Highwood Junction in Kananaskis Country, some 120 km to the north of Coleman. Along the way are many hiking and fishing opportunities and plenty of primitive Forest Service campgrounds. Highlights include **Livingstone Gap** (48 km north of Coleman)—where the Oldman River flows through a narrow gorge—and **Livingstone Falls** (65 km north of Coleman), which has a nearby campground.

Accommodations
Coleman has one motel, but this certainly isn't your only option. An old hotel has been restored as a budget accommodation, and outside of town are cabins, a ranch, and a B&B. The **Stop Inn Motel,** tel. (403) 562-7381, is on Hwy. 3 above town. Clean, basic rooms are $35 s, $40 d. The **Grand Union International Hostel,** 7719 17th Ave., tel. (403) 563-3433, was built in 1926.

Early advertising for the hotel boasted of "thirty rooms with electric light and furnished in first class style." Substantial restoration work has been undertaken by the Southern Alberta Hostelling Association, and although the rooms aren't first class they are of good hostel standard. The hostel is also central within Coleman—17th Ave. was originally the town's main street. Hostel rates are $12 members, $15 nonmembers. On Crowsnest Lake 12 km west of town is the **Rum Runner's Roost**, tel. (403) 563-5111. Rooms in this large country home are $35 s, $45 d including a hot breakfast. Self-contained cabins with fantastic mountain views are also available for $50. Also on the lake is **Kosy Knest Kabins**, tel. (403) 563-5155, where all rooms have kitchenettes and TVs; $35 s, $45 d.

Food

Most of Coleman's businesses have relocated from the main street to Hwy. 3, which bypasses town to the north. **Chris & Irvin's Cafe**, tel. (403) 563-3093, is one of the few businesses hanging on downtown. It serves hamburgers, cheeseburgers, bacon burgers, and loaded burgers. The menu might be limited but the burgers are good. They start at $2. It's open Mon.-Sat. 6 a.m.-10 p.m., Sunday 8 a.m.-8 p.m. Up on the highway is **Popiel's**, tel. (403) 563-5555, surprisingly nice inside and with a reasonably priced steak, chicken, and seafood menu. It's open Tues.-Sat. 7 a.m.-midnight, till 10 p.m. on Sunday and Monday.

Services and Information

Greyhound stops at the Kananaskis Mohawk gas station on Hwy. 3. Beside Popiel's is a grocery store and laundromat. The **post office** on Main St. has recently closed and now houses only the residents' post boxes. The best source of information in town is the **Crowsnest Museum**, 7701 18th Ave., tel. (403) 563-5434, open daily during summer 10 a.m.-noon and 1-4 p.m.; closed weekends the rest of the year.

WEST OF COLEMAN

Crowsnest Mountain

From Coleman, the British Columbia border is only 15 km. But there's no rush, you have a mountain to climb. Crowsnest Mountain (2,785 meters) is the symbol of the pass, and although it's a fairly difficult ascent with an elevation gain of 1,030 meters, it can be hiked by anyone with a good level of fitness. Snow may be encountered until July and a certain amount of scrambling across scree slopes is required. For the most part the trail is up the north-facing slope, so don't be perturbed by the cliff faces that face the highway. The Allison Creek Rd. spurs north three km west of Coleman past one of Alberta's few outcrops of igneous rock (to the north just before the junction). Follow this road for 10.5 km, staying right at the first fork. The trailhead is marked, and a little farther is the parking lot—well, a place to park your car anyway.

At first the trail climbs steadily through a subalpine forest of pine and spruce before crossing a stream. This is the last water source so fill up. At the first scree slope, below the north face of the mountain, is an impressive view of the Seven Sisters to the northeast. The trail through the scree slope is not always obvious, but try to follow it anyway—it's the easiest route. At the base of the cliff go right and climb up the wide gully to approximately 20 meters before the top of the rise, then veer sharply to the left. If you have difficulties scrambling up this section turn back; if not, continue up three more gullies (the route is fairly obvious) from where the trail levels out and continues to the summit. The view from here is spectacular, extending well into British Columbia to the west, and to the Porcupine Hills to the east. A canister attached to one of the summit markers contains a notepad in which to sign your name and prove you made it. It is only five km to the summit but you should allow between three and a half and five hours each way. Check the weather forecast before heading out.

To the Border

Also along Allison Creek Rd. is the **Allison Creek Brood Trout Station**, tel. (403) 563-3385, open to the public for tours and a self-guided walk. It's open daily in summer 10:30 a.m.-noon and 1-3:30 p.m., closed weekends Sept.-May. The road continues to a recreation area on **Allison Lake,** which has good fishing and nearby camping. During winter, cross-country ski trails are set around the lake. The **Travel Alberta Information Centre**, tel. (403) 563-

3888, on Hwy. 3 has a spectacular view of Crowsnest Mountain. The center is difficult to see coming from the east—look for a blue roof on the south side of the road opposite Crowsnest Lake. It's open mid-May to mid-June 10 a.m.-6 p.m. and mid-June to August 9 a.m.-6 p.m. Behind the information center an old road now accessible only on foot leads three km (one hour each way) to an abandoned mine. The road crosses a small creek several times before coming to an intersection. Continue straight ahead (follow the creek) past an old car and into a grassy meadow. Head one km farther to the mine slag heap and scramble to the top for a view of the mine and some log cabins.

Nearby are some interesting caves, also accessible by a short walk. They are not marked nor is there a set trail. The easiest way to get to them is from the roadside turnout on Crowsnest Lake (just west of the information center). Follow the lake's edge to the north, cross a small creek and follow the railway tracks to a point nearly opposite the roadside turnout. Look for a small stream to the north. The caves are here, and their walls bear petroglyphs (native rock carvings).

Crowsnest Lake is popular for fishing and windsurfing. From here Hwy. 3 crosses Island Lake and passes a small residential community known as **Crowsnest** before crossing the Continental Divide and entering British Columbia, which is another day and another book (Moon's *British Columbia Handbook*, to be precise).

Struthiomimus

BOB RACE

KAREN McKINLEY

DINOSAUR VALLEY

East of Calgary the Red Deer River flows past some of the world's richest dinosaur fossil beds; hundreds of specimens from the Cretaceous period—displayed in museums throughout the world—have been unearthed along a 120-km stretch of the river valley. One spot, **Dinosaur Provincial Park,** is the mother lode for paleontologists. This UNESCO World Heritage Site includes a "graveyard" of over 300 dinosaurs of 35 species, many of which have been found nowhere else in the world. As a comparison, Utah's Dinosaur Natural Monument has yielded just 12 species. The valley has more than just dinosaur skeletons; paleontologists have unearthed skin impressions, eggshells, dung, and footprints as well as fossilized insects, fish, amphibians, crocodiles, pterodactyls, and reptiles. And the valley's landforms are as enthralling as the prehistoric artifacts they entomb—spectacular badland formations make for a sight not easily forgotten.

Alberta's best-known dinosaur is the duck-billed hadrosaur. Remains of this creature have been found on all continents except South America and Australia, an item of interest to paleontologists. By comparing specimens found on different continents, they can prove that these ancient beasts roamed the greater part of the earth.

The major city in the valley, Drumheller, is home to the Royal Tyrrell Museum of Palaeontology. The museum is a research and display center with over 50 full-size dinosaurs exhibited, more than in any other museum in the world.

The Great Canadian Dinosaur Rush

For generations natives had regarded the ancient bones, which were always common in the valley, as belonging to giant buffalo. During early geographical surveys of southern Alberta by George M. Dawson, the first official dinosaur discovery was recorded. In 1884 one of Dawson's assistants, Joseph B. Tyrrell, collected and sent specimen bones to Ottawa for scientific investigation. Their identification initiated the first real dinosaur rush. For the first century of digging, all the dinosaur bones uncovered were transported to museums around the world for further study. Just over 100 years after Tyrrell's discovery, a magnificent museum bearing his name opened in the valley. The idea of the museum was promoted by dinosaur hunter Dr. Phil Currie, and since its opening the dinosaurs have stayed and the tourists have come.

DRUMHELLER AND VICINITY

Drumheller is one of Alberta's major tourist destinations. Over half a million people flock to this desolate part of Canada for one reason: dinosaurs. The city (pop. 6,500) is set in a spectacular lunarlike landscape in the Red Deer River Valley 138 km northeast of Calgary. Ancient glacial meltwaters gouged a deep valley into the surrounding rolling prairie, and wind and water have continued the erosion process ever since. The city's proximity to some of the world's premier dinosaur fossil beds has made it a mecca for paleontologists—scientists from around the globe come to Drumheller and environs to learn more about the prehistoric animals that roamed the earth millions of years ago.

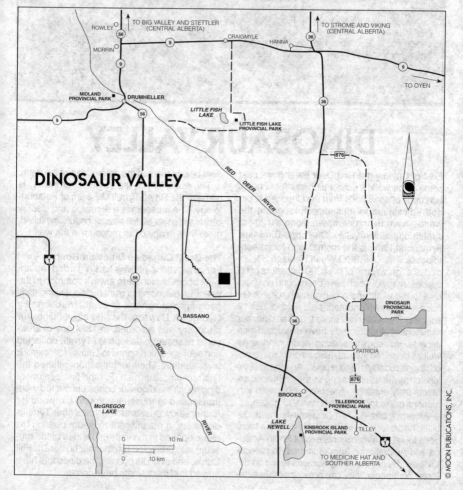

© MOON PUBLICATIONS, INC.

DINOSAUR DIGS

Become involved in the actual digging of dinosaur bones by participating in a museum-organized **Day Dig.** These take place at a site close to the Royal Tyrrell Museum of Palaeontology. The adventure begins at 8:30 a.m. with a behind-the-scenes look at specimens already collected by museum staff, then it's out to the dig site. After a brief lesson in excavation techniques, the day is spent digging up dinosaur bones under the guidance of museum paleontologists. Lunch is provided and you are returned to the museum by 4 p.m., free to wander around the displays. The work is not particularly strenuous, but it gets hot in the badlands, so bring plenty of sunscreen and a hat. Cost is $85 per person. Trips run July through August. Ask at the museum's reception desk for details or call (403) 823-7707.

For those with more time, the **Field Experience** program allows interested parties to totally immerse themselves in the world of paleontology. These weeklong programs take place within Dinosaur Provincial Park and at Devil's Coulee, south of Lethbridge. The week is spent prospecting for new finds, engaging in excavation work, and preparing specimens for further study. The program runs June through August, beginning each Sunday. Accommodations at the Dinosaur Provincial Park site are in trailers, while the Devil's Coulee site is more remote—participants must supply tents but a dining trailer is on site. The cost is $800 per person, which includes all meals. For further information write Field Experience Program, Royal Tyrrell Museum, P.O. Box 7500, Drumheller, AB T0J 0Y0; tel. (403) 823-7707.

The city was named after Samuel Drumheller, an early pioneer in the local coal industry. Coal deposits had been found in the area by early explorers, but it wasn't until 1911 that the first mine opened. In 1913, when the rail link was completed with Calgary, the town's population exploded. Coal dominated the economy until after WW II, when diesel replaced steam and demand for coal dwindled. Today the town is an agricultural and oil center, with 3,000 oil wells perforating the farmland within a close radius of town.

SIGHTS

Royal Tyrrell Museum of Palaeontology

So many of the world's great museums are simply showcases for natural history, yet nestled in the badlands six km northwest of Drumheller, the Royal Tyrrell Museum of Palaeontology, the world's largest museum devoted entirely to paleontology, is a lot more. It integrates display areas with fieldwork done literally on the doorstep, with specimens trans-

at the Royal Tyrrell Museum

DRUMHELLER

ported to the museum for research and cataloging. Even for those with little or no interest in dinosaurs it's easy to spend half a day in the massive 11,200-square-meter complex. The museum holds over 80,000 specimens, including 50 full-size dinosaur skeletons, the world's largest such display.

A "time line" of exhibits covers 3.8 billion years of life on this planet, beginning with early life forms and the development of Charles Darwin's theory. Before the age of the dinosaurs, the Precambrian and Paleozoic eras saw life on earth develop at an amazing rate. These periods are cataloged through numerous displays, such

as the one of British Columbia's Burgess Shale, where circumstances allowed the fossilization of a community of soft-bodied marine creatures 530 million years ago. But the museum's showpiece is Dinosaur Hall, where reconstructed skeletons and full-size replicas of dinosaurs are complemented by realistic dioramas of their habitat. Another feature is the two-story paleoconservatory, featuring over 100 species of plants, many of which flourished during the period dinosaurs roamed the earth. Nearing the end of the tour, the various theories for the cause of the dinosaurs' extinction, around 64 million years ago, are presented. The coming of the ice ages is described in detail, and humanity's appearance on earth is put into perspective.

The museum is also a major research center: a large window into the main preparation lab allows you to view the delicate work of technicians as they clear the rock away from newly unearthed bones.

The museum is in Midland Provincial Park (see below). It's open daily 9 a.m.-9 p.m. in summer, Tues.-Sun. 10 a.m.-5 p.m. the rest of the year. Admission is adult $6.50, senior $5.50, child $3. For further information, call (403) 823-7707.

Midland Provincial Park
This 595-hectare park covers the lower part of Fox Creek Coulee on the northern bank of the Red Deer River. **McMullen Island,** created by an old river meander, is a secluded day-use area shaded by willows and cottonwoods. Pathways lead along the riverbank, and barbecues and a generous supply of wood are available. On the opposite side of the highway the origins of the park become apparent. Slag heaps and building foundations are the only reminders of the three Midland Coal Mines that operated here until the late 1960s. The mine office is now the park visitor center where interpretive boards explain the history of the area, and a short trail leads through the old mining sites. Many visitors to the park are not even aware that they're in it. The Royal Tyrrell Museum (see above), from where rangers conduct short hikes during summer, is at the western end of the park. For more information on the park, call (403) 823-1749.

Homestead Antique Museum
This museum, featuring mostly pioneer artifacts, is housed in a Quonset hut two km west of the

DINOSAURS OF ALBERTA

Dinosaur bones found in the Red Deer River Valley play an important role in the understanding of our prehistoric past. The bones date from the late Cretaceous period, around 70 million years ago; for reasons that have mystified paleontologists for over a century, dinosaurs disappeared during this period, after having roamed the earth for 150 million years. A recent theory, put together largely through work done in Alberta, suggests that while larger species disappeared, some of the smaller ones evolved into birds.

The bones of 35 dinosaur species—around 10% of all those currently known—have been discovered in Alberta. Like today's living creatures, they are classified in orders, families, and species. Of the two orders of dinosaurs, both have been found in the Red Deer River Valley. The bird-hipped dinosaurs (order Ornithischia) were herbivores, while the lizard-hipped dinosaurs (order Saurischia) were omnivores and carnivores.

Apart from their sheer bulk, many herbivores lacked any real defenses. Others developed their own protection; the chasmosaurus had a bony frill around its neck, the pachycephalosaurus had a 25-centimeter-thick dome-shaped skull cap fringed with spikes, and the ankylosaurus was an armored dinosaur whose back was covered in spiked plates.

Among the most common herbivores that have been found in the valley are members of the family of duck-billed hadrosaurs. Fossilized eggs of one hadrosaur, the hypacrosaurus, were unearthed still encasing intact embryos.

Another common herbivore in the valley was a member of the horned ceratops family; over 300 specimens of the centrosaurus have been discovered in one "graveyard."

Of the lizard-hipped dinosaurs, the tyrannosaurs were most feared by herbivores. The 15-meter *Tyrannosaurus rex* is most famous among *Homo sapiens*. But the smaller albertosaurus, a remarkably agile carnivore weighing many tons, was the most common tyrannosaur found in the valley.

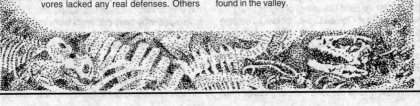

city, tel. (403) 823-2600. The collection includes Indian relics, pioneer clothing, mining equipment, musical instruments, a two-headed calf, and re-creations of an early beauty parlor and barber shop. Outside is an array of farm machinery, automobiles, and a buffalo rubbing stone. The museum is open July-Aug. 9 a.m.-9 p.m., and May, June, September, and October 9 a.m.-6 p.m. Admission is $4.

Drumheller Dinosaur and Fossil Museum

This small downtown museum at 335 1st St. E, tel. (403) 823-2593, has an interesting display of privately owned and donated prehistoric pieces, most of which have been collected from the Red Deer River Valley. Exhibits include interpretive boards explaining the geography of the ancient inland sea, the process of coal formation, and the fossilization process. Two items of particular interest are the mounted 10-meter-long skeleton of an edmontosaurus and the skull of a pachyrhinosaurus, the first of its species found. The museum is open in summer daily 10 a.m.-6 p.m., shorter hours in May and October. Admission is $3.

Prehistoric Park

For the complete Dinosaur Valley experience you need to visit at least one gimmicky attraction and this is the best of the bunch. Life-size dinosaur models are displayed among 50 hectares of natural badlands canyon scenery. A one-km trail leads through the park, finishing at **Ollie's Rock & Fossil Shop,** which sells stones, bones, and dinosaurs. The park is at the end of Premier Crescent off South Dinosaur Trail. It's open April-Sept. daily 10 a.m.-6 p.m. longer hours in summer. Admission is $5.

Little Fish Lake Provincial Park

Undulating hills of northern fescue grassland and the clear waters of Little Fish Lake provide the backdrop for this small park 40 km east of Drumheller via East Coulee. (For sights along the way, see "East Coulee Drive," below.) The park is also accessible off Hwy. 9, 40 km south from Craigmyle. Both access roads are gravel. The nearby **Hand Hills** were used by both Cree and Blackfoot as a viewpoint. Many indications of the area's prehistory have been found at the southeast end of the lake—mainly tepee rings

and campsites. The beach and cool water of the lake attract people from Drumheller, so it can get busy on weekends. The lake is also popular with vacationing waterfowl en route to their summer homes down south or returning in the fall. The primitive campground has pit toilets, a kitchen shelter, and firewood. Sites are $7.

Other Things to Do

The country's largest collection of reptiles is housed at **Reptile World** in Suncity Mall, 1222 Hwy. 9 S, tel. (403) 823-8623, where you can view and handle these much maligned creatures; admission $4. The **Horn and Antler Museum** and **Funland Amusement Park** are along Dinosaur Trail NW, tel. (403) 823-5201. It's easy to spend hours in the many shops selling fossils; the best in town is **The Fossil Shop** at 61 Bridge St., tel. (403) 823-6774. Pieces start at $10 for chunks of unidentifiable dinosaur bones and go to thousands of dollars for magnificent ammonites from the United States. The owner is a knowledgeable local man who has spent his life collecting fossils from around the world.

SCENIC DRIVES

The Dinosaur Trail

This 48-km circular route to the west of Drumheller starts and finishes in town and passes many worthwhile stops, including two spectacular viewpoints. After passing the access road to Royal Tyrrell Museum, the first point of interest is the **Little Church,** often described as being able to seat thousands—but only six at a time. The road then climbs steeply out of the valley onto the prairie benchland. Take the first access road on the left—it doubles back to **Horsethief Canyon Lookout** from where there are spectacular views of the badlands and the multicolored walls of the canyons. Slip, slide, or somersault down the embankment here into the mysterious lunarlike landscape and it's easy to imagine why early explorers were so intrigued by the valley and how easy it was for thieves to hide stolen horses along the coulees in the early 1900s.

The halfway point of the trail is the crossing of the Red Deer River on the **Bleriot Ferry,** one of the few remaining cable ferries in Alberta. It op-

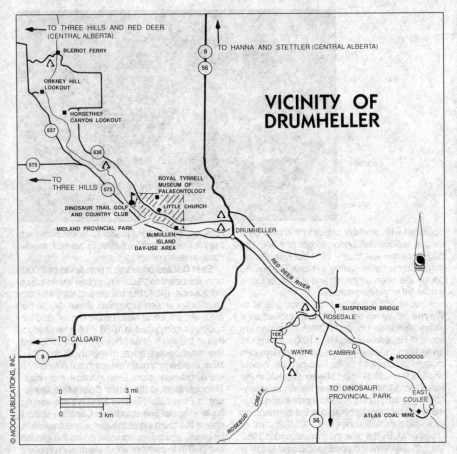

VICINITY OF DRUMHELLER

TO THREE HILLS AND RED DEER (CENTRAL ALBERTA)

BLERIOT FERRY

ORKNEY HILL LOOKOUT

HORSETHIEF CANYON LOOKOUT

837

838

575

TO THREE HILLS 575

DINOSAUR TRAIL GOLF AND COUNTRY CLUB

MIDLAND PROVINCIAL PARK

McMULLEN ISLAND DAY-USE AREA

ROYAL TYRRELL MUSEUM OF PALAEONTOLOGY

LITTLE CHURCH

DRUMHELLER

9

56

TO HANNA AND STETTLER (CENTRAL ALBERTA)

RED DEER RIVER

SUSPENSION BRIDGE

ROSEDALE

10X

WAYNE

CAMBRIA

HOODOOS

TO CALGARY

9

TO DINOSAUR PROVINCIAL PARK

EAST COULEE

ATLAS COAL MINE

56

ROSEBUD CREEK

© MOON PUBLICATIONS, INC.

0   3 mi

0   3 km

erates April-Nov. 7 a.m.-11 p.m. On the far side of the river is a primitive campground. Upstream from the campground a major dinosaur discovery was made in 1923 when the fossilized bones of a duck-billed edmontosaurus were unearthed. The road continues along the top of the valley to **Orkney Hill Lookout** for more panoramic views across the badlands and the lush valley floor below. A buffalo jump where Indians once stampeded great herds of bison off the edge of the cliff was nearby. But centuries of erosion have changed the clay and sandstone landscape so dramatically that the actual position of the jump is now impossible to define.

East Coulee Drive

This 25-km road, southeast from Drumheller, passes three historic coal-mining communities in an area dotted with mine shafts and abandoned buildings. The first town along this route is **Rosedale,** which at first looks prosperous. On closer inspection, however, you'll notice the distinct lack of businesses. In fact, the town's population dropped from 3,000 to less than 100 a few years ago. The community began on the opposite side of the Red Deer River around the Star Mine, but after the combined car and rail bridge was washed out, the town was moved to its present site. For many years the mine still

hoodoos

operated with workers crossing the river on a unique suspension bridge to get to work. The original bridge was built in 1931 but was later replaced by a cable-trolley system. Today the bridge has been upgraded and is safe for those who want to venture across.

A worthwhile detour from Rosedale is to **Wayne,** an almost-a-ghost town tucked up a valley alongside Rosebud Creek. It is nine km south of Rosedale along Hwy: 10X, which spurs away from the river just south of the town and crosses the creek 11 times. In its heyday, Wayne had 1,500 residents, most of whom worked in the Rosedeer Mine. It was never known as a law-abiding town. During Alberta's prohibition days many moonshiners operated in the surrounding hills, safe from the nearest RCMP patrol in Drumheller. By the time the mine closed in 1957 the population had dipped to 250 and today is probably a tenth of that. Many buildings remain, making it a popular setting for film crews. The only operating business in the sleepy hamlet is the **Rosedeer Hotel,** tel. (403) 823-9189, where the walls are lined with memorabilia from the town's glory days. The hotel's outside porch overlooking the creek is a great place to grab a beer and wallow in nostalgia.

From Rosedale Hwy. 10 continues southeast, crossing the Red Deer River at the abandoned mining town of Cambria and passing hoodoos to the left. These strangely shaped rock formations along the river valley have been carved by eons of wind and rain. The harder rock on top is more resistant to erosion than the rock beneath it, resulting in the odd, mushroom-shaped pillars.

East Coulee once had a population of 3,000; now it's down to 250. Mining has taken place here since 1924, but building a rail line from Drumheller proved expensive. Eventually part of the riverbank was blasted into the river, and the spur was completed in 1928. Full-time production at the main Atlas Mine ended in 1955, but the mine operated intermittently till the '70s. Most buildings remain standing but now only a hotel, grocery store, and garage are open. Through town is the **Atlas Coal Mine Museum,** a Provincial Historic Site. An ore-sorting tipple—the last one standing in Canada—towers above the mine buildings. It's a great place to just walk around, or you can go on the guided tour ($3) to learn more about the mining process. It's open in summer daily 9 a.m.-6 p.m.; tel. (403) 823-2220. In the center of East Coulee, in the East Coulee School Museum, is a cultural center featuring a restored schoolroom, a coal-mining room, art gallery, and tearoom. It's open daily 9 a.m.-5 p.m., closed weekends in winter; tel. (403) 822-3970.

RECREATION

Drumheller's popularity as a tourist destination is only recent and facilities for tourists reflect this. The local indoor pool is located on Riverside

Dr., tel. (403) 823-1321, and has a water slide; **Dinosaur Trail Golf and Country Club,** tel. (403) 823-5622, is past the Royal Tyrrell Museum and charges $28 for a round. In winter, ski the badlands at **Drumheller Valley Ski Club,** which boasts a vertical drop of 120 meters served by a chairlift. Lift tickets are $15 for a half day and $19 for a full day. Closed Monday and Tuesday. The hill is along South Dinosaur Trail, tel. (403) 823-2277.

Entertainment

The after-dark scene is not crash hot. Apart from the quiet lounge in the Drumheller Inn there is nowhere respectable to go. Many hostelers head downstairs to **The Zoo,** 30 Railway Ave. W, tel. (403) 823-2642, a lively rock 'n' roll bar where bands play most nights; cover charge Friday and Saturday. Go anywhere else and, if you're not careful, you'll finish up with more broken bones than an albertosaurus.

ACCOMMODATIONS

Motels

Outside of the cities and the Rocky Mountains, Drumheller is the province's next-largest tourist center, attracting over half a million visitors annually. Yet there are fewer than 350 motel beds in town (including the hostel). With increased demand over the last few years prices have risen, but the quality hasn't. Rooms (reserve in advance during summer) are full by early afternoon every day. Ask about off-season rates outside of summer. The two information centers have accommodation boards which post room availability. **Rockhound Motor Inn,** P.O. Box 2350, Drumheller T0J 0Y0, tel. (403) 823-5302, has large rooms for $60 s, $70 d. **Drumheller Inn,** P.O. Box 3100, tel. 403-823-8400, has an indoor pool, spa, and two restaurants; $80 s, $87 d. **Badlands Motel,** P.O. Box 2217, tel. (403) 823-5155, has a great pancake house next door; $48 s or d. The best asset of **The Lodge,** P.O. Box 1810, tel. (403) 823-3322, is that it's downtown; $60 s or d. **Dinosaur Motel,** 240 Riverside Dr., tel. (403) 823-3381, is beside the river; $40 s or d. **Hoo-doo Motel,** P.O. Box 310, tel. (403) 823-5662, is nothing special at $54 s, $58 d.

Each of the bed and breakfasts in town requires advance reservations. **Riverside Inn,** 501 Riverside Dr. W, tel. (403) 823-4746, is closest to downtown; also within walking distance is **Dinosaur Valley B&B,** 1103 Riverside Dr. E, tel. (403) 823-9250; farther out among the badlands, five minutes west of Drumheller on South Dinosaur Trail, is **Coles B&B,** tel. (403) 823-5844. Rates for the bed and breakfasts are $40-45 s, $45-55 d. The hotels along East Coulee Drive in **Rosedale, Wayne** (definitely worth checking out), and **East Coulee** are within 15 minutes of town and fill up last.

Hostel

After extensive renovations, a downtown hotel was reopened in 1991 as **Alexandra International Hostel.** The old hotel rooms have been given a coat of paint, and facilities include a modern kitchen area, TV room with pool table, coin laundry, and lockers. Most of the dorms are small—many have only two or four beds—and some have private baths. The downstairs hallway is lined with "things to do" brochures and schedules of current events. The hostel rents mountain bikes for $5 an hour or $18 a day—an excellent way to get out to the museum, but take plenty of water. Hostel rates are $12 for members, $15 for nonmembers. It's located at 30 Railway Ave. W, tel. (403) 823-6337—a 20-minute walk or $5 cab ride from the bus station.

Campgrounds

Three campgrounds are located on the north side of the river. **Shady Grove Campground,** 25 Poplar St., tel. (403) 823-2576, is in a well-treed spot beside the Red Deer River and offers welcome relief from the heat of the badlands. Serviced sites are semiprivate; tenters have more options and are able to disappear among the trees. The campground offers a nice beach (by Albertan standards), mini-golf, and an arcade, and town is just a short stroll away. Tent sites are $10, hookups $12-16. On the corner of Hwy. 9 and North Dinosaur Trail is **Dinosaur Trailer Park,** tel. (403) 823-3291. Also within walking distance of town, this private campground has full hookups, barbecues ($5 per night), and an owner who knows everything there is to know about bison—he owns the herd along Hwy. 576. Unserviced sites are $13, hookups $14-18. On the north side of the river, four km west of the Tyrrell Museum, is **Dinosaur Trail RV Resort,** tel. (403) 823-9333, which has a heated pool, groceries, laundry, and canoe rentals. Tent sites are $15, hookups $17.25-21.75. All three campgrounds are open April-October.

At the end of the Dinosaur Trail is **Bleriot Ferry Provincial Recreation Area** with 35 sites, plenty of firewood, a kitchen shelter, and a small beach on the river; $7 per night. **Rosedale,** east of town, has a small campground (free) with pit toilets and a kitchen. It's at the back of town along the road to Wayne. **Wayne,** with a population of around 25, has two campgrounds; one beside the saloon, the other over the green bridge. Each costs $5 and has limited facilities.

FOOD

Drumheller is probably the only place in the world where you can find a Chinese restaurant called **Fred & Barney's.** It's in the Suncity Mall at 1222 Hwy. 9 S beside Reptile World, tel. (403) 823-3803. A regular Chinese menu is offered between 11 a.m. and 10:30 p.m., but most people come for the excellent buffets served daily. Lunch (11:30 a.m.-2 p.m. year-round) is $6.95 and dinner (5-9 p.m., Fri.-Sun., summer only) is $8.95. **Sizzling House,** 160 Centre St., tel. (403) 823-8098, is a popular downtown eatery dishing up Sichuan and Beijing cuisine. Forget the lunch buffet and stick to the small (by Chinese standards) menu.

All dishes at the **Bridge Greek Restaurant–Steak & Pizza House,** 71 Bridge St. N, tel. (403) 823-2225, are made from scratch, and everything is excellent. Appetizers are $3-7; try the lemon soup or large Greek salad. Greek entrees start at $8.95. The house specialty is Kleftiko, juicy spring lamb baked with herbs and spices—have it with the Greek salad for the full effect, or try the generous portion of moussaka. The atmosphere is informal, an abundance of greenery hangs from the ceiling, and later in the evening the chef can often be seen chatting with satisfied patrons. It's open 10:30 a.m.-midnight.

SERVICES AND INFORMATION

Services
Greyhound has frequent service between Calgary and Drumheller ($19.63 one-way). The depot, 1222 Hwy. 9 S (at Suncity Mall), tel. (403) 823-7566 or (800) 661-8747, has a small cafe and lots of information on the area. For a cab call **Badlands Taxi,** tel. (403) 823-6552, or **Jack's Taxi,** tel. (403) 823-2220. **Tilden** is the only car rental agency in town, tel. (403) 823-3371 or (800) 387-4747.

The **post office** is at 96 Railway Ave. E. You can wash your dusty clothes at the **laundromat** in the Esso gas station on Hwy. 9 on the south side of town. It's open till 8 p.m. **Drumheller Regional Health Complex** is at 665 Riverside Dr. E, tel. (403) 823-6500. For the **RCMP** call (403) 823-2630.

Information
Drumheller has two information centers. One, operated in conjunction with the chamber of commerce, is beside the Red Deer River at the corner of Riverside Dr. and 2nd St. W. You can't miss it—look for a towering replica of a *Tyrannosaurus rex* in front. It's open daily 9 a.m.-9 p.m. during summer, Mon.-Fri. 9 a.m.-4:30 p.m. the rest of the year; tel. (403) 823-1331. The other center is in Suncity Mall on Hwy. 9 at the south end of town. This one is privately owned and run by friendly staff. The walls are lined with brochures of things to do and see, and it's open year-round Mon.-Sat. 6 a.m.-9 p.m., Sunday 9 a.m.-9 p.m.; tel. (403) 823-7566. **Drumheller Public Library** is at 224 Centre St., tel. (403) 823-5382.

HIGHWAY 9 EAST

Hanna
This is the heart of goose country. Giant replicas of the Canada grey goose grace the town entrances, and in fall the area is a mecca for hunters. **Hanna Museum,** at the east end of 4th Ave., tel. (403) 854-4244, is a re-creation of a 19th-century village with a church, railway station, jail cell, hospital, and schoolhouse. It's open daily 10 a.m.-6 p.m. during summer; admission $2.

PRONGHORN

BOB RACE

These agile and graceful animals (often mistakenly called antelope) which roam Alberta's shortgrass prairie have made a remarkable comeback after being hunted to near extinction in the first quarter of this century. They are easily recognized by their dark muzzles, tan bodies, and large white patches on the rump, cheeks, neck, and belly. Both sexes grow hollow, pronged horns that are shed annually.

Pronghorns have adapted well to life on the plains and are endowed with incredible attributes vital for their survival. Able to sustain speeds up to 80 kph over long distances, they are one of the fastest mammals in the New World. An oversized windpipe helps them to dissipate heat quickly as they breathe, allowing for large extended outbursts of energy. Telescopic eyesight enables them to detect movement over 1.5 km away. When a member of the herd senses danger, hairs on its white rump will stand erect, silently alerting comrades of the threat.

The pronghorn's diet consists primarily of sagebrush, but they'll eat weeds and sometimes grass as well. They obtain sufficient moisture from these plants to allow them to survive hot, dry summers without much to drink. And as a guard against the long and severe prairie winters, these amazing creatures have developed hollow body hairs to insulate against the cold.

Much of the bucking stock that throws the cowboys and woos the crowds at the Calgary Exhibition and Stampede is bred and raised at **Stampede Ranch,** 50 km south of Hanna. The ranch welcomes visitors (call ahead, tel. 403-566-2206), but don't let anyone talk you into going on a trail ride.

Campers have a few choices. Beside the museum are some electrical hookups ($8), north of town is **Fox Lake Campground** ($5-8), and 25 km south is **Prairie Oasis Park** ($5), which has a good beach and swimming. Rooms in the **Hanna Inn,** 113 Palliser Trail, tel. (403) 854-2400, are $47 s, $52 d; a restaurant, fitness center, and laundromat are on the premises. The inn's restaurant is a popular place to eat, serving steaks, seafood, and pasta until midnight. The **information center** is in a train caboose on the highway beside Petro-Canada.

Oyen

From Hanna, Hwy. 9 continues east through many small communities to Oyen and into Saskatchewan. Pronghorn have been the most distinctive animal on this part of the prairies for thousands of years and have adapted remarkably well to the environment. Due to overhunting and particularly harsh winters in the early 1900s, their numbers were devastated until three national parks were created to protect them. When their numbers rebounded the parks were abolished and today many thousand live on the prairies. At the north end of Main St. is a replica of a pronghorn. **Oyen Crossroads Museum,** 312 1st Ave. E, tel. (403) 664-2330, has many artifacts relating to the history of the area. It's open daily 9 a.m.-5 p.m. during summer. The campground in town is opposite the golf course; most sites are free, with power $5. At the junction of Hwys. 9 and 41 is a **Travel Alberta Information Centre,** handy for those entering the province here (this highway is the most direct route between Calgary and Saskatoon). It's open mid-May to mid-June 10 a.m.-6 p.m., mid-June through August 9 a.m.-6 p.m.; tel. (403) 664-2486.

Rowley's main street has been featured in a number of movies and commercials.

HIGHWAY 56 NORTH

As Hwy. 56 passes out of the Red Deer River Valley on the north side of Drumheller it climbs onto the prairie benchland and heads due north for 100 km to Stettler. Along the route the towns of Rowley and Big Valley are worth investigating, and **Morrin,** just off the highway, 22 km north of Drumheller, has an interesting sod house, similar to those that many of Alberta's earliest pioneers lived in.

Rowley

The first time we visited Rowley was late one evening. The streets were empty (as they are most of the time) and yet within a few minutes we were in the community hall having coffee and apple pie with members of the town's rapidly shrinking population. It's just that sort of town. Like other prairie towns, many of its residents have moved to larger centers and their houses stand empty, but residents of Rowley have made good from bad. They actively promote the town and its empty buildings as a site for TV commercials and movies. Most of the shopfronts along the main street are locked, but someone is always around to unlock them. In the back of the old cafe you can watch videos of clips filmed in town. A small museum is located near the rail line.

Big Valley

Located a few kilometers west of Hwy. 56, Big Valley is a quiet town of 300 with a restored Canadian Northern Railway Station that houses a museum. Farther west the Red Deer River has carved a canyon 120 meters into the surrounding prairie.

CALGARY TO DINOSAUR PROVINCIAL PARK

STRATHMORE

From Calgary, the TransCanada Hwy. parallels the Bow River (although it's never in sight) 100 km to Bassano. The only town along the way is Strathmore, home to the large stockyards which are a major center for livestock auctions in southern Alberta. To catch the action head down on Thursdays in summer (weekdays in fall). The yards are located on the west side of town, tel. (403) 240-7694. Good food is served at the **Little Village Cafe,** 755 Lakeside Blvd., tel. (403) 934-2828, next to the Shell station on the TransCanada Highway. The cafe looks like a truck stop but the omelettes and fruit pies are excellent.

Wyndham-Carseland Provincial Park

Visit this 178-hectare park for the fishing. Rainbow and brown trout, up to 60 centimeters, are caught in the Bow River where it flows through the park; the best fishing is in the deeper main channel. Also within the park is a large population of white pelicans, as well as prairie falcons, Canada geese, and great blue herons. The large campground is spread out along the river, and all sites are $11. The park is about 30 km south of Strathmore via Hwy. 24 or 817.

BASSANO

Bassano is located on the TransCanada Hwy. midway between Calgary and Medicine Hat. It's a thriving agricultural town of 1,200 people. Most visitors who stop in town are on their way to somewhere else.

Bassano Dam

Bassano Dam is six km southwest of town at Horseshoe Bend on the Bow River. It was built by the Canadian Pacific Railway between 1910 and 1914 to divert water from the Bow River into irrigation canals. Today those canals provide water for over 100,000 hectares of land pro-

ducing crops such as wheat, hay, potatoes, and beets. At the time of construction, the dam was known as the most important structure of its type in the world because of its great length and unique foundations. It consists of a 2.3-km earthen embankment with 24 steel sluices controlling the river's flow. At the dam is a picnic area.

BROOKS

Brooks (pop. 9,400) is in the heart of Alberta's extensive irrigated farmlands, 160 km east of Calgary along the TransCanada Highway. The town began as a railway stop in the 1880s. Canadian Pacific Railway officials soon realized the potential for homesteading in the area and developed a major irrigation system. Today, the **Eastern Irrigation District** includes two dams, over 2,000 kilometers of canals, and 2,500 control structures. Brooks offers all tourist services and is a good base for exploring Dinosaur Provincial Park (see below).

Sights

The **Brooks Aqueduct,** three km southeast of town, was a vital link in the development of agriculture in southeastern Alberta and was used until the 1970s. It carried water across a shallow valley to a dry prairie on the other side, opening up a massive chunk of otherwise unproductive land to farming. At the time of its completion in 1914, the 3.2-km aqueduct was the longest concrete structure of its type in the world and had

BOB RACE

been designed and built using unique engineering principles. Although now replaced by an earth-filled canal, the impressive structure has been preserved as a National Historic Site and now serves as a monument to those who developed the region. A small interpretive center is open in summer daily 10 a.m.-6 p.m.; tel. (403) 362-4451.

Brooks and District Museum on Sutherland Dr., tel. (403) 362-5073, catalogs the area's past from the era of dinosaurs to the heady days of a short-lived oil boom. Many restored buildings dot the grounds and the entrance is guarded by a four-ton replica of a bison. It's open in summer daily 10 a.m.-5 p.m.; admission $1.

Budding gardeners won't want to miss the **Alberta Special Crops and Horticultural Research Centre** east of town, tel. (403) 362-3391, where research is done on greenhouse crops, various fruits, ornamental flowers, vegetables, and weed control. The grounds are an oasis of flower beds and experimental plots, many of which are open to the public. Free guided tours are offered on weekdays throughout summer at 10:15 a.m. and 2 p.m. At **Brooks Pheasant Hatchery**, beside Tillebrook Provincial Park east of town, tel. (403) 362-4122, ring-necked pheasants are hatched from breeding stock, raised, and released into the wild. A small visitor center is open in summer daily 9 a.m.-4 p.m., weekdays only the rest of the year.

Kinbrook Island Provincial Park

Part of this 38-hectare park, 13 km south of Brooks, is an island in **Lake Newell,** the largest man-made body of water in Canada. Naturally, most activities revolve around the water—swimming, fishing, and boating are all popular. The large expanses of freshwater attract many species of gulls, pelicans, and cormorants, which nest on the islands. The campground has firewood and picnic shelters, and a concession operates during summer. Sites are $11; reservations are taken, tel. (403) 362-2962. Open year-round.

Accommodations

Vacant motel rooms can be difficult to find in Brooks. During the week they are filled by work crews, and on weekends there always seems to be a wedding in town. Most motels are along 2nd St. W and the best of the bunch is **Tel Star Motor Inn,** 813 2nd St. W, tel. (403) 362-3466 or (800) 260-6211. Each room has a microwave and fridge; $46 s, $52 d. Other options in town are **Plains Motel,** 1004 2nd St. W, tel. (403) 362-3367, $46 s, $50 d; and **Heritage Inn,** 1303 2nd St. W, tel. (403) 362-6666, with an indoor pool, coffee shop, and restaurant, $65 s, $72 d. **Douglas Country Inn,** P.O. Box 463, Brooks T0J 0J0, tel. 403-362-2873, is seven km north of Brooks on Hwy. 873. The large rooms are beautifully furnished, one with a fireplace and hot tub. Other amenities include a TV room, solarium, and lounge with fireplace. Rates are $60-77 s, $99 d including a hearty country breakfast.

Halfway between Brooks and Tilley is **Tillebrook Provincial Park,** one of a number of campgrounds built along the TransCanada Hwy. during that road's construction. Tillebrook is an excellent base for exploring Dinosaur Provincial Park and Lake Newell, and is one of the province's best developed parks. It has powered sites, enclosed kitchen shelters with gas stoves, showers, a laundromat, summer interpretive programs, and a trail to the aqueduct. Unserviced sites are $13, powered sites $15. It's open year-round.

Information

An **information center** is open in summer, daily 8 a.m.-8 p.m. It's beside Petro-Canada on the highway.

East to Medicine Hat

Continuing southeast from Brooks on the Trans-Canada Hwy., it's 100-some km across the prairies to Medicine Hat. For more information on Medicine Hat, see the Southern Alberta chapter.

DINOSAUR PROVINCIAL PARK

Badlands stretch along many river valleys throughout the North American plains, and some of the most spectacular are in 7,332-hectare Dinosaur Provincial Park, 200 km east of Calgary. But the park is best known for being one of the most important dinosaur fossil beds in the world. Thirty-five species of dinosaurs—from every known family of the Cretaceous period—have been unearthed here, along with the skeletal remains of crocodiles, turtles, fish, lizards, frogs, and flying reptiles. Not only is the diversity of specimens great, but so is the sheer volume; more than 300 museum-quality specimens have been removed and are exhibited in museums around the world.

The park's environment is extremely complex and is unique within the surrounding prairie ecosystem. Stands of cottonwoods, a variety of animal life, and most importantly the extensive bone beds, were instrumental in UNESCO's designation of the park as a World Heritage Site in 1979. In 1985 the opening of the **Royal Tyrrell Museum of Palaeontology,** 100 km upstream in Drumheller, meant that bones that had in the past been shipped to museums throughout the world for scientific analysis and display remained within the province. The Royal Tyrrell Museum operates a field station in the park where many of the bones are cataloged and stored. The displays, films, and interpretive programs offered at the center will best prepare you to begin your visit to the park.

Prehistory

Seventy-five million years ago during Cretaceous times, the area was a low-lying marsh at

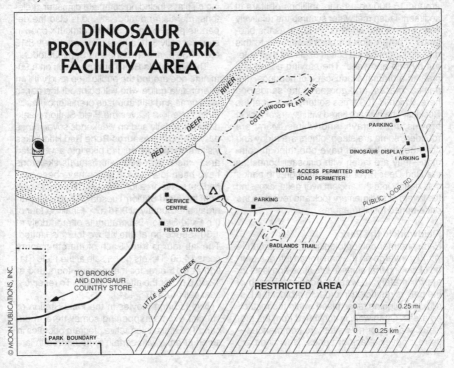

DINOSAUR PROVINCIAL PARK FACILITY AREA

RED DEER RIVER

COTTONWOOD FLATS TRAIL

PARKING

DINOSAUR DISPLAY PARKING

NOTE: ACCESS PERMITTED INSIDE ROAD PERIMETER

PARKING

PUBLIC LOOP RD.

SERVICE CENTRE

FIELD STATION

LITTLE SANDHILL CREEK

BADLANDS TRAIL

TO BROOKS AND DINOSAUR COUNTRY STORE

RESTRICTED AREA

0   0.25 mi
0   0.25 km

PARK BOUNDARY

© MOON PUBLICATIONS, INC.

the mouth of a river flowing into the Bearpaw Sea. The Bearpaw was the last in a succession of vast seas that covered the interior plains for 30 million years. Swamp grasses and reeds grew in the wetlands, while on higher ground, giant redwoods and palms towered over a dense forest. Dinosaurs flourished in this subtropical environment.

Over millions of years, great quantities of silt and mud were flushed downriver, building up a delta at the edge of the sea. In time this delta hardened and the countless layers formed sedimentary rock. Soon after, great pressures beneath the earth's surface pushed the crust upward, forming a jagged mountain range that we know today as the Rocky Mountains. This dramatically changed the climate of the plains region from tropical to temperate, probably killing off the dinosaurs around 64 million years ago. From then until a million years ago the climate changed many times until the first of many sheets of ice covered the plains. As the final sheet receded, around 15,000 years ago, millions of liters of sediment-laden meltwater scoured the relatively soft bedrock into an area we know as the badlands. The erosion process continues to this day, no longer by the action of glacial meltwater but by rain and wind. The carving action has created a dramatic landscape of hoodoos, pinnacles, mesas, and gorges in the sandstone here, which is 100 times softer than that of the Rockies. The hills are tiered with layers of rock in browns, reds, grays, and whites. Many are rounded, some are steep, others are ruddy and cracked, but they all have one thing in common—they are laden with dinosaur bones: as the Red Deer River curves through the park it cuts deeply into the ancient river delta, exposing the layers of sedimentary rock and revealing the once-buried fossil treasures.

Fieldwork in the Park

Each summer paleontologists from around the world converge on the park for an intense period of digging that starts in late June and lasts for approximately 10 weeks. Access to much of the park is restricted in order to protect the fossil beds. Digging takes place within the restricted areas. Often work is continued from the previous season, or new sites are commenced—there's never a lack of bones. New finds are often discovered with little digging, having been exposed by wind and rain since the previous season.

Excavating the bones is an extremely tedious procedure; therefore, only a limited number of sites are worked on at a time, with preference given to particularly important finds such as a new species. Getting the bones out of the ground is only the beginning of a long process that culminates with their scientific analysis and display by museums around the world.

EXPLORING THE PARK

Interpretive Programs and Tours

Even though much of the actual digging of bones is done away from public view, the **Field Station of the Royal Tyrrell Museum**, tel. (403) 378-4342, organizes enough interesting activities and tours to keep you busy for at least a full day. The Field Station offers many interesting displays including complete dinosaur skeletons, murals, and models, and is also the departure point for tours into the park. It's open in summer daily 8:15 a.m.-9 p.m., weekdays 8:15 a.m.-4:30 p.m. May-June and Sept.-October.

The **Badlands Bus Tour** takes you on a 90-minute ride around the public loop road with an interpretive guide who will point out the park's landforms and talk about its prehistoric inhabitants. This tour leaves the Field Station weekdays twice daily and on weekends seven times daily. The **Centrosaurus Bone Bed Hike** takes visitors on a short, guided hike into a restricted area where over 300 centrosaurus skeletons have been identified. Studies have been carried out in this area for 12 years. This tour leaves from the Field Station Tuesday, Thursday, Saturday and Sunday at 9:15 a.m. Finally, a tour of the Field Station Laboratory is offered daily at 1:30. Space on all the above tours is limited. The lab tour is free. Each of the other tours costs $4.50. Tickets go on sale at the Field Station at 8:15 a.m. for the morning tours and at 12:30 p.m. for the afternoon tours. To reserve a seat call (403) 378-4344.

Nights bring movies in the Field Station or special events happening somewhere in the park. The entire interpretive program operates in summer only, with certain tours offered in late

May and September. The Field Station is open in summer daily 9 a.m.-9 p.m., and weekdays only 9 a.m.-4 p.m. the rest of the year.

On Your Own

Much of the park is off-limits to unguided visitors, but you may explore two short interpretive trails and the area bounded by the public loop road on your own. The **Badlands Trail** is a 1.5-km loop that starts just east of the campground and passes into the restricted area. It's easy to ignore the nearby floodplains, but the large stands of cottonwoods you'll see were a contributing factor in the park being designated as a World Heritage Site. The **Cottonwood Flats Trail** starts from behind the campground, leading through the trees and into old river channels that lend themselves to good birdwatching. The cabin of black cowboy John Ware has been moved to the park and is open to the public. Many regard Ware—originally a southern slave who came north on a cattle drive—as the greatest horseman ever to ride in the Canadian West. The **loop road** passes through part of the area where bones were removed during the Great Canadian Dinosaur Rush. By staying within its limits hikers are prevented from becoming lost, although the classic badlands terrain is still littered with fragments of bones, and the area is large enough to make you feel "lost in time." It's a fantastic place to explore. Of special interest are two dinosaur dig sites excavated earlier this century, one of which contains a still-intact skeleton of a duck-billed hadrosaur.

The restricted area protects the bone beds and the valley's fragile environment. It also serves to keep visitors from becoming disoriented in the uniform landscape and ending up spending the night among the bobcats and rattlesnakes. The area is well posted and should not be entered except on a guided tour. One other important rule: *Surface collecting and digging for bones anywhere within the park is prohibited.*

PRACTICALITIES

Accommodations and Camping

The park's campground is in a low-lying area beside Little Sandhill Creek. It has pit toilets, a kitchen shelter, and a limited number of powered sites. Unserviced sites cost $13, powered sites $15. The campground fills up by early afternoon. To book a site call (403) 378-3700. Along the access road is **Dinosaur Country Store,** which has a grassy spot for camping; tents $7, powered $10. The next closest alternative is in Brooks. **Patricia Hotel** in Patricia, 15 km from the park, tel. (403) 378-4647, is known for its Western atmosphere. Many of the cattle brands on the walls date back over 50 years. The hotel has basic rooms with private baths; $35 s, $40 d. The bar downstairs gets fairly lively and there's a barbecue every Saturday night.

Services and Information

The only commercial facility within the park is the **Dinosaur Service Centre,** a fast-food place

badlands at Dinosaur Provincial Park

open limited hours each day. Within the center are laundry facilities and coin showers. No groceries are available in the park.

For information write to Dinosaur Provincial Park, P.O. Box 60, Patricia, AB T0J 2K0; or call the park at (403) 378-4342.

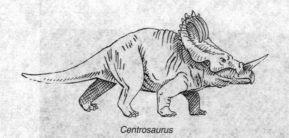

Centrosaurus

BOB RACE

BOB RACE

WEST OF CALGARY

While most people driving west from Calgary head straight for the famous Banff and Jasper National Parks, there are many worthwhile detours to consider.

Although nonrenewable resources such as oil and gas are the basis of Alberta's economy today, ranching was the province's first major industry. The first ranch established in Alberta was at Cochrane, just west of Calgary, but the entire southern foothills have been used for running cattle for over a century. Throughout the hills many well-established towns with interesting histories, quaint teahouses, holiday ranches, and sprawling properties have the inspiring Rocky Mountains as a backdrop.

Kananaskis Country is a vast tract of land set aside by the Alberta government as a multi-use recreation area. It's within easy day trip distance west of Calgary. Although the region's emphasis is on the outdoors and camping, luxurious accommodations are available in Kananaskis Village. The village and the modern ski resort of Nakiska at Mt. Allan nearby were built for the 1988 Winter Olympic Games. On the northern edge of Kananaskis Country, and at the entrance to Banff National Park, is the ever-growing mountain community of Canmore. The town provides an inexpensive alternative to staying deeper in the mountains and is an active outdoor center in itself; many mountaineers, climbers, hikers, and skiers take advantage of the mountains surrounding it.

RANCHLANDS

Between the snowcapped peaks of Kananaskis Country and the arid grassland of southern Alberta lies some of North America's best ranching country. From Cochrane in the north, through the ranching and farming communities of Okotoks and High River, to the Porcupine Hills northwest of Fort Macleod, these low, rolling hills have been home to many of western Canada's cowboy heroes and the setting for movies such as the Oscar-winning *Unforgiven* starring Clint

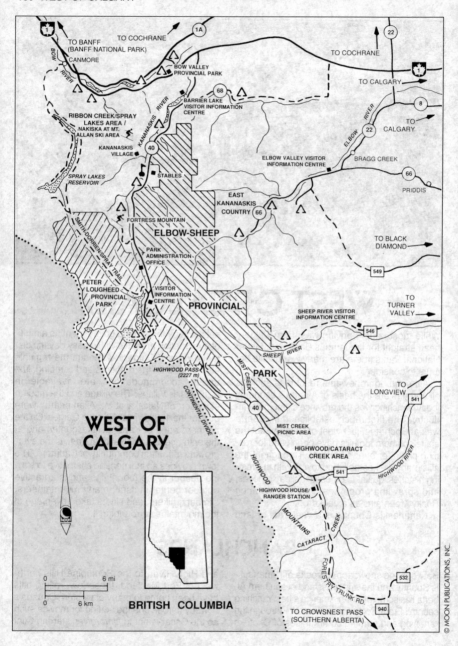

WEST OF
CALGARY

BRITISH COLUMBIA

0   6 mi

0   6 km

© MOON PUBLICATIONS, INC.

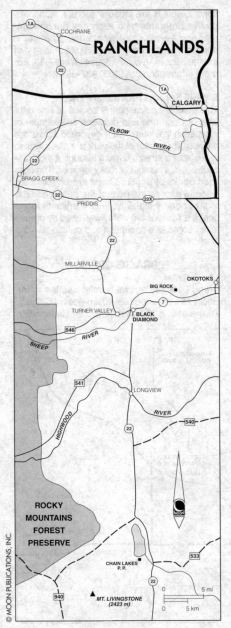

RANCHLANDS

Eastwood. Highway 2 follows the eastern flanks of these foothills south from Calgary. Other roads crisscross the region and lead to communities rich in heritage, many of which have recently been discovered by artisans and craftspeople who now call them home.

If you have ever dreamed of being a cowboy for a day or a week this is the place to do it. And the area offers enough museums, teahouses, antique emporiums, and events to keep even the most saddle-sore city slicker busy all summer.

History

The ranching tradition that Alberta so proudly claims started in the late 1800s. The massive herds of bison that once roamed the foothills had been devastated, the indigenous peoples had been moved to reservations, and the Canadian Pacific Railway had completed the link to the eastern provinces. A huge tract of land in the shadow of the Rocky Mountains now stood empty, and the Canadian government decided to lease it at a cent an acre. It didn't take long for word to get out. Cowboys from Montana, Wyoming, and Texas came hootin' and hollerin' as they drove thousands of head of cattle north. They brought with them a new spirit, craving the open spaces and the hardships associated with living on the land.

Many of those who invested in the land were wealthy Americans and eastern Canadians who rarely, if ever, visited their holdings. Even English royalty became involved. Edward Prince of Wales, who abdicated the throne to marry Wallis Simpson, purchased a 10,000-hectare spread in 1919. One of the first major landholdings was at Cochrane Ranche, west of Calgary, where today a Provincial Historic Site commemorates the history of ranching in Alberta.

In 1904 a farmer found a gas seepage on his land west of Okotoks; it turned out to be petroleum gas. This first discovery of oil on the prairies led to a boom that propelled Alberta into the forefront of world oil-and-gas production—a position it still holds today.

COCHRANE

The foundation of Alberta's cattle industry was laid down here last century, when Sen. Matthew

Cochrane established the first of the big lease-hold ranches in the province. Today's town of Cochrane is situated 22 km northwest of Calgary along Hwy. 1A in the Bow River Valley and has a population of 5,000. Although ranching is still important to the local economy, Cochrane is growing as a "bedroom" suburb of Calgary. The business district is in the older section of town between Hwy. 1A and the rail line. The only accommodations in town are at **Bow River Inn**, tel. (403) 932-7900, with rooms for $65 s or d, and **Rivers Edge Campground** off Hwy. 22, tel. (403) 932-4675. The campground has showers and charges $9 for unserviced sites, $14 for powered sites.

Western Heritage Centre
Although Matthew Cochrane's 76,500-hectare ranch had almost everything going for it, a number of harsh winters forced its closure in 1883. A 61-hectare site one km west of Cochrane was once the headquarters of this historic ranch and today is the site of a heritage center. The facility has state-of-the-art exhibits cataloging western Canada's cattle industry from its earliest frontier days to the world of computerized auc-

tions. Displays are indoors and out, with interpretive programs held each day during summer and events most weekends. The site is open in summer daily 9 a.m.-8 p.m., the rest of the year 9 a.m.-5 p.m. Admission is $7.50. For more information call (403) 932-3514.

Big Hill Springs Provincial Park
This small 26-hectare park is located 16 km northeast of Cochrane and provides an example of vegetation that was once widespread across the prairies. The center of the park is a steep-walled valley with a stream flowing through it that cascades over a number of rocky terraces. The tree-lined banks of Big Hill Creek are an excellent place to escape the heat of the prairie and the roar of nearby highways. From artifacts found here it is obvious the valley was used by prehistoric people as a habitation and buffalo-kill site.

BRAGG CREEK

Bragg Creek is a rural hamlet nestled in the Rocky Mountain foothills 40 km west of Calgary. To the east is the Sarcee Indian Reservation

and to the west is Kananaskis Country. The **Stony Trail,** an Indian trading route that passed through the area, had been in use for generations when the first white people arrived in the early 1880s. Much of the surrounding forest had been cleared by fire, encouraging farmers to settle in the isolated region and eke a living from the land. Improved road access in the 1920s encouraged families from Calgary to build weekenders in town. Today many of Bragg Creek's 500 residents commute daily to nearby Calgary. The ideal location and quiet lifestyle have attracted artists and artisans—the town claims to have more painters, potters, sculptors, and weavers than any similarly sized town in Alberta.

Sights

White Avenue, also known as **Heritage Mile** and originally the main commercial strip, is lined with craft shops, antique emporiums, and restaurants. The road continues southwest to 122-hectare **Bragg Creek Provincial Park,** a day-use area alongside the Elbow River, before continuing along the Elbow Valley into East Kananaskis Country (see "Kananaskis Country," below). North of Bragg Creek is the site of southern Alberta's first church. The earliest structure, built in 1873, was a crude cabin where an Irish minister devoted his time to ministering to the native Blackfoot people. A plaque, 12 km north of town along Hwy. 22, marks this historic spot. **Wintergreen Ski and Golf Resort** is a year-round sporting facility six km northwest of town. In summer golfers flock to the fairways of its 18-hole championship golf course ($38). In winter a small ski area with five lifts and a vertical rise of 190 meters operates. Night skiing is offered on Friday and Saturday. Lift tickets are $24. For more information call (403) 949-3333.

Accommodations and Food

Although lacking motels and campgrounds (closest camping is in East Kananaskis Country), Bragg Creek has bed and breakfasts and a restaurant that attracts folk from Calgary. **Four Point Crossing,** tel. (403) 947-2247, is a large country-style house nestled among stands of trees, yet is within walking distance of restaurants and shops. The home has a guest lounge with fireplace, and a hearty breakfast is included in the rates of $58 s, $68 d. Another, within walking distance of town, is **Bricket Wood B&B,** 36 White Ave., tel. (403) 949-2482, where rates are $48 s, $60 d.

The **Steak Pit,** 43 White Ave., tel. (403) 949-3633, is a fantastic restaurant. The decor is early Canadian, yet realistic and elegant. The dining room decorated with hand-hewn cedar furniture is only a small part of the restaurant, which also has a cafe, lounge, sports bar, and gift shop. Eating here isn't cheap but *is* comparable to Calgary restaurants. The menu features mostly Alberta beef but has enough choices to please everyone. Open daily from 11:30 a.m. Bragg Creek Shopping Centre has a wide variety of eateries as well as most services. **Pies Plus Cafe,** tel. (403) 949-3950, specializes in meat and fruit pies at reasonable prices. Also in the center are two saloons: **Powderhorn Saloon,** tel. (403) 949-3946, serves good food and has a few pool tables, including a Fusion pool table shaped like a double diamond and with 10 pockets. Ask the manager how to play and he'll probably buy you a game.

BRAGG CREEK TO OKOTOKS

Turner Valley

The name Turner Valley is synonymous with the oil-and-gas industry in Alberta. It was here in 1914 that Canada's first major crude-oil discovery was made. But it was gas, not oil, that first sparked interest in the valley. In 1903 a farmer named Bill Herron found gas seeping from fissures in his land. He had it tested and to his surprise was told it was petroleum gas. He was having trouble convincing anyone to back an oil-related enterprise and, so the story goes, he finally persuaded two oilmen to become involved by taking them to the site of the gas, lighting it and cooking them a fried breakfast on the flame. Shortly after, the Calgary Petroleum Products Company was formed and started sinking wells, which was the beginning of an economic boom. During the oil boom, gas was burned off in an area known as "Hell's Half Acre" northeast of Turner Valley. It is estimated that 28 billion cubic meters of excess gas was flared off in the first 10 years. Gas flares still burn 24 hours a day at an area known as the "Burning Ground." The best viewing point is from **Hell's**

Half Acre Bridge, which crosses the Sheep River southwest of downtown.

Turner Valley is now a quiet town of 1,400 straddling Sheep River. The **Discovery Centre** on the southeastern outskirts of town showcases the oil-and-gas industry in Alberta. Open in summer only 10 a.m.-6 p.m. The town has an 18-hole golf course and a swimming pool and is the gateway to the **Sheep River Valley** in Kananaskis Country.

Turner Valley Hotel, 112 Flare Ave., tel. (403) 933-7878, is the town's only motel; rooms are $40 s, $45 d. **Hell's Half Acre Campground,** downtown behind the information center, has limited services; unserviced sites $6, powered sites $8. Tenters would be better off heading west into Kananaskis Country to one of two Forest Service campgrounds. Eating out is limited. The Turner Valley Hotel has a popular buffet every Wednesday night ($10.95) and a Sunday brunch ($9.95). **Valley Rose Tea Room,** 146 Main St., tel. (403) 933-2972, serves breakfast from $4 and lunch $5-9, although most visitors stop only for tea and scones and to browse through the antiques. It's open year-round, daily 7 a.m.-5 p.m. A replica of an oil derrick on Main St. makes the **information center** highly visible.

Black Diamond

This town on the banks of the Sheep River, four km east of Turner Valley, was named for the coal once mined nearby. James A. McMillan, a government land surveyor, was digging an irrigation ditch when he uncovered a rich seam of coal. Within a few years a mine had become operational and the coal, of excellent quality, was used in households throughout the region. The coal mines have long since closed. Most residents work in the nearby oil fields or commute the 65 km to Calgary.

One of the year's highlights is the **Diamond Valley Parade** held on the first weekend of June. A colorful parade, pancake breakfast, mutton busting (a rodeo for children on wildly bucking sheep), and a fireworks display are among the event's activities. The town has limited visitor services. **Triple "A" Motel** on Hwy. 22, tel. (403) 933-4915, has basic rooms for $35 s, $42 d. A campground in **Centennial Park** by the Sheep River has showers, a kitchen shelter, and firewood; unserviced sites $10, pow-

ered sites $12. For further information, ask at the **town office,** tel. (403) 933-4348; open weekdays 8 a.m.-4:30 p.m.

OKOTOKS AND VICINITY

The rural retreat of Okotoks is in the Sheep River Valley 34 km south of Calgary and just minutes from Hwy. 2 to the east. It is the largest population base between Calgary and Lethbridge and many of its 7,500 residents commute into Calgary to work. The name Okotoks came from the Blackfoot word *okatak,* which means rock, probably in reference to the glacial erratics west of town. The town began as a rest stop along the Macleod Trail, which linked Fort Calgary to Fort Macleod last century. Many old buildings still stand and have been incorporated in a walking tour, with maps available at the Tourist Information Centre. **Okotoks Bird Sanctuary,** east of town, attracts ducks, geese, and other waterfowl that can be watched from a raised observation deck.

The Big Rock

But the town's most popular attraction isn't a museum or a park—it's a rock, the Big Rock, the largest glacial erratic in the world. During the last ice age a sheet of ice up to a kilometer thick crept forward from the north. A landslide in what is now Jasper National Park deposited large boulders on top. The ice continued moving south, carrying the boulders with it. Many thousands of years later, as temperatures warmed and the ice melted, the boulders were deposited far from their source (hence the name "erratic"). Big Rock, seven km west of Okotoks, weighs 18,000 tons.

Practicalities

The only motel in town is **Sheep River Motor Inn,** on the main drag, tel. (403) 938-1999; $52 s, $58 d. A good campground on the south side of Sheep River is linked to town by a nearby bridge; unserviced sites $10, powered sites $12.

Ginger Tea Room and Gift Shop, 43 Riverside Dr., tel. (403) 938-2907, is a large Victorian-style mansion that has become a local landmark. Inside it's crammed with two floors of crafts and antiques. At the back is a tearoom that is always busy. Okotoks's original creamery is now a restaurant, bistro, and pub all under one roof. Food in the bistro is served family style, and although the dining room is more expensive it's still casual. The Sunday brunch is especially good. Open daily 11 a.m.-11 p.m. Called **Foothills Cattle Co.**, it's at 35 Riverside Dr., tel. (403) 938-2855.

An **information center** in a restored train station at 53 N. Railway St., tel. (403) 938-3204, also has an interpretive display and art market. It's open in summer daily 9 a.m.-5 p.m.

HIGHWAY 22 SOUTH

Bar U Ranch National Historic Site
Established in 1882, the Bar U Ranch, 13 km south of Longview, was one of western Canada's top ranches late last century. A 145-hectare parcel of the original spread has been preserved and now features an interpretive center, general store, and restaurant. The site is open in summer Mon.-Fri. 8 a.m.-6 p.m., till 8 p.m. on weekends. For more information call (403) 395-2212.

Chain Lakes Provincial Park
Heading south, the next worthwhile stop is Chain Lakes Provincial Park, sitting in the Willow Creek Valley between the Rocky Mountains and Porcupine Hills. It was named because of a series of spring-fed lakes that have since been dammed and stocked with rainbow trout. The park is in a transition zone; therefore, plant and animal species are varied. In the north end of the park are some high bluffs, offering good views of the surrounding land. The campground and day-use area are at the southern end of the reservoir, close to a boat launch and beach. Camping is $11 on weekends and $9 weekdays.

East to Nanton
Views of the Rocky Mountains in the rear-view mirror are spectacular as you head east on Hwy. 533 from Chain Lakes Provincial Park through the northern reaches of the Porcupine Hills. At a high point in the hills is **Magnetic Hill,** where an optical illusion creates a bizarre misimpression: put your car in neutral and it will slowly roll *up* the hill! As you descend into a valley east from the hill you'll pass the old holdings of the A 7 Ranch, once one of Alberta's largest ranches. Its original owner, A.E. Cross, helped finance the first Calgary Stampede in 1912. The ranch has now been subdivided but remains in the same family. From this point it's 35 km to Nanton and Hwy. 2 where you can head north to Calgary or south to Fort Macleod.

HIGH RIVER

In the heart of the province's ranching country, 50 km south of Calgary, High River has grown steadily from its beginnings as a rest stop on the Macleod Trail. Originally it was known as "The Crossing" as it was the only possible place to ford the Highwood River. A period of severe drought at the turn of the century was followed by many years of ample rainfall, and slowly the community grew to its current population of 6,400.

The **Museum of the Highwood** is housed in a restored C.P.R. Station on 1st St. W, tel. (403) 652-7156. Its displays portray early western life. Of particular interest is the exhibit cataloging chuck-wagon racing, a sport that has special significance to locals as the area boasts many champions. It's open in summer 1-8 p.m. If you're in town on the last weekend of June don't miss the **North American Chuckwagon Championships** at the fairgrounds. Downtown are a number of interesting shops including **Eamor's Saddlery Ltd.** and **Olson Silver and Leather Company.** Both are on Centre Street.

Of the motels in town, **Foothills Motel,** 67 8th Ave., tel. (403) 652-1395, is the best value, with rooms starting at $40. Camping is in **George Lane Memorial Park** off Macleod Trail at 5th Ave. W; $10. Beside the museum is a rail car restored as a cafe.

KANANASKIS COUNTRY

During Alberta's oil-and-gas boom of the 1970s, oil revenues collected by the provincial government were channeled into various projects aimed at improving the lifestyle of Albertans. One lasting legacy of the boom is Kananaskis Country, a sprawling 4,250-square-km area west of Calgary that has been developed with an emphasis on providing recreation opportunities for as many people as possible.

Within the area are two distinct ecosystems: the high peaks of the Continental Divide to the west, and the lower, rolling foothills to the east. The glacier-carved **Kananaskis Valley** separates the two. The area contains four provincial parks, hundreds of kilometers of hiking trails, a complex network of bike paths, areas for horseback riding and some for ATVs, a world-class 36-hole golf course, and 40 lakes stocked with fish. The downhill-skiing events of the 1988 Winter Olympic Games were held at the specially developed Nakiska ski area, now open to the public. Fortress Mountain, located deeper in the mountains, provides more downhill skiing. And nordic skiers can glide over hundreds of cross-country skiing trails in the region. As well as the areas set aside for recreation, large tracts of land, such as the Elbow-Sheep Wildland Park, give full protection to wildlife.

Although Kananaskis Country lacks the famous lakes and glaciated peaks of Banff and Jasper National Parks, in many ways it rivals them. Wildlife is abundant and opportunities for observation of larger mammals are superb. The region has large populations of moose, mule and white-tailed deer, elk, black bear, bighorn sheep, and mountain goat. Wolves, grizzly bears, and cougars are present, too, but are less likely to be seen.

Services within the recreation area include an information center at each of the main entrances, high-class accommodations in Kananaskis Village, camping at one of many campgrounds, bike and boat rentals, and accommodations for the physically challenged at William Watson Lodge.

The main access to Kananaskis Country is 90 km west of Calgary off the TransCanada Highway. Other points of access are immediately south of Canmore; at Bragg Creek on the region's northeast border; west from Longview in the southeast; or along the Forestry Trunk Rd. from the south. For more information write to Kananaskis Country, P.O. Box 280, Canmore, AB T0L 0M0; tel. (403) 678-5508.

The Old Banff Road

The original route from Calgary into the mountains has long been bypassed, but for those with a little extra time it remains as a pleasant alternative to TransCanada Highway. Also known as Hwy. 1A, the easiest place to join it is at Cochrane, an important ranching center west of Calgary. From there Hwy. 1A follows the north side of the Bow River to Hwy. 40, the main entrance to Kananaskis Country. The first major junction is with Hwy. 940, which spurs northwest to **Ghost River Wilderness Area,** a remote reserve more easily accessible from Lake Minnewanka in Banff National Park. Soon after this junction the highway passes **Ghost Lake,** created by the damming of the Bow River for hydroelectricity. At the west end of the lake is a white church built in 1875. For the next 30 km the road passes through a large Stoney Indian Reserve and the town of **Morley,** where there's a handicraft store and a restaurant (Chief Chiniki's) known for traditional meals. It then leaves the reserve and passes the turnoff to the TransAlta town of **Seebe.** To the north is the impressive face of **Mt. Yamnuska,** a popular rock-climbing spot. From here Hwy. 1A continues west, entering the mountains (views are marred by a cement plant and limestone quarry at Exshaw) and continuing to Canmore and Banff. Along this road, at a major junction 10 km east of Seebe, Hwy. 40 crosses the TransCanada Hwy. and heads south into Kananaskis Country.

Bow Valley Provincial Park

This 935-hectare park at the north end of Kananaskis Country sits at the confluence of the Kananaskis and Bow Rivers and is bisected by the TransCanada Highway. Calgary is 80 km to the east and Canmore is 28 km to the west. It was originally part of Rocky Mountains Park (now Banff National Park) but the area became separated when park boundaries were reduced in 1930, excluding areas zoned for further industrial development.

The Bow Valley was gouged by glaciers during a succession of ice ages, leaving the typical U-shaped glacial valley surrounded by towering peaks. Three vegetation zones are found within the park, but evergreen and aspen forest predominates. To the casual motorist driving along the highway the park seems fairly small, but over 300 species of plants have been recorded and 60 species of birds are known to nest within its boundaries. The abundance of wildflowers, birds, and smaller mammals can be enjoyed along four short interpretive trails. Other popular activities in the park include fishing for a variety of trout and whitefish in the Bow River, bicycling along the paved trail system, and attending interpretive programs presented by park staff.

Facilities at the two campgrounds within the park, **Willow Rock** and **Bow Valley,** are as good as any in the province. They both have showers, flush toilets, and kitchen shelters. Willow Rock also has powered sites and a coin laundry and is open for winter camping but has a distinct lack of trees. Unserviced sites are $13, powered sites $15. Reservations can be made for both campgrounds at (403) 673-2163.

A **Visitor Information Centre** is located at the park entrance on Hwy. 1X. It offers general information on the park and Kananaskis Country, and interpretive displays. A 2.2-km hiking trail also begins here. The center is open in summer Mon.-Fri. 8 a.m.-8 p.m., the rest of the year Mon.-Fri. 8:15 a.m.-4:30 p.m.

RIBBON CREEK/SPRAY LAKES AREA

This is the most developed of K-country's five zones, yet summer crowds are minimal compared to Banff. Highway 40 follows the Kananaskis River through the zone to Peter Lougheed Provincial Park, and the Smith-Dorrien/Spray Trail parallels this road to the west. At the zone's north entrance is Barrier Lake Visitor Information Centre (open in summer daily 9 a.m.-6 p.m., the rest of the year daily 9 a.m.-4 p.m.), a good

place to start your trip into Kananaskis Country. Along Hwy. 40 are two ski areas; Kananaskis Village; horseback riding at Boundary Ranch, tel. (403) 591-7171; a 36-hole golf course; and some spectacular mountain scenery. Although the best hiking is farther south in Peter Lougheed Provincial Park, there are a few trails around the village area. In the village, **Peregrine Sports,** tel. (403) 591-7453, rents a wide variety of sporting equipment including mountain bikes ($6.25 per hour, $27 per day), scooters ($13 per hour, $60 per day), fishing rods ($9 per day), canoes ($35 per day), and various downhill and cross-country skiing equipment.

Kananaskis Country Golf Course

This 36-hole championship course opened in 1983 at a cost of almost $1 million for each hole. Renowned golf-course architect Robert Trent Jones, who designed the layout, described the Kananaskis River Valley as ". . . the best spot I have ever seen for a golf course." After marveling at the surrounding mountains, few will disagree with his statement. Just don't let the 136 sand traps, water that comes into play on over half the holes, or the large rolling greens distract you. Green fees are $45; for tee times call (403) 591-7272.

Nakiska at Mt. Allan

This state-of-the-art ski area was built on Mt. Allan as host site for the alpine skiing events of the 1988 Winter Olympic Games. The area has been surrounded by controversy ever since plans for the 25.3-million-dollar project were proposed. Originally the events were to be held on existing ski slopes in Banff National Park. Environmentalists succeeded in keeping the games out of the park, but the victory soon turned sour when plans for a new area on the slopes of Mt. Allan were unveiled. This was only the start of Nakiska's early problems. Anyone who had spent any time in this part of the mountains knew the effect chinook winds can have on the snow cover and how impractical it was to build a ski area there. The answer was snowmaking. A five-million-dollar computerized snowmaking system covering 85% of the runs was installed, with 40 km of piping and 343 hydrants capable of pumping 24 million liters of water a day. Great cruising and fast fall-line skiing on runs cut specially for racing will satisfy the intermediate-to-advanced crowd. And the Bronze Chairlift accesses a novice area below the main area. The area has a total of 28 runs and a vertical rise of 735 meters. Lift tickets are $35, children under five free. Packages are offered in Kananaskis Village, which is linked to Nakiska by shuttle from Canmore, 40 km to the northwest.

For more ski resort information call (403) 591-7777. For accommodation reservations call (800) 258-7669.

Fortress Mountain

Fortress is a sleeping giant as ski areas go. It's a 30-minute drive farther into Kananaskis Country than Nakiska but the rewards are uncrowded slopes, more snow, on-hill accommodations, and spectacular views. Runs are short, but with skiing on three distinct faces there's something for everyone. With a little hiking, experienced powderhounds can ski untracked snow days after a storm. Facilities include three chairlifts and three T-bars serving a vertical rise of 330

fresh tracks at Fortress

meters, and a large day lodge with cafeteria, restaurant, and bar. Lift tickets are $30 per day or $23 for the afternoon; seniors and students $13. Cat-skiing is also offered; $100 half day, $195 full day. On-hill lodging is $19 in a dorm or $65 s, $75 d in motel-style rooms. For more information call (403) 591-7108.

Cross-Country Skiing

The most accessible of Kananaskis Country's 200 km of cross-country trails are in the Ribbon Creek area. Most heavily used are those radiating from Kananaskis Village and those around the base of Nakiska ski area. Most trails are easy to intermediate, including a five-km track up Ribbon Creek. Rentals are available in the Village Centre in Kananaskis Village.

Kananaskis Village

This modern alpine resort 100 km from Calgary was built for the 1988 Winter Olympic Games. Today it serves as headquarters for those who want to experience Kananaskis Country while enjoying the comforts of hotels and fine restaurants. The village is located on a narrow plateau overlooking its golf course, with magnificent mountain vistas in all directions and two ski areas a short drive away. Of the three hotels in the village, **Best Western Kananaskis Inn,** tel. (403) 591-7500 or (800) 528-1234, is the least expensive. Some of the 96 rooms are bedroom lofts with fireplaces, kitchenettes, and sitting rooms ($165); the others are standard hotel rooms that begin at $135. The inn also offers an exercise room, indoor pool, and the Garden Cafe. The other two accommodations in the Village—**Lodge at Kananaskis** and **Hotel Kananaskis,** tel. (403) 591-7711 or (800) 441-1414 for both—are managed by Canadian Pacific Hotels & Resorts (which also runs the famous mountain resorts in Banff, Lake Louise, and Jasper). The lodge has 255 moderately large rooms, many with mountain views, balconies, and fireplaces. The hotel is much smaller, and each room has a mountain view, a luxurious bathroom complete with bathrobes, and extra large beds. Guests at both the hotel and lodge have use of a full-facility health club, an indoor swimming pool, whirlpool, steam room, sauna, and a beauty salon with tanning beds. Rates start at around $200 s or d but drop dramatically outside of summer. Good ski packages are offered all winter.

Restaurants in the lodge include **Peaks Dining Room** (open daily 6 a.m.-10 p.m.), with a casual atmosphere, floor-to-ceiling windows, and an adjoining outdoor patio used during summer; and **Bighorn Lounge,** offering a bistro-style menu with occasional live entertainment. In the hotel, **L'Escapade** is the village's most elegant restaurant. French-Canadian cuisine is served on sterling silver while a pianist plays through dinner. The hotel's **Fireside Lounge** is a warm, intimate bar with an Italian decor and a moderately priced pasta bar.

Village Centre in Kananaskis Village has a grocery store, post office, and information center (open in summer daily 9 a.m.-5 p.m.).

Hostel
Ribbon Creek Hostel is along the access road to Kananaskis Village, within walking distance. The hostel has hot showers, a kitchen, family rooms, a lounge room with fireplace, and an outdoor barbecue. Cost to members is $12, nonmembers $17. For reservations call (403) 762-4122.

Campgrounds
Mt. Kidd RV Park, tel. (403) 591-7700, is arguably the finest in Canada. It's nestled below the sheer eastern face of Mt. Kidd in a forest of spruce and lodgepole pine. The campground's showpiece is the Campers Centre. Inside are all the usual bathroom facilities as well as whirlpools, saunas, a wading pool, game room, lounge, groceries, a concession, and laundry. Outside are tennis courts, picnic areas by the river, and many paved trails. Tent sites are $14, hookups $18-23. It's open year-round.

Those who can survive without such luxuries have the choice of three other campgrounds along Hwy. 40 ($11).

PETER LOUGHEED PROVINCIAL PARK

This park, originally named Kananaskis Provincial Park, was renamed in 1986 after Peter Lougheed. Lougheed was the Albertan premier who, with the help of oil-money-based Heritage Savings

and Trust Fund, began the development of Kananaskis Country as a multiuse recreation area. The 500-square-km wilderness is the largest provincial park in Alberta. The high peaks of the Continental Divide form the eastern and southern boundaries of the park, making a spectacular backdrop for the Kananaskis River and the Kananaskis Lakes. These lakes are the center of boating and fishing in the park and opportunities abound for hiking and camping nearby.

Highway 40 is the main route through the park. In the southeastern corner it climbs to **Highwood Pass** (2,227 meters), the highest road pass in Canada. South of the park administration office, **Kananaskis Lakes Trail** heads into the main recreation area. The **Smith-Dorrien/Spray Trail** is a gravel road that follows Smith-Dorrien Creek north from Lower Kananaskis Lake to Spray Lakes, descending steeply into Canmore on the TransCanada Highway.

Recreation
Hiking is the most popular activity in the park (see "Hiking in Lougheed Park," below) but by no means the only one. The **Bike Trail** is a 20-km paved trail designed especially for bicycles that begins behind the Visitor Information Centre and follows Lower Kananaskis Lake to Mount Sarrail Campground. Many other trails are designated for mountain bike use; inquire at the Visitor Information Centre, tel. (403) 591-6345. **Boulton Creek Trading Post,** tel. (403) 591-7058, rents mountain bikes during summer; $7 per hour, $30 per day. Upper and Lower Kananaskis Lakes have fair fishing for a variety of trout and whitefish. A nightly interpretive program takes place in campground amphitheaters throughout the park. Look for schedules posted on bulletin boards or check with the Visitor Information Centre.

In winter Highwood Pass is closed to traffic, but Hwy. 40 into the park is cleared, and cross-country skiing is excellent.

William Watson Lodge
This special facility is available to disabled persons and Albertan seniors. Guests stay in private cabins, but the lodge operates like a hostel and you must supply your own bedding and food. The main lodge has a kitchen, lounge, library, laundry room, and gas barbecues on the sun-

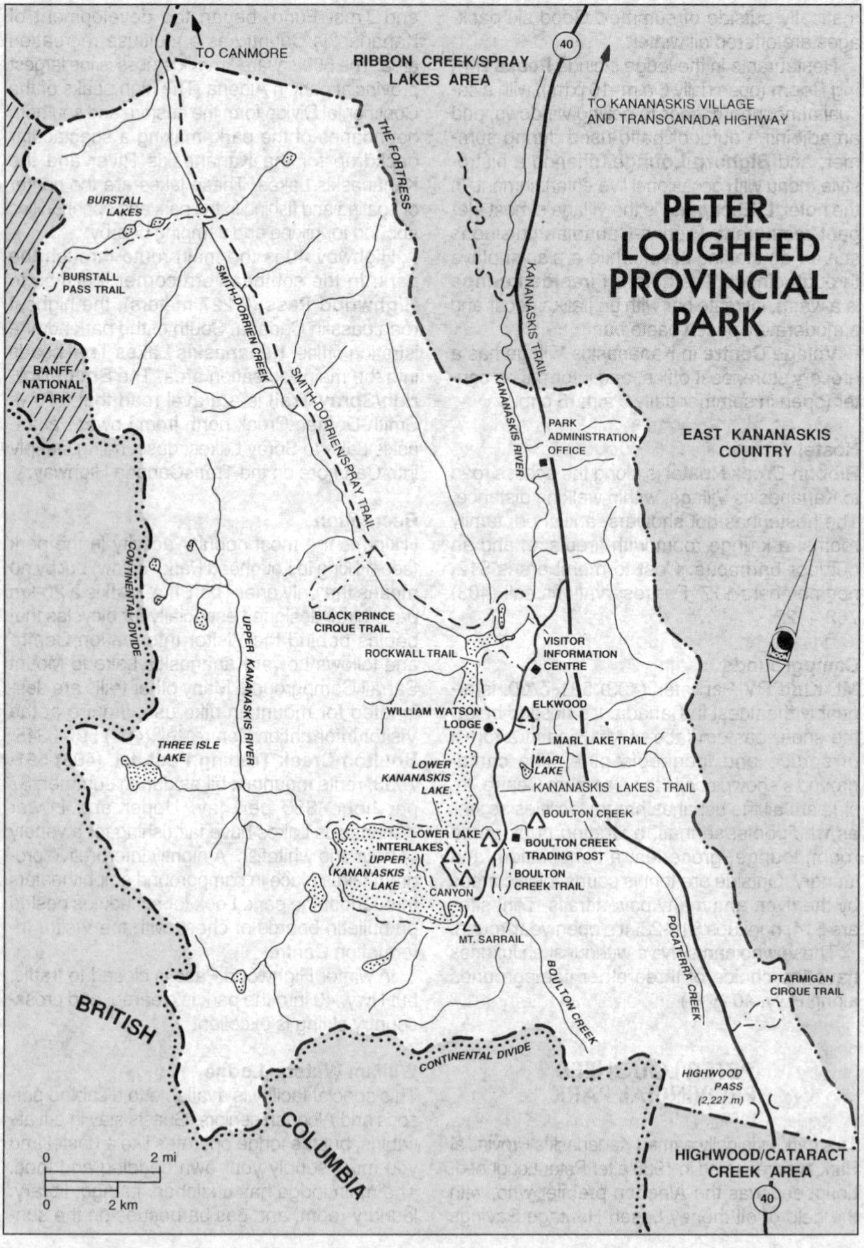

TO CANMORE

RIBBON CREEK/SPRAY
LAKES AREA

TO KANANASKIS VILLAGE
AND TRANSCANADA HIGHWAY

40

THE FORTRESS

BURSTALL
LAKES

BURSTALL
PASS TRAIL

BANFF
NATIONAL
PARK

SMITH-DORRIEN CREEK

SMITH-DORRIEN/SPRAY TRAIL

KANANASKIS TRAIL

KANANASKIS RIVER

PARK
ADMINISTRATION
OFFICE

PETER
LOUGHEED
PROVINCIAL
PARK

EAST KANANASKIS
COUNTRY

CONTINENTAL DIVIDE

UPPER KANANASKIS RIVER

BLACK PRINCE
CIRQUE TRAIL

ROCKWALL TRAIL

VISITOR
INFORMATION
CENTRE

ELKWOOD

WILLIAM WATSON
LODGE

THREE ISLE
LAKE

LOWER
KANANASKIS
LAKE

MARL LAKE TRAIL

MARL
LAKE

KANANASKIS LAKES TRAIL

BOULTON CREEK

LOWER LAKE

INTERLAKES

UPPER
KANANASKIS
LAKE

CANYON

BOULTON CREEK
TRADING POST

BOULTON
CREEK TRAIL

POCATERRA CREEK

MT. SARRAIL

BOULTON CREEK

PTARMIGAN
CIRQUE TRAIL

BRITISH

CONTINENTAL DIVIDE

HIGHWOOD
PASS
(2,227 m)

COLUMBIA

0   2 mi

0   2 km

HIGHWOOD/CATARACT
CREEK AREA

40

© MOON PUBLICATIONS, INC.

deck. Disabled guests may bring up to three family members or friends. The cost is $5-10 per person per night. Reservations are essential and can be made up to four months in advance. Write to William Watson Lodge, Peter Lougheed Provincial Park, P.O. Box 130, Kananaskis Village, AB T0L 2H0, or call (403) 591-7227.

Camping

The nearest hotels are to the north in Kananaskis Village. Within the park are six auto-accessible campgrounds that have a total of 507 sites. All are on the Kananaskis Lakes Trail and are linked by bicycle and hiking trails. **Mount Sarrail,** at the southern end of Upper Kananaskis Lake, is for tenters only and has pit toilets and firewood; $9 per night. **Canyon, Lower Lake,** and **Interlakes** have pit toilets and firewood; $11 per night. **Elkwood** has showers, flush toilets, powered sites, and an interpretive amphitheater; unserviced sites $13, powered sites $15. **Boulton Creek** has showers, flush toilets, powered sites, an interpretive amphitheater, and grocery store; $13-15 per night. For campground reservations call (403) 591-7226.

Services and Information

Boulton Creek Trading Post, a grocery store selling basic supplies, fishing tackle and souvenirs, is located on the Kananaskis Lakes Trail. The store also rents bikes. Next door is a small cafe serving hamburgers and light meals. The ice cream is good, although expensive.

The **Visitor Information Centre** is an excellent facility three km along Kananaskis Lakes Trail. The staff is very knowledgeable about the park and has hordes of literature hidden under the desk—but you have to ask for it. Ask them to put a movie or slide show on in the theater; most revolve around the park. The movie *Bears and Man* is a classic '70s flick dealing with public attitude toward bears, one of the first documentaries to do so. A large lounge that overlooks the valley is used mainly in winter by cross-country skiers but is always open for trip planning or relaxing on rainy afternoons. This center is the place to pick up fishing licenses and backcountry camping permits. It's open in summer daily 9 a.m.-7 p.m., the rest of the year Mon.-Fri. 9 a.m.-5 p.m. and Sat.-Sun. 9 a.m.-5 p.m.; tel. (403) 591-6345. For more information write to Kananaskis Country, P.O. Box 280, Canmore, AB T0L 0M0, or call (403) 678-5508.

HIKING IN PETER LOUGHEED PROVINCIAL PARK

The park has a number of interesting interpretive trails and more-strenuous hikes. Most trailheads are located along Kananaskis Lakes Trail. Many trails have interpretive signs along them; others require an interpretive booklet available from the Visitor Information Centre. **Rockwall Trail,** from the Visitor Information Centre, and **Marl Lake Trail,** from Elkwood Campground, are wheelchair accessible and barrier-free respectively. Below are some of the park's more popular interpretive and day hikes.

Boulton Creek

- Length: 4.9 km (90 minutes) roundtrip
- Elevation gain: minimal
- Rating: easy

This trail starts where Kananaskis Lakes Trail crosses Boulton Creek. A booklet, available at the trailhead or at the Visitor Information Centre, corresponds with numbered posts along the trail. The highlighted stops emphasize the valley's human history. After a short climb the trail reaches a cabin built in the 1930s as a stopover for forest ranger patrols. The trail then follows a high ridge and loops back along the other side of the creek to the trailhead.

Ptarmigan Cirque

- Length: 5.6 km (2 hours) roundtrip
- Elevation gain: 230 meters
- Rating: moderate

The trailhead for this steep interpretive walk is across the road from Highwood Meadows, 17 km south of Kananaskis Lakes Rd. on Hwy 40. A booklet, available at the trailhead or at the Visitor Information Centre, corresponds with numbered posts along the trail. As it climbs into the alpine zone, magnificent panoramas unfold. Along the trail you are likely to see numerous small mammals. Columbian ground squirrels, pikas, least chipmunks, and hoary marmots are all common. At higher elevations the meadows are home to bighorn sheep, mountain goats, and grizzly bears. Another short walk, the **Rock**

COUGARS

Elusive and rarely encountered by casual hikers, cougars (also known as mountain lions, pumas, or catamounts) measure up to 1.5 meters long with the average male weighing 75 kilograms and the female 40-55 kilograms. Their athletic prowess puts Olympians to shame. They can spring forward over eight meters from a standstill, leap four meters into the air, and safely jump from a height of 20 meters.

Cougars are versatile hunters whose acute vision takes in a peripheral span in excess of 200 degrees. They typically kill a large mammal such as an elk or deer every 12-14 days, eating part of it and caching the rest. Their diet also includes chipmunks, ground squirrels, snowshoe hares, and occasionally porcupines. Although attacks on humans are rare, they do occur, usually if the cougar has been surprised or if it's particularly hungry. Cases have been recorded of the animal stalking human prey, but there have been no recorded cougar attacks in Alberta for 30 years.

The cougar is a solitary animal with distinct territorial boundaries. This limits its population density, which in turn means that its overall numbers are low. As is the case with all North America's large mammals, the cougar's biggest threat is man and the diminishing range of its habitat due to development and ranching. An extensive study of the cougar took place throughout the 1980s in Alberta and the good news is that although its numbers are low they remain steady.

BOB RACE

Glacier Trail, two km north of Highwood Meadows, leads 150 meters to a unique formation of moraine rock.

Black Prince Cirque
- Length: 5.6 km (90 minutes) roundtrip
- Elevation gain: 210 meters
- Rating: easy/moderate

The trailhead is eight km from Kananaskis Lakes Trail along the Smith-Dorrien/Spray Trail. Numbered posts along the trail correspond to a booklet available at the trailhead or at the Visitor Information Centre. The trail climbs steadily to an area that was logged in the early 1970s, then winds through a forest of Engelmann spruce and subalpine fir, crosses Old Creek, and emerges at a high mountain cirque scoured out by a glacier. Each spring the cirque fills with water, forming a small emerald-green lake.

Burstall Pass
- Length: 7.4 km (2.5 hours) one-way
- Elevation gain: 480 meters
- Rating: moderate/difficult

The trailhead is on the west side of the Smith-Dorrien/Spray Trail at the south end of Mud Lake. For the first three km it climbs an old logging road to Burstall Lakes. After traversing the willow flats it begins climbing again through heavy forest and avalanche paths to a large cirque. The final ascent to the pass is a real slog, but the view across the Upper Spray Valley (which is in Banff National Park) is worth it. From the pass it is possible to continue to Palliser Pass (two days one-way) and Banff townsite (three days one-way).

EAST KANANASKIS COUNTRY

East Kananaskis Country is the largest and most diverse of the zones in K-country, spanning the Elbow, Sheep, Sibbald, and Jumpingpound Valleys. The valleys start in the west among the high peaks of the Rockies. As they cut east through the foothills, they gradually open up, ending at the prairie. At higher elevations elk, bighorn sheep, and bears make their home. In the foothills visitors are likely to see mule and white-tailed deer, elk, and moose. East Kananaskis also has a relatively high population of cougars, but these shy cats are rarely sighted.

The main access roads into the zone are from Bragg Creek on Hwy. 66, Millarville on Hwy. 549, and Turner Valley on Hwy. 546. **Sibbald Creek Trail** (Hwy. 68) crosses the northern reaches of the zone and is accessible from the TransCanada Hwy., intersecting Hwy. 40 south of the Barrier Lake Visitor Information Centre. Much of the zone is set aside for off-road vehicles and travel on horseback, although some hiking trails along Hwy. 66 are worthy of exploration.

Practicalities

From Bragg Creek, Hwy. 66 follows the Elbow River southwest past three campgrounds to a staging area for horses at the end of the road. Each campground is close to the river and has kitchen shelters, firewood, and picnic tables; $11-13 per night. Along Hwy. 546, west from Turner Valley, are two campgrounds. At each entrance are information centers; open in summer daily 9 a.m.-9 p.m. For more information write to Kananaskis Country, P.O. Box 280, Canmore, AB T0L 0M0; tel. (403) 678-5508.

HIGHWOOD/CATARACT CREEK AREA

The Highwood/Cataract Creek Area stretches from Peter Lougheed Provincial Park to the southern border of Kananaskis Country. This is the least developed zone in Kananaskis Country. The jagged peaks of the Highwood Mountains are its most dominant feature; high alpine meadows among the peaks are home to bighorn sheep, elk, and grizzlies. Lower down, lush spruce and lodgepole pine forests spread over most of the zone, giving way to rich grazing lands along its eastern flanks. Access to the area is via Hwy. 40 from the north, Hwy. 541 from Longview to the east, and Hwy. 940 from Crowsnest Pass to the south. In winter, the only access is from Hwy. 541.

The main summer activities are hiking, horseback riding, climbing, and fishing. Winter use is primarily by snowmobilers. Only two formal hiking trails are signposted. The rest are a complex system of traditional routes that are not well traveled; many require river crossings. One of the two marked trails, **Mist Creek Trail,** starts 21 km north of Highwood Junction at Mist Creek Picnic Area. It leads seven km one-way to Rickert's Pass, one of the most scenic vantage points in Kananaskis Country. The other marked route is **Cat Creek Interpretive Trail,** a short hike from Cat Creek Picnic Area. Some of the best hiking in the zone is only accessible after a difficult ford of the Highwood River, which runs parallel to Hwys. 40 and 541. Highlights include two Indian petroglyphs along Zephyr Creek and abandoned fire lookouts along Hwy. 940. For more information contact the ranger station at Highwood Junction, tel. (403) 558-2151, or read Joey Ambrosi's *Hiking Alberta's Southwest.*

Practicalities

All four campgrounds in the zone are south of Highwood Junction on Hwy. 940. Each has water, pit toilets, firewood, fire pits, and picnic tables; $7 per night. A fifth campground at Strawberry Creek is open during the hunting season. **Highwood House** is located at Highwood Junction and has gas and a grocery store. It's open May-June Fri.-Sun. 9 a.m.-5 p.m., July-Sept. daily 9 a.m.-8 p.m., and Oct.-April weekends only 9:15 a.m.-5 p.m. The **Highwood Ranger Station,** also located at the junction, is open in summer only Thurs.-Mon. 10 a.m.-6 p.m.; tel. (403) 558-2151. For more information write to Kananaskis Country, P.O. Box 280, Canmore, AB T0L 0M0; tel. (403) 678-5508.

CANMORE

Canmore (pop. 6,000) is nestled below the distinctive peaks of the Three Sisters in the Bow Valley between Calgary and Banff. It is the gateway to the mountain national parks and Kananaskis Country, and provides inexpensive lodging and dining alternatives. Its ideal mountain location and the freedom it enjoys from the strict development restrictions that apply in the nearby parks have made the town one of the fastest-growing resort areas in the country. Downtown Canmore, on the southwestern side of the TransCanada Hwy., has managed to retain much of its charm. Most of the development is taking place on the outskirts. Around $2.3 billion in resort and residential projects have been planned for the next two decades, and the town's population is estimated to reach 20,000 by the end of that period. One of the largest and most controversial developments, still in its infancy, is the Three Sisters Resort. When completed, it will include 4,000 residential units, two hotels, and two golf courses on an 840-hectare parcel of land in the environmentally sensitive Wind Valley.

Apart from being a service center, the town has much to offer. Many historical buildings line the downtown streets, nearby hiking is excellent, and Mt. Yamnuska has become the most developed rock-climbing site in the Rockies. Canmore also hosted the nordic events of the 1988 Winter Olympic Games and is the home of the Alpine Club of Canada.

History

The Hudson's Bay Company explored the Bow Valley corridor and attempted, without success,

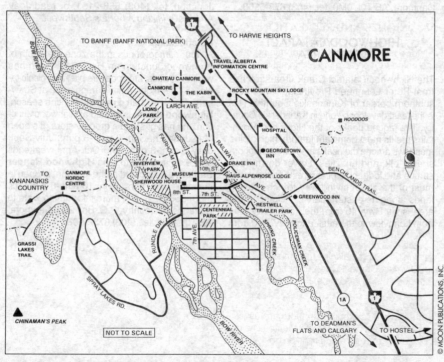

CANMORE

NOT TO SCALE

© MOON PUBLICATIONS, INC.

to establish a fur trade with the Stoney Indians for most of the 1840s. In 1958 an expedition from the east, led by John Palliser, sent back discouraging reports about the climate and prospects of agriculture in the valley. One of the conditions of British Columbian entry into the confederation of Canada was the completion of a rail line linking them to the east by 1881. The Canadian Pacific Railway chose the Bow Valley Corridor as the route through the mountains, and the first divisional point west of Calgary was established at what is now Canmore. Mining on the Three Sisters and Mount Rundle commenced soon after. Hotels and businesses were established, and a hospital, NWMP post, and opera house were built. The Canmore Opera House—reputed to be the only log movie house in the world—still stands and has been relocated to the Calgary Heritage Park. In 1899 the C.P.R. moved its divisional point to Laggan (now Lake Louise), but the mines continued to operate until 1979.

SIGHTS AND RECREATION

Historic buildings from the coal-mining days are being preserved at their original locations around town. The best way to get downtown from the TransCanada Hwy. is to take Benchlands Trail from Hwy. 1A and drive down 8th St., the main drag. The first building of interest at the east end of 8th St. is Canmore's original NWMP post, built in 1892. **Ralph Connor Memorial United Church,** opposite the bakery and a little farther down 8th St., was built in 1890 and is now a Provincial Historic Site. **Canmore Hotel** on the corner of 8th St. and 7th Ave. was built in 1891 (at a time when four hotels already operated) and is still open for thirsty travelers today. **Canmore Centennial Museum,** 801 7th Ave., tel. (403) 678-2462, has a collection of artifacts from the area's early coal-mining days and a display from the 1988 Winter Olympic Games. Open daily noon-4 p.m., extended hours in summer.

Hiking
The hiking trails around Canmore are usually passed by in favor of those of its famous neighbors. But some interesting trails do exist. Paved paths around town are suitable for walking, bicycling, and, in winter, skiing. They link Policeman's Creek with the golf course, nordic center, and Riverview Park on the Bow River.

Grassi Lakes Trail takes about three hours and climbs to a series of small lakes below Chinaman's Peak. To get to the trailhead follow Spray Lakes Rd. past the nordic center and take the first gravel road to the left after the reservoir. This leads to a parking lot and trailhead. The trail forks to the left by a gate and climbs to **Grassi Falls.** Stairs cut into a cliff face lead up to a bridge over Canmore Creek and to the lakes. A further scramble up a scree slope leads to four pictographs (native rock paintings) of human figures. They are on the first large boulder in the gorge.

A trail on the opposite side of the valley leads to hoodoos and a panoramic view of the Bow Valley and Canmore. To get there take the Benchlands Trail (an extension of Railway Ave.) across the TransCanada Hwy. and turn left on the first gravel road after the overpass. The trail starts at the cemetery (interesting itself with graves dating back to the 1890s) and climbs to the mysterious-looking columns carved from the soft sandstone by wind and rain. Past the hoodoos the trail continues climbing to a ridge with excellent views across the valley.

Canmore Nordic Centre
This remarkable complex was built at a cost of $15 million for the 1988 Winter Olympic Games. The cross-country skiing and biathlon (combined cross-country skiing and rifle shooting) events were held here, and today the center remains a world-class training ground for Canadian athletes. Even in summer, long after the snow has melted, the place is worth a visit. An interpretive trail leads down to the banks of the Bow River where Georgetown, an old coal-mining town, once stood. Many other trails lead around the grounds and it's possible to hike or bike to the Banff Springs Hotel. Mountain biking is extremely popular on the trails. Events are held throughout summer and bike rentals are available at **Trail Sports,** tel. (403) 678-6764, at the center. The day lodge has an information rack with maps and brochures, lockers, a lounge area, and a cafeteria. It's open daily 8 a.m.-4:30 p.m. For more information call (403) 678-2400.

Other Recreation

The Bow River has good fishing for rainbow and brook trout; Gap Lake for brown and brook trout; Grotto Lake for rainbow trout; and Ghost Lake for lake, rainbow, and brown trout. **Wapiti Sports,** 1506 Railway Ave., tel. (403) 678-5550, stocks bait and tackle and sells fishing licenses.

Canmore is home to many qualified mountain guides who operate both in and out of Banff National Park. Basic climbing courses cost $40-70 per day, and instruction is available for all ability levels. The main guiding companies are: **Ascent,** P.O. Box 1624, Canmore, AB T0L 0M0; tel. (403) 678-2815; **M.W. Guides Office,** P.O. Box 1913; tel. (403) 678-2642; and **Company of Canadian Mountain Guides,** P.O. Box 1149, tel. (403) 678-4662;

Canmore Golf Course, built in 1926, has developed into an 18-hole championship course with a clubhouse and driving range. Green fees are $35; for tee times call (403) 678-4784.

Once a traditional form of transportation, dogsledding is now a popular winter sport.

Festivals and Events

Canmore's annual **Winter Carnival** is a two-week celebration including an ice-sculpture demonstration, ice-fishing derby, and pancake breakfasts. The highlight is the **Alberta Sled Dog Championship** held at Canmore Nordic Centre, where teams of four, six, eight, and 10 dogs are harnessed up and compete in various heats (organizers are always looking for volunteers; ask around if you'd like to help). **Canada Day** is celebrated with a parade, midway, and fireworks display. The first weekend in August is a busy one. **Hobie's Howler** is a nationally sanctioned mountain bike race held at Canmore Nordic Centre. Events include downhill, uphill, and cross-country. Spectators are admitted free. The same weekend is the **Heritage Day Folk Festival,** which starts on Sunday and runs through Monday evening. This event features national and international acts performing in Centennial Park. The second Sunday of September is the traditional **Highland Games,** a day of dancing, eating, and tug-of-war.

ACCOMMODATIONS

Hotels and Motels

Most lodging is located on Hwy. 1A, just off the TransCanada Hwy. between the two Canmore exits. (Mailing addresses for the following accommodations are the listed P.O. Box followed by **Canmore, AB T0L 0M0.**)

Akai Motel, P.O. Box 687, tel. (403) 678-4664, is a little run-down but each room has a kitchenette; $48 s, $61 d. **Rocky Mountain Ski Lodge,** P.O. Box 3000, tel. (403) 678-5445 or (800) 665-6111, has large, modern rooms and some loft apartments with kitchenettes. Basic rooms start at $59 s, $63 d, making it the least expensive motel in town. Another inexpensive option is the **Drake Inn,** P.O. Box 2760, tel. (403) 678-5131 or (800) 461-8730, at the end of Canmore's main street. It has a sports bar, outdoor jacuzzi, and restaurant, and each room has a private balcony; from $79 s or d. **Rundle Mountain Motel,** P.O. Box 147, tel. (403) 678-5322 or (800) 661-1610, has small but comfortable rooms and an indoor pool and outdoor whirlpool; $68-93 s or d.

The old Viscount Motor Inn is now **Westridge Country Inn,** P.O. Box 790, tel. (403) 678-5221.

THE ALPINE CLUB OF CANADA

The Alpine Club of Canada, like similar clubs in the United States and Great Britain, is a nonprofit mountaineering organization whose objectives include the encouragement of mountaineering, the exploration and study of alpine and glacial regions, and the preservation of mountain flora and fauna.

The club was formed in 1906, mainly through the tireless campaign of its first president, A.O. Wheeler. A list of early members reads like a Who's Who of the Canadian Rockies—Bill Peyto, Tom Wilson, Byron Harmon, Mary Schäffer—names familiar to all Canadian mountaineers. The original clubhouse was near the Banff Springs Hotel, but in 1980 a new clubhouse was built in Canmore, serving as headquarters for over 3,000 members throughout Canada. The club's ongoing projects include operating the Lake Louise Hostel, maintaining a system of huts throughout the backcountry, and publishing the annual *Canadian Alpine Journal*—the country's only record of mountaineering accomplishments. A reference library of the club's history is kept at the Whyte Museum of the Canadian Rockies in Banff. For further information and membership details write to: P.O. Box 2040, Canmore, AB T0L 0M0, tel. (403) 678-3200.

WHYTE MUSEUM OF THE CANADIAN ROCKIES

The old rooms are still available ($59 s, $63 d), but the much more comfortable rooms in a new section facing Bow Valley Trail are better value at $80-125 s or d. Each has a balcony and fireplace. Another new accommodation is **Greenwood Inn,** P.O. Box 1140, tel. (403) 678-3625, which features many facilities and air-conditioning in each room. Rates are $119 s or d. In the same price range is **Best Western Green Gables Inn,** P.O. Box 520, tel. (403) 678-5488 or (800) 661-2133, which has a whirlpool in each room, private balconies, fireplaces, and a fine-dining restaurant. Rooms are $105 s or d and ski packages start at $65 per person. Similarly priced, and of the same high standard, is **Chateau Canmore,** P.O. Box 3451, tel. (403) 678-6699.

The **Georgetown Inn,** P.O. Box 3327, tel. (403) 678-3439 or (800) 657-5955, is run by a friendly English couple who have set the place up as an inn of times gone by. Each room has its own charm and a delicious cooked breakfast is included in the rate of $95 d ($75 in winter).

Lodging in Harvie Heights, west of Canmore and closer to Banff (same Canmore postal code as above), is generally more expensive, but most units have kitchens. Options are: **Banff Gate Mountain Lodge,** P.O. Box 525, tel. (403) 678-5251, from $69 s or d; **Gateway Inn Motor Lodge,** P.O. Box 585, tel. (403) 678-5396, $75 s, $90 d; **Rundle Ridge Chalets,** P.O. Box 1847, tel. (403) 678-5387 or (800) 332-1299, set in a pleasant wooded area, each chalet with its own fireplace, $89-124 s or d; and **Stockade Motel,** P.O. Box 575, tel. (403) 678-5212, $78-140.

Deadman's Flats, south of Canmore, is little more than a truck stop but has two motels; **Green Acres Motel,** P.O. Box 1770, tel. (403) 678-5344; and **Pigeon Mountain Motel,** P.O. Box 434, tel. (403) 678-5756. Both have rooms starting around $60.

Kananaskis Guest Ranch

This historic lodge, 10 minutes east of Canmore, has been owned and operated by five generations of the Brewster family—a name synonymous with tourism in Banff. The lodge is located on a picturesque lake in the Bow Valley, close to the mountain parks. Yet a traditional Western atmosphere prevails; the emphasis is on horseback riding and the outdoors, although they also have an indoor jacuzzi, dining room, and lounge. Chalets and cabins are basic but comfortable. Rates are $105 per person per day, which includes three meals and one hour of trail riding. For more information write to Kananaskis Guest Ranch, P.O. Box 964 Banff, AB T0L 0C0; tel. (403) 762-5454.

Bed and Breakfasts

Over a dozen bed and breakfasts operate in Canmore. Most are small, family-run affairs, with only one or two rooms. During summer they fill every night. Largest is **Haus Alpenrose Lodge,** P.O. Box 723, Canmore, AB T0L 0M0, tel. (403) 678-4134, a Bavarian-style chalet at 629 9th St. that is home to the Canadian School of Mountaineering. The hosts operate an extensive mountaineering program, making this the perfect place for climbers. Rates are $50 s, $60 d.

For a full list of B&Bs in the area, ask at the Travel Alberta Information Centre or check the *Alberta Accommodation and Visitors' Guide.*

Hostel

The **Alpine Club of Canada Clubhouse** is an excellent hostel-style accommodation at the base of Grotto Mountain. The clubhouse overlooks the Bow Valley and can sleep 30 in the dormitories. It has a kitchen, excellent library, laundry, lounge area with fireplace, bar, and a sauna. Rates are $12 per night for Alpine Club members, $20 otherwise. Club membership is inexpensive and includes a discount at the Lake Louise Hostel. For reservations and more information write to Canmore Clubhouse, Alpine Club of Canada, P.O. Box 2040, Canmore, AB T0L 0M0, or call (403) 678-3200. To get there from the east take the first Canmore exit and follow Hwy 1A to Exshaw (to the northeast). The clubhouse is signposted to the left.

Campgrounds

Restwell Trailer Park, off 8th St. in downtown Canmore, tel. (403) 678-5111, has showers and a laundry. It is mainly suited to RVs, but tents are allowed. Unserviced sites are $15, hookups $17-21. Behind Canmore, 16 km along the Smith-Dorrien/Spray Lakes Trail, is a primitive campground on Spray Lakes, $7 per night. East of Canmore are three government campgrounds, each with pit toilets, kitchen shelters, and firewood. **Bow Valley Campground** is located four km west of Deadman's Flats, **Three Sisters Campground** is in Deadman's Flats, and **Lac Des Arcs Campground** is seven km east. Rates are $9-15.

FOOD

Fireside Inn, 718 8th St., tel. (403) 678-6677, is a popular early morning hangout. Cooked breakfasts begin at $4. Open Sun.-Thurs. 6 a.m.-5 p.m., Fri.-Sat. 6 a.m.-9 p.m. Another option for breakfast is the **Drake Inn,** where a hearty breakfast will set you back around $5 and you can finish off with a beer or shooter. The best coffee in town is served up at the **Coffee Mine,** 802 8th St., tel. (403) 678-2241. **Sherwood House,** 738 8th St., tel. (403) 678-5211, on Canmore's busiest downtown corner, is open daily 11 a.m.-10 p.m. You can dine outdoor on a deck or inside in a simply furnished restaurant and lounge. The menu is mainly pasta, grills, and inexpensive fondues. **The Kabin,** 1702 Hwy. 1A, tel. (403) 678-4878, is a two-story log structure at the eastern end of a strip of restaurants. Although the menu is small it is varied and should appeal to all tastes. Expect to pay $12-20 for a main meal. On Sunday, 10:30 a.m.-2 p.m., an appetizing brunch buffet is served for $13.95, which includes dessert.**Des Alpes,** 702 10th St., tel. (403) 678-6878, is a simply furnished, upscale European restaurant. **Peppermill,** 726 9th St., tel. (403) 678-2292, serves excellent homemade pasta and lots of beef. Try daily specials such as lamb or arctic char, and finish with a bowl of delicious homemade ice cream. It's open daily 5-10 p.m.

SERVICES AND INFORMATION

The **post office** is on 8th St. at the corner of 7th Avenue. **Mountain Laundromat,** open 8 a.m.-9:30 p.m., is located in the mall on 7th Avenue. **Canmore Hospital** is along Hwy. 1A, tel. (403) 678-5536. For the **RCMP** call (403) 678-5516.

Canmore Public Library, 700 9th St., tel. (403) 678-2468, is open Tues.-Thurs. 11 a.m.-8 p.m., Fri.-Sun. 11 a.m.-5 p.m. A **Travel Alberta Information Centre** on the west side of town, just off the TransCanada Hwy., provides plenty of information on Canmore, Calgary, and the rest of the province. Open May-Sept. 8 a.m.-8 p.m. and October 9 a.m.-6 p.m.; tel. (403) 678-5277.

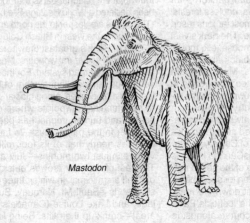

Mastodon

BOB RACE

KAREN MℂKINLEY

BANFF NATIONAL PARK

INTRODUCTION

This 6,641-square-km national park encompasses some of the world's most magnificent scenery. The snowcapped peaks of the Rocky Mountains form a spectacular backdrop for glacial lakes, fast-flowing rivers, endless forests, and two of North Americas's most famous resort towns, Banff and Lake Louise. The park's vast wilderness is home to deer, moose, elk, mountain goats, bighorn sheep, black and grizzly bears, wolves, and cougars. Many of these species are commonly sighted from roads in the park, others forage within town, and some remain deep in the backcountry. The human species is concentrated mainly in the picture-postcard town of Banff, located near the park's southeast gate, 128 km west of Calgary. Northwest of Banff, along the TransCanada Hwy., is Lake Louise, regarded as one of the seven natural wonders of the world, rivaled for sheer beauty only by Moraine Lake, just down the road. Just north of Lake Louise, the Icefields Parkway begins its spectacular course alongside

the Continental Divide to Jasper National Park.

Banff National Park is only one component of a complex geological and natural area consisting of four adjacent national parks that together have been declared a World Heritage Site by UNESCO. (The others are Jasper to the north and Kootenay and Yoho to the west in British Columbia.)

One of Banff's greatest drawcards is the accessibility of its natural wonders. Most highlights are close to the road system. For those more adventurous, an excellent system of hiking trails leads to alpine lakes, along glacial valleys, and to spectacular viewpoints where crowds are scarce and human impact has been minimal. Summer in the park is busy. In fact, the park receives nearly half of its four million annual visitors in just two months—July and August. The rest of the year crowds outside the town of Banff are minimal. In winter, three world-class ski resorts—Banff Mt. Norquay, Sunshine Village, and Lake Louise (Canada's largest ski area)—crank up their lifts. Being low season,

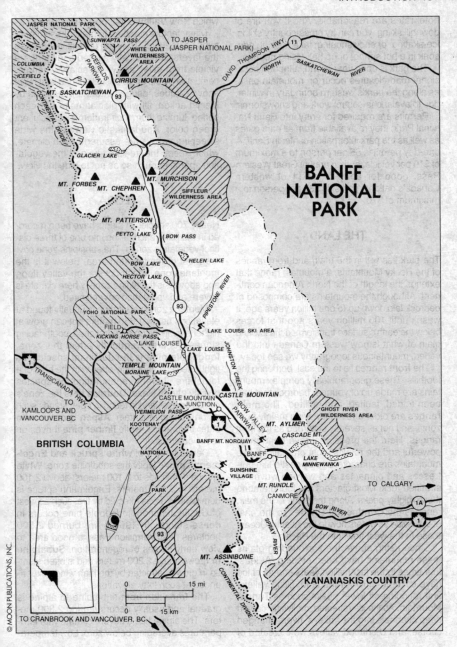

JASPER NATIONAL PARK
SUNWAPTA PASS
TO JASPER
(JASPER NATIONAL PARK)
COLUMBIA
ICEFIELD
WHITE GOAT WILDERNESS AREA
DAVID THOMPSON HWY
11
CIRRUS MOUNTAIN
ICEFIELDS PARKWAY
NORTH SASKATCHEWAN RIVER
MT. SASKATCHEWAN
93
CONTINENTAL DIVIDE
GLACIER LAKE
MT. FORBES
MT. CHEPHREN
MT. MURCHISON
SIFFLEUR WILDERNESS AREA

BANFF NATIONAL PARK

MT. PATTERSON
PEYTO LAKE
BOW PASS
HELEN LAKE
BOW LAKE
HECTOR LAKE
PIPESTONE RIVER
93
YOHO NATIONAL PARK
FIELD
KICKING HORSE PASS
LAKE LOUISE
LAKE LOUISE SKI AREA
JOHNSTON CREEK
TRANSCANADA HWY
TO KAMLOOPS AND VANCOUVER, BC
1
TEMPLE MOUNTAIN
MORAINE LAKE
CASTLE MOUNTAIN JUNCTION
CASTLE MOUNTAIN
BOW VALLEY PARKWAY
VERMILION PASS
KOOTENAY
BANFF MT. NORQUAY
MT. AYLMER
GHOST RIVER WILDERNESS AREA
CASCADE MT.
BRITISH COLUMBIA
NATIONAL
BANFF
SUNSHINE VILLAGE
PARK
LAKE MINNEWANKA
MT. RUNDLE
CANMORE
TO CALGARY
1A
BOW RIVER
1
93
SPRAY RIVER
MT. ASSINIBOINE
CONTINENTAL DIVIDE
KANANASKIS COUNTRY
0   15 mi
0   15 km
TO CRANBROOK AND VANCOUVER, BC

© MOON PUBLICATIONS, INC.

hotel rates are reasonable. And if you tire of downhill skiing, you can try cross-country skiing, ice-skating, or snowshoeing; take a sleigh ride; soak in a hot spring; or go heli-skiing nearby.

The park is open year-round, although occasional road closures occur on mountain passes along the park's western boundary in winter, due to avalanche-control work and snowstorms.

Permits are required for entry into Banff National Park; they're available from all park gates as well as the park information center in Banff. A one-day permit is $5 per person to a maximum of $10 per vehicle, and an annual Great Western Pass, good for entry to all 11 of western Canada's national parks, is $35 per person to a maximum of $70.

THE LAND

The park lies within the main and front ranges of the Rocky Mountains, a mountain range that extends the length of the North American continent. Although the mountains are composed of bedrock laid down up to one billion years ago, it wasn't until 100 million years ago that forces below the earth's surface transformed the lowland plain of what is now western Canada into the varied, mountainous topography we see today.

The **front ranges** lie to the east, bordering the foothills. These geographically complex mountains are made up of younger bedrock that has been folded, faulted, and uplifted. The **main ranges** are older and higher, lying mainly horizontal and not as severely disturbed as the front ranges. Here the pressures have been most powerful and the results most dramatic; these mountains are characterized by castle-like buttresses and pinnacles and warped waves of stratified rock. Most glaciers are found among these mighty peaks. Along the spine of the main range is the **Continental Divide.** To the east of the divide all waters flow to the Atlantic Ocean; those to the west flow into the Pacific.

Since rising above the surrounding plains these mountains have been eroding. At least four times in the last million years sheets of ice have covered much of the land, filling valleys and rounding off lower peaks such as **Tunnel Mountain.** As the ice retreated, meltwater carved deep channels into the valleys, rivers changed course, and U-shaped valleys were created of

which **Bow Valley** is the most distinctive.

Many factors combine to make these mountains so beautiful. They are distinctive because the layers of drastically altered sediment are visible from miles away, especially when accentuated by the angle of sunlight or a light fall of snow. Cirques, gouged into the mountains by glacial action, fill with glacial meltwater each spring, turning them their trademark translucent green color. And fantastic views of the wide sweeping valleys are assured by the climate, which keeps the treeline low and the vegetation sparse enough so as not to hide the view.

FLORA

Nearly 700 species of plants have been recorded in the park, each falling into one of three distinct vegetation zones. The subalpine zone covers most of the forested area. Below it is the montane zone, which covers the valley floor, and above it is the alpine zone, where climate is severe and vegetation cover limited.

Montane zone vegetation is usually found at elevations below 1,350 meters but can grow at higher elevations on sun-drenched, south-facing slopes. As fires frequently affect this zone, **lodgepole pine** is the dominant species; its tightly sealed cones only open with the heat of a forest fire, thereby regenerating the species quickly after a blaze. **Douglas fir** is the zone's climax species and is found in open stands such as on Tunnel Mountain. **Aspen** is common in older burn areas, while **limber pine** thrives on rocky outcrops.

Dense forests of **white spruce** and **Engelmann spruce** typify the subalpine zone. White spruce dominates to 2,100 meters; above 2,100 meters to 2,400 meters, Engelmann spruce is dominant. In areas affected by fire, such as west of Castle Junction, lodgepole pine occurs in dense stands. In 1968 a fire burned 2,500 hectares near Vermilion Pass, a good area to view early stages of regeneration. **Subalpine fir** grows above 2,200 meters and is often stunted in growth, affected by the high winds experienced at such lofty elevations.

The transition from subalpine to alpine is gradual and usually occurs around 2,300 meters. The alpine has a severe climate with temperatures averaging below zero. Low temperatures, strong winds, and a very short summer force alpine plants to adapt by growing low to the ground with long roots. Mosses, mountain avens, saxifrage, and an alpine dandelion all thrive in this environment. The best place to view the brightly colored carpet of alpine flowers is Sunshine Meadows or Parker's Ridge.

FAUNA

Viewing the park's abundant and varied wildlife is one of the park's most popular activities. During summer, with the onslaught of millions of visitors, many of the larger mammals tend to move away from the more heavily traveled areas. It then becomes a case of knowing when and where to look for them. Spring and fall are the best times of year for wildlife viewing. The big-game animals have moved below the snow cover of the higher elevations, and the crowds have thinned out. Winter also has its advantages. Although bears are hibernating, a large herd of elk winters in the town of Banff, coyotes are often seen roaming around town, bighorn sheep have descended from the heights, and wolf packs can be seen along the Bow Valley Corridor.

One of the biggest changes in the park over the last 60 years has been in the way that the complex relationship among higher-order mammals has been perceived by, and presented to, the visiting public. Only 20 years ago, hotels were taking guests to the Banff or Lake Louise dump to watch bears feeding on garbage; 30 years ago a predator-control program led to the slaughter of nearly every wolf in the park; 30-50 years ago it was deemed necessary to kill "surplus" elk; and it was only 60 years ago that Banff had a polar bear on display behind the Banff Park Museum. Amazingly enough, throughout these unsavory sagas, the park has remained a prime area for viewing the unique wildlife of the Canadian Rockies. Hopefully it will continue to be so for a long time to come.

Small Mammals
One of the first mammals you're likely to come in contact with is the **Columbian ground squirrel,** seen throughout the park's lower elevations. The **golden-mantled ground squirrel,** similar

in size but with a striped back, is common at higher elevations or around rocky outcrops. The one collecting Engelmann spruce cones is the **red squirrel.** The **least chipmunk** is striped, but smaller than the golden-mantled squirrel. It lives in dry, rocky areas throughout the park.

Short-tailed weasels are very common, **long-tailed weasels** are rare. Look for both in higher subalpine forests. **Pikas** (commonly called rock rabbits) and **hoary marmots** (well known for their shrill whistles) live among rock slides near high-country lakes—look for them around Moraine Lake and along Bow Summit Loop. **Porcupines** are widespread and are most active at night.

Vermilion Lakes is an excellent place to view the **beaver** at work; the best time is dawn or dusk. **Muskrats** and **mink** are common in all wetlands within the park. **Badgers** and **otters** are rare but do occur in the lower reaches of the Bow River watershed.

Banff's Elk
Few visitors leave Banff without having seen elk, easily distinguished by their white rump. Elk were reported passing through the park early this century but have never been indigenous. In 1917, 57 elk were moved to the park from Yellowstone National Park. Two years later 20 more were transplanted and the new herd multiplied rapidly. Coyote, cougars, and wolves were being slaughtered under a predator-control program, leaving the elk relatively free from predators. The elk proliferated and soon became a problem as they took to wintering in the range of bighorn sheep, deer, moose, and beaver. Between 1941 and 1969, controlled slaughters of elk were conducted in an attempt to reduce the population.

Today, with wolf packs returning to the park, the elk population has stabilized at about 3,500. In summer, look for them in open meadows along the Bow Valley Parkway, along the road to Two Jack Lake, or at Vermilion Lakes. In fall you'll find hundreds grazing on the golf course until the first snow flies. Fall is rutting season and the horny bull elk become dangerous as they gather their harems. In winter small herds roam in and around town. At any time of year you may see them in Central Park or walking proudly down Banff Avenue.

Other Hoofed Residents

Moose were once common around Vermilion Lakes, but competition from the expanding elk population caused their numbers to decline—now fewer than 100 live in the park. Look for them along the Icefields Parkway near Rampart Creek or at Waterfowl Lakes.

Mule deer, named for their large ears, are most common in the southern part of the park. Watch for them along the Mt. Norquay Rd. and Bow Valley Parkway. **White-tailed deer** are much less common but seen occasionally at Saskatchewan River Crossing. The park has a population of around 25 **woodland caribou.** The small herd remains in the Dolomite Pass area and Upper Pipestone Valley and is rarely seen.

Mountain goats occupy all mountain peaks in the park, living almost the entire year in the higher subalpine and alpine regions. The most accessible place to view these high-altitude hermits is along Parker's Ridge in the far northwestern corner of the park. The park's **Rocky Mountain bighorn sheep** have for the most part lost their fear of humans and often congregate at certain spots to lick salt from the road. Look for them at the south end of the Bow Valley Parkway, between switchbacks on the Mt. Norquay Rd., and just beyond Lake Minnewanka.

Predators

Coyotes are widespread along the entire Bow River watershed. They are attracted to Vermilion Lakes by an abundance of small game, and many have permanent dens there. The **lynx** population fluctuates greatly; look for them in the backcountry during winter. **Cougars,** the largest members of the cat family, are very shy and number less than 20 in the park. They are occasionally seen along the front ranges behind Cascade Mountain. **Wolves** had been driven close to extinction by the early 1950s, but today at least six wolf packs have been reported in the park. One pack winters close to the townsite and is occasionally seen on Vermilion Lakes during this period.

Where Can I Go to See a Bear?

This commonly asked question doesn't have an answer, but the exhilaration of seeing one of these magnificent creatures in its natural habitat is unforgettable. From the road you're most likely to see **black bears,** which range in color from jet black to a cinnamon brown. Try the Bow Valley Parkway at dawn or late in the afternoon. Farther north they are often seen near the road as it passes Cirrus Mountain. **Grizzly bears** spend most of the year in remote valleys, often on south-facing slopes away from the Bow Valley Corridor. During late spring they are occasionally seen in the area of Bow Pass.

The chance of encountering a bear face-to-face in the backcountry is remote. To lessen chances even further, a number of simple precautions should be taken. Never hike alone or at dusk, make lots of noise when passing through heavy vegetation, keep a clean camp, and read the pamphlet *You are in Bear Country,* available at all park visitor centers. At the Banff Visitor Centre, 224 Banff Ave., daily trail reports list all recent bear sightings. Report any bears you see to the Warden's Office, tel. (403) 762-4506.

Reptiles and Amphibians

The **wandering garter snake** is rare and found only near the Cave and Basin, where warm water from the mineral spring flows down a shaded slope into Vermilion Lakes. Amphibians found in the park are the widespread **western toad,** the **wood frog,** commonly found along the Bow River, the rare **spotted frog,** and the **long-toed salamander,** which spawns in shallow ponds and spends summer under logs or rocks in the vicinity of its spawning grounds.

Fish

Many of Banff's lakes and rivers have at some time been stocked with a variety of fish, usually with a low rate of success. **Rainbow trout** are widespread throughout most deep lakes and large streams. **Lake trout** to 15 kilograms are found in Lake Minnewanka. **Dolly Varden** (also called bull trout) are also found in most lakes. Whitefish have been introduced as have Atlantic salmon, Quebec red trout, brook trout, black bass, and golden trout.

Early residents of Banff released a variety of tropical fish into the marshes below the Cave and Basin where they quickly multiplied. Today many thrive, but the extremely rare **Banff longnose dace,** found nowhere else in the world, is in danger of extinction.

Birds

Although over 240 species of birds have been recorded in the park, most are shy and live in heavily wooded areas. One species that definitely isn't shy is the fearless **gray jay** that haunts all campgrounds and picnic areas. Similar in color, but larger, is the **Clark's nutcracker,** which lives in higher, subalpine forests. Another common bird is the black and white **magpie. Ravens** are frequently encountered, especially around campgrounds.

A number of species of **woodpeckers** live in subalpine forests. Several species of grouse are also in residence. Most common of the grouses is the **downy ruffled grouse** seen in montane forest. The **blue grouse** and **spruce grouse** are seen at higher elevations, as is the **white-tailed ptarmigan,** which lives above the treeline (watch for them in Sunshine Meadows or on the Bow Summit Loop). A colony of **black swifts** in Johnston Canyon is one of only two in Alberta.

Good spots to view **dippers** and migrating waterfowl are Hector Lake, Vermilion Lakes, and the wetland area near Muleshoe Picnic Area. A bird blind has been set up below the Cave and Basin but is only worth visiting at dawn and dusk when the hordes of human visitors aren't around. Part of the nearby marsh stays ice free during winter, attracting birds such as **killdeer.**

Although raptors are not common in the park, **bald eagles** and **golden eagles** are present part of the year, and Alberta's provincial bird, the **great horned owl,** lives in the park year-round.

HISTORY

Although the valleys of the Canadian Rockies became ice free nearly 8,000 years ago and native people periodically hunted and traded in the area since that time, the real story of the park began with the arrival of the railroad to the area.

In 1871, Canadian Prime Minister John A. MacDonald promised to build a rail line linking British Columbia to the rest of the country as a condition of the new province joining the confederation. It wasn't until early 1883 that the line reached Calgary, pushing through to **Laggan,** now known as Lake Louise, that fall. The rail line was one of the largest engineering jobs ever undertaken in Canada, eventually proving to also be one of the most costly.

On 8 November 1883, three young railway workers—Franklin McCabe, and William and Thomas McCardell—went prospecting for gold on their day off. After crossing the Bow River by raft they came across a warm stream and traced it to its source at a small log-choked basin of warm water that had a distinct smell of sulphur. Nearby, they detected the source of the foul smell coming from a hole in the ground. Nervously, one of the three men lowered himself

WHYTE MUSEUM OF THE CANADIAN ROCKIES

Feeding bears was one of the park's early attractions.

into the hole and came across a subterranean pool of aqua-green warm water. The three men had not found gold, but something just as precious—a hot mineral spring that in time would attract wealthy customers from around the world. Word of the discovery soon got out, and the government encouraged visitors to the Cave and Basin as an ongoing source of revenue to support the new railway.

A 25-square-km reserve was established around the springs on 25 November 1885, and two years later the reserve was expanded and renamed **Rocky Mountains Park.** It was primarily a business enterprise centered around the unique springs and catering to wealthy patrons of the railway. At the turn of the century Canada had an abundance of wilderness; it certainly didn't need a park to preserve it. The only goal of Rocky Mountains Park was to generate income for the government and the Canadian Pacific Railway. Luxurious hotels such as the Banff Springs were constructed, and golf courses, the hot springs themselves, and manicured gardens were developed. It soon became Canada's best known tourist resort, attracting visitors from around the world.

In 1902 the park boundary was again expanded to include 11,440 square km of the Canadian Rockies. This dramatic expansion meant that the park became not just a tourist resort but home to existing coal-mining and logging operations and hydroelectric dams. Government officials saw no conflict of interest, actually stating that the coal mine and township at **Bankhead** added to the park's many attractions. Many of the forests were logged, providing wood for construction, while other areas were burned to allow clear sightings for surveyors' instruments.

Most of the larger mammals were killed for food and by 1915 game was scarce. The Victorian concept of wildlife was that it was either good or evil. Although an early park directive instructed superintendents to leave nature alone, it also told them to ". . . endeavor to exterminate all those animals which prey upon others."

As attitudes began to change, the government set up a Dominion Parks Branch whose first commissioner, J.B. Hawkins, believed that land set aside for parks should be used for recreation and education. Gradually resource industries were phased out. Hawkins's work culminated in the National Parks Act of 1930, which in turn led Rocky Mountains Park to be renamed Banff National Park. Present boundaries, encompassing 6,641 square km, were established in 1964.

TOWN OF BANFF

Many visitors to the national park don't realize that the town of Banff is a bustling commercial center with 7,000 permanent residents. The town's location is magnificent. It is spread out along the Bow River, extending to the lower slopes of Sulphur Mountain to the south and Tunnel Mountain to the east. In one direction is the towering face of Mt. Rundle, and in the other, framed by the buildings along Banff Ave., is Cascade Mountain. A strip of hotels and motels lines the north end of Banff Ave., while a profusion of shops, boutiques, cafes, and restaurants hugs the south end. Also at the south end, just over the Bow River, is the Park Administration Building. Here the road forks—to the right is the

historic Cave and Basin Hot Springs, to the left the Banff Springs Hotel and Sulphur Mountain Gondola. Some people are happy walking along the crowded streets or shopping in a truly unique setting; those more interested in some peace and quiet can easily slip into pristine wilderness just a five-minute walk from town.

History
After the discovery in 1883 of the Cave and Basin, just a few kilometers from the railway station then known as **Siding 29,** many commercial facilities sprang up along what is now Banff Avenue. The general manager of the C.P.R. (later to become its vice president), William Cornelius Van Horne, was

If we can't export the scenery, we'll import the tourists.

—WILLIAM C. VAN HORNE,
vice president of the
Canadian Pacific Railway

instrumental in creating a hotel business along the rail line. His most recognized achievement was the Banff Springs Hotel, which opened in 1888—the world's largest hotel at the time. Enterprising locals soon realized the area's potential and began opening restaurants and offering guided hunting and boating trips. By 1900 the bustling community of Banff had eight hotels. It was named after Banffshire, the Scottish birthplace of George Stephen, the C.P.R.'s first president.

After a restriction on automobiles in the park was lifted in 1916, Canada's best-known tourist resort also became its busiest. More and more commercial facilities sprang up, offering luxury and opulence amid the wilderness of the Canadian Rockies. Calgarians built summer cottages and the town began advertising itself as a year-round destination.

For most of its existence, the town of Banff was run as a service center for park visitors by the Canadian Parks Service in Ottawa—a government department with plenty of economic resources but little idea about how to handle the day-to-day running of a midsized town. Any inconvenience this caused park residents was off-

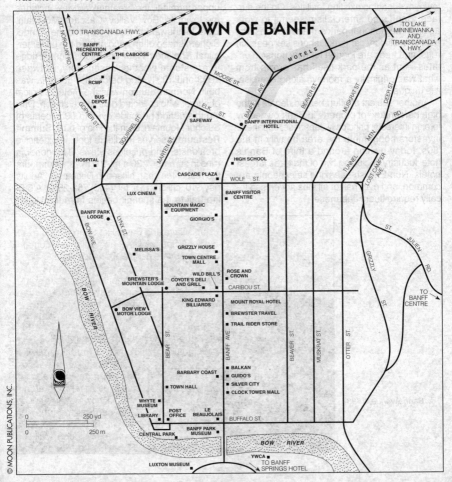

TOWN OF BANFF

set by cheap rent and subsidized services. In June 1988, Banff's residents voted to sever this tie and on 1 January 1990 Banff officially became an incorporated town, no different than any other in Alberta (except that Parks Canada controls environmental protection within the townsite).

Development and the Future
The town of Banff is the largest urban center in any national park in the world. Demand for housing continues to grow faster than development will allow, real estate prices are high, and each summer 50,000 visitors daily converge on the town, overloading existing facilities. On the surface, Banff's commercialism seems to work against the national park's mandate—visitors park in multistory car parks, shops sell bearskin rugs, and trees are logged for new housing estates—but as the park itself has grown from what was originally a moneymaking exercise, it is unique.

Another subject of often-heated debate is the high percentage of property in Banff owned by foreign interests, principally Japanese. Japanese investors bought into the area heavily in the '80s, today owning around a third of Banff's hotel industry, including two of the three largest hotels. Non-English-speaking salespeople are common, and over half of all jobs advertised locally require fluent Japanese.

These issues of continuing development, housing, and foreign ownership of property here in Canada's first national-park town will be debated well into the next century.

SIGHTS AND DRIVES

Sulphur Mountain Gondola
The easiest way to get high above town without raising a sweat is on this gondola, which rises 700 meters in eight minutes to an elevation of 2,285 meters. From the observation deck at the upper terminal, the breathtaking view includes the townsite, Bow Valley, Cascade Mountain, Lake Minnewanka, and the Fairholme Range. Bighorn sheep often hang around the upper terminal. The short **Vista Trail** leads along a ridge to a restored weather observatory. Between 1903 and 1931, long before the gondola was built, Norman Sanson was the meteorological observer who collected data at the station. During this period he made over 1,000 ascents of Sulphur Mountain, all in the line of duty. **Summit Restaurant** serves mediocre food, inexpensive breakfasts, and priceless views. The gondola runs in summer 7:30 a.m.-9 p.m., shorter hours the rest of the year; closed in December. Adults pay $10, children $5; tel. (403) 762-2523. A 5.5-km trail to the summit begins from the Upper

Banff Avenue, 1888

WHYTE MUSEUM OF THE CANADIAN ROCKIES

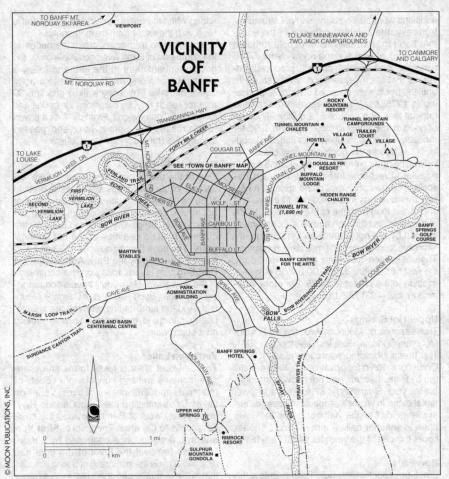

VICINITY OF BANFF

TO BANFF MT. NORQUAY SKI AREA

VIEWPOINT

TO LAKE MINNEWANKA AND TWO JACK CAMPGROUNDS

TO CANMORE AND CALGARY

MT. NORQUAY RD.

TRANSCANADA HWY.

ROCKY MOUNTAIN RESORT

TUNNEL MOUNTAIN CAMPGROUNDS

TUNNEL MOUNTAIN CHALETS

VILLAGE II

TRAILER COURT

VILLAGE

TO LAKE LOUISE

VERMILION LAKES DR.

FORTY MILE CREEK

BANFF AVE.

COUGAR ST.

TUNNEL MOUNTAIN RD.

HOSTEL

DOUGLAS FIR RESORT

SEE "TOWN OF BANFF" MAP

BUFFALO MOUNTAIN LODGE

FENLAND TRAIL

ECHO CREEK

GOPHER ST.

FIRST VERMILION LAKE

ELK ST.

MOOSE ST.

HIDDEN RANGE CHALETS

SECOND VERMILION LAKE

WOLF ST.

TUNNEL MTN. (1,690 m)

BOW RIVER

BOW AVE.

BANFF AVE.

CARIBOU ST.

ST. JULIEN RD.

TUNNEL MOUNTAIN DR.

BOW RIVER

BANFF SPRINGS GOLF COURSE

MARTIN'S STABLES

BIRCH AVE.

BUFFALO ST.

BANFF CENTRE FOR THE ARTS

MARSH LOOP TRAIL

CAVE AVE.

PARK ADMINISTRATION BUILDING

SPRAY AVE.

BOW FALLS

BOW RIVER

HOODOOS TRAIL

GOLF COURSE RD.

CAVE AND BASIN CENTENNIAL CENTRE

SUNDANCE CANYON TRAIL

BANFF SPRINGS HOTEL

SPRAY RIVER

SPRAY RIVER TRAIL

MOUNTAIN AVE.

0   1 mi
0   1 km

UPPER HOT SPRINGS

RIMROCK RESORT

SULPHUR MOUNTAIN GONDOLA

© MOON PUBLICATIONS, INC.

Hot Springs parking lot. Although it's a long slog, views on the way up are good and you'll be rewarded with a free gondola ride down—they don't check tickets at the top. From downtown the gondola is three km along Mountain Avenue. In summer **Brewster** provides shuttle service to the gondola from downtown hotels ($18 includes gondola ride). For details call (403) 762-6700.

Cave and Basin Centennial Centre
At the end of Cave Ave. is this historic site, the birthplace of Banff National Park and of the

Canadian National Parks system. It was here in 1883 that three men employed by the C.P.R. stumbled upon the hot springs now known as the Cave and Basin, and were quickly lounging in the hot water—a real luxury in the Wild West. They built a fence around the springs, constructed a crude cabin, and began the long process of establishing a claim to the site. But the government beat them to it, settling their claims for a few thousand dollars and acquiring the hot springs. Bathhouses were installed in 1887 and bathers paid 10 cents for a swim. The pools were eventually lined with concrete, and additions were built onto the original structures. Ironically, the soothing minerals in the water that had attracted millions of people to bathe here eventually caused the pools' demise. The minerals, combined with chlorine, produced sediments that ate away at the concrete structure until the pools were deemed unsafe. After closing in 1975, the pools were restored to their original look at a cost of $12 million. They reopened in 1985 only to close again in 1993 for the same reasons, coupled with flagging popularity. Although the pools are now closed for swimming, the center is still one of Banff's most popular attractions. Interpretive displays describe the hows and whys of the springs. A narrow tunnel winds into the dimly lit cave, and short trails lead from the center to the entrance of the cave and through a unique environment created by the hot water from the springs. Interpretive tours begin four times daily in summer. The site is open in summer daily 9 a.m.-6 p.m., the rest of the year daily 9:30 a.m.-5 p.m. Admission to the center is $2.25. For more information, call (403) 762-1557.

Upper Hot Springs

These springs on Mountain Ave., toward Sulphur Mountain Gondola, were first developed in 1901. The present building was completed in 1935. Once considered for privatization, they are still run by Parks Canada and are popular throughout the year. Swimming is $7, lockers and towel rental extra. In winter therapeutic massages are available for $17 per half hour. The facility is open in summer daily 9 a.m.-11 p.m., shorter hours the rest of the year; tel. (403) 762-1515.

Bow Falls

Small but spectacular, Bow Falls is below the Banff Springs Hotel, only a short walk from downtown. The waterfall is the result of a dramatic change in the course of the Bow River brought about by glaciation. At one time the river flowed north of Tunnel Mountain and out of the mountains via the valley of Lake Minnewanka. As the glaciers retreated they left terminal moraines, forming natural dams and changing the course of the river. Eventually the backed-up water found an outlet here between Tunnel Mountain and the northwest ridge of Mt. Rundle. The falls are most spectacular in late

spring when the entire Bow Valley watershed is filled with the water from melting snow.

To get there from town, cross the bridge at the south end of Banff Ave., scramble down the grassy embankment to the left, and follow a pleasant trail along the Bow River to a point above the falls. This easy walk is one km (30 minutes) each way. By car, cross the bridge and follow Golf Course signs. From the falls a paved road crosses the Spray River and passes through the Banff Springs Golf Course.

Cascade Gardens

One of the earliest entrepreneurs to take advantage of the hot springs was Dr. R.G. Brett. In 1886 he opened a private spa and hospital that became known as Brett's Sanatorium. It accommodated 90 guests, drawn to Banff by the claimed healing qualities of the hot springs' water. The hotel burned down in 1933 and was replaced in 1936 by the **Park Administration Building** that stands today on the south side of the Bow River. Here you'll have a commanding view along Banff Ave. and of Cascade Mountain. And the surrounding gardens are immaculately manicured, making for enjoyable strolling on a sunny day.

Vermilion Lakes

This series of shallow lakes forms an expansive montane wetland supporting a variety of mammals and 238 species of birds. Vermilion Lakes Dr., paralleling the TransCanada Hwy. immediately west of Banff, provides the easiest access to the area. The level of **First Vermilion Lake** was once controlled by a dam. Since its removal the level of the lake has dropped. This is the beginning of a long process that will eventually see the area evolve into a floodplain forest such as is found along the Fenland Trail. **Second** and **Third Vermilion Lakes** have a higher water level that is controlled naturally by beaver dams. Near First Vermilion Lake is an active osprey nest. The entire area is excellent for wildlife viewing, especially in winter when it provides habitat for elk, coyote, and the occasional wolf.

Mount Norquay Road

One of the best views of town accessible by car is on this road which switchbacks steeply to the

Vermilion Lakes in winter

base of **Banff Mt. Norquay,** the local ski area. On the way up are several lookouts, including one near the top where bighorn sheep often graze.

To Lake Minnewanka

Lake Minnewanka Rd. begins where Banff Ave. ends at the northeast end of town. An alternative to driving along Banff Ave. is to take Buffalo St., opposite the Banff Park Museum, and follow it around Tunnel Mountain, passing the hostel, campground, and a number of viewpoints of the north face of Mt. Rundle, rising vertically from the forested valley below. This road eventually rejoins Banff Ave. at the Rocky Mountain Resort. The first road to the right after passing under the TransCanada Hwy. leads to **Cascade Ponds,** a popular day-use area. The next turnout along this road is at **Lower Bankhead.** During the early 1900s, Bankhead was a booming mining town producing 200,000 tons of coal a year. The poor quality of coal and bitter labor disputes led to the mine's closure in 1922. Soon after, all the buildings were moved or demolished. Although for many years the mine had brought prosperity to the park, peoples' perceptions changed. The National Parks Act of 1930, which prohibited the establishment of mining claims in national parks, was greeted with little animosity. From the parking lot at Lower Bankhead, a 1.1-km interpretive trail leads through the industrial section of the town and past an old mine train. The town's 1,000 residents lived on the other side of the road at **Upper Bankhead.** Just before the Upper Bankhead turnoff the foundation of the Holy Trinity Church can be seen on the side of the hill to the right. Not much remains of Upper Bankhead. It is now a day-use area with picnic tables, kitchen shelters, and firewood. Through the meadow to the west of here are some large slag heaps, concealed mine entrances, and various stone foundations.

Lake Minnewanka

Meaning "Lake of the Water Spirit," Minnewanka is the largest body of water in Banff National Park. **Mt. Inglismaldie** (2,964 meters) and the **Fairholme Range** form an imposing backdrop. The reservoir was first constructed in 1912, and additional dams were built in 1922 and 1941 to supply hydroelectric power to Banff. Minnewanka Landing was a resort village that was submerged when the most recent dam went in. It's now a popular spot for scuba diving. The lake is great for fishing (lake trout to 15 kilograms) and is the only one in the park where motorboats are allowed. Easy walking trails lead along the western shore, and a 90-minute cruise departs from the dock every two hours. **Brewster** offers this cruise combined with a bus tour from Banff for $40 per person.

From Lake Minnewanka the road continues along the reservoir wall—passing a commemorative plaque to the Palliser Expedition and a herd of bighorn sheep—to **Johnson Lake,** with good fishing and swimming, as well as lakeside picnic facilities.

BOW VALLEY PARKWAY

Two roads link Banff to Lake Louise. The Trans-Canada Hwy. is the quicker route, more popular with through traffic. The other is the more scenic 51-km Bow Valley Parkway, which branches off the TransCanada Hwy. five km west of Banff. Cyclists will appreciate this road's two long divided sections and low speed limit (60 kph). Along this route are a number of impressive viewpoints, interpretive displays, picnic areas, good hiking, great opportunities for viewing wildlife, a hostel, three lodges, campgrounds, and one of the park's best restaurants (see "Accommodations" and "Food," below).

As you enter the parkway, you pass the quiet **Fireside** picnic area beside a creek and an interpretive display describing how the Bow Valley was formed. At **Backswamp Viewpoint,** you can look upstream to the site of a former dam, now a swampy wetland filled with aquatic vegetation. Farther along the road is another wetland at **Muleshoe.** This wetland consists of oxbow lakes that were formed when the Bow River changed its course and abandoned its meanders for a more direct path. Across the parkway is a one-km trail that climbs to a viewpoint overlooking the valley. (The slope around this trail is infested with wood ticks during summer so be sure to check yourself carefully after hiking in this area.) To the east, **Hole-in-the-wall** is visible. This large-mouthed cave was created by the Bow Glacier that once filled the valley and whose meltwater dissolved the soft limestone bedrock as it receded. It is known as a solution cave.

Beyond Muleshoe the road inexplicably divides for only a few meters. A large white spruce stood on the island until it blew down in 1984. The story goes that while the road was being constructed a surly foreman was asleep in the shade of the tree, and not daring to rouse him workers cleared the roadway around him. The road then passes through particularly hilly terrain, part of a mass rock slide that occurred around 8,000 years ago.

Continuing down the parkway you'll pass the following sights.

Johnston Canyon

Johnston Creek drops over a series of spectacular waterfalls here, deep within the chasm it has carved into the limestone bedrock. The canyon is not nearly as deep as Maligne Canyon in Jasper National Park (30 meters at its deepest, compared to 50 meters at Maligne), but the raised boardwalk that leads to the falls has been built through the depths of the canyon rather than along its lip, making it seem just as spectacular. The lower falls are one km from Johnston Canyon Resort. Other falls are passed along the trail as it continues to weave its way through the canyon to the **Ink Pots,** mineral springs whose sediments reflect sunlight, producing a brilliant aqua color. While in the canyon look for nesting great gray owls and black swifts.

Silver City

At the west end of **Moose Meadows** a small plaque marks the site of Silver City. At its peak this boomtown had a population of 2,000, more than Calgary had at the time. The city was founded by John Healy, who also founded the notorious Fort Whoop-Up in Lethbridge. During its heady days, five mines were operating, extracting not silver but ore rich in copper and lead. The town had a half dozen hotels, four or five stores, two real-estate offices, and a station on the transcontinental rail line when its demise began. Two men, named Patton and Pettigrew, salted their mine with gold and silver ore to attract investors. After selling 2,000 shares at $5 each they vanished, leaving investors with a useless mine. Investment in the town ceased, mines closed, and the people left. Only one man refused to leave. His name was James Smith but he was known to everyone as Joe. In 1887 when Silver City came under the jurisdiction of the National Parks Service, Joe was allowed to remain. And he did so, friend to everyone including Stoney Indians, Father Albert Lacombe who occasionally stopped by, well-known Banff guide Tom Wilson, and of course to the animals who grazed around his cabin. By 1926 he was unable to trap or hunt due to failing eyesight, and many people tried to persuade him to leave. It wasn't until 1937 that he finally moved to a Calgary retirement home where he died soon after.

Castle Mountain

Castle Mountain to Lake Louise

After leaving the former site of Silver City, the aptly named Castle Mountain comes into view. It's one of the park's most recognizable peaks and most interesting geographical features. The mountain consists of very old rock (approximately 500 million years old) sitting atop much younger rock (200 million years old). This unusual situation occurred as the mountains were forced upward by pressure below the earth's surface, thrusting the older rock up and over the younger rock in places.

The road skirts the base of the mountain, passes **Castle Mountain Village,** and climbs a small hill to **Storm Mountain Viewpoint,** which provides more stunning views and a picnic area. The next commercial facility is **Baker Creek Chalets and Bistro,** an excellent spot for a meal, then another viewpoint at **Morant's Curve,** from where **Temple Mountain** is visible. After passing another picnic area and a chunk of Precambrian shield, the road rejoins the TransCanada Hwy. at Lake Louise.

RAINY DAY BANFF

Banff Park Museum

Although displays of stuffed animals are not usually associated with national parks, this museum, at 93 Banff Ave., tel. (403) 762-1558, provides an insight into the park's early history. Visitors during the Victorian era were eager to see the park's animals without actually having to venture into the bush. A lack of roads and scarcity of large game due to hunting meant that the best way to see animals was either in the game paddock, the zoo, or here in the museum. It was built in 1903, before the park had electricity—hence its "railroad pagoda" design with use of skylights on all levels. Between 1904 and 1937 the grounds behind the museum were occupied by Banff Zoo and Aviary. The zoo kept over 60 species of animals, including a polar bear.

Under the supervision of a keen naturalist, Norman Sanson, the museum's extensive collection of specimens continued to grow. As times changed it was considered outdated, and plans for its demolition were put forward in the '50s. Fortunately this didn't occur and the museum was restored for the park's 100th anniversary in 1985. The exhibits are an interesting link to the park's past and provide insight into the intricate workings of various park ecosystems. The museum is open in summer daily 10 a.m.-6 p.m., the rest of the year Mon.-Fri. 1-5 p.m., Sat.-Sun. 10 a.m.-6 p.m. Admission is $2.25. **Wonderful Wildlife Tours** of the museum take place daily at 3 p.m. The museum also has a reading room stocked with books on the park.

Luxton Museum

Looking like a stockade, this museum, to the west of the Banff Bridge at 1 Birch Ave., tel. (403) 762-2388, is dedicated to the heritage of the Indians who once inhabited the Canadian

WILD BILL PEYTO

" . . . rarely speaking—his forte was doing things, not talking about them." These words from a friend sum up one of Banff's earliest characters. These attributes, combined with his knowledge of the Canadian Rockies, earned Bill Peyto status as one of Banff's greatest guides. In 1886, at the tender age of 18, Ebenezer William Peyto left England for Canada. After traveling extensively he settled in Banff and was hired as an apprentice guide for legendary outfitter Tom Wilson. Wearing a tilted sombrero, fringed buckskin coat, cartridge belt, hunting knife, and a six-shooter, he looked more like a gunslinger than a mountain man. As his reputation as a competent guide grew, so did the stories. While guiding clients on one occasion, he led them to his cabin. Before entering, Peyto threw stones in the front door until a loud snap was heard. It was a bear trap that he'd set up to catch a certain trapper who'd been stealing his food. One of the guests commented that if caught, the trapper would surely have died. "You're damned right he would have," Bill replied. "Then I'd have known for sure it was him."

In 1900 Peyto left to fight in the Boer War and was promoted to corporal for bravery. This was revoked before it became official after they learned he'd "borrowed" an officer's jacket and several bottles of booze for the celebration. Returning to a hero's welcome in Banff he established an outfitting business and continued prospecting for copper in Simpson Pass. Although his outfitting business thrived, the death of his wife left him despondent. He built a house on Banff Avenue. Its name, "Ain't it Hell," summed up his view of life. In his later years, after being wounded in WW I, he became a warden in the Healy Creek–Sunshine

district where his exploits during the 1920s added to his already legendary name. After 20 years of service he retired, and in 1943, at the age of 75, he passed away. One of the park's most beautiful lakes is named after him, as is a glacier and one of Banff's popular watering holes, **Wild Bill's,** a designation that he would have appreciated. His face also adorns the large signs welcoming visitors to Banff.

WHYTE MUSEUM OF THE CANADIAN ROCKIES

Rockies and surrounding prairies. It was named for prominent Banff resident Norman Luxton, who had a close relationship with the natives of the area and was involved in the Banff Indian Days. He operated a trading post on the site for many years before opening the museum in 1952 with the help of the Glenbow-Alberta Institute. The museum contains memorabilia from Luxton's 60-year relationship with the Stoney Indians, as well as an elaborately decorated tepee, hunting equipment, a few stuffed animals, a realistic diorama of a buffalo jump, peace pipes, and traditional clothing. The Indian Trading Post is now one of Banff's better gift shops and is definitely worth a browse. The museum is open in summer daily 9 a.m.-9 p.m., the rest of the year 11:30 a.m.-4:30 p.m. Admission is $5.

Whyte Museum of the Canadian Rockies

The Whyte Foundation was established in the mid-'50s by local artists Peter and Catherine Whyte to help preserve artistic and historical material relating to the Canadian Rockies. Their museum opened in 1968 and has continued to grow ever since. It now houses the world's largest collection of Canadian Rockies literature and art. Included in the archives are over 4,000 volumes, oral tapes of early pioneers and outfitters, antique postcards, old cameras, manuscripts, and a large photographic collection. The highlight is the photography of Byron Harmon, whose black-and-white studies of mountain geography have shown people around the world that the Canadian Rockies are one of the most beautiful mountain destinations in the world. The downstairs gallery features changing art and photographic exhibitions. The museum also houses the library and archives of the Alpine Club of Canada. On the grounds are a number of heritage homes formerly occupied by local pioneers. The Whyte Museum is open in summer Tues.-Sat. 10 a.m.-9 p.m. and Sun.-Mon. 10 a.m.-6 p.m., the rest of the year 1-5 p.m. Admission is adult $3, senior $2. It's beside the library at 111 Bear St., tel. (403) 762-2291. Don't miss this one.

Natural History Museum

Banff's smallest museum, located upstairs in the Clock Tower Mall at 112 Banff Ave., tel. (403) 762-4747, is crammed with exhibits displaying the geological evolution of the Canadian Rockies. Highlights include a replica of Castleguard Cave (one of the largest caves in North America), an interesting slide show, rock and fossil displays, and a tacky life-size model of Bigfoot—just what you came to Banff for. It's open daily 10 a.m.-6 p.m., till 10 p.m. in summer.

Banff Centre

Located on the lower slopes of Tunnel Mountain is the Banff Centre for the Arts, whose surroundings provide inspiration for some of Canada's finest postgraduate artists. Banff Centre, as it's usually called, first opened in the summer of 1933 as a theater school, and has grown to become a prestigious institution attracting artists of many disciplines from throughout Canada. The center's **Walter Phillips Gallery** on St. Julien Rd., tel. (403) 762-6281, has changing exhibits of visual arts from throughout the world. Open Tues.-Thurs. noon-5 p.m., Fri.-Sat. noon-8 p.m., and Sunday noon-5 p.m. Activities are held on the grounds year-round. Highlights include

concerts, displays, live performances, the Banff Arts Festival, Banff Television Festival, Banff Mountain Book Festival, and Banff Festival of Mountain Films, to name a few (see "Festivals and Events" below). Call (403) 762-6100 for a program or check the *Crag and Canyon* (published weekly on Wednesday).

Banff Springs Hotel

On a terrace above a bend in the Bow River is one of the largest, grandest, and most opulent mountain-resort hotels in the world. What better way could there be to spend a rainy afternoon than to explore this turreted 20th-century castle—finding a writing desk overlooking one of the world's most photographed scenes and penning a long letter to the folks back home?

"The Springs" has grown with the town and is an integral part of its history. William Cornelius Van Horne, vice president of the C.P.R., decided that the best way of encouraging customers to travel on the newly completed rail line across the Rockies was to build a series of luxurious mountain accommodations. The largest of these was begun in 1886, as close as possible to Banff's newly discovered hot springs. The location chosen had magnificent views and was only a short carriage ride from the train station. Money was no object and architect Bruce Price began designing a mountain resort the likes of which the world had never seen. At some stage of construction his plans were misinterpreted, and much to Van Horne's shock the building was built back to front. The best guest rooms faced the forested slopes of Sulphur Mountain while the kitchen had panoramic views of the Bow Valley.

On 1 June 1888 it opened, the largest hotel in the world with 250 rooms beginning at $3.50 per night including meals. Water from the nearby hot springs was piped into the hotel's steam baths. Rumor has it that when the pipes blocked, water from the Bow River was used, secretly supplemented by bags of sulphur-smelling chemicals. Overnight, the quiet community of Banff became a destination resort for wealthy guests from around the world, and the hotel soon became one of North America's most popular accommodations. Every room was booked every day during the short summer seasons. In 1903 a wing was added, doubling the hotel's capacity. The following year a tower was added to each wing.

Guest numbers reached 22,000 in 1911, and construction of a new hotel, designed by Walter Painter, began that year. The original design—an 11-story tower joining two wings in a baronial style—was reminiscent of a Scottish castle mixed with a French country chateau. It was completed in 1928. It is this concrete-and-rock-faced, green-roofed building that stands to this day.

Don't let the hotel's opulence keep you from spending time here. Sightseeing is actually encouraged. "Building of Banff" tours are offered daily at 5 p.m. in the summer. Guides take you through the hotel, explaining its history and influence on the community. Tickets are $5 per person. Call (403) 762-2211 for details. Otherwise wander through on your own (maps are available in the lobby), admiring the 5,000 pieces of furniture and antiques (most "antiques" in public areas are reproductions), paintings, prints, tapestries, and rugs. Take in the medieval atmosphere of Mt. Stephen Hall with its lime flagstone floor, enormous windows, and large oak beams, or relax in one of 16 eateries.

The hotel is a 15-minute walk southeast of town along Spray Ave., or via the trail along the south bank of the Bow River. Horse-drawn buggies take passengers from the Trail Rider Store at 132 Banff Ave. to the Springs for $35; **Banff Explorer** buses leave downtown twice an hour, $1.50.

Gifts and Galleries

Banff has a great selection of galleries displaying the work of mostly Canadian artists. **Art of the Wild**, tel. (403) 762-2999, and **Canada House**, 201 Bear St., tel. (403) 762-3757, are two galleries in one, featuring Canadian landscape and wildlife works and native art. **The Quest for Handcrafts**, 105 Banff Ave., tel. (403) 762-2722, **Marika Jewellery and Fine Art**, 94 Banff Ave., tel. (403) 782-2678, and the smaller **The Gallery**, 210 Bear St., tel. (403) 762-5990, contain a diverse range of affordable Canadian paintings and crafts.

HIKING

After experiencing the international thrills of Banff Avenue, many people will want to see the *real* Banff—the reason that millions of visitors

flock here, thousands take low-paying jobs just to stay here, and those who become severely addicted cut ties with the outside world, raise families, and live happily ever after here. Although many landmarks can be seen from the roadside, to really experience the park's personality you'll need to go for a hike. One of the best things about Banff's 80-odd hiking trails is the variety. From short interpretive walks originating in town, to easy hikes rewarded by spectacular vistas, to a myriad of overnight backcountry opportunities—Banff's trails offer something for everyone. Before attempting any hikes you should visit the **Banff Visitor Centre**, 224 Banff Ave., tel. (403) 762-1550, where staff can advise you on the condition of trails and closures. If you are planning an overnight trip into the backcountry you *must* pick up a permit from here before heading out; $6 per person per night.

Most of the trails listed below start in or near town; the last four start out of town, on the way toward Lake Louise.

Fenland
- Length: 2 km (30 minutes) roundtrip
- Elevation gain: none
- Rating: easy

This short interpretive trail begins at the Forty Mile Creek Picnic Area 300 meters north of the rail line along Mt. Norquay Road. A brochure, available at the trailhead, explains the various stages in the transition between wetland and a floodplain forest of spruce as you progress around the loop. This fen environment is prime habitat for many species of birds. The work of beavers can be seen along the trail and elk are here during winter. This trail is also a popular shortcut for joggers and cyclists heading for Vermilion Lakes.

Tunnel Mountain
- Length: 2.3 km (30-60 minutes) one-way
- Elevation gain: 300 meters
- Rating: easy/moderate

Accessible from town, this short hike is an easy climb to one of the park's lower peaks. The trailhead is on St. Julien Rd., 350 meters to the south of Wolf Street. The trail ascends the western flank of Tunnel Mountain through a forest of lodgepole pine, switchbacking past some viewpoints before reaching a ridge just below the summit. Here the trail turns northward, climbing through a forest of Douglas fir to the summit (which is partially treed, preventing 360-degree views).

Bow River/Hoodoos
- Length: 4.8 km (60-90 minutes) one-way
- Elevation gain: minimal
- Rating: easy

From the Bow River Viewpoint on Tunnel Mountain Dr., the trail descends to the Bow River, passing under the sheer east face of Tunnel Mountain. It then follows the river for a short distance before climbing into a meadow where deer and elk often graze. From this perspective the north face of Mt. Rundle is particularly imposing. As the trail climbs you'll hear the traffic on Tunnel Mountain Rd. long before you see it. The trail ends at **hoodoos,** strange limestone-and-gravel columns jutting mysteriously out of the forest. An alternative to returning the same way is to catch the **Banff Explorer** bus from Tunnel Mountain Campgrounds. It leaves every half hour ($1.50).

Sundance Canyon
- Length: 4.4 km (90 minutes) one-way
- Elevation gain: 100 meters
- Rating: easy

Sundance Canyon is a rewarding destination accessed from the Cave and Basin Centennial Centre. Unfortunately the first three km are along a paved road closed to traffic (but not bikes) and hard on your soles. Occasional glimpses of the Sawback Range are afforded by breaks in the forest. The road ends at a shaded picnic area from where the 2.4-km Sundance Loop begins. Sundance Creek was once a larger river whose upper drainage basin was diverted by glacial action. Its powerful waters have eroded into the soft bedrock, forming a spectacular overhanging canyon whose bed is strewn with large boulders that have tumbled in.

Spray River
- Length: 6 km (2 hours) one-way
- Elevation gain: 70 meters
- Rating: easy/moderate

This trail follows one of the many fire roads in the park. It is not particularly interesting, but it's accessible from Banff and makes a pleasant way to escape the crowds. For serious hikers this trail provides access to the rugged and remote southern reaches of the park. From the Bow Falls parking lot walk along Golf Course Rd. to the green of the first hole on the right. From there a trail heads uphill into the forest. It follows the Spray River closely—when not in sight the river can always be heard. For those so inclined, a river crossing one km from the golf course allows for a shorter loop. Continuing south, the trail climbs a bluff for a good view of the Banff Springs Hotel and Bow Valley. The return journey is straightforward with occasional views, ending at a locked gate behind the Banff Springs Hotel, a short walk to Bow Falls.

Western Slope of Mount Rundle
- Length: 5.4 km (2 hours) one-way
- Elevation gain: 500 meters
- Rating: moderate

At 2,950 meters, Mt. Rundle is one of the park's dominant peaks. Climbing to its summit is possible without ropes, but previous scrambling experience is advised. An alternative is to ascend the mountain's western slope along an easy-to-follow trail that ends just over 1,000 vertical meters before the summit. The trail follows the Spray River Trail (see above) before branching off left 700 meters from Golf Course Rd. and climbing steadily, breaking out of the enclosed forest after 2.5 km. The trail ends in a gully from where the undefined route to the summit begins.

Stoney Squaw
- Length: 2.4-km loop (1 hour roundtrip)
- Elevation gain: 180 meters
- Rating: easy

Stoney Squaw's 1,884-meter summit is dwarfed by Cascade Mountain, directly behind it. To get to the trailhead, follow Mt. Norquay Rd. to a parking lot at the ski area. Immediately to the right of the entrance, a small sign marks the trail. The narrow trail passes through a thick forest of lodgepole pine and spruce before breaking out into the open near the summit. The sweeping panorama includes Vermilion Lakes, the Bow Valley, Banff, Spray River Valley, Mt. Rundle, Lake Minnewanka, and the imposing face of Cascade Mountain (2,998 meters). The return trail follows the northwest slope of Stoney

Squaw to an old ski run at the opposite end of the parking lot.

Cascade Amphitheatre

- Length: 6.6 km (2-3 hours) one-way
- Elevation gain: 610 meters
- Rating: moderate/difficult

This enormous cirque and the subalpine meadows directly behind Cascade Mountain are one of the most rewarding destinations for hiking in the Banff area. The demanding trail begins by the Banff Mt. Norquay day lodge at the end of Mt. Norquay Road. From parking lot no. 3, the trail skirts the base of a number of ski lifts, following an old road to the floor of Forty Mile Valley. Keep right at all trail junctions. One km after crossing Forty Mile Creek the trail begins switchbacking up the western flank of Cascade Mountain through a forest of lodgepole pine. Along the way are breathtaking views of Mt. Louis's sheer east face. After the trail levels off it enters a magnificent U-shaped valley and the amphitheater begins to define itself. The trail becomes indistinct in the subalpine meadow, which is carpeted in colorful wildflowers during summer. Farther up the valley, vegetation thins out as the boulder-strewn talus slopes cover the ground. It you sit still long enough on these rocks, marmots and pikas will slowly appear, emitting shrill whistles before disappearing again.

The most popular route to the summit of 2,998-meter Cascade Mountain is along the southern ridge of the amphitheater wall. It is a long scramble up scree slopes—made more difficult by a false summit—and should be attempted only by experienced scramblers.

C Level Cirque

- Length: 4 km (90 minutes) one-way
- Elevation gain: 455 meters
- Rating: moderate

This trail begins from Upper Bankhead Picnic Area on the Lake Minnewanka Rd. and is named for an abandoned mine along its route. It climbs steadily through a forest of lodgepole pine, aspen, and spruce to a pile of tailings and broken-down concrete walls. Soon after is a panoramic view of Lake Minnewanka, then the trail reenters the forest before ending in a small cirque where there are views down the Bow Valley to Canmore and beyond. The cirque is

carved into the eastern face of Cascade Mountain where snow often lingers until July. When the snow melts, the lush soil is covered in a carpet of colorful wildflowers.

Aylmer Lookout

- Length: 12 km (4 hours) one-way
- Elevation gain: 810 meters
- Rating: moderate/difficult

The first eight-km stretch of this trail follows the northern shore of Lake Minnewanka from the day-use area to a junction. The right fork leads to a campground, the left climbs steeply to the site of an old fire tower on top of an exposed ridge. The deep blue waters of Lake Minnewanka are visible backed by the imposing peaks of Mt. Girouard (2,995 meters) and Mt. Inglismaldie (2,964 meters). Bighorn sheep are often seen grazing in this area. From here a trail forks left and continues climbing to the alpine tundra of Aylmer Pass.

Cory Pass

- Length: 5.8 km (2.5 hours) one-way
- Elevation gain: 920 meters
- Rating: moderate/difficult

This strenuous hike from the Fireside Picnic Area at the Banff end of the Bow Valley Parkway has a rewarding objective—a magnificent view of dogtoothed Mt. Louis. The towering slab of limestone rises over 500 meters from the valley below. Just over one km from the trailhead the trail divides. The left fork climbs steeply across an open slope to an uneven ridge that it follows before ascending yet another steep slope to Cory Pass—a wild, windy, desolate area surrounded in jagged peaks dominated by Mt. Louis. An alternative to returning along the same trail is continuing into **Gargoyle Valley,** following the base of Mt. Edith before ascending to Edith Pass and returning to the junction one km from the picnic area. Total distance for this trip would be 13 km, a long day considering the steep climbs and descents involved.

Bourgeau Lake

- Length: 7.6 km (2.5 hours) one-way
- Elevation gain: 730 meters
- Rating: moderate

This trail follows Wolverine Creek from a parking area three km west of Sunshine Village Junction on the TransCanada Hwy. to a small subalpine lake nestled at the base of an impressive limestone amphitheater. Although the trail is moderately steep, plenty of distractions along the way are worthy of a stop (and rest). Across the Bow Valley the Sawback Range is easy to distinguish. As the forest of lodgepole pine turns to spruce, the trail passes under the cliffs of Mt. Bourgeau and crosses Wolverine Creek (below a spot where it tumbles photogenically over exposed bedrock). After strenuous switchbacks, the trail climbs into the cirque containing Bourgeau Lake. As you continue around the lake's rocky shore you'll hear the colonies of noisy pikas, even if you don't see them.

Rock Isle Lake
- Length: 8 km (2.5 hours) one-way
- Elevation gain: 590 meters
- Rating: moderate

Sunshine Meadows, straddling the Continental Divide, is a unique and beautiful region of the Canadian Rockies. Large amounts of precipitation

ruffed grouse, commonly seen in subalpine forests

create a lush cover of vegetation during the short summer season—over 300 species of wildflowers alone have been recorded. For 60 years the meadows have been a favorite area for downhill skiing—it wasn't until 1984 that summer activities were promoted. Suddenly, instead of a few hundred adventurous souls willing to hike the 6.5-km road into the meadows, tens of thousands of visitors were whisked onto the fragile alpine tundra by gondola. In 1992 Sunshine Village terminated its summer gondola service and the meadows are quiet once again.

To get to the base station from Banff follow the TransCanada Hwy. nine km west to Sunshine Village Rd., which continues another nine km to the Gondola Base Station. The road to the meadows is closed to public traffic and climbs steadily for 6.5 km to Sunshine Village. From there the Rock Isle Lake Trail passes the Strawberry Chairlift and climbs out of the valley into an alpine meadow covered in a colorful carpet of fireweed, glacier lilies, mountain avens, white mountain heather, and forget-me-nots. Mount Assiniboine (3,611 meters), known as the "Matterhorn of the Rockies," is easily distinguished to the southeast. On the descent to the lake are various viewpoints and around the shoreline are benches and an observation deck.

In summer, **White Mountain Adventures** offers a shuttle service for a limited number of hikers from Banff (daily at 9:30 a.m., $35 roundtrip) and the Sunshine Village parking lot (daily at 10 a.m., 11 a.m., and 1 p.m., $15 roundtrip) to the village itself. If you take the 10 a.m. shuttle, a two-hour guided hike is included in the rate. Advance reservations are required: call (403) 678-4099.

Shadow Lake
- Length: 14.3 km (4.5 hours) one-way
- Elevation gain: 440 meters
- Rating: moderate

Shadow is one of the many impressive subalpine lakes along the Continental Divide but is also popular as a base for a great variety of day trips. The trail begins at the Redearth Creek Parking Area, 20 km west of Banff on the TransCanada Highway. It follows the old Redearth fire road for 11 km before forking right and climbing into the forest. The campground is two km beyond this junction and 500 meters farther is **Shadow Lake**

Lodge (see "Backcountry Huts and Lodges" in the "Accommodations" section, below, for details). The lake itself is nearly two km long, and from its southern shore trails lead to Ball Pass, Gibbon Pass, and Haiduk Lake.

Castle Lookout
- Length: 3.7 km (90 minutes) one-way
- Elevation gain: 520 meters
- Rating: moderate

However you travel through the Bow Valley you can't help but be impressed by Castle Mountain rising proudly from the forest below. This trail takes you above the treeline on the mountain's west face to the site of Mt. Eisenhower fire lookout, abandoned in the 1970s and burned in the 1980s. The trailhead is on the Bow Valley Parkway, five km northwest of Castle Junction. The trail follows a wide pathway for 1.5 km to an abandoned cabin in a forest of lodgepole pine and spruce. It then becomes narrower and steeper, switchbacking through a meadow before climbing through a narrow band of rock and leveling off near the lookout site. From here a magnificent panorama of the Bow Valley is afforded in both directions. Storm Mountain can be seen directly across the valley.

Rockbound Lake
- Length: 8.4 km (2.5 hours) one-way
- Elevation gain: 760 meters
- Rating: moderate/difficult

The trailhead for this strenuous hike is just east of Castle Junction on the Bow Valley Parkway. For the first five km it follows an old fire road along the southern flanks of Castle Mountain. Early in the season or after heavy rain, this section can be boggy. Glimpses of surrounding peaks ease the pain of the steady climb as the trail narrows. **Tower Lake** is reached after eight km. The trail skirts it to the right and climbs a steep slope. From the ridge Rockbound Lake comes into view and the reason for its name immediately becomes apparent. Good views can be achieved by scrambling up any of the nearby slopes.

OTHER RECREATION

Mountain Biking
Whether you have your own bike or you rent one from the many bicycle shops in town, cycling in

the park is for everyone. The roads to Lake Minnewanka, Mt. Norquay, and along the Bow Valley Parkway are all popular routes. A number of trails radiating from Banff townsite and ending deep in the backcountry have been designated as bicycle trails. These include Sundance (3.7 km one-way), Rundle Riverside (eight km one-way), Spray River Loop (43 km roundtrip), and Cascade Trail (nine km one-way). Other trails are at Redearth Creek, Lake Louise, and in the northeastern reaches of the park near Saskatchewan River Crossing. Before heading into the backcountry, pick up the *Trail Bicycling Guide* from the Banff Visitor Centre. Riders are particularly susceptible to sudden bear encounters. Be alert and make loud noises when passing through heavy vegetation.

Bactrax Bike Rentals, in the Banff Ptarmigan Inn, 339 Banff Ave., tel. (403) 762-8177, has high-quality mountain bikes for $5-7 per hour and $17-25 per day, the best deal in town. Rollerblade rentals are $10 per day. Bactrax also offers mountain bike tours, including an easy two-hour pedal along Vermilion Lakes in search of wildlife then to a lookout of Banff Springs Hotel for $20 per person. The shop is open daily 8 a.m.-8 p.m.

Horseback Riding
Jim and Bill Brewster led Banff's first paying guests into the backcountry on horseback over 100 years ago. Today visitors are still able to enjoy the park on this traditional form of transportation. **Warner Guiding & Outfitting,** P.O. Box 2280, Banff, AB T0L 0C0, tel. (403) 762-4551, offers a great variety of trips. Their main office is in the Trail Rider Store at 132 Banff Ave., although most trips depart from **Martin's Stables,** tel. (403) 762-2832, behind the recreation grounds on Birch Ave., and **Banff Springs Corral,** tel. (403) 762-2848, along Spray Avenue. One-hour rides are $21, two hours $36, three hours $46. Other day trips include the three-hour **Mountain Breakfast Ride** that includes a hearty breakfast along the trail, $49; **Explorer,** a six-and-a-half-hour ride up the Spray River Valley, $95; and the **Evening Steak Fry,** a three-hour ride with a steak dinner along the trail, $49. Overnight trips to established backcountry camps and lodges are also available; rates begin at $285 including all meals, one

night's accommodation at Sundance Lodge, and the horse, of course.

Whitewater Rafting and Canoeing
Anyone looking for whitewater-rafting action will want to run the Kicking Horse River, which flows down the western slopes of the Canadian Rockies into British Columbia. Many operators based in Banff offer exhilarating trips down this river, all of which include transportation from Banff. **Wild Water Adventures,** tel. (403) 522-2211, leads full-day trips beginning as far up river as possible. The price of $89 also includes a narrated bus trip and a gourmet lunch. Half-day trips begin from Lake Louise at 8:30 a.m. and 1:30 p.m. Other operators are: **Kootenay River Runners,** 204 Caribou St., tel. (403) 762-5385; **Rocky Mountain Raft Tours,** tel. (403) 762-3632; and **Whitewater Voyageurs,** 339 Banff Ave., tel. (403) 762-8177, who raft the exciting Lower Canyon of the Kicking Horse River. Rocky Mountain Raft Tours also offers one-hour ($21) and three-hour ($38) float trips down the Bow River. **Banff Canoe Rentals,** on the corner of Wolf St. and Bow Ave., rents canoes for use on the Bow River, Vermilion Lakes, or Lake Minnewanka. **Adrenalin Descents,** in the Banff Ptarmigan Inn at 339 Banff Ave., tel. (403) 762-8177, rents whitewater kayaks and operates varying kayaking courses.

Fishing and Boating
The finest fishing in the park is in Lake Minnewanka, where lake trout as large as 15 kilograms have been caught. One way to ensure a good catch is through **Minnewanka Tours,** tel. (403) 762-3473, which offers three-and-a-half-hour guided fishing expeditions; $150 for one or two persons. Fishing boats and tackle are also for rent. **Performance Ski and Sports,** 208 Bear St., tel. (403) 762-8222, also rents tackle. Before fishing anywhere in the park you need a National Park fishing license ($6 per week, $13 per year), available from the Banff Visitor Centre and sport shops around town.

Golfing
Banff Springs Golf Course, spread out along the Bow River between Mt. Rundle and Tunnel Mountain, is considered one of the world's most scenic. The original 18 championship holes were designed by Stanley Thompson in 1928 and have been extended to 27. Not only is the course breathtakingly beautiful, but it's also very challenging for all levels of golfer. Pick up a copy of the book *The World's Greatest Golf Holes,* and there'll be a picture of the fourth hole on the Rundle Nine. It's a par three, over Devil's Cauldron 70 meters below, to a small green backed by the sheer face of Mt. Rundle rising vertically over 1,000 meters above the putting surface. Another unique feature of the course is the abundance of wildlife. Each fall hundreds of elk gather on the course, and there's always the chance of seeing coyotes, deer, or black bears scurrying across in front of you.

Green fees are $74 for 18 holes including a cart, $30 for nine holes with no cart. Free shuttle buses run from the Banff Springs Hotel to the clubhouse, located in the middle of the course. There you'll find club rentals ($25), three putting greens, a driving range, pro shop, cafe, and restaurant. Booking tee times well in advance is essential; tel. (403) 762-6801.

Indoor Recreation
Banff Springs Hotel, tel. (403) 762-2211, has a four-lane bowling center; games are $2.50 per person. **King Edward Billiards,** upstairs at 137 Banff Ave., tel. (403) 762-4629, is a large, clean pool hall. Tables are $8 per hour. The **Lux Cinema** at 229 Bear St., tel. (403) 762-8595, shows new releases for $7.

Banff's only water slide is in the Douglas Fir Resort on Tunnel Mountain Dr., tel. (403) 762-5591. The two slides are indoors and the admission price of $7.50 (under six free) includes use of a jacuzzi and exercise room. It's open Mon.-Fri. 2-9:30 p.m., Sat.-Sun. 10 a.m.-9:30 p.m. If you have energy to burn, **Banff Rocky Mountain Resort,** tel. (403) 762-5531, has a small gym and pool open to nonguests, $6.50 per session. **Sally Borden Recreation Building** in the Banff Centre has an exercise room, gymnasium, squash courts, pool, and sauna; $8 per day, tel. (403) 762-6461; open daily 6:30 a.m.-11 p.m.

WINTERTIME

Of Alberta's six world-class ski resorts, three are in Banff National Park. Banff Mt. Norquay is a small but steep hill overlooking the town of Banff; Sunshine Village is located high in the mountains on the Continental Divide, catching more than its share of fluffy white powder; and Lake Louise, Canada's largest ski area, is spread over four distinct mountain faces providing something for everyone (for details of the Lake Louise ski area, see "Wintertime" under "Lake Louise," below). Apart from an abundance of snow the resorts have something else in common—spectacular views—alone worth the price of a lift ticket.

In fact the entire park transforms itself into a winter playground covered in an impossibly white blanket of snow from November till May. You'll always find something to do: cross-country skiing, ice-skating, snowshoeing, dogsledding, or just relaxing. Crowds are nonexistent and hotels reduce rates by up to 50%—reason enough to venture into the mountains.

Banff Mt. Norquay

The steep eastern slopes of Mt. Norquay had been attracting local skiers for 20 years before Canada's first chairlift was installed on its face in 1948. Ever since then, the resort has had an experts-only reputation, mainly because of terrain serviced by the North American Chair, including the famous double-black-diamond Lone Pine run. But an express quad installed in 1990 opened up new intermediate terrain and made the resort—located only six km from Banff—a favorite with shredders and cruisers alike. Lift tickets are $33 per day; lift, lesson, and rental packages cost about the same. Night skiing is offered on Wednesday. A free shuttle bus picks skiers up from Banff hotels for the short ride up the hill. For more information on the resort call (403) 762-4421, or in Calgary call the 24-hour Snowphone, tel. (403) 221-8259.

Sunshine Village

The skiing at Sunshine has lots going for it—over six meters of snow annually (no need for snowmaking up here), wide-open bowls, a season stretching for nearly 200 days, skiing in two provinces, and the only slope-side accommodations in the park.

The first people to ski the Sunshine Meadows were two local men, Cliff White and Cyril Paris, who became lost going over Citadel Pass in the spring of 1929 and returned to Banff with stories of deep snow and ideal slopes for skiing. In the following years, a C.P.R. cabin was used as a base for skiing in the area. In 1938 the Canadian National Ski Championships were held here, and in 1942 a portable lift was constructed. The White family was synonymous with the Sunshine area for many years, running the lodge and ski area while Brewster buses negotiated the steep narrow road that led to the meadows. In 1980 a gondola was installed to whisk skiers six km from the parking area in Bourgeau Valley to the alpine village. More recently, new high-speed quads have opened up the north face of Goats Eye Mountain and made the trip to the summit of 2,730-meter Lookout Mountain much quicker.

The area has a remarkable variety of terrain serviced by a gondola and nine lifts, including the fastest chairlift in the Rockies. Lift tickets are $42 per day, seniors $35, and those under six ski free. Two days of skiing and one night's lodging at slopeside Sunshine Inn costs from $80 per person per day.

The inn has a restaurant, lounge, game room, and jacuzzi. For more information call (403) 762-5561 or (800) 661-1676. Transportation from Banff to the hill is $15 roundtrip; call the hill or inquire at major hotels for the timetable.

Ski Rentals

Each resort has rental facilities, but getting your gear down in town is often easier. **Snowtips,** in the Banff Ptarmigan Inn at 339 Banff Ave., tel. (403) 762-8177, has a large selection. Basic packages—skis, poles, and boots—are $11 per day, but most skiers prefer the High Performance packages, which range $15-21 per day. Snowtips also has snowboards for $19 per day, cross-country skis for $7 per day, and full repair services at reasonable prices.

Heli-Skiing

Although there is no heli-skiing in Banff National Park, **R.K. Heli-ski** books trips to areas outside the park from desks in the Banff Springs Hotel, 304 Caribou St., tel. (403) 762-3771, and in the Chateau Lake Louise. Each morning during winter, the company's bus leaves Banff to take skiers to Panorama in British Columbia for a day of helicopter skiing high in the Purcell

Mountains. For further information call (604) 342-3889. Banff is also headquarters for the world's largest heli-skiing operation, **C.M.H. Heli-skiing,** founded by Hans Gmoser. Seven-day packages in BC's interior mountain ranges begin at around $2,800 per person. For more information write to C.M.H. Heli-skiing, P.O. Box 1660, Banff, AB T0L 0C0; tel. (403) 762-7100 or (800) 661-0252. **Mike Wiegele Helicopter Skiing,** whose lodge at Blue River is a base for heli-skiing in the Monashee and Cariboo Mountains, is also based in Banff. For information write to P.O. Box 249, Banff, call (403) 762-5548, or drop by the shop on the corner of Banff Ave. and Caribou Street.

Cross-Country Skiing

No better way of experiencing the park's winter delights exists than skiing through the landscape on cross-country skis. Many summer hiking trails are groomed for winter travel. The most popular areas are Johnson Lake, Golf Course Rd., Spray River, Sundance Canyon, and near Lake Minnewanka. The booklet *Cross-country Skiing—Nordic Trails in Banff National Park,* is available for $1 from the Banff Visitor Centre at 224 Banff Avenue. Weather forecasts (tel. 403-762-2088) and avalanche hazard reports (tel. 403-762-1460) are posted here also.

Rental packages are available from **Performance Ski & Sports** at 208 Bear St., tel. (403) 762-8222; **Snowtips,** with outlets in the Banff Ptarmigan Inn, tel. (403) 762-8177, and Travellers Inn; and **Mountain Magic Equipment** at 224 Bear St., tel. (403) 762-2591. Expect to pay $7-12 per day.

Ice-Skating

Rinks are located at **Banff High School** on Banff Ave. at Wolf St.; on the **Bow River** along Bow St.; and on the golf course side of the **Banff Springs Hotel.** The latter rink is lighted after dark and a raging fire is built beside it—the perfect place for a hot chocolate. Rent skates from **The Ski Stop** in the Banff Springs Hotel, tel. (403) 762-5333.

Other Winter Activities

Without the tourists, dogsledding probably wouldn't take place in the park—but there are tourists and there is dogsledding. **Mountain Mushers,** tel. (403) 762-3647, offers half-hour ($60), one-hour ($100), and half-day ($250) tours around the Banff Springs Golf Course.

Beside the Banff Springs Hotel ice-skating rink is an unofficial toboggan run; ask at your hotel for sleds. **Holiday on Horseback** has sleigh rides on the frozen Bow River throughout winter. For reservations call (403) 762-4551 or stop by the Trail Rider Store at 132 Banff Ave. ($10 per person). **Banff Fishing Unlimited** offers ice-fishing trips on nearby lakes, tel. (403) 762-4936. Anyone interested in ice climbing must register at the national park desk in the Banff Visitor Centre or call (403) 762-1550. The world famous (if you're an ice climber) **Terminator** is located just outside the park boundary. Curling bonspiels take place at the Banff Recreation Centre on Mt. Norquay Road. If none of the above appeals to you head to **Upper Hot Springs** for a relaxing soak; open Mon.-Fri. noon-9 p.m., Sat.-Sun. 10 a.m.-11 p.m. ($7). Camping might not be everyone's idea of a winter holiday but Tunnel Mountain Village II remains open year-round.

FESTIVALS AND EVENTS

Spring

First of the major spring events, on the third weekend of April, is the **Banff/Lake Louise Cowboy Jubilee,** a celebration of Western heritage through poetry readings and story-telling at venues throughout town. While spring sees the local golf courses begin to open, keen skiers are at higher elevations, swooshing down the slopes of some of North America's latest-closing resorts. At Sunshine Village on the first Saturday in May is the **Dummy Downhill**—ski racing with a difference. Enter your own dummy or just watch the fun. The **Slush Cup** also takes place at Sunshine Village, this event in late May. Events include kamikaze skiers who attempt to jump an ice-cold pit of water.

During the second week of June is the **Banff Television Festival,** a meeting and international competition for the television industry with limited public viewings. For information call (403) 678-9260. Also in early June is the **Jasper to Banff Relay,** attracting over 100 teams along the 300-km route.

Summer

Summer is a time of hiking and camping, so festivals are few and far between. The main event is the **Banff Arts Festival,** a summer-long extravaganza presented by professional artists studying at the Banff Centre. They perform dance, drama, opera, and jazz for the public at locations around town. Look for details in the *Crag and Canyon* or call (403) 762-6300. Late in June is **Parks Day.** On 1 July, Banff celebrates **Canada Day** with a parade, fireworks, and events for all the family.

Each summer the national park staff presents an extensive **Park Interpretive Program** at locations in town and throughout the park. All programs are free and include guided hikes, nature tours, slide shows, campfire talks, and lectures. For details consult *The Mountain Guide* available at the Banff Visitor Centre, tel. (403) 762-1550, or look for postings at campground bulletin boards.

Fall

Fall is the the park's quietest season, but busiest in terms of festivals and events. To help fill rooms **Winterstart** runs through November to mid-December and features a host of fun events, cheap lodging, and the opening of local ski hills.

First of the fall events, on the last Saturday in September, **Melissa's Mini Marathon** attracts over 2,000 runners. The following weekend is **Taste of Banff/Lake Louise,** when visitors can take advantage of the park's varied dining opportunities by "testing" samples of cuisine from local restaurants. In the same vein is a **wine and food festival** hosted by the Banff Springs Hotel at the end of October.

Banff Festival of Mountain Films

One of the year's biggest events is the Banff Festival of Mountain Films on the first weekend of November. Mountain-adventure filmmakers from around the world submit films to be judged by a select committee. Films are then shown throughout the weekend to an enthusiastic crowd of thousands. Exhibits and seminars are also presented, and the crème de la crème of climbers and mountaineers from around the world is invited as guest speakers; the 1994 special guest was Sir Edmund Hillary.

Tickets go on sale a year in advance and sell out in advance. Tickets for daytime shows start at $33 (for up to 10 films). Night shows are from $20, and all-weekend passes cost around $100. Films are shown in the two theaters of the Banff Centre for the Arts. For more information write to Banff Festival of Mountain Films, Banff Centre, P.O. Box 1020, Station 38, Banff, AB T0L 0C0; tel. (403) 762-6349 or (800) 298-1229.

Starting in the days leading up to the film festival, then run in conjunction with it, is the **Banff Mountain Book Festival,** which showcases the work of publishers, writers, and photographers whose work revolves around the world's great mountain ranges. Tickets can be bought to individual events ($8-15), but better value is the Book Festival Pass for $48.

Winter

By mid-December all local ski areas are operating. **Santa Claus** makes an appearance on Banff Avenue on November 30; if you miss him there, he usually goes skiing at the local resorts on Christmas Day. Events at the resorts continue throughout the long ski season, among them **World Cup Downhill** skiing. **First Night** is an alcohol-free New Year's celebration held downtown. **Banff Winter Festival** is a 10-day celebration at the end of January that has been a part of Banff's history for over 75 years. Look for ice sculpting, the Lake Louise Loppet, barn dancing, and the Town Party, which takes place in the Banff Springs Hotel.

ACCOMMODATIONS

Finding a room in Banff in summer is nearly as hard as trying to justify its price. By late afternoon just about every room and campsite in town will be occupied, and basic hotel rooms begin at around $100. Fortunately, many alternatives are available. Rooms in private homes begin at around $30 s, $40 d. Canmore, just outside the park boundary, has many hotels and strip motels considerably cheaper than anything in Banff. Banff International Hostel has dormitory-style accommodations from $17 per night. Bungalows or cabins can be rented, which can be cost-effective for families or small groups. And a thousand-odd campsites close to town accommodate campers. Wherever you decide to stay, it is vital to book well ahead during summer and the Christmas holidays. The park's off season is from October to May, and hotels offer huge rate reductions during this period; the Banff Springs Hotel leads the way with lift and lodging packages beginning from $70 per person. Shop around and you'll find many bargains. **Banff Central Reservations,** tel. (403) 762-5561 or (800) 661-1676, represents most hotels in the park and can make reservations for you.

When addressing written inquiries to the establishments listed below, follow the P.O. Box provided with: **Banff, AB T0L 0C0.** All rates quoted below are for a standard room in the high season (June-Sept.).

Downtown

While most accommodations are strung out along Banff Avenue, an easy walk from the shopping and dining precinct, other choices are right downtown. Newest of these is **Brewster's Mountain Lodge,** P.O. Box 2286, 208 Caribou St., tel. (403) 762-2900. It features an eye-catching log exterior with an equally impressive lobby in a prime downtown location. The Western theme is continued in the 63 upstairs rooms. Superior rooms feature two queen-size beds or one king-size bed ($170), deluxe rooms offer a private balcony ($190), and suites have private jacuzzis ($270-370). Rates here in the off season are slashed 50%. The only other hotel right downtown is **Mount Royal Hotel,** P.O. Box 550, 138 Banff Ave., tel. (403) 852-3146 or (800) 661-1528, which has a large health club and tastefully decorated rooms; $159 s or d.

Close to the river is **Bow View Motor Lodge,** P.O. Box 339, 228 Bow Ave., tel. (403) 762-2261 or (800) 661-1565; rooms are $105 or, with a view of the river, $125. Between this accommodation and the main drag is **Banff Park Lodge,** P.O. Box 2200, 222 Lynx St., tel. (403) 762-4433 or (800) 661-9266, a modern, full-service luxury hotel. Rooms begin at $195, suites with bedside jacuzzis are $255.

Banff Avenue

Least expensive accommodation along this strip is the **Spruce Grove Motel,** P.O. Box 471, 545 Banff Ave., tel. (403) 762-2112, offering basic rooms for $70; kitchenettes are $80 but are larger and sleep four (you can get rooms here for $40 in the off season). Also at this end of the strip is **Banff Voyager Inn,** P.O. Box 1540, 555 Banff Ave., tel. (403) 762-3301 or (800) 372-9288, which has a swimming pool and restaurant, $95 s or d, and, next door, **Bumper's Inn,** P.O. Box 1328, 603 Banff Ave., tel. (403) 762-3386, offering Banff's best steakhouse; $106 s, $112 d. **Red Carpet Inn,** P.O. Box 1800, 425 Banff Ave., tel. (403) 762-4184 or (800) 563-4609, could do with a coat of paint; $85 s, $100 d. **Irwin's Motor Inn,** P.O. Box 1198, 429 Banff Ave., tel. (403) 762-4566 or (800) 661-1721, has rooms of similar standard for $100. **Homestead Inn,** P.O. Box 669, 217 Lynx St., tel. (403) 762-4471 or (800) 661-1021, has rooms beginning at $110. **Rundle Manor Apartment Hotel,** P.O. Box 1077, 348 Marten St., tel. (403) 762-5544 or (800) 661-1272, offers one-bedroom suites for $115, two-bedroom suites for $175, each with a full kitchen. Closest to downtown is **High Country Inn,** P.O. Box 700, 419 Banff Ave., tel. (403) 762-2236 or (800) 661-1244, which has a restaurant and pool; $115 per room.

Rundlestone Lodge, P.O. Box 489, 537 Banff Ave., tel. (403) 762-2201 or (800) 661-8630, features a whirlpool, sauna, and laundry, and many rooms have balconies, fireplaces, and kitchenettes. Rooms begin at $105; some are wheelchair accessible. A few doors away, but still within easy walking distance of downtown, is **Banff Caribou Lodge,** P.O. Box 279, 521 Banff Ave., tel. (403) 762-5887 or (800) 563-8764, which opened in 1993. Its bright airy rooms go for $140 s, $155 d. The impressive log entrance is not easily missed. Close by is **Dynasty Inn,** P.O. Box 1018, at 501 Banff Ave., tel. (403) 762-8844 or (800) 667-1464, which also opened in 1993. Each room has a log-trimmed balcony, and the facade is Rundlestone (quarried locally and named for Mt. Rundle). Rooms are $140 s, $175 d, which includes a continental breakfast.

Charlton's Evergreen Court, P.O. Box 1478, 459 Banff Ave., tel. (403) 762-3307 or (800) 661-1379, has an outdoor pool and a limited number of kitchenettes; $145 s or d. One block north is **Charlton's Cedar Court,** P.O. Box 1478, 513 Banff Ave., tel. (403) 762-4485 or (800) 661-1225, with an indoor pool; basic rooms are $145, loft suites with a fireplace are

$165. **Traveller's Inn,** P.O. Box 1017, 401 Banff Ave., tel. (403) 762-4401 or (800) 661-8340, has larger rooms, many with mountain views. A buffet breakfast is served for guests each morning. Rates are $145 s or d. **Best Western Siding 29 Lodge,** P.O. Box 1387, 453 Marten St., tel. (403) 762-5575 or (800) 528-1234, is good value for small groups; rooms are $140 for up to four people.

Expensive hotels begin at $150, but between October and May it is these same lodgings that offer the deepest discounts. And you can usually receive a room upgrade for little or no extra. **Banff Ptarmigan Inn,** P.O. Box 1840, 337 Banff Ave., tel. (403) 762-2207 or (800) 661-8310, is a full-service hotel with tastefully decorated rooms, down comforters on all beds, and mountain views. Rooms are $164 s, $171 d. **Banff International Hotel,** P.O. Box 1040, 333 Banff Ave., tel. (403) 762-5666 or (800) 665-5666, has high-quality rooms for $145. The much larger lofts are $165, mountain-view rooms $175. Both these accommodations are at the downtown end of Banff Avenue. One of Banff's larger hotels, but a 10-minute walk to town, is **Inns of Banff Park,** P.O. Box 1077, 600 Banff Ave., tel. (403) 762-4581 or (800) 661-1272. Each room has a mini-bar, fridge, and balcony while near the lobby is a pool, lounge, and restaurant; $170 s or d.

Banff Rocky Mountain Resort, P.O. Box 100, at the northeast end of Banff Ave. on the corner of Tunnel Mountain Rd., tel. (403) 762-5531 or (800) 667-3529, is an ideal alternative for groups or families. Units are spread out across the well-manicured grounds while in the main building is a lounge, restaurant, pool, and exercise room. Tennis courts are available for guest use and cross-country ski trails are set during winter. Many of the one- and two-bedroom suites have kitchens, all have fireplaces; $159 and $209, respectively. A free shuttle runs into town from the resort each hour.

Tunnel Mountain

The four properties on Tunnel Mountain are all set on pleasant grounds and offer an alternative to the strip of hotels along Banff Avenue. Although similar in price to those on Banff Ave., all have individual chalets, making them good for families, small groups, or for those who want to cook their own meals. Town is a 15-minute walk away or a short ride on the **Banff Explorer** bus that runs along Tunnel Mountain Rd. twice an hour.

Douglas Fir Resort, P.O. Box 1228, tel. (403) 762-5591 or (800) 661-9267, has 133 large condo-style rooms. Each has a fully equipped kitchen and a lounge with fireplace. Facilities include an indoor pool, two water slides, a jacuzzi, weight room, squash and tennis courts, a grocery store, and laundromat. Rates begin at $145 s or d. **Hidden Ridge Chalets,** P.O. Box 519, tel. (403) 762-3544 or (800) 661-1372, is just that, hidden. The self-contained cabins are spread among stands of Douglas fir and spruce. Each has a kitchen and fireplace; $155 per night, $180 for larger chalets on the ridge.

The first things you'll notice at **Buffalo Mountain Lodge,** P.O. Box 1326, tel. (403) 762-2400 or (800) 661-1367, are the impressive log entrance, the hand-hewn construction of the lobby, and the huge stone fireplace. The rooms, chalets, and bungalows all have fireplaces; many have kitchens. And you won't need to go to town to eat—one of Banff's best restaurants, **Cilantro Mountain Cafe,** is adjacent to the main lodge. Rooms start at $170. Across the road is **Tunnel Mountain Chalets,** P.O. Box 1137, tel. (403) 762-4515 or (800) 661-1859. Each modern unit has a kitchenette, fireplace, and two TVs; some have a whirlpool. One-bedroom units go for $155, two-bedrooms $184.

Other Hotels

Elkhorn Lodge, P.O. Box 352, is located halfway up the hill to the Banff Springs Hotel at 124 Spray Ave., tel. (403) 762-2299. The small sleeping rooms are $80, while larger rooms with kitchens are $135. Nothing special. **Timberline Lodge,** P.O. Box 69, is located on the north side of the TransCanada Hwy. at the base of the Banff Mt. Norquay ski area road, tel. (403) 762-2281. Standard rooms are $120-130; those on the second floor have private balconies, those on the south-facing side have excellent views. Out in back are chalets that sleep six to eight in three bedrooms. Each chalet has a kitchen and fireplace; $250 per night.

Banff Springs Hotel

This famous landmark, one of the world's great mountain resort hotels, offers 846 guest rooms

Banff Springs Hotel

in 80 different configurations. Many rooms were built in the 1920s, and as is common in older establishments, many are small. But room size is only a small consideration when staying in this historic gem. With 16 eateries, a health club, pool, outdoor jacuzzi, library, 27-hole golf course, tennis courts, horseback riding, and enough twisting, turning hallways, boardwalks, towers, and shops to warrant a detailed map, you'll not be wanting to spend time in the room. Unless of course you are in the presidential suite, located in the central tower. It has eight rooms, a canopy bed, jacuzzi, baby grand piano, private pool, and your own glass elevator linking each of the three floors; $3,000 per night.

For the rest of us, staying at the hotel isn't as expensive as you might think. Standard rooms begin at $110 d during the low season, $165 in high season. Those with a view are $270-335, suites begin at $385, and if you bring your pet it's $15 extra. Reserve well in advance during summer, and request "the best room available" the rest of the year. The hotel is at the end of Spray Avenue. For reservations write to P.O. Box 960, Banff, AB T0L 0C0; tel. (403) 762-2211 or (800) 441-1414.

Rimrock Resort Hotel
Located on Mountain Ave. a short walk from the Upper Hot Springs is the Rimrock, P.O. Box 1110, tel. (403) 762-3356 or (800) 661-1587. The original hotel was constructed in 1903 but was fully rebuilt and opened as a 345-room full-

service luxury resort in August 1993. Each well-appointed room has a king-size bed, comfortable armchair, writing desk, mini-bar, and hair dryer. The staff is trained to pamper guests and answer all requests.

Since it's set high above the Bow Valley, views for the most part are excellent. Prices range from $225 to $300 depending solely on the views. Regular shuttle buses make the short run to town during summer.

Bow Valley Parkway
This is the original route between Banff and Lake Louise (see above). It is a beautiful drive in all seasons and along its length are three lodges, each a viable alternative to staying in Banff. A fourth lodge is located to the west of the parkway on Hwy. 93.

Johnston Canyon Resort, P.O. Box 875, tel. (403) 762-2971, is 26 km west of Banff at the beginning of a short trail that leads to the famous canyon. The rustic cabins are older, and some have kitchenettes. On the grounds are tennis courts, a barbecue area, and restaurant. No television. Rooms start at $59 s or d, two-person cabins $69, four-person cabins $89, and chalets with a kitchen and fireplace are $115-145. It's open May-October.

Six km farther northwest is **Castle Mountain Village,** P.O. Box 178, Lake Louise, AB T0L 1E0, tel. (403) 762-3868. Small summer cottages with kitchenettes are $58 s or d, $75 with two double beds. Log chalets that sleep four and have kitchenettes and a fireplace are $120. The newly built deluxe log chalets are one of the park's best bargains. They have high ceilings, beautifully handcrafted log interiors, three beds, a stone fireplace, full kitchen with dishwasher, and a bathroom with jacuzzi; $160 for up to four people, $170 for five or six.

Six km west of Castle Mountain Junction is **Storm Mountain Lodge,** P.O. Box 670, tel. (403) 762-4155, whose 12 original log cabins are among the nicest in the park. Each has a wood-burning fireplace, a private bathroom, cozy comforters, and antique furnishings. Only one has a kitchenette, but a restaurant is on the property. Rates are $110 s or d, extra people $10 each. The lodge is open May-September.

Baker Creek Chalets, P.O. Box 66, Lake Louise, AB T0L 1E0, tel. (403) 522-3761, is the next resort along the parkway. Each of the log cabins has a kitchenette, fireplace, and outside deck. Basic one-room cabins are $125 for two; one-bedroom cabins with loft (sleeps six) are $150; two bedroom cabins (sleeps six) are $180 for four. A new wing has motel-style rooms, each with a kitchen and jacuzzi, for $150 s or d. Each additional person $10. The restaurant here is highly recommended.

Inexpensive Options

The Banff/Lake Louise Tourism Bureau in the Banff Visitor Centre, 224 Banff Ave., tel. (403) 762-8421, has a list of bed and breakfasts and private homes that rent rooms or cabins. Standards range from fair to good, but the prices are lower than those of the hotels. **Mrs. Cowan,** 118 Otter St., tel. (403) 762-3696, has very sparsely furnished rooms for $30 s, $35 d, $50 s or d with a private bathroom. Continental breakfast is served in your room. Ask Mrs. Cowan about her emergency room for $15 per night—which also includes breakfast in bed.

Blue Mountain Lodge, 137 Muskrat St., tel. (403) 762-5134, has rooms for $65 and small cabins from $80. All guests have use of shared kitchen facilities. Better value is **Beaver St. Suites and Cabins,** 220 Beaver St., tel. (403) 762-5077, with rooms beginning at $65 and cabins at $75. Without a doubt, the best bed and breakfast in town is **Eleanor's,** 1225 Kootenay Ave., tel. (403) 760-2457, a lovely guesthouse on a quiet residential street. It has a library, and each luxuriously furnished room has a private bathroom. Rates are $85 s, $105 d.

Hostels

Banff International Hostel, P.O. Box 1358, tel. (403) 762-4122 or 237-8282 from Calgary, is located just off Tunnel Mountain Rd. three km from downtown. This large, modern hostel sleeps 154 in small two-, four-, and six-bed dormitory rooms. The large lounge area has a fireplace, and other facilities include a recreation room, bike and ski workshop, large kitchen, self-service cafe, and laundry. Members of Hostelling International pay $17 per night, nonmembers $22. During July and August reserve at least a month in advance to be assured of a bed. The hostel is open all day. To get there from town ride the **Banff Explorer** ($1.50), which passes the hostel twice an hour during summer. The rest of the year the only transportation is by cab, about $5 from the bus depot. Thirty-two km along the Bow Valley Parkway is **Castle Mountain Hostel,** near a number of interesting hikes. This hostel sleeps 36 and has a kitchen, common room, hot showers, and bike rentals; members $11, nonmembers $16. Make reservations through the Banff Hostel.

The **YWCA,** 102 Spray Ave., tel. (403) 762-3560, is convenient to town, but rooms are fairly barren. Bunk beds in the dormitory are $19 per person, and you'll need a sleeping bag. Private rooms begin at $51 s or d, and $55-69 for family rooms (sleeps four to six). Between October and May all prices (except bunk bed) are reduced by $12 and everyone is treated to a full breakfast. Other facilities include kitchen, cafe, and laundry.

Backcountry Huts and Lodges

In the backcountry of the national park are two distinct types of accommodations—rustic mountain huts and lodges. Each of the often historic huts has a stove, lantern, kitchen utensils, and foam mattresses. The extensive system of huts is managed by the Alpine Club of Canada. For locations and reservations, write to P.O. Box 2040, Canmore, AB T0L 0M0; tel. (403) 678-3200. No huts are located in the southern end of the park.

Shadow Lake Lodge and Cabins (Brewster Rocky Mountain Adventures, P.O. Box 964, Banff, AB T0L 0C0; tel. 403-762-5454) is located 13 km from the nearest road. Access is on foot, or in winter on skis. The lodge is located near a picturesque lake of the same name, and many hiking trails are nearby. The oldest structure here has been restored as a dining area. Guests sleep in newer, more cozy cabins. All meals and afternoon tea are included in the rate of $99 per person per day. The trailhead is along the TransCanada Hwy., 19 km from Banff, at the Redearth Creek parking area.

Campgrounds

Although Banff has seven campgrounds with well over 1,000 sites in its immediate vicinity, all fill by early afternoon. Closest to town are **Tunnel Mountain Village II** and **Tunnel Mountain Trailer Court**, 3.5 km along Tunnel Mountain Road. The former has electrical hookups and is the only campground in the park open year-round. The latter has full hookups. Both have hot showers but little privacy between sites. Sites are $17.50-20 and no tents are allowed. Less than one km farther along the road is **Tunnel Mountain Village I,** which has hot showers, private sites, firewood, and kitchen shelters, but no hookups. Sites are $15. Toward Lake Minnewanka northeast of town is **Two Jack Lakeside,** which has pit toilets, firewood, and lots of trees; $13 per night. In the same vicinity is **Two Jack Main;** $12. Along Bow Valley Parkway you'll find **Johnston Canyon Campground, Castle Mountain Campground,** and **Protection Mountain Campground.** Generally these don't open until June and fill up later than those in Banff; $12-15 per night.

FOOD

Banff has over 100 restaurants. That's more per capita than any town or city across Canada. From lobster to linguini, alligator to à la carte, and fajitas to fudge—anyone who spends time in the park will find something that suits his or her taste and budget, although not necessarily at the same place. Many have been around for decades and attract diners from as far away as Calgary (some of whom have been known to stay overnight just to eat at their favorite haunt). An eclectic mix of restaurants lines Banff Avenue—most have menus posted out front. The

less adventurous can try one of the eateries at the major hotels. The Banff Springs Hotel tops the list with a choice of 16. In July and August the most popular restaurants don't take reservations and you can expect a wait at most spots. Various dining guides are available throughout town.

Budget Stretchers

The best place to begin looking for cheap eats is the Food Court in the lower level of Cascade Plaza at 317 Banff Avenue. Here you'll find two bakeries and **Edo Japan,** which sells simple Japanese dishes for around $6 including a drink. A local bylaw prohibiting obtrusive signs and neon lights means that the fast-food chains are easily missed. For the most expensive Big Macs this side of the Toronto Skydome, **McDonald's** is at 116 Banff Avenue. **KFC** is at 202 Caribou St., and **Harvey's** is at 304 Caribou Street. **Smitty's,** 227 Banff Ave., tel. (403) 762-2533, is a popular breakfast spot and has many steak and chicken dishes for under $10. Another good spot for breakfast is **Craig's Way Station,** 461 Banff Ave., tel. (403) 762-4660.

Coffee Shops

The **Cake Company,** 220 Bear St., tel. (403) 762-2330, serves great coffee, as well as a delicious range of pastries, muffins, and cakes baked daily on the premises. Another Cake Company outlet is on the lower level of Cascade Plaza; a muffin and coffee is $2.50. **Evelyn's,** on Banff Ave. in the Town Centre Mall, has good coffee and huge sandwiches, and is a super place for socializing and people-watching. **Jump Start,** 206 Buffalo St., tel. (403) 762-0332, has a wide range of coffee concoctions as well as delicious homemade soups ($4) and sandwiches ($5).

Canadian

A town favorite that has faithfully served locals for many years is **Melissa's,** 218 Lynx St., tel. (403) 762-5511, housed in a log building that dates from 1928 (the original Homestead Inn). For breakfast the hotcakes piled high on your plate ($5) can't be beat. Or try the bran muffins made from scratch each morning. Lunch and dinner are casual affairs—choose from a wide variety of generously sized burgers, freshly prepared salads, and mouthwatering Alberta beef.

Melissa's also features an outside patio and rustic bar with well-priced drinks. Open daily 7 a.m.-10 p.m.

Even though **Bumper's,** 603 Banff Ave., tel. (403) 762-2622, is away from the center of Banff, it remains one of the town's busiest restaurants. And not just in summer; locals and visitors alike flock to this popular steak house year-round. Large cuts of Alberta beef, efficient service, and great prices keep people coming back. Favorite choices are the prime rib Pile-o-bones, Barbecue Beef Ribs, and of course slabs of juicy beef cooked to your taste. Main entrees are $11-19 and include a fresh salad bar. Upstairs is the **Loft Lounge,** a good place to wait for a table or relax afterwards with an inexpensive drink. It's open 4:30-10 p.m.

Closer to town in the Banff Caribou Lodge is **The Keg,** 521 Banff Ave., tel. (403) 762-4442, part of a western Canada chain noted for its consistently good steak, seafood, and chicken dishes at reasonable prices. All entrees include a 60-item salad bar. The Keg is open daily 7 a.m.-2 a.m. Another Keg location is downtown at 117 Banff Ave., tel. (403) 760-3030. The familiar **Earl's,** upstairs at 229 Banff Ave., tel. (403) 762-4414, has more of the same at slightly higher prices (but the usual parrot mascot out front is nowhere to be found).

If you are staying in the hostel or at Tunnel Mountain campgrounds, **Cilantro Mountain Cafe,** at Buffalo Mountain Lodge, tel. (403) 762-2400, is well worth trying. The menu is limited to a few Italian-style dishes, but each is well prepared and their outside deck is perfect for those hot summer nights. Another restaurant is in Buffalo Mountain Lodge itself. The distinctive interior of hand-hewn cedar beams and Old World elegance is the perfect setting for a moderate splurge. Expect to pay around $25 per person for soup, an entree, and dessert. Breakfast is also good. It's open daily 7 a.m.-11 p.m. One of Banff's only bistro-style restaurants is **Coyote's Deli and Grill,** 206 Caribou St., tel. (403) 762-3963. Meals are prepared in full view of diners, and the menu emphasizes the health conscious—broiled chicken, vegetarian lasagna, and tempting desserts are favorites. Entrees are $10-19.50. Coyote's is open daily 8 a.m.-10 p.m.

The romantic era of the railway is relived in **The Caboose,** located in the old C.P.R. station at the corner of Elk and Lynx Streets, tel. (403) 762-3622. Although not the original station, kings, queens, and millions of other visitors have passed through the building. The walls are lined with railway memorabilia, and the elegant atmosphere makes for a memorable dining experience. Seafood and steak dominate the menu; expect to pay $12-25 for entrees and around $5 for dessert. All meals include the self-service salad cart which is wheeled to your table. The Caboose is open daily 5-10 p.m.

Mexican and Cajun
The **Magpie & Stump,** 203 Caribou St., tel. (403) 762-4067, serves no-frills authentic Mexican food at reasonable prices. Lunch is from $5, dinner from $8, and a few outside tables catch the afternoon sun. It's open 11 a.m.-midnight. **Two Crows,** 205 Wolf St., tel. (403) 760-8221, has a similar menu.

Italian
Banff is blessed with fine Italian restaurants. **Guido's,** 116 Banff Ave., tel. (403) 762-4002, is known for its homemade pasta, which is cooked to perfection in a variety of sauces that appeal to all tastes and diets. Entrees are $8-17. It's open daily from 5 p.m. More trendy (reflected in the prices) is **Giorgio's,** 219 Banff Ave., tel. (403) 762-5114, which was fully remodeled in 1994 with stylish decor. Its five fully trained chefs prepare as many as 400 meals each afternoon, and the lineup for tables is ever-present. Pasta dishes begin at $10. It's open from 4:30 p.m.

Greek
The **Balkan,** 120 Banff Ave., tel. (403) 762-3454, is run by Greeks, but the menu blends their heritage with the cuisines of Italy, China, and Canada. Select from Greek ribs (pork ribs with a lemon sauce) for $14.95, the Greek chow mein (stir-fried vegetables, fried rice, and your choice of meat) for $9, or Greek spaghetti for $8.50. But the most popular dishes are souvlakia ($11.95) and an enormous Greek platter that includes a leg of lamb ($36 for two). The Balkan is open daily 11 a.m.-11 p.m.

Swiss-Italian
Once one of Banff's busiest restaurants, **Ticino,** has moved from downtown to the High Country

Inn at 415 Banff Ave., tel. (403) 762-3848. It's named for the southern province of Switzerland, where the cuisine has a distinctive Italian influence. The Swiss chef is best known for his beef and cheese fondues, veal dishes, and juicy steaks. Expect to pay around $6 for appetizers and from $11 for entrees; open daily 5-11 p.m.

Japanese
The large number of Japanese visitors in Banff has created the need for good Japanese restaurants. **Shiki Japanese Noodles** in Clock Tower Mall, 110 Banff Ave., tel. (403) 762-0527, has a choice of *donburi,* various meat cakes, teriyaki, and sushi. Dishes are $5-10 each. It's open daily 11 a.m.-9 p.m. A bit more expensive is **Suginoya,** 225 Banff Ave., tel. (403) 762-4773, which has a relaxed atmosphere. Choose from the sushi bar, *ozashiki* booths, or regular tables. Traditional *shabu-shabu* and seafood teriyaki are popular. The number of Japanese diners here is indicative of the quality. Expect to pay at least $10 for entrees, $18-21 for one of the combination dinners. Suginoya is open daily 11 a.m.-10:30 p.m.

French
Le Beaujolais, 212 Buffalo St., tel. (403) 762-2712, is a Canadian leader in French cuisine and has been one of Banff's most popular fine-dining restaurants for over a decade. Its second-floor location ensures great views of Banff, especially from window tables. The dishes feature mainly Canadian ingredients, prepared and served with a French flair. Entrees begin at $18, but the extent of your final tab depends on whether you choose à la carte items or the three-course table d'hôte menu ($36-40)—and also on how much wine you consume (at $20-250 a bottle). The restaurant is open daily from 6 p.m.; reservations are necessary.

The Grizzly House
This unique fondue restaurant at 207 Banff Ave., tel. (403) 762-4055, provides Banff's most unusual dining experience. The decor is, to say the least, eclectic (or should that be eccentric). Each table has a phone for across-table conversation, or you can call your waiter, the bar, a cab, diners in the private booth, or even those who spend too long in the bathroom. Through all

this the food is good and the service professional. Although traditional Swiss fondues are on the menu, the buffalo, seafood, oriental, rattlesnake, and alligator are the most popular. Of course it wouldn't be right to leave without having a chocolate fondue dipped with fresh fruit. Individual fondues are $17-25 (lunch a little cheaper), complete three-course dinners start at $37. Open 11:30 a.m.-midnight.

Baker Creek Bistro
Along the Bow Valley Parkway, towards Lake Louise, are the Baker Creek Chalets. The intimate restaurant here, housed in a log building, is definitely worth the drive from Banff. Next to the restaurant is a rustic lounge and large outdoor patio. The bistro is open in summer, daily 7 a.m.-10 p.m., shorter hours the rest of the year; tel. (403) 522-2182.

Banff Springs Hotel
Whether guests or not, most visitors to Banff drop by to see one of the town's biggest tourist attractions. And a meal here might not be as expensive as you think. The hotel itself has more eateries than most small towns—from a 24-hour deli serving pizza to the finest of fine dining.

Koffie Haus Restaurant is open all day serving reliable and reasonably priced meals; **Red Terrace** features outdoor summer barbecues; **Samurai Restaurant** fills every night with Japanese guests; **Clubhouse** on the golf course serves light breakfasts, lunch, and formal dinners; **Grapes** is a small wine bar noted for its fine cheeses and pâtés; **Henry VIII Pub** serves simple meals and delicious cappuccinos with panoramic views of the Bow River; **Pavilion Restaurant** serves pasta at good prices; **Alhambra Room** is a Spanish-style restaurant serving continental dishes; and the **Waldhaus** serves German specialties. The **Alberta Room** is the place to enjoy a breakfast buffet in Banff. The huge spread is $10.50 per person and definitely worth the splurge. But the most acclaimed restaurant at the hotel is the **Rob Roy Room,** named for a Scottish outlaw. This fine-dining restaurant is renowned for its excellently prepared Alberta beef (over 1,000 portions of beef are served in the hotel each day). Try the beef strip loin for two, broiled to order then carved at your table. Many lighter dishes such as chicken and seafood ($15-28) are also offered. It's open daily 6-10 p.m. For reservations call (403) 662-6860, or after 5 p.m. call (403) 762-2211. During the summer months a desk to the left of the main lobby has all menus posted and takes reservations for the hotel restaurants.

NIGHTLIFE

Like resort towns around the world, Banff has more than its fair share of bars and nightclubs. **Wild Bill's Legendary Saloon,** upstairs at 201 Banff Ave., tel. (403) 762-0333, is named for Banff guide Bill Peyto, and is truly legendary. Music is mostly country, but bands usually play a bit of everything. The food here is excellent. Just as popular is the **Barbary Coast,** 119 Banff Ave., tel. (403) 762-4616, which also serves good food and occasionally has live music in a clean, casual atmosphere. Across the road from Wild Bill's is the **Rose and Crown,** 202 Banff Ave., tel. (403) 762-2121, an English-style pub serving British beers. Below the Mount Royal Hotel is the **Buffalo Paddock,** 138 Banff Ave., tel. (403) 762-3331, with pool tables. **Silver City,** 110 Banff Ave., tel. (403) 762-3337, has cheap drinks and a disco open till 2 a.m. every night. Banff's newest night spot is **Outa Bounds,** 137 Banff Ave., tel. (403) 762-8434, with no cover charge, but watch for anyone diving off the bar. The lounge in the **Voyager Inn,** 555 Banff Ave., tel. (403) 762-3301, has drink specials every night. Just past the Voyager Inn is **Bumpers,** with a small bar and pool table upstairs.

Police patrol Banff all night, promptly arresting anyone who even looks like trouble, including anyone drunk or drinking on the streets.

SHOPPING

It may seem a little strange, but city folk from Calgary actually drive into Banff National Park to shop for clothes. This reflects the number of clothing shops in Banff rather than a lack of choice in one of Canada's largest cities. About the only clothing store that Banff lacks is an army-surplus outlet.

One of the best places to shop for outdoor apparel is **Outdoor Access** at 201 Banff Ave.;

downstairs is a factory outlet with big savings. Other recommended stores are **Monod Sports** at 129 Banff Ave., and **Helly Hansen,** in the back of the mall at 119 Banff Avenue. Pick up your Canadian-made Tilley Hat and other Tilley Endurables from **Piccatilley Square** on the main floor of the Cascade Plaza at 317 Banff Avenue. The **Rude Boys Snowboard and Skateboard Shred Shop,** on the lower level of 215 Banff Ave., is, well, rude. Take a look—their T-shirts are hilarious (and unlike anything on Banff Ave., original), but don't expect to find anything for your grandparents here.

Camping equipment and supplies can be found in **Home Hardware** at 208 Bear St. and **The Hudson's Bay Company** at 125 Banff Ave. (downstairs). More specialized needs are catered to at **Mountain Magic Equipment** located at 224 Bear St., tel. (403) 762-2591. The store has a large range of top-quality outdoor and survival gear (including climbing equipment) and rents tents ($15 per day), sleeping bags ($8), backpacks ($7.50), and boots ($7). The largest mountain-bike shop in Banff is **Park 'N Pedal,** which has a sales, repair, and rental outlet at 229 Wolf St., tel. (403) 762-3190. Mountain Magic Equipment also sells and repairs all types of bikes.

TRANSPORTATION

Getting There

Banff has no airport and no scheduled rail service. The closest airport is an hour and a half away in Calgary. **Brewster,** tel. (403) 762-6700, operates an airporter service that leaves Calgary International Airport daily at 12:30 p.m. (summer only), 3 p.m., 6 p.m., and 7:45 p.m.; $30 each way. This service terminates in Banff at the large **Brewster Transportation Depot** located at 100 Gopher Street. Buses leave at 8:30 a.m., 12:30 p.m., 4 p.m., and 7:30 p.m. (summer only) for Calgary International Airport. The depot has a ticket office, lockers, cafe, and gift shop. It is open daily 7:30 a.m.-10:45 p.m. From Jasper, Brewster has an express service departing the terminal on Connaught Dr. daily at 1:30 p.m.; $42 one-way. A longer alternative is the nine-hour Jasper-to-Banff tour, which stops at the Columbia Icefield and Lake Louise; $69

THE BREWSTER BOYS

Few guides in Banff were as well known as Jim and Bill (pictured) Brewster. In 1892, aged 10 and 12, respectively, they were hired by the Banff Springs Hotel to take guests to local landmarks. As their reputation as guides grew, they built a thriving business. By 1900, they had their own livery and outfitting company, and soon expanded operations to Lake Louise. Other early business interests included a trading post, the original Mt. Royal Hotel, the first ski lodge in the Sunshine Meadows, and the hotel at the Columbia Icefield.

Today, a legacy of the boys' savvy, **Brewster,** a transportation and tour company, has grown to become an integral part of many tourists' stays. The company operates some of the world's most advanced sightseeing vehicles, including a fleet of Snocoaches on Athabasca Glacier.

WHYTE MUSEUM OF THE CANADIAN ROCKIES

one-way, $95 roundtrip. In spring and fall the fare is $53 one-way, $69 roundtrip. No bus service runs between Banff and Jasper in winter.

Greyhound, tel. (403) 762-6767 or (800) 661-8747, offers scheduled service from the Calgary bus depot at 877 Greyhound Way SW, five times daily to the Brewster Transportation Depot; $17.92 one-way. Greyhound buses also leave Vancouver from the depot at 1150 Station St., three times daily for the scenic 14-hour ride to Banff; $97.32 one-way.

Getting Around

Most of the sights and many trailheads are within walking distance of town. The **Banff Explorer** is a transit service operated by the town of Banff. Two routes are served, one from the Banff Springs Hotel to the RV and trailer drop-off at the far end of Banff Ave., the other from the Luxton Museum to the hostel and Tunnel Mountain Campgrounds. Buses run June-Sept., twice an hour between 8 a.m. and 9 p.m. Fare is $1.50.

Cabs around town are reasonably priced—flag drop is $2.30, then it's $1.25 per kilometer. From the bus depot to the hostel will run around $5, same to the Banff Springs Hotel, more after midnight. Companies are: **Banff Taxi,** tel. (403) 762-4444; **Taxi Taxi,** tel. (403) 762-3111; and **Mountain Taxi,** tel. (403) 762-3351.

The days when a row of horse-drawn buggies eagerly awaited the arrival of wealthy visitors at the C.P.R. Station have long since passed, but the era is relived by the **Trail Rider Store,** 132 Banff Ave., tel. (403) 762-4551, offering visitors rides around town in a beautifully restored carriage ($7 per person for 15 minutes). Expect to pay around $35 per carriage between downtown and the Banff Springs Hotel.

Banff Rent-A-Car, 230 Lynx St., tel. (403) 762-3352, rents used cars for $50 per day with 100 free kilometers. Other agencies are **Avis,** tel. (403) 762-3222 or (800) 879-2847; **Budget,** tel. (403) 762-4565 or (800) 268-8900; **Discount,** tel. (403) 760-8262; **Hertz,** tel. (403) 762-2027 or (800) 263-0600; **Sears,** tel. (403) 762-4575; and **Tilden,** tel. (403) 762-2688 or (800) 387-4747. Reservations for cars in Banff should be made well in advance.

Persons with Disabilities

The **Banff Visitor Centre** is wheelchair accessible—its washrooms, information desks, and theater are all barrier free. Once inside, use the handy Touchsource monitor for a full listing of all barrier-free services within the park. An all-terrain wheelchair is available at the Cave and Basin Centennial Centre for use on park trails. To reserve call (403) 762-1557.

Tours

Brewster, tel. (403) 762-6700, offers a three-hour Discover Banff bus tour that takes in downtown Banff, Tunnel Mountain Dr., the hoodoos, the Cave and Basin, and Sulphur Mountain Gondola (gondola fare not included). This tour runs in summer only and departs from the bus depot daily at 8:30 a.m.; call for hotel pick-up times. Adult fare is $35, children half price. The rest of the year this tour runs five hours and includes a trip to Lake Louise with time for lunch at the chateau; $36, lunch extra. During summer other tours available are Sulphur Mountain Gondola ($18; includes gondola ride) and Lake Minnewanka ($40; includes two-hour boat cruise). From Calgary, Brewster has a nine-hour tour out to Banff for $65.

SERVICES

The **post office** is located on the corner of Buffalo and Bear Streets opposite Central Park; open Mon.-Fri. 9 a.m.-5:30 p.m. The general-delivery service here is probably among the busiest in the country, with the thousands of seasonal workers in the area, no home mail-delivery service, and a two-year wait for a post box. Address all mail to General Delivery, Banff, AB T0L 0C0. For all other postal services try the small and friendly full-service postal outlet in **Cascade Plaza Drug,** located in the Cascade Plaza at 317 Banff Avenue. **Mail Boxes Etc.,** 226 Bear St., is a privately run postal outlet and can send and receive facsimiles.

Major banks can be found along Banff Ave. and are generally open 9 a.m.-4 p.m. The **Bank of Montreal,** 107 Banff Ave., allows cash advances with MasterCard, while the **C.I.B.C.,** 98 Banff Ave., accepts Visa.

The **C.T.M. Currency Exchange** is in the Clock Tower Mall at 108 Banff Ave. and also has offices in the Cascade Plaza and Banff Springs Hotel.

Downtown laundromats are **Johnny O's Emporium,** at 223 Bear St., open Mon.-Sat. 8 a.m.-11 p.m., Sunday 10 a.m.-10 p.m., and **Cascade Coin Laundry,** on the lower level of the Cascade Plaza, open daily 7:30 a.m.-10 p.m. Located on Tunnel Mountain Rd. at the Douglas Fir Resort, and within walking distance of the hostel, is **Chalet Coin Laundry;** open daily 8 a.m.-10 p.m. Along Banff Ave. is a handful of one-hour film labs; check around for the cheapest as many have special offers. The most competitive and reliable is **Miles High Image Center** at 119 Banff Ave. (beneath the Barbary Coast), tel. (403) 762-5221. Drop slide film here on Wednesday and it will be ready for pick-up Friday morning. Get photographic supplies from **Wolf Street Cameras** at 203 Bear Street.

Mineral Springs Hospital is at 301 Lynx St., tel. (403) 762-2222. **Cascade Plaza Drug** on the lower level of the Cascade Plaza at 317 Banff Ave. is open till 9 p.m., as is **Harmony Drug** at 111 Banff Avenue. (Harmony Drug was once owned by noted Banff photographer Byron Harmon, whose prints, dating from around 1915, adorn the walls and adjacent mall.) **Gourlay's Pharmacy** at 229 Bear St. is open till 8 p.m. For the **RCMP** call (403) 762-2226.

INFORMATION

Banff Public Library

Banff's library is located opposite Central Park at 101 Bear St., tel. (403) 762-2661. The extensive collection of nonfiction books, many about the park and its environs, makes it an excellent rainy-day hangout. It also has a large collection of magazines and newspapers. It's open Mon.-Sat. 11 a.m.-6 p.m. (till 9 p.m. on Tuesday and Thursday) and Sunday 1-5 p.m.

Books and Bookstores

The Rockies are one of the most written about, and definitely the most photographed, regions in Canada. As a walk along Banff Ave. will confirm, there is definitely no lack of postcards, calendars, and books. For general reading, the guides and coffee-table books produced by **Altitude Publishing** in Canmore are the best. Look for them in all Banff bookstores. Ben Gadd's *Handbook of the Canadian Rockies* is the best all-around source of information for those interested in the geology, climate, ecology, flora, and fauna of the Canadian Rockies.

Banff Book & Art Den, in the Clock Tower Mall at 110 Banff Ave., has a large collection of park literature, wilderness guides, coffee-table books, travel guides, and relevant topographical maps for backcountry trips within the park. Open in summer daily 10 a.m.-9 p.m., till 7 p.m. rest of the year; tel. (403) 762-3919.

Look for the *Crag and Canyon* each Wednesday. It's been keeping Banff residents and visitors informed about park issues and town gossip for over 90 years.

Banff Visitor Centre

This large complex, at 224 Banff Ave., houses information desks for **Parks Canada** and the **Banff/Lake Louise Tourism Bureau.** The national park staff will answer all of your queries and questions regarding Banff's natural wonders and advise of trail closures. Anyone planning an overnight backcountry trip should register here and obtain a permit ($6 per person per night).

The brochure *Banff and Vicinity Drives and Walks* is a compact guide to things to see and do around Banff. At the back of the center is a free slide show, videos, updated trail reports, and copies of the best hiking books. Across the floor is the tourism bureau, tel. (403) 762-8421, which represents businesses and commercial establishments in the park. Here you can find out about accommodations and restaurants and have any other questions answered. To answer the most-often-asked question, the washrooms are downstairs. The center is open July-Aug. daily 8 a.m.-8 p.m., June and September daily 8 a.m.-6 p.m., the rest of the year daily 9 a.m.-5 p.m. For more information on the park write to: The Superintendent, Banff National Park, P.O. Box 900, Banff, AB T0L 0C0; tel. (403) 762-1550. For general tourism information write to: Banff/Lake Louise Tourism Bureau, P.O. Box 1298, Banff, AB T0L 0C0. The **Warden's Office** is located in the industrial park, tel. (403) 762-1470 or 762-4506.

Call the **weather office** at (403) 762-2088 for updated forecasts. A full weather synopsis is available by calling (403) 762-3091. Tune into Channel 10 on the television for park information.

LAKE LOUISE

As the first flush of morning sun hits Victoria Glacier, and the impossibly steep northern face of Mt. Victoria is reflected in the sparkling emerald-green waters of Lake Louise, you'll understand why this lake is regarded as one of the world's seven natural wonders. Overlooking the lake is one of the world's most photographed hotels, Chateau Lake Louise. Apart from staring, photographing, and videoing, the area has plenty to keep you busy. Some of the park's best hiking, canoeing, and horseback riding is nearby. And only a short distance away is Moraine Lake, not as famous as Lake Louise but rivaling it in beauty.

Lake Louise is located 51 km northwest of Banff along the TransCanada Hwy., or a little bit farther if you take the quieter Bow Valley Parkway. The hamlet of Lake Louise, composed of a small mall, hotels, and restaurants, is located in the Bow Valley, just west of the Trans-Canada Highway. The lake itself is 200 vertical meters above the valley floor, along a winding

four-km road. Across the valley is Canada's largest ski area, Lake Louise, a world-class facility renowned for its diverse terrain, abundant snow, and breathtaking views.

From Lake Louise the TransCanada Hwy. continues west, exiting the park over Kicking Horse Pass (1,647 meters) and passing through Yoho National Park to Golden. Highway 93, the famous Icefields Parkway, also begins at the townsite and heads northwest through the park's northern reaches to Jasper National Park.

History

During the summer of 1882, Tom Wilson, an outfitter, was camped near the confluence of the Bow and Pipestone Rivers when he heard the distant rumblings of an avalanche. He questioned Stoney Indian guides and was told the noises originated from "Lake of Little Fishes." The following day Wilson, led by a native guide, hiked to the lake to investigate. He became the first white

The lakes are such marvelous colors. What kind of chemicals do you use?

—ANONYMOUS, Lake Louise Visitor Centre

man to lay eyes on what he named Emerald Lake. Two years later the name was changed to Lake Louise, honoring Princess Louise Caroline Alberta, daughter of Queen Victoria.

A railway station known as Laggan was built where the rail line passed closest to the lake, six km away. Until a road was completed in 1926, everyone arrived by train. The station's name was changed to Lake Louise in 1913 to prevent confusion among visitors. In 1890 a modest two-bedroom wooden hotel replaced a crude cabin that had been built on the shore of the lake as word of its beauty spread. After many additions, a disastrous fire, and the addition of a concrete wing in 1925, the chateau of today took shape. A 51-square-mile reserve was set aside around the lake and this was incorporated as part of Rocky Mountains Park in 1902.

Recreational mountaineering has been popular in the park for over 100 years and most of the early climbing was done on peaks around Lake Louise. In 1893 Walter Wilcox and Samuel Allen, two Yale schoolmates, spent the summer climbing in the area, making two unsuccessful attempts to reach the north peak of Mt. Victoria. The following summer they made first ascents of Mt. Temple and Mt. Aberdeen, extraordinary achievements considering their lack of experience and proper equipment.

During the summer of 1896, P.S. Abbot slipped and plunged to his death attempting to climb Mt. Lefroy. In doing so he became North America's first mountaineering fatality. Following this incident, Swiss mountain guides were employed by the C.P.R. to satisfy the climbing needs of wealthy patrons of the railway and make the sport safer. During the period of their employment, successful climbs were made of Mt. Victoria, Mt. Lefroy, and Mt. Balfour.

SIGHTS AND RECREATION

Lake Louise

In summer, around 10,000 visitors a day make the journey from the Bow Valley floor up to Lake Louise. By noon the tiered parking lot is often full. An alternative to the road is one of two trails that begin at the townsite and end at the public parking lot (see "Hiking," below). From here a number of paved trails lead to the lake's eastern shore. From these vantage points the dramatic setting can be fully appreciated. The lake is 2.4 km long, 500 meters wide, and up to 90 meters deep. Its cold waters reach a maximum temperature of 4° C in August.

Chateau Lake Louise is a tourist attraction in itself. Built by the C.P.R. to take the pressure off the popular Banff Springs Hotel, the chateau has seen many changes in the last 100 years and remains one of the world's great mountain resorts. No one minds the hordes of camera-toting tourists who traipse through each day—and there's really no way to avoid them. The immaculately manicured gardens between the chateau and the lake make an interesting foreground for the millions of Lake Louise photographs taken each year.

The snow-covered peak at the back of the lake is **Mt. Victoria** (3,459 meters), which sits on the Continental Divide. Amazingly, its base is over 10 km from the eastern end of the lake. Mount Victoria, first climbed in 1897, remains one of the park's most popular peaks for mountaineers. Although the difficult northeast face (facing the chateau), was first successfully ascended in 1922, the most popular and easiest route to the summit is along the southeast ridge, approached from Abbot Pass.

Moraine Lake

Although less than half the size of Lake Louise, Moraine Lake is just as spectacular and wor-

thy of just as much film. It is located up a winding road 12.5 km off Lake Louise Drive. Its rugged setting, nestled in the Valley of the Ten Peaks among the towering mountains of the main ranges, has provided inspiration for millions of people from around the world since Walter Wilcox became the first white man to reach its shore in 1899. Wilcox's subsequent writings, such as "no scene has given me an equal impression of inspiring solitude and rugged grandeur . . ." guaranteed its future popularity. Although Wilcox was a knowledgeable man, he named the lake on the assumption that it was dammed by a glacial moraine deposited by the retreating Wenkchemna Glacier. In fact, the large rockpile that blocks its waters was deposited by major rockfalls from the Tower of

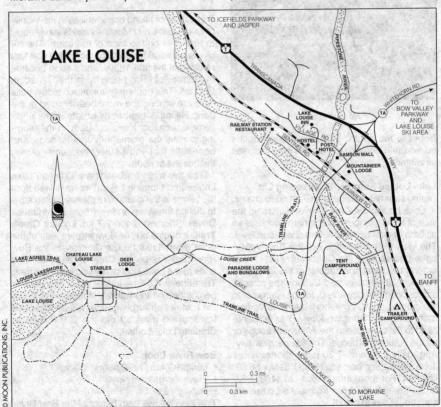

Moraine Lake

Babel to the south. The lake often remains frozen until June and the access road is closed all winter.

Lake Louise Summer Sightseeing Lift
During summer the Friendly Giant quad chairlift at Lake Louise Ski Area whisks visitors up the face of Mt. Whitehorn to Whitehorn Lodge, at an altitude of over two kilometers above sea level. The view from the lodge—of the Bow Valley, Lake Louise, and the Continental Divide—is among the most spectacular in the Canadian Rockies. Short trails lead through the forests, across open meadows, and, for the energetic, to the summit of Mt. Whitehorn over 600 vertical meters above. After working up an appetite head to the teahouse in the Whitehorn Lodge or try the outdoor barbecue. The lift operates July-Aug. daily 7:30 a.m.-7:30 p.m., shorter hours June and September; adult $9.50, senior $8.50, child $4. For more information call (403) 522-3555. Free shuttles run from Lake Louise accommodations to the lift.

Whitewater Rafting
Wild Water Adventures, tel. (403) 522-2211, operates two rafting adventures on the Kicking Horse River. Half-day trips depart from Lake Louise daily at 8:30 a.m. and 1:30 p.m. and the full-day trip leaves at 8:30 a.m. The prices are $59 and $89 respectively.

Horseback Riding
Brewster Lake Louise Stables, tel. (403) 522-3511, has hour-long rides (departing on the hour) for $21.40, rides to the end of Lake Louise for $32.10, half-day rides for $48.15, and all-day rides up Paradise Valley for $85.60.

HIKING

The variety of hiking opportunities in the vicinity of Lake Louise and Moraine Lake is surely equal to any area on the face of the earth. The region's potential for outdoor recreation was first realized in the late 1800s, and it soon became the center of hiking activity in the Canadian Rockies. This popularity continues today; trails here are among the most heavily used in the park. Hiking is best early or late in the short summer season. Head out early in the morning to miss the prams, high heels, dogs, and bear-bells that you'll surely encounter during the busiest periods.

The two main trailheads are Chateau Lake Louise and Moraine Lake. Two trails lead from the village to the chateau (a pleasant alternative to driving the steep and very busy Lake Louise Drive). Shortest is the 2.7-km **Louise Creek Trail.** It begins on the downstream side of the point where Lake Louise Dr. crosses the Bow River, crosses Louise Creek three times, and ends at the Lake Louise parking lot. The other, **Tramline,** is 4.5 km—longer but not as steep. It begins behind the railway station and follows the route of a narrow-gauge railway that once transported guests from the C.P.R. line to Chateau Lake Louise.

Bow River Loop
- Length: 7 km (1.5-2 hours)
- Elevation gain: minimal
- Rating: easy
This loop follows both banks of the Bow River

Chateau Lake Louise

southeast from the railway station. It links the station to the hostel, Post Hotel, Samson Mall, both campgrounds, and the Louise Creek and Tramline trails to Lake Louise. Interpretive signs along its length explain the ecosystem of the Bow River. It's used by joggers and cyclists to access various points in the village.

Louise Lakeshore

- Length: 2 km (30 minutes) one-way
- Elevation gain: none
- Rating: easy

Probably the park's busiest trail, it follows the north shore of Lake Louise, beginning in front of the chateau and ending at the west end of the lake. Numerous braided glacial streams here empty their silt-filled waters into Lake Louise. Along its length are benches to sit and ponder what English mountaineer James Outram once described as "a gem of composition and of coloring . . . perhaps unrivalled anywhere."

Plain of the Six Glaciers

- Length: 5.3 km (90 minutes) one-way
- Elevation gain: 370 meters
- Rating: easy/moderate

Hikers along this trail are not only rewarded with panoramic views of the glaciated peaks of the main range, but at the end of the trail is a rustic teahouse serving homemade goodies baked on a wooden stove. For the first two km the trail follows Louise Lakeshore Trail to the western end of the lake from where it begins a steady uphill climb through a forest of spruce and alpine fir. It enters an open area where an avalanche has come tumbling down (now a colorful carpet of wildflowers), then passes through a forested area into a vast wasteland of moraines produced by the advance and retreat of Victoria Glacier. Views of surrounding peaks continue to improve until the trail switchbacks through a stunted forest before arriving at the teahouse. Built by the C.P.R. at the turn of the century, the teahouse operates as it has since it was first built. Supplies are packed in by horse and all cooking is done in its rustic kitchen. It's open July-early September. After resting, it's worthwhile continuing one km to the end of the trail at the top of a narrow ridge of lateral moraine. From here the trail's namesakes are visible. From left to right the glaciers are Aberdeen, Upper Lefroy, Lower Lefroy, Upper Victoria, Lower Victoria, and Pope's. Between Mt. Lefroy (3,441 meters) and Mt. Victoria (3,459 meters) is Abbot Pass where it's possible to make out Abbot Hut on the skyline. When constructed in 1922 this stone structure was the highest building in Canada. The pass and hut are named for Phillip Abbot, who died attempting to climb Mt. Lefroy in 1896.

Lake Agnes

- Length: 3.6 km (90 minutes) one-way
- Elevation gain: 400 meters
- Rating: moderate

This strenuous hike is one of the park's most popular. It begins in front of the chateau, branching right near the beginning of the Louise Lakeshore Trail. For the first 2.5 km the trail climbs steeply, switchbacking through a forest of alpine fir and Engelmann spruce, crossing a horse trail, passing a lookout, and leveling out at tiny **Mirror Lake.** Here the old, traditional trail veers right (use if it's wet or snowy underfoot) while a more direct route veers left to the Plain of the Six Glaciers. Take a sharp right along a trail that climbs steeply below the Big Beehive. The final elevation gain along both trails is made easier by a flight of steps beside **Bridal Veil Falls,** ending beside a rustic teahouse that overlooks Lake Agnes, a subalpine lake nestled in a hanging valley carved out by a receding glacier. The teahouse offers homemade soups, healthy sandwiches, and a wide assortment of teas. From the teahouse a one-km trail leads to **Little Beehive** and impressive views of the Bow Valley. Another trail leads around the northern shore of Lake Agnes, climbing to Big Beehive (see below) or to the Plain of the Six Glaciers Trail (see above) 3.2 km from the chateau and 2.1 km from the teahouse at the end of that trail.

Big Beehive
- Length: 5 km (2 hours) one-way
- Elevation gain: 520 meters
- Rating: moderate

The lookout atop the larger of two "beehives" is one of the best places to admire the uniquely colored waters of Lake Louise, over half a kilometer directly below. The many variations in trails to the summit have one thing in common— all are steep. But the rewards are worth every drop of sweat along the way. The most popular route follows the Lake Agnes Trail for the first 3.6 km to Lake Agnes. From the teahouse, a trail leads to the western end of the lake, then switchbacks steeply up an exposed north-facing ridge. At the crest of the ridge, the trail forks. To the right it descends to the Plain of the Six Glaciers Trail, to the left it continues 300 meters to a log gazebo. This trail is not well defined but scrambling through the large boulders is easy. Across Lake Louise is Fairview Mountain (2,745 meters), and behind this peak is the distinctive shape of Mt. Temple (3,549 meters). Views also extend up the lake to Mt. Lefroy and northeast to Lake Louise Ski Area. Views from the edge of the cliff are spectacular but be very careful—

it's a long, long way down. By returning down the Lake Louise side of the Big Beehive the loop is 11.5 km (4-5 hours).

Saddleback
- Length: 3.7 km (90 minutes) one-way
- Elevation gain: 600 meters
- Rating: moderate

This trail climbs the lower slopes of Fairview Mountain from beside the boat shed on Lake Louise, ending in an alpine meadow with a view of Mt. Temple from across Paradise Valley. Four hundred meters from the trailhead the trail forks. Keep left and follow the steep switchbacks through a forest of Englemann spruce and alpine fir until reaching the flower-filled meadow. The meadow is actually a pass between Fairview Mountain (to the northwest) and Saddle Mountain (to the southeast). Although most hikers are content with the awesome views from the pass and return along the same trail, it is possible to continue to the summit of Fairview (2,745 meters), a further climb of 400 vertical meters. The barely discernible, switchbacking trail to the summit begins near a stand of larch trees above the crest of Saddleback. As you would expect, the view from the top is stupendous; Lake Louise is over one km directly below. This option is for strong, experienced hikers only. From the Saddleback the trail descends into **Sheol Valley,** then into **Paradise Valley.** The entire loop would be 15 km.

Paradise Valley
- Length: 18 km (6 hours) roundtrip
- Elevation gain: 380 meters
- Rating: moderate

This aptly named trail makes for a long day hike, but it can be broken up by overnighting at the backcountry campground at the far end of the loop. The trailhead is located 3.5 km along the Moraine Lake Rd. in a heavily forested area on the right. The trail climbs steadily for the first five km, crossing **Paradise Creek** numerous times and passing the junction of a trail that climbs the Sheol Valley to Saddleback (see above). After five km the trail divides again, following either side of the valley, forming a 13-km loop. **Lake Annette** is 700 meters along the left fork. It is a typical subalpine lake in a unique setting—nestled against the near-vertical 1,200-

meter north face of snow- and ice-capped **Mt. Temple** (3,549 meters), one of the 10 highest peaks in the Canadian Rockies. This difficult face was successfully climbed in 1966, relatively late for mountaineering "firsts." The lake is a worthy destination in itself—allow yourself four hours roundtrip from the trailhead. For those completing the entire loop, continue beyond the lake into an open avalanche area that affords views across Paradise Valley. Look and listen for pikas and marmots among the boulders. The trail then passes through **Horseshoe Meadow,** crosses Paradise Creek, and begins back down the valley. Keep to the left at all trail crossings and you'll quickly arrive at a series of waterfalls known as the **Giant Steps.** From the base of these falls it is eight km back to the trailhead.

Consolation Lakes
- Length: 3 km (1 hour) one-way
- Elevation gain: 65 meters
- Rating: easy/moderate

This short trail begins from the bridge over Moraine Creek near the Moraine Lake parking lot and ends at a pleasant subalpine lake. The first section of the trail traverses a boulder-strewn rock pile—the result of rock slides on the imposing Tower of Babel (3,101 meters)—before entering a dense forest of Engelmann spruce and alpine fir and following **Babel Creek** to the lower lake. The wide valley affords 360-degree views of the surrounding jagged peaks, including Mt. Temple back down the valley and Mt. Bident and Mt. Quandra at the far end of the lakes. After eating lunch while perched on one of many boulders, you could continue to Upper Consolation Lake by crossing Babel Creek and following a usually wet and muddy trail along the lake's eastern shore.

Larch Valley
- Length: 2.9 km (60-90 minutes) one-way
- Elevation gain: 450 meters
- Rating: moderate

In autumn, when the larch trees have turned a magnificent gold and the sun is shining, few spots in the Canadian Rockies can match the beauty of this valley. But don't expect to find much solitude. Although the most popular time for visiting the valley is fall, it is a worthy destination all summer. The trail begins just past

Moraine Lake Lodge and climbs fairly steeply with occasional glimpses of Moraine Lake below. After reaching the junction of the Eiffel Lake Trail, keep right, passing through an open forest of larch and into the meadow beyond. The range of larch is restricted within the park and this is one of the few areas where they are prolific. Mount Fay (3,235 meters) is the dominant peak on the skyline, rising above the other mountains that make up the Valley of the Ten Peaks.

Keen hikers will want to continue through the meadows to **Sentinel Pass** (2,608 meters), one of the park's highest passes. From the end of the meadow, the trail switchbacks for 1.2 km up a steep slope to the pass, sandwiched between Pinnacle Mountain (3,067 meters) and Mt. Temple (3,549 meters). From the pass most hikers opt to return along the same trail, although it is possible to continue into Paradise Valley.

Eiffel Lake
- Length: 5.6 km (2 hours) one-way
- Elevation gain: 400 meters
- Rating: moderate/difficult

Eiffel Lake is small, and looks even smaller in its rugged and desolate setting, surrounded by the famed Valley of the Ten Peaks. For the first 2.4 km, follow the Larch Valley Trail (see above), then fork left. Most of the elevation gain has already been made, and the trail remains relatively level before emerging onto an open slope from where each of the 10 peaks can be seen, along with Moraine Lake far below. From left to right the peaks are: Fay, Little, Bowlen, Perren, Septa, Allen, Tuzo, Deltaform, Neptuak, and Wenkchemna. The final two peaks are divided by **Wenkchemna Pass** (2,605 meters), a further four km and 360 vertical meters above Eiffel Lake. The lake itself soon comes into view. It lies in a depression formed by a rock slide from Neptuak Mountain. The lake is named for **Eiffel Peak** (3,085 meters), a rock pinnacle behind it, which with a little imagination could be compared to the Eiffel Tower in Paris.

Skoki Lodge
- Length: 14.4 km (5 hours) one-way
- Elevation gain: 775 meters
- Rating: moderate/difficult

The trail into historic Skoki Lodge is only one of the endless hiking opportunities tucked behind

Lake Louise Ski Area, across the valley from all hikes detailed above. Access to the Skoki Valley is from a parking lot on a gravel road that branches right from the ski area access road. The first four km of the trail are along a gravel access road leading to Temple Lodge, part of the Lake Louise Ski Area. From here, the trail climbs to **Boulder Pass,** passing a campground and Halfway Hut, above Corral Creek. The pass harbors a large population of pikas and hoary marmots. The trail then follows the north shore of Ptarmigan Lake before climbing again to **Deception Pass,** named for its false summit. It then descends into Skoki Valley, passing the Skoki Lakes and eventually reaching Skoki Lodge (see "Accommodations," below). Just over one km beyond the lodge is a campground, an excellent base for exploring the region.

WINTERTIME

Lake Louise is an immense winter playground offering one of the world's premier ski resorts, hundreds of kilometers of cross-country-ski trails, ice-skating, sleigh rides, nearby heli-skiing, and more. Between November and May, accommodation prices tumble by up to 70% (except Christmas holidays). Lift and lodging packages begin at $56 per person and you'll always be able to get a table at your favorite restaurant.

The most popular cross-country skiing areas are on Lake Louise, along Moraine Lake Rd., and in Skoki Valley at the back of Lake Louise Ski Area. For details and helpful trail classifications, pick up a copy of *Cross-country Skiing—Nordic Trails in Banff National Park* ($1) from the Lake Louise Visitor Centre. Before heading out check the weather forecast at the visitor center or call (403) 762-2088 for a recorded message. For avalanche reports call (403) 762-1460. On the first Sunday in March, the long-running **Lake Louise Loppet,** a Nordic-skiing competition, is held. Races are run at 10-km and 20-km distances, with prizes in 29 age categories. For details call the Calgary Ski Club at (403) 245-9496.

Of all the ice-skating rinks in Canada, the one on frozen Lake Louise, in front of the chateau, is surely the most spectacular. Spotlights allow skating after dark, and on special occasions hot chocolate is served. Skates are available in the chateau at **Monod Sports,** tel. (403) 522-3837; $8 for two hours.

The closest heli-skiing is a two-hour drive away in the Purcell Mountains. A bus from **R.K. Heli-ski** leaves the chateau each morning for a day of ultimate powder skiing. Their desk in the chateau is staffed daily, 4-9 p.m. For further information call (604) 342-3889.

Brewster Lake Louise Sleigh Rides, tel. (403) 522-3511, ext. 1210, or 762-5454, offers rides in traditional horse-drawn sleighs along the shores of Lake Louise beginning from in front of the chateau. Although blankets are supplied, you should still bundle up. The one-hour ride is $12 per person, $8 for children. Reservations are necessary. The rides are scheduled hourly from 11 a.m. on weekends, from 3 p.m. weekdays.

Lake Louise Ski Area

Canada's answer to the United States megaresorts such as Vail and Killington is Lake Louise. The nation's largest ski area comprises 40 square kilometers of gentle trails, mogul fields, long cruising runs, steep chutes, and vast bowls filled with famous Rocky Mountain powder.

The earliest skiing undertaken in the Lake Louise area was in the 1920s when groups from Banff went backcountry touring in the Skoki Valley. In 1930, Cliff White and Cyril Paris built a small ski chalet in the valley. The location of this chalet, 20 km from the nearest road, turned out not to be practical, so another, closer one was built on the site of today's Temple Lodge. In 1954, a lift was constructed next to Temple Lodge's back door, opening the slopes of Larch Mountain to the ever-increasing number of downhill enthusiasts in the area. A young Englishman who had inherited a fortune from his father saw the potential for a world-class ski resort here and made the completion of his dream a lifelong obsession. Norman Watson, known as the "Barmy Baronet," pulled together a group of financiers and constructed a gondola up the slopes of Whitehorn in 1958. More lifts were constructed and two runs—Olympic Men's Downhill and Olympic Ladies' Downhill—were cut on the south face of Whitehorn in anticipation of a successful bid for the 1968 Winter Olympics. The bid eventually failed due to the opposition of environmentalists (the same reasons that the alpine events of the Calgary Winter Olympics were held on a specially built hill outside of the park boundary). Huge development plans for the base area that included rooms for 6,500 guests were scuttled in 1972, but, under the supervision of one-time local mountain guide Charlie Locke, the area has continued to improve and grow, and often hosts World Cup skiing events.

The resort is made up of four distinct faces. The front side has a vertical drop of 1,000 meters and is served by eight lifts, including two high-speed quads. The four back bowls are each as big as many midsize ski areas and are all well above the treeline. Larch and Ptarmigan faces have a variety of terrain, allowing you to follow the sun as it moves across the sky or escape into trees for protection on windy days.

Each of the three day lodges has a restaurant and bar. Ski rentals, clothing, and souvenirs are available at the base area. Lift tickets are $42 per day, children and seniors $37. Lifts are open from early November to early May, 9 a.m.-4 p.m. Free guided tours of the mountain are available three times daily—inquire at customer service. Free shuttle buses run regularly from Lake Louise accommodations to the hill. From Banff you pay $15 roundtrip for transportation to Lake Louise. For more information on the ski area call (403) 522-3555.

ACCOMMODATIONS

In summer, for the price of the cheapest room in town, you could buy a tent, pay your campground fee with a smile, and sit around a campfire telling bear stories. If you must stay indoors it's essential to make reservations well in advance. Any rooms not taken by early afternoon will be the expensive ones. When making reservations for all lodging listed below, write to the establishment's P.O. Box followed by: **Lake Louise, AB T0L 1E0.**

Hotels
Originally called Lake Louise Ski Lodge, the **Post Hotel,** P.O. Box 69, tel. (403) 522-3989 or (800) 661-1586, is bordered to the east and south by the Pipestone River. It may lack views

of Lake Louise, but it is as elegant, in a modern, woodsy way, as the chateau. Each bungalow-style room is furnished with Canadian pine and has a balcony. Many have whirlpools and fireplaces, while some have kitchens. Other facilities include an indoor pool, steam room, and library. High tea is served in the lobby each afternoon. The hotel has 17 different room types, with 26 different rates depending on the view. Rates start at $155 s or d per night.

Across the road from the Post Hotel is **Lake Louise Inn,** P.O. Box 209, tel. (403) 522-3791 or (800) 661-9237, where rooms start at $120 per night. **Mountaineer Lodge,** P.O. Box 150, tel. (403) 522-3844, close to everything, is open in summer only. Rates start at $110 s or d. The historic **Deer Lodge,** P.O. Box 100, tel. (403) 522-3747 or (800) 661-1595, is located along Lake Louise Dr., just below Chateau Lake Louise, and has a good restaurant; $115-170. **Moraine Lake Lodge,** P.O. Box 70, tel. (403) 522-3733 or (800) 661-8340, is on the lake of the same name. Rooms are $175 per night; cabins with fireplaces start at $240.

Paradise Lodge and Bungalows
A much better deal, especially for those who like privacy or for families and small groups, is Paradise Lodge and Bungalows, P.O. Box 7, tel. (403) 522-3595. Spread out around the well-manicured gardens are self-contained cabins beginning at $125 per night. Bungalows with kitchens are $130 for one bedroom and $150 for two bedrooms. A few self-contained two-room units with large balconies boast views across the Bow Valley; $160. Newly built suites, each with a fireplace, TV, two rooms, and fabulous mountain view start at $180, $190 with a kitchen. Honeymoon suites, with all of the above as well as a jacuzzi, are $215. The lodge is open mid-May to mid-October. To get there from the valley floor, follow Lake Louise Dr. toward Chateau Lake Louise for two kilometers.

Chateau Lake Louise
This historic 520-room hotel, on the shore of Lake Louise, has views equal to any mountain resort in the world. But all this historic charm and mountain scenery comes at a price. During the summer season (June to mid-October), a standard room is $185, mountainside $261, and

Paradise Lodge and Bungalows

lakeside $349. Rates drop 40% outside of summer and many ski packages are advertised in winter. Children under 17 sharing with parents are free, but if you bring a pet it'll be an extra $20. For reservations—and you'll need one— write to P.O. Box 96; tel. (403) 522-3511 or (800) 441-1414.

Skoki Lodge

Skoki is a rustic lodge, deep in the backcountry, north of Lake Louise Ski Area. Getting there requires an 11-km hike or ski depending on the season. The lodge is an excellent base for exploring nearby valleys and mountains. For information and reservations write to P.O. Box 5; tel. (403) 522-3555.

Hostel

At around $90 less than any other bed in town **Lake Louise International Hostel** fills up quickly each day. Of log construction, with large windows and high vaulted ceilings, the hostel was a joint venture between the Alpine Club of Cana-

da and the Southern Alberta Hostelling Association. It opened early in the summer of 1992 with extensions in 1995 bringing the total number of beds to 150. Downstairs is a large reception area and **Bill Peyto's Cafe,** the least expensive place to eat in Lake Louise. Upstairs is a large lounge area and guides room—a quiet place to plan your next hike or browse through the large collection of mountain literature. Hostel members pay $18 per night in a four- or six-bed dorm, or $22.50 in a two-bed dorm. Nonmembers pay $25 and $29, respectively. The hostel is open year-round. In summer and on weekends during the ski season, advance bookings (up to six months) are essential. Write P.O. Box 115, Lake Louise, AB T0L 1E0; tel. (403) 522-2200. The hostel is located along Village Rd., one km from Samson Mall.

Campgrounds

Lake Louise Campground, within easy walking distance of the village, is divided into two areas by the Bow River. One side has unserviced sites, the other serviced. Individual sites are close together, but some privacy and shade are provided by towering lodgepole pines. The unserviced (tent camping) sites have flush toilets, kitchen shelters, fire rings, and free firewood; $12 per night. Serviced (trailer camping) sites have power and flush toilets; $16. A dump station is located near the entrance to the campground. An interpretive program runs throughout summer, nightly at 9 p.m. in the outdoor theater. **Bow River Loop** leads into the village along either side of the Bow River, crossing at the southern end of the serviced sites and again behind Samson Mall. To get to the campground take Lake Louise Dr. under the railway bridge, turn left on Fairview Dr., and continue past the impressive log staff accommodations to the fee station. The campground is open year-round.

FOOD AND DRINK

On the Cheap

Samson Mall is the center of much activity each afternoon as campers descend on the grocery store to stock up on supplies for the evening meal. Prices are high and by the end of the day stocks are low. **Laggan's Mountain Bakery,**

in the mall, is *the* place to hang out with a coffee and one of their delicious freshly baked cakes or muffins. If the tables are full and you manage to somehow reach the cake cabinet, order takeout and enjoy your feast on the grassy bank behind the mall. The chocolate brownie ($1.30) is delicious. Order two slices to save having to line up again. It's open daily 6 a.m.-7 p.m.

Forget the Bar and Grill in the mall—much better is **Bill Peyto's Cafe** in the hostel on Village Road. The food is consistent and well priced. A huge portion of nachos is $7. You don't have to be staying in the hostel to eat there. Open daily 7 a.m.-9 p.m. The **Lake Louise Inn,** tel. (403) 522-3791, has a barbecue buffet in a gazebo (7-8 p.m.), $18 per person. Other inexpensive alternatives are the **Mountain Restaurant,** in the Esso station, and **Lake Louise Trading Post,** beside Deer Lodge on Lake Louise Drive.

Lake Louise Station Restaurant

One hundred years ago visitors departing trains at Laggan Station were keen to get to the Chateau Lake Louise as quickly as possible to begin their adventure. Today, guests from the chateau, other hotels, and even people from as far away as Banff are returning to the restored station to dine in this unique restaurant. Although the menu is not extensive, the ample variety satisfies most tastes. Open for lunch and dinner. For reservations call (403) 522-2600.

Chateau Lake Louise

Within this famous hotel are a choice of eateries and an ice-cream shop. The **Poppy Room** has obscured lake views and is the most casual place for a meal. A continental buffet breakfast is served 7-9 a.m.; $9. For dinner a pizza and pasta buffet is offered ($15), or order off the menu. It's open till 8:30 p.m. **Walliser Stube** is an elegant two-story wine bar decorated with oak furniture. It offers a simple menu of German dishes from $13.95 as well as cheese fondue. **Lakeside Terrace** is an open-front grill. Victorian afternoon tea of crumpets, sandwiches, desserts, and drinks is served each afternoon; $14.95. **Glacier Saloon** is a Western-style saloon serving light meals; open noon-1 a.m. **Edelweiss Room** has the best view of Lake Louise and offers the chateau's most ele-

gant dining. Appetizers start at $4.50 while entrees from the fish, game, chicken, and meat menu start at $17.

Post Hotel

In 1987, the Post Hotel was expanded to include a luxurious new wing. The original log building was renovated as a rustic, timbered, dining room, linked to the rest of the hotel by an intimate bar. Although eating here is not cheap, it's a favorite of locals and visitors alike. The chef specializes in European cuisine—preparing a number of Swiss dishes (such as veal Zurichoise) to make owner George Schwarz feel homesick—but he's also renowned for his presentation of Alberta beef, Pacific salmon, and Peking duck. Main meals start at $20. The restaurant is open daily 7 a.m.-2 p.m. and 5-9:30 p.m. Reservations are essential for dinner; call (403) 522-3989.

Drink

Hang out with seasonal workers at **Lake Louise Bar and Grill,** upstairs in Samson Mall, or head to rowdy **Charlie's Pub** in the Lake Louise Inn for dancing to recorded music. Although the bar in the Post Hotel doesn't have mountain views, it has light food, a fireplace, and a distinctive mountain atmosphere. In the Chateau Lake Louise is **The Glacier Saloon,** where on most summer nights a DJ plays music ranging from pop to western.

TRANSPORTATION

Getting There

Calgary International Airport is the closest major airport to Lake Louise. **Brewster,** tel. (403) 762-6700, operates a bus service leaving the airport three times daily, stopping at Banff, Samson Mall, and the chateau. The bus arriving at 1:10 p.m. continues to Jasper (April-Oct. only). The earliest service back to the airport departs at 7:40 a.m. Lake Louise to Banff is $12.50, to Calgary and Jasper $36.

Greyhound, tel. (403) 522-2121 or (800) 661-8747, leaves the Calgary Bus Depot at 877 Greyhound Way SW five times daily for Banff and Lake Louise, $19.45. Banff to Lake Louise is $7.35. Buses leave Vancouver from 1150

Station St., tel. (604) 662-3222, three times daily for the 13-hour haul to Lake Louise; $93.57.

Getting Around

The campground, hostel, and hotels are all within easy walking distance of Samson Mall. Chateau Lake Louise is a 2.7-km walk from the valley floor. The only car rental agency in the village is **Tilden,** tel. (403) 522-3870 or (800) 387-4747. The agency doesn't have many cars; you'd be better off picking one up in Banff or at Calgary International Airport. **Lake Louise Taxi & Tours** is located in Samson Mall, tel. (403) 522-2020; flag drop is $2.30, then $1.25 per km. From the mall to Chateau Lake Louise runs around $9, to Moraine Lake $16, and to Banff $85. **Wilson Mountain Sports,** in Samson Mall, tel. (403) 522-3636, has mountain bikes for rent for $7 per hour or $28 per day (includes a helmet, bike lock, and water bottle). Inquire here about canoe rentals for float trips along the Bow River to Banff.

Tours

No tours of the area are offered for visitors staying in Lake Louise. For those staying in Banff, **Brewster Transportation and Tours,** tel. (403) 762-6700, has a four-hour tour departing select Banff hotels daily 1:15-1:40 p.m. to Lake Louise; $38. In winter this tour departs in the morning, runs five hours, and includes Banff sights; $36.

SERVICES AND INFORMATION

Services

Located in Samson Mall is a small postal outlet serving as a bus depot and car rental agency. Although Lake Louise has no banks, there's a currency exchange in the Chateau Lake Louise and a cash machine in the grocery store. The mall also has a laundromat that's always busy, and downstairs are military-style showers; $2.50. Open in summer, daily 8 a.m.-8 p.m., shorter hours the rest of the year. Camping supplies are available from **Wilson Mountain Sports** and photographic supplies from **Pipestone Photo.** Pipestone has a one-hour photo-developing service and is the only place in the park offering overnight slide developing; tel. (403) 522-3617. The closest **hospital** is in Banff, tel. (403) 762-2222. For the **RCMP** call (403) 522-3811.

Information

Woodruff & Blum, located in the Samson Mall, tel. (403) 522-3842, has an excellent selection of books on the natural and human history of the park, animal field guides, hiking guides, and general western Canadiana.

The **Lake Louise Visitor Centre,** tel. (403) 522-3833, is located beside Samson Mall on Village Road. This excellent facility has interpretive displays, slide and video displays, and park staff on hand to answer questions, issue backcountry camping permits, and recommend hikes suited to your ability. Look for the stuffed (literally) female grizzly and read her fascinating, but sad, story.

ICEFIELDS PARKWAY/BANFF

The 230-km Icefields Parkway, between Lake Louise and Jasper, is one of the most scenic, exciting, and inspiring mountain roads ever built. From Lake Louise it parallels the Continental Divide, following in the shadow of the highest, most rugged mountains in the Canadian Rockies. The first 122 km to Sunwapta Pass (the boundary between Banff and Jasper National Parks) can be driven in two hours, and the entire parkway in four. But it's likely you'll want to spend at least a day, probably more, stopping at each of the 13 viewpoints, hiking the trails, watching the abundant wildlife, and just generally enjoying one of the world's most magnificent landscapes. Along the section within Banff National Park are two lodges, three hostels, three campgrounds, and one gas station.

Although the road is steep and winding in places, it has a wide shoulder, making it ideal for an extended bike trip. Allow seven days to pedal north from Banff to Jasper, staying at hostels or camping along the route. This is the preferable direction to travel by bike as the elevation of Jasper townsite is more than 500 meters lower than either Banff townsite or Lake Louise.

History
Natives and early explorers found the swampy nature of the Bow Valley difficult for foot and horse travel. They used instead the Pipestone River Valley, farther east, when heading north. Banff guide Bill Peyto led American explorer Walter Wilcox up the Bow Valley in 1896, to the high peaks along the Continental Divide northeast of Lake Louise. The first complete journey along this route was made by Jim Brewster in 1904. Soon after, A.P. Coleman made the arduous journey, becoming a strong supporter for the route aptly known as "The Wonder Trail." During the Great Depression of the 1930s, as part of a relief-work project, construction began on what was to become the Icefields Parkway. It was completed in 1939 and the first car traveled the route in 1940. In tribute to the excellence of the road's early construction, when upgraded to its present standard in 1961 the original roadbed was followed nearly the entire way.

The parkway remains open year-round, although winter brings with it some special considerations. The road is often closed for short periods for avalanche control—check road conditions in Banff or Lake Louise before setting out. And fill up with gas—no services are available between November and April.

SIGHTS

The Icefields Parkway forks right from the TransCanada Hwy. just north of Lake Louise. The impressive scenery begins immediately. Just three km from the junction is **Herbert Lake,** formed during the last ice age when retreating glaciers deposited a pile of rubble—known as a moraine—across a shallow valley and water filled in behind it. The lake is a perfect place for early morning or evening photography when the **Waputik Range** and distinctively shaped **Mt. Temple** are reflected in its waters.

Traveling north, you'll notice numerous depressions in the steep, shaded slopes of the Waputik Range across the Bow Valley. The cooler climate on these north-facing slopes makes them prone to glaciation. Cirques were cut by small "local glaciers." On the opposite side of the road, **Mt. Hector** (3,394 meters), easily recognized by its layered peak, soon comes into view.

Hector Lake Viewpoint is 16 km from the junction. Although the view is partially obscured by trees, the emerald-green waters nestled below a massive wall of limestone form a breathtaking scene. **Bow Peak,** seen looking northward along the highway, is only 2,868 meters high but is completely detached from the Waputik Range, making it a popular destination for mountain climbers. As you leave this viewpoint look across the northeast end of Hector Lake for glimpses of **Mt. Balfour** (3,246 meters) on the distant skyline.

Crowfoot Glacier
The aptly named Crowfoot Glacier can best be appreciated from north of Bow Lake. From the

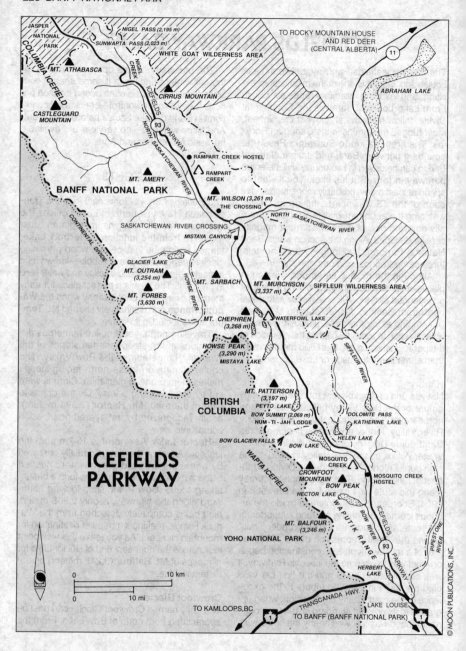

TO ROCKY MOUNTAIN HOUSE
AND RED DEER
(CENTRAL ALBERTA)

JASPER NATIONAL PARK

COLUMBIA ICEFIELD

MT. ATHABASCA

CASTLEGUARD MOUNTAIN

NIGEL PASS (2,195 m)
SUNWAPTA PASS (2,023 m)

WHITE GOAT WILDERNESS AREA

ABRAHAM LAKE

CIRRUS MOUNTAIN

NIGEL CREEK

ICEFIELDS PARKWAY

93

NORTH SASKATCHEWAN RIVER

MT. AMERY

BANFF NATIONAL PARK

RAMPART CREEK HOSTEL
RAMPART CREEK

MT. WILSON (3,261 m)
THE CROSSING

SASKATCHEWAN RIVER CROSSING

NORTH SASKATCHEWAN RIVER

MISTAYA CANYON

CONTINENTAL DIVIDE

GLACIER LAKE
MT. OUTRAM (3,254 m)

MT. FORBES (3,630 m)

MT. SARBACH

HOWSE RIVER

MT. MURCHISON (3,337 m)

SIFFLEUR WILDERNESS AREA

MT. CHEPHREN (3,268 m)

WATERFOWL LAKE

HOWSE PEAK (3,290 m)
MISTAYA LAKE

SIFFLEUR RIVER

MT. PATTERSON (3,197 m)
PEYTO LAKE
BOW SUMMIT (2,069 m)

BRITISH COLUMBIA

NUM-TI-JAH LODGE

BOW GLACIER FALLS

BOW LAKE

DOLOMITE PASS
KATHERINE LAKE

HELEN LAKE

ICEFIELDS PARKWAY

WAPTA ICEFIELD

MOSQUITO CREEK

CROWFOOT MOUNTAIN
BOW PEAK

HECTOR LAKE

MOSQUITO CREEK HOSTEL

WAPUTIK RANGE

BOW RIVER

MT. BALFOUR (3,246 m)

YOHO NATIONAL PARK

ICEFIELDS PARKWAY

93

PIPESTONE RIVER

HERBERT LAKE

0   10 km
0   10 mi

TRANSCANADA HWY.
LAKE LOUISE

TO KAMLOOPS, BC

1

TO BANFF (BANFF NATIONAL PARK)

1

© MOON PUBLICATIONS, INC.

viewpoint, 17 km north of Hector Lake, it is easy to see how this and other glaciers are formed. It sits on a wide ledge near the top of Crowfoot Mountain from where its glacial "claws" cling to the mountain's steep slopes. The retreat of this glacier has been dramatic. It was only 50 years ago that two of the claws extended to the base of the lower cliff.

Bow Lake

The sparkling, translucent waters of Bow Lake are among the most beautiful that can be seen from the Icefields Parkway. The lake was created when moraines, left behind by retreating glaciers, dammed subsequent meltwater. On still days, the water reflects the snowy peaks, their sheer cliffs, and the scree slopes that run into the lake. You don't need to take a photography class to take good pictures here! At the southeast end of the lake is a day-use area with waterfront picnic tables and a trail that leads to a swampy area at the lake's outlet. At the upper end of the lake is a lodge and the trailhead for a walk to Bow Glacier Falls (see "Hiking," below).

The road leaves Bow Lake and climbs to **Bow Summit.** Looking back, the true color of Bow Lake becomes apparent and the Crowfoot Glacier reveals its unique shape. At an elevation of 2,069 meters, this pass is one of the highest points crossed by a public road in Canada. It is also the beginning of the Bow River, the one you camped beside at Lake Louise, photographed flowing through the town of Banff, and strolled along in downtown Calgary.

Peyto Lake

From the parking lot at Bow Summit, a short paved trail leads to one of the most breathtaking views that you could ever imagine. Far below the viewpoint is Peyto Lake, an impossibly intense green-colored lake whose hues change according to season. Before heavy melting of nearby glaciers begins (June to early July), the lake is dark blue. As summer progresses, meltwater flows across a delta and into the lake. This water is laden with fine particles of ground-rock debris known as "rock flour," which remains suspended in the water. It is not the mineral content of the rock flour that is responsible for the lake's unique color, but rather the particles reflecting the blue-green sector of the light spectrum. Hence, as the amount of suspended rock flour changes, so does the color of the lake.

The lake is one of many park landmarks named for early outfitter Bill Peyto. In 1898 he was part of an expedition camped at Bow Lake. Seeking solitude (as he was wont to do), he slipped off during the night to sleep near this lake. Other members of the party coined the name "Peyto's Lake," and it stuck.

A further three km along the parkway is a viewpoint from where **Peyto Glacier** is visible at the far end of Peyto Lake Valley. This glacier is part of the extensive **Wapta Icefield** that straddles the Continental Divide and extends into the north-

spectacular Bow Lake and Crowfoot Glacier

ern reaches of **Yoho National Park** in British Columbia.

Beside the Continental Divide

From Bow Pass the parkway descends to a viewpoint directly across the Mistaya River from **Mt. Patterson** (3,197 meters). **Snowbird Glacier** clings precariously to the mountain's steep northeast face, and the mountain's lower, wooded slopes are heavily scarred where rock and ice slides have swept down the mountainside.

As the parkway continues to descend and crosses **Silverhorn Creek,** the jagged limestone peaks of the Continental Divide can be seen to the west. **Mistaya Lake** is a three-km-long body of water that sits at the bottom of the valley between the road and the divide, but it can't be seen from the parkway. The best place to view this panorama is from the **Howse Peak Viewpoint** at Upper Waterfowl Lake. From here the high ridge that forms the Continental Divide is easily distinguishable. Seven peaks can be seen from here including **Howse Peak** (3,290 meters). At no point along this ridge does the elevation drop below 2,750 meters. From Howse Peak the Continental Divide makes a 90-degree turn to the west. One dominant peak that can be seen from Bow Pass to north of Saskatchewan River Crossing is **Mt. Chephren** (3,268 meters). Its distinctive shape and position away from the main ridge of the Continental Divide make it easy to distinguish (directly north of Howse Peak).

To Saskatchewan River Crossing

Numerous trails lead around the swampy shores of **Upper** and **Lower Waterfowl Lakes,** providing one of the park's best opportunities to view moose, who feed on the abundant aquatic vegetation that grows in Upper Waterfowl Lake. Rock and other debris that has been carried down nearby valley systems has built up, forming a wide alluvial fan, nearly blocking the **Mistaya River** and creating Upper Waterfowl Lake.

Continuing north is **Mt. Murchison** (3,337 meters), on the east side of the parkway. Although not one of the park's highest mountains, this gray-and-yellow massif of Cambrian rock includes 10 individual peaks, covering an area of 30 square km.

From a parking lot 14 km northeast of Waterfowl Lake Campground, a short trail descends

into the montane forest to **Mistaya Canyon.** Here, the effects of erosion can be appreciated as the Mistaya River leaves the floor of Mistaya Valley, plunging through a narrow-walled canyon into the North Saskatchewan Valley. The area is scarred with potholes where boulders have been whirled around by the action of fast-flowing water, carving deep depressions into the softer limestone bedrock below.

The **North Saskatchewan River** posed a major problem for early travelers and later for the builders of the Icefields Parkway. This swiftly running river eventually drains into Hudson Bay. In 1989 it was named a Canadian Heritage River. A panoramic viewpoint of the entire valley is located one km past the bridge. From here the Howse and Mistaya Rivers can be seen converging with the North Saskatchewan at a silt-laden delta. This is also a junction with Hwy. 11 (also known as David Thompson Hwy.), which follows the North Saskatchewan River to Rocky Mountain House and Red Deer. From this viewpoint numerous peaks can be seen to the west. Two sharp peaks are distinctive. **Mount Outram** (3,254 meters) is the closer. The farther is **Mt. Forbes** (3,630 meters), highest peak in Banff National Park (and sixth-highest in the Canadian Rockies).

To Sunwapta Pass

On the north side of the North Saskatchewan River is the towering hulk of **Mt. Wilson** (3,261 meters), named for Banff outfitter Tom Wilson. The Icefields Parkway passes this massif on its western flanks. A pullout, just past Rampart Creek Campground, has good views of Mt. Amery to the west and Mounts Sarbach, Chephren, and Murchison to the south. Beyond here is the **Weeping Wall,** a long cliff of gray limestone where a series of waterfalls tumbles over 100 meters down the steep slopes of **Cirrus Mountain.** In winter this wall of water freezes, becoming a mecca for ice climbers. After climbing quickly, the road drops again, before beginning the long climb to Sunwapta Pass. Before ascending to the pass the road makes a sweeping curve over an alluvial plain of the North Saskatchewan River. Halfway up the 360-vertical-meter climb is a viewpoint well worth stopping for. Cyclists will definitely appreciate a rest. From here views extend down the valley to the slopes of Mt. Saskatchewan and, on the other side of the parkway, Cirrus Mountain. Another viewpoint, farther up the road, has the added attraction of **Panther Falls** across the valley. A cairn at **Sunwapta Pass** (2,023 meters) marks the boundary between Banff and Jasper National Parks. It also marks the divide between the North Saskatchewan and Sunwapta Rivers, whose waters drain into the Atlantic and Arctic oceans, respectively.

HIKING

Helen Lake
- Length: 6 km (2.5 hours) one-way
- Elevation gain: 455 meters
- Rating: moderate

The trail to Helen Lake is one of the easiest ways to access true alpine environment from the southern end of the Icefields Parkway. The trailhead is opposite Crowfoot Glacier Lookout, 33 km from the junction with the TransCanada Highway. The trail climbs steadily through a forest of Engelmann spruce and alpine fir for the first 2.5 km to an avalanche slope, reaching the treeline after three km. The view across the valley is spectacular, with Crowfoot Glacier visible to the southwest. As the trail reaches a ridge, it turns 180 degrees and descends into the glacial cirque where Helen Lake lies. Listen and look for hoary marmots around the scree slopes along the lakeshore. For those with the time and energy, it's possible to continue an additional three km to **Dolomite Pass**. The trail to the pass switchbacks steeply a further 100 vertical meters before descending to Katherine Lake and Dolomite Pass.

Bow Glacier Falls
- Length: 3.4 km (1 hour) one-way
- Elevation gain: 130 meters
- Rating: easy/moderate

This hike skirts one of the most beautiful lakes in the Canadian Rockies before ending at a narrow but spectacular waterfall. The trail begins beside Num-ti-jah Lodge at the north end of Bow Lake and follows the shore through Willow Flats to a gravel outwash area at the end of the lake. Across the lake are reflected views of Crowfoot Mountain and, farther west, a glimpse of Bow

Glacier among the jagged peaks of the Waputik Range. The trail then begins a short but steep climb up the rim of a canyon before leveling out at the edge of a vast moraine of gravel, scree, and boulders. This is the end of the trail, although it's possible to reach the base of Bow Glacier Falls by picking your way through the 800 meters of rough ground that remains.

Peyto Lake
- Length: 1.4 km (30 minutes) one-way
- Elevation loss: 100 meters
- Rating: easy

Without doubt the best place to view Peyto Lake is from the popular viewpoint accessible via a short trail from Bow Summit. From here a trail drops nearly 300 meters in 2.4 km to the lake. For those wanting to reach the lake's shore there is an easier alternative. From a small parking lot 2.4 km north of Bow Summit an unmarked trail leads 1.4 km to the shore of this famous lake. The pebbled beach, strewn with driftwood, is the perfect setting for picnicking, painting, or admiring the lake's quieter side.

Chephren Lake
- Length: 4 km (60-90 minutes) one-way
- Elevation gain: 100 meters
- Rating: easy/moderate

This pale-green body of water is hidden from sight of those traveling the Icefields Parkway. The trailhead is located within **Waterfowl Lakes Campground,** where the Mistaya River flows into the lake. The trail crosses the Mistaya River, 400 meters from the trailhead, then dives headlong into a subalpine forest until reaching the lake, nestled under the buttresses of Mt. Chephren. To the left is Howse Peak. The trail to **Cirque Lake** (4.5 km from trailhead) branches left after 1.7 km and is less heavily used.

Glacier Lake
- Length: 9 km (2.5-3 hours) one-way
- Elevation gain: 220 meters
- Rating: moderate

This three-km-long lake is one of the largest backcountry lakes in the park. Although not as scenic as the more accessible lakes along the parkway, it's a pleasant destination for a full-day or overnight trip. The trailhead is in an old gravel pit on the west side of the highway, one km north of the Saskatchewan River Crossing service center. For the first kilometer the trail passes through an open forest of lodgepole pine to a fancy footbridge across the rushing North Saskatchewan River. It then climbs gradually to a viewpoint overlooking Howse River and the valley beyond before turning away from the river for a long slog through a dense forest to Glacier Lake. A primitive campground is located just over 300 meters from where the trail emerges at the lake.

Saskatchewan Glacier
- Length: 7.3 km (2 hours) one-way
- Elevation gain: 150 meters
- Rating: moderate

The Saskatchewan Glacier, a tongue of ice from the great Columbia Icefield, is visible from various points along the Icefields Parkway. This hike will take you right to the toe of the glacier. The trailhead is an old concrete bridge located on the gravel flats just before the road begins its "big bend," 35 km north of the Saskatchewan River Crossing service center. The trail begins across the bridge, disappearing into the forest to the right, joining an old access road, and continuing up the valley along the south bank of the river. When the toe of the glacier first comes into sight it looks deceptively close. It is still a long hike over rough terrain to the actual glacier.

Nigel Pass
- Length: 7.4 km (2.5 hours) one-way
- Elevation gain: 365 meters
- Rating: moderate/difficult

On the east side of the Icefields Parkway, 2.5 km north of the switchback on the "big bend," is a gravel road that leads to a locked gate. Turn right here and cross Nigel Creek on the bridge. The trail is obvious, following open avalanche paths up the east side of the valley. In a stand of Engelmann spruce and alpine fir two km from the trailhead is an old campsite used first by native hunting parties, then by mountaineers exploring the area around the Columbia Icefield. Look for carvings on trees recording these early visitors. From here the trail continues to climb steadily, only increasing in gradient for the last one km to the pass. The pass (2,195 meters) marks the boundary between Banff and Jasper National Parks. For the best view, scramble over the rocks to the left. To the north, the view extends down the Brazeau River Valley, surrounded by a mass of peaks. To the west (left) is **Nigel Peak** (3,211 meters) and southwest are views of Parker's Ridge and the glaciated peaks of Mt. Athabasca.

Parker's Ridge
- Length: 2.4 km (1 hour) one-way
- Elevation gain: 210 meters
- Rating: easy/moderate

This short trail into the alpine begins from a parking lot at the north end of the park, just four km south of Sunwapta Pass. From the trailhead on the west side of the road, the wide path gains elevation quickly through open meadows and scattered stands of alpine fir. This fragile environment is easily destroyed, so it's very important that you stay on the trail. During the short alpine summer, these meadows are carpeted with red heather, white mountain avens, and blue alpine forget-me-nots. From the summit of the ridge, you look down on the two-km-wide Saskatchewan Glacier spreading out below. Beyond is **Castleguard Mountain,** renowned for its extensive cave system.

ACCOMMODATIONS

Lodging
Pioneer guide and outfitter Jimmy Simpson built **Num-ti-jah Lodge** on the north shore of Bow Lake in 1920. In those days, the route north from Lake Louise was nothing more than a horse trail. The desire to build a large structure when only short timbers were available led to the unusual octagonal shape of the main lodge. Simpson remained at Bow Lake, a living legend, until his death in 1972. Today the lodge continues to offer facilities for travelers along the highway. Rooms here cost $70 s, $100 d; most units have private baths. A small coffee shop is open daily 9 a.m.-5:30 p.m., and **Elkhorn Dining Room** is open for dinner. Horseback rides are offered for guests and nonguests. A one-hour ride along Bow Lake is $20, a three-hour ride to Peyto Lake is $41, and a full-day ride to Helen Lake is $85. Write to the lodge at P.O. Box 39, Lake Louise, AB T0L 1E0; tel. (403) 522-2167.

Just north of Saskatchewan River Crossing, 45 km south of the Columbia Icefield, is **The Crossing** (Mail Bag 333, Lake Louise, AB T0L 1E0; tel. 403-761-7000), with rooms for $73 s, $78 d (40% discount in spring and fall), a restaurant, cafeteria, lounge, large gift shop, and gas.

Hostels

From Lake Louise, hostels are located at Km 24, 88, and 118 of the Icefields Parkway. The first is **Mosquito Creek Hostel,** which has good hiking nearby, accommodations for 38 in four cabins, and a large common room with fireplace, a kitchen, and a wood-heated sauna. **Rampart Creek Hostel** is located 12 km north of Saskatchewan River Crossing, a long day's bike ride from Mosquito Creek. Accommodation for 30 is in two cabins, and there's a kitchen, sauna, and good hiking nearby. After the long climb up to Sunwapta Pass, **Hilda Creek Hostel** will be a welcome sight for cyclists. This hostel is located just below the glacial moraines left by the re-

treating Columbia Icefield and has a variety of hikes beginning from the doorstep. It has 21 dorm beds, kitchen, sauna, and a common room. Members $10-11, nonmembers $15-16. Mosquito Creek is open year-round; the latter two, nightly mid-May to mid-October and weekends only mid-December to mid-May (closed the rest of the year). It's recommended to book ahead during July and August as these hostels fill each night. Rampart Creek requires reservations between November and May. Reservations can be made at the hostels in Banff (tel. 403-762-4122), Lake Louise (tel. 403-522-2200), or Calgary (tel. 403-237-8282).

Campgrounds

Campgrounds are located at **Mosquito Creek** (Km 24; $9), **Waterfowl Lake** (Km 57; $12), and **Rampart Creek** (Km 88; $9). Each has pit toilets, kitchen shelters, firewood, and fire rings, but no showers or hookups, and each is open from mid-June to early September. Mosquito Creek also remains open for winter camping.

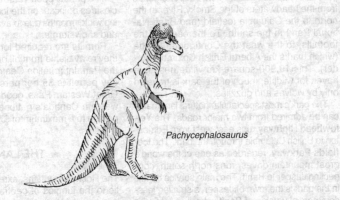

Pachycephalosaurus

BOB RACE

KAREN M°KINLEY

JASPER NATIONAL PARK
INTRODUCTION

Snowcapped peaks, vast icefields, beautiful glacial lakes, soothing hot springs, thundering rivers, and the most extensive backcountry trail system of any Canadian national park make Jasper a stunning counterpart to its sister park, Banff. A three-and-a-half-hour drive west of the provincial capital of Edmonton, Jasper extends from the headwaters of the Smoky River in the north to the Columbia Icefield (and Banff National Park) in the south. To the east are the foothills, to the west the Continental Divide (which marks the Alberta/British Columbia border). This 10,900-square-km wilderness is a haven for wildlife; much of the park is traveled only by wolves and grizzlies.

The park's most spectacular natural landmarks can be admired from two major roads. The **Yellowhead Highway** runs east-west from Edmonton to British Columbia through the park. The **Icefields Parkway,** regarded as one of the world's great mountain drives, runs north-south, connecting Jasper to Banff. The main service center in the park is the town of Jasper, a smaller, less-commercial version of Banff, where you'll find a number of motels and restaurants. Many of the park's campgrounds are accessible by road, while others are located throughout the backcountry. Also popular in the park are fishing, boating, downhill skiing, golfing, horseback riding, and white-water rafting.

The park is open year-round, although road closures do occur on the Icefields Parkway during winter months due to avalanche-control work and snowstorms.

Permits are required for entry into the park; they're available from all park gates as well as the Park Information Centre in Jasper. A one-day permit is $5 per person, and an annual Great Western Pass, good for entry to all 11 of western Canada's national parks, is $35 per person to a maximum of $70 per vehicle.

THE LAND

The Rocky Mountains, extending from the Arctic to the jungles of central Mexico, form the backbone of North America. Although the peaks of Jasper National Park are not particularly high, they are among the most spectacular along the range's entire length. About 100 million years ago, layers of sedimentary rock—laid down here up to a billion years ago—were forced upward, folded, and twisted under tremendous pressure into the mountains seen today. The land's contours were further altered during four ice ages that began around a million years ago. The last ice age ended about 10,000 years ago, and the vast glaciers began to retreat. A remnant of this final sheet of ice is the huge Columbia Icefield; approximately 325 square km and up to 400 meters deep, it's the most extensive icefield in the Rocky Mountains. As the glaciers retreated, piles of rock melted out and were left behind. Meltwater from the glaciers flowed down the valleys and was dammed up behind the moraines. Maligne Lake, like many other lakes in the park, was created by this process. The glacial silt suspended in the lake's waters produces amazing emerald, turquoise, and amethyst colors; early artists who painted these lakes had trouble convincing people that their images were real.

In addition to creating the park's gemlike lakes, the retreating glaciers carved out the valleys that they ever-so-slowly flowed through. The **Athabasca River Valley** is the park's largest watershed, a typical example of a U-shaped, glacier-carved valley. The Athabasca River flows north through the valley into the Mackenzie River System and ultimately into the Arctic Ocean. The glacial silt that paints the park's lakes is also carried down streams into the Athabasca, giving the river a pale-green "milky" look. Another beautiful aspect of the park's scenery is its abundance of waterfalls. They vary from the sparkling tumble of Mountain Creek as it cascades down a limestone cliff into a picturesque pool at Punchbowl Falls, to the roar of Athabasca Falls where the river is forced through a narrow gorge.

FLORA

Vegetation zones in the park range from montane in the valleys, through subalpine evergreen forests higher up, to alpine tundra above the treeline.

Only a small part of the park is montane. It is characterized by stands of Douglas fir, as well as savannah-like grasslands that occur on drier sites in valley bottoms. Well-developed stretches of montane can be found along the floors of the Athabasca and Miette River valleys, providing winter habitat for larger mammals such as elk.

The subalpine zone, heavily forested with evergreens, extends from the lower valley slopes up to the treeline. The dominant species in this zone is lodgepole pine, although Engelmann spruce, alpine fir, poplar, and aspen grow here. Lodgepole pine has adapted to make use of fire. Its hard seed cones are sealed by a resin that is melted only at high temperatures. When fire races through the forest, the resin melts and the cones release their seeds. As a result, these are the first conifers to regenerate in burned-out areas. The park's extensive stands of lodgepole pine are inhabited by few large mammals as the understory is minimal. Wildflowers are common in this zone and can be found by the roadside, in clearings, or on riverbanks.

Timberline here lies at an elevation between 2,050 and 2,400 meters above sea level. At this height, only a few stunted trees survive. Above this point is the alpine zone, where the climate is severe; the average yearly temperature is below freezing, and summer is brief. The zone's plant species grow low to the ground, with extensive root systems to protect them during high winds and through the deep snow cover of winter. During the short summer these open slopes and meadows are carpeted with a profusion of flowers such as golden arnicas, bluebells, pale columbines, and red and yellow paintbrush. Higher still are brightly colored heathers, buttercups, and alpine forget-me-nots.

FAUNA

Wildlife is abundant in the park, and can be seen throughout the year. During winter many larger mammals move to lower elevations where food is accessible. February and March are particularly good for looking for animal tracks in the snow. By June most of the snow cover at lower elevations has melted, the crowds haven't arrived, and animals can be seen feeding along the valley floor. In fall, tourists move to warmer

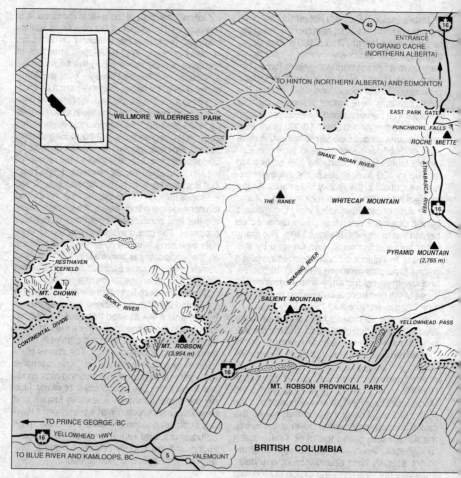

climates, the rutting season begins, bears go into hibernation, and a herd of elk moves into Jasper townsite for the winter.

While the park provides ample opportunities for seeing numerous animals in their natural habitat, it also leads to human/animal encounters that are not always positive. For example, less than 10% of the park is made up of well-vegetated valleys. These lower areas are essential to the larger mammals for food and shelter but are also the most heavily traveled by visitors. Game trails used for thousands of years

are often bisected by roads—hundreds of animals are killed each year by speeding motorists. Please drive slowly in the park.

Another problem occurs when people leave food where animals can get at it (inside a cooler isn't secure enough) or try to feed them directly—a well-meaning gesture that creates as much of a problem for the animals as does traffic. Some of them become accustomed to the taste of human food and become reliant on this easily obtained food source. Then after summer, when everyone has gone home, they have no

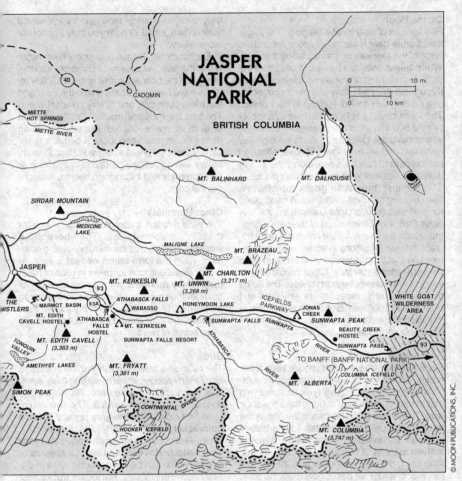

JASPER NATIONAL PARK

BRITISH COLUMBIA

0   10 mi

0   10 km

CADOMIN

MIETTE HOT SPRINGS
MIETTE RIVER

SIRDAR MOUNTAIN

MT. BALINHARD   MT. DALHOUSIE

MEDICINE LAKE

MALIGNE LAKE   MT. BRAZEAU

JASPER

MT. KERKESLIN   MT. CHARLTON (3,217 m)
MT. UNWIN (3,268 m)

THE WHISTLERS

MARMOT BASIN
MT. EDITH CAVELL HOSTEL

ATHABASCA FALLS
WABASSO

HONEYMOON LAKE

ICEFIELDS PARKWAY

JONAS CREEK   SUNWAPTA PEAK

WHITE GOAT WILDERNESS AREA

ATHABASCA FALLS HOSTEL
MT. KERKESLIN

SUNWAPTA FALLS   SUNWAPTA

BEAUTY CREEK HOSTEL

MT. EDITH CAVELL (3,363 m)

SUNWAPTA FALLS RESORT

SUNWAPTA PASS

TONQUIN VALLEY
AMETHYST LAKES

SIMON PEAK

MT. FRYATT (3,361 m)

CONTINENTAL DIVIDE

TO BANFF (BANFF NATIONAL PARK)

MT. ALBERTA

COLUMBIA ICEFIELD

HOOKER ICEFIELD

MT. COLUMBIA (3,747 m)

ATHABASCA RIVER

RIVER

© MOON PUBLICATIONS, INC.

---

supply of food. Some of these animals lose their
fear of humans and start demanding or stealing
food. The familiar moral of the story: Please
Don't Feed the Animals.

Campground Critters
Several species of small mammals thrive around
campgrounds, thanks to an abundance of humans
who are careless with their food. **Columbian
ground squirrels** are very bold and will demand
scraps of your lunch. **Golden-mantled ground
squirrels** and **red squirrels** are also common.

The **least chipmunk** (often confused with the
golden-mantled ground squirrel thanks to similar
stripes) can also be seen in campgrounds; they'll
often scamper across your hiking trail then sit
boldly on a rock waiting for you to pass.

Aquatic Species
Beaver dams are common between the townsite and the park's east gate. Dawn and dusk are
the best times to watch these intriguing creatures at work. Also common in the park's wetlands are **mink** and **muskrat**.

On the Hoof
Five species of deer inhabit the park. The large-eared **mule deer** is commonly seen around the edge of the townsite or grazing along the road. **White-tailed deer** can be seen throughout the park. A small herd of **woodland caribou** roams throughout the park; they are most commonly seen during late spring, feeding in river deltas. The town of Jasper is in the home range of around 500 **elk**, which can be seen most of the year around the townsite or along the highway northeast and south of town. **Moose,** although not common, can be seen along the major drainage systems feeding on aquatic plants.

In summer, **mountain goats** can often be seen feeding in alpine meadows. A good place for goat watching is Goat Lookout on the Icefields Parkway. Unlike most of the park's large mammals, these surefooted creatures don't migrate to lower elevations in winter, but stay sheltered on rocky crags where wind and sun keep the vegetation snow free. Often confused with the goat is the darker **bighorn sheep.** The horns on the males of this species are very thick and often curl 360 degrees. Bighorns are common in the east of the park at Disaster Point and will often approach cars.

Reclusive Residents
Several of the park's resident species keep a low profile, usually out of sight of humans. Populations of the shy and elusive **lynx** fluctuate with that of their primary food source, the snowshoe hare. The largest of the big cats in the park is the **cougar** (also called the mountain lion), a solitary carnivore that inhabits remote valleys. Jasper's **wolves** are one of the park's success stories. After being driven to near extinction, the species has rebounded. Five packs now roam the park, but they are rarely seen—keeping to the deep wilderness rarely traveled by people. While not common in the park, **coyotes** can be seen in cleared areas alongside the roads; usually at dawn and dusk.

Bears
Black bears are common throughout the park and occasionally wander into campgrounds looking for food. **Grizzly bears** are occasionally seen crossing the Icefields Parkway at higher elevations early in summer. For the most part

they remain in remote mountain valleys, and if they do see, smell, or hear you they'll generally move away.

Each summer, human/bear encounters occur within the park, with the most common outcome being that the bear will amble away. Very few attacks have been recorded within the park and there has been only one fatality in recent years. The best ways to avoid trouble? Don't hike alone or at dusk; make lots of noise when passing dense brush; and keep a clean camp. It is imperative that you read *You are in Bear Country* before setting out; the pamphlet is available at campgrounds and information centers throughout the park.

Other Mammals
The **pine marten** is common, but shy; look for them in subalpine forests. The **short-tailed weasel**—a relative of the marten—is also common, while the **long-tailed weasel** is rare. At higher elevations look for **pikas** in piles of fallen rock. **Hoary marmots** live near the upper limits of vegetation growth, where their shrill warning whistles carry across the open meadows. **Porcupines** are widespread in all valleys and are most active at night.

Birds
The extensive tree cover in the lower valleys hides many species of birds, making them seem less abundant than they are. A total of 248 species have been recorded. The two you're most likely to see are the **gray jay** and **Clark's nutcracker,** which regularly joins picnickers for lunch. Also common are black-and-white **magpies,** raucous **ravens,** and several species of **ducks,** which can be seen around lakes in the Athabasca River Valley. **Harlequin ducks** nest in the park during early summer. A stretch of the Maligne River is closed during this season to prevent human interference.

The colony of **black swifts** in Maligne Canyon is one of only two in Alberta. Their poorly developed legs make it difficult for them to take off from their nests in the canyon walls—they literally fall before becoming airborne. High alpine slopes are home to **white-tailed ptarmigans,** a type of grouse that turns white in winter. Also at this elevation are flocks of **rosy finches** that live under overhanging cliffs. In subalpine forests the songs of **thrushes** and the tapping of **wood-peckers** can be heard.

At dusk, **great horned owls** swoop silently through the trees, their eerie call echoing through the forest. **Golden eagles** and **bald eagles** can be seen soaring high above the forests, and 12 pairs of **ospreys** are known to nest in the park, many along the Athabasca River between town and the east park gate.

HISTORY

The first white man to enter the Athabasca River Valley was David Thompson, one of Canada's greatest explorers. He was looking for a pass through the mountains to use as access to the Pacific Ocean. The gap he eventually found— **Athabasca Pass,** south of Mt. Edith Cavell—became famous as the route used by the North West and Hudson's Bay Companies to cross the Rockies.

Meanwhile, the North West Company built a post named Jasper's House near the present townsite of Jasper. In time, an easier passage through the mountains was discovered farther north (at what is now called **Yellowhead Pass**), displacing Thompson's original, more difficult route to the south.

Leading up to the end of the fur-trading era, many visitors to the area returned home with accounts of the region's natural splendor. In 1858, Irish-Canadian artist Paul Kane published the book *Wanderings of an Artist,* which gave the outside world its first glimpse of the Jasper area.

At the turn of this century only seven homesteaders lived in the valley, but the Grand Trunk Pacific Railway was pushing westward, bringing with it the possibility of multitudes of settlers coming to live there. In 1907, the federal government officially declared the boundaries of Jasper Forest Park and bought all the land within, save for one homestead owned by Lewis Swift. (This parcel remained privately owned until 1962, long after the stubborn Mr. Swift had passed away.) The threat of oversettlement of the valley had been abated, but as a designated forest park, mining and logging were still allowed. In 1908, Jasper Park Collieries staked claims in the park. By the time the railway came through in 1910, mining activity was centered at **Pocahontas** (near the park's east gate), where a township was established and thrived. During an extended miners' strike, the men spent their spare time constructing log pools at Miette Hot Springs, which were heavily promoted to early park visitors. The mine closed in 1921 and many families relocated to Jasper, which had grown from a railway camp into a popular tourist destination. Jasper was officially designated a national park in 1930. This was followed by the construction of many roads including the Icefields Parkway, which opened in 1940.

ICEFIELDS PARKWAY/JASPER

Sunwapta Pass, at the boundary between Banff and Jasper National Parks, is just over halfway between Lake Louise and Jasper townsite along the 230-km Icefields Parkway, one of the world's great mountain drives. From the pass it is 108 km to Jasper, passing first the Columbia Icefield then following the Athabasca River for the rest of the way. The scenery along this stretch of road is no less spectacular than the other half through Banff National Park, and it's easy to spend a few days en route. Along this section of the parkway are lodges, hostels, campgrounds, and a gas station.

SIGHTS

Columbia Icefield

The largest and most accessible of 17 glacial areas along the Icefields Parkway is 325-square-km Columbia Icefield at the south end of the park. It's a remnant of the last major glaciation that covered most of Canada 20,000 years ago, and it has survived because of the elevation (1,900-2,800 meters above sea level), cold temperatures, and heavy snowfalls. From the main body of the ice cap, which sits astride the Continental Divide, glaciers creep down three main valleys. Of these, **Athabasca Glacier** is the most accessible and can be seen from the Icefields Parkway. A path to the toe of the glacier traverses a mixture of rock, sand, and gravel, known as "till," deposited by the glacier as it retreats. The speed at which glaciers advance and retreat varies with the long-term climate. Athabasca Glacier has retreated to its current position from across the highway, a distance of over 1.5 km, in 100 years. Currently it retreats two to three meters per year.

The icefield is made more spectacular by the impressive peaks that surround it. **Mt. Athabasca** (3,491 meters) dominates the skyline, and three glaciers cling to its flanks. **Dome Glacier**

is also visible from the highway. Although part of Columbia Icefield it is not actually connected. It is made of ice that breaks off the icefield 300 meters above, supplemented by the large quantities of snow the area receives each winter.

Exploring the Icefield

The icefield can be very dangerous for unprepared visitors, especially the broken surface of Athabasca Glacier where often-deep crevasses are uncovered as the winter snows melt. The safest way to experience it firsthand is on specially developed vehicles with balloon tires that can travel over its crevassed surface. These Snocoaches are operated by **Brewster**, tel. (403) 762-6700. The 90-minute tour of Athabasca

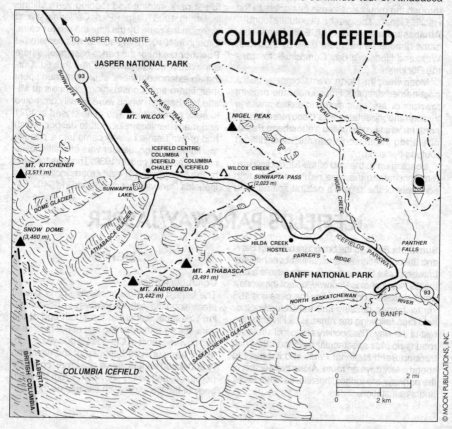

COLUMBIA ICEFIELD

TO JASPER TOWNSITE

JASPER NATIONAL PARK

93

SUNWAPTA RIVER

WILCOX PASS TRAIL

MT. WILCOX

NIGEL PEAK

BRAZEAU RIVER

MT. KITCHENER
(3,511 m)

ICEFIELD CENTRE/
COLUMBIA
ICEFIELD
CHALET

COLUMBIA
ICEFIELD

WILCOX CREEK

SUNWAPTA PASS
(2,023 m)

NIGEL CREEK

SUNWAPTA
LAKE

DOME GLACIER

SNOW DOME
(3,460 m)

ATHABASCA GLACIER

HILDA CREEK
HOSTEL

PARKER'S   RIDGE

ICEFIELDS PARKWAY

PANTHER
FALLS

MT. ATHABASCA
(3,491 m)

MT. ANDROMEDA
(3,442 m)

BANFF NATIONAL PARK

NORTH SASKATCHEWAN RIVER

TO BANFF

93

SASKATCHEWAN GLACIER

COLUMBIA ICEFIELD

ALBERTA
BRITISH COLUMBIA

0   2 mi

0   2 km

BREWSTER

Brewster's Snocoaches drive right onto the icefield for a close look.

Glacier includes time spent walking on the surface of the glacier. The tour, which begins from the Icefield Centre opposite the icefield, is adult $21.50, child $5 and operates from May to early October. Early in the season the glacier is still covered in a layer of snow and is therefore not as spectacular as during the summer months.

The magnificent Icefield Centre opened in the summer of 1996. As well as accommodations, it features the **Parks Canada Exhibit Hall,** a large display area cataloging all aspects of the frozen world including the story of glacier formation and movement. It's open May and September daily 10 a.m.-5 p.m., June-Aug. daily 10 a.m.-7 p.m.

To Sunwapta Falls

Sunwapta Lake—at the toe of the Athabasca Glacier—is the source of the **Sunwapta River,** which the Icefields Parkway follows for 48 km to Sunwapta Falls. Eight km north from the Icefield Centre, the road descends to a viewpoint for **Stutfield Glacier.** Most of the glacier is hidden from view by a densely wooded ridge, but at its toe till left by the glacier's retreat litters the valley floor. The main body of the Columbia Icefield can be seen along the clifftop high above. To the south of the glacier is **Mt. Kitchener.** Six km farther down the road is **Tangle Ridge,** a grayish-brown wall of limestone over which Beauty Creek cascades. At this point the Icefields Parkway runs alongside the Sunwapta River, following its course through the **Endless Range,** the eastern wall of a classic glacier-carved valley.

A further 40 km along the road a one-km gravel spur to the left leads to **Sunwapta Falls.** Here, the Sunwapta River changes direction sharply and drops into a deep canyon. Two km downstream the river flows into the much-wider Athabasca Valley.

Goat Lookout

After following the Athabasca River for 17 km, the road ascends to a lookout. Below the lookout is a steep bank of glacially ground material containing natural deposits of salt. The local mountain goats spend most of their time on the steep slopes of Mt. Kerkeslin, to the northeast, but occasionally cross the road and can be seen searching for the salt licks along the riverbank.

Athabasca Falls

At Athabasca Falls, the Athabasca River is forced through a narrow gorge and over a cliff into a cauldron of roaring water below. Old river channels can be seen along the west bank. As the river slowly erodes the center of the riverbed, the falls will move upstream. Trails lead from a day-use area to various viewpoints above and below the falls.

Continuing north, the road passes a parking lot used by hikers heading to Horseshoe Lake. Two km further north are a couple of lookouts with spectacular views across the Athabasca River to the Athabasca Pass, used by David Thompson on his historic expedition across the continent. To the north of the pass lies Mt. Edith Cavell. From this lookout it is 26 km to Jasper townsite.

HIKES ALONG ICEFIELDS PARKWAY

Wilcox Pass

- Length: 4 km (90 minutes) one-way
- Elevation gain: 340 meters
- Rating: moderate

This trail was once used by northbound outfitters because, 100 years ago, Athabasca Glacier covered the valley floor and had to be bypassed. The trail begins from the north side of Wilcox Creek Campground, three km south of the Icefield Centre. It climbs through a forest of Engelmann spruce and alpine fir to a ridge with panoramic views of the valley, Columbia Icefield, and surrounding peaks. Ascending gradually from there, the trail enters a fragile environment of alpine meadows. From the pass, most hikers return along the same trail, although it is possible to continue north, descending to the Icefields Parkway at Tangle Ridge, 11.5 km from the trailhead.

Fortress Lake

- Length: 24 km (7-8 hours) one-way
- Elevation gain: minimal
- Rating: moderate

The trail to this seldom-visited lake straddling the Continental Divide begins from the Sunwapta Falls parking lot. For the first 15 km the trail meanders along the east bank of the Athabasca River, then crosses it. Beyond the main bridge you'll need to ford the braided Chaba River, then continue southwest along the river flats for six km to the east end of Fortress Lake. The lake lies within British Columbia in Hamber Provincial Park. Its shores are difficult to traverse as they lack established trails.

Geraldine Lakes

- Length: 5 km (2 hours) one-way
- Elevation gain: 410 meters
- Rating: moderate

The first of the four Geraldine Lakes is an easy two-km hike from the trailhead (located 5.5 km along the Geraldine Fire Rd., which spurs south off Hwy. 93A west of Athabasca Falls). The for-est-encircled lake reflects the north face of Mt. Fryatt (3,361 meters). The trail continues along the northwest shore, climbs steeply past a scenic 100-meter waterfall, and traverses some rough terrain where the trail becomes indistinct; follow the cairns. At the end of the valley is another waterfall. The trail climbs east of the waterfall to a ridge above the second of the lakes, five km from the trailhead. Although the trail officially ends here, it does continue to a campground at the south end of the lake. Two other lakes, accessible only by bush-bashing, are located farther up the valley.

ACCOMMODATIONS

Lodging

Columbia Icefield Chalet, tel. (403) 852-6550, part of the newly opened Icefield Centre, features 32 standard rooms each with private facilities. Rates June-Sept. range $115-145 s or d while in May and the first couple of weeks of October rates are from $55. The facility is closed the rest of the year. **Sunwapta Falls Resort,** P.O. Box 97, Jasper, AB T0E 1E0, tel. (403) 852-4852, is 55 km south of Jasper townsite. It has 40 rooms, a restaurant, and a gift shop; $118 s or d. **Becker's Roaring River Chalets,** P.O. Box 579, tel. (403) 852-3779, just six km from the townsite, was established in the 1940s. One-bed sleeping rooms are $60, chalets—each with a kitchenette, fireplace, and double bed— are $95 (or $100 for those on the riverfront).

Hostels

Along this section of the Icefields Parkway, hostels are located at Km 144 and 198 (from Lake Louise). **Beauty Creek Hostel,** 17 km from Columbia Icefield, is nestled in a small stand of Douglas fir between the Icefields Parkway and the Sunwapta River. It has two separate male and female cabins; each sleeps 13 and has a woodstove. A third building holds a well-equipped kitchen and dining area. Members of Hostelling International pay $9, nonmembers $14. Open May-September. **Athabasca Falls Hostel** is a further 60 km toward Jasper townsite. It is larger and has electricity. Athabasca Falls is only a few minutes' walk away; members $9, nonmembers $14. Reservations for the above hostels can be made at all major hostels or by calling (403) 852-3215.

Campgrounds

Wilcox Creek and **Columbia Icefield Campgrounds** are within two km of each other at the extreme southern end of the park. Both are primitive campgrounds with toilets, cooking shelters, and fire rings; sites are $10. Traveling north, **Jonas Creek, Honeymoon Lake,** and **Mt. Kerkeslin Campgrounds** are located along the next 50 km stretch of road. Each is $10 per site, per night. **Wabasso Campground** is along Hwy. 93A, 16 km south of Jasper townsite; $12.

JASPER TOWNSITE

The townsite of Jasper is Banff's northern counterpart, linked to its neighbor by a similar history and, today, by the Icefields Parkway. The town—run by Parks Canada—has just over half the population of Banff, and its setting is less dramatic. But it's also less commercialized than Banff and its streets a little quieter. Part of the town's charm is its location at the confluence of the Athabasca and Miette Rivers, surrounded by the rugged, snowcapped peaks of Jasper National Park. From town it's a three-and-a-half-hour drive to Edmonton, the closest city. The town of Banff is 280 km to the southeast, and to the west is the vast wilderness of the Monashee, Cariboo, and Columbia ranges of the British Columbia interior.

Connaught Drive, the town's main street, parallels the rail line as it curves through town. Along here you'll find the Park Information Centre, bus depot, rail terminal, restaurants, motels, and a parking lot. Behind Connaught Drive is Patricia Street (one-way), which has more restaurants and services and leads to more hotels and motels on Geikie Street. Behind this main core are rows of neat houses—much less pretentious than those in Banff—and all the facilities of a regular town, including a library, school, post office, museum, swimming pool, and hospital.

History

In the winter of 1810-11, when David Thompson was making the first successful crossing of the Continental Divide, some of his party remained in the Athabasca River Valley and constructed a small settlement east of the present townsite. The settlement was named Henry House and was used for many years by the North West Company as a supply depot for fur traders. The post was run by a clerk named Jasper Hawes, and in time the settlement became known as Jasper's House. Over the years, stories of the area's natural beauty filtered east. Gold seekers commonly stopped by on their way to the Cariboo goldfields. But when the fur-trading era ended in the mid-1880s, the post closed.

In 1911 a construction camp was established for the Grand Trunk Pacific Railway near the present townsite of Jasper. The company had dreamed of a transcontinental rail line to rival the C.P.R. line that crossed the Rockies farther south. When the northern line was completed, visitors flocked into the remote mountain settlement, and its future was assured. The first accommodation for tourists was 10 tents on the shore of Lac Beauvert that became known as Jasper Park Camp. In 1921 the tents were replaced and the original Jasper Park Lodge was constructed. By the summer of 1928, a road was completed from Edmonton and a golf course was built. As the number of tourists to the park continued to increase, existing facilities were expanded. In 1940 the Icefields Parkway opened and in the '60s Marmot Basin Ski Area opened and the downtown core of the townsite was developed.

SIGHTS AND DRIVES

Downtown

With all the things to do and see in the park it's amazing how many people hang out in town. July and August are especially busy; much-needed improvements to the parking problem have had little impact on the traffic. The best way to avoid the problem is to avoid town during the day. The Park Information Centre, on Connaught Dr., is the only real reason to be in town. The shaded park in front of the center is a good

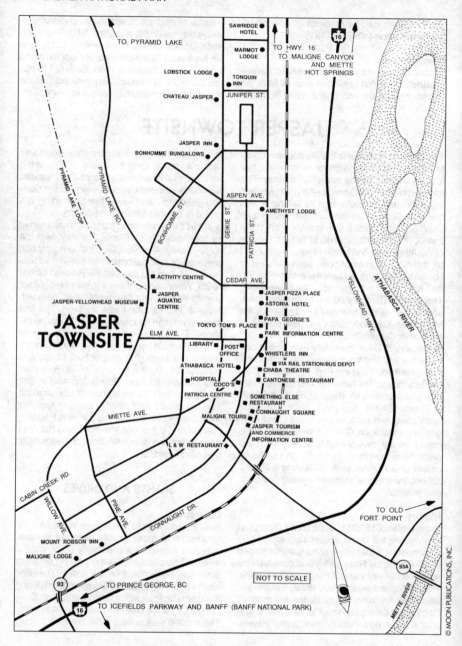

TO PYRAMID LAKE

SAWRIDGE HOTEL

MARMOT LODGE

LOBSTICK LODGE

TONQUIN INN

CHATEAU JASPER

JUNIPER ST.

TO HWY. 16
TO MALIGNE CANYON AND MIETTE HOT SPRINGS

JASPER INN

BONHOMME BUNGALOWS

ASPEN AVE.

AMETHYST LODGE

PATRICIA ST.

GEIKIE ST.

BONHOMME ST.

PYRAMID LAKE RD.

PYRAMID LAKE LOOP

CEDAR AVE.

ACTIVITY CENTRE

JASPER AQUATIC CENTRE

JASPER-YELLOWHEAD MUSEUM

JASPER TOWNSITE

JASPER PIZZA PLACE
ASTORIA HOTEL
PAPA GEORGE'S
PARK INFORMATION CENTRE

TOKYO TOM'S PLACE

ELM AVE.

LIBRARY

POST OFFICE

WHISTLERS INN

CHABA THEATRE

VIA RAIL STATION/BUS DEPOT

ATHABASCA HOTEL

CANTONESE RESTAURANT

HOSPITAL

COCO'S

SOMETHING ELSE RESTAURANT

PATRICIA CENTRE

MIETTE AVE.

CONNAUGHT SQUARE

MALIGNE TOURS

JASPER TOURISM AND COMMERCE INFORMATION CENTRE

L & W RESTAURANT

YELLOWHEAD HWY.

ATHABASCA RIVER

TO OLD FORT POINT

CABIN CREEK RD.

WILLOW AVE.

PINE AVE.

CONNAUGHT DR.

MOUNT ROBSON INN

MALIGNE LODGE

93

TO PRINCE GEORGE, BC

16

TO ICEFIELDS PARKWAY AND BANFF (BANFF NATIONAL PARK)

NOT TO SCALE

93A

MIETTE RIVER

© MOON PUBLICATIONS, INC.

place for people-watching—but you may get clobbered by a wayward Hacky Sack.

At the back of town is the excellent, relatively new **Jasper-Yellowhead Museum and Archives,** 400 Pyramid Lake Rd., tel. (403) 852-3013, which has a collection of artifacts cataloging the human history of the park. The museum also features extensive archives, including photos, documents, and maps. It's open June-Sept. daily 10 a.m.-9 p.m.

If you like taxidermy, visit **The Den Wildlife Museum,** which exhibits stuffed animals in their "natural setting." It's located down a dark stairway beneath the Whistlers Inn. Yep, they even charge you for it; $2.50. Open year-round daily 9 a.m.-10 p.m.

Patricia and Pyramid Lakes

A winding road heads through the hills at the back of town to these two picturesque lakes, formed when glacial moraines dammed shallow valleys. The first, to the left, is Patricia, the second, farther along the road, is Pyramid, backed by **Pyramid Mountain** (2,765 meters). Both lakes are popular spots for picnicking, fishing, and boating. Boat rentals are available at **Pyramid Lake Resort,** tel. (403) 852-4900. Canoes, rowboats, paddleboats, and kayaks are $12 for the first hour and $8 for each additional hour. The resort also rents windsurfers ($16 per hour), motorboats and catamarans ($22 per hour), and jet skis ($70 per hour). From the resort the road continues around the lake to a bridge, which leads to an island popular with picnickers. The road ends at the quieter end of the lake.

Jasper Tramway

This tramway climbs over 1,000 vertical meters up the steep north face of **The Whistlers,** named after the hoary marmots that live on the summit. The tramway operates two 30-passenger cars that take seven minutes to reach the upper terminal, during which time the conductor gives a narrated lecture about the mountain and its environment. From the upper terminal, a one-km trail leads to the summit (2,470 meters). The view is breathtaking; to the south is the Columbia Icefield, and on a clear day you can see Mt. Robson (3,954 meters)—the highest peak in the Canadian Rockies—to the northwest. Roundtrip fare is $14.95; allow two hours on

top and, on a clear summer's day, two more hours in line at the bottom. The tramway is located three km south of town on Hwy. 93 (Icefields Parkway) and then three km up Whistlers Road. It operates in summer daily 8 a.m.-10 p.m., shorter hours April-May and Sept.-Oct., closed the rest of the year. For more information call (403) 852-3093.

Mount Edith Cavell

The original Icefields Parkway (Hwy. 93A), which followed the southeast bank of the Athabasca River, has been bypassed by a more direct route on the other side of the river. Along the original route, known also as the Athabasca Parkway, a 14.5-km road leads to a parking area below the northeast face of Mt. Edith Cavell (3,363 meters). This peak can be seen from many vantage points in the park, including the townsite, but none is more impressive than directly below it. On this face, **Angel Glacier** lies in a saddle on the mountain's lower slopes. From the parking area the **Path of the Glacier Trail** (one hour roundtrip) traverses moraines deposited by the receding Angel Glacier and leads to some great viewpoints. For other hiking opportunities in the vicinity of Mt. Edith Cavell see "Hikes near Mount Edith Cavell" below.

Edith and Annette Lakes

These two lakes along the road to Jasper Park Lodge—across the Athabasca River from town—are perfect for a picnic, swim, or pleasant walk. They are remnants of a much larger lake that once covered the entire valley floor. The lakes are relatively shallow, therefore the sun warms the water to a bearable temperature; in fact they have the warmest waters of any lakes in the park. The 2.5-km **Lee Foundation Trail** encircles Lake Annette and is wheelchair accessible. Both lakes have day-use areas with beaches and picnic areas.

Jasper Park Lodge

Accommodations are not usually considered "sights" but then this is the Rockies, where three grand railway hotels attract as many visitors as the more legitimate natural attractions. Jasper Park Lodge has been the premier accommodation in the park since it opened in 1921. Back then it was a single-story structure, reputed to be

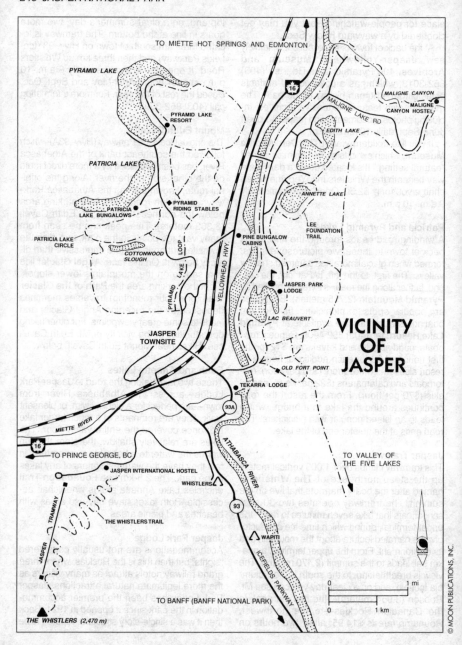

TO MIETTE HOT SPRINGS AND EDMONTON

PYRAMID LAKE

MALIGNE CANYON

MALIGNE CANYON HOSTEL

PYRAMID LAKE RESORT

MALIGNE LAKE RD

EDITH LAKE

PATRICIA LAKE

ANNETTE LAKE

PATRICIA LAKE BUNGALOWS

PYRAMID RIDING STABLES

LEE FOUNDATION TRAIL

PATRICIA LAKE CIRCLE

PINE BUNGALOW CABINS

COTTONWOOD SLOUGH

PYRAMID LAKE LOOP

YELLOWHEAD HWY.

JASPER PARK LODGE

JASPER TOWNSITE

LAC BEAUVERT

VICINITY OF JASPER

OLD FORT POINT

TEKARRA LODGE

93A

MIETTE RIVER

ATHABASCA RIVER

TO PRINCE GEORGE, BC

TO VALLEY OF THE FIVE LAKES

JASPER INTERNATIONAL HOSTEL

WHISTLERS

93

WAPITI

JASPER TRAMWAY

THE WHISTLERS TRAIL

ICEFIELDS PARKWAY

THE WHISTLERS (2,470 m)

TO BANFF (BANFF NATIONAL PARK)

0   1 mi

0   1 km

© MOON PUBLICATIONS, INC.

the largest log building in the world. It burned to the ground in 1952 but was rebuilt. Additional bungalows were erected along Lac Beauvert, forming a basis for today's lodge. Rows of cabins radiate from the main lodge, which contains restaurants, lounges, and the town's only covered shopping arcade. Today up to 900 guests can be accommodated in 442 rooms. A large parking area for nonguests is located on Lodge Rd., behind the golf clubhouse; you're welcome to walk around the resort, play golf, dine in the restaurants, and of course, browse through the shopping promenade—even if you're not a registered guest. From the main lodge, a hiking trail follows the shoreline of Lac Beauvert and links up with other trails from Old Fort Point. To walk from town will take one hour.

Maligne Canyon

To get here head northeast from town and turn right onto Maligne Lake Road. The canyon access road veers left 11 km from Jasper. This unique geological feature has been eroded out of the easily dissolved limestone bedrock by the fast-flowing Maligne River. Surface water here is augmented by underground springs, therefore it seems that more water flows out of the canyon than into it. The canyon is up to 50 meters deep, yet so narrow that squirrels often jump across. At the top of the canyon, opposite the teahouse, are large potholes in the riverbed. These potholes are created when rocks and pebbles become trapped in what begins as a shallow depression, and under the force of the rushing water carve jug-shaped hollows into the soft bedrock.

An interpretive trail winds down from the parking lot, crossing the canyon six times. The most spectacular sections of the canyon can be seen from the first two bridges, at the upper end of the trail. In summer a teahouse operates at the top of the canyon. To avoid the crowds at the upper end of the canyon, an alternative would be to park at Sixth Bridge, near the confluence of the Maligne and Athabasca Rivers, and walk *up* the canyon (see "Hiking around Town," below). The **Maligne Lake Shuttle** stops at the canyon eight times daily. For reservations call (403) 852-3370; fare is $6 one-way from town. In winter guided tours of the frozen canyon are an experience you'll never forget (see "Wintertime" below).

To Maligne Lake

From the canyon, Maligne Lake Rd. climbs to **Medicine Lake,** which does a disappearing act each year. The water level fluctuates due to an underground drainage system. At the northwest end of the lake, where the outlet should be, the riverbed is often dry. In fall, when runoff from the mountains is minimal, the water level drops and, by November, the lake has almost completely dried up. Early Indians believed that spirits were responsible for the phenomenon, hence the name.

At the end of the road, 48 km from Jasper, is Maligne Lake, the largest glacier-fed lake in the Canadian Rockies and second largest in the world. The first paying visitors were brought to the lake in 1929, and it has been a mecca for camera-toting tourists from around the world ever since. Once at the lake, activities are plentiful. But other than taking in the spectacular vistas, the only thing you won't need your wallet for is hiking one of the numerous trails in the area.

The most popular tourist activity at the lake is a 90-minute narrated cruise on a glass-enclosed boat up the lake to oft-photographed **Spirit Island.** Cruises leave in summer, every hour on the hour 10 a.m.-5 p.m., with fewer sailings in May and September; $35 per person. Many time slots are block-booked by tour companies, therefore reservations are suggested; make them at the Maligne Tours office, 626 Connaught Dr., tel. (403) 852-3370. The lake also has excellent trout fishing; Alberta's record rainbow trout was caught here. Fishing tackle and bait is available at the Boathouse, by Parking Lot 2. The Boathouse also rents rowboats and canoes for $12 the first hour, $6 each additional hour. Again, for reservations contact Maligne Tours in Jasper. Horseback riding is also available at the lake.

The Maligne River, a class III river and the wildest whitewater trip in the park, is run by three companies. **Maligne River Adventures,** tel. (403) 852-3370, **Rocky Mountain River Guides,** tel. (403) 852-3777, and **White Water Rafting,** tel. (403) 852-7238, offer three-hour trips, including transfers from Jasper for $55.

The **Maligne Lake Shuttle** runs from the Maligne Tours office at 626 Connaught Dr., tel. (403) 852-3370, and from various hotels out to the lake. Tickets can be bought in conjunction with a cruise ($50), raft trip ($70), or horseback ride ($70), or for the bus only ($25 roundtrip). The shuttle makes eight trips daily.

Miette Hot Springs

Near the park's east gate is Miette Hot Springs Rd., which leads to the warmest springs in the Canadian Rockies. One km along the road is **Punchbowl Falls,** where a small river cascades through a narrow crevice in a cliff to a pool of turbulent water. After curving, swerving, rising, and falling many times the road ends at the hot springs. In the early 1900s, the springs were one of the park's biggest attractions. In 1910, a packhorse trail was built up the valley and the government constructed a bathhouse. The original hand-hewn log structure was replaced in the '30s with pools that remained in use until new facilities were built in 1985. Water that flows into the pools is artificially cooled from 54° C to a soothing 39°. A swim in the pools is $4.50, a towel $1, and lockers 25 cents. It's open mid-May to mid-June daily 10:30 a.m.-9 p.m., mid-June to September daily 8:30 a.m.-10:30 p.m. For more information call (403) 866-3939.

Many hiking trails begin from the hot springs complex; the shortest is from the picnic area to the source of the springs (200 meters). Below the springs is a restaurant and lodging.

HIKING AROUND TOWN

The 1,000 kilometers of hiking trails in Jasper are significantly different than those in the other mountain national parks. The park has an extensive system of interconnecting backcountry trails that, for experienced hikers, can provide a wilderness adventure rivaled by few areas on the face of this earth. For casual day-hikers, on the other hand, opportunities are more limited. Most trails in the immediate vicinity of the townsite have little elevation gain and lead through montane forest to lakes. The trails at the base of Mt. Edith Cavell, in the Tonquin Valley, around Maligne Lake, and along the Icefields Parkway have more rewarding objectives and are more challenging.

The most popular trails for extended backcountry trips are the **Skyline Trail,** between the townsite and Maligne Lake (44.5 km, three days each way); the trails to **Amethyst Lakes** in the

Tonquin Valley (19 km, one day each way) and **Athabasca Pass** (50 km, three days each way), which was used by fur traders for 40 years as the main route across the Rockies; and the **South Boundary Trail,** which traverses a remote section of the front ranges into Banff National Park (160 km, 10 days each way).

Before setting off on any hikes, whatever the length, go to the **Park Information Centre** in Jasper townsite for trail maps, trail conditions, and trail closures. To prevent overuse, many longer trails operate on a quota system and you *must* pick up a permit before heading out; $6 per person per night.

Pyramid Lake Loop

- Length: 17 km (5 hours) roundtrip
- Elevation gain: 150 meters
- Rating: easy/moderate

A myriad of official and unofficial hiking trails is located on the benchland immediately west of Jasper townsite. From the parking lot opposite the Aquatic Centre on Pyramid Lake Rd., a well-marked trail climbs onto the benchland. Keep right, crossing Pyramid Lake Rd., and you'll emerge on a bluff overlooking the Athabasca River Valley. Bighorn sheep can often be seen grazing here. If you return to the trailhead from here, you will have hiked seven km. The trail continues north, disappearing into the montane forest until arriving at Pyramid Lake. Various trails can be taken to return to town; ask at the Park Information Centre before setting out for a map of the entire area.

Patricia Lake Circle

- Length: 5 km loop (90 minutes roundtrip)
- Elevation gain: minimal
- Rating: easy

This trail begins across the road from the riding stables on Pyramid Lake Road. It traverses a mixed forest of aspen and lodgepole pine, prime habitat for a variety of larger mammals such as elk, deer, and moose. The second half of the trail skirts Cottonwood Slough where you'll see a number of beaver ponds.

The Whistlers

- Length: 8 km (2.5-3 hours) one-way
- Elevation gain: 1,220 meters
- Rating: moderate/difficult

BIGHORN SHEEP

Bighorn sheep are some of the most distinctive mammals of the Canadian Rockies. Easily recognized by their impressive horns, they are often seen grazing on grassy mountain slopes or at salt licks beside the road. The color of their coat varies with the season; in summer it is a brownish gray with a cream-colored belly and rump, turning lighter in winter. At seven years of age, males are fully grown and can weigh up to 120 kilograms. Females generally weigh around 80 kilograms.

Both sexes possess horns, rather than antlers like moose, elk, and deer. Unlike antlers, horns are not shed each year and can grow to astounding sizes. The horns of rams are larger than those of ewes and curve up to 360 degrees. The spiraled horns of an older ram can measure 115 centimeters and weigh as much as 15 kilograms. As the horns grow, they become marked by an annual growth ring. By counting the rings it is possible to determine the approximate age of the animal. In fall, during the mating season, a hierarchy is established among them for the right to breed ewes. As the males face off against each other to establish dominance, their horns act as both a weapon and a buffer against the head-butting of other rams. The skull structure of the bighorn, rams in particular, has become adapted to these clashes, avoiding heavy concussion.

These animals are particularly tolerant of humans and often approach parked vehicles; although they are not dangerous, as with all mammals in the park, you should not approach or feed them.

BOB RACE

This steep ascent, one of the most arduous in the park, is unique in that it passes through three distinct vegetation zones in a relatively short distance. From the trailhead on Whistlers Rd., 200 meters below the hostel, the trail begins climbing and doesn't let up until you merge with the crowds getting off the tramway at the top. The trail begins in a montane forest of aspen and white birch, climbs through a subalpine forest of Engelmann spruce and alpine fir, then emerges onto the open, treeless tundra, inhabited by pikas, hoary marmots, and a few hardy plants. Carry water—none is available before the upper tramway terminal.

Old Fort Point
- Length: 6.5 km loop (2 hours roundtrip)
- Elevation gain: 60 meters
- Rating: easy

Old Fort Point is a moderately sized knoll above the Athabasca River, to the east of Jasper townsite. Although it is not likely a fort was ever located here, the first fur-trading post in the Rockies, Henry House, was located just downstream, and it is easy to imagine fur traders and early explorers climbing to this summit for 360-degree views of the Athabasca and Miette Rivers. To get to the trailhead from town, take Hwy. 93A and turn left to Lac Beauvert. The trail begins just over the Athabasca River. Climb the wooden stairs, take the left trail to the top of the knoll, then continue back to the parking lot along the north flank of the hill.

Valley of the Five Lakes
- Length: 2.3 km (1 hour) one-way
- Elevation gain: 60 meters
- Rating: easy

These lakes, nestled in an open valley, are small but make a worthwhile destination. From the trailhead, 10 km south of Jasper townsite along the Icefields Parkway, the trail passes through a forest of lodgepole pine, crosses a stream, and climbs a ridge from where you'll have a panoramic view of surrounding peaks. As the trail descends to the lakes, turn left at the first intersection to a point between two of the lakes. These lakes are linked to Old Fort Point by a tedious 10-km trail through montane forest.

Maligne Canyon
- Length: 3.7 km (90 minutes) one-way
- Elevation gain: 125 meters
- Rating: moderate

Maligne Canyon is one of the busiest places in the park, yet few visitors hike the entire length of the canyon trail. By beginning from the lower end of the canyon, at the confluence of the Maligne and Athabasca Rivers, you'll avoid starting your hike alongside the masses and you'll get to hike downhill on your return (when you're tired). To get to the trailhead head east from the townsite, turn right on Maligne Lake Rd., and follow it 2.5 km to the warden's office, from where a one-km access road leads to Sixth Bridge. Crowds will be minimal for the first three km, to Fourth Bridge, where the trail starts climbing. By the time you get to Third Bridge, you start encountering "adventurous" hikers coming down the canyon, and soon thereafter you'll meet the real crowds, bear-bells and all. Upstream of here the canyon is deepest and most spectacular. See "Maligne Canyon" under "Sights and Drives," above, for details of the hike starting from the *top* of the canyon.

HIKES NEAR MOUNT EDITH CAVELL

Mount Edith Cavell Rd. begins from Hwy. 93A and winds through a subalpine forest, ascending 300 meters in 14.5 km. Trailheads are located at the end of the road (Cavell Meadows Trail and a short interpretive trail) and across from the hostel two km from the end (Astoria River Trail). A third trailhead is on Marmot Basin Rd. where it crosses Portal Creek (Maccarib Pass Trail).

Cavell Meadows
- Length: 4 km (1 hour) one-way
- Elevation gain: 350 meters
- Rating: easy/moderate

This trail, beginning from the parking lot beneath Mt. Edith Cavell, provides easy access to an alpine meadow and panoramic views of Angel Glacier. The trail climbs steadily through a subalpine forest of Engelmann spruce and alpine fir to emerge facing the northeast face of Mt. Edith Cavell and Angel Glacier. The trail continues to higher viewpoints and an alpine meadow which, in mid-July, is filled with wildflowers.

Astoria River
- Length: 19 km (6-7 hours) one-way
- Elevation gain: 450 meters
- Rating: moderate

Beginning opposite the hostel on Mt. Edith Cavell Rd., this trail descends through a forest on the north side of Mt. Edith Cavell for five km, then crosses the Astoria River and begins a long ascent into spectacular Tonquin Valley. Amethyst Lakes and the 1,000-meter cliffs of the Ramparts first come into view after 13 km. At the 17-km mark the trail divides. To the left it climbs into Eremite Valley where there is a campground. The right fork continues following Astoria River to Tonquin Valley, Amethyst Lakes, and a choice of four campgrounds.

Maccarib Pass
- Length: 21 km (7-8 hours) one-way
- Elevation gain: 730 meters
- Rating: moderate

This trail is slightly longer and gains more elevation than the trail along Astoria River but is more spectacular. From 6.5 km up Marmot Basin Rd., the trail strikes out to the southwest. It follows Portal Creek and passes under Peveril Peak before making a steep approach to Maccarib Pass, 12.5 km from the trailhead. The full panorama of the Tonquin Valley can be appreciated as the path gradually descends from the pass. At Amethyst Lakes it links up with the Astoria River Trail, and many options for day hikes head out from campgrounds at the lakes.

HIKING IN THE MALIGNE LAKE AREA

Maligne Lake, 48 km from Jasper townsite, provides more easy hiking with many opportunities to view the lake and explore its environs. The first two hikes detailed are along the access road to the lake; the others leave from various parking lots located at the northwest end of the lake.

Watchtower Basin

- Length: 10 km (3.5 hours) one-way
- Elevation gain: 630 meters
- Rating: moderate/difficult

Watchtower is a wide, open basin high above the crowds of Maligne Lake Road. The trailhead is 24 km from Jasper townsite. All the elevation gain is made during the first six km, through a dense forest of lodgepole pine and white spruce. As the trail levels off and enters the basin it continues to follow the west bank of a stream, crossing it at km 10, and officially ending at a campground. To the west and south the **Maligne Range** rises to a crest three km beyond the campground. From the top of this ridge, at the intersection with the Skyline Trail, it is 17.5 km northwest to Maligne Canyon, or 27 km southeast to Maligne Lake. By camping at Watchtower Campground, day trips can be made to a small lake in the basin or to highlights of the Skyline Trail such as the Snowbowl, Curator Lake, and Shovel Pass.

Jacques Lake

- Length: 12 km (3-3.5 hours) one-way
- Elevation gain: 100 meters
- Rating: moderate

The appeal of this trail, which begins from a parking lot at the southeast end of Medicine Lake, is its lack of elevation gain and the numerous small lakes it skirts as it travels through a narrow valley. On either side, the severely faulted mountains of the Queen Elizabeth Ranges rise steeply above the valley floor, their strata tilted nearly vertical.

Lake Trail (East Side)

- Length: 3.2-km loop (1 hour roundtrip)
- Elevation gain: minimal
- Rating: easy

This short trail begins from the back of Parking Lot 2, following the eastern shore of Maligne Lake to a point known as **Schäffer Viewpoint,** named for the first white person to see the valley. After dragging yourself away from the spectacular panorama, follow the trail into a forest of spruce and subalpine fir before looping back to the trailhead.

Opal Hills

- Length: 8.2-km loop (3 hours roundtrip)
- Elevation gain: 455 meters
- Rating: moderate

This trail begins at the back of Parking Lot 1, climbing steeply for 1.5 km to a point where it divides. Both options end in the high alpine meadows of the Opal Hills; the trail to the right is shorter and steeper. Once in the meadow, the entire Maligne Valley can be seen below. Across Maligne Lake are the rounded Bald Hills, the Maligne Range, and to the southwest, the distinctive twin peaks of Mt. Unwin (3,268 meters) and Mt. Charlton (3,217 meters).

Bald Hills

- Length: 5.2 km (2 hours) one-way
- Elevation gain: 495 meters
- Rating: moderate

MARY SCHÄFFER

In the early 1900s, exploration of mountain wilderness areas was considered a man's domain. However, a spirited and tenacious woman entered that domain and went on to explore areas of the Canadian Rockies that no white man ever had. Mary Sharples was born in 1861 in Pennsylvania and raised in a strict Quaker family. Mary was introduced to Dr. Charles Schäffer on a trip to the Rockies, and in 1889 they were married. His interest in botany drew them back to the Rockies, where Charles collected, documented, and photographed specimens until his death in 1903. Mary also became apt at these skills. After hearing Sir James Hector (the geologist on the Palliser Expedition) reciting tales of the mountains, her zest to explore the wilderness returned. In 1908, with Billy Warren guiding, Mary, her dog, and a small party set out for a lake that no white man had ever seen but that the Stoney Indians knew as Chaba Imne, or "Beaver Lake." After initial difficulties, they succeeded in finding the elusive body of water now known as Maligne Lake. In Mary's words, "there burst upon us . . . the finest view any of us have ever beheld in the Rockies. . . ." In 1915 Mary married Billy Warren, continuing to explore the mountains until her death in 1939. Her success as a photographer, artist, and writer were equal to any of her male counterparts. But it was her unwavering love of the Rockies—her "heaven of the hills"— for which she is best remembered.

Maligne Lake

BREWSTER

From a picnic area at the very end of Maligne Lake Rd., this trail follows an old fire road for its entire distance, entering an open meadow near the end. This was once the site of a fire lookout. The 360-degree view includes the jade-green waters of Maligne Lake, the Queen Elizabeth Ranges and the twin peaks of Mt. Unwin and Mt. Charlton. The Bald Hills extend for seven km, their highest summit not exceeding 2,600 meters. A herd of caribou summers in the hills.

Moose Lake
- Length: 1.4 km (30 minutes) one-way
- Elevation gain: minimal
- Rating: easy

This trail begins 200 meters along the Bald Hills trail, spurring left along the Maligne Pass Trail (signposted). One km along this trail a rough track branches left, leading 100 meters to Moose Lake—a quiet body of water where moose are sometimes seen. To return, continue along the trail as it descends to the shore of Maligne Lake, a short stroll from the picnic area.

OTHER RECREATION

Mountain Biking
Bicycling in the park continues to grow in popularity: the ride between Banff and Jasper, along the Icefields Parkway, attracts riders from around the world. As well as the paved roads, many designated unpaved bicycle trails radiate from

the town. One of the most popular is the Athabasca River Trail, which begins at Old Fort Point and follows the river to a point below Maligne Canyon. Cyclists are particularly prone to sudden bear encounters—a couple of years ago a rider was pulled from his bike by a grizzly, within screaming distance of Jasper Park Lodge. Fit bear-bells to your bike, or make noises when passing through heavily wooded areas. The brochure *Trail Bicycling Guide* lists designated trails and is available from Freewheel Cycle at 611 Patricia St., tel. (403) 852-3898.

Horseback Riding
Pyramid Riding Stables is on Pyramid Lake Rd., tel. (403) 852-3562. The stables offer one-, two-, and three-hour guided rides for $18.50, $30, and $40, respectively. The one-hour trip follows a ridge high above town, providing excellent views of the Athabasca River Valley. **Sunrider Stables,** at the Jasper Park Lodge, tel. (403) 852-4215, offers guided rides around Lake Annette; the one-hour trip is $22. **Ridgeline Riders,** at Maligne Lake, offers three-and-a-half-hour guided rides high into the Bald Hills for $45. Book through Maligne Tours at 626 Connaught Dr., tel. (403) 852-3370.

Overnight pack trips consist of four to six hours of riding per day, with a few nights spent at a remote mountain lodge where you can hike, boat, fish, or ride. Rates start at $140 per person per day. For details write to Skyline Trail Rides, P.O. Box 207, Jasper, AB T0E 1E0, tel. (403) 852-

4215; or Tonquin Valley Packtrips, P.O. Box 550, Jasper, AB T0E 1E0, tel. (403) 852-3909.

Canoeing and Whitewater Rafting

Running Jasper's raging rivers is the "in" thing to do. Half a dozen outfitters offer trips ranging from an easy float down the Athabasca River to shooting the boulder-strewn rapids of the Maligne River. Most companies offer a choice of rivers and provide transportation to and from downtown hotels. Expect to pay $35-45 for a two-hour trip on the Athabasca and $55 for a three-hour trip on the Maligne. For details and reservations contact **Jasper Adventure Centre** in the Chaba Theatre, tel. (403) 895-5595; **Jasper Raft Tours,** tel. (403) 852-3612; **Maligne Tours,** tel. (403) 852-3370; **Rocky Mountain River Guides,** tel. (403) 852-3777; or **White Water Rafting,** tel. (403) 852-7238.

For a different, more relaxing, and historically linked adventure, try a trip down the Athabasca River in a stable 10-meter voyageur canoe, similar to those used by early explorers and fur traders. These trips are offered by **Rocky Mountain Voyageurs** starting at Old Fort Point and floating downstream for two to three hours. The cost, including transfers, is $45. For reservations call (403) 852-3343 or drop by Jasper Adventure Centre in the Chaba Theatre.

Fishing

Fishing in the many alpine lakes—for rainbow, brook, Dolly Varden, cutthroat, and lake trout, as well as pike and whitefish—is excellent. Guided fishing trips are offered by many outfitters. Whether you fish with a guide or by yourself, you'll need a National Park fishing license ($6 per week, $13 per year), available from the Park Information Centre or On-line Sport & Tackle at 600 Patricia Street. Maligne Lake is the most popular fishing hole; in 1981 a 10-kilogram rainbow trout was caught in its deep waters, a provincial record. Boats, bait, and tackle are available from the Boathouse at Maligne Lake, tel. (403) 852-3370. Guided fishing trips on the lake are offered by **Maligne Tours,** tel. (403) 852-3370; half day $80, full day $150. **Currie's Guided Fishing,** 414 Connaught Dr., tel. (403) 852-5650, offers trips to Maligne Lake (full day $149) and other lakes requiring a 30-60 minute hike to access (from $139). Their shop on Connaught Dr. sells and rents tackle and also has canoe and boat rentals. **On-line Sport & Tackle,** 600 Patricia St., tel. (403) 852-3630, offers similar trips, sells tackle, and rents canoes and boats (from $25 per day).

Climbing and Mountaineering

Jasper Climbing Schools & Guide Service runs two-day beginner's rock-climbing classes that deal with use of equipment, technique, and safety. Everything is supplied except lunch, gloves, boots, and Band-Aids; $80. The service also leads two-day courses for intermediates ($110), snow- and ice-climbing trips to Columbia Icefields ($90), and various courses that include climbs of nearby summits. For dates and details write to Hans Schwarz, P.O. Box 452, Jasper, AB T0E 1E0; tel.(403) 852-3964.

Golfing

The world-famous **Jasper Park Lodge Golf Course** was designed by renowned golf-course architect Stanley Thompson. The 18-hole championship course takes in the contours of the Athabasca River Valley as it hugs the banks of turquoise-colored Lac Beauvert. The 6,598-meter course is a true test of accuracy, and with holes named "The Maze," "The Bad Baby," and "The Bay" you'll need lots of balls, literally. Green fees for 18 holes vary with the season; $75 in summer, $60 mid-May through June and mid-Sept. to mid-October. Club rentals are $30 and an electric cart is $32. Tee times can be reserved by calling (403) 852-6090.

Indoor Recreation

Jasper Aquatic Centre, with an Olympic-size swimming pool, is at 401 Pyramid Lake Rd., tel. (403) 852-3663; admission is $3.74. The **Activity Centre,** next door, tel. (403) 852-3381, has squash courts, indoor and outdoor tennis courts, and a weight room; admission $6.

WINTERTIME

Winter is certainly a quiet time in the park, but that doesn't mean there's a lack of things to do: Marmot Basin offers world-class alpine skiing; many snow-covered hiking trails are groomed for cross-country skiing; portions of Lac Beauvert

Maligne Canyon in winter

ALBERTA TOURISM

and Pyramid Lake are cleared for ice-skating; horse-drawn sleighs travel around town; and Maligne Canyon is transformed into a magical, frozen world. Hotels reduce rates by 40-70% through winter and many offer lodging and lift tickets for under $50 per person.

Marmot Basin Ski Area

The skiing at Marmot Basin is highly underrated; the terrain is good, there's plenty of the dry fluffy stuff, and the mountain scenery is breathtaking, to say the least. A fellow by the name of Joe Weiss saw the potential for skiing in the basin in the 1920s and began bringing skiers up from the valley. A road was constructed from the highway in the early '50s, and the first paying skiers were transported up to the slopes in a Sno-Cat. The first lift, a 700-meter rope tow, was installed on the Paradise face in 1961 and the area has continued to expand ever since. Marmot Basin now has seven lifts servicing 400 hectares of terrain and a vertical rise of 701 meters. It doesn't get the crowds of Banff, so lift lines are uncommon. The season runs from early December to late April. Lift tickets are $35. Rentals are available at the resort or in town at **Totem Ski Shop,** 408 Connaught Dr., tel. (403) 852-3078. For more information on the resort write to Marmot Basin Ski-lifts, P.O. Box 1300, Jasper, AB T0E 1E0; tel. (403) 852-3816 or, from Edmonton, (403) 488-5909.

Buses depart three times daily for Marmot Basin (the first departure is 8-8:30 a.m.) from most Jasper hotels; $5 one-way, $9 roundtrip.

Cross-Country Skiing

For many, traveling Jasper's hiking trails on skis is just as exhilarating as on foot. An extensive network of summer hiking trails is groomed for cross-country skiing. The four main areas of trails are along Pyramid Lake Rd., around Maligne Lake, in the Athabasca Falls area, and at Whistlers Campground. The booklet *Cross-country Skiing in Jasper National Park,* available at the Park Information Centre, details each trail and its difficulty. Weather forecasts and avalanche-hazard reports are posted here also.

Rental packages are available from **Spirit of Skiing Ski Rentals** in the Jasper Park Lodge, tel. (403) 852-3433; **Sports Shop** at 414 Connaught Dr., tel. (403) 852-3654; or **Totem Ski Shop,** with rentals, repairs, and sales, at 408 Connaught Dr., tel. (403) 852-3078.

Maligne Canyon

By late December the torrent that is the Maligne River has frozen solid. Where it cascades down through Maligne Canyon the river is temporarily stalled for the winter, creating remarkable formations through the deep limestone canyon. **Maligne Tours,** 626 Connaught Dr., tel. (403) 852-3370, offers exciting two-hour guided tours into the depths of the canyon throughout winter, daily at 9 a.m. and 1 p.m.; adult $22, child $11.

FESTIVALS AND EVENTS

Summer is prime time on the park's events calendar. The first weekend of June is the **Jasper to Banff Relay.** Every second year (even years), at the end of July, the town hosts the **Jasper Heritage Folk Festival.** The **Jasper Lions Pro Indoor Rodeo,** on the third weekend of August, dates back 60 years and attracts pro cowboys from across North America. Apart from the traditional rodeo events, the fun includes dances, a casino, the Miss Jasper contest, and jail-and-bail, where pedestrians are thrown in the slammer until friends bail them out. On the other side of the calendar, winter is not totally party-less—**Jasper in January Winter Festival** is a two-week celebration that includes fireworks, special evenings at local restaurants, and all the activities associated with winter.

Park Interpretive Program
Parks Canada offers a wide range of interpretive talks and hikes throughout summer. Each night in the **Whistlers Campground Outdoor Theatre** a different slide and movie program is shown. The theater is located near the shower block. The **Wilcox Campground Campfire Talk** takes place each Tuesday and Friday at 8 p.m.; hot tea is supplied while wardens and various speakers talk about the park. Wilcox Campground is on the Icefields Parkway at the southern end of the park. Each Wednesday at 7:30 p.m. a slide show on hiking in Jasper is shown at the museum located at 400 Pyramid Lake Road. Many different guided hikes are offered (all free) throughout summer; check bulletin boards at the Park Information Centre and campgrounds, or call (403) 852-6176.

ACCOMMODATIONS

Motel and hotel rooms here are expensive. Most of the motels and lodges are within walking distance of town and have indoor pools and restaurants. Luckily, alternatives to staying in $100-plus places do exist. Many private residences have rooms for rent in summer; two hostels are close to town (and many more are down the Icefields Parkway), bungalows are available that can be a good deal for families or small groups, and there's always camping in the good ol' outdoors. The park has nearly 2,000 campsites, and camping is virtually unlimited in the backcountry. When addressing written inquiries to the establishments listed below, follow the listed P.O. Box with **Jasper, AB T0E 1E0.**

Hotels and Motels
Aside from the famous Jasper Park Lodge, all accommodations discussed here are within walking distance of downtown Jasper. Rates quoted are for a standard room in summer. Outside the busy June-Sept. period most lodgings reduce rates drastically (ask also about ski packages during winter).

The least expensive, and also the most central, is the **Athabasca Hotel,** 510 Patricia St., P.O. Box 1420, tel. (403) 852-3386, with rooms above a honky-tonk bar. Some of the rooms have private bathrooms, but most share one down the hall. Rates are $46-81 s, $48-119 d (the least expensive rooms share bathrooms). One block away is the **Astoria Hotel,** 404 Connaught Dr., P.O. Box 1710, tel. (403) 852-3351 or (800) 661-7343, a European-style lodging built in 1924 and kept in the same family since. It is close to town, and all rooms have a fridge; from $104 s or d. The only other lodging right downtown is **Whistlers Inn,** 105 Miette Ave., P.O. Box 250, tel. (403) 852-3361 or (800) 282-9919, which features spacious rooms and a rooftop jacuzzi; $109 s, $119 d.

Mountain Park Lodges operates three high-quality accommodations north of downtown. Best value of these is **Marmot Lodge,** 84 Connaught Dr., P.O. Box 687, tel. (403) 852-4471 or (800) 661-6521, featuring modern and stylishly decorated rooms, many with mountain views. On the main level is a good restaurant. Some rooms and the indoor pool are fully wheelchair accessible. In summer, rates begin at $123 s or d, from $80 the rest of the year. Another, **Lobstick Lodge,** P.O. Box 1200, tel. (403) 852-4431 or (800) 661-9317, has extra-large, simply furnished rooms and a range of modern amenities; $126 s, $131 d. Closest of the three to downtown is **Amethyst Lodge,** 200 Connaught

Dr., P.O. Box 1200, tel. (403) 852-3394 or (800) 661-9935, named after a lake in the Tonquin Valley. It offers large rooms and an outdoor hot tub; $141 s or d.

Immediately north of the Marmot Lodge is **Sawridge Hotel,** 82 Connaught Dr., P.O. Box 2080, tel. (403) 852-5111 or (800) 661-6427, an older-style lodging with a large indoor atrium and indoor pool; rooms start at $120 s, $126 d (discounts here in the off season aren't as large as at other places). One block west, away from the main road is another bunch of accommodations. Least expensive of these is **Tonquin Inn,** Juniper St., P.O. Box 658, tel. (403) 852-4987 or (800) 661-1315. Guests enjoy luxurious rooms, a beautiful indoor pool, an outdoor hot tub, and laundry facilities; $144 s or d. **Jasper Inn,** 98 Geikie St., P.O. Box 879, tel. (403) 852-4461 or (800) 661-1933, is a modern chateau-style lodging of brick and red cedar. Many rooms have kitchenettes and fireplaces; $158 s, $184 d, chalet with kitchen $131. **Chateau Jasper,** 96 Geikie St., P.O. Box 1418, tel. (403) 852-5644 or (800) 661-9323, is one of Jasper's nicest lodgings. Rooms are large and the low ceilings give them a cozy feel. Downstairs is an excellent restaurant; $225 s or d.

On Connaught Dr. southwest of downtown you'll find two more accommodations. **Mount Robson Inn,** P.O. Box 88, tel. (403) 852-3327 or (800) 587-3327, has a fridge in each room; $136 s or d. **Maligne Lodge,** P.O. Box 757, tel. (403) 852-3143 or (800) 661-1315, has medium-size rooms; $149 s or d.

Jasper Park Lodge, P.O. Box 40, tel. (403) 852-3301 or (800) 441-1414, on Lac Beauvert, is the park's original resort and its most famous. It has four restaurants, three lounges, horseback riding, tennis courts, a championship golf course, and Jasper's only covered shopping arcade. The main lodge features stone floors, carved wooden pillars, and a high ceiling. The 442 rooms vary in configuration; some are modern while others are elegantly rustic. Most are in cottages spread around Lac Beauvert, each with a porch or balcony; basic rooms start at $316 s or d; off-season rates begin at $97.

A few kilometers from town is **Pyramid Lake Resort,** Pyramid Lake Rd., P.O. Box 388, tel. (403) 852-4900, the only lodging away from town, besides Jasper Park Lodge, open year-round.

Plenty of water-based activities make the resort a good choice for families; $115-195 per unit.

Summer Lodging
The following lodgings all open for the summer months only (generally May to late September). **Bonhomme Bungalows,** on Bonhomme St., P.O. Box 700, tel. (403) 852-3209, offers the only accommodation of this type in the townsite. Cabins are basic, but each has a TV, bathroom, and coffee-making facilities; $72-82 s or d. **Patricia Lake Bungalows,** P.O. Box 657, tel. (403) 852-3560, is located on the lake of the same name, a five-minute drive north from Jasper along Pyramid Lake Road. Small motel-style rooms are $49, cottages with kitchens are $92-156 depending on the size.

With your own transportation, you can seek out a number of good options along the Athabasca River, which flows past town to the east of the Yellowhead Highway. At the northern entrance to town is **Pine Bungalow Cabins,** P.O. Box 7, tel. (403) 852-3491, on a secluded section of the Athabasca River. Motel-style units with kitchenettes are $90 s or d, individual cabins with fireplaces begin at $95. **Tekarra Lodge,** P.O. Box 669, tel. (403) 852-3058, is located 1.5 km southeast of the townsite at the confluence of the Miette and Athabasca Rivers. Rooms in the lodge are $65 s or d; cabins, each with a kitchenette and wood-burning fireplace, begin at $105. Down on the Icefields Parkway, four km south of the townsite, is **Jasper House Bungalows,** P.O. Box 817, tel. (403) 852-4535, offers basic sleeping units for $70; those with cooking facilities begin at $148. A couple of kilometers further south, spread along a picturesque bend on the Athabasca River is **Becker's Roaring River Chalets,** P.O. Box 579, tel. (403) 852-3779. One-bed sleeping rooms run $60, chalets with kitchenette, fireplace, and double bed $95 (or $100 for those on the riverfront).

Other summer-only choices lie east of the townsite. **Pocahontas Bungalows,** P.O. Box 820, tel. (403) 866-3732, is near the park's east gate at the bottom of the road that leads to Miette Hot Springs; $65-73 s or d. **Miette Hot Springs Bungalows,** P.O. Box 907, tel. (403) 866-3750, is within walking distance of the park's only hot springs. Motel units are $65 s or d, $70 with a kitchenette; bungalows begin at $105.

Tonquin Valley Lodge

The only backcountry accommodation in the park is Tonquin Valley Lodge, P.O. Box 550, Jasper, AB T0E 1E0, tel. (403) 852-3909. The lodge is southwest of Jasper in the spectacular Tonquin Valley. Getting there involves a 23-km hike or, in winter, cross-country ski trip, from a trailhead opposite Mt. Edith Cavell Hostel. Cabins have wood-burning heaters, bunk beds, oil lanterns, and a spectacular view. The rate, $90 per person per night, includes accommodations, three meals, and use of small boats.

Private Home Accommodations

At last count, Jasper had over 70 residential homes offering accommodations. Often they supply nothing more than a room with a bed (and, officially, park by-laws prohibit them serving breakfast), but the price is right—$35-60 s or d. Usually the bathroom is shared with other guests or the family; few have kitchens, and breakfast is not included. The positive side, apart from the price, is that your hosts are usually knowledgeable locals and town is only a short walk away. The Jasper Tourism and Commerce Information Centre has a board listing each accommodation, but in summer, by early afternoon, there is a big red "full" plastered across it. Most have signs out front so you could cruise the streets (try Connaught, Patricia, and Geikie), but checking with the information center is easier. For a full listing that includes the facilities at each, write to Jasper Home Accommodation Association, P.O. Box 758, Jasper, AB T0E 1E0; use their brochure to book ahead.

Hostels

On the road to the Jasper Tramway, seven km from town, is **Jasper International Hostel,** which has 80 beds in men's and women's dorms, a large kitchen, a common room, showers, an outdoor barbecue area, and mountain bike rentals. Members of Hostelling International pay $15, nonmembers $20. For hostel reservations call (403) 852-3215. In the summer months this hostel fills up every night. Check-in time is in the evening, but the hostel is open all day. A cab between downtown Jasper and the hostel is $10.

Mt. Edith Cavell Hostel has a million-dollar view for the price of a dorm bed. It's located 13 km up Mt. Edith Cavell Road. Because of the location there's usually a spare bed. Opposite the hostel are trailheads for hiking in the Tonquin Valley, and it's just a short walk to the base of Mt. Edith Cavell. The hostel is rustic but has a kitchen, dining area, and outdoor wood sauna. Members pay $9 per night, nonmembers pay $14. It's closed November to mid-June. For reservations call (403) 852-3215.

Maligne Canyon Hostel is on Maligne Lake Rd., beside the Maligne River and a short walk from the canyon. Although rustic, it is in a beautiful setting. The 24 beds are in two cabins; other facilities include a kitchen and dining area. Rates are members $9, nonmembers $14. For reservations call (403) 852-3215. The hostel is closed Wednesday Oct.-April. The **Maligne Lake Shuttle,** 626 Connaught Dr., tel. (403) 852-3370, costs $6 from town. It makes eight trips daily.

Campgrounds

Whistlers Campground, at the base of Whistlers Rd., three km south of Jasper townsite, has 781 sites, making it the largest campground in the Canadian Rockies. It is divided into three sections; prices vary with the services available—unserviced sites $15, powered sites $17, full hookups $19. Each section has showers. The campground is open June to mid-October. A further two km south is **Wapiti Campground,** which stays open year-round and has showers; unserviced sites $14, powered sites $16. Northeast of the townsite, along Hwy. 16, are two smaller, more primitive campgrounds. **Snaring River Campground,** 17 km from Jasper, is $10; **Pocahontas Campground,** 45 km northeast, is $12. Both are open mid-May to early September.

Backcountry campgrounds are located throughout the park. For a full list as well as a camping permit ($6 per person per night) head for the Park Information Centre.

FOOD AND DRINK

Coffeehouses and Cafes

Soft Rock Cafe, in Connaught Square at 622 Connaught Dr., tel. (403) 852-5850, starts the day by dishing up plates of waffles topped with cream and your choice of fresh fruit for $3.95. If the cinnamon buns are still in the oven you'll have to come back later in the day—they're gigantic! The variety of coffee concoctions here is mind-boggling; prices are reasonable. It's open 7 a.m.-11 p.m. **Spooner's,** in the Patricia Centre at 610 Patricia St., tel. (403) 852-4046, is a second-floor cafe with stunning mountain views and a good range of coffees and light meals. A couple of doors away, at 608 Patricia St., is **Coco's Cafe,** tel. (403) 852-4550, another coffee-lover's meeting place. **Dano's,** 604 Patricia St., tel. (403) 852-3322, will satisfy any ice cream or cappuccino cravings. The cappuccino bar in the Athabasca Hotel is also a good hangout on rainy days.

Cool and Casual

For pizza, you won't be able to miss **Jasper Pizza Place,** 402 Connaught Dr., tel. (403) 852-3225. It's a large and noisy restaurant with bright furnishings and walls lined with photos from Jasper's earliest days. Pizza from the wood-fired oven starts at $8.75 while smaller pita pizzas, perfect for a lunchtime snack, cost just $3.25. **Papa George's,** 406 Connaught Dr., tel. (403) 852-3351, is a locals' favorite and one of Jasper's oldest restaurants. Breakfast is $3-6, lunch and dinner feature burgers, pasta, and steaks; daily specials are $10-15 and include soup and salad. Hours are 7 a.m.-11:30 p.m. **O'Shea's Restaurant,** 510 Patricia St., tel. (403) 852-4229, also has a good selection of pasta dishes.

The best Greek meals in town are served at **Something Else Restaurant,** 621 Patricia St., tel. (403) 852-3850. Portions are generous, service is friendly, the prices are right, and you'll find plenty of alternatives if the Greek dishes don't appeal to you. Greek favorites are $10-15, pasta dishes $10-13, pizza from $10. It's open daily 11 a.m.-midnight.

L&W Restaurant, on the corner of Hazel and Patricia Streets, tel. (403) 852-4114, has an outside patio, a strangely sloping roof, and plenty of greenery that brings to life an otherwise ordinary restaurant—a good place to take the family for an inexpensive meal. **Tramway Restaurant,** tel. (403) 852-5352, high above town on the Whistlers has, without a doubt, the best views in town. Daily lunch and dinner buffets complement the à la carte menu.

Middle of the Road

The Cantonese Restaurant, 608 Connaught Dr., tel. (403) 852-3559, is the place to go for Chinese; combo specials are $9-13 and set menus for two start at $23. It's open daily noon-10 p.m. **Miss Italia Ristorante,** 610 Patricia St., tel. (403) 852-4002, upstairs in the Patricia Centre, features mountain views from tables indoors and out. Pastas average $10, while Taste of Italy choices, featuring a sampling of cuisines from three regions, run $15. The place to go for Alberta beef is **Tonquin Prime Rib Village,** on Juniper St. beside the Tonquin Inn, tel. (403) 852-4966, which specializes in charbroiled steaks and prime rib but also offers a good choice of seafood. Five km south of town is **Becker's Gourmet Restaurant,** tel. (403) 852-3535, where the atmosphere is intimate and relaxing, the views of Mt. Kerkeslin and the Athabasca River are inspiring, and the steak and seafood dishes are well prepared. With a bottle of wine expect to pay $70 for two. **Tokyo Tom's Place,** 410 Connaught Dr., tel. (403) 852-3780, features a traditional sushi bar and eight tatami booths for eating the very best Japanese cuisine; combination dinners average $17 per person. It's open 5-11:30 p.m. **Walter's Dining Room** in the Sawridge Hotel, 82 Connaught Dr., tel. (403) 852-5111, features a menu of Alberta beef, Rocky Mountain trout, and British Columbia salmon in an elegant but relaxed atmosphere.

Top End

The **Inn Restaurant** in the Jasper Inn, 98 Geikie St., tel. (403) 852-3232, sits within a glass-enclosed atrium and features a menu of Alberta beef, ribs, fondue, and seafood. Entrees start at $15. Diners are offered complimentary limo service to the restaurant. The same menu is served in the just-as-elegant lounge for half the price. **Fiddle River Seafood Company,** 620 Connaught Dr., tel. (403) 852-3032, upstairs in Connaught Square, has fresh seafood, but expect to pay around $40 per person for a three-course meal. If you can't afford to eat here, at least stick your head in the door and admire the decor. The award-winning **Beavallon Dining Room** at Chateau Jasper, tel. (403) 852-5644, ext. 179, offers an extensive menu emphasizing continental cuisine prepared by a Swiss chef. All the chairs are upholstered, and the blue tablecloths and wood-trimmed crimson walls provide an air of elegance—elegance you pay for. It's expensive. The Sunday brunch here is worth the splurge.

Jasper Park Lodge

The lodge offers a choice of casual or elegant dining in four restaurants and three lounges. **Meadows Cafe,** in the Beauvert Shopping Promenade, is open for breakfast, lunch, and dinner. **Obsessions,** also in the arcade, has tempting French pastries, gourmet coffee, and homemade truffles and chocolates. Drinks and light snacks are served at the **Spike Lounge Deck** overlooking the golf course. At lunchtime the smell of sizzling steaks from **La Terrasse** wafts across Lac Beauvert; this outdoor eatery is open only in summer. The least expensive dining room is **Moose's Nook,** whose rustic atmosphere serves as a good place to enjoy some fine Canadian fare. **Beauvert Room,** a huge dining room overlooking Lac Beauvert, features a menu of European cuisine. The **Edith Cavell Room** is the finest fine-dining restaurant in Jasper. Its dark oak walls are contrasted by white linens and large, bright windows overlooking Lac Beauvert and the mountains beyond. The classic cuisine is served with a French flair and price tag; if you need to ask the price you can't afford it. For all lodge restaurant reservations call (403) 852-3301.

Drinking and Dancing

The most popular nightspot in town is the **Atha-b,** in the Athabasca Hotel. Bands play most nights and it gets pretty rowdy with all the seasonal workers but is still enjoyable; minimal cover charge. **The Pub,** in the Whistlers Inn, has great atmosphere with a classic wooden bar and memorabilia everywhere. Most of Jasper's larger hotels have lounges.

TRANSPORTATION

Getting There

The closest domestic and international airports are in Edmonton, three and a half hours to the east. The **VIA rail station** and the **bus depot** (both Greyhound and Brewster's) are in the same building, central to town at 607 Connaught Drive. The building is open 24 hours daily in summer, the rest of the year Mon.-Sat. 7:30 a.m.-10:30 p.m., Sunday 7:30-11 a.m. and 6:30-10:30 p.m. Lockers are available for $1 per day, and also here are a travel agent and a Tilden car rental agency.

Jasper is on the "Canadian" route, the only remaining transcontinental passenger rail service in the country. Trains run either way three times weekly. To the west the line divides going to both Prince Rupert and Vancouver; to the east it passes through Edmonton ($81 one-way from Jasper) and all points beyond. For all rail information call (800) 561-8630. Another rail option is offered by **Rocky Mountaineer Railtours,** tel. (800) 665-7245. This company operates a luxurious summer-only rail service between Vancouver and Jasper with an overnight in Kamloops (British Columbia). The one-way fare is $565-965 depending on the class of travel, with

Early guests to the Jasper Park Lodge, then a remote mountain retreat, were treated to all the luxuries of the day.

a $100 per person discount for travel in May and October.

Greyhound buses, tel. (403) 852-3926 or (800) 661-8747, depart Jasper for all points in Canada, including Vancouver (three times daily, 12-13 hours, $97.50 one-way), Edmonton (five times daily, four and a half hours, $47.08 one-way) with connections to Calgary, and Prince Rupert (once daily, 18 hours, $123.64 one-way).

Between June and the end of September **Brewster,** tel. (403) 852-3332 or (800) 661-1152, operates an airporter service between Jasper and Calgary International Airport. Buses depart the airport daily at 12:30 p.m. ($56 one-way to Jasper), pick up passengers in Banff at 3:15 p.m. ($42 one-way) and Lake Louise at 4:15 p.m. ($36 one-way), and arrive in Jasper at 8 p.m. The return service departs daily from Jasper Park Lodge at 12:50 p.m. and from the downtown bus depot at 1:30 p.m. Brewster also runs a nine-hour (one-way) tour between Banff and Jasper departing daily mid-April through October from the Banff and Jasper depots at 8 a.m.; if the bus picks you up at your lodging, departure time is earlier. The tour costs $69 one-way ($53 in spring and fall), $95 roundtrip ($69 in spring and fall). The roundtrip requires an overnight in Jasper. No bus service between Banff and Jasper is available November to mid-April. The Winter Tour, which includes a detour to Emerald Lake Lodge (Yoho National Park, British Columbia), runs November to mid-December and mid-January through April, departing Banff Tuesday at 9:45 a.m. and Jasper Thursday at 8:30 a.m.; $46 one-way, $81 roundtrip.

The **Rocky Express** is the only other transportation option for reaching Jasper. This six-day tour, which leaves from hostels in Calgary, Banff, and Lake Louise each Sunday and Wednesday through the summer, takes in sights along the Icefields Parkway and around Jasper. The tour costs $175 per person, including return transportation to Calgary but not including accommodations. The accommodations, in hostels, are provided at hostel member rates—approximately $75-80. Make reservations through Banff International Hostel at (403) 762-4122.

Getting Around

Although the town is compact, getting out to see the sights can be a problem without your own transportation. **Hiker's Wheels** is a shuttle service to popular trailheads, but it also does pick-ups and drop-offs at hostels and campgrounds. The departure point in town is Hava Java House at 407 Patricia Street. For details and reservations call (403) 852-2188.

The **Maligne Lake Shuttle** runs out to Maligne Lake eight times daily ($20 roundtrip) and will make drops at Maligne Canyon and Maligne Canyon Hostel ($6 one-way); tel. (403) 852-3370.

Rental cars start at $53 per day with 100 free kilometers. The following companies have agencies in town: **Avis,** tel. (403) 852-3970 or (800) 879-2847; **Budget,** tel. (403) 852-3222 or (800) 268-8900; and **Tilden,** tel. (403) 852-4972 or (800) 387-4747.

Mountain bikes can be rented from: **On-line Sport & Tackle,** 600 Patricia St., tel. (403) 852-3630; **Beyond Bikes,** 14 Cedar Ave., tel. (403) 852-5922; **The Sports Shop,** 414 Connaught Dr., tel. (403) 852-3654; **Freewheel Cycle,** 618 Patricia St., tel. (403) 852-3898; and **Sandy's at Jasper Park Lodge** (tel. 403-852-3301). Expect to pay $4-5 per hour or $12-20 per day.

Cabs in town are not cheap; most drivers will take you on a private sightseeing tour or to trailheads if requested: try **Jasper Taxi,** tel. (403) 852-3600 or 852-3146. **Heritage Cabs,** tel. (403) 852-5558, has a fleet of antique cars.

Tours

Brewster, tel. (403) 852-3332, offers a three-hour Discover Jasper tour taking in Patricia and Pyramid Lakes, Maligne Canyon, and Jasper Tramway (ride not included in fare). It departs April-Oct. daily at 8 a.m.; $32. A shortened version of this tour operates daily in spring and fall and each Wednesday through winter departing daily at 9:30 a.m.; $25.

Maligne Tours has a variety of tours including one to Maligne Lake ($50, includes cruise); the office is at 626 Connaught Dr., tel. (403) 852-3370. **Jasper Adventure Centre,** in the Chaba Theatre at 604 Connaught Dr. in summer (at 306 Connaught in winter), tel. (403) 852-3127, is the agent for a number of operators. Tours travel to Mount Edith Cavell (departs 2 p.m.; three hours), Maligne Canyon (departs 10 a.m.; three hours), and Miette Hot Springs (departs 7 p.m.; four hours); $30 per person per tour. The Jasper Adventure Centre is also an agent for rafting trips, guided hikes, heli-hiking, fishing trips, and just about everything else; open in summer daily 7:30 a.m.-9 p.m.

SERVICES AND INFORMATION

Services

The **post office** is at 502 Patricia St., opposite the Park Information Centre. Mail to be picked up here should be addressed General Delivery, Jasper, AB T0E 1E0. The two laundromats on Patricia St. are open 6 a.m.-11 p.m. and offer showers that cost $2 for 10 minutes (quarters). **On-line Sport & Tackle** sells a wide range of camping gear and fishing tackle. It's located at 600 Patricia St., tel. (403) 852-3630. The **hospital** is at 518 Robson St., tel. (403) 852-3344. For the **RCMP** call (403) 852-4848.

Books and Bookstores

The small **Jasper Municipal Library,** on Elm Ave., tel. (403) 852-3652, holds just about everything ever written about the park. It's open Mon.-Thurs. 2-5 p.m. and 7-9 p.m., Friday 2-5 p.m., Saturday 10 a.m.-3 p.m.

Head to the Park Information Centre or the museum for a good selection of books on the park's natural and human history. **Maligne Lake Books,** in the Jasper Park Lodge, has a good selection of coffee-table books.

Information

The Parks Canada **Park Information Centre** is in a beautiful old stone building in Athabasca Park on Connaught Drive. The staff at the first desk provides general information on the park and can direct you to hikes in the immediate vicinity. Then they whip out another map and a fluorescent marker and quicker than you can say "bear-bells" they've marked all the trail closures. The next desk is for those going into the backcountry—save your questions that you don't want a canned answer for, for here. This is also the place to register for backcountry camping permits. In the far corner is a **Parks and People** outlet selling maps, books, and local publications. Look out for notices posted out front with the day's interpretive programs. The center is open in summer, daily 8 a.m.-8 p.m., the rest of the year, daily 9 a.m.-5 p.m.; tel. (403) 852-6786.

At 632 Connaught Dr. is the **Jasper Tourism and Commerce Information Centre,** tel. (403) 852-3858, where the friendly staff never seems to tire of explaining that all the rooms in town are full. They will happily ring around to find accommodations for you and can provide general information on the town. They also have a large collection of brochures on activities, shopping, and restaurants in town. It's open in summer daily 8 a.m.-8 p.m., the rest of the year Mon.-Fri. 9 a.m.-5 p.m. Jasper's weekly newspaper *The Booster* (70 cents) is available throughout town on Wednesday. For a list of park-related items including publications and topographic maps write to Parks and People, P.O. Box 992, Jasper, AB T0E 1E0; or call (403) 852-4767. For more information on the park write to The Superintendent, Jasper National Park, P.O. Box 10, Jasper, AB T0E 1E0. For general tourist information write to Jasper Tourism and Commerce, P.O. Box 98, Jasper T0E 1E0, or call (403) 852-3858. **Jasper National Park Radio** is on the AM band at 1490. For weather conditions in the park call (403) 852-3185.

KAREN McKINLEY

CENTRAL ALBERTA

The central sector of the province is a diverse region extending from the peaks of the Canadian Rockies in the west through the foothills and aspen parkland to the prairies in the east. **Rocky Mountain Forest Reserve** occupies much of the the heavily forested western foothills, nestled against the folded and faulted front ranges of the Rocky Mountains. Most of this large coniferous forest is committed for nonrenewable resource development, although two designated wilderness areas in the reserve are totally protected from development. The entire reserve is a recreation playground: perfect for camping, fishing, hiking, and other outdoor activities. Rocky Mountain House, a medium-size town on Hwy. 11, is the gateway to the foothills. The North West and Hudson's Bay Companies once used trading posts here as a jumping-off point into the mountain wilderness to the west. The original site of these posts is now Alberta's only National Historic Park.

The 290-km route between Calgary and Edmonton through central Alberta on Hwy. 2 takes about three hours to drive straight through. Those with a little more time can explore the many historic towns along the way or visit a buffalo jump used by natives to stampede herds of bison to their deaths. Halfway between Calgary and Edmonton is Red Deer, a city of 60,000 that was once an important way station for travelers on the Calgary Trail (or Edmonton Trail, depending on which direction they were going).

North and east of Red Deer is the aspen parkland, a biome with characteristics unique to Canada's prairie provinces. Long, straight country roads link primarily agricultural towns along three main highways that extend into the neighboring province of Saskatchewan. Highlights of this section of parkland include five provincial parks, one of Canada's last remaining passenger steam trains at Stettler, and a fantastic museum dedicated to machinery at Wetaskiwin.

WEST-CENTRAL ALBERTA

Highway 2 between Calgary and Edmonton skirts the edge of the prairie—just west of the highway a region of foothills begins. The hills rise gradually, eventually reaching the lofty peaks of the front ranges adjoining Banff and Jasper National Parks. Several rivers—among them the North Saskatchewan, Red Deer, Clearwater, and Brazeau—slice through the foothills on their cascading descent from sources high in the Rockies. Fur trading was once a booming industry here, but the greatest human impact on the area came from coal mining earlier this century. Rocky Mountain House, located on the bank of the North Saskatchewan River, is the largest town in the region and a good base for exploring. The cities of Calgary and Edmonton are also close by.

This little-traveled region of the Canadian Rockies attracts outdoor enthusiasts year-round. Here you can hike in two wilderness areas, camp in many Forest Service campgrounds, fish in fish-filled lakes and rivers, explore historic sites, run the North Saskatchewan River, take horseback trips into the hills, cross-country ski in winter, or just admire the spectacular mountain scenery.

HIGHWAY 22 NORTH

This highway follows the eastern flanks of the foothills from Cochrane, northwest of Calgary, through the small communities of Cremona, Sundre, and Caroline, and the larger town of Rocky Mountain House. The Rockies dominate the western horizon for much of the route and are especially imposing around Sundre.

Sundre

This town of 1,800, on the banks of the Red Deer River, is a good jumping-off point for trips into the Rocky Mountain Forest Reserve. Nearby rivers provide excellent whitewater-rafting opportunities for those with their own craft. Highway 584, heading west from town, links up with Forestry Trunk Rd., providing access to many campgrounds and fishing spots. In town, Sun-

dre's **Pioneer Village Museum,** 130 Centre St., tel. (403) 638-4768, displays a large collection of artifacts from early pioneer days, including farm machinery, a blacksmith shop, and an old schoolhouse. It's open in summer Wed.-Sat. 10 a.m.-4:30 p.m. and Sunday noon-4:30 p.m. A canoe race is held on the Red Deer River on the last weekend of May, and the **Sundre Pro Rodeo** comes to town on the third weekend of June.

Sundre has four motels, all on Main Ave.; the least expensive is **Bulldogs Inn,** on the town's western outskirts, tel. (403) 638-4748; $33 s, $35 d. **Greenwood Park,** on the west bank of the Red Deer River, has no hookups, but the clean facilities include showers; $9. East of town is **Tall Timber Leisure Park,** tel. (403) 638-3555, a full-service RV park where tenters aren't welcome; powered sites $19, full hookups $21. **Outlaw's Bar and Grill,** 250 Main Ave., tel. (403) 638-2882, is the only place in town to get a decent meal. Lunch specials are $5-7 including a salad bar, and the weekend hot breakfast buffet, served till noon, is $5.95. The **Tourist Information Centre** is located on the east bank of the Red Deer River; open in summer Thurs.-Mon. 10 a.m.-8 p.m.

Caroline

Named after the daughter of one of the town's earliest settlers, Caroline depended on agriculture and forestry to support its economy until recently, when Alberta's largest sour gas discovery was made south of town. Now Shell Canada's plant at the site also contributes to the area's economy.

Multiple-time world figure-skating champion Kurt Browning was born and raised on a ranch just west of town. His portrait adorns local tourist literature, and the town's Kurt Browning Arena, on 48th Ave., houses Kurt's Korner, a display of Browning memorabilia.

The two motels in town are inexpensive, and **Caroline Municipal RV Park,** at the east end of town, tel. (403) 722-2210, has showers, kitchen shelters, and firewood. Unserviced sites are $10 a night, powered sites are $12.

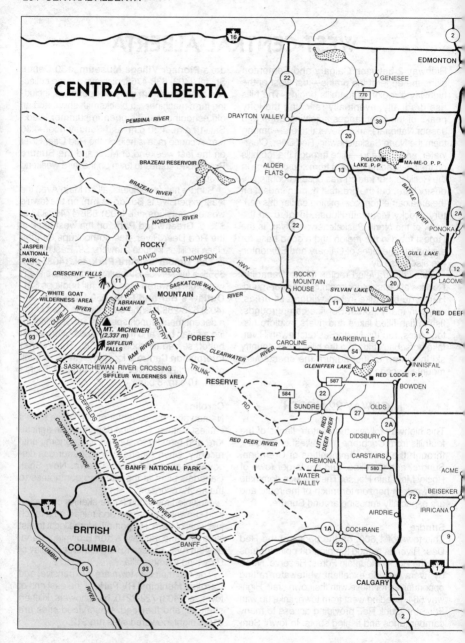

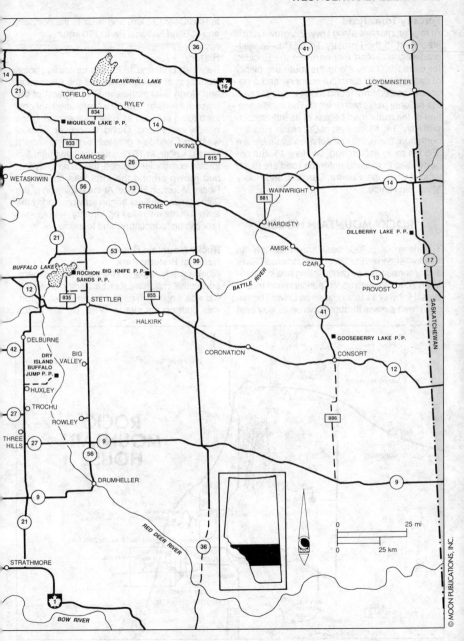

Forestry Trunk Road

At regular intervals along Hwy. 22, gravel roads lead west to the Forestry Trunk Rd.—a well-graded gravel road that parallels the Rockies for over 1,000 km. Along the route are plenty of campgrounds, beautiful scenery, and a degree of solitude not found along roads through the national parks farther west. The middle section of the trunk road begins at its intersection with Hwy. 1A, 13 km west of Cochrane. Heading north from there, the first services available are 265 km away at Nordegg, on Hwy. 11. But opportunities to exit and enter the road are found west of Cremona, Sundre, Caroline, and Rocky Mountain House.

ROCKY MOUNTAIN HOUSE

This town of 5,700, best known simply as "Rocky," straddles the North Saskatchewan River and is surrounded by gently rolling hills in a transition zone between aspen parkland and mountains. Highway 11 (also known as David Thompson Hwy.) passes through town on its way east to Red Deer (82 km) and west to the northern end of Banff National Park (170 km).

History

Between 1799 and 1875, four fur-trading posts were built at the confluence of the Clearwater and North Saskatchewan Rivers, west of the present townsite. The forts were used not only for trading but also as bases for exploring the nearby mountains. David Thompson, one of western Canada's greatest explorers, was a regular visitor. In 1821, after the two major fur-trading companies merged, the community that had grown around the forts was christened Rocky Mountain House. At the beginning of the 20th century, settlers began arriving. Today the town's economy relies on forestry, natural-gas processing, agriculture, and tourism.

Rocky Mountain House
National Historic Park

Alberta's only National Historic Park commemorates the important role fur trading played in Canada's history. The first trading post, or fort, was built on the site in 1799. By the 1830s

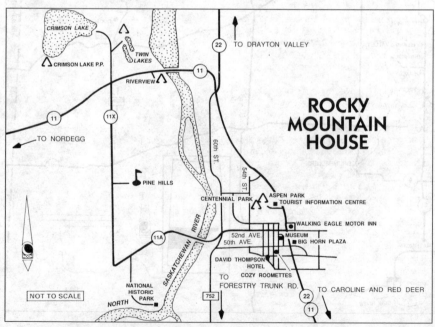

NOT TO SCALE

Natives built dome-shaped sweat lodges out of brush and covered them in buffalo robes.

beaver felt was out of fashion in Europe and traders turned to buffalo robes. By the 1870s, the massive herds of buffalo that had roamed the plains for thousands of years were gone. This signaled an end to the fur trade—an industry that had opened up the West and had been the Indians' main source of European goods such as clothing, horses, and guns. The last post at Rocky Mountain House closed soon after and, by the early 1900s, was reduced to two brick chimneys. In 1926 the forts were declared National Historic Sites. Today the protected areas include the sites of four forts, a buffalo paddock, and a stretch of riverbank where the large voyageur canoes would have come ashore to be loaded with furs bound for Europe.

The **visitor center** is the best place to begin a visit to the site; its interpretive displays detail the history of the forts, the fur trade, and exploration of the West. Two trails lead along the north bank of the river. The longer of the two, a 3.2-km loop, passes the site of the two original forts. Frequent "listening posts" along the trail play a lively recorded commentary on life in the early 1800s. All that remains of the forts are depressions in the ground, but through the commentary and interpretive displays it is easy to get a good idea of what the forts looked like. To the north of the fort site is an observation deck for viewing a herd of 25 buffalo that may, or may not, be visible. The other trail leads to two chimneys, remnants of the later forts.

The park is open year-round, although the visitor center is only open May-Sept., daily 9:30 a.m.-6 p.m. It's located five km west of Rocky Mountain House on Hwy. 11A. Admission is by donation. For more information write to Rocky Mountain House, P.O. Box 2130, AB T0M 1T0; tel. (403) 845-2412.

Other Sights

The **Rocky Mountain House Museum,** 4604 49th Ave., tel. (403) 845-2332, located in a 1927 schoolhouse, exhibits an array of pioneer artifacts, including an early Forest Service cabin. It's open in summer Mon.-Sat. 10 a.m.-7 p.m. and Sunday 1-7 p.m. Admission is $2. Another collection of pioneer memorabilia is housed at **Mandelin Eldon Museum,** tel. (403) 845-6144, 15 km southwest of Rocky on Hwy. 752; admission $2. It's open in summer Mon.-Sat. 10 a.m.-7 p.m. and Sunday 1-7 p.m., the rest of the year Mon.-Fri. 10 a.m.-3 p.m. The Canadian chapter of the **Rocky Mountain Elk Foundation** is based in Rocky. The foundation's main objective is to preserve critical wildlife habitat by buying large chunks of land; members are mostly hunters. It's located in the Big Horn Plaza; tel. (403) 845-6492.

Recreation

The best way to appreciate the history of the area, see some great river scenery, and generally have a good time is to take a float trip with **Voyageur Adventure Tours,** 4804 63rd St., tel.

(403) 845-7878, on the North Saskatchewan River. The voyageur canoes used are replicas of those used by early explorers; they are large and stable, requiring little paddling skill. Half-day trips, which include a stop at the National Historic Park and lunch, are $40; a full day with cooked lunch—prepared along the riverbank while you take a short hike or rest in the sun—is $60. Overnight tours start at $140, and a five-day trip—including three days on horseback—is $395.

Pine Hills Golf Course offers linksters an 18-hole course eight km west of town, tel. (403) 845-7400; green fees are $24.

Accommodations

Many motels are spread out along Hwy. 11 east of town, among them: **Voyageur Motel,** tel. (403) 845-3381, which has large, clean rooms for $36 s, $44 d; **Big Horn Motel,** tel. (403) 845-2871, in the Big Horn Plaza, $35 s, $39 d; and **Walking Eagle Motor Inn,** tel. (403) 845-2804, easily recognized by its striking log exterior, $57 s, $63 d. Downtown, **Cozy Roomettes,** 4917 49th St., tel. (403) 845-2270, aren't particularly cozy but offer cheap backpacker rooms, each with kitchenette, cable TV, and shared bathroom; $28 s, $32 d.

Both the municipal campgrounds within town limits have toilets, showers, and firewood; unserviced sites $10. **Aspen Park,** behind the Tourist Information Centre, is the larger of the two and has powered sites ($14). The other, **Centennial Park,** is along 54th Street. **Riverview Campground,** tel. (403) 845-4422, on the North Saskatchewan River is the only commercial facility in town. The unserviced sites are tucked in among a grove of trees on the riverbank and above them are serviced sites, with spectacular views along the valley. The campground has a small grocery store, laundromat, showers, and free firewood; unserviced sites $10, full hookups $15.

In **Crimson Lake Provincial Park,** northwest of town along an access road off Hwy. 11, you'll find two campgrounds; sites along the bank of Crimson Lake are $15 while those on **Twin Lakes** (good rainbow trout fishing) are $13.

Food and Drink

The only restaurants in town are those in the strip of family-style and fast-food places along Hwy. 11 and 52nd Avenue. **Walking Eagle Motor Inn,** on the east side of the highway, serves a good lunch buffet for $8.95. A wild honky-tonk bar in the **David Thompson Hotel,** 4834 50th St., tel. (403) 845-3123, cranks out live music most nights.

Services and Information

The **Greyhound** bus depot is in the Shell gas station at 4504 47th Ave. Greyhound operates a daily service between Calgary and Rocky ($30.07 one-way), but you must change buses in Red Deer. For further information call (800) 661-8747. For a taxi call **Rocky Cabs** at (403) 845-4000.

The **post office** is downtown at 5011 50th Avenue. **Happy's Laundromat** is located at 4507 47th Ave., open daily 8 a.m.-10 p.m. **Rocky Mountain House General Hospital** is at 5016 52nd Ave., tel. (403) 845-3347. For the **RCMP** call (403) 845-2881, and if you spot a forest fire call (403) 845-8211.

The **Tourist Information Centre,** located in a small trailer north of town on Hwy. 11, offers free coffee and good information on the forestry roads farther west. Don't buy the town map—many shops in town give them away. The center is open in summer daily 9 a.m.-8 p.m.; tel. (403) 845-2414. The chamber of commerce, located in the Town Hall, also has information; open year-round weekdays only, tel. (403) 845-5450.

NORDEGG

Westbound Hwy. 11 climbs slowly from the aspen parkland around Rocky Mountain House into the dense forests on the eastern slopes of the Rockies. The only community between Rocky and Banff National Park is Nordegg, 85 km west of Rocky. Nordegg was once a booming coal-mining town of 3,500. But the town was abandoned when the mines closed; now fewer than 100 hardy souls call the town home. Below the old townsite, just off Hwy. 11, various tourist facilities have sprung up, including an excellent interpretive center. And the town is near many fine fishing rivers and the Forestry Trunk Road.

History

Early this century, Martin Nordegg staked a claim at a site near where his namesake town is today.

Soon after, he established **Brazeau Collieries** and struck a deal with the Canadian National Railway; if they would extend the line to his mines, he would have 100,000 tons of coal waiting. He kept his side of the deal and the railway kept theirs, completing the rail line in 1914. Until then, miners had been housed in makeshift quarters. But the railway brought construction supplies, and permanent structures were soon erected. The town of Nordegg became the first "planned" mining town in Alberta. The streets were built in a semicircular pattern, centered around the railroad station and shops. Fifty miners' cottages were built, all painted in pastel colors. Gardens were planted and two churches and a modern hospital were built; miners had never had it better. In 1923 production peaked at nearly half a million tons of coal. By the '30s, most of the coal was being converted to briquettes, which were easy to handle and burned better than raw coal. By the early '40s, with four briquette presses, Nordegg had one of the largest such operations in North America. But the success soon turned to ash. In 1941 an explosion killed 29 men, and in 1950 fire destroyed many structures. Then trains began converting to diesel fuel and home heating went to natural gas. Brazeau Collieries ceased operations in January 1955. Many miners had spent their entire lives working the mine and had raised families in the remote mining community. By the summer of '55, the town had been abandoned. A minimum security prison has operated on the site since 1963 and only a few of the original buildings remain.

The **Nordegg Historic Heritage Interest Group,** made up of many former residents of the mining community, has commenced restoration of some of the buildings. The townsite is not open to the general public. To visit the area, you must either take a guided tour or do a short stint in the slammer. We recommend the tour. For more information, write to the group at P.O. Box 2039, Rocky Mountain House, AB T0M 1T0.

In Town

Tourist services are on an access road south of Hwy. 11. The **Nordegg Heritage Centre** is housed in the old schoolhouse, just up the hill from "downtown." Among many interesting displays are newspaper articles telling of the town's ups and downs. Tours of the abandoned townsite and mine leave from here in summer, daily at 1 p.m. They last about two and a half hours and cost $4. The museum, tel. (403) 721-3950, is open in summer daily 9 a.m.-5 p.m. and is a good source of information about the area. The Fish and Wildlife office, tel. (403) 721-3949, has information on current **road conditions.** The office is open year-round Mon.-Fri. 8:30 a.m.-midday.

Recreation

Nearby fishing is excellent—inquire at the **Fish and Wildlife office,** tel. (403) 721-3949, for details. Nordegg, with a population of under 100, has a nine-hole golf course; $5.

Accommodations and Food

Nordegg Resort Lodge, tel. (403) 721-3757, is the town's only motel, but it's usually full with mineral exploration crews (so much so that there's a temporary helipad beside it); basic rooms are $50 s, $60 d. If you must have a roof over your head, don't despair; Nordegg has its own hostel. **Shunda Creek Hostel** is a huge log chalet in a bush setting that has a fully equipped kitchen, dining room, fireplace, hot showers, and some private rooms. Members of Hostelling International pay $14 per night, nonmembers $19. For reservations call (403) 721-2140, or book through the Edmonton Hostel at (403) 439-3139. The hostel is located along Shunda Creek Recreation Area Rd., just west of Nordegg. If you've never stayed in a hostel, check this one out.

Campers are spoiled for choice with Forest Service campgrounds north and south along the Forestry Trunk Road, and provincial recreation areas east and west along Hwy. 11. All are primitive but have pit toilets, firewood, and kitchen shelters and are usually beside a creek or lake. Expect to pay $7-9 per night. Closest to town is **Upper Shunda Creek,** west of Nordegg.

The only place to eat in town is the restaurant in the **Nordegg Resort Lodge,** open 7 a.m.-9 p.m.

WEST FROM NORDEGG

The **Forestry Trunk Rd.** crosses Hwy. 11 three km west of Nordegg. This road, used mainly to maintain the forest, is well traveled by those going fishing, hiking, and camping. From Hwy.

11 it is 190 km north to Hinton and 265 km south to Cochrane. There are no services along either route but the scenery is spectacular, the fishing great, and the crowds nonexistent.

From this junction Hwy. 11 veers southwest. Twenty-three km from Nordegg it passes a gravel parking area at the trailhead for **Crescent Falls** and **Bighorn Canyon**. A further five km, a gravel road leads south to the eastern end of **Abraham Lake** on the North Saskatchewan River, one of Alberta's largest reservoirs. An information center at the dam is open in summer daily 8:30 a.m.-4:30 p.m.; tel. (403) 721-3952. Back on the highway, the main body of Abraham Lake quickly comes into view, its brilliant turquoise water reflecting the front ranges of the Rockies. Don't stop for a photo session just yet—the views improve farther west. Across the lake is **Michener Mountain** (2,337 meters).

David Thompson Resort, tel. (403) 721-2103, provides the only services along the highway west of Nordegg. Its full-service RV park charges $13 for unserviced sites, $15-17 for hookups. Motel rooms are available for $58 s, $65 d. A cafe serves hearty breakfasts from $4, lunch and dinner from $6. The resort also rents bikes for $12 per day and has a heated pool and a Frisbee golf course. **Helicopter Adventures** is based at the resort and takes people on a seven-minute spin for $30, worthwhile if it's clear. To the south of the resort is the main access point into White Goat Wilderness Area (see below).

Kootenay Plains Ecological Reserve/Siffleur Falls

Located at the south end of Abraham Lake, this reserve protects a unique area of dry grasslands in the mountains. The climate in this section of the valley is unusually moderate, the warmest in the Rockies. Vegetation such as June grass and wheat grass, usually associated with the prairies of southeastern Alberta, thrives here. The valley is a prime wintering area for elk, but due to the dry microclimate and its associated vegetation, mammals are not abundant in summer.

Two km farther west along the highway is the trailhead for a five-km hike (allow 90 minutes one-way) to spectacular Siffleur Falls. Along the first section the trail crosses the North Saskatchewan River via a swinging bridge. From the falls, this trail continues into the Siffleur Wilderness Area (see below).

Highway 11 then continues climbing, past a parking area (from where a trail leads to a whirlpool on the North Saskatchewan River) and on into Banff National Park at Saskatchewan River Crossing. From here it is 153 km north to Jasper and 127 km south to Banff.

White Goat Wilderness Area

The region's three designated wilderness areas—White Goat, Siffleur to the south, and Willmore to the north, afford hikers the chance to enjoy the natural beauty and wildlife of the Cana-

DAVID THOMPSON

David Thompson, one of Canada's greatest explorers, was a quiet, courageous, and energetic man who drafted the first comprehensive and accurate map of western Canada. He arrived in Canada from England as a 14-year-old apprentice clerk for the Hudson's Bay Company. With an inquisitive nature and a talent for wilderness navigation, he quickly acquired the skills of surveying and mapmaking. Natives called him Koo-koo-sint, which translates as "the man who looks at stars."

Between 1786 and 1808 Thompson led four major expeditions into what is now Alberta—the first for the Hudson's Bay Company and the last three for its rival, the North West Company. The most important one was the fourth, from 1806 to 1808, during which he traveled up the North Saskatchewan River and discovered the Athabasca Pass through the Continental Divide. For many years, this was the main route across the Rockies to the Pacific Ocean.

In 1813 Thompson began work on a master map covering the entire territory that the North West Company controlled. It was four meters long and two meters wide, detailing over 1.5 million square miles. On completion it was hung out of public view in the council hall of a company fort in the east. It was years later, after his death in 1857, that the map was "discovered" and Thompson became recognized as one of the world's greatest land geographers.

dian Rockies away from the crowds associated with the mountain national parks. No horses or motorized vehicles are allowed within wilderness area boundaries; hunting and fishing are prohibited, as is all construction. This, ironically, gives these lightly traveled regions (an unnamed 15-year resident of adjoining Banff National Park had never heard of them) more protection than national parks. The drawback, and the reason so few people explore these areas, is that wilderness really means *wilderness,* sans roads, bridges, or campsites. With one exception at Willmore, no roads even lead to the areas' boundaries; the only access is on foot.

White Goat is the largest of the three wilderness areas, comprising 445 square km of high mountain ranges, wide valleys, hanging glaciers, waterfalls, and high alpine lakes. The area's vegetation zones are easily recognizable: subalpine forests of Engelmann spruce, subalpine fir, and lodgepole pine; alpine tundra higher up. Large mammals here include a large population of bighorn sheep, as well as mountain goats, deer, elk, woodland caribou, moose, cougars, wolves, coyotes, black bears, and grizzly bears.

The most popular hike is the **McDonald Creek Trail,** which first follows the Cline River, then McDonald Creek to the creek's source in the heart of the wilderness area. McDonald Creek is approximately 12 km from the parking area on Hwy. 11, but a full day should be allowed for this section as the trail crosses many streams. From where McDonald Creek flows into the Cline River it is 19 km to the McDonald Lakes but allow another two full days; the total elevation gain for the hike is 1,224 meters. Other hiking possibilities include following the Cline River to its source and crossing Sunset Pass into Banff National Park, 17 km north of the Saskatchewan River Crossing, or heading up Cataract Creek and linking up with the trails in the Brazeau River area of Jasper National Park. White Goat Wilderness Area has no services and is for experienced hikers only. For more information write to Alberta Environmental Protection, Main Floor, 9920 108th St., Edmonton, AB T5K 2M4, tel. (403) 944-0313. The park is covered by topographic maps 83 C/2 and 83 C/7 and, for those traveling in the remote northwestern corner of the area, 83 C/6.

Siffleur Wilderness Area

Siffleur, like White Goat Wilderness Area, is a remote region of the Canadian Rockies, completely protected from any activities that could have an impact on the area's fragile ecosystems, including road and trail development. No bridges have been built over the area's many fast-flowing streams, and the few old trails that do exist are not maintained. Elk, deer, moose, cougars, wolverines, wolves, coyotes, black bears, and grizzly bears roam the area's four main valleys, while higher, alpine elevations harbor mountain goats and bighorn sheep.

The area is located on the opposite (south) side of Hwy. 11 from White Goat Wilderness and borders Banff National Park to the west and south. The main trail into the 412-square-km wilderness begins from a parking area two km south of the Two O'clock Creek Campground at Kootenay Plains (see above)..The area's northeastern boundary is a seven-km hike from here. Once inside the wilderness area, the trail climbs steadily alongside the Siffleur River and into the heart of the wilderness. Ambitious hikers can continue through to the Dolomite Creek Area of Banff National Park, finishing at the Icefields Parkway, seven km south of Bow Summit. Total length of this trail is 68 km (five to seven days). Another access point for the area is opposite Waterfowl Lakes Campground in Banff National Park. From here it is six km up Noyes Creek to the wilderness area boundary; the trail peters out after 4.5 km and requires some serious scrambling before descending into Siffleur. This trail— as with all others in the wilderness area—is for experienced hikers only. For more information write to Alberta Environmental Protection, Main Floor, 9920 108th St., Edmonton, AB T5K 2M4, tel. (403) 944-0313. Siffleur Wilderness Area is covered by topographic maps 82 N/15 and 82 N/16.

NORTH FROM ROCKY MOUNTAIN HOUSE

Alder Flats

Alder Flats is 61 km north of Rocky and six km west of Hwy 22. Through town, along a gravel road, is Alberta's only privately owned ghost town, **Em-te.** It was built completely from scratch and includes a saloon, jailhouse, harness shop, stables, a bank, emporium, and a church. Rose's Cantina serves meals throughout the day. A campground at the ghost town has hot showers, but sites are unserviced; $8.60 per night. Admission to Em-te is $4.25; tel. (403) 388-2166.

Pigeon Lake Provincial Park

On the shore of Pigeon Lake east of Alder Flats, this park is a popular recreation area for residents of Edmonton (60 km to the northwest). The lake is reputed to be the best swimming lake in Alberta and offers good fishing for walleye, pike, and whitefish. At the main campground you'll find a beach, showers, kitchen shelters, firewood, and the start of a short hiking trail; unserviced sites $13. **Zeiner Campground,** a little farther north, has powered sites, kitchen shelters, firewood, and canoe rentals, but no showers; unserviced sites $13. Reservations are taken for both these campgrounds; call (403) 586-2644. Also on Pigeon Lake is Alberta's smallest provincial park, **Ma-me-o Provincial Park** (1.5 hectares), which sits at the south-

eastern end of the lake among a colorful array of summer cottages. It is a day-use area only.

Drayton Valley and Vicinity

Drayton Valley is a town of 5,000 at the base of the foothills and at the western edge of Alberta's extensive oil and gas fields, 110 km north of Rocky Mountain House. It is located on what is known as the **subcontinental divide:** a high point of land dividing the Arctic Ocean–bound Pembina River System from the Atlantic-bound North Saskatchewan River System. To the southwest, along Hwy. 620, is **Brazeau Reservoir,** whose waters are used to supply hydroelectric power to nearby industry. To the east, 40 km along Hwy. 39, then 25 km north on Hwy. 770, are the **Genesee Fossil Beds.** Each year the North Saskatchewan River erodes its banks here, exposing often perfectly preserved 60-million-year-old fossilized plants. To get to the site from the hamlet of Genesee head west three km, south 1.5 km, then west again 1.5 km to a small creek. A partially defined trail leads down to the much larger river and to the fossil beds.

CALGARY TO RED DEER

The main route out of Calgary is the Deerfoot Trail, which becomes Hwy. 2 as it heads through outlying suburbs and onto the prairies. To the west are the foothills and, over 100 km away, dominating the horizon, the Canadian Rockies. They remain in view for much of the 145-km run to the city of Red Deer, located halfway to Edmonton. The Calgary and Edmonton Railway Company built the first permanent link between Alberta's two largest centers in 1891, following a trail used for generations by natives, early explorers, traders, and missionaries. With the coming of the automobile, a road was built. The original road (Hwy. 2A) is now paralleled the entire length by Hwy. 2, a four-lane divided highway that makes the trip an easy three-hour drive. Highway 2A is still maintained in some sections, passing through small ranching and farming communities. A longer but more interesting alternative is to take Hwys. 9 and 21, to the east of Hwy. 2, passing through the southern edge of the aspen parkland to a buffalo jump used by natives 2,000 years ago.

VIA HIGHWAY 2A

Airdrie

This fast-growing city is mostly residential. Folks from Calgary who become disenchanted with city living need only move to this rural town—only 10 minutes from Calgary International Airport—to escape the hustle. It began as the first stopping house on the Calgary and Edmonton Railway and has grown ever since. The town's **Nose Creek Valley Museum,** 1701 Main St. S, tel. (403) 948-6685, has an interesting exhibit of artifacts from the Blackfoot and Shoshoni tribes who fought many battles in the area, vying for dominance as buffalo herds declined. It's open in summer daily 10 a.m.-5 p.m.

Beside the main highway is **Airdrie Driftwood Inn,** 121 Edmonton Trail, tel. (403) 948-3838, convenient to Calgary International Airport and a handy alternative to Calgary lodgings during Stampede Week. Rooms are $70 s, $80 d, and there is a restaurant on site.

Carstairs

Carstairs is a farming, dairy, and ranching center 67 km north of Calgary. The town's tree-lined streets are dotted with grand old houses, while the grain elevators associated with all prairie towns stand silhouetted against the skyline. Although there is a small museum at 1138 Nanton St., the main attractions are outside of town. **Pasu Farm,** 10 km west of town (follow the signs), displays a wide variety of sheepskin, Albertan wool products, and weavings from Africa. The farm's Devonshire Tea Room serves scones, homemade apple pie, and various teas each afternoon. The farm is open year-round Tues.-Sat. 10 a.m.-5 p.m., Sunday noon-5 p.m.; tel. (403) 337-2800.

On the other side of Carstairs, 20 km east on Hwy. 581 and 4.5 km north on Hwy. 791, is **Custom Woollen Mills,** tel. (403) 337-2221, open Mon.-Fri. 8 a.m.-5 p.m. Here raw wool is processed on strange-looking machines—some of which date to the mid-1800s—into the finished product ready for knitting. Call ahead to arrange a tour.

Didsbury

From its beginnings as a Dutch Mennonite settlement, Didsbury has grown into a thriving agricultural community. Cheese lovers should stop for a tour of **Neapolis Dairy Products,** tel. (403) 335-4485. You can camp on the east side of town at **Rosebud Valley Campground,** which has showers and kitchen shelters; unserviced sites $10, powered sites $12.

Olds

Olds is located just over halfway between Calgary and Red Deer. Surrounded by rich farmland, it's the home of **Olds Agriculture College,** which has been a leader in the development of Canadian agriculture for most of this century. The school's landscaped gardens provide a welcome break from the seemingly endless farms that surround the town. The campus is located between Hwys. 2 and 2A.

Red Lodge Provincial Park

This small park is located 14 km west of **Bowden** on the **Little Red Deer River.** An English settler built a large log house on the river's edge and then painted the logs red, hence the name.

The park is within a heavily wooded strip of land that extends east from the foothills well into central Alberta, an ideal habitat for deer and moose. The campground has a kitchen shelter and firewood, and the river is good for swimming. It can get busy on weekends; $13.

Innisfail

Innisfail (pop. 6,000) is the largest town between Calgary and Red Deer. From Antler Ridge, north of town, Anthony Henday in 1754 became the first white man to see the Canadian Rockies. Highway 54, named the Anthony Henday Hwy. in his honor, begins in town and branches west, passing the turnoff to Markerville and continuing to Caroline and the Forestry Trunk Road. The large **Innisfail Historical Village,** in the fairgrounds at 42nd St. and 52nd Ave., tel. (403) 227-2906, has re-created historic buildings including a stopping house, school, store, C.P.R. Station, and blacksmith's shop. It's open in summer daily 8 a.m.-5 p.m. Afternoon tea is served on Friday ($1.50). The **RCMP Dog Training Centre,** located four km south of town on the east side of the highway, is the only one of its type in Canada. Canine cops receive training here in obedience, agility, and criminal apprehension. Tours of the facility are given year-round, weekdays 9 a.m.-4 p.m.; tel. (403) 227-3346.

Innisfail has two inexpensive motels, and just west of town is **Anthony Henday Campground,** with showers and kitchen shelters; unserviced sites $8, powered sites $12.

Markerville

This town, 16 km west then three km north of Innisfail, was originally settled by Icelandic people in the late 1800s; today their heritage lives on through the work of the local Icelandic Society. In town is **Historic Markerville Creamery.** Between 1897 and the time of its closure in 1972, the creamery won many awards for its fine quality butters. Tours of the factory explain how butter is made. It's open in summer daily 10 a.m.-5:30 p.m.; tel. (403) 728-3006. Just north of Markerville is **Stephansson House,** once home to Stephan A. Stephansson, one of the western world's most prolific poets. He spent the early part of his life in Iceland but most of his poetry was written here. The house has been restored with displays about the man and his work. Open May-Sept. daily 10 a.m.-6 p.m. For more information call (403) 728-3929.

THE BACK WAY

The area east of Hwy. 2, immediately north of Calgary, was once covered in aspen. But over time, the trees have given way to cereal agriculture and large dairy farms. Stands of trees are now limited to the valleys of tributaries of the Red Deer River, the region's main watershed. The landscape is generally flat, but along the main route north (via Hwys. 9 and 21) are interesting towns and a buffalo jump.

To Three Hills

Highway 9 intersects Hwy. 1 31 km east of Calgary and heads north to **Irricana**. Two km northwest of town, **Pioneer Acres Museum** displays a large collection of working farm machinery and holds a festival the second weekend each August, with demonstrations of pioneer farming and homemaking activities. It's open May to September daily 9 a.m.-5 p.m. Admission is $5. For more information call (403) 935-4357.

North of Irricana is **Beiseker,** where a C.P.R. Station, built in 1910, has been restored and now houses a museum. From here Hwy. 9 heads east, passing the junction with Hwy. 21 and continuing on to Drumheller (see the Dinosaur Valley chapter). North up Hwy. 21 is **Three Hills,** home of **GuZoo Animal Farm.** The farm, tel. (403) 443-7463, keeps a collection of exotic animals such as Siberian tigers, as well as cougars and bobcats—native to Alberta but rarely seen. It's open year-round daily from 9 a.m. Admission is $4. To get there from Three Hills head 1.5 km west, then six km north.

Trochu

The **Arboretum,** just off Hwy. 21, showcases the flora of southern Alberta. Pathways lead through the gardens, where over 100 different plant species attract a variety of birds. The arboretum is open in summer daily 10 a.m.-6 p.m.;

tel. (403) 442-2111. **St. Ann Ranch Trading Co.** was established in 1905 by a group of aristocratic French settlers and is now a Provincial Historic Site. A French settlement including a school, church, and post office grew around it. The thriving community suffered a blow during WW II when many townsmen returned to France to defend their country. Descendants of one of the men now operate the ranch, which has been partly restored. A small museum displays many historic items, and a large tearoom serves, among other delicacies, delicious fruit pies; open in summer daily 2-5 p.m. Two rooms are available for guest use; rates run $45-75 s or d including breakfast. For information or room reservations call (403) 442-3924.

Dry Island Buffalo Jump

This 1,180-hectare park is named for both an isolated mesa in the Red Deer River Valley and the site where natives stampeded bison over a cliff around 2,000 years ago. The buffalo jump—a 50-meter drop—is much higher than other jumps in Alberta and is in an ideal location; the approach to the jump is uphill, masking the presence of a cliff until the final few meters. Below the prairie benchland, clifflike valley walls and banks of sandstone have been carved into strange-looking badlands by wind and water erosion. A great diversity of plantlife grows in the valley; over 400 species of flowering plants have been recorded. The park is a day-use area only—apart from a picnic area and a few trails, it is undeveloped. Access is along a gravel road east from Huxley on Hwy. 21. From the park entrance, at the top of the buffalo drop, the road descends steeply into the valley. (It can be extremely slippery after rain.)

RED DEER

This city of 60,000 is located on a bend of the Red Deer River, halfway between the cities of Calgary and Edmonton (which are 145 km south and 148 km north, respectively). From the highway, Red Deer seems all in-

The bison was once king of the plains.

BOB RACE

dustrial estates and suburban sprawl. But an extensive park system runs through the city and many historic buildings have been restored.

History

The name Red Deer was mentioned on maps by explorer David Thompson in the early 1800s. The Cree name for the river is Waskasoo, which means "Elk"; scholars believe Thompson translated the word incorrectly, confusing these animals with the red deer of Scotland.

Permanent settlement began in 1882 at a site where the busy trail linking Calgary to Edmonton crossed the Red Deer River. Most of the early settlement was centered around Fort Normandeau, at the river crossing. But the Calgary and Edmonton Railway Company built its line and a station farther east, and the town slowly grew in around it. Initially the economy was based on agriculture, but it enjoyed the oil-and-gas boom after WW II. By the '70s, Red Deer was one of Canada's fastest growing cities.

Waskasoo Park and Fort Normandeau

Red Deer's sights are spread out along the Red Deer River, connected by 11-km-long, 1,000-

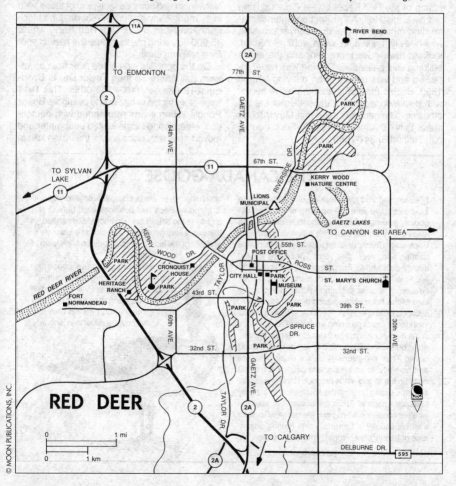

hectare Waskasoo Park. The park has an extensive trail system, good for walking or biking in summer and cross-country skiing in winter. The best place to start is **Heritage Ranch,** tel. (403) 346-0180, located at the end of Cronquist Drive (also accessible directly from Hwy. 2). The ranch is primarily an equestrian center offering trail rides but is also a year-round Tourist Information Centre. From the ranch, walk upstream through the wooded river valley, or drive back out along 32nd St., crossing Hwy. 2, to Fort Normandeau. This replica is built on the site of the original fort, constructed in the spring of 1885 in anticipation of the Reil Rebellion—a Cree uprising led by Louis Reil. As protection against marauding natives, a hotel by the river crossing was heavily fortified. Its walls were reinforced, lookout towers were erected, and the entire building was palisaded. The fort was never attacked and was moved to an outlying farm in 1899. Beside the fort is an interpretive center with displays depicting early settlement at the crossing. The center is open mid-May through June daily 10 a.m.-5 p.m., July-Sept. noon-8 p.m.; tel. (403) 347-7550.

Other Sights

The **Red Deer and District Museum,** 4525 47A Ave., tel. (403) 343-6844, tells the story of the area from prehistoric times to the present, with emphasis on the growth and development of the last 100 years. It's open July-Aug. Mon.-Fri. 10 a.m.-9 p.m. and Sat.-Sun. 1-5 p.m., the rest of the year daily 1-5 p.m. The museum is also the starting point for two historical walking tours—ask here for a map. Adjacent to the museum is **Heritage Square,** a collection of historic structures including the Stevenson-Hall Block, Red Deer's oldest building, and a re-created Norwegian sod farmhouse, typical of those lived in by many early settlers in Alberta. One block north, on Ross St., is **City Hall Park,** where 45,000 flowering plants create the perfect spot for a relaxing stroll.

On the opposite side of the river from downtown (take 55th St. then Taylor Dr.) is **Cronquist House,** tel. (403) 346-0055. This 1911 three-story Victorian farmhouse overlooks Bower Ponds. When it was threatened with demolition, enterprising locals waited until winter and moved it piece by piece across the frozen lake to

THE CANADA GOOSE

Each spring and fall the skies of central Alberta come alive with the honking of the Canada goose, a remarkable bird whose migratory path takes it clear across the North American continent. Each spring family units migrate north to the same nesting site, year after year. These are spread throughout Canada, from remote wetlands of northern Alberta to desolate islands in the Arctic Ocean. Groups of families migrate together in flocks, the size of the flock varying according to the region, subspecies, and season. Preparation for long flights includes hours of preening and wing-flexing. Once in the air they navigate by the sun, moon, and stars, often becoming disoriented in fog or heavy cloud cover. They are intensely aware of air pressure and humidity. In spring Canada geese hitch a ride north on the strong winds produced by low-pressure systems rolling up from the southwest. In fall they take advantage of Arctic fronts that roar south. If weather conditions aren't right, the geese will rest for a while, usually in farmers' fields (taking advantage of freshly sown crops). The "V" formation, for

which the geese are famous, serves a very specific purpose. Each bird positions itself behind and slightly to the side of the bird immediately ahead. In this way every goose in the flock has a clear view, and all but the leader benefit from the slipstream of the birds ahead.

If, during migration, a goose becomes ill or is crippled by a hunter's bullet, family members will remain with the bird, delaying their flight and only leaving the injured bird if it dies or if their own survival is in jeopardy.

BOB RACE

its present site. Open Mon.-Fri. 9 a.m.-4 p.m. and Sunday 1-4 p.m.

Kerry Wood Nature Centre is north of downtown at 6300 45th Ave., tel. (403) 346-2010. The center has various exhibits and videos on the natural history of the river valley and provides access to the adjacent **Gaetz Lakes Sanctuary,** home to 128 species of birds and 25 species of mammals. On the east side of town, at the junction of 30th Ave. and Ross St., is the distinctive **St. Mary's Church,** designed by renowned architect Douglas Cardinal. The church is open to the public weekdays 10 a.m.-4 p.m.

Recreation

The city's park system provides a range of recreational facilities. Paddleboats and canoes can be rented at Bower Ponds; tel. (403) 347-9777. At Heritage Ranch, trail riding, horseback riding lessons, and wagon and sleigh rides are offered; tel. (403) 347-8058. **River Bend Golf Course** (tel. 403-343-8311) couples an 18-hole championship course with a driving range, pro shop, and club rentals; green fees are $25. To get there follow 30th Ave. four km north of the city.

Canyon Ski Area, nine km east of town along Hwy. 11, tel. (403) 346-5589, has 11 runs on a 164-vertical-meter slope, and night skiing on weekday nights. Lift tickets are $22.50 for adults, $16 for children six to 12, and $5 for toddlers five and under. Half-day rates are available.

Sylvan Lake

This lake, 16 km west of Red Deer, has been a popular summer resort since the turn of the century. It has sandy beaches, a large marina, and plenty of recreation facilities. **Wild Rapids Waterslides,** on Lakeshore Dr., tel. (403) 887-3636, offers two 110-meter-long water slides, nine other slides, a heated pool, and windsurfer and paddleboat rentals; admission $15, children under 12 $11. Other facilities at the lake include boat rentals from **Rev's Hover Sports,** tel. (403) 887-2220, or **Sylvan Marina,** tel. (403) 887-2950; three golf courses; and a greyhound racetrack (racing each Saturday), tel. (403) 887-5782.

Festivals and Events

The **Silver Buckle Rodeo,** held the third week of April, kicks off Red Deer's summer festival season and attracts rodeo stars from throughout

North America. For more information call (403) 343-7800. The town celebrates **Canada Day** (1 July) with a parade and the **International Folk Festival. Westerner Days** begin in mid-July, the weekend the Calgary Stampede ends; festivities include a parade, midway, livestock displays, chuck wagon races, an art display, and a casino. Most events are held at the Agriplex, tel. (403) 343-7800. The **Red Deer International Air Show** on the weekend closest to 1 August is one of Canada's most spectacular aerial events. For information call (403) 340-2333.

Accommodations

Red Deer's location between Alberta's two largest cities makes it a popular location for conventions and conferences. As a result, the city has a lot of hotels. On the south side of the city are some inexpensive strip motels: try **Holiday House Motel,** tel. (403) 346-4188, $36 s, $42 d; or **Rest E-Z Inn,** tel. (403) 343-8444, $39 s, $44 d, where a continental breakfast is included in the price. Other clusters of motels are south and north of the city along Gaetz Avenue. Two of the best are: **Friendship Inn,** 4124 Gaetz Ave., tel. (403) 342-6969, $43 s, $52 d; and **Renford Inn,** 2803 Gaetz Ave., tel. (403) 343-2112 or (800) 661-6498, which has nicer rooms than the Friendship, many designated nonsmoking, $46 s, $51 d. The following hotels are generally full of conventioneers during the week; ask about reduced rates on weekends. **North Hill Inn,** 7150 Gaetz Ave., tel. (403) 343-8800, has a restaurant, lounge, and indoor pool; $54-65 s or d. **Holiday Inn Red Deer,** 6500 67th St., tel. (403) 342-6567, has slightly larger rooms and similar facilities as well as an exercise room; $60 s or d. The city's largest hotel, with over 200 rooms, is **Red Deer Lodge,** 4311 49th Ave., tel. (403) 346-8841 or (800) 661-1657, a full-service establishment with rooms beginning at $75 s, $85 d.

Lions Municipal Campground stands on the west side of the river at 4723 Riverside Dr., tel. (403) 342-8183. To get there follow Gaetz Ave. north through town and turn right after crossing the Red Deer River. The campground has showers, full hookups, and a laundry; unserviced sites $13, hookups $16. Open in summer only.

Food and Drink

Downtown, head to **City Roast Coffee,** 4940 Ross St., tel. (403) 347-0893. It's a big-city style coffeehouse offering coffees from around the world and light snacks. It's open Mon.-Sat. 7:30 a.m.-6 p.m. Around the corner a very different type of eatery, the **Jerry Can,** at 5005 50th Ave., tel. (403) 347-9417, attracts a strange collection of locals who come for the inexpensive meals and to catch up on gossip. Fast-food restaurants line Hwy. 2 as it passes by town; Gaetz Ave. has additional fast-food choices, as well as a range of family-style dining places. **Willy's Hamburgers,** on the east side of Hwy. 2 S, tel. (403) 347-5444, has daily breakfast specials and is open from 6:30 a.m. **Snifters Dining Lounge,** in the Red Deer Lodge, opens daily at 5 p.m. for fine dining.

Brandon County Saloon, 4608 50th Ave., tel. (403) 341-6060, plays country music seven nights a week, while **Tom Sawyer's** at 4605 Gaetz Ave., tel. (403) 347-4386, favors rock.

Transportation

Two scheduled bus services link Red Deer to Calgary and Edmonton. **Greyhound** departs from the depot at 4303 Gaetz Ave., tel. (403) 343-8866, throughout the day for both cities; $19.52 one-way to either one. **Red Arrow** offers a more luxurious service with fewer departures but with free onboard beverages and snacks. Their buses depart Red Deer Lodge four times daily for Calgary and Edmonton; $20 one-way. For more information call (403) 343-2356 or (800) 232-1958.

For a cab call **City Cabs,** tel. (403) 346-4444, or **Alberta Gold Taxi,** tel. (403) 341-7777.

Services and Information

The **post office** is at 4909 50th Street. The **Laundry Basket,** at 5511 50th Ave., is open Mon.-Fri. 8 a.m.-10 p.m. and Sat.-Sun. 8 a.m.-9 p.m. **Red Deer Regional Hospital** is at 3942 50th Ave., tel. (403) 343-4422 (for emergencies, call 403-343-4448). For the **RCMP** call (403) 341-2000.

Red Deer Book Exchange features a wide variety of used books and magazines at 6791 50th Ave., tel. (403) 342-4883. For a good place to laze away a rainy afternoon head to **Red Deer Public Library** at 4818 49th St., tel. (403) 346-4576. A **Tourist Information Centre** is located at Heritage Ranch. To get there from Hwy. 2 northbound, use the exit bearing the center's name. If you're southbound on the highway, take the 32nd St. exit and follow the signs onto Cronquist Drive. It's open year-round Mon.-Fri. 9 a.m.-5 p.m., Sat.-Sun. 10 a.m.-5 p.m. and until 6 p.m. in summer; tel. (403) 346-0180 or (800) 215-8946.

EAST OF HIGHWAY 2: THE ASPEN PARKLAND

The aspen parkland lying east of Hwy. 2, between Red Deer and Edmonton, is a transition zone between the prairies to the south and the boreal forest to the north. Here groves of aspen and, to a lesser degree, balsam poplar, grow around sloughs and pothole-like depressions left by the retreating ice sheet at the end of the last ice age. Much of the original vegetation was burned by native peoples in order to attract grazing bison. And in the last 100 years, the land has been given over to agriculture, changing its ecological makeup forever. Although much of the forest has been cleared and cultivated, the region is still home to mammals such as fox, coyote, lynx, white-tailed deer, beaver, and muskrat. The lakes and sloughs attract over 200 species of birds, including literally millions of ducks that can be seen in almost all bodies of water.

From Red Deer, halfway between Calgary and Edmonton, Hwy. 2 continues north, providing access to outdoor recreation opportunities along the way. Sylvan, Gull, and Pigeon Lakes are popular summer resort areas west of the highway. To the east are the historic towns of Lacombe, Ponoka, and Wetaskiwin, home of the large Reynolds-Alberta Museum. Highways 12, 13, and 14 are the main routes east. Along each are many small towns with interesting museums and quiet provincial parks. Camrose, on Hwy. 13, hosts one of North America's largest gatherings of country-music superstars each August.

HIGHWAY 12 EAST

Lacombe
Lacombe, located 30 km north of Red Deer, is a historic town of 7,000 that is the site of provincial and federal agricultural stations. At the turn of the century, the town was a bustling commercial center of 1,000 where an important spur of the Calgary and Edmonton Railway headed east. Today many Edwardian buildings from this era stand in the main business district. One block from the main street (50th Ave.) is the **Mitchener House Museum,** birthplace of a former Canadian governor-general. It's open in summer Wed.-Sun. 10 a.m.-4 p.m.; 5036, tel. (403) 782-3933.

Rochon Sands Provincial Park
This small 99-hectare park is located on a peninsula on the south shore of Buffalo Lake, 14 km north of Erskine. The lake is used by migrating waterfowl each spring and fall and also supports a large population of northern pike. Camping is $11 per night. The west side of the lake is part of the Buffalo Lake Moraine, a hummocky area created by receding ice during the last ice age.

Stettler
Stettler (pop. 5,300) is located 72 km east of Hwy. 2 in the middle of a farming and ranching area well known for its purebred livestock. One of Canada's last remaining passenger steam trains operates from a historic railway station at the end of the main street. **Alberta Prairie Steam Tours** runs these trains each weekend May through October between Stettler and small prairie towns such as Big Valley, Rowley, Donalda, and Consort. Onboard entertainment is provided, and a hearty smorgasbord lunch or dinner is served at the destination. The fare is adult $53, senior $49, child $29.50. For more information call (403) 742-2811. Stettler also offers the **Stettler Town and Country Museum,** comprising a courthouse, railway station, and schoolhouse spread over three hectares along 44th Ave., tel. (403) 742-4534. Admission $3. Open summer only, daily 9 a.m.-5 p.m.

The best of six motels in town is **Grandview Motel,** 5720 44th Ave. (at the south end of town), tel. (403) 742-3391; $38 s, $46 d. **Stettler Lions Campground** is located on the west side of town off Hwy. 12 on 62nd Street. It has showers and hookups for $9-14 per night. Most restaurants are along Hwy. 12; try **White Goose Restaurant,** tel. (403) 742-2544, a family-style eatery with inexpensive seafood dishes. **Kala-**

mata, 4920 50th St., tel. (403) 742-3520, is a pleasant downtown Greek restaurant; entrees are $10-13. A tepee-shaped **Tourist Information Centre** is at the junction of Hwys. 12 and 56.

Big Knife Provincial Park

Legend has it that Big Knife Creek was named after a fight between two long-standing enemies—one Cree, the other Blackfoot—that resulted in the death of both men. Recent history is no less colorful. A local farmer named One-eyed Nelson ran a moonshine operation here. His hooch was in demand the length of the prairies; he even exported the popular brew to Montana. Thirty years after he'd left the area, park rangers found the remains of his still in the side of the creek bank.

The small campground at the park has no services, but the Battle River flows through the park making for good swimming and boating. Sites are $13. To get to the park from Stettler, head east along Hwy. 12 40 km to Halkirk then north on Hwy. 855 another 29 km.

Gooseberry Lake Provincial Park

This small park, 14 km north of Consort, is on the shore of a tree-encircled lake and is made up of rolling grassland and a series of alkaline ponds. Many birds—including the northern phalarope—use the lake as a staging area along their migratory paths. The campground is between the lake and a nine-hole golf course and has powered sites, a kitchen shelter, and firewood. Unserviced sites are $13, powered sites $17. To the north are the **Neutral Hills,** which, according to legend, the Great Spirit raised to prevent Cree and Blackfoot from fighting. Nearby **Consort** is the birthplace of music star k.d. lang.

northern phalarope

WETASKIWIN

This town, halfway between Red Deer and Edmonton on Hwy. 2A, was founded as a siding on the Calgary and Edmonton Railway and has developed into a wheat-farming and cattle-ranching center of 10,800. In the language of the Cree, Wetaskiwin means "Hills of Peace," a reference to nearby hills where a treaty between Cree and Blackfoot was signed in 1867.

Reynolds-Alberta Museum

Usually museums of this caliber are located in major cities. But here in the rolling hills two km west of Wetaskiwin, a world-class facility cataloging the history of all types of machinery rises like a mirage from the rural prairie landscape. Surrounding the main exhibition hall, the complete history of transportation in Alberta is recreated, from horse-drawn carriages to luxurious 1950s automobiles. Most have been fully restored, but some, such as the handmade snowmobile, are in their original condition. At the end of the display, you can peer into a large hall where the restoration takes place. The transportation displays encircle a large area where traditional farm machinery is on show, from the most-basic plow to a massive combine harvester. The museum is open year-round daily 9 a.m.-5 p.m. Admission is adult $6.50, senior $5.50, child $3. For further information call (403) 361-1351 or (800) 661-4726.

Behind the museum lies an airstrip and a large hangar that houses **Canada's Aviation Hall of Fame.** The Hall of Fame recognizes those who have made contributions to the history of aviation and contains a number of vintage aircraft. Admission is included with a ticket to the Reynolds-Alberta Museum. Hours are also the same. Operating out of the Hall of Fame, **Central Aviation,** tel. (403) 352-9689, offers a 10-minute flight in an old biplane for $35; weekends only.

BOB RACE

Reynolds Antique Machinery Museum

After donating one collection of antique machinery to the government for display in the Reynolds-Alberta Museum, Stan Reynolds went right on pursuing his favorite hobby. A legacy of his work is this outdoor museum—hundreds of old cars, tractors, military vehicles, aircraft, steam engines, and assorted farm machinery strewn about in varying states of repair. The collection is halfway between town and the Reynolds-Alberta Museum at 4110 57th St., tel. (403) 352-6201. Open in summer daily 10 a.m.-5 p.m.; admission is $2.

This display at the Reynolds-Alberta Museum shows the amount of work it takes to restore an antique vehicle.

Accommodations and Food

The least expensive and most convenient motel in town is the newly restored **Rose Country Inn,** 4820 50th St., tel. (403) 352-3600. Rooms are basic; $39 s, $49 d including breakfast. Another two options are **Fort Ethier Lodge,** 3802 56th St., tel. (403) 352-9161, $48 s or d; and **Wayside Inn,** 4103 56th St., tel. (403) 352-6681, which has a restaurant, $53 s, $56 d. **Wetaskiwin Community Campground,** located 2.5 km east of town along Hwy. 13, has showers, laundry, and mini-golf; unserviced sites $10, hookups $14.

MacEachern Tea House, 4719 50th Ave., tel. (403) 352-8308, built by one of the district's early pioneers, is a distinctive two-story green and yellow building. It's open for breakfast, lunch, and afternoon tea. Everything served is made on the premises, including delicious cheesecakes ($4 per slice). It's open Mon.-Sat. 9 a.m.-5 p.m. **Blair Originals,** 5116 50th Ave., tel. (403) 352-6035, is a European-style cafe serving coffees and desserts. Other restaurants can be found along all main routes into town.

Information

The **Tourist Information Centre** is in the chamber of commerce at the corner of 50th St. and 50th Ave., tel. (403) 352-4636. It's open in summer daily 9 a.m.-5 p.m., the rest of the year Mon.-Fri. 8 a.m.-4:30 p.m.

CAMROSE

Camrose, 40 km east of Wetaskiwin, is a town of 13,000 that has greatly benefitted from the oil-and-gas boom yet retains its agricultural base. The area was first settled by Scandinavians, primarily Norwegians, late last century. As a tribute to their success in breaking the land and developing the community, a 10-meter Viking longship is on display in the **Bill Fowler Centre,** 5402 48th Ave., overlooking Mirror Lake. A **Tourist Information Centre,** tel. (403) 672-4217, is also in the Fowler Centre. It's open in summer daily 9 a.m.-9 p.m., the rest of the year Mon.-Fri. 8:30 a.m.-4:30 p.m.

Camrose hosts the **Big Valley Jamboree,** one of North America's largest gatherings of country-music superstars, each August.

Sights

One of western Canada's most recognizable breakfast cereals is Sunny Boy, manufactured here in Camrose by **Prairie Sun Grains.** The mill is located at 4601 51st Ave., tel. (403) 672-3675. Tours are given and are not very official; call ahead or just roll up and you'll be taken through each process of the 50-year-old operation, then given some samples to try. **Camrose & District Museum** on 53rd St. at 46th Ave., tel. (403) 672-5456, presents a working model of a steam threshing machine and many other outdoor displays; it's open in summer daily 10 a.m.-6 p.m.

Accommodations

Camrose Motel, 6116 48th Ave., tel. (403) 672-3364, has newly renovated rooms, each with a fridge; $34 s, $36 d. The much larger **Camrose Country Inn,** 3911 48th Ave., tel. (403) 672-7741, has large rooms, a cafe, restaurant, and lounge. Rates are $35 s, $39 d.

Valleyview Campground has powered sites, showers, a kitchen shelter, and firewood. Sites overlook the ski hill and ski jump, and a trail links the campground to downtown Mirror Lake. Unserviced sites are $10, powered $12. To get there follow 53rd St. two km and turn left on 39th Avenue.

Food

The **Feed Mill Dining Lounge,** 4919 47th St., tel. (403) 672-9502, is in a historic building downtown. The relaxed atmosphere and excellent food are popular with locals and visitors alike. The menu is fairly standard and prices are good; entrees range $9.75-15. It's open daily 11 a.m.-10 p.m. Downtown, a two-tiered movie theater has been transformed into a unique restaurant called **The Old Cinema,** 4917 48th St., tel. (403) 672-4809. Downstairs is a lounge and stage where live entertainment is presented on weekends. The dining area is upstairs on the balcony, surrounded in greenery. Expect to pay $20 for a three-course meal.

HIGHWAY 13 EAST

This part of Alberta is dominated by the **Battle River,** which flows from Pigeon Lake, in the foothills west of Wetaskiwin, through heavily developed agricultural land to Wainwright, then

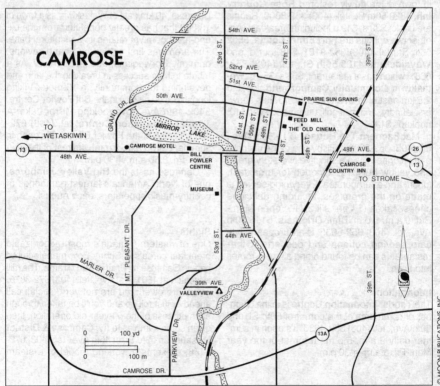

CAMROSE

© MOON PUBLICATIONS, INC.

into Saskatchewan where it drains into the North Saskatchewan River. Buffalo herds once congregated along the banks of the river, drawing Cree from the north and Blackfoot from the south, who fought over the right to hunt them—hence the river's name.

In **Strome,** the **Sodbuster's Museum,** on Main St., tel. (403) 376-3688, is dedicated to the ingenuity of pioneer families who homesteaded the region. The museum also has various Indian artifacts and a six-meter-long chunk of petrified wood. It's open in summer, daily 9 a.m.-4 p.m. **Hardisty** is located in the Battle River Valley, just north of Hwy. 13. Two local companies offer tours of their plants; in each case you should call ahead. **Home Oil Ltd.,** tel. (403) 888-3565, liquefies petroleum gas, while **Hi-grade Feed Lot,** tel. (403) 888-3540, is the largest feedlot in the province, with the capacity to feed 15,000 cattle. **Hardisty Lake** at the west edge of town is stocked with rainbow trout and has a beach, golf course, and campground; $11-14.

From Hardisty the highway continues east through **Amisk** (a nearby Hutterite colony welcomes visitors) to **Czar** and the **Prairie Panorama Museum,** tel. (403) 857-2155, which is known throughout the land for its collection of over 1,000 salt and pepper shakers; open Sunday 2-6 p.m. The town of **Provost** (pop. 1,800) is 20 km from the Alberta/Saskatchewan border. Ten km south of town is **St. Norbert's Church,** a magnificent Gothic structure built in 1926. If viewing the church from the outside doesn't satisfy you, call (403) 753-6687 or 753-6503 to get a key.

HIGHWAY 14 EAST

Miquelon Lake Provincial Park
Originally a bird sanctuary, this 906-hectare park lies 30 km north of Camrose on Hwy. 833. It is part of the 650-square-km Cooking Lake Moraine, a hummocky, forested region dotted with lakes that extends north to Elk Island National Park. At the end of the last ice age, as the sheet of ice that covered much of the continent receded, it occasionally stalled, as it did in this area. Chunks of ice then broke off and melted, depositing glacial till in mounds. Be-

tween the mounds are hollows, known as kettles, that have filled with water. The **Knob and Kettle Trail System** is a series of short interconnecting trails through this remarkable landscape; it starts behind the baseball diamond. Being heavily wooded, the area attracts many birds and animals; most ponds house a resident beaver family, and moose and deer can often be seen feeding at dawn and dusk. The main body of water is fed by underground springs and has no streams running into it. This means that the level of the lake in summer is largely dependent on winter snowfall which, in recent years, has been low. During summer, rangers conduct guided hikes (Thurs.-Sun. at 10:30 a.m.) and present evening shows in the amphitheater (Wed.-Sat.). A visitor center is open in summer Wed.-Sun. 1-5 p.m. The campground has showers, kitchen shelters, and firewood; unserviced sites $13, powered sites $15. For more information on the park, or to reserve a campsite, call (403) 672-7274.

Tofield
Western Canada's only shorebird reserve, **Beaverhill Natural Area,** is located 10 km east of Tofield. Beaverhill Lake, with its unspoiled islands and rich marshes, is a haven for over 250 species of birds. Many species use the lake as a stopover on their migratory path, attracting birders from around Canada during spring and fall. The natural area is relatively undeveloped. A paved road from Tofield turns to gravel four km from town and ends at **Beaverhill Bird Observatory,** operated by the Edmonton Bird Club; biologists and club members are often present—feel free to ask questions. Before the road turns to gravel you'll see a turnoff to the north (left). At the end of this road a short trail leads to **Francis Viewpoint** and a bird blind on the lakeshore. On the eastern shore of the lake is another undeveloped area with access to a beach. Walking north along the beach you can see pelicans, cormorants, and swans on **Pelican Island.** Farther north are the **Dekker Islands,** another nesting area for a variety of bird species.

With all this great birdwatching, you'd expect a bird-related celebration at some point. The last weekend of April is the **Snow Goose Festival,** a celebration of the town's ornithological neighbors.

Beaverhill Motel, tel. (403) 662-3396, has basic rooms for $36 s, $44 d. The closest campground is in Ryley, east of town (free), or at **Ministik Recreation Area,** on the highway 24 km west of town (much nicer, $9). **That Place** on 50th St. is where the locals gather to eat and gossip—not necessarily in that order. At the entrance to the town of Tofield is the **Beaverhill Lake Nature Centre,** an interpretive center with maps of the area and bird checklists. It's open in summer daily 8 a.m.-8 p.m.; tel. (403) 662-3191.

Ryley

If you need an excuse to stop in Ryley, visit **George's Harness & Saddlery,** tel. (403) 663-3611, a working museum that produces saddles, chuck wagon harnesses, and other equine accessories. Most artifacts are made with antique tools and stitching machines. The goings-on in the large workshop are visible from the shop, but if George isn't busy filling orders he'll happily show you around. The store is on the main street; closed Sunday.

Viking

Southeast of Viking in a farmer's field are the **rib stones,** two stones carved with a design resembling bison ribs. The stones held special significance for generations of plains Indians, whose lives revolved around the movement of bison herds. They believed that by conducting certain ceremonial rites and by leaving gifts of beads or tobacco around the stones their luck in hunting would improve. The site is not well marked. Fourteen km east of Viking on Hwy. 14 is a historical sign. A little farther east is a gravel road to the south; follow this road a short way to Hwy. 615, turn east (left), then take the first gravel road to the south (right) and follow it for three km. A provincial historic cairn marks the site.

Wainwright

Best known for a large combined forces base, Wainwright is the last town along Hwy. 14 before Saskatchewan. The military's **Camp Wainwright** is on the site of what once was Buffalo National Park, the site of probably the most unusual chain of events ever to take place in a Canadian national park. Originally created in 1908 to protect 3,000 plains bison, Buffalo National Park was also home to elk, moose, and deer. Experiments within the park cross-bred bison with cattle, trying to create a more resilient farm stock. Meanwhile bison parts were sold for pemmican. All that may seem odd enough to begin with. But then a Hollywood film crew paid officials to stampede a herd of bison and slaughter part of the herd for a movie scene. Shortly afterward the bison were struck by tuberculosis and were secretly shot along with every ungulate in the park. This sad and sorry story ended with the land being handed over to the Department of National Defence. Today it is Canada's second-largest military training facility, able to house 15,000 troops at one time. On its 400 square kilometers are 22 weapons ranges, two airfields, and yes, a small herd of bison, which can be viewed in **Bud Cotton Buffalo Paddock** beside the base's main gate. The base is two km south of town along 1st Street.

Also in Wainwright, the Canadian Wildlife Service operates a **Peregrine Falcon Hatchery,** where individuals of the endangered species are raised and released into the wild. During summer, tours can be arranged through the Tourist Information Centre at the west end of town; the rest of the year contact the facility, tel. (403) 842-3115. **Wainwright Museum** is a restored Canadian National Station at the end of Main St., with displays on the railway and the ill-fated national past. Open daily 9 a.m.-5 p.m.; tel. (403) 842-3115.

Dillberry Lake Provincial Park

This park is on the Alberta/Saskatchewan border, 50 km southeast of Wainwright in the transition zone between aspen parkland and prairie. Of the many lakes within the park, Dillberry is the largest. It's surrounded by sandy beaches and low sand dunes (the biggest dunes are at the southeastern end of the lake), and its clear spring-fed waters are good for swimming. The diverse habitat creates excellent birdwatching opportunities—140 species have been recorded. The large campground is right by the best beach and has showers, kitchen shelters, and firewood; unserviced sites $13, powered sites $15. For more information on the park or to reserve a site call (403) 858-3824.

KAREN McKINLEY

EDMONTON

INTRODUCTION

Edmonton, Alberta's capital, sits in the center of the province, surrounded by the vast natural resources that have made the city unabashedly wealthy. It's a vibrant cultural center and a gateway to the north, but its reputation as a boomtown may be its defining characteristic. Boomtowns are a phenomenon unique to the West—cities that have risen from the surrounding wilderness, oblivious to hardship, pushed forward by dreams of the incredible wealth to be made overnight by pulling riches from the earth. Most boomtowns disappear as quickly as they rise, but not Edmonton. The proud city has seen not one, but three major booms in the past century and has grown to become one of the world's largest northerly cities. Its population has mushroomed 800% in 50 years to 820,000, making it the fifth-largest city in Canada. While Calgary is the administrative and business center of the province's billion-dollar petroleum industry, Edmonton is the technological, service, and supply center.

The **North Saskatchewan River Valley** winding through the city has been largely preserved as a 27-km greenbelt of parks—the largest urban park system in Canada. Rather than the hodgepodge of slums and streets you might expect in a boomtown, the modern city of Edmonton has been extremely well designed and well built, with an eye toward the future. The downtown area sits on a spectacular bluff overlooking the river valley park system. Silhouetted against the deep-blue sky a cluster of modern glass-and-steel high-rises makes a dynamic contrast to the historic granite Alberta Legislature Building and lush valley floor below.

Edmonton is home to the University of Alberta, and it's hosted events such as the 1978 Commonwealth Games, 1983 World University Games, and 1996 World Figure Skating Championships. So it comes as no surprise that Edmonton has some of Canada's best cultural facilities. Each week during summer, a festival of some sort takes place within the city. But the

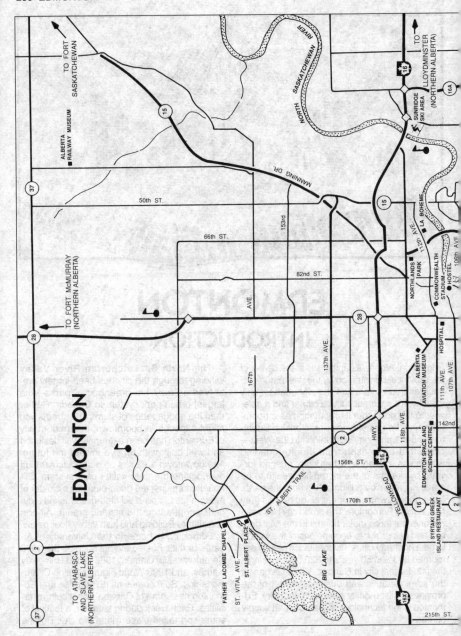

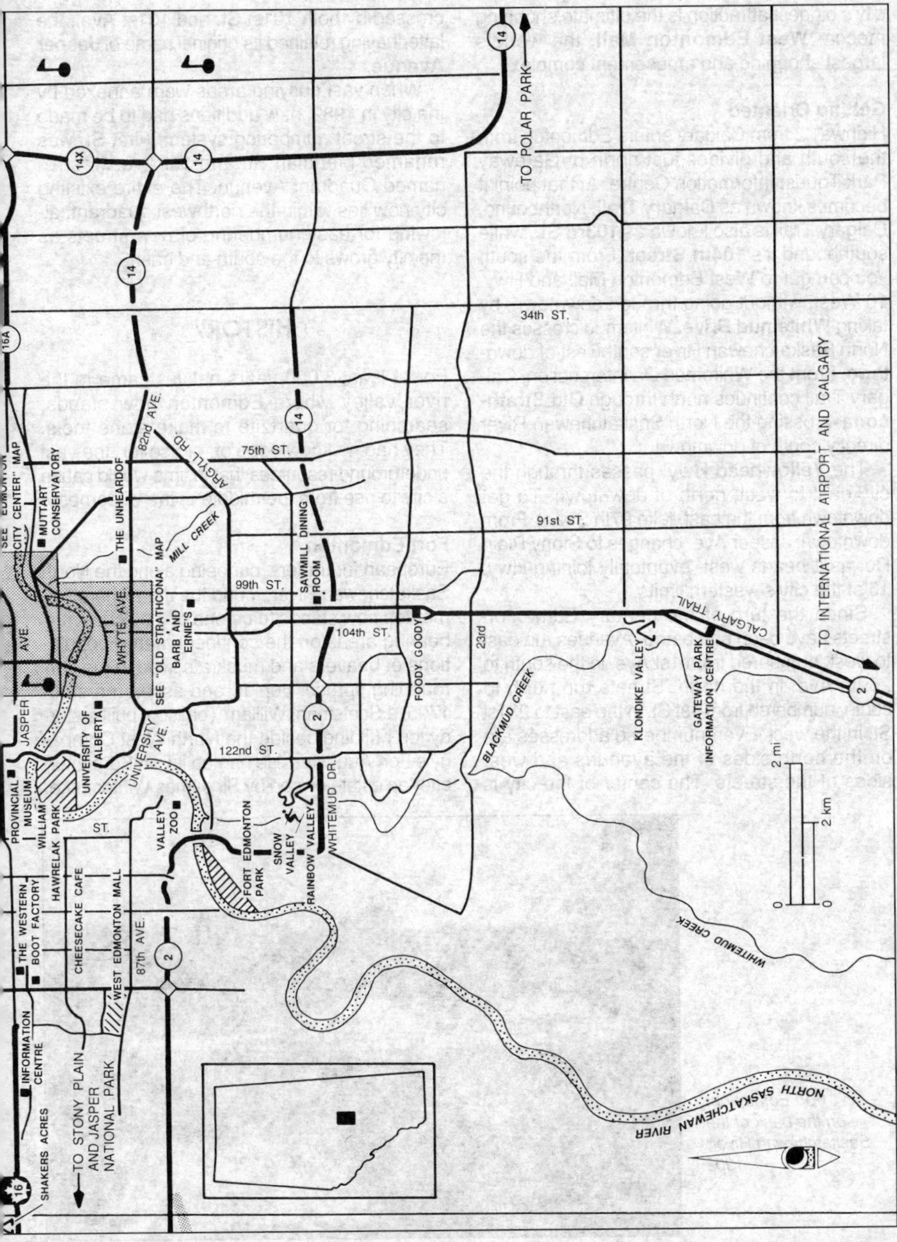

TO POLAR PARK

14

14

14X

14

16A

SEE "EDMONTON CITY CENTER" MAP

MUTTART CONSERVATORY

THE UNHEARDOF

82nd AVE.

ARGYLL RD.

MILL CREEK

75th ST.

34th ST.

91st ST.

SAWMILL DINING ROOM

99th ST.

SEE "OLD STRATHCONA" MAP

BARB AND ERNIE'S

WHYTE AVE.

104th ST.

FOODY GOODY

23rd

CALGARY TRAIL

TO INTERNATIONAL AIRPORT AND CALGARY

2

16A

JASPER AVE.

PROVINCIAL MUSEUM

WILLIAM HAWRELAK PARK

UNIVERSITY OF ALBERTA

UNIVERSITY AVE.

122nd ST.

2

WHITEMUD DR.

BLACKMUD CREEK

KLONDIKE VALLEY

GATEWAY PARK INFORMATION CENTRE

ST.

THE WESTERN BOOT FACTORY

CHEESECAKE CAFE

WEST EDMONTON MALL

87th AVE.

VALLEY ZOO

FORT EDMONTON PARK

SNOW VALLEY

RAINBOW VALLEY

2

WHITEMUD CREEK

2 mi

2 km

0

0

INFORMATION CENTRE

SHAKERS ACRES

16

TO STONY PLAIN AND JASPER NATIONAL PARK

NORTH SASKATCHEWAN RIVER

© MOON PUBLICATIONS, INC.

city's biggest attraction is the ultimate shopping mecca, **West Edmonton Mall,** the world's largest shopping and amusement complex.

Getting Oriented

Highway 2 from Calgary enters Edmonton from the south and divides just north of Gateway Park Tourist Information Centre. At that point it becomes known as **Calgary Trail.** Northbound, Calgary Trail is also known as **103rd St.,** while southbound it's **104th Street.** From the south you can get to West Edmonton Mall and Hwy. 16 West, without going through downtown, by taking **Whitemud Drive.** Whitemud crosses the North Saskatchewan River southwest of downtown. From the Whitemud Dr. intersection, Calgary Trail continues north through **Old Strathcona,** crossing the North Saskatchewan River directly south of downtown.

The **Yellowhead Hwy.** passes through the city east to west, north of downtown. To get downtown from the east, take 97th Street. From downtown, Jasper Ave. changes to Stony Plain Rd. as it heads west, eventually joining Hwy. 16 at the city's western limits.

Since the turn of the century Edmonton streets have been numbered. Avenues run east to west, numbered from 1st Ave. in the south to 259th Ave. in the north. Streets run north to south, numbered from 1st St. in the east to 231st St. in the west. Even-numbered addresses are on the north sides of the avenues and west sides of the streets. The center of the city is crossed by both 101st St. and 101st Ave., the latter having retained its original name of **Jasper Avenue.**

When vast outlying areas were annexed by the city in 1982, new additions had to be made to the street numbering system. First St. was renamed Meridian St. and 1st Ave. was renamed Quadrant Avenue. The entire existing city now lies within the northwest quadrant, allowing for easy numbering of new streets as the city grows to the south and east.

HISTORY

For at least 3,000 years natives came to the river valley where Edmonton now stands, searching for quartzite to make stone tools. They had no knowledge of, or use for, the vast underground resources that in time would cause a city to rise from the middle of the wilderness.

Fort Edmonton

European fur traders, canoeing along the North Saskatchewan River, found the area where Edmonton now stands to be one of the richest fur-bearing areas on the continent. Large populations of beavers and muskrats lived in the surrounding spruce, poplar, and aspen forest. In 1795, a Scotsman, William Tomison, built a sturdy log building beside the North West Company's Fort Augustus. He named it Fort Edmonton after an estate owned by Sir James Winter Lake,

Fort Edmonton, on the bank of the Saskatchewan River, 1902

PROVINCIAL ARCHIVES OF ALBERTA

deputy governor of the Hudson's Bay Company. Both forts stood on the site of the present Legislature Building grounds. It was an ideal location for trading. Cree and Assiniboine could trade beaver, otter, and marten pelts in safety, without encroaching on the territory of fierce plains Indians, such as the Blackfoot. Yet the fort was far enough south to be within range of the Blackfoot—peaceable when outside their own territory—who came north to buy muskrat, buffalo meat, and other natural resources, which they later traded with Europeans.

After 100 years the fur trade ended abruptly. Many of the posts throughout the west were abandoned, but Edmonton continued to be an important stop on the route north. Goods were taken overland from Edmonton to Athabasca Landing, where they were transferred to barges or steamers and taken north on the Athabasca River. Around this time there was an increased demand for grains, and improving technology made agriculture more viable. This attracted settlers who arrived through the 1880s to farm the surrounding land. Edmonton suffered a setback when the Canadian Pacific Railway chose a southerly route through Calgary for the TransContinental Railway. A branch built by the Calgary and Edmonton Railway Company arrived in 1891, but it ended on the south side of the North Saskatchewan River, at Strathcona.

The Klondike Gold Rush

The most common images of the Klondike Gold Rush in the Yukon are of miners climbing the Chilkoot or White Pass trails in a desperate attempt to reach Dawson City. Often for financial reasons, various other routes were promoted as being superior. The merchants of Edmonton led a patriot cry to try the "All-Canadian Route," which would allow prospectors to buy their supplies in a Canadian city rather than Seattle. The proposed route followed the Athabasca Landing Trail north to Athabasca, continued by boat down the Athabasca, Slave, and Mackenzie Rivers to just south of the Mackenzie Delta, and ended with a short overland trip to the goldfields. The route was impractical and very difficult. About 1,600 people were persuaded to attempt the route. Of these, 50 died, many turned back, and only 700 reached the Yukon. None reached the gold-

fields before 1899 when the main rush was over, and few, if any, found gold. It is this slim connection to the gold rush that is now celebrated in the annual **Edmonton's Klondike Days,** much to the displeasure of Yukoners.

Selecting the Capital

The provinces of Alberta and Saskatchewan were both inaugurated on 1 September 1905. As Regina had been the capital of the Northwest Territories, it was only natural that it continued as the capital of Saskatchewan. The decision on Alberta's capital did not come as easily. The Alberta Act made Edmonton the temporary capital but it had plenty of competition. Other contenders were Athabasca Landing, Banff, Calgary, Cochrane, Lacombe, Red Deer, Vegreville, and Wetaskiwin. Each thought it had a rightful claim: Banff because it could be fortified if war ever broke out; Vegreville for the clean air and a climate free of chinook winds. But the strongest claims were from the citizens of Calgary, who believed their city to be the financial and transportation center of the province. Heated debates on the subject took place in the Canadian capital of Ottawa and between rival newspaper editors, but Edmonton has remained the capital to this day. In 1912 Edmonton merged with Strathcona, giving the city a total population of 55,000. For the next 35 years the city grew and declined according to the fortunes of agriculture.

Oil and a Growing City

Fur was Edmonton's first industry and coal was its second. Commercial coal-mining operations began as early as 1880, with mining concentrated in three areas of the city. The last of over 150 operations closed in 1970, and much of the coal seam remains unmined below the downtown area. But Edmonton's future lay not in coal, but oil. Since the discovery of "black gold" in 1947 at nearby Leduc, Edmonton has been one of Canada's fastest-growing cities. The building of pipelines and refineries created many jobs and the city became the center of western Canada's petrochemical industry. As demand continued to rise, hundreds of wildcat wells were drilled around Edmonton. Farmers' fields were filled with derricks, valves, and oil tanks, and by 1956 over 3,000 producing wells were pumping within 100 kilometers of the city.

Edmonton experienced the same postwar boom of most major North American cities, as a major population shift from rural areas to the city began. By 1956 Edmonton's population had grown to 254,800, doubling in size since 1946. A 20-square-km area east of the city was filled with huge oil tanks, refineries, and petrochemical plants. Changes were also taking place within the city as the wealth of the oil boom began to take hold. Restaurants improved and cultural life flourished. The city's businesses were jazzed up, and the expanding business community began moving into the glass-and-steel skyscrapers that form the city skyline today. Although the boom is over, oil is still a major part of the city's economy. Also important are the various service industries; West Edmonton Mall alone employs 15,000 people.

SIGHTS

DOWNTOWN

Looking at Edmonton's dynamic skyline, it's hard to believe that less than 100 years ago the main drag was lined with dingy saloons and rowdy dance halls. Since those heady days, the city has seen many ups and downs—its present look is a legacy of the 1970s oil boom. The well-planned city center, on the northern bank of the North Saskatchewan River, is a conglomeration of skyscrapers that seemingly rose overnight when oil money flooded the city. The downtown core is fairly compact and is within walking distance of many hotels, the bus depot, and the train station. **Jasper Avenue** (101st Ave.) is downtown's main thoroughfare, lined with restaurants and shops. One block north is the large and popular **Eaton Centre** shopping complex. On 102nd St. is 36-story ManuLife Place, Edmonton's tallest building. A few blocks east are the provincial government buildings, including the futuristic **City Hall,** which opened in August 1992.

The **pedway** system is unique and necessary this far north. It's a complex system of enclosed walkways linking office buildings, hotels, plazas, the Civic Centre, and public transportation stops. Using the pedways, you can get virtually anywhere downtown, without ever having to step outside into the elements. At first it all seems a bit complicated, but if you're armed with a map the system soon becomes second nature. Pedways are below, above, or at street level and the excellent signage makes it easy to find your way. The walkways are spotlessly clean, well lit, and relatively safe, although you wouldn't want to loiter around the Central LRT (Light Rail Transit) Station at night.

The streets immediately east of 97th St. are a skid row with sleazy bars and suspicious-looking characters—not the place to linger at night. Throughout all the development, a number of historic buildings managed to survive. Many can be seen along **Heritage Trail,** a route taken by early fur traders that linked the old town to Fort Edmonton. Today the trail begins at the Convention Centre, at the corner of Jasper Ave. and 97th St., and ends at the legislature grounds. The route is easy to follow—the sidewalk is paved with red bricks and lined with period benches, replica lampposts, and old-fashioned street signs. The **High Level Bridge** crosses the North Saskatchewan River at the bottom end of 109th Street. It was built in 1913, linking the new capital to Strathcona. The bridge is 775 meters long and 53 meters above the river. It has been used as a tramway, railway, sidewalk, and roadway. In 1980, the **Great Divide Waterfall** was added to the bridge. When turned on, a curtain of water higher than Niagara Falls cascades down along the entire length of the bridge. It usually operates during special events such as Edmonton's Klondike Days. For operating times call (403) 496-8416.

Edmonton Civic Centre

This complex, in the heart of downtown, occupies six square blocks and is one of the city's showcases. Within its limits are the Centennial Library, Edmonton Art Gallery, Sir Winston Churchill Square, City Hall, the Law Courts Building, Convention Centre, Concert Hall, and the performing arts community's pride and joy, the magnificent Citadel Theatre.

The **Edmonton Art Gallery** houses an extensive collection of modern Canadian paintings as well as historical and contemporary art in all media. Various traveling exhibitions are presented throughout the year. The exhibit *From Sea to Sea: The Development of Canadian Art* catalogs the entire history of the country's art through well-laid-out displays. The gallery is open Mon.-Wed. 10:30 a.m.-5 p.m., Thurs.-Fri. 10:30 a.m.-8 p.m., and Sat.-Sun. 11 a.m.-5 p.m. Admission is $3, free on Thursday after 4 p.m. The gallery is located northeast of Sir Winston Churchill Square on 99th St.; tel. (403) 472-6223.

The new **City Hall,** built on the site of the old, is designed to be the centerpiece of the Civic Centre. The main public areas are located on the main floor. An Edmonton Tourist Information Centre is in the South Plaza. Tours of City Hall leave from this center Monday, Wednesday, and Friday at 10:30 a.m. and 2:30 p.m. Immediately behind this area is the City Room, the building's main focal point. Its ceiling is a glass pyramid that rises eight stories. To the east are various displays cataloging the city's short but colorful history.

On the lower pedway level of the Convention Centre is the **Canadian Country Music Hall Of Honour,** with plaques and memorabilia in recognition of Canadian entertainers who have made contributions to the development of this popular style of music.

Chinatown

An elaborate gateway designed by a master architect from China welcomes visitors to where Edmonton's small Chinatown *used* to be. The gate spans 23 meters across 102nd Ave. (also known as Harbin Rd.) at 97th Street. It is supported by eight steel columns painted in the traditional Chinese color of red. Stretched across the center of the arch's roof is a row of ornamental tiles featuring two dragons, the symbol of power in China. The 11,000 tiles used in the gate were each handcrafted and glazed in China. In the last few years Chinatown has moved up the road a few blocks. The archway now leads into an area of cheap boardinghouses and deserted parking lots, but also forms a colorful break from the pawnshops of 97th Street.

Edmonton Police Museum

This museum is located on the second floor of the Police Service Headquarters at 9620 103A Ave., tel. (403) 421-2274. Displays of uniforms, photographs, and equipment tell the story of the Royal Canadian Mounted Police (originally called the North West Mounted Police) and the now defunct Alberta Provincial Police who existed 1917-32. The museum is open Mon.-Sat. 9 a.m.-3 p.m. Admission is free.

Hotel Macdonald

This hotel overlooking the river valley, at 10065 100th St., has long been regarded as Edmonton's premier luxury accommodation. For many years it was the social center of the city. It was built in 1915 by the Grand Trunk Railway in the same chateau-style used for many of the Canadian Pacific hotels across the country. After closing in 1983, plans to tear it down were aborted. After $28 million was spent on refurbishing, the hotel reopened, as grand and elegant as ever. The main lobby has been totally restored and opens to the Confederation Lounge and The Library, a bar overlooking the river that has the feel of an Edwardian gentlemen's club. Ask at reception for a map of the hotel.

Edmonton Public Schools Archives and Museum

Built in 1904, **McKay Avenue School** is Edmonton's oldest standing brick schoolhouse. It was the venue of the first two sittings of the provincial legislature in 1906. The building contains reconstructions of early classrooms and of the historic legislature assembly. Also on the grounds is Edmonton's first schoolhouse, built in 1881 and looking much as it would have looked to 19th-century students. Admission to both is free. The school is located on Edmonton's Heritage Trail at 10425 99th Ave., tel. (403) 422-1970. It's open Tues.-Fri. 12:30-4 p.m., Sunday 1-4 p.m.

Alberta Legislature Building

Home of the provincial government, this elegant Edwardian building overlooking the North Saskatchewan River Valley is surrounded by 24 hectares of formal gardens and manicured lawns. It officially opened in 1912 and for many years stood beside the original Fort Edmonton. Today it remains as one of western Canada's best examples of architecture from that era. Its 16-story vaulted dome is one of Edmonton's most recognizable landmarks. Many materials

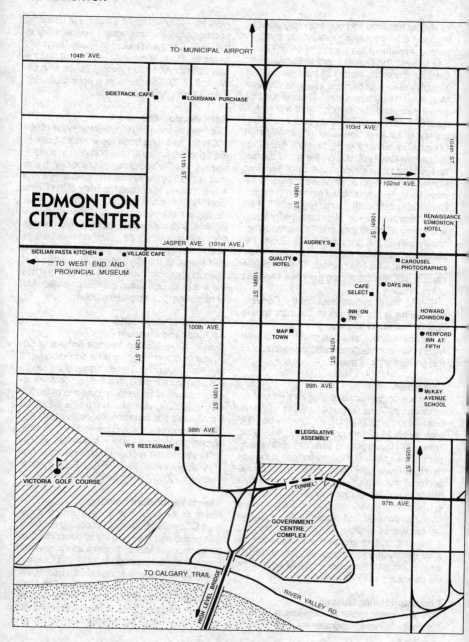

TO MUNICIPAL AIRPORT

104th AVE.

SIDETRACK CAFE ■ ■ LOUISIANA PURCHASE

103rd AVE.

111th ST.

102nd AVE.

108th ST.

104th ST.

106th ST.

EDMONTON CITY CENTER

JASPER AVE. (101st AVE.)

AUDREY'S ■

RENAISSANCE EDMONTON HOTEL

SICILIAN PASTA KITCHEN ■ ■ VILLAGE CAFE

TO WEST END AND PROVINCIAL MUSEUM

QUALITY HOTEL ●

■ CAROUSEL PHOTOGRAPHICS

109th ST.

CAFE SELECT ■

● DAYS INN

INN ON 7th ●

HOWARD JOHNSON ●

100th AVE.

MAP TOWN ■

● RENFORD INN AT FIFTH

112th ST.

110th ST.

107th ST.

99th AVE.

■ McKAY AVENUE SCHOOL

98th AVE.

■ LEGISLATIVE ASSEMBLY

VI'S RESTAURANT ■

105th ST.

VICTORIA GOLF COURSE

TUNNEL

97th AVE.

GOVERNMENT CENTRE COMPLEX

TO CALGARY TRAIL

RIVER VALLEY RD.

HIGH LEVEL BRIDGE

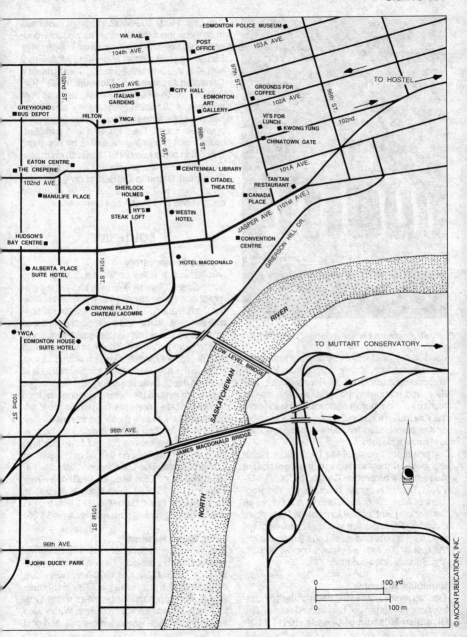

St. Josephat's Ukrainian Catholic Cathedral

used in its construction were imported: sandstone from near Calgary; granite from Vancouver; marble from Quebec, Pennsylvania, and Italy; and mahogany from Belize. The interior features a wide marble staircase that leads from the spacious rotunda in the lobby to the chamber and is surrounded by stained-glass windows and bronze statues.

Immediately north of the Legislature Building, beyond the fountains, is the **Legislative Assembly Interpretive Centre,** tel. (403) 427-7362. This new center recounts the development of Alberta's political history and serves as the starting point for free tours of the Legislature Building. Tour hours in summer are weekdays 8:30 a.m.-5 p.m. and weekends 9 a.m.-5 p.m., the rest of the year weekdays noon-4:30 p.m. and Sunday noon-5 p.m.

Ukrainian Museums

Two museums, just to the north of the city center, honor Albertans of Ukrainian descent. The **Ukrainian Museum of Canada,** 10611 110th Ave., tel. (403) 483-5932, displays costumes from throughout the Ukraine, as well as woodcarvings, tapestries, and a small collection of Easter eggs. It's open May-Aug., Mon.-Fri. 9 a.m.-4 p.m., Sunday 2-5 p.m. The **Ukrainian Canadian Archives and Museum,** 9543 110th Ave., tel. (403) 424-7580, exhibits artifacts from the lives of Ukrainian Pioneers in Canada and has one of the largest archives in the country. It's open year-round, Tues.-Fri. 10 a.m.-5 p.m., Saturday noon-5 p.m. Admission is by donation. Edmonton has a number of Ukrainian churches. One of the most impressive is **St. Josephat's Ukrainian Catholic Cathedral** on 97th St. at 108th Ave., well worth a look for its elaborate decorations and pastel wall paintings.

SOUTHSIDE

Muttart Conservatory

Nestled in the valley on the south side of the North Saskatchewan River are four large pyramid-shaped greenhouses that make up the Muttart Conservatory. Three contain the flora of specific climates. In the arid pyramid are cacti and other hardy plants found in desertlike conditions. The tropical pyramid holds a humid jungle and one of North America's largest orchid collections. In the tropical pyramid jungle colorful and raucous exotic birds live among the palms. The temperate pyramid features plant species from four continents—none of which would grow naturally in Edmonton's harsh environment. Displays in the fourth pyramid change with the season but always feature colorful floral displays such as red, white, and yellow poinsettias at Christmastime. The conservatory is located at 9626 96A St. off 98th Ave.; tel. (403) 496-8755. Take bus no. 45 or 51 south along 100th Street. It's open year-round, Sun.-Wed. 11 a.m.-9 p.m., Thurs.-Sat. 11 a.m.-6 p.m. Admission is $4.25.

John Walter Museum

This historic site located near the Kinsmen Sports Centre consists of three houses—dating from 1875, 1884, and 1900—that were built by John Walter for his family. The first house was a stopping point for travelers using Walter's ferry service to cross the river. Walter also opened a carriage works, lumber mill, and coal mine, and at one time even built a steamship. For a time the area was known as Walterdale, but with the completion of the High Level Bridge, the need for a ferry service ended. Today, all that remains are Walter's houses. Each house holds exhibits corresponding to the period of its construction and depicts the growth of Edmonton and the importance of the North Saskatchewan River. The buildings are only open in summer, Sunday 1-5 p.m., but the grounds are pleasant to walk through at any time. The museum is located at 10627 93rd Avenue. From downtown, take 101st St. south down Bellamy Hill and cross the river at the Walterdale Bridge. On foot allow 30-60 minutes. By bus, jump aboard no. 43 west along 102nd Ave. or south along 103rd Street. For further information call (403) 496-7275.

Rutherford House

This elegant Edwardian mansion was built in 1911 for Alexander C. Rutherford, Alberta's first premier. The Rutherford family lived in this house for 30 years. It was then used as a University of Alberta frat house before being restored to its original condition and furnished with antiques from the Edwardian period. You can wander throughout the two-story house and ask questions of the costumed interpreters. The covered sunporch operates as a tearoom in summer (Wed.-Sun.), serving lunch ($7) and afternoon tea (from $4), using historical recipes from 1915 or earlier. The house is open in summer daily 10 a.m.-6 p.m., the rest of the year

daily noon-5 p.m. It's located on the University of Alberta campus at 11153 Saskatchewan Dr., tel. (403) 427-3995. Admission is $1. The easiest way to get there by public transport is on the LRT from downtown.

Fort Edmonton Park

An authentic reconstruction of the early trading post from which Edmonton grew is only a small part of this exciting park, Canada's largest historic park. From the entrance, a 1919 steam locomotive takes you through the park to the Hudson's Bay Company Fort, which has been built much as the original fort would have looked in 1846—right down to the methods of carpentry used in its construction. Outside the fort is 1885 Street, re-creating downtown Edmonton between 1871 and 1891 when the west was opened up to settlers. The street is lined with wooden-facaded shops such as a bakery, blacksmith, and Egges Stopping House (where there is always a game of horseshoes on). As you continue down the road, you round a corner and are on 1905 Street, in the time period 1892-1914 when the railway had arrived and Edmonton was proclaimed provincial capital. **Reed's Tea Room,** near the far end of the street, serves English teas and scones 12:30-5 p.m. in a traditional atmosphere. By this time you're nearly on 1920 Street, representing the years 1914-1929—a period of social changes when the business community was developing and the city's industrial base was expanding.

Muttart Conservatory

ALBERTA TOURISM

A constant variety of activities is offered; a weekly program is available from the main entrance or by calling (403) 428-2992. An authentic streetcar travels the park picking up passengers along the way. You can take a wagon ride or a pony ride, or rent a canoe.

The park is located in the North Saskatchewan River Valley off the Whitemud Freeway near Fox Drive. By public transport, take the LRT to the University Transit Centre, then bus no. 32 or 132. It's open May-June Mon.-Fri. 10 a.m.-4 p.m. and Sat.-Sun. 10 a.m.-6 p.m., July-Sept. daily 10 a.m.-6 p.m., closed in winter except for special events (such as sleigh rides) over the Christmas break. Admission is adult $6.50, senior $5, child $3.25. For more park information call (403) 496-8787 or the Talking Yellow Pages at (403) 493-9000; enter 4229.

John Janzen Nature Centre
Beside Fort Edmonton Park (use the same parking lot) is John Janzen Nature Centre, which has hands-on exhibits, displays of local flora and fauna—both dead and alive—and a four-km self-guided interpretive trail that leads through the river valley and loops back to the center. In one room various natural environments have been simulated with displays of frogs, fish, snakes, salamanders, and a working beehive made from glass. Throughout the year special events are held, films are shown, and Sunday nature walks are conducted. The center is open year-round Mon.-Fri. 9 a.m.-4 p.m., longer hours and weekends in summer. Admission is free. For more information call (403) 496-2939.

Valley Zoo
Across the river from Fort Edmonton Park is the city zoo, which holds around 350 animals, representing all seven continents. It is designed mainly for kids, with a petting zoo, camel and pony rides, a miniature train, and cut-out storybook characters. The zoo is open daily May-June 10 a.m.-6 p.m., July-Aug. 10 a.m.-9 p.m., the rest of the year noon-4 p.m. It's located at the end of Buena Vista Rd., off 142nd St., tel. (403) 496-6911. To get there by bus take no. 12 from west along 102nd Ave. to Buena Vista Rd. and walk 1.5 km down to the park. On Sunday, buses leave on the hour from the University Transit Centre and go right to the zoo. Admission is $4.75 adults, $2.50 children.

OLD STRATHCONA

When the Calgary and Edmonton Railway Company completed a rail line between the province's two largest cities, it decided to end it south of the North Saskatchewan River and establish a townsite there, rather than build a bridge and end the line in Edmonton. The town was named Strathcona, and it grew to a population of 7,500 before merging with Edmonton in 1912. Because of an early fire-prevention bylaw, buildings were built of brick. Today many still remain, looking much as they did at the turn of the century. Old Strathcona is Edmonton's best-preserved historical district. In addition to the old brick buildings, the area has been refurbished with brick sidewalks and replica lampposts. The commercial core of Old Strathcona is centered along Whyte (82nd) Ave. west of the rail line. Over 75 residential houses built prior to 1926 are scattered to the north and west of Whyte Avenue. The easiest way to get around is on foot, and the best place to start walking from is the **Caboose Tourist Information Centre** on the corner of Whyte Ave. and 103rd Street. Opposite is the **Strathcona Hotel,** one of the few wood-framed buildings surviving from the pre-1900 period. Before Strathcona had permanent churches, congregations worshipped in the hotel, and during prohibition it was used as a ladies' college. One block north, on 83rd Ave., is **Old Strathcona Farmer's Market** with plenty of fresh produce, crafts, and homemade goodies for sale. It's open year-round Saturday 8 a.m.-3 p.m. and in summer Tuesday noon-5 p.m. and Thursday 4-8 p.m. Many of the historic buildings have plaques at street level but the brochures *A Walk through Old Strathcona* and *Historical Walking and Driving Tour: Strathcona,* available at the information center, make a stroll much more interesting. The caboose is open in summer Wed.-Sun. 10 a.m.-6 p.m. For more information on the district write to Old Strathcona Foundation, 4th Floor, 10324 82nd Ave., Edmonton, AB T6E 1Z8, tel. (403) 433-5866. Within walking distance of Whyte Ave. are several small museums detailed below. By

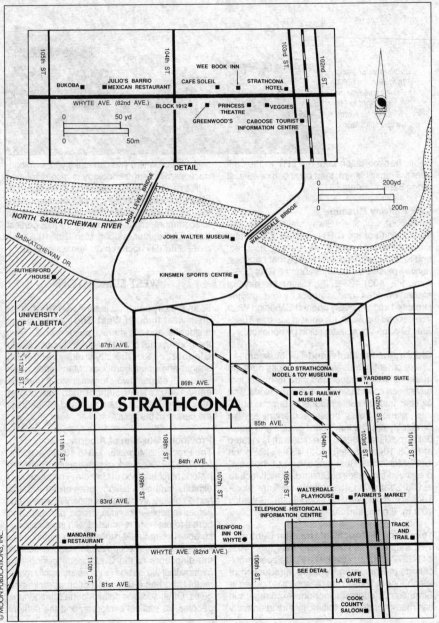

DETAIL

WEE BOOK INN
BUKOBA
JULIO'S BARRIO
MEXICAN RESTAURANT
CAFE SOLEIL
STRATHCONA
HOTEL

105th ST.
104th ST.
103rd ST.
102nd ST.

WHYTE AVE. (82nd AVE.)
BLOCK 1912
PRINCESS THEATRE
VEGGIES
GREENWOOD'S
CABOOSE TOURIST INFORMATION CENTRE

0   50 yd
0   50m

NORTH SASKATCHEWAN RIVER
HIGH LEVEL BRIDGE
WALTERDALE BRIDGE

0   200yd
0   200m

SASKATCHEWAN DR.
RUTHERFORD HOUSE

JOHN WALTER MUSEUM

KINSMEN SPORTS CENTRE

UNIVERSITY OF ALBERTA

87th AVE.

S 112th ST.

86th AVE.

OLD STRATHCONA MODEL & TOY MUSEUM
YARDBIRD SUITE

C & E RAILWAY MUSEUM

OLD STRATHCONA

85th AVE.

102nd ST.
104th ST.
103rd ST.
101st ST.

111th ST.
108th ST.
109th ST.
107th ST.
105th ST.

84th AVE.

83rd AVE.

WALTERDALE PLAYHOUSE
FARMER'S MARKET

TELEPHONE HISTORICAL INFORMATION CENTRE

MANDARIN RESTAURANT

RENFORD INN ON WHYTE

TRACK AND TRAIL

110th ST.
81st AVE.
106th ST.

WHYTE AVE. (82nd AVE.)

SEE DETAIL

CAFE LA GARE

COOK COUNTY SALOON

© MOON PUBLICATIONS, INC.

Looking west along Whyte Ave. in 1903. The large building on the right is the Strathcona Hotel, which still stands.

PROVINCIAL ARCHIVES OF ALBERTA

public transportation take the LRT to the University Transit Centre, then bus no. 8 or 46 east along 82nd Avenue.

C&E Railway Museum

Strathcona's original railway station was located just north of the C.P.R. Station. It was later moved farther along the line, then demolished, and replaced with a partial replica that houses a railway museum. The museum, at 10447 86th Ave., tel. (403) 433-9739, relives the days of steam engines and settlers, when people streamed into the newly opened Canadian West from around the world. It's open in summer Tues.-Sat. 10 a.m.-4 p.m.; admission by donation.

Old Strathcona Model and Toy Museum

Unlike other toy museums, all exhibits here are made entirely of paper and card from kits that have been collected from around the world. The exhibits include scale models of famous buildings, planes, trains, boats, and animals. Also on display are children's card games and paper dolls from last century. The museum is located at 8603 104th St., tel. (403) 433-4512, in the 1907 McKenzie Residence, one of the best-preserved examples of Edwardian architecture in Old Strathcona. It's open in summer Mon.-Tues. 1-5 p.m., Wed.-Fri. noon-8 p.m., Saturday 10 a.m.-6 p.m., and Sunday 1-5 p.m.

Telephone Historical Information Centre

This museum, at 10437 83rd Ave., tel. (403) 441-2077, catalogs the history of telecommunications in Edmonton from the introduction of telephones in 1885 to the present. It is housed in Strathcona's original telephone exchange and has many hands-on exhibits, including an early

switchboard where you can make your own connections. Current technology is also displayed with exhibits of digital switching, fiber-optic cables, and cellular phones. A multimedia presentation in the small **Alex Taylor Theatre** traces telecommunications technology from its earliest days. The center is open Mon.-Fri. 10 a.m.-4 p.m., Saturday noon-4 p.m. Admission is $2.

WEST EDMONTON

From the city center, Jasper Ave. (101st Ave.) goes west through **West End**—where many residential and commercial buildings date from the boom years of 1912-14—and continues to **Glenora,** one of the city's oldest and most sought-after neighborhoods. Many streets are lined with elegant two-story mansions from the early 1900s. The neighborhood fountain in Alexander Circle, at 103rd Ave. and 133rd St., is the center of the area.

Provincial Museum of Alberta

The Provincial Museum, 12845 102nd Ave., tel. (403) 453-9100, overlooks the river valley in the historic neighborhood of Glenora. The museum's exhibits catalog a billion years of natural and human history. In the habitat gallery Alberta's four natural regions—mountain, prairie, parkland, and boreal forest—are re-created with incredible accuracy. The natural-history section explains the forces that have shaped Alberta's land, describes the dinosaurs of the Cretaceous period and mammals of the ice age (such as the woolly mammoth), and has a large collection of rocks and gems. Other sections detail Alberta's indigenous peoples, its earliest explorers, and the settlers who came from around the world to eke out a living in the harsh environment. The museum also has a gift shop and cafeteria. It's open in summer Sun.-Wed. 9 a.m.-9 p.m. and Thurs.-Sat. 9 a.m.-5 p.m., the rest of the year Tues.-Sun. 9 a.m.-5 p.m. Admission is $5.50; half price on Tuesday in winter. To get there, take bus no. 1, 2, or 10 along Jasper Ave; or bus no. 115, 116, or 120 west along 102nd Avenue.

The museum houses the **Provincial Archives,** containing photographs, maps, government records, and other documents pertaining to Alberta's history. The archives are open to the public Tues.-Sat. 9 a.m.-5 p.m.; for more information call (403) 427-1750. Beside the museum is **Government House,** an impressive structure used for conferences.

Edmonton Space and Science Centre

Completed in 1984, this multipurpose complex in Coronation Park at 11211 142nd St., tel. (403) 452-9100 (weekdays) or 451-7722 (recorded information), is one of Edmonton's major attractions and most recognizable landmarks. It houses various science displays including an IMAX Theatre, Star Theatre, observatory, Challenger Centre, and a science shop. The complex is open Tues.-Sun. 10 a.m.-10 p.m. The IMAX theatre, a cafe, and science shop occupy the **Lower Gallery.** In the **Middle Gallery** you'll see changing science and technology exhibits and photos as well as an audiovisual of the deadly tornado that hit Edmonton in the summer of 1987. Displays in the **Upper Gallery** include a look into the future of communications and a chunk of the moon. Also in the upper gallery, the **Challenger Centre** allows you to make a simulated minimission through the universe. Times for missions vary; charge is adult $7, child $4.50.

Science demonstrations take place throughout the day, the Dow Computer Lab showcases modern technology, and laser light shows are presented in the **Margaret Zeidler Star Theatre,** daily 11 a.m.-7 p.m. with a different show each hour. A Day Pass (adult $6.50, child $4.25) includes all shows in this theater and admission to all galleries.

The **IMAX Theatre** presents spectacular video productions—seemingly always of an interesting nature—projected onto a 13- by 19-meter screen; adults $7, children $5 for the theater only; $12 and $8 respectively for admission to one IMAX feature and the other displays. Laser light shows featuring music of the world's most popular bands are presented each evening at 8 p.m., with three later shows on Friday and Saturday nights; $4.95-11 per show.

Beside the complex is an **observatory,** open to the public Friday 8 p.m.-midnight, Sat.-Sun. 1-5 p.m. then 8 p.m.-midnight (weather permitting) for star-, moon-, and planet-gazing; no charge.

By bus, from downtown, take no. 5 or 22 west along Jasper Ave. to the Westmount Transfer Centre and hoof it through Coronation Park or transfer to bus no. 96.

Edmonton Space and Science Centre

West Edmonton Mall

Feel like a trip to the beach to do some sunbaking and surfing? Would you like to play a round of golf? How about a submarine trip through a coral reef? Do you like eating at Parisian cafes? Does watching a National Hockey League team in training seem like a good way to spend the afternoon? Do the kids like dolphin shows? And at the end of the day would you like to sink into a jacuzzi, surrounded by a lush tropical forest? This is all possible under one roof at West Edmonton Mall, the largest shopping and indoor amusement complex in the whole wide world. Calgary may have the greatest *outdoor* show on earth but Edmonton has what can surely be billed as the greatest *indoor* show on earth, a place that attracts 20 million people a year. Much more than an oversized shopping mall, Edmonton's top tourist attraction is a shop-and-play four-season wonderland, where many visitors check into the 355-room luxury Fantasyland Hotel, stay a weekend, and never step a foot outside the mall's 58 entrances.

Shopping is only one part of the mall's universal appeal. Prices are no less than anywhere else in the city, but the experience of having over 800 stores (including over 200 women's-wear stores, 35 men's-wear stores, and 55 shoe shops) under one roof is unique. Aside from the shops, five other major attractions fill the mall. **Galaxyland Amusement Park** is the world's largest indoor amusement park, with 22 rides including "Mindbender"—a fourteen-story, triple-loop roller coaster (world's largest indoor roller coaster)—and "Drop of Doom," where you're strapped into a cage, hauled up thirteen stories, then dropped, free falling back to earth in seconds. Admission is free, but the rides cost money. A Galaxyland Day Pass, allowing unlimited rides, is adult $22.95, child $16.95, senior $9.

In the two-hectare **World Waterpark** you almost feel as though you're at the beach; the temperature is set at a balmy 30° C, and a long sandy beach (with special non-slip sand), tropical palms, change houses, a beach bar, and waves crashing on the shore all emulate the real thing. The computerized wave pool holds 12.3 million liters of water and is programmed by computer to eject "sets" of waves at regular intervals. Behind the beach are 22 water slides that rise to a height of 26 meters. The World Waterpark also has the world's only indoor bungee jump ($59.95 per jump; $89.95 with a t-shirt and video), three whirlpools, and a volleyball court. On the second floor of the mall is a water park viewpoint. Admission to World Waterpark is $22.95 adults, $16.95 children under 10, $7.95 seniors.

At the same end of the mall as World Waterpark is the world's largest indoor lake and a series of attractions, known collectively as **Deep Sea Adventure.** You can gawk at the area along its entire

---

WEST EDMONTON MALL TRIVIA

West Edmonton Mall is:
- the world's largest shopping and amusement complex, encompassing 483,000 square meters (that's equivalent to 48 city blocks)

West Edmonton Mall has:
- over 800 stores
- over 100 eateries
- 58 entrances
- 19 movie theaters
- 235,000 light bulbs
- five postal codes
- the world's largest car park (parking for 20,000 vehicles)
- the world's largest indoor amusement park
- the world's largest water park, covering two hectares and containing 50 million liters of water
- the world's largest indoor lake (122 meters long)
- the world's only indoor bungee jump
- more submarines than the Canadian Navy

West Edmonton Mall:
- cost over a billion dollars to construct
- employs 15,000 people
- uses the same amount of power as a city of 50,000
- attracts 20 million people a year (nearly 55,000 per day)

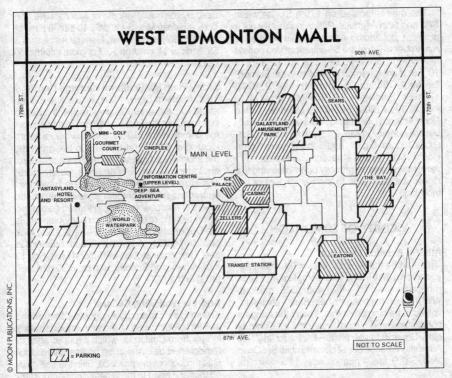

WEST EDMONTON MALL

90th AVE.

178th ST.

170th ST.

MINI - GOLF

GOURMET COURT

CINEPLEX

MAIN LEVEL

GALAXYLAND AMUSEMENT PARK

SEARS

INFORMATION CENTRE (UPPER LEVEL)

ICE PALACE

THE BAY

FANTASYLAND HOTEL AND RESORT

DEEP SEA ADVENTURE

CASINO

WORLD WATERPARK

ZELLERS

EATONS

TRANSIT STATION

87th AVE.

NOT TO SCALE

= PARKING

© MOON PUBLICATIONS, INC.

122-meter length from either the main or second floor of the mall. The most dominant feature of the lagoon is a full-size replica of Christopher Columbus's flagship, *Santa Maria*. It was built in False Creek, Vancouver, and shipped across the Rockies to its new indoor home. You can descend into the depths in one of four self-propelled submarines that cruise the lake, passing 200 different types of marine life, including real coral (adults $12, children under 10 $5). The lake is also the site of regular dolphin shows ($2, or watch from above for free), scuba-diving courses, canoe rentals, and an underwater aquarium with seals, penguins, and sharks ($2.50).

Other major attractions in the mall include **Cinema Ride Edmonton,** a hydraulic capsule that simulates on-screen movements ($6 per ride), a mini-golf version of Pebble Beach Golf Course ($9), and, smack in the middle of the

mall, **The Ice Palace.** This NHL-size skating rink is the second home of the Edmonton Oilers, who often practice here. It's open to the public year-round; $4.50 per session, senior $2.25, child $2.50, skate rentals $2.25.

Other sights include an aviary with various exotic birds, a Chinese pagoda hand-carved by four generations of the same family, replicas of the British crown jewels, bronze statues commissioned especially for the mall, and a couple of aquariums. Two theme streets, **Europa Boulevard** and the glitzy New Orleans–style **Bourbon Street** hold some of the mall's 110 restaurants and eateries, including a Hard Rock Café.

Throughout the mall, information booths can supply maps and answer all commonly asked questions. When your legs tire, **scooter rentals** are available; $5.50 for the first hour, $3.25 for each additional hour.

The mall is located on 170th St., between 87th and 90th Avenues. Parking is usually not a problem, but finding your car again can be, so remember which of the 58 entrances you parked near. From downtown take bus no. 12, 115, or 10. For more information write to West Edmonton Mall Tourism Department, #2472, 8770 170th St., Edmonton, AB T5T 4M2, or call (403) 444-5200 or (800) 661-8890 (toll-free within North America). Shopping hours vary seasonally but are generally Mon.-Fri. 10 a.m.-9 p.m., Saturday 10 a.m.-6 p.m., and Sunday noon-5 p.m. Hours of the various attractions and restaurants vary. Many restaurants stay open later, and the nightclubs stay open to the early hours of the morning.

VICINITY OF EDMONTON

Alberta Aviation Museum
Operated by the Alberta Aviation Museum Association (AAVIAM), this complex at 11410 Kingsway Ave., tel. (403) 453-1078, dates to WW II, when the hangars held British aircraft involved in training programs. Today the hangars contain restored aircraft, including a favorite of early Canadian bush pilots—the Fairchild 71-C. Admission is adult $3, senior and child $2. Open Mon.-Sat. 9 a.m.-4 p.m., Sunday 11 a.m.-4 p.m.

Devonian Botanic Garden
These gardens developed by the University of Alberta are southwest of the city and five km north of the small town of Devon, which was named for the Devonian rock formation in which nearby oil strikes were made during the late 1940s. The 70-hectare site has been developed around the natural contours of the land. The highlight is **Kurimoto Japanese Garden,** one of the world's northernmost authentic Japanese gardens. The various natural elements are complemented by an ornamental gate, arched bridge, and ornamental lanterns. Other features are the large Alpine Garden, with examples of plants from mountainous regions; the Herb Garden, where in August the aroma is almost overpowering; the Peony Collection, at its most colorful in July; a greenhouse filled with plants unique to the Southern Hemisphere; and the Native People's Garden, surrounded by water and showcasing plants used by the native people of Alberta. The gardens are open May-Sept. daily 10 a.m.-6 p.m., till 8 p.m. in July and August. General admission is $5, seniors $4, children $3. For more information call (403) 987-3054.

Stony Plain Multicultural Heritage Centre
The streets of Stony Plain, which was homesteaded before 1900, are lined with historic buildings, but the best place to learn more about the community's history is this living museum located at 5411 51st Street. On the grounds, the town's first high school houses a museum, craft store, library and archives, candy store, and **Homesteader's Kitchen**—a basement restaurant serving pioneer-style home-cooked meals at reasonable prices. Housed next door, in the historic residence of an early pioneer, is the **Oppertshauser Gallery,** Alberta's first rural public art gallery. Admission to both buildings is free. The center is open year-round Mon.-Sat. 10 a.m.-4 p.m. and Sunday 10 a.m.-6:30 p.m.; tel. (403) 963-2777.

Andrew Wolf Wine Cellars
Known to the French as a *négociant,* this winery, at Stony Plain west of the city, imports wines in bulk from California, which it further ages in handcrafted oak vats, then bottles and distributes throughout the province. Skip the self-guided tour and head to the winetasting bar for samples of the remarkably well-rounded wines. Bottles in the gift store are priced from $6—as inexpensive as you'll find anywhere in Canada. It's open in summer Mon.-Fri. 10 a.m.-8 p.m., Saturday 10 a.m.-6 p.m., Sunday noon-5 p.m.; tel. (403) 963-7717.

St. Albert
The city of St. Albert (pop. 42,000)—northwest of Edmonton along the St. Albert Trail—is one of Alberta's oldest settlements but has today become part of Edmonton's sprawl. Albert Lacombe, a pioneering western Canadian priest, built a mansion overlooking the Sturgeon River in 1861, when Fort Edmonton was only a small trading post. A sawmill and gristmill were constructed, and by 1870 St. Albert was the largest agricultural community west of Winnipeg. Father Lacombe's first log chapel, built in 1861, had a brick structure built around it in 1927. It was

used as a museum until the mid-'70s when it was declared a Provincial Historical Site and restored to its original appearance. Father Lacombe Chapel, west of Hwy. 2 on St. Vital Ave., tel. (403) 427-3995, is open in summer daily 10 a.m.-6 p.m. Beside the chapel is a cast-iron statue of Father Lacombe that was made in France and brought to Canada in 1929. Also on Mission Hill is **Grandin House,** an imposing three-story structure built in 1887 as a hospital.

In stark contrast to the historic buildings overlooking the Sturgeon River is City Hall in **St. Albert Place** on St. Anne Street, a contoured brick building designed by Douglas Cardinal. Inside is the **Musée Heritage Museum,** tel. (403) 459-1528, with displays telling the story of St. Albert's history and the people that made it happen. It's open in summer daily 9:30 a.m.-8 p.m., the rest of the year Tues.-Sun. noon-5 p.m.

A **Tourist Information Centre** is located in a log cabin by the river, just off Hwy. 2 at Sturgeon Road. It's open in summer Mon.-Tues. 9 a.m.-6 p.m., Wed.-Fri. 9 a.m.-8 p.m., and Sat.-Sun. 11 a.m.-8 p.m.; weekdays only the rest of the year. From downtown Edmonton, take the St. Albert bus east along 102nd Avenue.

Alberta Railway Museum

Featuring Canada's largest collection of N.A.R. (Northern Alberta Railway) equipment, this museum also has rolling stock from C.N.R. (Canadian National Railway) and C.P.R. (Canadian Pacific Railway). Over 70 locomotive, passenger, and freight cars from 1877-1950 are displayed. Also exhibited are various railway artifacts, equipment, and machinery. Admission is adult $3, senior $2, child $1, and train rides ($1) are offered on long weekends. The museum,

tel. (403) 472-6229, is open in summer, Tues.-Sun. 10 a.m.-6 p.m. To get there, take 97th St. (Hwy. 28) north to Namao, turn east on Hwy. 37 for seven km, then south on 34th St. for two km. It is well signposted.

Fort Saskatchewan Historic Site

In 1875—long after the fur-trading post of Fort Edmonton had been established—the NWMP marched north and established its northern divisional fort on the North Saskatchewan River, 30 km northeast of Fort Edmonton. Fort Saskatchewan Historic Site overlooks the river from along 101st St. in the present-day town of Fort Saskatchewan. It consists of various historic buildings moved to this picturesque site where the original post was situated. Structures include Fort Saskatchewan's first courthouse, a restored log homestead, a blacksmith shop, and a one-room schoolhouse. A cairn marking the site of the NWMP guard room has been built from stones used in the original structure. Admission $2. It's open July-Aug. daily 10 a.m.-6 p.m., the rest of the year daily 11 a.m.-3 p.m. For more information call (403) 998-1750.

Polar Park

Located 22 km east of the city on Hwy. 14, Polar Park, tel. (403) 922-3401, is a 600-hectare park designed to preserve and breed cold-climate animals, many of which are endangered. All animals are outdoors, so the park is open year-round. Hay rides are offered on summer weekends, sleigh rides during winter. Extensive cross-country-ski trails are set during winter. Also within the park are a restaurant (summer only), picnic area, and hiking trails. It's open daily 8 a.m. till dusk. Admission is adult $5, senior $4, child $3.

RECREATION

River Valley Park System

One of the first things you'll notice about Edmonton is its large amount of parkland. The city has more land set aside for parks, per capita, than any other city in the country. Most parks interconnect along the banks of the North Saskatchewan River and in adjoining ravines, encompassing 7,400 hectares and comprising the largest stretch of urban parkland in North America. Within these parks are picnic areas, swimming pools, historic sites, golf courses, and many kilometers of walking and biking trails. The map *·Cycle Edmonton,* available from Tourist Information Centres, details all routes and trail lengths. One of the larger individual parks is **William Hawrelak Park,** which has a man-made lake with boat rentals and fishing. It is west of the university along Groat Road. **River Valley Cycle,** 9124 82nd Ave., tel. (403) 465-3863, rents mountain bikes for $7 per hour, $28 per day, and leads guided tours during summer. **Sport & Ski Rentals,** 6430 104th St., tel. (403) 435-7547, also rents bikes at similar rates.

Swimming

Edmonton's outdoor swimming season lasts around three months beginning at the end of May. Of the five outdoor pools owned by the city, the one in **Queen Elizabeth Park** is in a particularly picturesque location among poplar trees and with a view of the city skyline over the river; access is from 90th Avenue. Another, close to the city center, is in **Mill Creek Park,** north of Whyte Ave. (82nd Ave.) on 95A Street. Admission to all outdoor pools is $3.50. When the weather gets cooler, or to take advantage of more facilities, head to one of the city's many indoor pools, where admission includes the use of saunas, a jacuzzi, weight rooms, and water slides. The most famous of these is **World Waterpark** in the West Edmonton Mall, which has 22 water slides, a wave pool, a nonslip sandy beach, and bungee jump (additional cost); admission is $22.95 adults, $16.95 children under 10, $7.95 seniors. Swimming events of the 1978 Commonwealth Games were held at the **Kinsmen Sports Centre,** 9100 Walterdale Hill, tel.

(403) 496-7300, in Kinsmen Park on the south bank of the North Saskatchewan River. Admission of $4.25 includes use of the pools, fitness center, sauna, and jogging track. Towel rental is $1.10. The cafeteria here has reasonably priced meals. For information on all outdoor and indoor pools call the Swim Line at (403) 428-7946.

Golfing

Edmonton has so many golf courses you could play a different one each day for a month. Three are within a five iron of the city center while others are located along the North Saskatchewan River Valley and throughout outlying suburbs. The municipal **Victoria Golf Course,** tel. (403) 496-4900, is a challenging 18-hole course, over 6,000 meters in length, located just west of the Legislature Building along River Road. Green fees are $20 weekdays, $23 weekends. Slightly longer and situated on a sweeping bend of the river is **Riverside Golf Course** at 8630 Rowland Rd., tel. (403) 496-8700; weekdays $20, weekends $23. **Kinsmen Pitch & Putt** is located behind the Kinsmen Sports Centre, a tree-covered area close to the city; 18 holes $9.50, seniors $7. For tee times call (403) 432-1626.

Ballooning and Skydiving

Recreational and competition ballooning is popular in Edmonton throughout the year. One company offering flights is **Windship Aviation,** 5615 103rd St., tel. (403) 438-0111. Flights depend entirely on weather conditions. Launch sites and landing sites change with the wind direction; most often the grounds of Muttart Conservatory are used for launching. Flight time is 60-90 minutes and the $150 cost includes transportation back to the launch site, a celebration drink on landing, and a framed picture of your flight.

Edmonton Skydive Centre has a shop at 10588 109th St., but they do their jumping from the small airport at Westlock, 85 km north of the city. Experienced skydivers pay $16-21.50 per jump, depending on the altitude; $35-39 with gear rental. A six-hour training program for first-timers includes a jump from 1,200 meters and costs $120. These courses begin each Saturday and Sunday at 9 a.m. For more information contact the center at P.O. Box 358, Morinville, AB T0G 1P0, tel. (403) 444-5867, or drop into their Edmonton shop.

Climbing

The **Vertically Inclined Rock Gym,** 8523 Argyll Rd., tel. (403) 496-9390, is Edmonton's best such facility with a total of 2,000 meters of climbing wall. A day pass costs $12, equipment rental an additional $8. Climbing instruction courses are offered from $30 per person. It's open Monday 4-11 p.m., Tues.-Sat. 11 a.m.-11 p.m., Sunday noon-8 p.m.

WINTERTIME

Downhill Skiing

Edmonton has three ski hills within the city limits and one just outside. All are small and great for beginners but won't hold the interest of other skiers for very long. **Edmonton Ski Club** runs the hill closest to the city at 9613 96th Ave., tel. (403) 465-0852. It's on the south side of the North Saskatchewan River, facing downtown. Lift tickets are $10 midweek, $13 on weekends. It's open from December to early March, Mon.-Thurs. 9 a.m.-9 p.m., Fri.-Sun. 9 a.m.-5:30 p.m. To get there follow signs to the Muttart Conservatory. Farther upstream, where Whitemud Dr. crosses the river, is **Snow Valley,** which has a chairlift, T-bar, and rope tow. Lift tickets are $15, $13 half day. Hours are weekdays 9:30 a.m.-9:30 p.m., weekends 9 a.m.-6 p.m. For information call (403) 434-3991. **Sunridge Ski Area** is downstream of downtown and has four lifts. Tickets are $15 per day, $13 half day. It's open Mon.-Fri. 9:30 a.m.-10 p.m., Sat.-Sun. 9:30 a.m.-5 p.m.; tel. (403) 449-6555. To get there follow the Yellowhead Hwy. to 17th St., then turn south and follow the signs. **Rabbit Hill Ski Area** is south of Edmonton. Take Calgary Trail south to Nisku, then follow the signs west for 13 km. The hill has a chairlift, two T-bars, and four rope tows. Lift tickets are $21 per day, $14 after 6 p.m. It's open Mon.-Fri. 10 a.m.-10 p.m., Sat.-Sun. 9 a.m.-6 p.m.; tel. (403) 955-2440.

Cross-Country Skiing

The River Valley Park System provides ample opportunity for cross-country skiing. Over 75 km of trails are groomed from December to early March. The most popular areas are in William Hawrelak Park, up Mill Creek Ravine, and through Capilano Park. For details of trails pick up the brochure *Cross-country Ski Edmonton* from Tourist Information Centres or call (403) 493-9000 and enter the code 3446. The **Kinsmen Sports Centre** has cross-country ski rentals; $10 for two hours, or $15 per day including boots and poles. **Sport & Ski Rentals,** 6430 104th St., tel. (403) 435-7547, has similar packages for $12 per day and $25 for three days.

SPECTATOR SPORTS

Ice Hockey

Alberta's first major-league hockey team was the Alberta Oilers, who played in both Calgary and Edmonton. The team finally settled in Edmonton permanently for the '73-74 season. During the '80s, when Wayne Gretzky was leading the **Edmonton Oilers,** the National Hockey League's Stanley Cup resided just as permanently in Edmonton, "City of Champions." Since 1988, when Gretzky was sold to the L.A. Kings, the team has floundered. Most talk on the streets these days is about the politics of the team rather than performances on the ice. Home games are played Sept.-April in Edmonton Coliseum adjacent to **Northlands Park,** 7300 116th Avenue. Tickets cost $15-60. For more information call (403) 471-2191 or Ticketmaster at (403) 451-8000.

Baseball

The **Edmonton Trappers** are a farm team for the Florida Marlins. They play in the AAA, Pacific Coast League. Home games are played April-Sept. at **Telus Field.** Tickets are priced from $7; for details call (403) 429-2934 or Ticketmaster at (403) 451-8000.

Football

The **Edmonton Eskimos** have a distinguished record in the Canadian Football League (C.F.L.), having won the Grey Cup 11 times—including five straight (1978-82)—since joining the league in 1910. "Eskimos" was originally an insult, given to the team by a Calgary sportswriter in its early days. But the name stuck. Since 1948 the team has played in, and won, more Grey Cup games than any other team in the league. Two former Albertan premiers, Peter Lougheed and Don Getty, once starred for the team. The "Esks" play June-Nov. at Commonwealth Stadium, 9021 111th Avenue. Tickets are $18-28. For more information call (403) 448-1525 or Ticketmaster at (403) 451-8000.

Horse Racing

Harness racing takes place at Northlands Park from spring to mid-December. Thoroughbred racing takes place throughout summer at the same track. During Edmonton's Klondike Days, a full racing program is presented. General admission is $2, $3.25 for the Clubhouse. The track is located at 7300 116th Ave.; for information call (403) 471-7379 or the Event Hotline at (403) 471-8111.

ARTS AND ENTERTAINMENT

For details on theater events throughout the city, a listing of art galleries, what's on where in the music scene, cinema screenings, and a full listing of festivals and events pick up a free copy of *See Magazine* or *Vue Weekly*. Both are published every Thursday and available all around town.

Art Galleries

Scattered throughout the city are commercial art galleries, many of which exhibit and sell Canadian and native art. A group of galleries close together on Jasper Ave. between 123rd and 124th Streets downtown form what is known as **The Gallery Walk.** Other galleries of note include **Northern Images,** in West Edmonton Mall, tel. (403) 444-1995, with a good collection of native and northern arts and crafts, and **Bearclaw Gallery,** 10403 124th St., tel. (403) 482-1204 (closed Sunday).

Theater

Edmonton's 13 professional theater companies present productions at various locations all year long. For most companies, Sept.-May is the main season.

The **Citadel Theatre,** 9828 101A Ave., tel. (403) 426-4811 or 425-1820, is Canada's largest theater facility, taking up an entire downtown block. From the outside it looks like a gigantic greenhouse; one entire side is glass, enclosing a magnificent indoor garden complete with waterfall. The complex houses five theaters: the Maclab Theatre showcases the work of teens and children; the Rice Theatre features mainly experimental and innovative productions; Zeidler Hall hosts films, lectures, and children's theater; Tucker Amphitheatre presents concerts and recitals, and often puts on small lunchtime stage productions; and Shoctor Theatre is the main stage for the Citadel's long-running subscription program ($18-40 per production). Tickets are available from the Citadel Box Office.

The **Phoenix Theatre** company, 9638 101A Ave., tel. (403) 429-4015, typically stages powerful and thought-provoking productions at the Kaasa Theatre in the University of Alberta's Jubilee Auditorium. Their season runs Sept.-June. For tickets call Ticketmaster, tel. (403) 451-8000. For slightly more adventurous productions and occasional international imports, see what's on at the **Northern Light Theatre,** 11516 103rd St., tel. (403) 471-1586. Tickets are $9-18. Edmonton's oldest theater is **Walterdale Playhouse,** 10322 83rd Ave., tel. (403) 439-2845, located in the heart of Old Strathcona, which presents historical and humorous material throughout the year. Ticket prices begin at $8. **Celebrations,** 102-13103 Fort Rd., tel. (403) 448-9339, is a popular dinner theater; the ticket price of $40 includes dinner. Open Wed.-Sun., reservations necessary, no jeans, and you must be seated by 6 p.m.

Music and Dance

Edmonton Opera, tel. (403) 429-1000, **Edmonton Symphony Orchestra,** tel. (403) 428-1414, and **Alberta Ballet,** tel. (403) 428-6839, all perform at the Jubilee Auditorium in the University of Alberta, 11455 87th Ave., between October and March. For performance dates and ticket information call the above numbers or Ticketmaster, tel. (403) 451-8000.

Cinemas

Famous Players Cinemas are located throughout the city, including 10233 Jasper Ave., tel. (403) 428-1307, and 2950 Calgary Trail S, tel. (403) 436-6977. The historic **Princess Theatre,**

10337 82nd Ave., tel. (403) 433-0979, is an old-time movie house showing revivals, experiments, and foreign films. **Metro Cinema,** 10136 100th St., tel. (403) 425-9212, in Canada Place, shows classics, imports, and brave new films.

Casinos
Casinos in Alberta are strange places. They are all privately owned and lack the glamour of Las Vegas, and all the profits must go to charity. They offer blackjack, roulette, baccarat, Red Dog, and Sic Bo—no slot machines. **Casino A.B.S.** has locations at 10549 102nd St., tel. (403) 497-7657, and on the south side at 7055 Argyll Rd., tel. (403) 466-0199. **Palace Casino,** in West Edmonton Mall, is located by Entrance 45, tel. (403) 444-2112.

Bars and Nightclubs
The **Sidetrack Cafe,** 10333 112th St., tel. (403) 421-1326, is central to downtown, serves excellent food, and presents live entertainment nightly from 9 p.m. Shows change dramatically—one night it might be stand-up comedians, the next a blues band, then jazz—the only thing you can rely on is that it will be busy. Monday is usually comedy night and Sunday variety night. Cover charges vary, $3-8 is normal. Downtown, the **Sherlock Holmes,** 10012 101A Ave., tel. (403) 426-7784, serves a large selection of British and Irish ales and is the place to head on St. Patrick's Day (17 March). The rest of the year, drinkers are encouraged to join in nightly sing-alongs with the pianist. Sherlock Holmes has opened a new location in Old Strathcona at 10341 82nd Ave., tel. (403) 433-9676. **The Rose and Crown,** 10235 101st St., tel. (403) 428-7111, in the Hilton Hotel, is another English-style pub with a great atmosphere and evening sing-alongs.

Cook County Saloon, 8010 103rd St., tel. (403) 432-2665, is consistently voted Canada's No. 1 Country Nightclub by the Canadian Country Music Association. Its mellow honky-tonk ambience draws crowds, and Canadian and international performers occasionally play here. Free two-step lessons are offered on Tuesday and Wednesday nights, while on Wednesday and Thursday nights "Twister" the mechanical bull bucks into action. On Friday and Saturday nights the action really cranks up with live entertainment and a DJ spinning country Top 40 discs. On these two nights, the cover is $6 after 8 p.m. Other country nightclubs are **Denim and Diamonds,** 10812 Kingsway Rd., tel. (403) 479-4266; **Longriders Saloon,** 11733 78th St., tel. (403) 479-8700, which has a jam session on Wednesday, cheap drinks for the ladies on Thursday, and a cover charge of $5 after 9 p.m. on Friday and Saturday; and **Mustang Saloon,** 16648 109th Ave., tel. (403) 444-7474.

Top 40 and dance nightclubs change names, reputations, and locations regularly. But some are reliable fixtures. **Chase Nightclub,** downstairs in the Scotia Centre at 10060 Jasper Ave., tel. (403) 426-0728, plays Top 40 and is one of the busiest clubs in the city. **Club Malibu** attracts the under-25 crowd to its locations at 10310 85th Ave., tel. (403) 432-7300 ($4 cover charge); 10045 109th St., tel. (403) 429-0404 ($3 cover charge); and in West Edmonton Mall ($4 cover charge). **Barry T's Grand Central Station,** 6111 104th St., tel. (403) 438-2582, plays a unique mix of Top 40 and country.

Personally, I'd prefer to hammer nails in my head than listen to alternative music. But if you're into Gothic and punk, head to **Peoples,** 10620 82nd Ave., tel. (403) 433-9411, Thurs.-Saturday. Another popular spot for alternative music is **Rebar,** 10551 82nd Ave., tel. (403) 433-3600. You won't find me at either place.

Jazz and Comedy
The Edmonton Jazz Society is based at the **Yardbird Suite** at 10203 86th Ave., tel. (403) 432-0428. Live jazz fills the air every night of the week 10 p.m.-2 a.m. Tuesday night jam sessions are $2, other nights admission is $5-18. Friday is nonsmoking night. Another jazz venue is **Figgs,** 12520 102nd Ave., tel. (403) 452-5130. Look for live performances each Saturday night.

Blues on Whyte, 10329 82nd Ave., tel. (403) 439-5058, has live entertainment most nights, including a Saturday night jam session; minimal cover charge.

Yuk Yuk's International is located at West Edmonton Mall, tel. (403) 481-9857. Show times vary, but generally there are two shows nightly Thursday through Saturday. Sunday is variety night, and Wednesday is amateur night. Tickets are $7-14.

SHOPPING

Plazas and Malls

Downtown's major shopping centers are **Eaton Centre, Edmonton Centre,** and **ManuLife Place.** Apart from **West Edmonton Mall** at 87th Ave. and 170th St. other malls are located along Stony Plain Rd., Calgary Trail South, and north of the city at 137th Ave. and 66th St. (Londonderry Mall). In the Eaton Centre, 10200 102nd Ave., tel. (403) 426-4613, the **Edmonton Store** specializes in souvenirs of the city.

Camping Gear and Western Wear

Across the railway tracks from Old Strathcona is **Track and Trail,** 10148 82nd Ave., tel. (403) 432-1707, which carries a wide variety of camping and climbing gear. In the same general area is **Totem Outdoor Outfitters,** 7430 99th St., tel. (403) 432-1223, with more of the same as well as kayaks, canoes, and some secondhand gear. **Gear up for the Outdoors,** 17309 107th Ave., tel. (403) 484-3066, is a climbing specialty store with a climbing wall; lessons are $20 per person per hour. Nearby is the large **Campers Village,** 10951 170th St., tel. (403) 484-2700, with camping equipment, fishing tackle, books, boots, and scuba diving equipment. **Budget Sports Rentals,** 10344 63rd Ave., tel. (403) 434-3808, rents backpacks, tents, sleeping bags, and canoes.

The **Western Boot Factory,** 10007 167th St., tel. (403) 489-0594, stocks thousands of styles of cowboy boots. You can't miss it—out front is the world's largest cowboy boot. This store has another location at 3414 Calgary Trail N, tel. (403) 435-3702. High-quality boots are also sold by **Diablo Boots,** at 3440 Calgary Trail N, tel. (403) 435-2592. **J.R. Austin Western Wear** in the lower level of West Edmonton Mall (near the Fantasyland Hotel lobby), tel. (403) 444-1511, always has specials on their extensive range of Western wear.

FESTIVALS AND EVENTS

Spring

Mid-March is the **Alberta Book Festival,** a three-day event with public workshops, readings, book signings, and a small midway. Many of the events are held in the Convention Centre. For details call (403) 426-5892. The rodeo season kicks off at Northlands Park the third weekend of March with Cody Snyder's **World Champion Bull Bustin'.** Call (403) 471-7210 for details. **Northern Alberta International Children's Festival** takes place the last week of May in the Arden Theatre, St. Albert. Acts from around the world include theater, music, dance, storytelling, and puppetry; tel. (403) 459-1692.

Dreamspeakers Festival, on the last weekend of May, celebrates the art, culture, and film-mak-

the world's largest cowboy boot

ing of the First Nation's People—the native Canadians. For more information call (403) 439-3456.

Edmonton's Klondike Days

This 10-day event beginning on the third Thursday of each July celebrates a somewhat infamous chapter in Edmonton's history. In 1898, when the rush to the Yukon goldfields was in full swing, city merchants persuaded around 1,600 miners that the best route north was to Edmonton and north along the Mackenzie River. The route turned out to be an impractical and difficult one. Few made it, many died trying, and when they reached the Klondike the rush was nearly over. Today that rush for gold is relived on the streets of the city. Events include a massive parade through downtown, an 1890s-style he-man contest at Hawrelak Park, the World Championship Sourdough Raft Race down the river, nonstop entertainment on downtown streets, and a bathtub road-race that always gets a laugh. Edmonton's finest restaurants offer samples of their cuisine in a Taste of Edmonton, and each morning, throughout the city, pancake breakfasts are given away. At Northlands Park, 7300 116th St., is the Edmonton's Klondike Days Exposition, open every day, featuring a midway, Klondike Days Casino, a British Pavilion, free concerts, racing pigs, vaudeville shows, thoroughbred racing, and a crafts and country fair. Future dates of the festival are: 17-26 July 1997 and 16-25 July 1998. For more information write to Edmonton's Klondike Days, P.O. Box 1480, Edmonton, AB T5J 2N5, tel. (403) 471-4653.

Other Summer Festivals

During the last week of June the **Jazz City International Festival** is held at various indoor and outdoor venues. Many foreign stars make special appearances. Call (403) 432-7166 for details. **The Works: A Visual Arts Celebration** features art exhibitions on downtown streets, in parks, and in art galleries for two weeks from late June; tel. (403) 426-2122. For 10 days in early July the streets and parks come alive during the **Edmonton International Street Performers Festival,** with nearly 1,000 performances by magicians, comics, jugglers, musicians, and mimes; tel. (403) 425-5162. Fifty outdoor ethnic pavilions are just a small part of the **Edmonton Heritage Festival,** on the last weekend of July. Visitors to the festival have the opportunity to experience international singing and dancing, arts and crafts displays, costumes, and cuisine representing over 60 cultures; tel. (403) 488-3378. During the **Edmonton Folk Music Festival** the first weekend of August, Gallagher Park comes alive with the sound of blues, jazz, country, celtic, traditional, and bluegrass music. Tickets are cheaper if bought in advance; tel. (403) 429-1999.

Quickly becoming one of the city's most popular festivals is the 10-day **Fringe Theatre Event,** which begins on the second Friday in August. It is held in parks, on the streets, in parkades, and in theaters throughout Old Strathcona. With over 1,200 performances, the festival has become North America's largest alternative-theater event, attracting artists from around the world. Tickets are generally inexpensive; for details call (403) 448-9000.

Symphony under the Sky, on the last weekend of August, is the last gasp in Edmonton's busy summer festival schedule. This five-day extravaganza of classical music takes place in William Hawrelak Park. For ticketing details call (403) 428-1108.

Winter

Farmfair brings livestock exhibits to Northlands Park the second week of November. Call (403) 471-7210 for details. The city celebrates the end of the year during the **First Night** festival, an alcohol-free celebration on the streets of downtown Edmonton; tel. (403) 448-9200. That same week, Edmonton Coliseum hosts the **Canadian Finals Rodeo,** tel. (403) 471-7210.

ACCOMMODATIONS

Nearly all of Edmonton's best hotels are located downtown. Other concentrations of motels can be found along Calgary Trail (south from downtown) and scattered along Stony Plain Rd. in the west. The towns of Leduc and Nisku have a number of motels close to Edmonton International Airport. Other options include many bed and breakfasts, a centrally located YHA hostel, and camping (just five minutes from downtown, or in campgrounds west, east, or south of the city).

HOTELS AND MOTELS

Downtown—Moderate

Generally, midpriced downtown hotels lie just a few blocks from the core of the city. One of the best values is the **Quality Hotel,** five blocks west of the Hudson's Bay Centre at 10815 Jasper Ave., tel. (403) 423-1650 or (800) 463-7666. Rooms are $55 s, $60 d, which includes breakfast in the downstairs restaurant. Four other motels stand within a few blocks of the Quality Hotel. Least expensive is **Days Inn,** 10041 106th St., tel. (403) 423-1925 or (800) 267-2191, newly renovated and with rooms from $54 s, $59 d. Otherwise try: **Renford Inn at Fifth,** 10425 100th Ave., tel. (403) 423-5611 or (800) 661-6498, $59 s or d (indoor pool); the recently renovated **Howard Johnson Plaza Hotel,** 10010 104th St., tel. (403) 423-2450 or (800) 446-4656, $69-99 s or d; or **Inn on 7th,** 10001 107th St., tel. (403) 429-2861 or (800) 661-7327, with rooms a bit overpriced at $99-109 s or d.

If you plan to be in the city for a few days and cook your own meals, suite hotels (also called apartment hotels) offer good value. **Alberta Place Suite Hotel,** 10049 103rd St., tel. (403) 420-4000 or (800) 661-3982, is one of the best. The rooms are large and each has a well-equipped kitchen. Continental breakfast and daily papers are complimentary and Jasper Ave. is only half a block away. Rates range $75-99 s or d. **Edmonton House Suite Hotel,** 10205 100th Ave., tel. (403) 424-5555 or (800) 661-

6562, is slightly more expensive, but each room has a balcony with views of the valley or city, and there's an indoor pool; $97-125 s or d.

Downtown—Expensive

Hotel Macdonald, 10065 100th St., tel. (403) 424-5181 or (800) 441-1414, is an Edmonton landmark and has the same historic charm as other Canadian Pacific hotels such as the Palliser in Calgary. The smallish rooms are decorated with a subtle elegance and the hotel has an excellent restaurant, a health club, and a beautiful lounge overlooking the river valley. Rates start at $139 s, $159 d, but deals are offered, including a golf package ($89 per person), a weekend package ($129 d per night), a bed and breakfast package for guests over 55 ($89 s or d), and upgrade packages including suite accommodation with all the trimmings (from $275 d).

Joined to the pedway system and very central, but still affording great river views is **The Westin Hotel,** 10135 100th St., tel. (403) 426-3636 or (800) 228-3000. Rooms are large and reasonably priced at $89-134 s or d. Hotel facilities include a large pool, exercise room, and one of Edmonton's favorite restaurants. Luxuriously appointed **Renaissance Edmonton Hotel,** 10155 105th St., tel. (403) 423-4811 or (800) 268-8998, features an indoor pool, exercise room, laundry service, lounge, restaurant, and complimentary limo service around downtown. Rates are $120 s, $140 d. Part of the Eaton Centre is **Delta Edmonton Centre Suite Hotel,** 10222 102nd St. (access it from 103rd Ave.), tel. (403) 429-3900 or (800) 661-6655, with a private lounge for guests. Rates for a standard room run $125; a two-room suite is $140. The **Edmonton Hilton,** 10235 101st St., tel. (403) 428-7111 or (800) 263-9030, is in the financial district, linked to other buildings by the pedway system. In each elegantly furnished room you'll find marble tabletops, walnut furniture, brass trimmings, and a bay window. Rooms are priced from $135 s or d. The 24-story **Crowne Plaza Chateau Lacombe,** 10111 Bellamy Hill, tel. (403) 428-6611 or (800) 465-4329, sits on Bellamy Hill; its unusual cylindrical design distinguishes it against the skyline. The Crowne Plaza features a fitness center, boutiques, a cocktail lounge, and a revolving restaurant; $160 s or d, but ask for specials when booking.

Calgary Trail

Prices at the 20-odd motels south of downtown along Calgary Trail begin at $32 s, $35 d. Entering Edmonton from the south, at the city limits and just north of Gateway Park, a few are on the west side of the highway. Best value of these is the **Ellerslie Motel,** 1304 Calgary Trail S, tel. (403) 988-6406. Rooms are basic but clean and comfortable, free airport shuttles are offered, some rooms have kitchenettes, and there's a laundry; $32 s, $35 d. Next door, the **Chateau Motel,** 1414 Calgary Trail S, tel. (403) 988-6661, offers similar rates.

Beyond Gateway Park, the first motel you'll encounter on Calgary Trail northbound is **Trailway Motel,** 3815 Calgary Trail N, tel. (403) 435-3863, where the rooms have been recently renovated; $34 s, $38 d. Next door is the **Derrick Motel,** 3925 Calgary Trail N, tel. (403) 434-1402, similarly priced. Continuing north, the **Holiday Inn The Palace,** 4235 Calgary Trail N, tel. (403) 438-1222 or (800) 565-1222, resembles a modern Banff Springs Hotel from the road. This place features large modern rooms and a tropical atrium with restaurant and lounge; from $85 s or d. **Cedar Park Inn,** 5116 Calgary Trail N, tel. (403) 434-7411 or (800) 528-1234, is a Best Western property with a very symmetrical design. Rooms are spacious and reasonably comfortable. Guest facilities include a pool, exercise room, and shuttles to West Edmonton Mall. Rates are $72 s or d (look for discount vouchers on their brochures at Gateway Park Tourist Information Centre). Behind this property is **Southbend Motel,** 5130 Calgary Trail N, tel. (403) 434-1418, where guests have access to the recreation facilities at Cedar Park Inn; $40 s, $44 d.

In the heart of Old Strathcona is **Renford Inn on Whyte,** 10620 82nd Ave., tel. (403) 433-9411 or (800) 661-6498, not particularly good value at $59 s or d but handy to the attractions and restaurants of this historic area of the city.

Fantasyland Hotel

Within West Edmonton Mall is 355-room Fantasyland Hotel, 17700 87th Ave., tel. (403) 444-3000 or (800) 661-6454, famous for theme rooms that attract folks from around the world. No catching a cab back to your hotel after a day shopping here—just ride the elevator to the room of your wildest fantasy. The lavish marble-floored lobby and two life-size lion statues surrounded by glittering lights are only a taste of what's to come upstairs.

Each floor has a theme: the choice is yours—Hollywood, Roman, Polynesian, Victorian, African, Arabian, Igloo, Canadian Rail, or Truck. Each theme is carried out in minute detail. The Polynesian-room fantasy, for example, begins as you walk along a hallway lined with murals depicting a tropical beach, floored with grass matting. You'll walk through a grove of palm trees before reaching your room. In the room, an enormous jacuzzi is nestled in a rocky grotto, and the bed is shaped like a warrior's catamaran, with a sail as the headboard.

All of this escapism comes at a cost, with the theme rooms ranging $195-225 per night. Regular guest rooms—without jacuzzis and mirrors on the ceiling—are $130 per night. Despite the price, the theme rooms are very popular and book up far in advance. Make reservations early.

West of Downtown

The closest accommodation to West Edmonton Mall is **Royal Inn West Edmonton,** 10010 178th St., tel. (403) 484-6000 or (800) 661-4879, featuring modern furnishings in all rooms, a health spa, a couple of restaurants, and a lounge. This place is good value at $57 s, $77 d. Back along Stony Plain Road, the three-story **West Harvest Inn,** also close to the mall at 17803 Stony Plain Rd., tel. (403) 484-8000, has slightly smaller rooms and fewer amenities for $53 s, $63 d. If you're on a budget and want to stay out by the mall consider **Yellowhead Motor Inn,** 15004 Yellowhead Trail, tel. (403) 447-2400, where rooms start at $40 s or d.

You'll find another bunch of motels along 111th Ave. just west of Edmonton Space and Science Centre. The best of these are the **Royal Western Motel,** 15335 111th Ave., tel. (403) 489-4911, $35 s, $45 d, and **Aurora Motel,** 15145 111th Ave., tel. (403) 489-2581, $35 s, $40 d. Farther west is **Mayfield Inn,** 16615 109th Ave., tel. (403) 484-0821 or (800) 661-9804, a large complex with exercise room, squash court, restaurant, and lounge. Rooms here cost $78 s or d.

BED-AND-BREAKFAST INNS

B&Bs start at $35 s, $45 d and are scattered throughout the city. Tourist Information Centres keep current listings, and you can make bookings through **Edmonton Bed & Breakfast,** 13824 110A Ave., Edmonton, AB T5M 2M9, tel. (403) 455-2297.

La Boheme, 6427 112th Ave., tel. (403) 474-5693, is located in the historic Gibbard building, which originally held Edmonton's first luxury apartments. Today, the La Boheme restaurant downstairs is one of the city's best, and a number of upstairs rooms have been refurnished and are run as a B&B. The building is certainly charming, right down to its creaky floors. Each of the simply furnished rooms has a kitchenette. Rates are $45-70 s or d.

HOSTELS

Edmonton International Hostel, 10422 91st St., tel. (403) 429-0140, is located in a suburban cul-de-sac, a few blocks east of downtown. It has 58 beds in male and female dorms. Facilities include a kitchen, laundry, and deck. The hostel rents bikes and issues bus passes. It's only open 8 a.m.-midnight but the curfew isn't strictly enforced. Rates are $13 for members and $18 for nonmembers.

The **YMCA** has an outstanding location, right downtown at 10030 102A Ave.; tel. (403) 421-9622. The rooms are small and sparsely furnished, and are available to men, women, couples, and families. Also here is a cafe and fitness center. Rooms are $27 s, $45 d. The **YWCA,** 10305 100th Ave., tel. (403) 429-8707, is for women only and has an exercise room and cafe. Dorm beds are $12, private rooms $38.

CAMPGROUNDS

The only camping within city limits is at **Rainbow Valley Campground,** 13204 45th Ave., tel. (403) 434-5531. The location is excellent and, as far as city camping goes, the setting pleasant. Facilities include showers, laundry, barbecue, and cooking shelter. In summer all sites are full by midday; phone reservations aren't taken. Grassed tent sites are $13, powered sites $16. To get there, turn south off Whitemud Freeway at 119th St., then take the first right and follow it into the valley. It's open 15 April to 30 September.

West

Shakers Acres, 21530 103rd Ave., tel. (403) 447-3564, on the north side of Stony Plain Rd., is fairly unprotected if the wind blows but has the advantage of being open year-round. Unserviced sites are $14 and full hookups are $21. Farther out, in Spruce Grove, is **Glowing Embers Travel Centre,** 26309 Hwy. 16, tel. (403) 962-8100. All facilities are modern, and although tents are allowed, they may look out of place among the satellite-toting RVs; all sites are $20.

East

Half Moon Lake Resort, 21524 Hwy. 520, tel. (403) 922-3045, is on the shore of a shallow lake, 30 km from Edmonton. It has a large area set aside for tents ($13.50) and RVs and trailers ($16.50-19.50), but the emphasis is mainly on activities such as fishing, swimming, boating, and horseback riding. To get them, head east on 82nd Ave. to Hwy. 21, three km east of Sherwood Park, then south to Hwy. 520, then 10 km east.

South

Klondike Valley Campground, 1660 Calgary Trail SW, tel. (403) 988-5067, is located along Blackmud Creek, to the west of Hwy. 2, at the southern edge of city limits. The sites are large and all facilities modern. Walk-in tent sites are $12.50, hookups $16-19. In the town of Devon, a 20-minute drive southwest of the city, is **Devon Lions River Valley Resort,** tel. (403) 987-4777; sites are $12-18.

FOOD

Eating out in Edmonton had always been identified with the aroma of good ol' Alberta beef wafting from the city's many restaurants. But things are changing. Today, 2,000 restaurants offer a balance of international cuisine and local favorites in all price brackets. From the legendary home-style cooking of Barb and Ernie's to the French sophistication of Claude's, there's something to suit everyone's taste and budget. Restaurants are concentrated in a few main areas. Downtown in the plazas are food courts that fill with office workers, shoppers, and tourists each lunchtime. This part of the city also has some of Edmonton's finest dining establishments. Old Strathcona offers a smorgasbord of choices, with cuisine from all corners of the world. Southbound and northbound along Calgary Trail are family restaurants, buffets, and inexpensive steak houses.

DOWNTOWN

Breakfast
The best city location for breakfast is the **Village Cafe,** 11223 Jasper Ave., tel. (403) 488-0955; the atmosphere is pleasant and the service friendly. The Breakfast Special—eggs, bacon, hash browns, and toast—is just $2.99. It opens Mon.-Fri. at 7 a.m., Sat.-Sun. at 9 a.m. **Howard Johnson Plaza Hotel,** 10010 104th St., tel. (403) 423-2450, serves up a good breakfast buffet each Sunday; $8.95 per person.

Coffeehouses
Zenari's in ManuLife Plaza East, at 10180 101st St., tel. (403) 425-6151, is a trendy lunchtime hangout known for its variety of sandwiches and freshly prepared soups, as well as coffee, ground fresh to order. It's closed on Sunday.

Near the sights around Edmonton Civic Centre, **Grounds for Coffee,** 10247 97th St., tel. (403) 429-1920, occupies a good location. In addition to coffee, patrons enjoy sandwiches, ice cream, and the daily newspapers. More cafes line Jasper Avenue west of downtown,

including **Grabbajabba,** at no. 11203 and **Second Cup,** at no. 11210.

Cheap Eats
Most of the city's downtown high-rises have food courts on their lower levels, where lunch dishes offered by many ethnic outlets begin at around $3. For the widest choice try the food courts in the Eaton Centre, Edmonton Centre, or Canada Place.

Surrounded by the city's highest high-rises is the **Sherlock Holmes,** 10012 101A Ave., tel. (403) 426-7784, a charming English-style pub with a shingled roof, whitewashed walls with black trim, and a white picket fence surrounding it. At lunchtime it is packed with the office crowd from above. Try traditional British dishes such as Mrs. Hudson's Steak and Kidney Pie ($7), ploughmans ($7.50), liver and onions ($7.50), or fish and chips ($7.50), washed down with a pint of English ale or Guinness stout. It's open Mon.-Sat. from 11:30 a.m.

Village Cafe, 11223 Jasper Ave., tel. (403) 488-0955, features inexpensive soups and pastas (most around $5) as well as build-your-own sandwiches at lunchtime. All dinner choices are under $10. Open Mon.-Fri. 7 a.m.-8 p.m., Sat.-Sun. 9 a.m.-2 p.m.

Many of the least-expensive restaurants downtown lie in the vicinity of 97th Street. **Vi's for Lunch,** 10221 97th St., tel. (403) 424-3890, offers lunch dishes ranging $3-6 in a diner-style atmosphere. Beyond the Chinatown archway is **Kwong Tung,** 9630 102nd Ave., tel. (403) 424-1595, the only Chinatown restaurant that's made an effort to reflect Chinese architecture (and even then, it's rather ordinary). Stick to the set menus, from $7.25 per person. Closed Sunday. Also try the Vietnamese **Tan Tan Restaurant,** 9640 Jasper Ave., tel. (403) 422-6862, which features some beautiful, fake wood paneling. East of Kwong Tung and Tan Tan, along 95th St., are a few more Asian restaurants and tavern cafes, but the numerous signs reading "No Knifes" serve as a reminder that you've wandered into a seedy part of town.

Italian

Among the dozens of Italian restaurants in the city, one of the most highly regarded is **Italian Gardens,** 10015 103rd Ave., tel. (403) 424-5454, tucked away down a lane beside the Centennial Building. All the pasta is made daily, in time for the regular lunchtime crush. Pastas on the regular dinner menu are $6.50-11, specialties begin at $9, and the lunch menu is slightly less expensive. Anything the chef puts out as a daily special will always be good—many of the regulars don't even bother looking at the menu, opting always for the special. It's closed on Sunday.

Sicilian Pasta Kitchen, on the western outskirts of downtown at 11239 Jasper Ave., tel. (403) 488-3838, has a bright breezy atmosphere, an open kitchen, and bar. Main dishes at lunch average $8, at dinner $11-18.

The Creperie

As you descend the stairs to this restaurant below the Boardwalk Market, 10220 103rd St., tel. (403) 420-6656, a great smell, wafting from somewhere in the depths of this historic building, hits you in the face. It will take a minute for your eyes to adjust to the softly lit dining area, but once you do, its inviting atmosphere will become apparent. Entree crepes begin at $8, including rice and vegetables. Dessert crepes begin at $5. It's open weekdays for lunch and daily for dinner.

Oysters at Midnight

Cafe Select, 10018 106th St., tel. (403) 423-0419, nestled below a parkade just off Jasper Ave., gives the first impression of being an upscale, trendy eatery, and to a degree it is. The restaurant is elegant, soft music is played, and a bunch of intellectuals sip wine and eat oysters till two in the morning. But the food is well priced ($10-15 for pasta, steak, or fondue dishes) and no one seems to mind if you stick to just coffee and dessert. Try the chocolate torte ($4.50). The cafe is open daily till 2 a.m.

Upscale

Located at the lower pedway level of the Edmonton Convention Centre, **Claude's on the River,** 9797 Jasper Ave., tel. (403) 429-2900, overlooks the North Saskatchewan River. The formal service, warm and comfortable atmosphere, soft music, well-prepared French dishes,

and a long and informative wine list make this restaurant a city favorite. Entrees are $18-26, a five-course table d'hôte is $35. Claude's is open Mon.-Fri. for lunch and Mon.-Sat. for dinner.

One of Canada's most renowned steak houses, **Hy's Steak Loft,** 10013 101A Ave., tel. (403) 424-4444, is probably also one of Canada's most expensive. The elegant setting, centered around a Tiffany-style skylight, is the perfect place for a splurge. The house specialty is New York strip steaks ($22); only the chicken dishes are less expensive. Also offered is a three-course table d'hôte for $35.95. It's closed on Sunday. **The Carvery of Edmonton,** in the Westin Hotel at 10135 100th St., tel. (403) 426-3636, is another popular steak house at the top end of the market. Professional service. **La Ronde,** 10111 Bellamy Hill, tel. (403) 428-6611, atop the Crowne Plaza Chateau Lacombe, is the city's only revolving restaurant.

WEST END

Vi's

This popular eatery is located in a refurbished house overlooking the North Saskatchewan River at 9712 111th St., tel. (403) 482-6402. Small groups of tables are located in various rooms throughout the house; many tables have river views. Upstairs is a lounge with some outside tables. Start with one of the thick homemade soups ($3.95) or a fresh salad (from $3.25). The wide variety of entrees ($8-14) should suit everyone's taste, and you'd better save room for a piece of chocolate-glazed pecan pie ($3). Vi's is open daily 11:30 a.m.-11 p.m.

A Southern Delight

Louisiana Purchase, 10320 111th St., tel. (403) 420-6779, serves Cajun and Creole cuisine without overdoing the blackened bit. All the fish and meat are carefully trimmed, doing away with the fat that is so much a part of Southern cooking. Prices are reasonable; entrees begin at $6.95. Open Mon.-Fri. 11:30 a.m.-midnight and Sat.-Sun. 5 p.m.-midnight.

Sidetrack Cafe

Directly behind Louisiana Purchase is the Sidetrack Cafe, 10333 112th St., tel. (403) 421-1326.

In addition to some of the city's best live entertainment, the cafe has a reputation for excellent food. Big, hearty breakfasts cost $3-7. Soups, salads, burgers, sandwiches, pizza, and world fare are all on the menu. The soup-and-sandwich lunch deal includes a bottomless bowl of soup. Dinners are served 5-10 p.m. and include such delicacies as Buffalo Meatloaf ($7.95). The cafe is open Mon.-Fri. from 7 a.m.and on weekends from 9 a.m.; expect a wait for a table on Saturday and Sunday mornings and most nights.

Saigon Terrace

One of Edmonton's premier Vietnamese restaurants, Saigon Terrace is at 11607 Jasper Ave., tel. (403) 488-8383. The elegant atmosphere and piped classical music distinguish it from other inexpensive Asian restaurants.

OLD STRATHCONA

Coffeehouses

The cavernous **Block 1912,** 10361 82nd Ave., tel. (403) 433-6575, offers a great variety of hot drinks, cakes, and pastries in an inviting atmosphere, which includes several comfortable lounges. Newspapers from around the world are available. **Cafe La Gare,** 10308 81st Ave., is beside Calgary Trail South on one of the busiest sidewalks in Old Strathcona, making it a prime people-watching location. It is bright, airy, gets the morning sun, and is nonsmoking. Another popular spot for coffee is **Bukoba,** 10460 82nd Ave., tel. (403) 433-1848, which has a large antique coffee-bean roaster in the front and a long coffee bar extending way down the back. Try an oatmeal cookie with your coffee.

Casual French Dining

An unobtrusive entrance, opening to a flight of rickety stairs, leads to **Cafe Soleil,** 10360 82nd Ave., tel. (403) 438-4848, one of Old Strathcona's best eateries. The food is excellent, the casual atmosphere appealing. The menu, presented by knowledgeable wait staff, consists of typical French fare at atypical prices. All lunches costs under $9 and dinners are only slightly more expensive. The restaurant is open Tues.-Sunday.

Mexican and Cajun

Julio's Barrio Mexican Restaurant, 10450 Whyte Ave., tel. (403) 431-0774, is decorated with earthy colors and southwestern-style furniture, and has a true south-of-the-border ambience. The menu is appealing but limited. If you just want a light snack, try the warm corn chips with Jack cheese and freshly made Ultimate Salsa for $5.25. Main meals are $9-15. Julio's is open daily till midnight.

For Cajun cuisine (main dishes $6-16) and a variety of fritters, head to **Da-de-o,** 10548 Whyte Ave., tel. (403) 433-0930. This place attracts a wide cross section of Old Strathcona residents, such as students and artists; it can get pretty loud when the jukebox is cranked up.

A Chinese Favorite

West of Old Strathcona, toward the University of Alberta, is **Mandarin Restaurant,** 11044 82nd Ave., tel. (403) 433-8494, consistently voted as having the best Chinese food in the city. You'd never know it by looking at it. It's informal, noisy, family-style dining, and the walls are plastered with sporting memorabilia donated by diners. Most dishes are from northern China, known for traditionally hot food. But enough Cantonese dishes are offered to please all tastes. Expect to pay under $20 per person for a three-course meal. It's open daily 11:30 a.m.-2 p.m. and 4:30-10 p.m.

Vegetarian

The dishes at **Veggies,** 10331 82nd Ave., tel. (403) 432-7560, should intrigue even the most ardent meat eaters. The choice is extreme— Eggplant Enchilada's Oriental Stir Fry, Hummus Ieladel (pureed chickpeas seasoned with garlic and lemon juice) from Arabia, or the more traditional tofu burgers. Dishes begin at $6. Veggies is open Sun.-Thurs. 11 a.m.-9 p.m., Fri.-Sat. 11 a.m.-10 p.m.

The Unheardof

This unusual restaurant has no windows and no regular menu. Despite this, it's harder to get a table here than just about anywhere else in town. The Unheardof, 9602 82nd Ave., tel. (403) 432-0480, is located in a renovated house filled with Victorian antiques. The seven-course table d'hôte costs $42.50 per person. The menu changes weekly, featuring fresh game, homemade chutneys, and relishes during fall, and chicken and beef dishes the rest of the year. Desserts such as Grapefruit Cheesecake with Grand Marnier top it off. The food is absolutely mouthwatering. Hours are Tues.-Sat. 6:30-8:30 p.m. Reservations are essential.

CALGARY TRAIL

Buffet

Everything a buffet lacks in atmosphere it usually makes up for in value. Along the city's main southern artery is the Chinese buffet **Foody Goody,** 3318 Calgary Trail N, tel. (403) 998-8113. A huge restaurant with over 100 choices, Foody Goody features all the usual Chinese fare, fried chicken, pizza, and a wide variety of desserts including a dozen or so flavors of ice cream. Dinner is more expensive but includes salmon, roast beef, and mussels or prawns. The food is never very hot, so only take small portions (easier said than done). Weekdays the lunch buffet is $6, dinner $10, weekend brunch $7, and weekend dinner $11. Drinks are extra, but wine and beer are well priced. It's open daily 11 a.m.-10 p.m., closed 3-4 p.m. to prepare for the evening crush.

Sawmill Dining Room and Pub

The menu at this popular south-of-the-river eatery, 4745 Calgary Trail N, tel. (403) 436-1950, will suit everyone. An array of seafood, beef, chicken, and pasta dishes (from $10) is complemented by one of the city's best small salad and oyster bars (an extra $3.95). Most tables are partitioned from each other, and the restaurant is filled with antiques and greenery. The pub next door has live entertainment Thurs.-Saturday. The Sawmill is open Mon.-Thurs. 11:30 a.m.-2:30 p.m. and 4:30-10 p.m., Fri.-Sat. till midnight, and for Sunday brunch 10:30 a.m.-2 p.m.

OTHER PARTS OF THE CITY

La Boheme

La Boheme, 6427 112th Ave., tel. (403) 474-5693, seems a little out of place, being in the same part of town where Wayne Gretzky made the Edmonton Oilers famous. But here just a

five-minute drive east of the city center is one of Edmonton's best restaurants. The restaurant is an ever-changing gallery of French prints. Fresh flowers are placed on every table, the windows are bordered by lace curtains, and above are Edwardian tin ceilings. The classic French menu features fresh game; appetizers begin at $3.50 (for the thick, healthy soups) or $4.50 (for the salads); entrees are $9-20. The six-course table d'hôte is $30 per person. The restaurant is open daily 11:30 a.m.-10:30 p.m.

Cheesecake Cafe

Anyone with a sweet tooth would be proud to be seen at this restaurant. The long, well-presented menu is fine, and many come for the main meals, but to our way of thinking, the main meals here are the desserts. A cabinet is filled with mouthwatering cheesecakes ($3.95 per slice) and foot-high cakes that come in all imaginable flavors ($4.25 per slice). Like all the good spots in town, expect a wait during the usual busy periods. It's open daily 11 a.m.-11 p.m., till 1 a.m. Fri.-Saturday. The cafe's two locations are 17011 100th Ave., tel. (403) 486-0440, and just off Calgary Trail S at 10390 51st Ave., tel. (403) 437-5011.

Greek

Syrtaki Greek Island Restaurant, 16313 111th Ave., tel. (403) 484-2473, is bright and airy, with four split-level dining areas, whitewashed walls, and a colorful Greek village mural encompassing one wall. A belly dancer dances up the aisles on Friday and Saturday nights. The extensive menu features dishes from northern Greece and Crete with entree prices ranging $8-17.50. Combination platters for two begin at $24. It's open for lunch and dinner Mon.-Saturday.

Barb and Ernie's: A Local Legend

It's hard to believe that here in the cultural capital of Canada, getting a table at this restaurant sandwiched between auto-body shops and backing onto an abandoned rail line nearly always entails a wait. But such is the case at Barb and Ernie's, 9906 72nd Ave., tel. (403) 433-3242, an unpretentious southside restaurant with vinyl seats, silver chrome chairs, and photos of Ernie with his hockey heroes. The home-style cooking is hearty and reasonably priced. Ernie will always make you feel welcome. Breakfast is the busiest time of day; omelettes begin at $4 and weekend breakfast specials are $4.50. The rest of the day hamburgers begin at $2.50,

main meals such as roast duck with red cabbage run around $12. It's open Mon.-Fri. 6 a.m.-8 p.m., Sat.-Sun. 9 a.m.-8 p.m.

TRANSPORTATION

GETTING THERE

Air
Edmonton International Airport is 29 km south of the city center along Calgary Trail (Hwy. 2). The airport is open 24 hours (the observation platform is a good place to catch some z's). On the **arrivals** level is a small information booth; open year-round, daily 7 a.m.-11 p.m. Also at the airport are car rental desks, hotel courtesy phones, a restaurant, and a currency exchange. The **Sky Shuttle**, tel. (403) 465-8515, departs the airport for downtown hotels every 20 minutes. One-way to downtown is $11, roundtrip $18. A cab to downtown runs $30-35, but if trade is slow, haggling the price is worthwhile. Long-term parking is possible at places nearby. For a regular-size car, **Airport Parking** charges $6 per day, $30 per week, and $90 per month; tel. (403) 890-7690.

Airlines operating out of the International Airport include: **Air Canada**, tel. (403) 423-1222 or (800) 332-1080; **Air B.C.**, tel. (403) 423-1222 or (800) 332-1080; **American Airlines**, tel. (800) 433-7300; **Canada 3000**, tel. (403) 429-3420; **Canadian**, tel. (403) 421-1414 or (800) 665-1177; **Canadian North**, tel. (403) 421-1414 or (800) 665-1177; **Canadian Regional**, tel. (403) 421-1414 or (800) 665-1177; **Delta**, tel. (403) 426-5990 or (800) 221-1212; **Lufthansa**, tel. (403) 563-5954 or (800) 665-2282; **NWT Air**, tel. (403) 423-1222 or (800) 661-0789; and **Northwest Airlines**, tel. (800) 225-2525.

Edmonton Municipal Airport, north of downtown, closed in May 1996. All flights now depart and arrive from the International. Though simpler, this means a longer travel time between the airport and downtown.

Rail
The **VIA Rail Station** is located close to the city center, downstairs in the CN Tower at 10004 104th Ave., tel. (800) 561-8630. The ticket office

is generally open 8 a.m.-3:30 p.m., later when trains are due. Trains leave Vancouver (1150 Station St.) and Prince Rupert three times weekly for the grueling 23-and-a-half-hour trip to Edmonton (via Jasper), continuing on the "Canadian" route to the eastern provinces. Sample one-way fares from Edmonton are: to Jasper $81, to Vancouver $192. Before paying full price for your ticket inquire about off-season discounts (up to 40%) and the Canrailpass.

Bus
The **Greyhound Bus Depot** is at 10324 103rd St., tel. (800) 661-8747, within walking distance of the city center, VIA Rail Station, and many hotels. A cab to Edmonton International Hostel from the depot is $5. Within the depot is an A&W Restaurant, a small paper shop, cash machine, and large lockers ($2). The depot is open 5:30 a.m.-midnight. Buses leave daily for all points in Canada including Vancouver (15-17 hours, $112.89 one-way), Calgary (three and a half hours, $33.17), and Jasper (four and a half hours, $47.09). No reservations are taken—just turn up, buy your ticket, and hop aboard. Discounts apply if tickets are bought seven days in advance. For extensive travel, the Canrailpass is a good deal (see "Getting There" under "Transportation" in the On the Road chapter).

Red Arrow buses leave Edmonton four times daily for Red Deer ($20) and Calgary ($33) and once daily for Fort McMurray ($42). Buses leave Edmonton from the Howard Johnson Plaza Hotel at 10010 104th St. and on southbound runs pick up at the Cedar Park Inn on Calgary Trail. For more information call (403) 424-3339 or (800) 232-1958.

GETTING AROUND

Bus
Edmonton Transit System operates an extensive bus system that links the city center to all

parts of the city and many major sights. Not all routes operate on Sunday. For many destinations south of the North Saskatchewan River you'll need to jump aboard the LRT to the University Transfer Point. Bus fare anywhere within the city is $1.60 during peak hours (5-9 a.m. and 3-6 p.m.), $1.35 at other times; exact fare only. Transfers are available on boarding and can be used for additional travel in any direction within 90 minutes. A day pass good for one day's unlimited travel is $4.25. For more information and passes, go to the Customer Services Outlet at Churchill LRT Station on 99th St. (weekdays 8:30 a.m.-4:30 p.m.) or the Tourist Information Centre in City Hall. For route and schedule information and a list of locations where day passes are sold, call (403) 496-1611. Another handy information service for bus timetables is **Bus Link,** which appears at the beginning of the Edmonton White Pages.

Light Rail Transit

The LRT has 10 stops (Canada's smallest subway system) running east-west along Jasper Ave. (101st Ave.), south to the University, and northeast as far as 139th Street. The LRT runs underground through the city center, connecting with many pedways. Travel between Grandin and Churchill is free Mon.-Fri. 9 a.m.-3 p.m. and Saturday 9 a.m.-6 p.m. LRT tickets are the same price as the bus, and tickets, transfers, and day passes are valid for travel on either the LRT or bus system.

Passengers with Disabilities

Edmonton Transit operates Disabled Adult Transportation System (D.A.T.S.), which provides access to various points of the city for physically disabled passengers who are unable to use the regular transit system. The door-to-door service costs the same as Edmonton Transit adult tickets. Priority is given to those heading to work or for medical trips; tel. (403) 496-4567. A Pedway Information Sheet, detailing accessibility, is available from City Hall or by calling (403) 424-4085.

Taxi

Standard flag charge for cabs is $2.25 plus around $1.40 per km, but most companies have flat rates for major destinations within the city. Major companies are: **Checker Cabs,** tel. (403) 484-8888; **Co-op Taxi Line,** tel. (403) 425-8310; **Skyline Cabs,** tel. (403) 468-4646; and **Yellow Cab,** tel. (403) 462-3456.

Car Rental

If you've just arrived in Edmonton, call around and compare rates. Lesser-known agencies are often cheaper, and all rates fluctuate with the season and demand. Many larger agencies have higher rates for unlimited mileage and built-in drop-off charges to nearby centers (otherwise to drop in Jasper is usually $70 extra, and Calgary is $80 extra). All agencies provide free pickup and drop-off at major Edmonton hotels and have outlets at both airports. Rental agencies are: **Avis,** tel. (403) 423-2847 or (800) 879-2847; **Budget,** tel. (403) 448-2000 or (800) 268-8900; **Discount Car Rentals,** tel. (403) 448-3892 or (800) 263-2355; **Dollar,** tel. (403) 413-8929 or (800) 800-4000; **Enterprise,** tel. (403) 424-1105 or (800) 325-8007; **Hertz,** tel. (403) 423-3431 or (800) 263-0600; **Rent-A-Wreck,** tel. (403) 448-1234 or (800) 327-0116; **Thrifty,** tel. (403) 428-8555 or (800) 367-2277; and **Tilden,** tel. (403) 422-6097 or (800) 387-4747.

Tours

If you are short on time, or just want to see Edmonton's major attractions, **Royal Tours** has just the answer. The two-and-a-half-hour Ecological Tour (Provincial Museum, University of Alberta, river valley, downtown, and West Edmonton Mall; $24) and three-and-a-half-hour Historical Tour (Legislature Building, river valley, and Fort Edmonton Park; $26.50) leave between 8:30 and 9:30 a.m. from all major hotels. Tours operate mid-May through October. For more information and details of ticketing call (403) 488-9040. **Nite Tours,** tel. (403) 453-2134, offers theme tours—such as comedy, country, dance, and pub crawls—of the city's nightlife in English double-decker buses; $20 per person.

SERVICES AND INFORMATION

SERVICES

The main **post office** is downtown at 9808 103A Avenue. Main branches of most banks in the downtown area will handle common foreign-currency exchange transactions. **Thomas Cook Foreign Exchange**, tel. (403) 448-3660, is located at 10165 102nd St. in ManuLife Place. **Currencies International**, tel. (403) 484-3868, is located in West Edmonton Mall at Entrance Nine beside the Fantasyland Hotel lobby. Edmonton International Airport has a foreign exchange on the departures level. **Carousel Photographics**, 10525 Jasper Ave., tel. (403) 424-7161, develops print film in an hour and E6 slide film in five hours; it's open Mon.-Fri. 7 a.m.-5:30 p.m. and Saturday 10 a.m.-4 p.m. For onward travel plans, **Travel Cuts**, at 12304 Jasper Ave., tel. (403) 488-8487, has the best deals.

On the south side of the river is **Clean Easy**, 10441 80th Ave., tel. (403) 439-5012, one of Edmonton's largest laundromats. On the west side of the city is **LaPerle Homestyle Laundry**, 9756 182nd St., tel. (403) 483-9200, handy to the hotels in the area and with large washers and dryers for sleeping bags. Toward the city is **Silver Coin Laundry**, at 15220 Stony Plain Rd., tel. (403) 481-9455. **Soap Time Laundromat**, 7626 104th St., tel. (403) 439-3599, is open till 11:30 p.m.

Emergency Services
For medical emergencies call 911 or one of the following hospitals: **Edmonton General Hospital**, 11111 Jasper Ave., tel. (403) 482-8111; **Charles Camsell Provincial General Hospital**, 12804 114th Ave., tel. (403) 453-5311; **Royal Alexandra Hospital**, 10240 Kingsway Ave., tel. (403) 477-4111; **University of Alberta Hospital**, 8440 112th St., tel. (403) 492-8822. For the **RCMP** call (403) 945-5330.

INFORMATION

Downtown Bookstores
Audrey's, 10702 Jasper Ave., tel. (403) 423-3487, has the city's largest collection of travel guides, western Canadiana, and general travel writing on two vast floors. Open Mon.-Fri. 9 a.m.-9 p.m., Saturday 9:30 a.m.-5:30 p.m., Sunday noon-5 p.m. **Map Town**, 10815 100th Ave., tel. (403) 429-2600, stocks the provincial 1:50,000 and 1:250,000 topographical map series along with city maps, world maps, Alberta wall maps, travel guides, atlases, and a huge selection of specialty maps. It's open Mon.-Fri. 9 a.m.-6 p.m., Saturday 10 a.m.-2 p.m.

Old Strathcona Bookstores
Old Strathcona is an excellent place for browsing through secondhand bookstores. **Wee Book Inn**, 10310 82nd Ave., tel. (403) 432-7230, is the largest and stocks more recent titles and a large collection of magazines. **Alhambra Books**, 10309 82nd Ave., tel. (403) 439-4195, specializes in Canadiana and has an extensive collection of Albertan material, including pamphlets and newspapers. **Athabasca Books**, 8228 105th St., tel. (403) 431-1776, stocks mostly history and literature books. **Bjarne's Books** has older books, including a large selection of hard-to-find western Canadiana and Arctic region material. **Edmonton Bookstore**, 8530 109th St., tel. (403) 433-1781, also has a large stock of out-of-print books from the region.

Old Strathcona's lone new-book store is **Greenwood's**, 10355 82nd Ave., tel. (403) 439-2005, which stocks a lot of everything.

Libraries
The Edmonton Public Library System has 13 libraries spread throughout the city. Largest is **Centennial Library** located at 7 Sir Winston

Churchill Square, tel. (403) 496-7000. It's open Mon.-Fri. 9 a.m.-9 p.m., Saturday 9 a.m.-6 p.m., and Sunday 1-5 p.m. This large two-story facility, connected to the downtown core by pedways, is a great place to spend a rainy afternoon. It carries newspapers, magazines, and phone books from all corners of the globe, as well as rows and rows of western Canadiana. Throughout the week, author readings take place on the main level. Other locations are: **Jasper Place Library,** 9010 156th St.; **Millwoods Library,** 2331 66th St.; **Strathcona Library,** 8331 104th St. (closed Wednesday); and **Highlands Library,** 6710 118th Avenue.

Information Centers
Edmonton Tourism has information centers at four locations in the city. The largest is in Gateway Park, south of town on Calgary Trail (Hwy. 2). Within this complex you'll find interpretive displays on the oil industry as well as direct-dial phones for Edmonton accommodations; open in summer daily 8 a.m.-9 p.m., the rest of the year Mon.-Fri. 8:30 a.m.-4:30 p.m. and Sat.-Sun. 9 a.m.-5 p.m.

The most central tourism office, in City Hall at 1 Sir Winston Churchill Square, doesn't offer much; open in summer daily 8:30 a.m.-4:30 p.m., weekdays only the rest of the year. On the arrivals level of Edmonton International Airport is a small booth open year-round daily 7 a.m.-11 p.m. A seasonal center operates at 19001 Stony Plain Road. It's open summer only

daily 9 a.m.-5 p.m. For more information on the city write to Edmonton Tourism, 9797 Jasper Ave., no. 104, Edmonton, AB T5J 1N9, tel. (403) 496-8400 or (800) 463-4667.

Alberta Tourism runs an information center at 10155 102nd St. that has general information on the province, including maps and guides to camping and accommodations. It's open in summer Mon.-Fri. 8:15 a.m.-4:30 p.m.; tel. (403) 427-4321 or (800) 661-8888.

The **Caboose Tourist Information Centre** on the corner of Whyte Ave. and 103rd St., run by the Old Strathcona Foundation, is open in summer Wed.-Sun. 10 a.m.-6 p.m. For more information on the district write to Old Strathcona Foundation, 4th Floor, 10324 82nd Ave., Edmonton, AB T6E 1Z8, tel. (403) 433-5866.

An excellent source of information on Alberta's provincial parks, forest reserves, and other protected areas is the **Environmental Protection Information Centre,** north of the Legislature Building at 9920 108th St., tel. (403) 422-2079.

On the Internet
For the latest news about Edmonton's recreation and entertainment, along with a full listing of sights, accommodations, restaurants, and transportation, access **U.Wanna.What** at http://www.UWannaWhat.com. The site is updated regularly—many listings daily—and has details of all the events during the city's busy summer festival season.

Edmontosaurus

KAREN MCKINLEY

NORTHERN ALBERTA

The northern half of Alberta, from Hwy. 16 north to the 60th parallel, is a sparsely populated land of unspoiled wilderness, home to deer, moose, coyotes, foxes, lynx, black bears, and the elusive Swan Hills grizzly bear. For the most part it is heavily forested, part of the boreal forest ecoregion that sweeps around the Northern Hemisphere broken only by the Atlantic and Pacific Oceans. Much of the world's boreal forest has been devastated by logging. But here in northern Alberta, a good portion of the land is muskeg—low-lying bogs and marshes that make logging difficult and expensive. Only a few species of trees are adapted to the long, cold winters and short summer growing seasons characteristic to these northern latitudes. Conifers such as white spruce, black spruce, jack pine, fir, and larch are the most common.

This vast expanse of land is relatively flat, the only exceptions being the Swan Hills—which rise to 1,200 meters—and, farther north, the Birch and Caribou Mountains. The Athabasca and Peace River Systems are the region's largest waterways. Carrying water from hundreds of tributaries, they merge in the far north-eastern corner of the province and flow north into the Arctic Ocean. A third major water-course, the North Saskatchewan River, flows east from the Continental Divide, crossing northern Alberta on its way to Hudson Bay. It was along these rivers that Alberta's earliest explorers arrived, opening up the Canadian west to the trappers, missionaries, and settlers who followed.

Northeast of Edmonton is the Lakeland region, where many early fur-trading posts were established. From there, Hwy. 63 heads north through boreal forest to Fort McMurray, an isolated city of 35,000, 437 km north of its closest sizable neighbor, Edmonton. Oil is Fort McMurray's raison d'être—oil sands, to be precise. The Athabasca Oil Sands are the world's largest such deposit. To extract just 33 billion barrels will take 500 years at current extraction rates.

North-central Alberta extends from Edmonton's outer suburbs north to the towns of Athabasca and Slave Lake, jumping-off points into the vast boreal forest. This area is a paradise for birdwatchers; it's at the confluence of three major flyways.

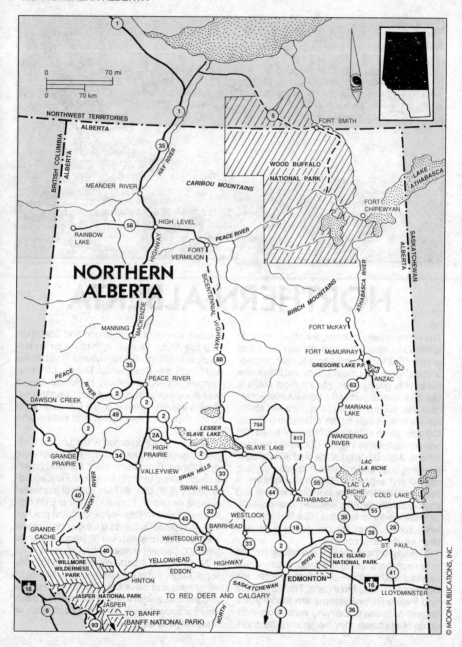

NORTHERN ALBERTA

© MOON PUBLICATIONS, INC.

West of Edmonton the Yellowhead Hwy. climbs into the Rockies, passing through Hinton, a town surrounded by natural wonders. From Hinton, travelers can continue on Hwy. 16 into Jasper National Park, or take Hwy. 40 northwest to Willmore Wilderness Park, a park usually ignored by tourists in favor of the neighboring national parks to the south. Continuing north on Hwy. 4 you come to Grande Prairie, one of northern Alberta's largest cities and a regional agriculture and service center. The Peace River Valley, north of Grande Prairie, leads travelers into the Northwest Territories via the Mackenzie Hwy. (Hwy. 35), which parallels the Peace and Hay Rivers.

With few regular "sights," northern Alberta receives fewer tourists than the rest of the province. Those who do venture north find solitude in a vast, untapped wilderness with abundant wildlife and plenty of recreation—lakes and rivers to fish, historic sites to explore, rivers to float, and gravel roads to drive just for the sake of it.

LAKELAND

Highway 16, east from Edmonton, follows the southern flanks of a region containing hundreds of lakes formed at the end of the last ice age by a retreating sheet of ice nearly one km thick. From its headwaters beneath the Columbia Icefield on the Continental Divide, the **North Saskatchewan River** flows east through Edmonton and the Lakeland region before eventually draining into Hudson Bay.

History buffs appreciate the legacies of early white settlers that dot the landscape here—restored fur-trading posts, missions, and the Ukrainian Village near Vegreville. Other visitors are attracted by the region's vast areas of unspoiled wilderness, including seven provincial parks. Anglers will feel right at home among the area's countless lakes, and wildlife watchers are drawn to Elk Island National Park, which rivals Tanzania's Serengeti Plains for the population densities of its animal inhabitants.

The region's major population centers are Lloydminster (250 km east of Edmonton), Canada's only town in two provinces; St. Paul, which has the world's only UFO landing pad; and the tri-towns of Grand Centre, Medley, and Cold Lake, at the edge of the boreal forest, surrounded by vast reserves of untapped oil.

ELK ISLAND NATIONAL PARK

Heading east from Edmonton on Hwy. 16, you'll soon come to Elk Island National Park. This small, fenced 194-square-km park preserves a remnant of the transitional grassland ecoregion—the aspen parkland—that once covered the entire northern flank of the prairie. It's also one of the best spots in Alberta for wildlife-watching; with around 3,000 large mammals, the park has one of the highest concentrations of big game in the world.

The park was originally set aside in 1906 to protect a herd of elk; it's Canada's only national park formed to protect a native species. The elk here have never been crossbred and are probably the most genetically pure in the world. In addition to the elk, resident mammals include moose, two species of bison, white-tailed and mule deer, coyotes, beavers, muskrats, mink, and porcupines. The many lakes and wetland areas in the park serve as nesting sites for waterfowl, and around 230 species of birds have been observed here.

A mosaic of mixed-wood forest—predominantly aspen and balsam poplar—covers the low, rolling Beaver Hills here, slowly taking over the grassland. One slow-moving stream winds its way through the park, and many shallow lakes dot the landscape.

Park entry for one day is $4 per person to a maximum of $8 per vehicle, an annual permit for Elk Island is $28 per person to a maximum of $50, and a Great Western Pass, valid for all Alberta and British Columbia national parks, is $35 per person to a maximum of $70.

Bison in the Park
Two different species of bison inhabit the park, and to prevent interbreeding they are separated. All bison on the north side of Hwy. 16 are **plains bison,** while those on the south side are **wood bison.**

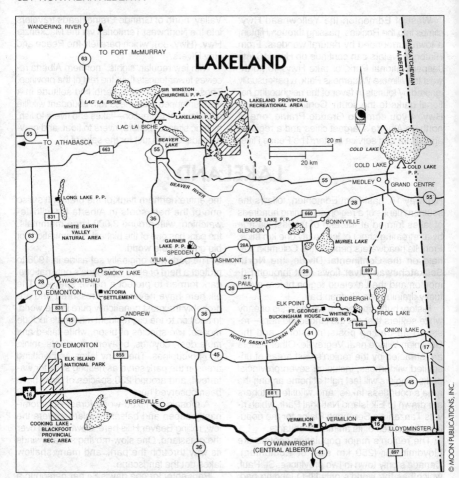

LAKELAND

Before the late 1700s, 60 million plains bison lived on the North American plains. In less than a century humanity brought these shaggy beasts to the brink of extinction. By 1880, incredibly, only a few hundred plains bison remained. A small herd, owned by ranchers in Montana, was brought north in 1907. They were held at what was then Elk Island Reserve until Buffalo National Park (since closed) at Wainwright was fenced. When it came time to move the animals from Elk Island, some couldn't be found—today's herd descended from those well-hidden progenitors. A small part of the herd is kept in a large enclosure just north of the Park Information Centre while others are free to roam through the north section of the park.

The wood bison, largest native land mammal in North America, was for many years thought to be extinct—a victim of hunting, severe winters, and interbreeding with its close relative, the plains bison. In 1957 a herd of 200 was discovered in the remote northwestern corner of Wood Buffalo National Park. Some were captured and transported to the Mackenzie Bison

Sanctuary in the Northwest Territories and to Elk Island National Park. The herd at Elk Island has ensured the survival of the species, and today it is the purest herd in the world. It is used as breeding stock for several captive herds throughout North America. To view the herd, look south from Hwy. 16 or hike the Wood Bison Trail.

Hiking

Twelve trails, ranging in length from 3.5 to 18.5 km, cover all areas of the park and provide excellent opportunities to view wildlife. A park information sheet details each one. Make sure to carry water with you—surface water in the park is not suitable for drinking. The **Shoreline Trail** (three km one-way) follows the shore of Astotin Lake from the golf course parking lot. The **Lakeview Trail** (3.3 km roundtrip) begins from the northern end of the recreation area and also provides good views of the lake. Hike this trail in the evening for a chance to see beavers. The only trail on the south side of Hwy. 16 is the **Wood Bison Trail** (18.5 km roundtrip), which has an interpretive display at the trailhead. In winter the trails provide excellent cross-country skiing and snowshoeing.

Other Recreation and Events

Canoes, rowboats, sailboards, and small sailboats can be rented at Astotin Lake. **Elk Island Golf Course,** an interesting nine-hole layout, is located beside Astotin Lake. Green fees are $22 for 18 holes; call (403) 998-3161 for reservations.

In summer an array of interpretive talks and walks are held at various locations; ask for details at the Park Information Centre or Astotin Interpretive Centre. Early August brings the **Great Buffalo-Chip Flip,** where contestants throw the organic frisbees and win prizes for accuracy and distance.

Practicalities

Sandy Beach Campground is the only overnight facility within the park. It has firepits, picnic tables, flush toilets, and showers; $13 per night. This facility is open in summer only; the rest of the year primitive camping (no water, chemical toilets) is available at the boat-launch area. A concession selling fast food and basic

ELK ISLAND NATIONAL PARK

camping supplies operates May-Oct. at Astotin Lake, and the golf course has a restaurant; tel. (403) 998-3161.

The **Park Information Centre,** tel. (403) 992-5790, is located less than a km north of Hwy. 16 on the Elk Island Parkway; it's open in summer Mon.-Sat. 10 a.m.-6 p.m., Sunday 8 a.m.-8 p.m. The **Astotin Interpretive Centre,** tel. (403) 992-6392, farther along the parkway, has interpretive programs; open daily in summer, weekends only the rest of the year. Another source of information is the park radio station (1540 AM). For further information on the park write: Superintendent, Elk Island National Park, R.R. No. 1, Site 4, Fort Saskatchewan, AB T8L 2N7.

EAST ALONG THE YELLOWHEAD HIGHWAY

Blackfoot Recreation Area

South of Elk Island National Park is the 97-square-km Cooking Lake–Blackfoot Recreation, Wildlife, and Grazing Area. It is an integrated resource management unit, meaning that it can be used for many purposes, including grazing, mineral exploration, hunting, and recreation. It is part of the massive Cooking Lake Moraine, formed during the last ice age as the retreating sheet of ice stalled for a time, leaving mounds and hollows which have since filled with water. Large natural areas of wetland and forest provide

the world's largest pysanka

habitat for abundant wildlife including moose, elk, white-tailed deer, coyotes, beavers, and over 200 species of birds. Much of the well-posted trail system is for hikers only, but some parts are open to horses and mountain bikes. **Blackfoot Staging Area,** off Hwy. 16, is the trailhead for a good selection of short hiking trails, but to really get into the heart of the area head south along the southwestern border of Elk Island National Park to three other staging areas.

Ukrainian Cultural Heritage Village

This site, 50 km east of Edmonton, is a realistic replica of a Ukrainian settlement, common in the rural areas of east-central Alberta at the turn of the century. It was in this region that the first, and largest, Ukrainian settlement in Canada was located. Driven from their homeland in Eastern Europe, Ukrainians fled to the Canadian prairies where for many years they dressed and worked in the ways of the Old World. These traditions are kept alive at the heritage village. It's open in summer daily 10 a.m.-6 p.m. Admission is $7. For more information call (403) 662-3640.

Vegreville

Although first settled by French farmers from Kansas, this town of 5,200 is best known for its Ukrainian heritage. Today Vegreville's biggest attraction is the world's largest *pysanka,* a giant, traditionally decorated Ukrainian Easter egg located at the east end of town. It measures eight meters long, weighs 2,270 kilograms, and can turn in the wind like a giant weathervane.

Vegreville celebrates its multicultural past on the Canada Day (1 July) weekend with the **Ukrainian Folk Festival.**

Vermilion

The reddish-colored iron deposits in a nearby river gave this town of 4,200 at the junction of Hwys. 16 and 41 its name. **Vermilion Provincial Park** is one of only two urban-area provincial parks in Alberta. The park encompasses 771 hectares of aspen parkland and grassland along the banks of the Vermilion River, an ancient glacial meltwater channel. To date, 20 species of mammals and 110 species of birds have been documented here. The park also has 15 km of hiking trails and a campground. **Vermilion Heritage Museum,** on 50th Ave., tel. (403) 853-

6211, features a pioneer home, an extensive photographic collection, and native artifacts; it's open in summer daily 10 a.m.-5 p.m. Across from the town office is a cast-iron mill wheel, one of the only relics retrieved from the Frog Lake Settlement after the massacre in 1885 (see "Southeast to St. Paul and Beyond," below).

LLOYDMINSTER

North America has a number of "twin cities" that straddle borders (such as Minneapolis and St. Paul), but Lloydminster is the only one that has a single corporate body in two provinces (or states, depending on the case). About 60% of the city's 18,000 residents live on the Alberta side, separated from their Saskatchewan neighbors by the main street.

Lloydminster was settled in 1903 by 500 immigrants from Britain, who followed the Reverend George Lloyd to the site of Lloydminster in search of good agricultural land. The community thrived, and when the provinces of Alberta and Saskatchewan were created out of the Northwest Territories in 1905, the town was divided by the new border, which ran along the fourth meridian. It functioned as two separate communities until 1930, when community leaders requested that the two halves be amalgamated

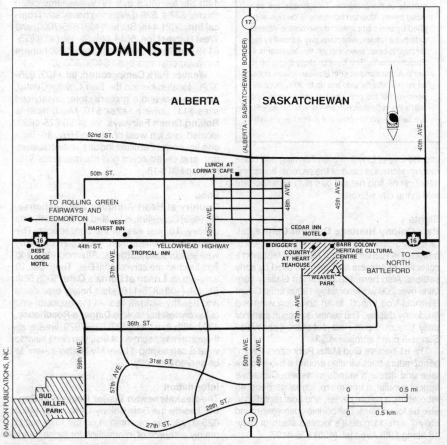

LIVING IN LLOYDMINSTER

Living in a town in two provinces can be confusing. The liquor store on the Alberta side is always busier—Alberta's booze is cheaper—except, of course, during one of Alberta's all-too-frequent beer strikes, when the Saskatchewan store gets the trade. The minimum drinking age is 19 in Saskatchewan, but 18-year-olds can just cross the road into Alberta to drink. The minimum wage is higher in Saskatchewan and vacations are longer, but income tax is higher. In theory Saskatchewan retailers charge five percent tax on many goods, unless of course you can prove they will be used or consumed outside of the province. Telephones are serviced by an Albertan company. Power is supplied by two companies; those on the Alberta side get a rebate. Albertans pay a monthly fee for health care, even though the hospital is in Saskatchewan. The best strategy might be to live in Alberta and work in Saskatchewan; houses on the Alberta side are up to 30% more expensive, but the province has lower taxes, and with a job in Saskatchewan—where the benefits are better—you'd come out in front eventually.

into the City of Lloydminster. Farming and cattle ranching form the base of the regional economy, although oil and natural gas play an important role in the city's future.

Sights

Barr Colony Heritage Cultural Centre, tel. (403) 825-5655, in Weaver Park on Hwy. 16, houses the Richard Larsen Museum featuring a collection of artifacts and antiques used by early settlers. Also here, the Imhoff Art Gallery contains over 200 works of early-1900s artist Count Berthold Von Imhoff. In an adjoining wing is a taxidermy display. The center is open in summer daily 10 a.m.-7 p.m., the rest of the year Wed.-Sun. 1-5 p.m.; admission $3.

The 81-hectare **Bud Miller Park** offers a number of nature trails winding around a two-hectare lake and through stands of aspen. Canada's largest sundial, a tree maze, formal gardens, an arboretum, a nature center, and boat rentals can also be found here. The park is open year-round daily 7 a.m.-11 p.m. It's located south of Hwy. 16 along 59th Ave.; tel. (403) 875-4497.

Events and Recreation

On the second weekend of July, Lloydminster hosts **Colonial Days.** Its **Heritage Day Festival** takes place mid-August, and the last week of October is the **Canadian Cowboys Association Rodeo Finals.** All winter you can go downhill skiing, prairie-style, south of town at **Mt. Joy Ski Area,** tel. (403) 745-2547.

Accommodations

Motels are located along Hwy. 16 (44th St.), mostly on the Alberta side of the border. **Cedar Inn Motel,** on the Saskatchewan side, 4526 44th St., tel. (403) 825-6155, is the least expensive; $27 s, $32 d. **Best Lodge Motel,** 6301 44th St., tel. (403) 875-1919, has large clean rooms; $37 s, $39 d including breakfast. **Tropical Inn,** 5621 44th St., tel. (403) 825-7000, and **West Harvest Inn,** 5614 44th St., tel. (403) 875-6113, are larger, with more facilities, but are more expensive, around $46 s, $55 d.

Weaver Park Campground, tel. (403) 825-3726, located behind the Barr Colony Centre, has showers and a grocery store; unserviced sites $11, powered sites $16. Much nicer is **Rolling Green Fairways,** tel. (403) 875-4653, located two km west of city on Hwy. 16, then one km north. Facilities include showers, laundry, and an adjacent golf course; tents $10, hookups $16-18.

Food

Country at Heart Antiques and Teahouse, tel. (403) 825-9498, is located on the south side of Hwy. 16, just east of the border post. The teahouse was built in 1942 and is surrounded by well-established gardens. Afternoon tea and light lunches are served April-Dec. Tues.-Sat. 10 a.m.-6 p.m. **Lunch at Lorna's Cafe,** 5008 50th St., tel. (403) 875-1152, has hearty breakfasts and healthy sandwiches. At the opposite end of the cholesterol scale is **Digger's Roadhouse,** 4301 49th Ave., tel. (403) 825-7979, where, although it may seem so at first, you don't have to wear a cap saying "I Love My Mother-in-law" to be served promptly.

Information

The **Saskatchewan Visitor Reception Centre,** beside the Barr Colony Centre, tel. (403) 825-0173, has information on the town but is mainly a source of information for those heading east; open in summer daily 8 a.m.-8 p.m. A **Travel Alberta Information Centre,** for those entering the province from the east, is located one km east of town on the north side of the highway; it's open mid-May to mid-June daily 9 a.m.-6 p.m. and through summer daily 8 a.m.-7 p.m.

HIGHWAY 28 TO ASHMONT

Highway 28 leaves Edmonton heading north through the suburbs. After a series of 90-degree turns—first one way, then the other, then back again—it comes to **Waskatenau,** where it straightens out to pursue an easterly heading toward Cold Lake.

Long Lake Provincial Park
During the last ice age, the low-lying area occupied by this 764-hectare park was a part of a glacial meltwater channel. Today it's surrounded by boreal forest, though aspens predominate in the park because of fires over the years. Fishing is great here; the main body of water holds some lunker northern pike. Right on the lake is a campground with flush toilets, showers, a grocery store, and canoe rentals; unserviced sites $11; powered sites $13. To get there from Hwy. 28 head north from Wasketenau on Hwy. 831 for 48 km.

Immediately to the south of the park is **White Earth Valley Natural Area,** a 2,055-hectare tract of land set aside to protect the habitat of the abundant wildlife and waterfowl.

World Championship Pumpkin Weigh-In
Smoky Lake, named for a lake 93 km west of St. Paul where natives once rested and smoked pipes during hunts, is home to an annual competition to find the world's largest pumpkin. Weigh-offs are held the same weekend at select locations around the world, with the winner from Smoky Lake winning $1,000 and the world's heaviest winning $3,500. But don't waste time scanning the vegetable section at your local supermarket for a winner; you'll need a pumpkin at least 300 kilograms (670 pounds) to take the day at Smoky Lake (the world record is 449.5 kilograms). For those who don't consider size

important, there's always a prize for the ugliest pumpkin and the pumpkin that's traveled the farthest. Celebrations take place the first weekend of October, with the official weigh-in Saturday at 10 a.m. For details, call (403) 656-3674.

Victoria Settlement
Victoria Settlement is 21 km south and east of Smoky Lake, on the north bank of the North Saskatchewan River. Founded as a mission in 1862, the settlement originally consisted of a small house, church, and school. In 1864 the Hudson's Bay Company established a fur-trading post at the site. The clerk's 1864 log house still stands, 100 years after the last beaver pelt changed hands. The trading post closed in 1897 and was abandoned until early this century, when groups of Ukrainian settlers moved to the area and the settlement became known as Victoria-Pakan. When the railway bypassed the settlement in 1918, businesses moved north to Smoky Lake and the area was abandoned once again. The Pakan Church is open in summer daily 10 a.m.-6 p.m. and presents a short slide show about the settlement. Paved trails lead to the clerk's house, to the river (where traders came ashore), and to the site of the McDougall Mission and the graves of the founder's three daughters. Picnic tables are set among broad maple trees, planted during the fur-trading days. For more information on the site call (403) 656-2333.

From Victoria Settlement, you can continue south on Hwy. 855, which eventually intersects Hwy. 16 west of Vegreville. Along the way, you'll pass by **Andrew,** home of the world's largest mallard duck. Careful you don't rip your jeans climbing the fence to touch it.

East to Ashmont
East from Smoky Lake, Hwy. 28 passes **Vilna**— home of the world's largest mushrooms—and skirts many lakes with excellent swimming, fishing, and boating. **Garner Lake Provincial Park,** four km north of Spedden, is a 74-hectare park with a sandy beach and fishing for northern pike, perch, and pickerel; camping is $13. At **Ashmont,** Hwys. 28 and 28A split, with Hwy. 28 dipping south to St. Paul and 28A continuing east to Bonnyville and Cold Lake (see "Northeast toward Cold Lake," below).

SOUTHEAST TO
ST. PAUL AND BEYOND

St. Paul

This town of 5,000 gets very few visitors from outer space. Ordinarily, that wouldn't be surprising—except that here they are encouraged to drop by. You guessed it (or maybe you didn't), St. Paul has the world's only UFO landing pad—a raised platform beside the main road forlornly waiting for its first visitor. The town's origins date to 1896 when Father Albert Lacombe, the famed western missionary, established a settlement where Métis people—who had been largely ignored by the government during treaty talks—could live and learn farming skills. Lacombe extended an open invitation to all Métis in western Canada, but fewer than 300 responded. After 10 years of hardship he opened the settlement to whites, attracting people from many cultures. The town's diverse background is cataloged at the **St. Paul Culture Centre,** 4537 50th Ave., tel. (403) 645-4800; open in summer Mon.-Sat. 9 a.m.-5 p.m. The **Old Rectory,** at 5015 47th St., looks much as it would have when built in 1896. At the south end of town (head down 47th St.) is **Upper Therien Lake.** Over 200 species of birds have been recorded around this and other nearby lakes. A large stretch of land along Lakeshore Dr. has been set aside as a park with picnic shelters and paths leading out to the lake.

The **King's Motel,** 5638 50th Ave., tel. (403) 645-5656 or (800) 265-7407, has good rooms for $35 s, $40 d; ask if that includes breakfast at the restaurant next door. The **Municipal Campground,** which has showers, is located on 55th St. at 49th Ave., a short walk from the golf course; unserviced sites $6, powered sites $9. **Westcove Municipal Recreation Area,** 16 km north of St. Paul, is beside a beach and has all facilities; unserviced sites $5-8, powered sites $10; tel. (403) 645-6688.

Corfou Restaurant, 5010 50th Ave., tel. (403) 645-2948, has a pleasant atmosphere and is managed by a friendly character. Pasta and other southern European dishes range $6.85-13.95; seafood and grills start at $8.75 but tend to be smaller portions. The **Tourist Information Centre** is on 50th Ave. at 53rd St., tel.

(403) 645-6800. It's a raised, circular structure behind the UFO landing pad; if approaching from outer space, look for the green flashing light on top. Hours are daily 9 a.m.-5 p.m.

Twenty-eight km east of St. Paul, Hwy. 28 makes a 90-degree left turn at its junction with Hwy. 41 and resumes its northeasterly course toward Cold Lake (see "Northeast toward Cold Lake," below). Those heading back to Hwy. 16 can turn right at this junction and either beeline directly south on Hwy. 41 to Vermilion or wind around the backwoods to Lloydminster, taking in the following sights.

Fort George/Buckingham House

Nine km south of Hwy. 28 is the junction of Hwys. 41 and 646 at **Elk Point** (look for a large mural outlining the history of the area along 50th Ave. and an 11-meter statue of explorer Peter Fidler at the north end of town). Turn left (east) onto Hwy. 646 and soon you'll come to Fort George and the Buckingham House.

The site of these two fur-trading posts on the north bank of the North Saskatchewan River, 13 km east of Elk Point, has been designated a Provincial Historical Site. In 1792, soon after the North West Company had established Fort George, the Hudson's Bay Company followed suit a few hundred meters away with Buckingham House. Both posts were abandoned in the early 1800s and have long since been destroyed; depressions in the ground, piles of stone, and indistinct pathways are all that remain. Above the site is an interpretive center with audio and visual presentations explaining the rivalry between the two companies and the history of the forts. Interpretive trails lead from the center down to the river. It's open mid-May to September daily 10 a.m.-6 p.m. Admission is $3. For more information call (403) 724-2612.

Whitney Lakes Provincial Park

Whitney, Ross, Laurier, and Borden Lakes are the namesake attractions at this 1,490-hectare park on Hwy. 646. The fishing is excellent in all but Borden. Because the park is located in a transition zone, plant, mammal, and bird species are diverse. A mixed forest of aspen, white spruce, balsam poplar, and jack pine grows on the uplands while black spruce and tamarack grow in lower, wetter areas. Beavers are common—look for their ponds on the north side of Laurier Lake. Other resident mammals include porcupines, white-tailed deer, coyotes, and, during berry season, black bears. Birds are abundant, especially waterfowl and shorebirds. A 1.5-km interpretive trail starts at the day-use area at the northeast corner of Ross Lake. Fishing is best for northern pike, perch, and pickerel. **Ross Lake Campground** has 149 unserviced sites ($13 per night) on six short loops around the south and eastern shore of the lake. A trail along the shore links each loop. Showers are located between loops "A" and "B".

Vast reserves of salt, west of Whitney Lakes, are harvested by the **Canadian Salt Company,** based at Lindbergh. Tours of the factory are available on weekdays; call ahead to (403) 724-3745.

Frog Lake Massacre

On 2 April 1885, a band of Cree led by Chief Big Bear massacred nine whites in a remote Hudson's Bay Company post on Frog Lake. It was an act of desperation on the part of the Cree. The great buffalo herds had been devastated and the fur trade was coming to an end. Big Bear had been forced into signing land treaties to prevent his people from starving. Life on reserves didn't suit the nomadic Cree and they yearned to return to the old ways. Exactly what sparked the massacre remains unknown, but word of confrontations farther east may have encouraged the Cree. Historians believe the natives originally planned to take hostages, but when Tom Quinn, the post's Indian agent, refused native orders a shooting spree took place.

The site is marked by a small graveyard and a series of interpretive panels outlining the events leading up to the massacre. To get there from Whitney Lakes, continue east on Hwy. 646 to its junction with Hwy. 897. Follow 897 north to the small hamlet of **Frog Lake.** At the Frog Lake General Store head east for three km to a slight rise, then south at the crest.

To Lloydminster

From Frog Lake get back on Hwy. 646 and follow it east to Hwy. 17 at the native community of **Onion Lake.** Highway 17 parallels the border 26 km south to Lloydminster.

NORTHEAST TOWARD COLD LAKE

Highway 28A

Highway 28A leaves Ashmont and bisects Upper and Lower Mann Lakes (best fishing is in Upper Mann Lake on the *south* side of the road).

A farther 25 km east is a turnoff to **Glendon.** Glendon's claim to fame takes the cake, or actually the pyrogy—it has the world's largest *pyrogy.* This indigestible part of the Ukrainian diet (something like boiled potato, or onion-filled ravioli) can be sampled next to Pyrogy Park in the Pyrogy Park Cafe, opposite the Pyrogy Motel on Pyrogy Drive.

Bonnyville

Originally called St. Louis de Moose Lake, this town of 5,000 is an agriculture center surrounded by many good fishing and swimming lakes including **Moose Lake,** to the west, and **Muriel Lake,** to the south. The town is located on the north shore of **Jessie Lake,** where over 300 species of waterfowl and shorebirds have been recorded. Spring and fall are the best viewing times although many species are present year-round, nesting in the marshes and aspen parkland surrounding the lake. Numerous viewing platforms, linked by the **Wetlands Nature Trail,** are scattered along Lakeshore Dr. and Hwy. 41.

All Bonnyville's tourist facilities, including motels, are located along the main highway. The **Tourist Information Centre** is at the west end of town. It's open in summer Mon.-Sat. 10 a.m.-8 p.m., Sunday 10 a.m.-5 p.m.; tel. (403) 826-7807.

Moose Lake Provincial Park

Moose Lake is a large, shallow body of water between Hwys. 28A and 660. One of Alberta's earliest trading posts was built in 1789 on the shore of Moose Lake by Angus Shaw, of the North West Company. All that remains of the post is a pile of rocks and a depression just west of Moose Lake River (which forms the park's western boundary). In 1870 a smallpox epidemic wiped out the local Cree—they're buried on the west side of Deadman's Point. Access to the lake is possible from many directions, but the 736-hectare provincial park is on the lake's north shore. All but Deadman's Point has been affected by fire and is reforested with jack pine and dense forests of aspen and birch. Ground squirrels and coyotes are common and occasionally black bears wander through. The park's namesake, moose, are long gone. The lakeshore is a good place to explore, with trails leading either way from the day-use area to good sandy beaches. Another trail leads to the tip of Deadman's Point and to a bog that is home to many species of birds. Fishing in the lake is best for pike, perch, and walleye. The small campground has 59 sites on two loops, both of which have access to the beach; unserviced sites $13, powered sites $15.

TRI-TOWN AREA

At the end of Hwy. 28, a little under 300 km northwest of Edmonton, are **Cold Lake, Grand Centre,** and **Medley.** The only one of these you'll want to visit is Cold Lake, located on the south shore of Alberta's seventh-largest lake. This historic town has a large marina and is close to Cold Lake Provincial Park. The town marked on most maps as "Medley" is, in fact, only the name of the post office at **Canadian Forces Base Cold Lake**— Canada's largest jet-fighter base, whose training range occupies a large tract of wilderness to the north. Over 5,000 military personnel and their families live on the base. Grand Centre, at the entrance to the base, is a service center consisting of a long strip of modern shopping facilities and industrial estates. At the town's main intersection is a CF-104 Starfighter donated by the base in recognition of the ties between the communities.

Generations of Chipewyan Indians hunted and trapped in the area and both major fur-trading companies had established posts on the lake, but it wasn't until after WW II that the population boomed. In 1952 C.F.B. Cold Lake was established. The base continues to expand, but the area's future economic growth is tied to its large deposits of oil sands.

Cold Lake Oil Sands

The heavy oil found northwest of Cold Lake is similar to that of the Athabasca Oil Sands at Fort McMurray, but the extraction process is different. The oil-rich sands lie in a 50-meter-thick band nearly a half km underground, making surface mining impractical. Instead, steam is pumped into the reservoir, thinning out the tar-like bitumen, which is then pumped to the surface and piped to Edmonton. This process, known as cyclic-steam simulation, is still in its developmental stages and is very expensive, but many of the major players in the North American oil market have leases around Cold Lake.

Alberta's Seventh-Largest Lake

Cold Lake is part of what was once a much larger lake, a remnant of the last ice age. Today the lake is approximately 22 km wide, 27 km long, has a surface area of 370 square km, and reaches depths of 100 meters. Its surface is frozen for five months of the year and doesn't break up till early May; the tackle shop at the marina has a sheet pinned to the wall showing break-up dates for the last 50 years. Fishing in the lake is best for northern pike, lake trout, and walleye.

The town of Cold Lake, on the south shore, is the center of most activity on the lake. The marina at the end of the main street rents boats and fishing tackle; four-meter boats with small outboard engines are $10 per hour and $70 per day; tel. (403) 639-3535. **Hook, Line, and Sinker Fishing Tours,** tel. (403) 594-3474, offers varying packages in a modern 5.5-meter fishing boat. Charters are from $10 per person per hour for two people, but it's least expensive for four, when a full day of guided fishing is a reasonable $42.50 per person. The best beaches are on the northwestern shore of the lake at **English Bay. Kinosoo Beach,** along Lakeshore Dr., is also popular.

Cold Lake Fish Hatchery is one of five facilities in Alberta that hatches fish eggs for the stocking of lakes throughout the province. It's open for self-guided tours daily 10 a.m.-3 p.m.; tel. (403) 639-4087. To get there, take Hwy. 55 eight km west of Cold Lake, then Primrose Rd. 15 km north, then head two km east.

Cold Lake Provincial Park

This 399-hectare park is located on a low isthmus of land east of town along 16th Avenue. Although the beaches are much nicer on the northwestern shore of the lake, fishing is excellent here and the park holds many interesting places to explore. A diversity of plant species grows in the park, thanks to its location in a transition zone between boreal forest and aspen

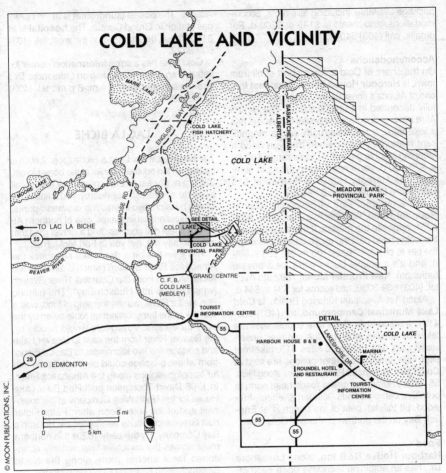

COLD LAKE AND VICINITY

MARIE LAKE

COLD LAKE
FISH HATCHERY

ENGLISH BAY RD.

COLD LAKE

ALBERTA · SASKATCHEWAN

MEADOW LAKE
PROVINCIAL PARK

MOORE LAKE

PRIMROSE RD.

TO LAC LA BICHE

55

SEE DETAIL

COLD LAKE
PROVINCIAL PARK

COLD LAKE

BEAVER RIVER

C.F.B.
COLD LAKE
(MEDLEY)

GRAND CENTRE

TOURIST
INFORMATION CENTRE

55

TO EDMONTON

28

© MOON PUBLICATIONS, INC.

0   5 mi

0   5 km

MOON

DETAIL

LAKESHORE DR.

COLD LAKE

HARBOUR HOUSE B & B

MARINA

ROUNDEL HOTEL
AND RESTAURANT

TOURIST
INFORMATION
CENTRE

55

parkland. Balsam fir and white spruce dominate the northern end of the peninsula while stands of aspen and birch can be found to the south. The dominant natural feature of the park is **Hall's Lagoon,** on the northwest side of the isthmus. The lagoon is very shallow and thick vegetation lines its banks. This is the best place for viewing birdlife. Over 40 species of mammals also inhabit the area, including muskrats, mink, water shrews, and moose. Within the park are many short hiking trails, most radiating from the campground and day-use area. The camp-

ground has showers, a beach, summer interpretive programs, and is open year-round; unserviced sites $13, powered sites $15.

Call of the Wild Horn Music Festival
Each year, on the first weekend of September at a time when thousands of birds are migrating over Cold Lake and fall colors are at their most spectacular, the town hosts a weekend-long festival of horn music. Festivities include performances—by solo artists as well as groups—and a dinner featuring the best in local game. A

package available, including all events, accommodations, and meals is $145 s, $200 d. For details, call (403) 840-8000.

Accommodations

On the shore of Cold Lake, a short stroll from town, is **Harbour House Bed & Breakfast Inn,** one of Alberta's finest B&Bs. Each room is tastefully decorated in a unique theme. The Hearts Afire room is decorated in pastel colors and has a lake view, a fireplace, bath, and a magnificent mahogany canopy bed that you need a stepping stool to get into. Rooms range $60-80 s, $70-100 d; you'll need reservations in summer. The Harbour House is located at 615 Lakeshore Dr., tel. (403) 639-2337.

For a different kind of hospitality stay at **Roundel Hotel,** 902 8th Ave., tel. (403) 639-3261, opposite the marina. If there is no one in the lobby, head past the exotic dancer posters to the bar to check in. Basic rooms are $25 s, $30 d, and it's a couple bucks extra for a private bathroom. **New Frontier Motel,** 1002 8th Ave., tel. (403) 639-3030, has rooms for $34 s, $44 d.

Along 1st Ave., past Kinosoo Beach, is **Cold Lake Municipal Campground,** tel. (403) 639-4121, a resort-style place where most sites are taken by families who stay the summer; unserviced sites $11, powered sites $13, lakefront sites with power $15. Other options are east at **Cold Lake Provincial Park** and west along Hwy. 55, where numerous gravel roads head north to primitive campgrounds (kitchen shelters, firewood, pit toilets); best of the bunch is at **English Bay** on the northwest shore of Cold Lake.

Food

Harbour House B&B Inn, along Lakeshore Dr., has an adjoining teahouse open each afternoon with a changing menu of mouthwatering desserts to accompany tea and coffee. The only place serving full meals is **Roundel Restaurant,** 902 8th Ave., tel. (403) 639-3261. Breakfast starts at $3, main meals at $6.50, and a huge bowl of clam chowder is $3. It's open daily 6 a.m.-10 p.m.

Services and Information

Greyhound buses depart daily from the Roundel Hotel for the five-hour run to Edmonton; $39.22 each way. The **post office** is at 913 8th

Avenue. The closest **laundromat** is at the Husky gas station in Grand Centre. The **hospital** is at 314 25th St., through town to the west; tel. (403) 639-3322.

Cold Lake has a small **information center** located in an A-frame building on Lakeshore Dr.; open in summer daily 9 a.m.-8 p.m., tel. (403) 639-2999.

LAC LA BICHE

The historic town of Lac La Biche (pop. 2,600) is located on the southern flanks of the boreal forest, 225 km northeast of Edmonton. The town itself has little of interest, but nearby you'll find a restored mission, two interesting provincial parks, many excellent fishing lakes, one of northern Alberta's finest golf courses, and a gravel road that may, or may not, get you to Fort McMurray.

The town lies on a divide that separates the Athabasca River System (which drains into the Arctic Ocean) from the Churchill River System (which drains into Hudson Bay). The historic Portage La Biche, across this strip of land, was a vital link in the transcontinental route taken by the early fur traders. Voyageurs would paddle up the Beaver River from the east to Beaver Lake and portage the five kilometers to Lac La Biche, from where passage could be made to the rich fur-trapping regions along the Athabasca River. In 1798 David Thompson built Red Deer Lake House for the North West Company at the southeast end of the lake. Soon after, Peter Fidler built Greenwich House nearby for the Hudson's Bay Company. By the early 1820s this northern route across the continent was virtually abandoned for a shorter route along the North Saskatchewan River via Edmonton House.

Lac La Biche Mission

The mission was established beside the Hudson's Bay Company post in 1853 and was moved to its present site, 11 km northwest of Lac La Biche, in 1855. It became a base for priests who had missions along the Athabasca, Peace, and Mackenzie Rivers and was used as a supply depot for voyageurs still using the northern trade route. The parish expanded, adding a sawmill, gristmill, printing press, and boat-building yard. Today the original buildings

half of the province. From its southern terminus (at the junction of Hwy. 55, between Lac La Biche and Athabasca) to Fort McMurray, only two small communities hug the highway. The first is **Wandering River,** a small lumber and service town with gas, a motel, and a 24-hour restaurant. The Alberta Forest Service maintains campgrounds 13, 58, and 76 km north of Wandering River. Each has a water source, pit toilets, kitchen shelter, and firewood; $7 a night. Along the route are many roadside fens and areas ravished by fire, where the cycle of natural reforestation has just begun.

Mariana Lake, a little over halfway to Fort McMurray, has the same services as Wandering River. Just south of town is **Mariana Lake Recreation Area,** which, although beside the highway, has a good campground; also $7 per night.

History
Natives and early explorers first reported oil oozing from the sand here, but it took a long time for anyone to gain commercial success from extracting it. Fort McMurray started out as a trading post along the Athabasca River, and for the first half of this century, the town experienced little growth. But in 1964, the first oil-sands plant was built, and 10 years later a second company began operation. Between 1974 and 1994, the population mushroomed from 1,500 to 36,000 as personnel from around the world came to work at the plants, attracted by high wages. At first the population was young and transient; they made their money then left. But today the city has an air of permanence about it. As new subdivisions are carved into the boreal forest, suburbs of respectable three-bedroom homes are springing up, and downtown looks similar to hundreds of midsize cities across Canada.

Athabasca Oil Sands
Only 800 billion barrels of conventional crude oil are known to remain on this planet. But trapped in the Athabasca Oil Sands surrounding Fort McMurray are one trillion barrels of bitumen. As conventional crude-oil reserves are depleted the sands will become essential to the world's future energy needs. At current production rates (187,000 barrels a day or 15% of Canada's petroleum needs) it will take 500 years to extract just three percent of the deposit.

As the name implies, the deposits are of highly compacted sand containing heavy oil or bitumen. The oil-rich sand is found both close to the surface—beneath a layer of clay and silt—and deeper down, requiring a more expensive extraction technique. Rather than being drilled for oil, the sands are mined. Once on the surface, hot water and steam are used to separate the sand from the bitumen, which is then diluted with naphtha to make it flow more easily. The bitumen is heated to 500° C, producing vapors that, when cooled, condense at three levels. While the sulphur and the gases produced during the process are all drawn off and put to use, it is the liquid products that are the most precious. By blending them and increasing the hydrogen content of the mix to make it "lighter," a high-quality synthetic crude oil is produced. This is piped to Edmonton and distributed around North America for use in cars, airplanes, and derivative products such as plastics.

Two companies are involved in the mining of the oil sands. **Suncor Inc.,** the smaller of the two, began production in 1967 after taking over the company that had initiated mining in the area three years earlier. The Suncor operation became the world's first commercially successful oil-sands plant. **Syncrude Canada Ltd.,** the world's largest producer of synthetic crude oil, was established in 1978. Both operations are located north of Fort McMurray. The size of machinery used to scrape off the surface layer of muskeg and excavate the oil sands below it is mind-boggling. Syncrude's walking draglines are the largest pieces of land-bound machinery in the world. Each moves slowly, dropping buckets as large as a two-car garage into the ground and dragging them back on a boom the length of a football field. The process continues around the clock with a constant stream of 170-ton heavy haulers taking the overburden to reclamation sites and the oil sands to conveyor belts bound for the processing plants.

SIGHTS

Oil Sands Interpretive Centre
For an insight into the history, geology, and technology of the Athabasca Oil Sands mining process, head to this large interpretive center at

the south end of the city (on the corner of Hwy. 63 and Mackenzie Blvd.). Start your visit by watching *Quest for Energy,* a multimedia, big-screen presentation about the industry that has grown around the resource. The center houses an interesting collection of machinery and has interactive displays, hands-on exhibits, and interpretive presentations. Outside is the Industrial Equipment Garden where an older-style bucketwheel excavator and other machinery is displayed. To move the excavator to this site it had to be disassembled, with some sections requiring a 144-wheel 45-meter-long trailer for the 45-km trip from the mine. The center is open in summer daily 10 a.m.-6 p.m.,the rest of the year daily 10 a.m.-4 p.m. Admission is $2.25. For information call (403) 743-7167.

Syncrude/Suncor Plant Tours

Touring the oil-sands plants is the best way to experience the operation firsthand. Syncrude is the larger, more imposing operation of the two, but it imposes more rules and keeps you farther from the action; tours depart July-Aug. Wed.-Sat. at 9 a.m. The Suncor tour gives you a better feel for the sheer size of the equipment; tours depart mid-June to August Sun.-Tues. at 9 a.m. Both tours are operated by the Fort McMurray Visitors Bureau and depart from the Oil Sands Interpretive Centre. Tour cost is $9.50; reservations are essential and can be made at the Visitors Bureau or by calling (403) 791-4336.

To Fort McKay

Fort McKay is a small native settlement on the west bank of the Athabasca River. The town itself has little of interest (and no services) but the drive out to the end of Hwy. 63 is pleasant and gives you a chance to view the mining operations, albeit at a distance. The **Oil Sands Viewpoint** is 40 km from Fort McMurray and looks out over tailing ponds and reclaimed land from the Suncor operation. The road north of the viewpoint has been rerouted so that Syncrude can continue work at what is known as East Mine. In the next stage of mining, the road will again be rerouted along a causeway over **Mildred Lake,** Canada's largest reservoir.

A farther five km north and the road forks. To the left is Fort McKay and to the right Hwy. 63 crosses the Athabasca River and continues 10

km to a dock. Here, supplies such as petroleum and building materials are loaded onto barges and transported downstream (north) to the communities of Fort Chipewyan, Uranium City, and Fond-du-lac on Lake Athabasca.

This is the end of the summer road. Between December and March a winter road is built over the frozen muskeg and river 225 km to Fort Chipewyan and up the Slave River to Fort Smith in the Northwest Territories.

Heritage Park

This two-hectare village, 1 Tolen Dr., tel. (403) 791-7575, is made up of historic buildings linked by a boardwalk and housing artifacts that reflect the importance of fishing, trapping, and transportation to the city. Other displays include boats used on the river, a Northern Alberta Railway passenger car, and an early log mission. The park is open in summer Mon.-Fri. 10 a.m.-5 p.m., Sat.-Sun. 1-5 p.m. Admission is by donation.

Gregoire Lake Provincial Park

Southeast of the city 34 km is Gregoire Lake, the only accessible lake in the Fort McMurray area. The 690-hectare park on the lake's west shore is a typical boreal forest of mixed woods and black-spruce bogs. Many species of waterfowl nest on the lake, and mammals such as moose and black bears are relatively common. Some short hiking trails wind through the park and canoes are rented in the day-use area.

Farther around the lake is the small community of **Anzac;** many people camp free on the beach here.

RECREATION AND EVENTS

Hiking

An extensive network of trails links downtown to all parts of the city, the Athabasca River, small parks, and picnic areas; ask for a map at the visitors bureau.

A self-guided interpretive trail demonstrating forestry management practices begins at the Alberta Forestry Ranger Station across the highway from the Fort McMurray Visitors Bureau.

In summer, each Sunday at 1 p.m., members of the **Field Naturalists Society** lead a walk through the nearby wilderness, pointing out the flora and fauna of the area. The walk starts from Heritage Park and ends with a slide show.

Wilderness Tours
Majic Country Wilderness Adventures offers tours from Fort McMurray. The most popular are their jet-boat tours to a wilderness camp along the river for fishing or birdwatching. Three-night packages, including accommodations, transportation, and meals, start at $350 per person. Other options include overnight horseback trips, fishing and sightseeing charters on the Athabasca River, and floats by canoe down the Clearwater River. For details write to Chuck Graves, P.O. Box 5242, Fort McMurray, AB T9H 3G3, tel. (403) 743-0766.

Other Recreation
Over 60 sports, ranging from scuba diving to skydiving, are organized locally. The city's original **golf course** is on MacDonald Island, north of downtown. It's a challenging 18-hole course with plenty of hazards. Green fees are $25; tel. (403) 790-1812. **Fort McMurray Golf Club,** located on the north side of the Athabasca River off Thickwood Blvd., is a new course carved out of the forest. Green fees are $24; tel. (403) 743-5577.

MacDonald Island Recreation Complex, tel. (403) 791-0070, north of downtown, has a modern exercise room, tennis courts, squash courts, and a swimming pool; it's open daily 8 a.m.-11 p.m.

Entertainment and Events
Fort McMurray has over 20 bars and lounges. The legendary **Oil Can Tavern,** 10007 Franklin Ave., tel. (403) 791-1300, occasionally presents live entertainment but is best known as a hard-drinking pub. At **Bronco Billy's,** in the Mackenzie Park Inn, 424 Gregoire Dr., tel. (403) 791-4770, a DJ plays country tunes Tues.-Saturday. **Keyano Theatre** puts on a season of live performances Sept.-March, with top country and pop acts appearing throughout the year. It's located in Keyano College at 8115 Franklin Ave., tel. (403) 791-4990.

Canada Day is celebrated on MacDonald Island with multicultural performers and ethnic foods. At **Heritage Park** on the second Sunday of each month you'll find a barbecue and displays of pioneer arts and crafts. **Heritage Day,** the first

Monday in August, is also celebrated at the park. A **Beerfest** takes place on MacDonald Island on the last Saturday in July; many out-of-town musicians perform in an outdoor concert.

ACCOMMODATIONS AND FOOD

Hotels and Motels
Peter Pond Inn, 9713 Hardin St., tel. (403) 743-3301, has small, basic rooms but is right downtown; $40 s, $45 d. **Twin Pine Motor Inn,** 10024 Biggs Ave., tel. (403) 743-3391, is also downtown and many rooms have a fridge; $42 s, $46 d. **Nomad Motor Inn,** 10006 MacDonald Ave., tel. (403) 791-4770 or (800) 661-5029, has well-kept rooms and a restaurant and lively bar; $69 s or d.

Sawridge Hotel, 530 Mackenzie Blvd., tel. (403) 791-7900, is geared for business travelers but usually has rooms on the weekend; $64 s or d. **Mackenzie Park Inn,** 424 Gregoire Dr., tel. (403) 791-7200 or (800) 582-3273, is the pick of the bunch but is four km south of downtown. It features a good restaurant, lounge, and indoor swimming pool; $64 s or d. **Rusty's Motor Inn,** 385 Gregoire Dr., tel. (403) 791-4646, is across the road from the Mackenzie Park Inn; $45 s, $49 d.

Campgrounds
Two campgrounds are located south of the city limits. **Rotary Park Campground,** tel. (403) 790-1581, 11 km south, offers showers, cooking facilities, and powered sites and is open year-round; all sites are $12. The park is signposted but easy to miss; turn east along Hwy. 69 and look for the entrance to the left. **Fort McMurray Centennial Park,** 9909 Franklin Ave., tel. (403) 743-7925, doesn't have showers or hookups but is along Hwy. 63, closer to the city. Sites are $8.

Food
Peter Pond Shopping Centre has a fast-food court, while **Grandma Lee's Bakery** slaps up a daily breakfast special of bacon, eggs, hash browns, and toast for $3.75. The **Mapletrees Pancake House,** in the Mackenzie Park Inn, 424 Gregoire Dr., tel. (403) 791-7200, serves well-prepared dishes at reasonable prices and offers the best Sunday brunch buffet in town ($8). Daily dinner specials, which include soup or salad, run around $8; open daily 6 a.m.-11 p.m.

For steaks try **Cedar Steak House,** 10020 Biggs Ave., tel. (403) 743-1717, where entrees start at $10. The **Garden Cafe,** 9924 Biggs Ave., tel. (403) 791-6665, is bright, full of greenery, and always busy; it's open 24 hours.

TRANSPORTATION

Getting There
Although the road out of Fort McMurray is excellent and always seems to be busy, many people prefer to fly. The **airport** is located nine km south then six km east of downtown. **Canadian Regional,** tel. (403) 743-2491 or (800) 665-1177, and **Air B.C.,** tel. (800) 222-6596, fly daily to Edmonton; $213 one-way, $232 roundtrip if purchased 14 days in advance. A cab from the airport to downtown runs around $17.

Greyhound has services three times daily to Edmonton ($41.65). The depot is located at 8220 Manning Ave., tel. (403) 791-3664. **Red Arrow,** 8316 Fraser Ave., tel. (403) 791-2990 or (800) 232-1958, offers a more luxurious service than Greyhound, with fewer stops, more legroom, and free coffee and snacks ($42 one-way). Either way, it's a five-hour trip to Edmonton.

Getting Around
Diversified Transportation, 460 MacAlpine Crescent, tel. (403) 743-4157, operates a transit service around town and to outlying suburbs; $1.10 per sector. From downtown, a cab will run $8 to the Oil Sands Interpretive Centre and

$17 to the airport. Taxi companies include: **Sun Taxi,** tel. (403) 743-5050; and **United Class Cabs,** tel. (403) 743-1234. The following car rentals are available in town and all have airport counters: **Avis,** tel. (403) 743-4773; **Budget,** tel. (403) 790-1440; **Hertz,** tel. (403) 743-2894; and **Tilden,** tel. (403) 743-6393.

SERVICES AND INFORMATION

The **post office** is at 9702 Hardin Street. **D Laundromat** is in the Park Plaza Mall on Franklin Ave.; open daily 8 a.m.-10:30 p.m. **Fort McMurray Public Library** is housed in a large, rust-colored building at 9907 Franklin Ave., tel. (403) 743-7800; closed Monday. **Fort McMurray Regional Hospital** is at 7 Hospital St., tel. (403) 791-6161. For the **RCMP** call (403) 799-8888.

Fort McMurray Visitors Bureau is located south of downtown, just north of the Oil Sands Interpretive Centre, tel. (403) 791-4336. As well as having a wealth of information on the city they represent many northern fly-in fishing lodges and offer overnight accommodation packages. It's open May-Aug. Mon.-Fri. 9 a.m.-7 p.m. and Sat.-Sun. 10 a.m.-7 p.m., the rest of the year Mon.-Fri. 9 a.m.-5 p.m.

FORT CHIPEWYAN

When the Hudson's Bay Company established a post on the west shore of Lake Athabasca in

Originally, fur-trading posts were heavily fortified, hence the name "fort." Later, the fortifications weren't necessary, but the name stuck. Today the names of many northern towns reflect this early heritage.

PROVINCIAL ARCHIVES OF ALBERTA

1788, what is now Alberta was a wild land with no white settlers. Today, Fort Chipewyan, on the site of the original trading post, holds the title of Alberta's most remote community. In summer, the only access is by river or air. After freeze-up, a winter road connects the community to the outside world. For fur traders, Fort Chip, as it's best known, was the ideal location for a post. The confluence of the Athabasca and Peace Rivers was nearby and to the north were the Slave and Mackenzie Rivers. It became a way station for some of Canada's great explorers—Alexander Mackenzie, David Thompson, Simon Fraser, and Sir John Franklin—who rested and replenished supplies at the post.

Things to See and Do
Perched on a south-facing slope overlooking the lake, the town itself is not particularly inspiring but is a good base for trips into nearby Wood Buffalo National Park and fishing on the lake and nearby rivers. In town, on Mackenzie Ave., is **Bicentennial Museum**, tel. (403) 697-3844, modeled on the original fur-trading post. The second floor is dedicated to the fur trade, while the lower floor catalogs the native history of the region, the RCMP, and local industries. Open year-round Mon.-Fri. 9 a.m.-5:30 p.m., Sat.-Sun. 1-5 p.m.

Athabasca Delta Interpretive Tours, P.O. Box 178, Fort Chipewyan, AB T0P 1B0, tel. (403) 697-3521, operates a lodge a short boat ride from Fort Chip on Jackfish Lake. The emphasis is on the traditional lifestyle of the local Dene people; activities include wilderness trips, fishing, wildlife viewing, and native cooking. Rates are $160 per person per day or $1,570 for a seven-day package departing from Fort McMurray.

Practicalities
The only accommodation in town is **Fort Chipewyan Adventure Lodge**, P.O. Box 347, Fort Chipewyan, AB T0P 1B0, tel. (403) 697-3679. The lodge has 10 rooms and a spectacular view over the lake. Rates are $85 s, $95 d, but many package deals, including meals and tours into the delta, are offered. The closest camping is 17 km northeast of town at **Dore Lake.**

Contact Air, tel. (403) 697-3753, departs twice daily from Fort McMurray for Fort Chipewyan. The 50-minute flight is $140 one-way, $245 roundtrip. If you are up in Fort Smith (NWT), there are two options for visiting Fort Chipewyan. **Northwestern Air**, tel. (403) 872-2216, has scheduled flights between the two towns for $95 each way or you can charter a five-seater plane for $610 roundtrip from **Loon Air**, tel. (403) 872-3030.

NORTH-CENTRAL ALBERTA

The area immediately north of Edmonton is a varied region that extends north out of the provincial capital's suburbs through rich agricultural land and into the wilderness of the boreal forest. The **Athabasca River** flows southwest to northeast through the region. It is linked to Edmonton by Hwy. 2, which follows the historic Athabasca Landing Trail—a supply route used by early explorers and traders for travel between the North Saskatchewan and Athabasca River Systems. From Athabasca, Hwy. 2 heads northwest to the city of Slave Lake, on the southeast shore of Lesser Slave Lake. From there it continues along the lake's southern shore to High Prairie and into the Peace River Valley. Other major roads in the region include Hwy. 18, which runs east-west through the southern portion of the region and through the farming

and oil towns of Westlock and Barrhead; Hwy. 33, which climbs into the Swan Hills, home to a subspecies of the now-extinct plains grizzly bear; and Hwy. 43, the main thoroughfare northwest from Edmonton to Grande Prairie. Adventurous souls driving to the Northwest Territories will want to travel the Bicentennial Highway (Hwy. 88) at least one-way. This gravel road opens up a remote part of the province otherwise accessible only by floatplane.

EDMONTON TO ATHABASCA

From downtown Edmonton, Hwy. 2 (called the St. Albert Trail in the vicinity of Edmonton) heads north into a once-forested land, now heavily developed as farm and ranch country. The first

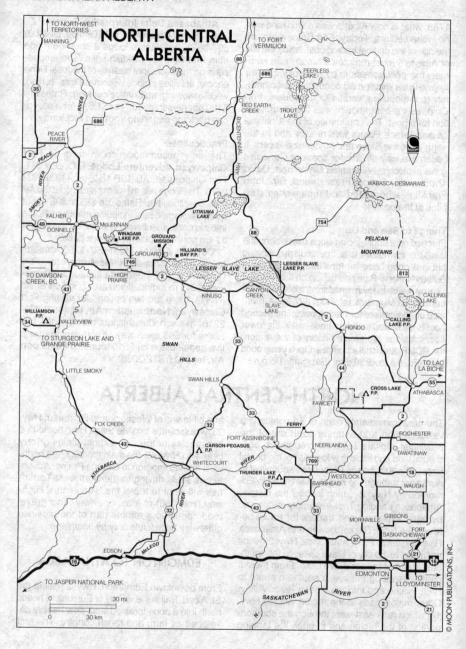

NORTH-CENTRAL ALBERTA

TO NORTHWEST TERRITORIES

MANNING

35

TO FORT VERMILION

88

686

PEERLESS LAKE

RED EARTH CREEK

TROUT LAKE

BICENTENNIAL HWY.

686

PEACE RIVER

2

PEACE RIVER

SMOKY RIVER

FALHER

49

DONNELLY

McLENNAN

WINAGAMI LAKE P.P.

GROUARD MISSION

GROUARD

HILLIARD'S BAY P.P.

UTIKUMA LAKE

WABASCA-DESMARAIS

88

754

PELICAN MOUNTAINS

813

HIGH PRAIRIE

749

LESSER SLAVE LAKE

LESSER SLAVE LAKE P.P.

TO DAWSON CREEK, BC

43

KINUSO

CANYON CREEK

SLAVE LAKE

2

CALLING LAKE

CALLING LAKE P.P.

WILLIAMSON P.P.

34

VALLEYVIEW

TO STURGEON LAKE AND GRANDE PRAIRIE

SWAN HILLS

33

HONDO

TO LAC LA BICHE

55

LITTLE SMOKY

SWAN HILLS

ATHABASCA

44

FAWCETT

CROSS LAKE P.P.

ATHABASCA

FOX CREEK

43

33

32

FERRY

FORT ASSINIBOINE

NEERLANDIA

ROCHESTER

2

TAWATINAW

CARSON-PEGASUS P.P.

WHITECOURT

ATHABASCA RIVER

769

WESTLOCK

WAUGH

18

THUNDER LAKE P.P.

18

BARRHEAD

32

43

33

MORINVILLE

GIBBONS

37

FORT SASKATCHEWAN

21

EDSON

McLEOD RIVER

16

TO JASPER NATIONAL PARK

EDMONTON

SASKATCHEWAN RIVER

N. SASKATCHEWAN RIVER

16

TO LLOYDMINSTER

21

2

21

0   30 mi

0   30 km

© MOON PUBLICATIONS, INC.

town north of the city limits is **Morinville,** a farming community founded by French and German settlers over 100 years ago. **St. Jean Baptiste Church,** built by the town's founders, is an imposing structure that has been declared a Provincial Historical Site. **Heritage Lake,** at the junction of Hwys. 2 and 642, is a popular recreation and camping area.

Athabasca Landing Trail

The Athabasca Landing Trail was a historic trade route plied first by indigenous people and later used by the Hudson's Bay Company to carry goods between Fort Saskatchewan and Athabasca. Bits and pieces of the original trail can still be seen today, interspersed among the small towns and hamlets east of Hwy. 2. Travelers wandering through this area will find a variety of other sights in addition to the old trail.

At one time the trail passed through **Gibbons,** a small town of 2,800 on the banks of the Sturgeon River. Sites of interest here include **Gibbons Anglican Church,** whose unique interior is shaped like a ship, and **Sturgeon River Historical Museum,** located in Oliver Park, which features a two-story log house. The museum is open in summer daily noon-8 p.m. Golfers will want to head to **Goose Hummock Golf Course,** four km north of town, one of Alberta's better courses. Green fees are $22-27; tel. (403) 921-2444.

Old St. Mary's Ukrainian Catholic Church is 1.5 km west of the hamlet of **Waugh.** It was the first church of its denomination to be built

north of Edmonton and is located adjacent to the original trail. The trail disappears north of Hwy. 18, but historic markers and buildings are accessible by following gravel roads east through **Tawatinaw** and **Rochester** (look for historic markers and log buildings on the roadside approaching the crest of the first ridge east of these towns).

ATHABASCA AND VICINITY

Located on the banks of the Athabasca River, 147 km north of Edmonton, this town of 2,000 was probably the most famous of the many communities that formed vital links to the north. The town is on a gently sloping hill on the river's south bank with the steep-sided Muskeg Creek Valley on one side and the Tawatinaw River on the other. Many historic buildings still stand in town and the surrounding area is pristine wilderness, excellent for fishing, boating, and camping.

History

Athabasca Landing was founded by the Hudson's Bay Company in 1874 on the southernmost bend of the Athabasca River. Goods from the east were shipped to Fort Saskatchewan and transported north along the Athabasca Landing Trail from where they were distributed throughout northern Canada. A thriving boat-building business began at the landing. Once the paddlewheelers and scows reached their destination along the river system many were

Athabasca Landing in 1898

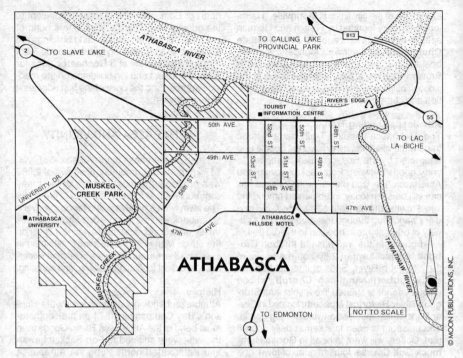

© MOON PUBLICATIONS, INC.

broken up and used for housing, while others were loaded with furs for the return journey. Passengers who boarded the paddlewheelers from the landing were from all walks of life— traders, trappers, land speculators, settlers, North West Mounted Police, geologists, missionaries, and anyone looking for a new life and adventure in Canada's great northern wilderness. Robert Service, the renowned poet, lived at Athabasca Landing for a time; much of his early work was about trappers and people of the Athabasca River.

Sights
Although the Hudson's Bay Company buildings have long since disappeared, many later buildings from the days of the paddlewheelers remain. On the riverfront is the railway station, built in 1912. Next to it is a 1915 steam engine. The Union Hotel, overlooking the river, was built in 1913. Behind it, up the hill on 48th St., is an old brick schoolhouse. Next door is the library that

houses the Athabasca Archives, a comprehensive collection of photographs and newspapers.

Muskeg Creek Park, on the west side of town, offers hiking trails and good fishing during spring. The creek flows through a heavily forested ravine into a floodplain, then drains into the Athabasca River. Wildlife abounds, berry picking is good in late summer, and cross-country skiing trails are laid in winter. Access to the park is from the elementary school on 48th Avenue.

Athabasca University has a 12,000-square-meter facility on a 180-hectare site, with a staff of over 500, a library with 100,000 books, and an annual budget exceeding $22 million—but no on-campus students. It's one of the largest correspondence universities in North America, open to students regardless of their geographical location or previous academic levels. The 12,000 enrolled students work from home, communicating with their tutors through the post and by phone, fascimile, and e-mail. The campus is open to the public and has some unique artworks commissioned especially for the building. For more information call (403) 675-6111.

Accommodations and Food
A number of motels are located on Hwy. 2, south of town. Try **Athabasca Hillside Motel,** 4804 46th Ave., tel. (403) 675-5111, with good views of the river and kitchenettes in each room; $42 s, $47 d. **Our Log Cabin,** tel. (403) 675-3381, a bed and breakfast 12 km south of town, has a pleasant outdoor area in quiet surroundings; from $50 s, $60 d. **River's Edge Campground,** on 50th Ave. where the Tawatinaw River drains into the Athabasca, is the site of the original landing; unserviced sites $9, powered sites $14.

Green Spot, 4820 51st St., tel. (403) 675-3040, serves breakfast for under $5 and sandwiches, hamburgers, and other dishes the rest of the day. **Giorgio's,** 4901 49th St., tel. (403) 675-5418, is a pizza, pasta, and steak place; the pizza is especially well priced.

Services and Information
Greyhound, tel. (403) 675-2112, stops three times daily at the Athabasca Inn on its run between Edmonton and Fort McMurray. The **Tourist Information Centre** is beside the railway station on 50th Ave., tel. (403) 675-2055; it's open mid-May to mid-September daily 10 a.m.-6 p.m.

Calling Lake Provincial Park
Lying along the south shore of one of Alberta's larger lakes, this 741-hectare park is on Hwy. 813, 55 km north of Athabasca. A boreal forest of aspen surrounds the lake, giving way to a marshy area nearer the shore. Look for deer, moose, and black bears, as well as the occasional white pelican and blue heron. Fishing for northern pike, walleye, perch, and whitefish is the park's main attraction, although swimming and canoeing on the lake are also possible. Camping is $13.

From the park, Hwy. 813 follows the east shore of Calling Lake to a hamlet of the same name. The road turns to gravel and continues 130 km north to **Wabasca-Desmarais,** a native settlement between South and North Wabasca Lakes, then loops back and follows the Willow River for much of the way to Lesser Slave Lake. This is a remote region of Alberta; services are few and far between. But wildlife is abundant and fishing is excellent in the many roadside lakes and rivers.

Amber Valley
This small hamlet just east of Athabasca was first settled in 1910 by 200 blacks from Oklahoma. They moved from their homeland to escape racial persecution, led north by 22-year-old Jefferson Davis Edwards. The prejudice continued in Alberta with locals suggesting they should head south because the climate wouldn't suit them. Despite the hard times, the community thrived and remained virtually all black. Since WW II the population has declined and today only a few black families remain.

ATHABASCA TO SLAVE LAKE

From Athabasca, Hwy. 2 heads northwest to Slave Lake, passing many summer communities along the shores of **Baptiste** and **Island Lakes.** This section of the highway is known as the **Northern Woods and Water Route.** Just before **Hondo,** the route intersects Hwy. 44, which heads south 106 km to Westlock and Hwy. 18 (see "Highway 18 West," below). At Hondo, 72 km from Athabasca, Hwy. 2A leads to **Fawcett Lake,** known for its good walleye fishing. At the lake are two campgrounds, cabins, and boat rentals.

SLAVE LAKE

The town of Slave Lake (pop. 5,600) is located on the southeastern shore of **Lesser Slave Lake,** 250 km northwest of Edmonton. It began as an important staging point for steamboat freight and passengers heading for the Peace River Country and Yukon goldfields. The arrival of a rail line in 1914 meant a boom time for the fledgling community and the beginning of a lumber industry that continues today. In 1935 disastrous floods destroyed many of the buildings on the main street. Following that debacle, the town was relocated, 3.5 km to the south. Only a few foundations remain of the original settlement. Today the town has little to interest the visitor, but Lesser Slave Lake has some of the best fishing in the province with northern pike to 10 kilograms, walleye to five kilograms, whitefish to 2.5 kilo-

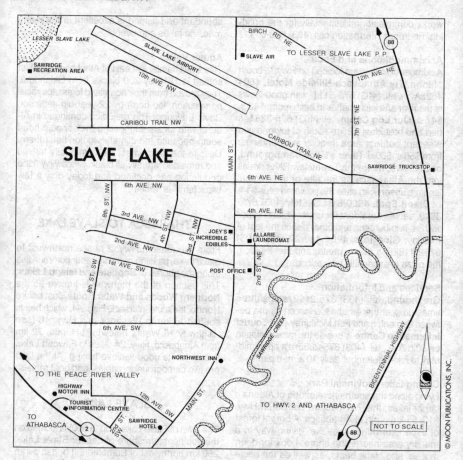

SLAVE LAKE

grams, and perch to one kilogram—enough to make any self-respecting fisherman quit his job, pack the rod and reel, and head north.

But Isn't Slave Lake in the Arctic?
Well, no, but an explanation is in order. Lesser Slave Lake is one of *two* Slave lakes in northwestern Canada. Both lakes are at the same longitude, but they're about 600 km apart as the crow flies. The bigger one—the one that many people *think* is in the Arctic—is north of Alberta in the Northwest Territories (but still south of the Arctic Circle). The smaller, more southerly of the two is here in northern Alberta. Both

are named after the Slavey Indians who traveled south up the Athabasca River from the big Slave Lake to the smaller Slave Lake on hunting and fishing expeditions. In early writings, and on maps, both lakes were denoted as Slave Lake. This led to confusion, especially since both were in what was then the Northwest Territories. To remedy the problem, the larger, northern body of water was renamed Great Slave Lake, and its Albertan counterpart, Lesser Slave Lake. Lesser Slave Lake is the third largest in Alberta (only Lakes Athabasca and Claire are larger) and the largest accessible by road. It is 90 km long, 20 km wide, has an area of 1,150 square km, and is relatively shallow, especially along the south shore where deltas have formed from the many northward-flowing Swan Hills watersheds.

And Why Are So Many Things Named "Sawridge"?

The original settlement on Lesser Slave Lake was named Sawridge, for the jagged range of hills to the north. Many prominent residents didn't like the name; in 1922 they changed it to Slave Lake. But the original name lives on. Today it's the name of the local Indian band and a creek flowing through town. And many local businesses use the name as well.

Lesser Slave Lake Provincial Park

At this 7,290-hectare park north of town you'll find a campground, long sandy beaches, unique sand dunes, and wetland and boreal forest habitats supporting diverse wildlife. Offshore is **Dog Island,** the lake's only island, home to a pair of bald eagles, pelicans, and other shorebirds. North of the Lesser Slave River are many access roads leading to **Devonshire Beach,** a seven-km stretch of sandy beach popular for sunbaking and swimming. The sunsets from this beach are spectacular (at the north end is a viewing platform). The **North Shore,** to the north of Devonshire Beach, has a picnic area and provides access to the 23-km **Freighter Lakeshore Trail,** which runs the entire length of the park. North Shore beaches are nonexistent, but a gravel road heading back toward Devonshire

leads to a quiet one. **Gilwood Golf Club,** tel. (403) 849-4389, with a challenging nine-hole course, is also on the North Shore. Green fees are $15 per round. At the north end of the park a steep eight-km road leads through a dense forest of lodgepole pine to the plateaulike summit of 1,030-meter Marten Mountain. The views are spectacular from this vantage point 500 meters above the lake. A three-km trail from the summit winds through an old-growth forest of balsam fir that has escaped major fires. The trail ends up at **Lily Lake,** a small, secluded lake from where Lily Creek flows into Lesser Slave Lake.

Fishing

Although fishing from the lake's edge and in nearby rivers can be productive, the big ones are hooked out on the lake, where pike grow to nine kilograms and walleye to four kilograms. Sawridge Recreation Area, on Caribou Trail, rents small motorboats for $20 per hour, $50 half day, or $100 full day. **Oglow Tours,** tel. (403) 849-2020, takes guided fishing and sightseeing tours onto the lake; $60 per hour or $300 per day for four people. Oglow can also arrange accommodations for its clients.

Pilots at **Slave Air,** tel. (403) 849-5353, based at the airport in town, will fly you to their favorite fishing lakes. Orloff Lake is a half hour to the east and has a campsite ($205 for up to five people), and God's Lake is one hour north ($429). If the pilot knows that the fishing is good he won't charge you ground time.

Fishing in northern lakes is nearly always productive.

ALBERTA TOURISM

Accommodations

Highway Motor Inn, on Hwy. 2 by the Tourist Information Centre, 600 14th Ave. SW, tel. (403) 849-2400, has basic rooms for $46 s, $52 d. **Sawridge Hotel,** 200 Main St. S, tel. (403) 849-4101 or (800) 661-6657, has rooms in an older section ($50 s, $55 d) and larger ones in a new wing ($62 s, $67 d). Just down Main St. is **Northwest Inn,** 801 Main St., tel. (403) 849-3300, which offers an exercise room and indoor pool; rates are $59 s, $69 d.

Worth the drive 30 km west of Slave Lake is **Canyon Creek Hotel,** tel. (403) 369-3784, in a small village of the same name. It's the only accommodation right on Lesser Slave Lake and although basic it's comfortable and clean. Out front is a sandy beach and meals are available. Rates are $35 s, $45 d, which includes breakfast.

Lesser Slave Lake Provincial Park's **Marten River Campground** (at the extreme northern end of the park) has showers, a beach, and a summer interpretive program; unserviced sites $13, powered sites $15. Immediately north, outside the park boundary, is **Diamond Willow Resort,** tel. (403) 849-2292, a private campground with coin showers, a grocery store, pitch-and-putt golf course, and nature trail; unserviced sites $13, powered sites $16. **Sawridge Recreation Area,** in town, is used mainly by noisy families who stay the entire summer.

Food

The **Sunrise Cafe** in the Sawridge Hotel, tel. (403) 849-4101, serves a good lunch buffet with a wide selection of dishes; $7. Also in the hotel is **Sweet Grass Cafe,** tel. (403) 849-4101, a casual dining room with bright decor and a great atmosphere. Expect to pay $5-7 for lunch and a few dollars more for the pasta, ribs, steak, and chicken on the dinner menu. Right downtown is **Joey's Incredible Edibles,** 101 3rd Ave. NW, tel. (403) 849-5577, which isn't that incredible but has a fairly standard menu of pasta, chicken, and beef from $9 at dinner. The **Sawridge Truckstop** on the corner of Hwy. 88 and Caribou Trail NE, tel. (403) 849-4030, is just that—a truckstop with vinyl seats, hearty meals, inexpensive prices, and waitresses as busy as Beirut bricklayers. It's open 24 hours.

Services and Information

The **Greyhound Bus Depot,** tel. (403) 849-4003, is in the Sawridge Truckstop on Hwy. 88 at the east end of town. The **post office** is on 2nd St. NE. **Allarie Laundromat,** at 116 3rd Ave. NE, is open 8:30 a.m.-10 p.m.

The **Tourist Information Centre** is located on Hwy. 2, just west of Main Street. It's open May-Sept. Mon.-Fri. 9 a.m.-9 p.m., Sat.-Sun. 10 a.m.-9 p.m.; tel. (403) 849-4611 or (800) 661-2594.

Bicentennial Highway

This 430-km road (also known as Hwy. 88) connects Slave Lake with Fort Vermilion to the north and is an excellent alternative to the Mackenzie Hwy. for those traveling in that direction. It was renamed and renumbered to commemorate the bicentenary of Fort Vermilion in 1988. Services (gas, rooms, and restaurant) are available at the only community along the road, **Red Earth Creek**—a semipermanent oil-fields town 130 km north of Slave Lake. From there, Hwy. 686 heads east to **Peerless** and **Trout Lakes,** named for the excellent fishing, and west to the town of Peace River.

At Red Earth Creek, the Bicentennial Hwy. turns to gravel and parallels the Loon and Wabasca Rivers, following the eastern flanks of the **Buffalo Head Hills.** Seventy km from Fort Vermilion a turnoff to the west leads to **Wadlin Lake,** home to one of Alberta's four colonies of white pelicans. They nest on an island during summer, migrating south to the Gulf of Mexico each winter. The island is a Prohibited Access Wildlife Area, as the birds should not be disturbed during the breeding season as they are prone to abandoning their nests if approached. The lake has good fishing for northern pike and whitefish, and a primitive campground with sites for $7 a night.

(For Fort Vermilion see "Mackenzie Highway" under "The Peace River Valley," later in this chapter.)

TO THE PEACE RIVER

From Slave Lake, Hwy. 2 follows the southern shore of Lesser Slave Lake past the small resort towns of Widewater and Canyon Creek. Take the turnoff to Wagner to follow the historic route to High Prairie along the lake. Mink farming was big business in the early 1900s and many mink cages remain, scattered along the shore. The hotel at Canyon Creek was once a fish hatchery where fish were raised as food for the mink. At **Kinuso** there is a museum with a stuffed grizzly bear that stands over 2.5 meters tall; the museum is open Mon.-Fri. 10 a.m.-4 p.m. A little farther along the highway, a nine-km gravel road leads to a marina, camping, and a beach at 144-hectare **Spruce Point Park,** tel. (403) 775-2117.

Grouard

A town of 350 on Buffalo Bay near the west end of Lesser Slave Lake, Grouard grew up around the St. Bernard Mission, founded in 1884 by Father Emile Grouard. The town was destined to become the center of the north. It had a few thousand people and a rail line on the way when, due to an unfortunate set of circumstances, everything changed. A sample of water from a nearby lake was sent to the railway headquar-

ters to ensure that it was fit for the steam engines. Along the way it was either dropped, lost, or emptied and replaced by a sample of water from muskeg wetland. The new sample was tested and found to be of poor quality. The proposed route for the railway changed and the once-thriving town collapsed. **Grouard Native Cultural Arts Museum** is dedicated to promoting a better understanding of North American native cultures through exhibition of native arts, crafts, and historic artifacts. It's open Mon.-Fri. 10 a.m.-4 p.m. in the Moosehorn Lodge Building of the Alberta Vocational College; tel. (403) 751-3915.

Hilliard's Bay Provincial Park is 13 km east of Grouard on the northwest shore of Lesser Slave Lake. It is a 2,330 hectare park with mixed woods, two sandy beaches, and a one-km spit framed by a stand of gnarled paper birches. The **Boreal Forest Interpretive Trail** meanders through a forest habitat where many species of mammals are present—look for

FATHER ALBERT LACOMBE

Dressed in a tattered black robe and brandishing a cross, Father Albert Lacombe, known to natives as "the man with the good heart," dedicated his life to those with native blood—to the Assiniboine, Blackfoot, Cree, and, in particular, to the Métis. His travels, mainly associated with northern Alberta, took him as far south as Calgary, but his reputation extended to every corner of the province. He was a spokesman for the church, an effective influence on government policies, and, most importantly, he had a hand in just about every advance in the often-tense relationship between warring tribes and white men.

Father Lacombe originally came to what is now Alberta in 1852 to serve the Métis and natives who had moved to Fort Edmonton. In his time there he founded missions at what are now St. Albert and Brosseau. After a short stint in Manitoba, he returned as a traveling missionary, instigating Canada's first industrial school for natives. He also mediated a dispute between the C.P.R. and angry leaders of the Blackfoot over rights to build a rail line through a reserve, and he wrote the first Cree dictionary. The trust he built up with native leaders was great; during one rebellion of the

PROVINCIAL ARCHIVES OF ALBERTA

Blackfoot Confederacy, it is claimed that his influence prevented the slaughter of every white man on the prairies.

tracks along the top of the ridges at the east end of the park. The campground has showers, kitchen shelters, and firewood; sites are $13-15 a night.

Shaw's Point Lakeside Resort, tel. (403) 751-3900, is a full-service campground located just outside the provincial park. It caters mainly to families and fishing enthusiasts. Facilities include showers, laundry, general store, two marinas, boat launches, and boat rentals; unserviced sites $13, powered sites $15.

High Prairie

This town of 3,000 hosts the **Golden Walleye Classic** the third week of August. It is North America's richest walleye tournament, boasting $100,000 in prize money. Walleye fishing is not the world's most exciting spectator sport, but amateur anglers are welcome to enter. For details call (403) 523-5566.

High Prairie and District Museum, tel. (403) 523-2601, has some material on the early settlement of Grouard. The museum is located in the library on 53rd Ave.; open Tues.-Sat. 11:30 a.m.-5 p.m.

High Prairie Lions Campground, at the east end of town, has showers; unserviced sites $9, powered sites $12. The **Tourist Information Centre** is open in summer daily 9 a.m.-5 p.m.

Winagami Lake Provincial Park

Winagami Lake, north of High Prairie on Hwy. 749, is ringed by a riot of paper birch, aspen, balsam fir, and poplar trees. The park is on the lake's eastern shore and is an excellent place for birdwatching; two platforms have been built for this purpose (the best time of year is May-June). The day-use area has been planted with ornamental shrubs, and a short hiking trail leads along the lakeshore. The campground has pit toilets, firewood, and kitchen shelters; sites are $13.

Winagami Conservation Area, located along the northeastern arm of the lake (turn off nine km south of McLennan), is also good for birdwatching. It's undeveloped except for a few short trails.

McLennan

Known as the "Bird Capital of Canada," this town of 1,000 is located on **Kimiwan Lake** at the confluence of three major bird migration paths—

the Mississippi, Pacific, and Central. An estimated 27,000 shorebirds and 250,000 waterfowl reside or pass through here; over 200 different species are sighted annually. An excellent interpretive center overlooking the lake has information on the many species sighted and comprehensive bird lists; it's open in summer daily 10 a.m.-7 p.m. From the center, a boardwalk leads through a wetland area to a gazebo and a bird blind. Panels along the boardwalk provide pictures and descriptions of commonly sighted species. For more information write to P.O. Box 489, McLennan, AB T0H 2L0, tel. (403) 324-2004.

Continuing West

The small hamlet of **Donnelly,** 14 km west of McLennan, is best known for the annual **Smoky River Agriculture Society Fair** on the first weekend of August. The fair features home cooking, a parade, demonstrations of country skills, a country-style beauty contest (the best looking tractor wins), and the highlight of the weekend—the Antique Tractor Pull.

From west of Donnelly, Hwy. 2 heads north 63 km to the town of Peace River. Highway 49 continues west to Spirit River and the turnoff to Grande Prairie. The first town along this route is **Falher,** known as the "Honey Capital of Canada." One million bees in 25,000 hives produce 2.5 million kilograms of honey annually. Naturally, this industry has created a need for the town to construct the world's largest honey bee; located in a small park on Third Avenue. At the east end of town are two strange-smelling alfalfa-processing plants. The alfalfa is dehydrated and pressed into pellets—over 50,000 tons annually. You can watch all the action from across the road.

HIGHWAY 18 WEST

Seventy-three km north of Edmonton on Hwy. 2, Hwy. 18 heads west through some of Canada's most productive mixed farming land. Major crops include wheat, barley, oats, canola, and hay. Livestock operations include cattle, hogs, poultry, dairy cows, and sheep; the area is home to several large feedlots and Alberta's two largest livestock auctions. At the junction of Hwys. 2

and 18, a gravel road leads north to **Nilsson Bros. Inc.,** Canada's largest privately owned cattle exchange. Live auctions are held in summer on Tuesday and Thursday mornings, more frequently the rest of the year. Buyers come from throughout North America but anyone is welcome to attend. The auctioneer is lightning fast—Alberta's best beef cattle are sold hundreds at a time by gross weight. The facility is open every day; ask to have a look around. The staff restaurant, open for an hour at lunchtime, serves hearty meat-and-potato meals for a reasonable price. Just don't ask for lamb. For details and auction times call (403) 348-5893.

Westlock

Westlock is an agricultural service center 11 km west of Hwy. 2. The small **District Museum** is at 10216 100th St., tel. (403) 349-2887 (open Fri.-Sun. 1-5 p.m.), and a private museum is located on the south side of Hwy. 18, just west of town. Look for colorful wooden animals alongside the road and head down the driveway to a collection of antiques gathered over many years by the friendly owner. **Tawatinaw Ski Hill** is a small, municipally operated ski club 31 km northeast of town with one rope tow, two T-bars, and groomed cross-country trails. The town also has a good golf course. One of the best-value motels in the entire province is **Southview Motel,** 9919 100th St., tel. (403) 349-2700, which has rooms with bath, kitchen, and cable TV for $28 s or d and is only a one-hour drive from West Edmonton Mall.

Highway 44 North

From Westlock it is 106 km north along Hwy. 44 to Hondo, halfway between Athabasca and Slave Lake. Along the way are two worthwhile detours. **Long Island Lake Municipal Park** (go 22 km north from Westlock, then turn right at Dapp Corner and follow the signs) is a recreation area with fishing, swimming, canoeing, and camping; sites are $8. Farther north, near the hamlet of Fawcett, is a turnoff to 2,068-hectare **Cross Lake Provincial Park.** Deer and moose are common here, and in late summer black bears often feed among the berry patches. The shallow lake is good for swimming, canoeing, and fishing for northern pike. The campground has pit toilets, firewood, kitchen shelters, and

a concession; unserviced sites are $13, powered sites $15.

Barrhead and Vicinity

Continuing west on Hwy. 18 takes you to Barrhead, an agriculture and lumber town of 4,100 located an hour and a half northwest of Edmonton. **Centennial Museum,** with displays depicting the town's agricultural past, is located along Hwy. 33 at 57th Avenue. The museum is open in summer Mon.-Sat. 10 a.m.-4 p.m., Sunday 1-5 p.m. The town's symbol is the great blue heron; you can see a model of one at the top end of 50th St., or head out to Thunder Lake Provincial Park for the chance to see a real one. The biggest event of the year is the **Wildrose Rodeo Association Finals** in mid-September.

Barrhead has many motels; most are on Hwy. 33 at the north end of town. Camping is free at **Rotary Park,** on the south side of town. The **Tourist Information Centre** is located in the museum.

An interesting loop drive from Barrhead is to take Hwy. 769 north to **Neerlandia** (settled by the Dutch in 1912 and named after their homeland), the small hamlet of **Vega,** and the Athabasca River. On the bank of the river is **Misty Ridge Ski Hill,** tel. (403) 674-4242, with a rope tow and T-bar. The river crossing is on the **Klondike Ferry,** one of the province's few remaining ferries. The next community along this route is **Fort Assiniboine,** which was a vital link in the Hudson's Bay Company chain of fur-trading posts. The original fort was built in 1824, making it one of the oldest settlements in Alberta. Although furs were traded at the fort, its main role was as a transportation link across the then-uncharted wilderness. A reconstruction of the original fur-trading post is located in the center of town; open in summer daily 1-5 p.m. From Fort Assiniboine it is 38 km southeast back to Barrhead, completing the loop, or 62 km northwest to Swan Hills.

Thunder Lake Provincial Park

Colonies of great blue herons reside at this 208-hectare park 21 km west of Barrhead on Hwy. 18. The park is on the northeast shore of Thunder Lake, set among stands of aspen and balsam fir. Birdwatching, especially for waterfowl, is excellent; look for herons on the islands in the quiet northwest corner of the lake. Grebes and black terns are also common. The lake's water level is artificially controlled to prevent flooding of cottages and beaches. This results in poor fishing, although the lake is stocked annually with northern pike and perch. Four short hiking trails begin from the day-use area including one along the lakeshore. The campground is beside the beach and is open year-round. It has pit toilets, showers, a concession, firewood, kitchen shelters, and canoe rentals; unserviced sites $15, powered sites $17.

SWAN HILLS

The town of Swan Hills (pop. 2,400) is located in the hills of the same name 100 km northwest of Barrhead. The hills were named, according to Indian legend, for giant swans that nested in a nearby river estuary. Oil was discovered in 1957 and the town grew quickly thereafter. Today, five major companies extract 260,000 barrels of oil and 250 million cubic meters of gas daily from 2,000 wells. North of town is the world's most modern special-waste treatment plant, which treats material that cannot be disposed of in a landfill, incinerator, or sewage system. Corrosive, combustible, and environmentally unfriendly materials such as lead, mercury, and pesticides are broken down into nontoxic compounds and either burned off or safely stored. Up to 55,000 tons of waste are treated annually. Tours of the plant are available; call (403) 333-4197 for details. The surrounding hills are wetter than the Rocky Mountain Foothills, creating a unique environment of rainforest, boreal, and subarctic zones. The best place to observe this blend is at **Goose Mountain Ecological Reserve,** 24 km west of town. Hiking and fishing are popular activities throughout the hills; the easiest area to access is **Krause Lake Recreation Area,** south of town. Old logging roads crisscross the entire region, making exploration (with a full tank of gas and a map from the Alberta Forest Service Office) easy. Moose, deer, and coyotes are common, while the **Swan Hills grizzly bear,** a subspecies of the now-extinct plains grizzly, is rare.

The **Grizzly Trail** (Hwy. 33), linking Barrhead and Swan Hills, offers two interesting stops along its route. **Trapper Lea's Cabin** is 30 km southeast of Swan Hills. It consists of two buildings constructed on the trapline of the "Wolf King of Alberta," the man who trapped the largest number of wolves in the province during the early '40s. Five km farther south is a highway rest area from where a three-km trail leads to the geographic center of Alberta. Follow the brown and yellow signs along an old seismic road to the center, indicated by an orange marker.

Accommodations and Food
Swan Hills has several motels, but each is usually full with work crews. Try **Derrick Motor Inn,** tel. (403) 333-4405, in the plaza; $43 s, $48 d. Instead of staying at the unappealing campground in town, head southeast to Trapper Lea's Cabin ($7), 15 km north to Chrystina Lake ($7), or 16 km south to Freeman River ($9). The only place to get a meal in town is the Chinese place in the plaza.

Information
The **Tourist Information Centre** is located on Hwy. 33, opposite the Grizzly Motel; open in summer daily 9 a.m.-5 p.m. For a good map of the surrounding area go to the **Alberta Forest Service Office** at 4831 Plaza Ave., tel. (403) 333-2229.

Carson-Pegasus Provincial Park
This 1,178-hectare park is located on the southern edge of the Swan Hills, 49 km south of the town of Swan Hills and 25 km north of Whitecourt. Because of its location in a transition zone, it contains forest typical of both the foothills (lodgepole pine and spruce) and the boreal forest (aspen, poplar, birch, and fir). Over 40 species of mammals have been recorded here including deer, moose, and black bear. Fishing is excellent for rainbow trout, and northern pike and whitefish are also caught. The day-use area offers canoe, rowboat, and motorboat rentals ($6, $7, and $11 per hour, respectively) and a sandy beach. The general store sells groceries, fishing tackle, bait, and hot food, and has a laundry; it's open in summer daily 9 a.m.-9 p.m. The campground has flush toilets, showers, firewood, and kitchen shelters; unserviced sites $15, powered sites $17.

WHITECOURT

Many of Whitecourt's earliest settlers had been Yukon-bound in search of gold when they reached this lushly forested region and decided to settle here instead. To them, the area held plenty of opportunities that wouldn't require an arduous trek to the Klondike. When the railroad arrived, so did many homesteaders. They took to cutting down trees to sell for firewood and railroad ties. Thus began Whitecourt's lumber industry; today the town is the "Forest Centre of Alberta."

Whitecourt sits at the confluence of the Athabasca, McLeod, and Sakwatamau Rivers on Hwy. 43, 177 km northwest of Edmonton and 341 km southeast of Grande Prairie. Highway 32 also passes through town; Swan Hills is 74 km north, and the Yellowhead Hwy. is 72 km south. If you're coming in from the southeast, you'll pass a strip of motels and restaurants before descending to the Athabasca River and the older part of town, off to the right. The **Tourist Information Centre** is by the traffic lights at the top of the hill, tel. (403) 778-5363; it's open in summer daily 8 a.m.-7 p.m., the rest of the year Mon.-Fri. 9 a.m.-5 p.m.

Sights

Industrial tours are run by the chamber of commerce Mon.-Fri. in summer. Each of the four tours is to a forestry-related industry—a pulp mill, newsprint plant, sawmill, and a medium-density fiberboard plant. For reservations call the Tourist Information Centre, tel. (403) 778-5362.

Medi-save Drugs, in Valley Centre Mall on 51st St., has North America's longest suspended railway, a large display of Coca-Cola memorabilia, a fudge machine, and a '50s-style diner.

The **E.S. Huestis Demonstration Forest,** five km north of Hwy. 43 on Hwy. 32, contains several stages of forest development. A seven-km road leads through various ecosystems including an old-growth coniferous forest and a deciduous forest, and past aspen and spruce cut blocks, a beaver dam, and an exotic plantation. Each site has interpretive signs; additional information is available from a kiosk at the entrance to the forest.

Accommodations and Food

Most of Whitecourt's dozen motels are on Hwy. 43 as it enters town from the southeast. All are priced $35-55 s, $40-60 d. Best value of the bunch is **Glenview Motel,** tel. (403) 778-2276. **Green Gables Inn,** tel. (403) 778-4537, at the top end of the scale, has large, modern rooms and a good restaurant. **Lions Club Campground,** at the south end of the service strip, is set in a heavily forested area and has a laundry and showers; unserviced sites $10-13, powered sites $15. On the opposite side of town, one km along Hwy. 43, is the full-service **Sagitawah Tourist Park,** tel. (403) 778-3734. Sites with hookups are $15-17. Camping is also possible at **Carson-Pegasus Provincial Park,** 30 km north of Whitecourt on Hwy. 32.

Mountain Pizza & Steak House, tel. (403) 778-3600, has great pizza from $6.75 and broiled steaks from $11. Next to the Tourist Information Centre is **Ken's Kitchen,** tel. (403) 778-4338. It is small, but the meals are excellent and all breads and pastries are baked on the premises. The Green Gables Inn has a cafe open all day and a restaurant with dishes starting at $10, which includes a salad bar.

HIGHWAY 43 WEST

From Whitecourt, Hwy. 43 continues northeast to **Fox Creek,** a small town surrounded by a wilderness where wildlife is abundant and the fishing legendary. If you don't believe the local fishing stories, head to the Home Hardware Store to see a 12-kilogram northern pike caught in a nearby lake. **Smoke** and **Iosegun Lakes** are two of the most accessible and offer excellent fishing for northern pike, walleye, perch, and whitefish. Both lakes have primitive camping.

Moose are abundant between Fox Creek and **Little Smoky,** 47 km northwest, from where gravel roads lead to small lakes. This area is not noted for fossils, but a few years back a mammoth tusk was found in Waskahigan River, west of Little Smoky.

Valleyview

Valleyview is an agricultural and oil-and-gas center that also serves travelers who pass through heading north to the Northwest Territories and west to Alaska. It is also one of the largest towns in Alberta without a pioneer museum. Instead, it has **Text Garden,** a series of miniature gardens with paths, benches, and a small chapel. It's located beside the Four Seasons Flower Centre at 4909 50th St.; open daily 10 a.m.-6 p.m.

The town's four motels fill up each night with road-weary travelers. **Horizon Motel,** tel. (403) 524-3904, has large rooms, a laundry, and restaurant; $46 s, $51 d. **Lions Den Campground** is on Hwy. 34, just west of Hwy. 43, and has showers; sites are $10. **Sherk's RV Park,** tel. (403) 524-4949, is a full-service campground on the south side of town (head west from Esso); full hookups $18. The large **Tourist Information Centre,** located five km south of town in a shaded rest area, is open in summer daily 8 a.m.-9 p.m.

Sturgeon Lake

Sturgeon Lake, west of Valleyview, is known for its excellent northern pike, perch, and walleye fishing and two interesting provincial parks. Located along the south side of the lake is the

Sturgeon Lake Indian Band Reserve whose members are from the Cree Nation. While many still pursue a traditional lifestyle, the band has built, of all things, a chopstick factory, from where the finished product is exported throughout the world, including to China.

Williamson Provincial Park is only 17 hectares but has a sandy beach, good swimming, and a campground with flush toilets and showers; unserviced sites $13, powered sites $15.

On the lake's northwest shore is 1,090-hectare **Young's Point Provincial Park.** Here you'll find good birdwatching for forest birds and waterfowl, and good fishing among the dense aquatic growth close to the shore. Much of the park is forested with a blend of aspen, white spruce, and lodgepole pine. Porcupines, deer, and coyotes wander the woods here, and if you're lucky, you might see red foxes, lynx, and black bears. Hiking trails begin at the day-use area and lead along the lake and to an active beaver pond. The campground has flush toilets, showers, and is near a sandy beach; unserviced sites $13, powered sites $15.

Lambeosaurus

BOB RACE

WEST OF EDMONTON

From the provincial capital, the Yellowhead Hwy. (Hwy. 16) heads west through a region of aspen parkland and scattered lakes to the Rocky Mountain Foothills and the border of Jasper National Park. The region's other main thoroughfare, Hwy. 40, spurs north off the Yellowhead Hwy. to Grande Cache and Willmore Wilderness Park. An area of frenzied oil activity during the early 1970s, the region west of Edmonton is the center for a large petroleum industry, as well as for farming, coal mining, forestry, and the production of electricity. The major service centers are Edson and Hinton, both on the Yellowhead Highway.

FROM EDMONTON TO EDSON

Long after leaving Edmonton's city limits, the Yellowhead Hwy. is lined with motels, industrial parks, and housing estates. The towns of Spruce Grove and Stony Plain (see "Vicinity of Edmonton" under "Sights" in the Edmonton chapter) flash by and farming begins to dominate the landscape.

Wabamun and Nearby Lakes
Wabamun is the name of a town, lake, and provincial park 32 km west of Stony Plain. The skyline around Wabamun Lake is dominated by high-voltage power lines coming from the three coal-fired generating plants that supply over two-thirds of Alberta's electrical requirements. Fuel for the plants is supplied by nearby mining operations—the largest coal extraction sites in Canada. Tours of the plants, mines, and the relocated hamlet of **Keephills** can be arranged through TransAlta Utilities, tel. (403) 498-7020 (Edmonton).
   Wabamun Lake Provincial Park is located on Moonlight Bay at the lake's eastern end. The fishing is good, a manmade beach is

Waterfowl flock to Wabamun Lake.

BOB RACE

the perfect spot for a swim, and the hiking trail is a good spot for wildlife viewing. Two geothermal outlets create a perfect environment for waterfowl in winter; expect to see up to 40 species at each. The easiest to get to is at the end of the wharf. The campground has showers, firewood, kitchen shelters, and is close to the beach; $13 per night.
   On the west side of Wabamun Lake is the busy resort community of **Seba Beach. Pier Boat Rentals,** on the main pier, rents canoes, paddleboats, and fishing boats. Seba Beach has no motels. Those red-backed, inflatable-toy-waving crowds either come out from Edmonton for the day or own a cottage in town. **Shadybrook Campground,** tel. (403) 797-5433, south of town, is a good place to escape the mob. It has showers and groceries and is close to the lake for fishing; unserviced sites $14, with power and water $16. North of the Yellowhead Hwy. are other lakes good for swimming, boating, and fishing including **Lac Ste. Anne.**

Pembina River Provincial Park and Vicinity
The Pembina River Valley is the first true wilderness area west of Edmonton. The small towns of Entwistle and Evansburg straddle either side of the valley where the park lies. The only structures you'll see in this 167-hectare park are an old single-lane road bridge and the concrete foundations of what once was a railroad trestle. White spruce and aspen blanket the park and provide a habitat for many mammals including beavers, mule deer, white-tailed deer, and moose. Fishing in the river is particularly good for northern pike and walleye, and those who don't fish might appreciate the deep swimming hole behind a weir, or the hiking trails in the northern part of the park. The campground, on the eastern side of the river, has flush

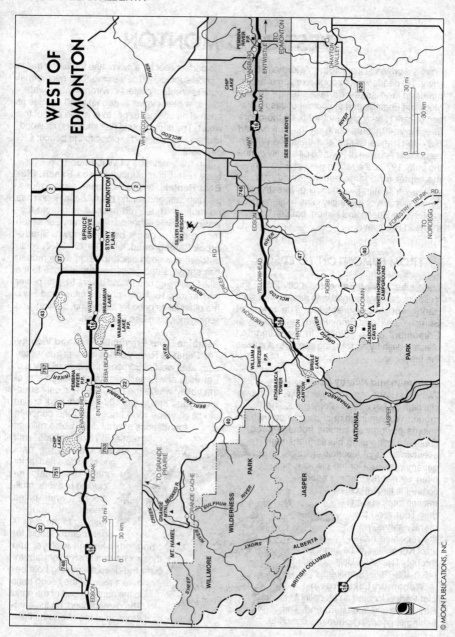

WEST OF EDMONTON

© MOON PUBLICATIONS, INC.

toilets, showers, kitchen shelters, and firewood; unserviced sites $13, powered sites $15.

Highway 16 bypasses **Entwistle,** but the town's main street is worth a look for its historic buildings. Out on the highway are all the services you'll need; motels ($35-40 s, $38-45 d), restaurants, gas, and, of course, mini-golf.

Continuing west on Hwy. 16 toward Edson, you'll pass **Chip Lake,** interesting primarily for the scatological story behind its name. It used to be called Buffalo Chip Lake, but the name was shortened for aesthetic reasons.

Edson

The site of today's town of Edson was once the starting point of a trail early settlers used to access the Peace River Valley to the north. Later, the site was picked as a divisional point of the Grand Trunk Pacific Railway and the town sprang up around it. Today this town of 7,500, 199 km west of Edmonton, relies on natural-resource-based industries such as forestry and oil-and-gas to fuel its economy.

The **Galloway Station Museum** is in RCMP Centennial Park at 5433 3rd Avenue. The museum houses artifacts reflecting the importance of transportation and industry to the town's growth. Also on display in the park are a restored caboose and a 1964 Lockheed jet. The museum is open in summer daily 9:30 a.m.-4:30 p.m. **Silver Summit Ski Resort,** 51 km north of town, has a rope tow, T-bar, and chairlift. Lift tickets are $25. The ski area is open Thurs.-Sun.; tel. (800) 667-2546.

Most motels are along 2nd Ave. (heading west) and 4th Ave. (heading east). **Castle Motel,** 5604 4th Ave., tel. (403) 723-3279, is best value; $35 s, $42 d. **Lions Park Campground,** tel. (403) 723-3169, at the east end of town, has treed sites far enough from the highway to be relatively quiet. Facilities include extra hot (and fast) showers and plenty of free firewood, which is just as well—you need a bonfire to cook anything on the oversized fire rings; unserviced sites $12, powered sites $14. Primitive campgrounds are signposted east and west of town; most are a short drive from Hwy. 16 along gravel roads and have a water source, pit toilets, and firewood.

Ernie O's, 4340 2nd Ave., tel. (403) 723-3600, is one of the best places in town to eat breakfast ($3-7). Nightly specials are $10. **Mountain**

Pizza & Steakhouse, 5102 4th Ave., tel. (403) 723-3900, is a classy pizza joint where the food and prices are excellent. The Mountain Extra Special Pizza ($15) is worth the extra bucks.

The **Tourist Information Centre** is in RCMP Centennial Park at 5433 3rd Ave., tel. (403) 723-3339. It's open in summer daily 8 a.m.-6 p.m., the rest of the year weekdays 9 a.m.-5 p.m.

HINTON AND VICINITY

Located on the south bank of the Athabasca River, at the base of the front ranges of the Canadian Rockies, this town of 9,800 makes an ideal base for exploring the northern reaches of Jasper National Park. But before speeding off into the mountains, take time out to explore Hinton's immediate vicinity. To the south are well-maintained roads leading into the historic Coal Branch; to the north, lakes, streams, canyons, hoodoos, and sand dunes. The town itself has some interesting sights and the motels and restaurants have prices you'll appreciate after spending time in Jasper.

Hinton began as a coal-mining and forestry town. These industries still play a major role in the town's economy, although the town now also benefits from being an important service along the Yellowhead Highway.

On the campus of the **Environmental Training Centre,** 1176 Switzer Dr., tel. (403) 865-8236, you'll find a small museum dedicated to the history of forestry in the province. It's open year-round, weekdays 8:15 a.m.-4:30 p.m. Outside, the **Forestry School Trail**—a 1.5-km interpretive path—winds around the perimeter of the school, passing various forest environments, an old rangers' cabin, Edna the erratic, and a viewpoint with magnificent views of the Athabasca River Valley and Rocky Mountains. If you're interested in seeing aspects of the forestry industry up close, **Weldwood** offers summer tours of its sawmill (Mon.-Fri. at 9:30 a.m.) and pulp mill (Mon.-Fri. at 1:30 p.m.). Book tours at (403) 865-8586.

The Coal Branch

An area of heavily forested foothills south of Hinton has been the scene of feverish coal-mining activity for 80 years. Most of the mines, along with the towns of Mountain Park, Luscar,

Leyland, Coal Spur, and Mercoal, have been abandoned. Two mines still operate, and two towns survive, although the populations of **Cadomin** and **Robb** have dwindled to around 100 apiece. This area, so rich in history, is also a wilderness offering hiking, fishing, and spectacular views of the Rockies. The best way to access the region, known as the Coal Branch, is via Hwy. 40. The active mines are Cardinal River Coal's pit-mining operation and another at Gregg River. A viewpoint overlooks one of the largest pits. Look for bighorn sheep at natural salt deposits on the cliff above the viewpoint, oblivious to the rumbling trucks below. As the highway approaches Cadomin, Genstar Cement's Cadomin Quarry and its "giant's staircase" come into view. The quarry is the only thing that keeps Cadomin—once a town of 2,500—alive. The town has a motel (tel. 403-692-3663), restaurant, and general store.

From the highway, **Cadomin Caves** can be seen in the mountain face west of town. These caves are the best known and most accessible in Alberta. A short trail leads up to them. Anyone serious about exploring the caves can find out more from the Tourist Information Centre in Hinton.

A campground five km south of Cadomin is nestled between **Whitehorse Creek** and a sheer rock wall. Sites are $7.50 per night. A trail from this campground leads 10 km to **Whitehorse Falls,** another four km to **Whitehorse Pass,** then continues to Miette Hot Springs in Jasper National Park, a total of 40 km one-way. Farther along the road, above the treeline, lies what's left of **Mountain Park,** once a thriving community of 1,000 connected by rail to Coal Spur to the east. The mine at Mountain Park closed in 1950, and residents dismantled their houses and moved to new locations. Today all that remains is a cemetery, some foundations, and remnants of the narrow-gauge railway.

From here you can continue south to Nordegg, across the Cardinal Divide (the division between the Athabasca River System, which flows north, and the North Saskatchewan River System, which flows east). Or you can return to Cadomin and take Hwy. 40 northeast to Hwy. 47, passing through the coal-mining hamlet of Robb and rejoining Hwy. 16 just west of Edson. This 250-km loop through the Coal Branch will take at least one day.

Ogre Canyon

This unique natural feature, between **Brûlé Lake** and the front ranges of the Rockies, was created by underground streams that dried up, creating sinkholes. Huge chunks of the treed surface above have dropped down, just like an elevator. In most cases the trees have continued growing, their tops barely reaching the level of the surrounding ground. Between the canyon and the lake is an old packhorse trail that switchbacks steeply up a hill (look for it near the C.P.R. tunnel). At the top of the ridge a cairn marks the boundary of Jasper National Park. The trail continues into a lush valley and to a hidden stream that cascades into a canyon below. A dry gully of eroded rock, across the canyon, marks the stream's former route. Camping is possible at Brûlé Lake although there are no facilities. To get to Ogre Canyon head north of Hwy. 16 on Hwy. 40 and take the first left after crossing the Athabasca River. Continue through Brûlé; the road is rough but passable and ends by Brûlé Lake. The canyon, at the base of the cliffs, is obvious.

Athabasca Tower

Fire towers are spread at regular intervals throughout the foothills. The Athabasca Tower is one of the few that can be reached by two-wheel drive. The access road turns west off of Hwy. 40, 14 km north of Hwy. 16. The gravel road passes a nordic center and finishes at the tower. Before attempting to climb the structure, holler for the warden or call (403) 865-2400 in advance. The 360-degree view from the 15-meter tower is fantastic. Anyone who doesn't like heights can appreciate the view from a platform a little farther up the road. This is also a popular hang gliding spot—many record-breaking flights have been made here, thanks to the updrafts that sweep through the valley.

Emerson Creek Road

Of the many logging roads that radiate from Hinton, Emerson Creek Rd. is one of the most interesting. It passes a small canyon, hoodoos similar to those found in the badlands, and a series of emerald-green lakes stocked with fish, before eventually rejoining Hwy. 16 at Edson. To access the road from Hinton, take Switzer Dr. and turn left on Weldwood Bridge Access Rd., then cross the Athabasca River and continue for five km. The Emerson Creek Rd. to the east (right) is marked by a sign. It is maintained primarily as a logging road, so drive with care and yield to trucks. (Yellow signs along the road are not kilometer markers.) A short hiking trail, between signs 18 and 19, follows **Canyon Creek** to a point where it cascades dramatically into a series of canyons. **Emerson Lakes,** at sign 52 (around 55 km from Hinton), were formed as the sheet of ice from the last ice age receded. A nature trail winds around the lakes to an old trapper's cabin and past some active beaver dams. A small campground at the lakes has sites with no services for $7.50. At sign 60 is **Wild Sculpture Trail,** where wind and rain have carved mysterious-looking hoodoos into the sandstone cliffs. Along the trail are three glacial lakes, each with a campground.

Accommodations

The strip of motels, hotels, restaurants, fast-food places, and gas stations along Hwy. 16 reflects the importance of Hinton as a service center. The cost of motel rooms here is considerably less than in Jasper, an hour west, making the town an ideal alternative for budget-conscious travelers. The **Hinton Hotel,** tel. (403) 865-2658, has the least expensive rooms in town, above the loudest bar in town; $32 s, $38 d with shared bathrooms. The dowdy-looking **Big Horn Motel,** tel. (403) 865-1555, beside the Husky gas station, has surprisingly good rooms, some larger than others; $64 s, $69 d, kitchenettes an extra $10. Other choices are **Pines Motel,** tel. (403) 865-2624, beside the golf course, $55 s or d; **Tara Vista Motel,** tel. (403) 865-3391, with the best views in town, $65 s, $68 d; and, in the Jasper price range, **Greentree Lodge,** tel. (403) 865-3321, which has a restaurant, pool, and jacuzzi, $77 s, $87 d. Hinton's newest accommodation is the **White-wolf Inn,** west of town on Hwy. 16, tel. (403) 865-7777, where rooms are $75 s, $80 d.

  Black Cat Guest Ranch, P.O. Box 6267, Hinton, AB T7V 1X6, tel. (403) 865-3084, is a mountain retreat west of Hinton. All the rooms have private baths and views of the mountains. Horseback riding is available during the day ($15 per hour), and in the evening, guests can relax in the large living room or hot tub. The rate, $79 per person, includes three delicious home-cooked meals. To get to the ranch take Hwy. 40 north for six km, turn left to Brûlé and continue for 11 km, then turn right and follow the signs.

  Hinton Campground, at 813 Switzer Dr., has flush toilets, kitchen shelters, and firewood; $10 per night. A much nicer alternative is to stay at a forest service campground (Emerson Lakes or along the Coal Branch Rd.) or in William A. Switzer Provincial Park toward Grande Cache.

Food

Apart from the fast-food restaurants that line the highway from one end of town to the other, Hinton has little to offer the hungry traveler. The **Husky Restaurant** does, as usual, serve filling meals at good prices; open 24 hours. If gas-station dining isn't your style, try **Greentree Cafe** in the Greentree Lodge. Continental breakfast is $3, the lumberjack breakfast of steak, bacon, eggs, and hotcakes is $9.50. Lunch specials are $4.50-6 and dinner specials start at $8. Also in the Lodge is the elegant **Fireside Dining Room,** tel. (403) 865-3321. Along the same strip is **Eagle Steakhouse,** tel. (403) 865-4074, serving chicken, pasta, and beef dishes for $10-14 in a comfortable setting. **Athens Corner,** tel. (403) 865-3956, in the Hill Shopping Centre, serves reasonable Greek, Italian, and Western food.

Services and Information

The **Greyhound Bus Depot,** 128 North St., tel. (403) 865-2367, is served daily by buses from Edmonton and Jasper. **Tilden** car rental has an office in the Greentree Lodge, tel. (403) 865-3321. For **Hinton Taxi** call (403) 865-5500.

  The **post office** is on Park Street. **Koin Spin and Dry Laundromat** is at 220 Pembina Avenue. The **Tourist Information Centre** is on Gregg Ave., which parallels the highway, tel. (403) 865-2777; open in summer daily 8 a.m.-7 p.m., the rest of the year weekdays 8 a.m.-4 p.m.

William A. Switzer Provincial Park

This 2,688-hectare park, in the foothills northwest of Hinton on Hwy. 40, encompasses a series of shallow lakes linked by Jarvis Creek. Most of the park is heavily forested with lodgepole pine, spruce, and aspen. The northern section, however, is more wide open, and elk and deer can often be seen grazing there. An ill-fated attempt at beaver ranching was made in the 1940s (cement lodges built for the purpose can be seen near Beaver Ranch Campground). Soon after, Entrance Provincial Park was established, renamed Switzer in 1958. The lakes are excellent for canoeing and bird and wildlife viewing; fishing is considered average. The park has various hiking trails, four day-use areas, and five campgrounds. Sites at **Graveyard, Halfway,** and **Cache Campgrounds** are $7 per night, **Jarvis Lake Campground** is $11, and **Gregg Lake Campground,** which has showers, powered sites, winter camping, and an interpretive program, is $13-15. For more information on the park call (403) 865-5600.

Also within the park boundary is **Blue Lake Adventure Lodge,** tel. (403) 865-4741 or (800) 582-3305, comprising chalets and cabins in a natural bushland setting. The emphasis is on activities, with canoes, kayaks, mountain bikes, and fishing tackle for rent as well as nearby hiking trails, a spa and sauna, and a game room. Rates for the smallest cabins are $37, those with two rooms are $57, and the more luxurious chalets are $67. Meals are available on site. Open year-round.

On to Grande Cache

From Switzer park it is 118 km to Grande Cache. A 32-km gravel spur to **Rock Lake,** a staging area for hikes into Jasper National Park and a worthwhile destination in itself, is 15 km north of the park. Ever since a Hudson's Bay Company post was established at the lake the area has drawn hikers and anglers, attracted by mountain scenery, the chance of viewing abundant big game, and the remote location. Hiking trails lead around the lake and three km to the remote northern reaches of Jasper National Park. Fortunately you don't have to travel far to appreciate the rugged beauty of the lake and surrounding mountainscapes. The large campground has kitchen shelters, firewood, and pit toilets; sites are $9 a night.

From Rock Lake Rd., Hwy. 40 continues to climb steadily, crossing Pinto Creek and Berland River (small campground), then following Muskeg River for a short while. The road passes **Pierie Grey Lakes** (fishing, boating, and camping) before making an arc around the shoulder of Grande Mountain and entering downtown Grande Cache, one of the most remote towns in the Canadian Rockies.

GRANDE CACHE

Grande Cache is a remote town of 3,700, 450 km west of Edmonton and 182 km south of Grande Prairie. The surrounding wilderness is totally undeveloped, offering endless opportunities for hiking, canoeing, kayaking, fishing, and horseback riding. Immediately to the south is Willmore Wilderness Park, an unspoiled region of snowcapped mountains, rivers, and over 700 km of hiking trails. The town is located on the side of Grande Mountain above the Smoky River. This river flows from its source in Jasper National Park through Willmore Wilderness Park and north, through the valley in which Grande Cache lies, to the Peace River whose waters drain into the Arctic Ocean.

The first Europeans to explore the area were fur trappers and traders. They cached furs near the site of the present town before taking them to major trading posts. At one point there was a small trading post on a lake south of town, remains of which can still be found.

Grande Cache is a planned town. Construction started in 1969 in response to a need for services and housing for miners and their families working at the McIntyre Porcupine Coal Mine. The town was developed 20 km south of the mine to maintain a scenic environment.

BOB RACE

Elk are frequently seen in Switzer Provincial Park.

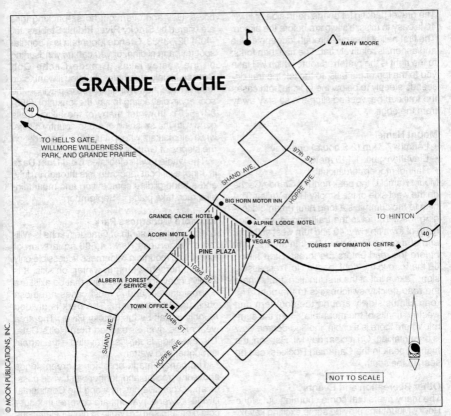

GRANDE CACHE

TO HELL'S GATE,
WILLMORE WILDERNESS
PARK, AND GRANDE PRAIRIE

40

MARV MOORE

97th ST.

SHAND AVE.

HOPPE AVE.

BIG HORN MOTOR INN

GRANDE CACHE HOTEL

ALPINE LODGE MOTEL

ACORN MOTEL

VEGAS PIZZA

PINE PLAZA

103rd ST.

ALBERTA FOREST
SERVICE

TOWN OFFICE

104th ST.

SHAND AVE.

HOPPE AVE.

TO HINTON

40

TOURIST INFORMATION CENTRE

MOON

NOT TO SCALE

© MOON PUBLICATIONS, INC.

Hiking

The main attraction of the Grande Cache area is the great outdoors. Hiking is excellent both inside and outside Willmore Wilderness Park—many short trails lead to lakes or along the banks of mountain rivers. Climbing the surrounding peaks usually requires at least a half-day of walking, and to access the most spectacular areas of Willmore will require an overnight trip. The Tourist Information Centre has brochures detailing each hike. Below are a few favorites.

Grande Mountain

- Length: 3.5 km (90 minutes) one-way
- Elevation gain: 730 meters
- Rating: moderate

The town of Grande Cache sits on the southern shoulder of Grande Mountain, which, at 2,000 meters, is not particularly imposing. But from the summit, the view across the Smoky River Valley to the Rocky Mountains is spectacular. The trail follows a power line the entire way to the peak and is easy to follow. To get to the trailhead, head northwest of town one km and turn right at the cemetery gate. Park, walk along the road to the power line, veer right, and start the long slog to the summit.

Muskeg Falls Trail

- Length: 1.5 km (30 minutes) one-way
- Elevation gain: minimal
- Rating: easy

The trailhead for this pleasant, easy hike to Muskeg Falls is 16 km east of Grande Cache.

The gravel parking lot on the north side of Hwy. 40 is easy to miss. It's two km before the airport. The first half of the trail, through lodgepole pine and aspen, is relatively flat. The trail then forks; to the right is the preferred route which will take you to the top of the falls, to the left the trail descends steeply to below the falls. In both cases the trail can be wet and slippery, so stay away from the edge.

Mount Hamel

- Length: 7.5 km (2-3 hours) one-way
- Elevation gain: 1,110 meters
- Rating: moderate/difficult

Mount Hamel is the peak north of Grande Cache on the west side of the Smoky River Valley. The hike to the summit is a long haul up an old logging road. To get to the trailhead, drive 10 km north of town on Hwy. 40 and turn west at the far end of a grassy meadow. Park in an area just before the road enters the forest. Start hiking up the road to the right, past a No Trespassing sign. Take a left at the first junction, from where the road quickly switchbacks to the right. The road climbs slowly around the southern and western flanks of the mountain. From the summit, where there is a cabin, the 360-degree view is breathtaking. On a clear day Mt. Robson, the highest peak in the Canadian Rockies, can be seen to the south.

Other Recreation and Events

The many rivers that come churning out of the Rocky Mountains provide some exciting kayaking and rafting possibilities. The most popular rivers are Muskeg River (class I-II), Sheep Creek (class III-V), and the Smoky River (class I-II). The first two flow into the Smoky, which can be navigated on a multiday trip to Grande Prairie, Peace River, or even to Inuvik and the Arctic Ocean. For guided tours contact **Wilderness River Adventure Tours,** tel. (403) 827-3377. For those who don't need an adrenaline rush to enjoy themselves, the lakes to the south of town are good for exploring by canoe and harbor large populations of waterfowl. These same lakes are good for fishing, with rainbow and brook trout, whitefish, and arctic grayling commonly caught. Many of the forestry roads are suitable for mountain biking; **Grande Cache Adventure Sports,** tel. (403) 827-3764, rents

bikes. Day and overnight horse-packing trips are offered by **Smoky River Riding Stables,** tel. (403) 827-3233. Grande Mountain is a popular spot for hang gliding, or you can go windsurfing on the nearby lakes. **Grande Cache Golf Course** is only nine holes, but you'll want to go around twice, however badly you're playing—the scenery is distracting to say the least; tel. (403) 827-5151. In winter many of the hiking trails echo with the swishing of cross-country skiers, while telemarkers whoop it up in fresh powder on the slopes of Grande Mountain.

The whole town celebrates **Coal Dust Daze** in June, a jet boat race thunders through in July, and a hang gliding competition and mountain-bike race take place in September.

Willmore Wilderness Park

To the west and south of Grande Cache is Willmore Wilderness Park, 4,600 square km of foothill and mountain wilderness accessible only on foot, horseback, or, in winter, on skis. It is totally undeveloped—the trails that do exist are not maintained, and in most cases are those once used by trappers. The park is divided roughly in half by the Smoky River. The area west of the river is reached from Hell's Gate. The east side is far less traveled—the terrain is rougher and wetter.

The park is made up of long, green ridges above the treeline and, farther west, wide passes and expansive basins along the Continental Divide. Lower elevations are covered in lodgepole pine and spruce, while at higher elevations the cover changes to fir. The diverse wildlife is one of the park's main attractions; white-tailed and mule deer, mountain goats, bighorn sheep, moose, elk, caribou, and black bears are all common. The park is also home to wolves, cougars, and grizzly bears.

The easiest way to access the park is from Hell's Gate Staging Area, six km north of town off Hwy. 40. From there, follow a gravel road the same distance farther in. Even for those not planning a trip into the park, the cliffs at **Hell's Gate** are only a short walk. These 70-meter cliffs are at the confluence of the Sulphur and Smoky Rivers. The color difference between the glacial-fed Smoky River and spring-fed Sulphur River is apparent as they merge. One of the most popular overnight trips is to Clarke's

Cache, an easy 16-km hike to the remains of a cabin where the original Grande Cache fur caches were made. Anyone planning an extended trip into the park should be aware that no services are available within the park, most trails are unmarked, and certain areas are heavily used by horse-packers. Topographical maps are available from **Alberta Forest Service** on Shand Avenue. The book *Willmore Wilderness Park,* published by the Alberta Wilderness Association, is available at **Grande Books** in the Pine Plaza Shopper's Mall on Hoppe Avenue. Two outfitters offer trips into the park on horseback: **Smoky River Riding Stables,** tel. (403) 827-3233, and **Sheep Creek Backcountry Experiences,** tel. (403) 827-2829.

Accommodations

Most motels are busy in summer so make reservations in advance. All addresses below are Grande Cache, AB T0E 0Y0. **Big Horn Motor Inn,** P.O. Box 208, tel. (403) 827-3744, is the best value. Each room has a fridge, some have kitchenettes, and a laundry and restaurant are on the premises; $30-40 s, $40-50 d. The other choices are **Alpine Lodge Motel,** P.O. Box 1349, tel. (403) 827-2450, $38 s, $48 d; **Acorn Motel,** P.O. Box 188, tel. (403) 827-2412, $36 s, $50 d; and **Grande Cache Hotel,** beside the mall, P.O. Box 600, tel. (403) 827-3377, which has suites, a restaurant, and a lounge with country bands on weekends; $49 s, $53 d.

Marv Moore Campground, tel. (403) 827-2404, has semiprivate, well-treed sites and showers, kitchen shelters, and firewood; unserviced sites $10, hookups $13-15. It's located at the north end of town on Shand Ave. beside the golf course. Forest service campgrounds are located

at regular intervals the entire length of Hwy 40. Of special note are the ones at **Hell's Gate Staging Area,** north of town, which makes a good base for exploring Willmore Wilderness Park ($7), and on **Grande Cache Lake,** five km south of town, which has good swimming, canoeing, and fishing ($7).

Food

On a clear day, the view from **Mountainview Cafe,** in the Grande Cache Hotel, is worth at least the price of a coffee. Soup and sandwich lunch specials are around $6 and pizza and pasta dishes start at $7. A dining room in the hotel opens at 5 p.m.; dinner entrees range $10-14, and on Friday night there's a prime rib buffet. Call (403) 827-3377 for reservations and information. **Vegas Pizza and Spaghetti House,** 207 Pine Plaza, tel. (403) 827-5444, is an inexpensive place to go for a meal; portions are large and the atmosphere pleasant.

Services and Information

The **post office** is in the plaza, as is a **laundromat** (beside IGA). **Home Hardware,** in the Pine Plaza, stocks camping and fishing gear. The **Tourist Information Centre** is east of town, toward Hinton; open in summer daily 8 a.m.-8 p.m. The **town office,** in the provincial building, is another good source of information. It's open year-round weekdays 9 a.m.-4 p.m.

To Grande Prairie

From Grande Cache a 181-km gravel road follows the Smoky River out of the foothills and into the wide valley in which Grande Prairie lies. Along the route are service campgrounds and good opportunities for wildlife viewing.

Black bears inhabit Willmore Wilderness Park.

BOB RACE

GRANDE PRAIRIE AND VICINITY

Grande Prairie, a city of 28,000, is located in a wide, gently rolling valley surrounded by large areas of natural grasslands. Grasslands are something of an anomaly at such a northern latitude. To the south and west are heavily forested mountains and to the north and east are boreal forests and wetlands. But it was the grasslands here, *la grande prairie,* that provided the stimulus for growth in the region. While so many of Alberta's northern towns began and grew as trading posts beside rivers, Grande Prairie grew as a result of the land's agricultural potential.

In the late 1800s, when the first settlers began making the arduous journey north to Peace River Country, the area had no roads and no communication to the outside world. Families had to be entirely self-sufficient. But that didn't deter the first immigrants from journeying through 300 km of dense forests and boggy muskeg to the prairie—isolated from southern farmland, but highly suited to agriculture. When the Grand Trunk Pacific Railway reached Edson, to the south, settlers arrived over the **Edson Trail.** When the railway arrived from Dunvegan in 1916, the settlement—then on the floodplains of Bear Creek—boomed. The population continued to climb slowly but steadily until 1976, when the discovery of Alberta's largest gas reserve nearby boosted it to over 20,000. Now the largest city in northwestern Alberta, Grande Prairie is a major service, cultural, and transportation center.

SIGHTS

Although malls, motels, restaurants, and other services are spread out along Hwy. 2 west and north of town, the center of the city has managed to retain much of its original charm. A short walk west of downtown on 100th Ave. is **Bear Creek,** along which most of Grande Prairie's sights lie.

Grande Prairie Museum
Located in Muskoseepi Park and overlooking Bear Creek, this excellent museum, tel. (403) 532-5482, houses artifacts from the area's early development, a natural history display, and dinosaur bones from a nearby dig site. Historic buildings outside include a church, schoolhouse, blacksmith shop, and fire station. It's open in summer daily 10 a.m.-6 p.m., the rest of the year Sun.-Fri. 1-4 p.m.; admission $3. The easiest access from downtown is east along 102nd Avenue.

Muskoseepi Park
The name of this 446-hectare city park means "Bear Creek" in the Cree language. The valley through which Bear Creek flows has always been used for recreation and is now preserved as a natural area within city limits. At the north end of the park is **Bear Creek Reservoir,** the focal point of the park. Here you'll find an interpretive pavilion, heated outdoor pool, tennis courts, mini-golf, and canoe rentals ($6 per hour; tel. 403-539-9397). Grande Prairie's main information center is also here. From the lake, 40 km of hiking and biking trails follow both sides of Bear Creek to the city's outer edge.

Overlooking the reservoir (access from the Hwy. 2 bypass) is **Grande Prairie Regional College.** Designed by renowned architect Douglas Cardinal, the flowing curves of this brick building are the city's most distinctive landmark.

Prairie Art Gallery
Housed in the original Grande Prairie High School, 10209 99th St., tel. (403) 532-8111, this large facility has three main galleries displaying permanent and temporary exhibitions of work by artists from throughout Canada. It's open year-round Tues.-Fri. 10 a.m.-6 p.m., Sat.-Sun. 1-5 p.m.

Kleskun Hill Natural Area
Kleskun Hill is located 20 km east of Grande Prairie along Hwy. 34. It rises 100 meters above the surrounding prairie and is the most northern badlands in North America. Plant species normally associated with southern latitudes, such as prickly pear cactus, are found here. The only facility is a picnic area at the south end.

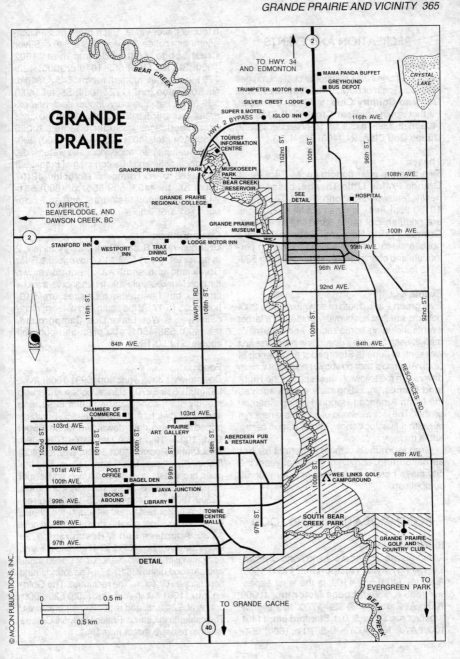

GRANDE PRAIRIE

BEAR CREEK

CRYSTAL LAKE

TO HWY. 34
AND EDMONTON

MAMA PANDA BUFFET

GREYHOUND
BUS DEPOT

TRUMPETER MOTOR INN

SILVER CREST LODGE

SUPER 8 MOTEL

IGLOO INN

116th AVE.

HWY 2 BYPASS

TOURIST
INFORMATION
CENTRE

GRANDE PRAIRIE ROTARY PARK

MUSKOSEEPI
PARK

BEAR CREEK
RESERVOIR

108th AVE.

102nd ST.

100th ST.

96th ST.

SEE DETAIL

HOSPITAL

GRANDE PRAIRIE
REGIONAL COLLEGE

TO AIRPORT,
BEAVERLODGE, AND
DAWSON CREEK, BC

GRANDE PRAIRIE
MUSEUM

100th AVE.

STANFORD INN

WESTPORT
INN

TRAX
DINING
ROOM

LODGE MOTOR INN

99th AVE.

96th AVE.

116th ST.

WAPITI RD.

108th ST.

100th ST.

92nd AVE.

92nd ST.

84th AVE.

84th AVE.

100th ST.

RESOURCES RD.

CHAMBER OF
COMMERCE

103rd AVE.

PRAIRIE
ART GALLERY

ABERDEEN PUB
& RESTAURANT

68th AVE.

102nd ST.

103rd AVE.

101st ST.

102nd AVE.

100th ST.

103rd ST.

99th ST.

98th ST.

101st AVE.

POST
OFFICE

100th AVE.

BAGEL DEN

JAVA JUNCTION

99th AVE.

BOOKS
ABOUND

LIBRARY

WEE LINKS GOLF
CAMPGROUND

98th AVE.

TOWNE
CENTRE
MALL

SOUTH BEAR
CREEK PARK

97th AVE.

97th ST.

GRANDE PRAIRIE
GOLF AND
COUNTRY CLUB

DETAIL

0   0.5 mi

0   0.5 km

TO GRANDE CACHE

TO
EVERGREEN PARK

BEAR CREEK

© MOON PUBLICATIONS, INC.

RECREATION AND EVENTS

Golfing

Grande Prairie has a number of challenging golf courses. South of downtown is **Grande Prairie Golf and Country Club,** tel. (403) 532-0340. Farther south are **Bear Creek Golf Club,** tel. (403) 538-3393, a difficult 18-hole course, and **Dunes Golf Club,** tel. (403) 538-4333.

Theater

Two theaters offer performances Sept.-April. **Grande Prairie Little Theatre,** based at the newly renovated Second Street Theatre at 10130 98th Ave., is small but all productions are popular; call (403) 538-1616 for details. **Grande Prairie Regional College Theatre** hosts amateur dramas as well as touring performers and country-music stars; call (403) 539-2916 for details.

Events

Evergreen Park, south of downtown, is a 200-hectare site that hosts many of the city's larger events including horse racing and a farmer's market each Saturday during summer. The first weekend of June is **Stompede,** a gathering of North America's best cowboys and chuck wagon drivers. On the following weekend are the **Highland Games,** including zany events such as the North American Haggis Hurling Championship. The last weekend of July is the regional fair with a livestock show, chuck wagon races, and a midway.

Grande Prairie's climate is perfect for **hot air ballooning,** and every couple of years the city plays host to a national or international competition.

ACCOMMODATIONS AND FOOD

Hotels and Motels

All motels are located west and north of downtown along Hwy. 2. **Westport Inn,** 11301 100th Ave., tel. (403) 532-4100, is the least expensive; $35 s, $38 d. **Lodge Motor Inn,** 10909 100th Ave., tel. (403) 539-4700, has slightly larger rooms; $38 s, $50 d. **Stanford Inn,** 11401 100th Ave., tel. (403) 539-5670 or (800) 661-

8160, is better value. Each room has a kitchenette with coffee supplied; $38 s, $46 d. **Silver Crest Lodge,** north of downtown at 11902 100th St., tel. (403) 532-1040 or (800) 422-7791, has clean, modern rooms; $45 s, $48 d. Nearby, **Igloo Inn,** 11724 100th St., tel. (403) 539-5314, has a laundry, indoor pool, and exercise room; $55 s, $58 d. Newest of the city's accommodations is **Super 8 Motel,** 10050 116th Ave., tel. (403) 532-8288 or (800) 800-8000, featuring an indoor pool and water slide, laundry facility, and free continental breakfast; $60 s, $68 d. And **Trumpeter Motor Inn,** 12102 100th St., tel. (403) 539-5561 or (800) 661-9435, has a good restaurant and an indoor pool; $61 s, $69 d.

Campgrounds

Grande Prairie Rotary Park, along the Hwy. 2 bypass, tel. (403) 532-1137, overlooks Bear Creek and is a short walk from downtown through Muskoseepi Park. It has showers and a laundry but few trees; tent sites are $10, hookups $15-17. At the south end of town, along 68th Ave., is **Wee Links Golf Campground,** tel. (403) 538-4501, at a pitch-and-putt golf course; $14.50-15.50.

Food

Downtown is **Java Junction,** 9931 100th Ave., tel. (403) 539-5070, a small coffee shop with friendly staff; coffee and a muffin is $2, and soup, sandwich, and coffee is $5. Similarly priced and also right downtown is the **Bagel Den,** 10024 100th Ave., tel. (403) 538-0080. **Trax Dining Room,** 11001 100th Ave., tel. (403) 532-0776, is open daily 6 a.m.-11 p.m. and has good breakfasts from $4 and lunch and dinner from $8. This joint is always busy. **Mama Panda,** 12309 100th St., tel. (403) 538-1600, is a reasonable buffet restaurant although the choice of hot dishes is not great; lunch is $7.35, dinner $9.35. **Aberdeen Pub & Restaurant,** 9728 Montrose Ave., tel. (403) 539-4720, has a warm, cozy atmosphere and reasonably priced steak and seafood dishes ($10-17). The lounge next door is open till 2 a.m. The restaurant **The Golden Inn,** 11201 100th Ave., tel. (403) 539-6000, opens at 5:30 a.m. and is popular for breakfast. The cafeteria in Grande Prairie Regional College has inexpensive meals from $4.

SERVICES AND INFORMATION

Transportation

Grande Prairie Regional Airport is located two km west of downtown, then north along Airport Road. It is served by **Air B.C.,** tel. (800) 222-6596, and **Canadian Regional,** tel. (403) 532-8001 or (800) 665-1177, who both have daily flights to Edmonton.

The **Greyhound Bus Depot,** 9918 121st Ave., tel. (403) 539-1111 or (800) 661-8747, has a cafe and lockers. Buses leave four times daily to Edmonton ($51.28 one-way), once daily to Peace River ($17.32), and twice daily to Dawson Creek in British Columbia ($14.98).

For a taxi call **Prairie Cabs,** tel. (403) 532-1060, or **Swan Taxi,** tel. (403) 539-4000.

Other Services

The **post office** is at 10001 101st Avenue. **Towne Centre Laundry** is in the Towne Centre Mall on 99th Ave. (another is located to the north in the Prairie Haven Motel at 12002 100th St.). **Queen Elizabeth II Hospital** is at 10409 98th St., tel. (403) 538-7100.

Information

Grande Prairie Public Library, 9910 99th Ave., tel. (403) 532-3580, is an excellent facility open Tues.-Thurs. 10 a.m.-9 p.m., Fri.-Sat. 10 a.m.-6 p.m., and Sunday 1-5 p.m. **Books Abound,** at 10017A 100th Ave., has a good selection of books about western Canada.

The **Tourist Information Centre** is off the Hwy. 2 bypass and overlooks Bear Creek Reservoir, tel. (403) 539-7688. Staffed by friendly volunteers, it's open in summer daily 8:30 a.m.-8:30 p.m. The **chamber of commerce,** 10011 103rd Ave., tel. (403) 532-5340, is open year-round Mon.-Fri. 8:30 a.m.-4:30 p.m.

VICINITY OF GRANDE PRAIRIE

Saskatoon Island Provincial Park

For thousands of years natives have come to this area to collect, as the name suggests, saskatoons (serviceberries). The berries are still abundant and cover nearly a third of the 102-hectare park. Late July and August are the best times for berry picking (although park rangers don't encourage the activity). **Little Lake,** with its abundant aquatic vegetation, provides ideal habitat for **trumpeter swans,** North America's largest waterfowl. This park is one of the few areas in Canada where the majestic bird can be viewed during the nesting season. Vegetation in the park is classified as northern aspen parkland, the only park in Alberta to be representative of this biome.

The campground has showers, groceries, a food concession, and mini-golf, and is beside a beach; unserviced sites are $13, powered sites $15. The park is 19 km west of Grande Prairie on Hwy. 2, then three km north.

Beaverlodge and Vicinity

This small town, 40 km west of Grande Prairie along Hwy. 2, is a northern agricultural center at the gateway to **Monkman Pass,** a pass through the Canadian Rockies found earlier this century. The only access to the pass is by 4WD. **Beaverlodge Hotel** houses a collection of over 20,000 historical artifacts, including a mechanical stuffed animal. **South Peace Centennial Museum,** tel. (403) 354-8869, started as a farmer's hobby and has grown into a working museum cataloging the agricultural history of Alberta with displays housed in 15 buildings. It's open in summer daily 10 a.m.-6 p.m.; admission is $3. On **Pioneer Day,** the third Sunday of July, all the farm machinery is started up and operated.

West of Beaverlodge on Hwy. 671, just west of **Goodfare,** is **Driftwood Ranch and Wildlife Haven.** The ranch functions as both an animal sanctuary and a working farm of exotic animals. Among the odd creatures are a joose (a cross between a Jersey cow and a moose); llamas; Vietnamese pigs; highland cattle; Siberian tigers, one of which appeared in the movie *Bird on a Wire;* and a jaguar. Part of the farm is a Ducks Unlimited bird sanctuary where many shorebirds and waterfowl nest. The farm is open in summer daily 10 a.m.-6 p.m.; tel. (403) 356-3769.

Sexsmith

North of Grande Prairie, the small town of Sexsmith—once known as "Grain Capital of the British Empire"—has undergone extensive restoration. Its main street is now a pleasant

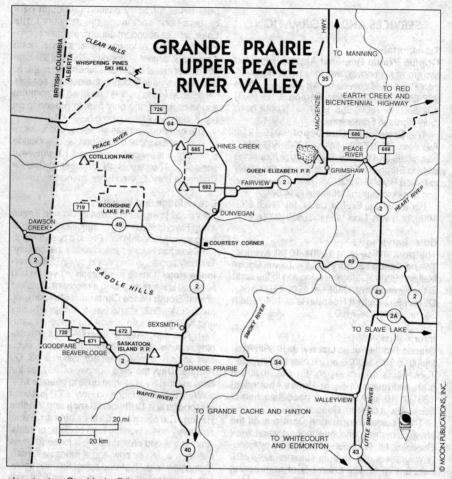

GRANDE PRAIRIE / UPPER PEACE RIVER VALLEY

place to stop. One block off the main street is the **Sexsmith Blacksmith Shop**, tel. (403) 568-3668, a working shop restored to its original 1916 condition. Inside the log structure are over 10,000 artifacts including caches of moonshine, hidden in the log walls to prevent detection by the North West Mounted Police. The shop is open in summer daily 9 a.m.-5 p.m.

From Sexsmith, Hwy. 2 climbs slowly through a mixed-wood forest connecting the Saddle Hills, to the west, and the Birch Hills, to the northeast. After crossing a low, indistinguishable summit the road begins descending into the Peace River Valley.

THE PEACE RIVER VALLEY

From its source in the interior of British Columbia, the Peace River has carved a majestic swath across the northwestern corner of Alberta's boreal forest. Explorers, trappers, settlers, and missionaries traveled upstream from Fort Chipewyan on Lake Athabasca and established trading posts along the fertile valley and surrounding plains. The posts at Fort Vermilion and Dunvegan have slipped into oblivion and are now designated historical sites, but the town of Peace River has grown from a small post into an agriculture and distribution center that serves the entire Peace River region. The river—so named because on its banks peace was made between warring Cree and Beaver Indians—and the surrounding land is often referred to as Peace Country. This moniker is a throwback to the 1930s, when the government refused to build a rail link and many local residents favored seceding from Alberta and creating their own country.

UPPER PEACE VALLEY

The Upper Peace Valley extends 230 km from the Alberta/British Columbia border to the town of Peace River. From Hwy. 49, on the south side of the river, and Hwys. 64 and 2 on the north side, roads lead down to the river and nine recreation and camping areas, initially developed for the bicentennial of Alexander Mackenzie's historical passage to the Pacific Ocean. The best way to start a visit to the region is to visit **Courtesy Corner,** at the junction of Hwys. 2 and 49. An enormous red-and-white tepee houses a Tourist Information Centre and sells local arts and crafts; open in summer daily 9 a.m.-8 p.m.

Moonshine Lake
Provincial Park and Vicinity

Over 100 species of birds and, in winter, high concentrations of moose call Moonshine Lake Provincial Park home. Occupying 850 hectares 42 km west of Courtesy Corner, the park is best known for its rainbow trout fishing. Some people

claim the lake is named for the moon's reflection on its still water, although it more likely came from a fellow who sold moonshine to travelers en route to Dawson Creek. Campsites are scattered among stands of aspen, poplar, and white spruce, and have pit toilets, kitchen shelters, and firewood; unserviced sites $13, powered sites $15.

From south of the park, Hwy. 49 continues 54 km to the Alberta/British Columbia border and a further 19 km to Dawson Creek at Mile Zero of the Alaska Highway. **Cotillion Park,** on the southern banks of the Peace River, is accessible along 35-km Pillsworth Rd. (Hwy. 719), eight km from the border. Many large mammals frequent this secluded park, and sandstone cliffs here have been eroded into strange-looking pinnacles called hoodoos. Camping, with showers, is $9.

Historic Dunvegan

As Hwy. 2 descends into the Peace River Valley from the south, it crosses Alberta's longest suspension bridge at Dunvegan—a point that has been the site of many trading posts and an Anglican mission. On the east side of the road are the restored buildings of St. Charles Roman Catholic Mission, built in 1885. A gravel road leads under the bridge to the site of the original settlement. Just past the bridge are truck farms that date back over 100 years. Beside them, hidden in the trees, the Hudson's Bay Company factor's house dates to the fur-trading era. A small provincial park on the east side of the bridge has a campground; unserviced sites $13, powered sites $15. Downstream from the fort is **Dunvegan Tea Room,** tel. (403) 835-4459, in an old greenhouse, which, naturally, means it's a well-lit place and surrounded by plenty of greenery.

Highway 64

From **Fairview,** 26 km northeast of Dunvegan, Hwy. 64 heads north then west, roughly following the Peace River into British Columbia. To the west, on the banks of the Peace River, are two campgrounds that form part of the Upper Peace Valley Recreation Area. **Pratt's Landing** is along Hwy. 682, and to the north, at the mouth of Montagneuse River, is **Carter Camp.**

Before 1916, Peace River had no rail line and was just one of many remote posts throughout the north.

Back on Hwy. 64 is the town of **Hines Creek** and its **End of Steel Heritage Park and Museum** featuring a caboose, church, trapper's cabin, and a Russian pioneer home; open in summer, Mon.-Fri. 9 a.m.-5 p.m., weekends 1-7 p.m. From Hines Creek it is 98 km to the border. To the north rise the flat-topped Clear Hills, which offer forest-service campgrounds, and **Whispering Pines,** a small ski hill with one lift and a vertical rise of 140 meters.

PEACE RIVER

From all directions, the final approach into the town of Peace River is breathtaking. This town of 7,000 straddles the majestic Peace River below the confluence of two other rivers, the Smoky and Heart. Alexander Mackenzie was one of the earliest white men to visit the region. He established a post, named Fort Forks, on the south bank of the river, upstream of the present town. It was from here, after the winter of 1792-93, that he completed his historic journey to the Pacific Ocean—the first person to cross the North American continent north of Mexico. The first permanent settlers were missionaries who, apart from their zealous religious work, promoted the region for its agricultural potential and as a service center and distribution point for

river transportation. When the rail link with Edmonton was completed in 1916, land was opened for homesteading and settlers poured into town. The farming traditions they began continue today.

Sights
High above town (access from 100th Ave., and under Hwy. 2), overlooking the valley, is the grave of **12 Foot Davis.** Davis was not a giant of a man. In fact, he was short. But he got his name from a claim he staked in the Cariboo goldfields in British Columbia. He noticed that two very successful claims had a 12-foot strip between them, so he staked the area and made a fortune. He then headed to Peace River Country and opened up trading posts along the river. Another excellent view is afforded from **Sagitawa Lookout** on Judah Hill. From here you can see town, valley, and the confluence of the Peace and Smoky Rivers.

Many historic buildings line the main street (100th St.), and many have plaques with historical facts. The wide street is typical of early boomtowns; its width allowed wagons to turn around. At the southern end of the street, across the mouth of the Heart River is **Peace River Centennial Museum,** 10302 99th St., tel. (403) 624-4261, which has displays on native clothing, the fur trade, early explorers, the development of

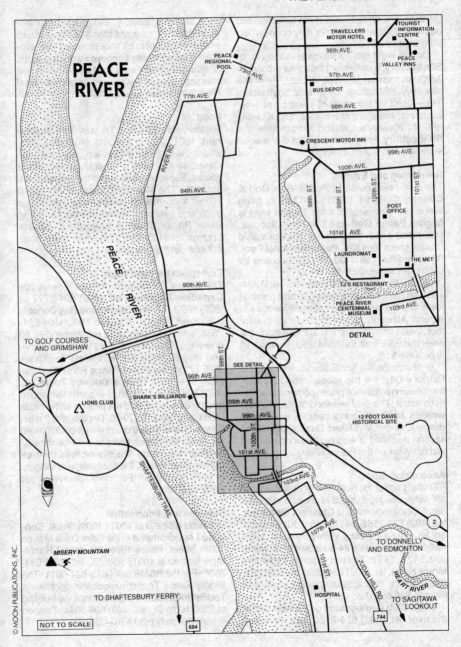

PEACE RIVER

PEACE RIVER

TO GOLF COURSES AND GRIMSHAW

DETAIL

TRAVELLERS MOTOR HOTEL

TOURIST INFORMATION CENTRE

PEACE REGIONAL POOL

73rd AVE.

96th AVE.

PEACE VALLEY INNS

97th AVE.

BUS DEPOT

98th AVE.

77th AVE.

RIVER RD.

CRESCENT MOTOR INN

99th AVE.

100th AVE.

POST OFFICE

84th AVE.

101st AVE.

LAUNDROMAT

THE MET

90th AVE.

TJ'S RESTAURANT

PEACE RIVER CENTENNIAL MUSEUM

103rd AVE.

98th ST.

96th AVE.

SEE DETAIL

SHARK'S BILLIARDS

98th AVE.

99th AVE.

100th ST.

101st AVE.

12 FOOT DAVIS HISTORICAL SITE

LIONS CLUB

103rd AVE.

SHAFTESBURY TRAIL

TO DONNELLY AND EDMONTON

107th AVE.

MISERY MOUNTAIN

101st ST.

JUDAH HILL RD.

HEART RIVER

TO SAGITAWA LOOKOUT

TO SHAFTESBURY FERRY

HOSPITAL

NOT TO SCALE

© MOON PUBLICATIONS, INC.

the town, and an extensive photo collection and archives. It's open in summer daily noon-5 p.m.; admission is $2.50.

On the west side of the river is the site of **Shaftesbury,** a settlement that grew around an Anglican mission founded in 1887. From the site, Hwy. 684 follows the historic Shaftesbury Trail—used for hundreds of years by natives, explorers, traders, missionaries, and Klondikers—to Blakely's Landing from where the **Shaftesbury Ferry** now crosses the river all summer, daily 7 a.m.-midnight.

Recreation and Events
The nine-hole course at **Peace View Golf & Country Club,** tel. (403) 624-1164, is along Weberville Rd., west of town. Farther west is **Mighty Peace Golf and Country Club,** tel. (403) 332-4653, an 18-hole championship course; green fees $24. **Peace Regional Pool,** 9810 73rd Ave., tel. (403) 624-3720, opens for public swimming each day; $4.

Misery Mountain Ski Centre, tel. (403) 624-4881, off Hwy. 684, is visible from most points in town. It's the largest nonmountain ski area in Alberta. Although the lifts don't operate in summer, views from the summit are well worth the one-hour walk from the base area. In winter lift tickets are $15.

In March, on the first Saturday following St. Patrick's Day, the **pig races** come to town—two-person teams race prized porkers down the main street. The third weekend of July the **Jaywalkers Jamboree** brings parades and a street dance to town. And **River Daze** floats by the second weekend of August, featuring wild and wet activities on the Peace River.

Accommodations
All motels are at the north end of downtown but still within walking distance of shops and restaurants. Least expensive is **Crescent Motor Inn,** tel. (403) 624-2586, $41 s, $45 d. Kitchenettes are an extra $7. **Peace Valley Inns,** tel. (403) 624-2020, is beside a 24-hour Smitty's Restaurant, $42 s, $49 d. The last option is **Travellers Motor Hotel,** tel. (403) 624-3621 or (800) 661-3227, which has a sauna, restaurant, and lounge; $46 s, $51 d.

Lions Club Campground on the west side of the river, tel. (403) 624-2120, has well-treed sites, showers, laundry, and groceries; unserviced sites $12, powered sites $12. Other places where you ought to be able to pitch a tent without a hassle include **Tangent Park,** beside the Shaftesbury Ferry south of town; at both golf courses (west of town); and west of town off Hwy. 2 at **Queen Elizabeth Provincial Park.**

Food
Restaurants are limited. Try busy **TJ's Restaurant,** 10011 102nd Ave., tel. (403) 624-3427, where the Chinese dishes are better than the Canadian and there's generally a daily pasta special. Especially delicious is the Seafood Hotpot, $15. **The Met** department store, 10010 102nd Ave., has an inexpensive cafe where eggs and bacon is 'round two bucks. Along River Rd. is **Shark's Billiards & Sports Lounge,** tel. (403) 624-5007, which offers meals at lunch- and dinnertime.

Transportation and Tours
The **airport,** 13 km west of town, is served by **Canadian Regional,** tel. (403) 624-1777 or (800) 665-1177. The **Greyhound Bus Depot** is downtown at 9801 97th Ave., tel. (403) 624-2558, with daily services to Edmonton ($52.68 one-way), Grande Prairie ($17.32 one-way), and Hay River in the Northwest Territories ($75.77 one-way). For **Peace River Taxi** call (403) 624-3020. **Town & Country Tours,** tel. (403) 624-2554, runs tours around town and to nearby attractions and will pick up at the Lions Club Campground; $20-36. Departing at 2 p.m., **Peace Island Tours** operates jet-boat trips 60 km down the Peace River to a 14-hectare island with log cabins. The overnight journey, including three meals, the boat ride, and lodging, is $130 per person. For more information call (403) 624-4295.

Services and Information
The **post office** is at 10031 100th Street. **Conveno Laundromat** is in the River Drive Mall on 100th Street. **Peace River Municipal Hospital** is located at 10915 99th St., tel. (403) 624-7500. For the **RCMP** call (403) 624-6611. The Mighty Peace Tourist Association operates a **Tourist Information Centre** from a log building at 9309 100th St., tel. (403) 624-2044; it's open in summer daily 8:30 a.m.-4:30 p.m.

MACKENZIE HIGHWAY

Named for 18th-century explorer Alexander Mackenzie, this route, also known as Hwy. 35, extends from Grimshaw, 24 km west of Peace River, for 473 km north to the Northwest Territories. It passes through a vast, empty land, dominated by the Peace River and a seemingly endless forest of spruce, poplar, and jack pine. The main population centers are Manning and High Level. Along the way are many stump-filled fields, carved out of the boreal forest by farmers who, for the last 100 years, have eked a living from some of the world's northernmost farmland. The only access to the Peace River is at Notikewin Provincial Park and at **Tompkin's Landing,** a ferry crossing east of Paddle Prairie.

When you're through exploring this wild northland, you have two alternatives to backtracking along Mackenzie Highway. One is to continue into the Northwest Territories and complete what is known as the **Deh Cho Connection,** which links the Mackenzie with the Liard and Alaska Highways—an 1,800-km loop that finishes in Dawson Creek, British Columbia. The other option is to follow Hwy. 58 east from High Level and head south on the Bicentennial Hwy. 430 km to Slave Lake (see "Slave Lake" in the "North-central Alberta" section above).

Grimshaw

Best known as Mile Zero of the Mackenzie Hwy., this town of 2,700 has grown around the railway as a farming center. For many years after the railway arrived it was a jumping-off point for farmers, trappers, and homesteaders in Peace Valley Country. Northwest of Grimshaw, on the eastern shore of Lac Cardinal, is **Queen Elizabeth Provincial Park.** The lake is very shallow and no streams flow from it. This creates an ideal habitat for many species of waterfowl. Beavers, moose, and black bears are also present. The camping area has pit toilets, kitchen shelters, and firewood; unserviced sites $13, powered sites $15.

To Manning

From Grimshaw it is 40 km north to the small hamlet of **Dixonville.** Here you'll find a trading post and the turnoff to Sulphur Lake (55 km northwest along Hwy. 689), where camping is available. A further 23 km north, along the access road to Deadwood, a turnoff south leads to **Bradshaw Bird Sanctuary,** a privately owned exotic bird farm with geese, peacocks, pheasants, and a pair of trumpeter swans. The Bradshaws also sell crafts made from bird feathers.

A homestead built by a Latvian settler in 1918 is located three km south of **North Star,** on the old Hwy. 35. It has been declared a Provincial Historical Site, and although it's locked you can stick your nose against the windows and see homemade wooden beds and a sauna, and appreciate the work that has gone into the hand-hewn log buildings.

Manning

As the highway descends into the picturesque Notikewin Valley it passes through the relatively new town of Manning. Formerly called Aurora, this town of 1,100 is a service center for the region's agricultural and petroleum industries. At the south end of town, one km east on Hwy. 691, is the excellent **Battle River Pioneer Museum,** which has a large collection of antique wrenches, stuffed animals (including a rare albino moose), carriages and buggies, farm machinery, a birch necklace carved out of a single piece of wood, and a collection of prehistoric arrowheads—ask to see the one embedded in a whalebone. The museum is open in summer daily 10 a.m.-6 p.m.; tel. (403) 836-2374.

Manning Motor Inn, tel. (403) 836-2801, $49 s, $62 d, is at the south end of town and has a restaurant. **Manning Municipal Campground** is located just west of the Tourist Information Centre in a shaded spot beside the Notikewin River. The campground is small but free and has showers and powered sites. It is also possible to camp at the golf course, north of town, which offers powered sites ($7-10 per night) and a restaurant. The **Tourist Information Centre,** tel. (403) 836-3875, is on the main street, by the river; it's open from May to mid-September daily 9 a.m.-5 p.m.

Notikewin Provincial Park

Twenty-one km north of Hotchkiss, Hwy. 692 turns east off Hwy. 35 and leads to Notikewin Provincial Park, a 970-hectare preserve at the confluence of the Notikewin and Peace Rivers.

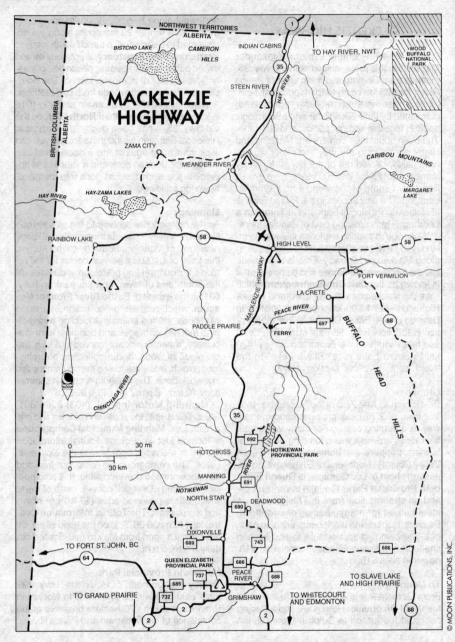

NORTHWEST TERRITORIES
ALBERTA

TO HAY RIVER, NWT

WOOD
BUFFALO
NATIONAL
PARK

INDIAN CABINS

BISTCHO LAKE

CAMERON
HILLS

STEEN RIVER

HAY RIVER

MACKENZIE
HIGHWAY

CARIBOU MOUNTAINS

ZAMA CITY

MEANDER RIVER

MARGARET
LAKE

HAY-ZAMA LAKES

HAY RIVER

RAINBOW LAKE

58

HIGH LEVEL

58

FORT VERMILION

LA CRETE

88

PEACE RIVER

697

PADDLE PRAIRIE

FERRY

BUFFALO

35

MACKENZIE HIGHWAY

CHINCHAGA RIVER

HEAD

HILLS

692

NOTIKEWAN
PROVINCIAL PARK

HOTCHKISS

RIVER

MANNING

NOTIKEWAN

691

NORTH STAR

DEADWOOD

690

DIXONVILLE

743

689

686

QUEEN ELIZABETH
PROVINCIAL PARK

686

737

685

688

TO FORT ST. JOHN, BC

64

732

2

PEACE
RIVER

TO SLAVE LAKE
AND HIGH PRAIRIE

TO GRAND PRAIRIE

2

GRIMSHAW

TO WHITECOURT
AND EDMONTON

88

© MOON PUBLICATIONS, INC.

0   30 mi
0   30 km

BRITISH COLUMBIA
ALBERTA

AURORA BOREALIS

The aurora borealis, or northern lights, is an emotional experience for some, spiritual for others, and without exception is unforgettable—an exhibition of color that dances across the sky like a kaleidoscope.

Auroral light is created through a complex process—a spontaneous phenomenon with no pattern and no "season"—that occurs within the earth's atmosphere and starts with the sun. Essentially a huge, atomic fusion reactor, the sun emits the heat and light that keep us alive, and also emits electronically charged ions that are thrust through space at high speeds. When these ions reach the earth's rarefied upper atmosphere—about 180 km above the earth's surface—they are captured by the earth's magnetic field and accelerated toward the poles. Along the way they collide with the atoms and molecules of the gases in the atmosphere, which in turn become temporarily charged or "ionized." This absorbed energy is then released by the ionized gases, often in the form of light. The color of the light varies from red to yellow to green, depending on the gas; nitrogen atoms produce a violet and sometimes red color, oxygen a green and, at higher altitudes, an orange.

Because the magnetic field is more intense near the north and south magnetic poles the lights are best seen at high latitudes. In northern Alberta the light show takes place up to 160 nights annually, with displays best north of Peace River. They generally start as a faint glow on the northeastern horizon after the sun has set, improving as the sky becomes darker.

The 30-km road to the park is partly paved and occasionally steep. "Notikewin" is the Cree word for battle—many were fought in the region. Here a stand of 200-year-old spruce presides over Spruce Island, at the mouth of the Notikewin River. The island also supports an abundance of ostrich ferns growing to a height of two meters. Beavers, mule deer, moose, and the occasional black bear can be seen in the area. Bird species are diverse and include sandhill cranes, which rest at the mouth of the Notikewin River on their southern migration in September. The river offers good fishing for gold-eye, walleye, and northern pike. Camping is $9.

A Short Detour

The largest of eight Métis settlements, established throughout the province during the 1930s, is **Paddle Prairie**, 65 km north of Twin Lakes. From 10 km north of here a gravel road (Hwy. 697) leads east to Tomkin's Landing and one of only eight ferry crossings in the province (operates in summer, daily 24 hours). It then continues to La Crete and Fort Vermilion, crosses the Peace River, and intersects Hwy. 58, which heads west, rejoining the Mackenzie Hwy. at High Level.

La Crete (pop. 1,000) has grown into an agricultural center on the northern fringe of the continent's arable land. Most residents are Mennonites who moved to the region in the 1930s. They are from a traditional Protestant sect originating in Holland, whose members settled in remote regions throughout the world and established self-sufficient agricultural lifestyles, in hopes of being left to practice their faith in peace. On the streets and in the local restaurants you'll hear their language, Plattdeutsch (Low German), which is spoken by Mennonites throughout the world.

To the southeast of this flat, prairielike area, the Buffalo Head Hills rise nearly 700 meters above the surrounding land. The only way into the hills is along an 18-km gravel road that spurs east from Hwy. 697 18 km south of La Crete. To the west, an eight-km road from town leads past a golf course to one of the Peace River's many natural sandbars, and to Etna's Landing where there is good swimming.

Fort Vermilion

This town of 840, on the south bank of the Peace River, 77 km east of High Level, vies with Fort Chipewyan as the oldest settlement in Alberta. It was named for the red clay deposits present in the banks of the river. The first trading post here was established a few kilometers downstream of present-day Fort Vermilion by the North West Company in 1788. Trade with Beaver, Cree, and Dene Indians was brisk, and by 1802 the Hudson's Bay Company had also established a post. In 1821 the companies merged, and in 1830, they moved operations to the town's present site. The area's agricultural potential gained worldwide attention when locally grown wheat, transported along the river highway, won a gold medal at the 1876 World Fair in Philadelphia. For 150 years, supplies arrived by riverboat or were hauled overland from the town of Peace River. When the Mackenzie Hwy. was completed the river highway became obsolete. The last riverboat arrived in Fort Vermilion in 1952, but it wasn't until 1974, when a bridge was built across the Peace River, that the town was linked to the outside world. Many old buildings and cabins, in varying states of disrepair, still stand. Pick up a *Fort Vermilion Heritage Guide* from the Tourist Information Centre to help identify the many historical sites in town. The **Mary Batt & Son General Store** was constructed from logs removed from the 1897 Hudson's Bay Company post.

The **Sheridan Lawrence Hotel,** tel. (403) 927-4400, is the only place to stay in town and has a small restaurant and bar; $45 s, $50 d. North and west of town are campgrounds. The summer-only **Tourist Information Centre** is located in a dove-tailed log home built by hand in 1923; tel. (403) 927-3216.

High Level

Located 279 km north of Grimshaw, this town of 3,000 is at the center of a vast region rich in natural resources. The town expanded during the oil boom of the 1960s and has prospered ever since. The grain elevators, serving agricultural communities to the east, are the northernmost in the world. Forestry is also a major local industry; the town boasts one of the world's most productive logging and sawmill operations, turning out over 250 million board feet of lumber annually.

Fortunately, much of the surrounding forest is safe from loggers; the 7.5-million-hectare **Footner Lake Forest** has poor drainage, forming major bogs and permafrost that make timber harvest commercially unviable. The forest encompasses the entire northern part of the province west of Wood Buffalo National Park.

Northeast of High Level are the Caribou Mountains, which rise to a plateau 800 meters above the Peace River. At that altitude, and being so far north, the fragile environment is easily disturbed. The mountains are blanketed in white spruce, aspen, and pine, and two major lakes—Margaret and Wentzel—offer excellent fishing and sandy beaches. Northwest of High Level are the Cameron Hills and **Bistcho Lake** (where many Albertan fish hatcheries harvest walleye spawn). The most accessible part of the forest is **Hutch Lake,** 32 km north of town. The lake is surrounded by aspen and poplar and is the source of the **Meander River.** The dominant feature here is **Watt Mountain** (780 meters), which you can see to the northwest of High Level. From Hutch Lake, a service road leads 11 km to the summit. The recreation area at the north end of the lake has a large picnic area, an interpretive trail, and camping. Maps are available at the Tourist Information Centre.

Motel prices in High Level are just a warm-up for those in the NWT, so don't be surprised at $60 rooms that you'd prefer to pay $30 for. The six motels in town are usually full throughout the year with work crews. Least expensive is **Family Motel,** tel. (403) 926-3395; $35 s, $40 d. The largest is **Sunset Motel,** tel. (403) 926-2272, which has a restaurant and bar; $55 s, $65 d. A free municipal campground is located east of town on Hwy. 35, and a primitive campground lies farther north at **Hutch Lake Recreation Area,** $9 per night. **Aspen Ridge Campground,** tel. (403) 926-4540, three km south of town, is privately owned and has coin showers and a laundry; unserviced sites $14, powered sites $17.

Hazems Family Restaurant, in front of the Family Motel, offers a Chinese buffet lunch ($7.95) and a regular dinner menu with main meals from $8. Another Chinese place is the **Canton Restaurant,** 100th Ave., tel. (403) 926-3053; the combo dinners seem like a good deal, but portions are small—stick to the main meals. The restaurant in the Sunset Motor Inn serves dishes starting at $10 including a salad bar (which also offers soup and fresh fruit). Also here is a lounge and nightclub open Friday and Saturday nights with occasional live bands.

Footner Lake Airport, north of town, is served by **Canadian Regional;** tel. (403) 926-3031 or (800) 665-1177. The **Greyhound Bus Depot** is located at 10101 95th St., tel. (403) 926-3233. Buses depart daily for Peace River ($36.45), continuing to Edmonton ($85.61).

The post office, banks, library, and a number of laundromats are located on 100th Street. The large **Tourist Information Centre,** tel. (403) 926-4811, is located at the south end of town (look for the excellent 3D map of northwestern Alberta). It's open in summer daily 9 a.m.-5 p.m., weekdays only the rest of the year.

Rainbow Lake

Rainbow Lake is an oil field community of 1,100, 141 km west of High Level along Hwy. 58. The town grew around oil-and-gas exploration during the 1960s. Vast reservoirs of these resources still lie underneath the ground, untapped until oil prices rise. **Husky Oil Operations** offers tours of its plant; call ahead at (403) 956-3757 for details. The town has a golf course, two motels, and two restaurants. A campground 24 km southwest of town has a few primitive sites; free. The other option is **Rainbow Lake Recreation Area**, 48 km south of town, where there's a beach with swimming, fishing, and campsites for $9.

Hay-Zama Lakes

This complex network of lakes, marshes, and streams is one of Canada's largest freshwater wetlands. It covers 800 square km and is home to over 200 species of birds. It's also the main source of the Hay River, which flows north to Great Slave Lake. This fragile ecosystem, 160 km northwest of High Level, is relatively remote, and would have remained that way except for the large reservoirs of oil that lay beneath its surface. Oil and birds do not mix, but drilling has gone ahead and the small community of **Zama City**, north of the lakes, has grown around the drilling project. The town is also the southern terminus for an interprovincial pipeline from the oil fields at Norman Wells (NWT). Strict environmental guidelines mean that most of the mining activity takes place during winter, after the many thousands of geese, ducks, and other shorebirds have migrated south. Although there are no designated roads or camping areas around the lakes, many gravel roads used by the natives and oil-exploration personnel lead through the area.

The Border or Bust

From High Level it is 191 km to the Alberta/ Northwest Territories border. The road follows the Meander River to a town of the same name at the confluence of the Hay River, which the road then parallels to the border. The settlement of **Meander River** is on a Dene Tha Indian Reserve and is noted for its many local artists. Watch for the local rabbit population living beside the road. North of the community, where the highway crosses the Hay River, a gravel road leads 63 km to the oil town of Zama City. Campgrounds are located north of Meander River and just south of the small community of **Steen River**, a base for forest-fire-fighting planes. Alberta's northernmost community is **Indian Cabins**, 14 km from the border. The cabins that gave the town its name are gone, but a traditional native cemetery with spirit houses covering the graves is located 200 meters north of the gas station. In the trees is the scaffold burial site of a child whose body was placed in a hollowed-out log and hung between the limbs of two trees.

NORTHWEST TERRITORIES
INCLUDING
NUNAVUT

KAREN McKINLEY

INTRODUCTION

As the world's last great wilderness frontiers slowly disappear, Canada's vast northlands—north of the 60th parallel—remain relatively untouched, unspoiled, and uninhabited. Once these lands were home only to small populations of indigenous Dene and Inuit people who had adapted to the harsh environment. But explorers, whalers, missionaries, and governments eventually found their way here, bringing rapid changes to native lifestyles. Today, travelers, adventurers, writers, artists, and scientists come in search of the territories' unlimited opportunities for naturalist and wilderness pursuits.

Within the region's borders are two of the world's 10 largest lakes, one of the world's longest rivers, a waterfall twice the height of Niagara, two UNESCO World Heritage Sites, five national parks, the glaciated peaks of Baffin and Ellesmere Islands, and an amazing abundance of wildlife.

THE LAND

The territories' 3.4 million square km take up a third of Canada—an area nearly half the size of the United States, with a population of only 64,500, just 0.2% of Canada's total population. Its borders stretch from the 60th parallel to the 84th, and from the Yukon to Davis Strait (just 50 km from Greenland)—over 3,200 km in each direction. The land can be divided into two regions: below the treeline and above it. The treeline is marked on most NWT maps as a single line that snakes from the southern reaches of Hudson Bay northwest to the Mackenzie Delta near Inuvik. The "line" provides a rough idea of where the boreal forest stops and the treeless tundra starts. But the actual transition takes place gradually across many kilometers and varies in latitude depending on the topography and climate of the particular area.

Apart from the **Mackenzie Mountains,** which form the NWT/Yukon border, the dominant natural feature of the mainland is the glacially scarred bedrock of the Canadian Shield. As ice from four or five ice ages receded north, it scoured the bedrock, carving hundreds of depressions—now lakes—and creating meltwater streams that today flow throughout the land. In the west is the **Mackenzie River,** 10th-longest river in the world. North and east of the Mackenzie River Valley the land is relatively flat. Only lakes, rivers, and low rolling hills break the monotonous landscape, which ends at the west coast of Hudson Bay and, farther north, at the Arctic coast. The tidal zone here is devoid of sessile life, which would be crushed by annual movement of pack ice. North of the Arctic coast are the lower Arctic islands, which are generally less than 300 meters above sea level, their gently rolling landscapes broken only by occasional bluffs. Finally, to the northeast are the islands of the high Arctic, where you'll find the classic Arctic landscape of mountains, icefields, glaciers, and icebergs. Here sheer cliffs rise thousands of meters out of the ice-choked waters of **Baffin Bay,** incised by steep-walled fiords that end at massive glaciers spilling over from the inland ice cap.

Climate

In general, the human species lives in the middle latitudes and is accustomed to the particular set of natural phenomena common to those latitudes—the sun rises in the east each morning and sets in the west each evening; night follows day; vegetation is lush; and water most often occurs as a liquid. But here in the north, these comfortable patterns don't exist. Here in winter, the sun doesn't rise for days (or, in some places, even months), while in summer, it circles endlessly around the horizon. And for over half the year, lakes, rivers, and the ocean aren't free-flowing water but solid ice.

The region's climate is harsh, but the image of the Canadian North being a land of eternal ice and snow is a misconception. During the summer months, from late May to September, the weather can be quite pleasant. Precipitation is slight, and the average July temperature in Yellowknife is 16° C—only three degrees cooler than Calgary. Farther north, the average July temperature in Inuvik is 13° C, and in Iqaluit 8° C. The highest temperature recorded in the territories was 41° C in Kugluktuk (Coppermine); the lowest, -57° C in Inuvik. In January, Yellowknife's average of -28° C is colder than that of Iqaluit, -26° C.

Much of the north is covered by **permafrost**— ground with an average annual temperature below freezing. In much of the mainland the top-soil melts each summer. This is known as an active layer of permafrost. But farther north, and in the Arctic archipelago, the ground remains continuously frozen in a layer two to 500 meters deep. This is called continuous permafrost.

Parks

Many of the territories' most spectacular landscape, wildlife concentrations, and sites of historical importance have been set aside as national, territorial, and historic parks. The western section of the territories possesses four national parks. These are **Wood Buffalo,** south and west of Fort Smith, and the second-largest national park in the world; **Nahanni,** in the rugged Mackenzie Mountains; **Aulavik,** on Banks Island, representative of Canada's Arctic lowlands and supporting one of the world's greatest concentrations of musk oxen; and **Tuktut Nogait,** between Paulatuk and Kugluktuk, the breeding ground of the Bluenose caribou herd. Nunavut boasts just two national parks, but both are spectacular. **Auyuittuq** is in the rugged mountains of Baffin Island while **Ellesmere Island,** the world's northernmost national park, lies at the tip of the North American continent. Proposals are currently under consideration to protect several additional areas as national parks, including the dramatic **East Arm of Great Slave Lake,** wildlife-rich **Wager Bay** on Hudson Bay, and the nesting grounds of millions of seabirds on **North Baffin Island.**

Territorial parks preserve and protect sites with historic or scenic value. The largest is **Katannilik,** stretching across Baffin Island's Meta Incognita Peninsula. The **Soper River** running through the park has been designated a **Canadian Heritage River.**

Among the 17 migratory bird sanctuaries in the territories are **Queen Maud Gulf,** the world's largest such sanctuary, and **McConnell River,** where one million lesser snow geese gather during the fall migration. **Thelon Game Sanctuary,** the only such area in Canada, is primarily for the conservation of wildlife but is also a popular area for wilderness river trips.

The Regions

On 1 January 1996 the Northwest Territories was divided to accommodate the political boundaries of Canada's newest territory, **Nunavut.** The name Nunavut is already widely used in the north, and in preparation for the change the Department of Economic Development and Tourism has incorporated the changes into current tourism literature. This Handbook does likewise.

As well as dividing the Northwest Territories in two, the following chapters break down the region even further. The **Accessible North** is immediately north of Alberta and has a good road system linking Hay River, on the south shore of Great Slave Lake, to Fort Smith and Wood Buffalo National Park. Across the lake to the north is the territorial capital, **Yellowknife**, and outlying Dene communities. The spectacular mountainous region in the southwest corner of the NWT, including Nahanni National Park, has for generations been known as **Rivers of Myth, Mountains of Mystery.** These mountains and Great Slave Lake form part of the watershed that drains into the **Mackenzie River Valley.** The Mackenzie flows into the Arctic Ocean in the **Western Arctic,** north of Inuvik, at the end of North America's northernmost public road.

The massive territory of Nunavut will encompass three distinct areas of Canada's far north. West of Nunavut is the **Arctic coast,** a barren, treeless land where small Inuit communities rely on the abundance of marine mammals and arctic char for survival. Traditionally known as the Keewatin, the west coast of **Hudson Bay** is an area rich in human history and wildlife. Finally, the mountainous islands of the eastern and high Arctic, including Baffin and Ellesmere, offer some of the continent's premier wilderness adventures, and are covered under **Baffin and Beyond.**

FLORA

The Northwest Territories include two main biomes. The **subarctic** biome, below the treeline, is predominantly evergreens interspersed with tundra vegetation. **Black spruce, white spruce, jack pine** (the most northerly of the pines), and **aspen** are the most common trees found here. **White birch** is the only deciduous tree able to withstand the region's climate. Due to little precipitation and a short growing season (70-80 frost-free days annually), tree growth is slow and stunted, especially closer to the treeline.

Above the treeline, in an area of continuous permafrost, is the **arctic** biome—the tundra. Here a unique selection of vegetation has successfully adapted to the region's extreme seasonal changes of temperature and sunlight, as well as its lack of precipitation (less than the Sahara Desert). Where water and wind have deposited soil—usually in depressions or along the banks of rivers—the vegetation is more varied. Almost all plants are perennials, able to spring to life quickly after a winter of hibernation. Brightly colored flowers such as **yellow arctic poppies, purple saxifrage, pink rhododendrons,** and **white heather** carpet entire landscapes during the short summer. **Willows** are one of the few woody plants to survive on the otherwise treeless tundra—they're found across the Arctic mainland along with **ground birch** and **Labrador tea.** Other areas are almost completely void of soil, supporting little more than **arctic ferns, lichens,** and **mosses.** Low temperatures here restrict bacterial action, and as a result, the soil is lacking in the nitrogen necessary for plant growth. Occasional oases of lush vegetation mark spots where the soil received a nitrogen boost—as from a rotting animal carcass or the detritus of an ancient Inuit campsite.

The sparse plantlife of the Arctic is inadequate as a human food source, but all the region's plants are edible. A popular Inuit drink is made by boiling **sorrel grass** then adding sugar. When chilled, this concoction is cool and refreshing.

FAUNA

Species *diversity* in the Northwest Territories is relatively low compared to other parts of the world. Species *concentrations* here, however, are enormous, including some of the world's largest populations of caribou, musk oxen, polar bears, whales, and seabirds. The same species are found below the treeline in the Mackenzie River Basin as are found in the mountainous and northern parts of Alberta. Of note are the high numbers of **black bears** and **moose,** especially prevalent along the Liard Hwy.; the **Dall's sheep** that roam the Mackenzie Mountains; and the hybrid **bison** of Wood Buffalo National Park.

Caribou

Caribou, standing 1.5 meters tall at the shoulder, seem ungainly but have adapted superbly to life in the Arctic. Those on the mainland normally live in small groups, but congregate each fall for a migration west to the boreal forest. As many as 400,000 of the animals may band together into a single herd. Each spring the process is reversed as they head east to summer calving grounds, high above the treeline. Caribou are also found on islands of the Arctic archipelago, as far north as Ellesmere Island.

Grizzly Bears

Although there is only one species of grizzly bear— whether they be on the tundra of the Northwest Territories, on Alaska's Kodiak Island, or in the forests of northern Russia—populations in different parts of the world have each made unique adaptations to their particular environment. The grizzlies inhabiting lands north of the treeline feed mostly on the vegetation alongside Arctic streams but occasionally hunt down other animals. One was spotted hunting seals on pack ice north of Victoria Island, 500 km north of the bears' usual range.

MIKE WELLINS

Musk Oxen

These shaggy beasts, hunted to near extinction by 1900, are now restricted to the Arctic archipelago and Thelon Game Sanctuary and number approximately 80,000. The image of them in a defensive circle, protecting the young from predators or the cold, is an endearing symbol of the north. Known to the Inuit as *oomingmak*, meaning "bearded one," they are covered with an underlayer of short, fine wool and a topcoat of shaggy hair up to 60 centimeters long. This gives the animals their characteristic prehistoric appearance and helps protect them from frequent blizzards and winter temperatures that in some areas average -30° C.

Polar Bears

Evolving from the grizzly bear 250,000-400,000 years ago, the polar bear may weigh up to 600 kilograms and measure 3.5 meters from head to tail. Its most distinctive feature is a pure white coat, but it also has a long body with a large neck.

The bear's scientific name, *Ursus maritimus*, aptly describes its habitat, that of the permanent pack ice of the Arctic Ocean and the eastern coastline down to Hudson Bay. Polar bears are at home in the sea and have been known to swim hundreds of kilometers. Their most common hunting strategy is to wait at a hole in the ice, days at a time, for a seal that needs to take a breath.

Whales

Only three of the world's 80 species of whales are widespread in the waters of the Canadian Arctic. **Belugas**—also called white whales for their coloring—are most common. They winter in the Bering Sea and off the west coast of Greenland, and migrate to estuarine areas such as the Mackenzie Delta in the western Arctic for summer calving season. **Bowheads** were the most intensely hunted of all whales, mainly due to their slow speed and great yield of blubber. The bowhead weighs as much as 50,000 kilograms and may reach 20 meters in length. Two separate populations inhabit these waters—one spends summer in the Beaufort Sea, the other in Lancaster Sound and Davis Strait.

The **narwhal** got its name from the Old Norse word *nar,* meaning "corpse"—a reference to the whale's mottled gray color. Distinguished by an ivory tusk that spirals from the male's head—an extension of a tooth—it was probably from this mammal that the European legend of the unicorn was born. It is one of the least understood of all whale species, wintering under the pack ice of Baffin Bay and Davis Strait and migrating north in pods of up to 300 each spring. Its remarkable circulatory system allows it to dive to great depths without suffering from the bends upon surfacing.

A fourth species, the **killer whale,** is occasionally seen in the Beaufort Sea and Davis Strait.

Walruses

With its massive build and sabrelike tusks, the walrus presents a formidable and intriguing

NWT ECONOMIC DEVELOPMENT & TOURISM

walrus

sight. They spend the summer months sunning themselves on pack ice or on isolated shorelines, and spend winter at the edge of the pack ice or at recurring polynyas in the high Arctic. Their main diet consists of mollusks, but they've also been known to eat fish and seals. Males can weigh up to 1,400 kilograms.

Seals

Five types of seals inhabit the Canadian Arctic. The most abundant, smallest, and most important to the Inuit are **ringed seals,** the name referring to the cream-colored circular markings on their backs. Largest are the **bearded seals,** which weigh up to 250 kilograms and have facial whiskers resembling a beard. **Harp seals** are found primarily around the coastline of Baffin Island. In the early 1980s, they were the focus of an emotional campaign aimed at ending hunting of the species. **Harbour seals** and **hooded seals,** although common, are found only in Hudson Bay and the waters of Davis Strait.

Fish

Arctic grayling are found in all watersheds on the mainland and are particularly common in the Mackenzie River Basin. **Inconnu,** a member of the whitefish family, inhabit the Hay River and are occasionally caught in the Big Buffalo and Taltson Rivers. **Lake whitefish** occur mainly in lakes and are bottom feeders. They are also the most valuable commercial fish in the territories; Great Slave Lake is the center of the industry. **Pickerel,** known as walleye in the south, inhab-

it small lakes in the southwest. **Northern pike** live around aquatic vegetation in slow-moving rivers and have been recorded weighing up to 18 kilograms. **Lake trout** are common in Great Slave and Great Bear Lakes but also occur in fast-flowing rivers and small lakes.

The most dominant fish of the Arctic is the **arctic char,** a member of the salmon family. It weighs an average of three to four kilograms but can grow to seven. The char spends most of its life in the freshwater of inland lakes, but each summer it makes a run to the ocean, returning after only a few weeks. They occur throughout the Arctic archipelago and in rivers and lakes along the coast.

Birds

Around 280 species of birds have been recorded in the territories, of which 70 nest exclusively north of the 60th parallel. These figures do no justice to the many millions of shorebirds, waterfowl, and seabirds that migrate north each spring to breed. Birds from six continents and 30 countries flock here each year, including species such as **gulls, kittiwakes, terns, fulmars, eiders,** and **geese.** Other species, such as **ptarmigan** and **ravens,** spend all year in the region. The winner for the longest migration goes to the **arctic tern,** which flies here from Antarctica. Many of Canada's endangered species spend summer here; the **Ross gull** prefers Queen Maud Gulf, while the **whooping crane,** for many years thought to be extinct, nests in Wood Buffalo National Park.

HISTORY

Prehistory

Two distinct groups of natives lived in the Canadian north for thousands of years before European exploration in the region. About 15,000 years ago, at the end of the last ice age, a group of people migrated from Siberia across the Bering Strait—then solid ice—and fanned out across North and South America. At first, the northern extent of their range was limited by the polar ice cap. But as the ice cap retreated, the people spread north. Over the generations, some of them eventually found their way to the Mackenzie River Basin, where they lived as hunters and gatherers. These people were known as the **Dene.**

The second group crossed the Bering ice bridge much later—around 10,000 years ago—and settled in Alaska. Eventually, people from this group would mi-

grate across the Arctic coast in two major waves. The first wave occurred around 4,000 years ago when the people known as the **Dorset culture** began to move east. They lived in skin tents in summer, and snow houses—previously unknown in Alaska—in winter. The second eastward migration, that of the **Thule culture,** occurred about 1,000 years ago and picked up elements of the Dorset culture—such as snow houses and intricate carvings—as it progressed. The Thule lived in semipermanent villages and specialized in hunting sea mammals. It is the Thule who are ancestors of the Inuit.

European Contact

The first European contact with the Inuit was recorded by expeditions searching for the **Northwest Passage.** (Vikings probably encountered the Inuit earlier, but no written record is available to prove it.) European contact with the Dene occurred much later but was more extensive, and the results more dramatic. Many Dene died of diseases brought by the white settlers, and the Dene lifestyle changed forever as they gave up their nomadic existence to settle around trading posts. Rivalry between the Hudson's Bay Company and the North West Company pushed traders farther north in search of furs. By 1900, the whaling industry was in decline and the fur trade of the Mackenzie was finished, but posts remained throughout the north. In 1905, when the provinces of Alberta and Saskatchewan were created, administration of the NWT remained with Ottawa. Local issues were left to the RCMP while the church was responsible for medical and education services.

The Twentieth Century

While many Inuit and Dene continued a nomadic way of life into the 20th century, rapid changes were soon to come. The WW II-instigated construction of military installations such as airfields and Distant Early Warning Line stations

BOB RACE

WHOOPING CRANES

The whooping crane, *Grus americana*, has become a symbol of human efforts to protect endangered species in North America. Whoopers, as they are commonly called, have never been prolific. Their naturally low reproduction rate, coupled with severe degradation of their habitat, caused their numbers at one point to dip as low as 21. This small flock wintered along the Texas coast in Aransas National Wildlife Refuge, but no one knew where their summer breeding grounds were. The last time infant whoopers had been seen in the wild was 1922, when a Saskatchewan game warden found a nesting couple and preserved a newly hatched chick for posterity. The mystery was solved in 1954 when a helicopter pilot spotted nesting whoopers in Wood Buffalo National Park. Ever since, a concerted effort has been made to increase their population, including an intense captive-breeding program. The birds arrive in the park in late April, with some pairs nesting in the same area for up to 15 years. Each pair produces two eggs but raises only one chick, leaving the other to die. By late September the young chicks have learned to fly and the flock migrates south, taking 20-40 days to cover the 4,000 km to the Texas coast.

PROVINCIAL ARCHIVES OF ALBERTA

The first bank in the NWT was erected at Fort Smith in the 1870s.

created an economic boom and a wage economy for many natives, while the construction of schools and hospitals throughout the 1950s gradually led natives to move into towns.

Mining has played an important role in the development of the north since Martin Frobisher took 1,000 tons of fool's gold back to England in 1576. Mineral and oil exploration had taken place for decades, but the introduction of aircraft opened the north up for mining. In the last 60 years, versatile bush planes—capable of carrying heavy loads and landing on short strips—have contributed to the expansion of the north.

GOVERNMENT

The NWT is one of Canada's two territories (the other is the Yukon). Its government is led by a commissioner with the advice of a legislative assembly. Unlike in Canada's provinces, natural resources remain sole responsibility of the federal government. The legislative assembly does not operate on a party system and a majority of members are of Dene or Inuit descent.

Nunavut
On 1 April 1999 the map of Canada will have to be redrawn when Canada's third territory, Nunavut, is born. Nunavut, meaning "Our Land," encompasses the Keewatin, Arctic coast, and Baffin regions—over two million square km—and is home to 22,000 people, of whom 18,000

are Inuit. While native groups around the world dragged issues of land claims through courts, held demonstrations, and, in parts of Canada, took up arms, the Inuit led a low-profile 15-year campaign that in July 1993 culminated in the passage in Canadian Parliament of the historic bill creating Nunavut. But Nunavut is a lot more than the world's largest land claim. It is an enormous step for the Inuit. One hundred years ago, many of them had never seen a white person; now they will assume responsibility for a chunk of land twice as big as Ontario—Canada's largest province—and will have outright ownership of about 18% of the land, including subsurface mineral rights. The capital of the new territory will be **Iqaluit**. The working language of the government will be **Inuktitut**.

Although Nunavut is a victory for the Inuit, it won't automatically solve the many social problems experienced in the region—unemployment is three times the national average, cost of living is twice the national average. Only 21 km of government-maintained roads cross the region, and only five percent of its population has completed high school. Nevertheless, after 100 years, the Inuit will once again have control of their land.

ECONOMY

Those communities accessible by road have a cost of living comparable to other areas of Canada, while those in the remote Arctic regions are up to 100% higher. Most consumer goods are imported from other parts of Canada, and all transportation costs must be added. Higher prices are offset by higher wages (the Northwest Territories has Canada's highest average weekly earnings—around $700), but visitors should arrive well prepared. The economy of the Northwest Territories relies heavily on non-renewable resources and less so on renewable resources. Although the federal and territorial governments are the largest employers, mining is the mainstay of the economy.

Mining

Apart from the government, mining is the territories' largest employer, employing 10% of the total NWT workforce and paying over $100 million in wages annually. In addition to the money mining companies spend in the north, they pay the government millions in taxes and royalties, which helps the local economy. Seven mines in the territories produce $1 billion worth of minerals annually. The principal minerals extracted are zinc and gold, with yields totaling 25% and 10%, respectively, of all Canadian production. Although Yellowknife has two gold mines within its city limits, **Lupin,** on the barrenlands 400 km northeast, is Canada's largest gold mine. Lupin and four other mines produce a total of 15,000 kilograms of gold annually while the territories' other two mines, at Nanisivik and on Little Cornwallis Island, combined extract 20,000 kilograms of silver, 32,000 tons of lead, and 176,355 tons of zinc.

Rumors of diamonds on the barrenlands had been rife for many years, but until 1991 no serious attempt was made to confirm the viability of mining the remote tract of land between Great Slave Lake and the Arctic Ocean. That summer and the following two summers 13,000 claims were staked totaling 11.8 million hectares. The rush confirmed the gems were there, but extraction is a long and expensive process. On 21 June 1996 BHP Minerals, a subsidiary of BHP, one of the world's mining giants, was granted approval by an Environmental Assessment Review Panel to commence mining 300 km northeast of Yellowknife at Lac de Gras. The mine will employ over 700 workers and projected revenue is $500 million annually (to reach this goal requires the extraction of 9,000 carats—about five cupfuls—daily).

While the approval of the territories' first diamond mine grabbed all the headlines in June 1996, it was the end of an era at **Norman Wells,** on the Mackenzie River, when, after over 70 years, the north's only producing oil field closed. But the oil under Norman Wells is only a tiny fraction of the vast reserves located in the Mackenzie Delta and islands of the high Arctic. In the future, as oil prices rise and supplies elsewhere in the world decline, extraction will become commercially viable.

Mineral exploration is also a major component of the economy. In 1993 $60 million was spent looking for diamonds, alone, and BHP spent $170 million in the territories even before being granted approval to commence mining.

Other Industry

Fishing has long been important to the economy of Hay River, the territories' second-largest town. Commercial fishing began in 1945, when 10 companies had dozens of boats trawling the farthest reaches of Great Slave Lake. The industry continues to this day, with lake trout, inconnu, pickerel, and northern pike transported from out on the lake to Hay River for packaging and processing.

Hunting and trapping had, until WW II, been the staple of the territorial economy; today they remain an important part of native lifestyle.

Tourism has grown quickly to become the second-largest slice in the NWT economic pie. Its importance to the economy will continue to rise as more people become aware of the region's potential.

PEOPLE

In 1994 the population of the Northwest Territories was 63,000, and it's been growing in recent years at four percent annually. Roughly half the population is of native descent. Three groups of indigenous northerners inhabit the NWT. The Dene and Métis peoples are found along the Mackenzie River Basin, while the Inuit live north of the treeline, along the Arctic coast, and in the Arctic archipelago.

The native peoples of the Arctic are often called Eskimos. This term comes from the French *esquimau,* a word derived from the Algonquin *esquimantsic* meaning "eater of raw fish." Although not derogatory, the natives of the Arctic feel it puts them in poor light. They prefer to use more specific terms. The most widely used of these is "Inuit," referring to those people of the Arctic coast and eastern Arctic regions of Canada. "Inuvialuit" refers to people of the Mackenzie Delta, and "Inupiat" and "Yup'ik" to those of the Alaskan coastlines.

Dene
The Dene (DEN-ay) people comprise of seven groups—Chipewyan, Dogrib, Gwich'in, Hare, Loucheux, Nahanni, and Slavey—that are part of the Athabascan family. As ice from the last ice age receded, North American Indians whose ancestors had migrated from Siberia moved north in small groups. They were nomadic hunters whose survival depended on their ability to fish and hunt in a harsh environment. This pattern of life changed dramatically with the coming of Europeans; the old trading systems and nomadic lifestyles were given up for life in settlements around trading posts. Today many Dene live a traditional lifestyle, while others have moved into a wage economy. All have developed influential political organizations such as the Dene Nation to seek increased control of their own affairs.

Métis
The Métis, numbering around 7,000 in the territories, are of mixed French Canadian and Cree or Dene descent. They were traditionally employed as workers for the major fur-trading companies and settled along the Mackenzie and Slave Rivers in the 18th and 19th centuries. They were well suited for positions with trading companies as they were bilingual. The Métis were responsible for bringing commerce to the north, and they continue to play an integral role in the territories' commercial world. Like the Dene, culture plays an important role in their lives and they have formed a political organization known as the Métis Nation.

Inuit
The Inuit live mainly above the treeline and along the coast and are the largest group of native people in the NWT, numbering around 19,000. Their distant ancestors, the Thule, specialized in hunting whales. While the Inuit's physical adaptation to Arctic conditions has been phenomenal, their recent Asian origins can be seen in the epicanthic eyefold. They are a short, stocky people, with small hands and feet. Their survival depended on insulated clothing and a diet high in saturated fats. Traditionally the Inuit hunted marine mammals in the spring, moved inland to hunt caribou in summer, and spent fall preparing for the long winter. By the end of the 1800s they had developed a dependence on white man's goods, brought by whalers. Diseases devastated their numbers in the 1940s, and when the fur-trading economy collapsed, the federal government began settling the Inuit in communities. Today, most still have strong ties to the land, living a traditional lifestyle hunting and fishing. They are also heavily involved in their own political and economic future, having successfully negotiated the world's largest land claim.

RECREATION

Although the vast wilderness of the NWT is the perfect destination for adventure, the climate can be unpredictable, severe, and dangerous for the ill-prepared. Help may be hundreds of kilometers away; you must be able to take care of yourself. Before setting out you should file travel plans with local authorities. In some areas, you are required to travel with a local guide—these arrangements should be made well in advance. Those planning their own adventure should first write to Arctic Expeditions Secretariat, Circumpolar and Scientific Affairs, Department of Indian and Northern Affairs Canada, Ottawa, ON K1A 0H4, for their booklet *Guide for Expeditions to Northern and Arctic Canada.*

Hiking
For all the wilderness in the north, opportunities for extended hikes along established trails are limited. The **Canol Heritage Trail** is a 372-km hike from the NWT/Yukon border to the Mackenzie River along a service road established in WW II. The most popular area for wilderness hiking is **Auyuittuq National Park** on Baffin Island. To explore either of these areas requires much advance planning and a big budget. **Katannilik Territorial Park,** near Lake Harbour, also has excellent hiking.

Canoeing and Kayaking

A number of adventure outfitters offer whitewater trips down some of the territories' most exciting rivers. For those with experience in both river *and* wilderness travel there are some excellent opportunities for extended river trips. The legendary **Nahanni River** is at the top of many people's to-do list. It provides unrivaled wildlife viewing, the excitement of fast-flowing water, and beautiful scenery. Other popular rivers include the **Burnside**, which bisects the vast barrenlands; the **Coppermine**, which combines isolation, wildlife, and history; the **Thomsen**, the world's northernmost navigable river; and the **Soper**, on Baffin Island. All of these rivers are run by outfitters. Experienced paddlers who can handle the challenging logistics can organize their own expedition and save some money.

Whitney & Smith, P.O. Box 2097, Banff, AB T0L 0C0, tel. (403) 678-3052, fax. (403) 678-5176, features sea kayaking adventures through the high Arctic. Led by trained biologists, the trips offer the unique perspective of viewing marine mammals from sea level. The trips, along with a sea kayaking expedition through the remote waters of Polar Inlet, northwestern Greenland, depart from Resolute in July and August. **Canadian River Expeditions**, P.O. Box 1023, Whistler, BC V0N 1B0, tel. (800) 898-7238, has an eight-day trip in mid-June to Lancaster Sound on Baffin Island. From an onshore base camp, sea kayaks are used to search out marine mammals congregating at the retreating floe edge. **Subarctic Wilderness Adventures**, P.O. Box 685, Fort Smith, NT X0E 0P0, tel. (403) 872-2467, rents just about everything you'd need for a northern adventure, right down to bug-proof clothing and microscopes. Canoes and rafts are $25 per day, $125 per week, and kayaks are $30 per day, $150 per week. **Peter Clarkson**, P.O. Box 1554, Inuvik, NT X0E 0T0, tel. (403) 979-2594, rents canoes for travel along the Mackenzie River and central Arctic. He has canoes in Inuvik, Norman Wells, and Cambridge Bay but can help with logistics for canoe dropoffs just about anywhere. The rate of $200 per week includes life jackets, paddles, and spray jackets. Peter also sells used canoes and will buy them from paddlers pulling off the Mackenzie River at Inuvik.

Fishing

The NWT has countless rivers, streams, and lakes teeming with fish that are both exciting to catch and delicious to eat. Inland lakes and rivers are the domain of trophy-size **lake trout, arctic grayling, pickerel,** and **northern pike.** Great Bear Lake holds world records in *every* class of lake trout and arctic grayling. The **arctic char,** caught in rivers, lakes, and the open ocean of the Arctic coast and Arctic archipelago, is famous as a fighting fish and as an acclaimed northern delicacy. The NWT also holds the overall world record for this species—an arctic char weighing a whopping 14.7 kilograms was caught in the Tree River.

Plummer's, 950 Bradford St., Winnipeg, MB R3H 0N5, tel. (204) 774-5775 or (800) 665-0240, operates fishing lodges on Great Slave and Great Bear Lakes. Rates for six days including charter flights from Winnipeg or Edmonton, professionally equipped boats, accommodations, and all meals are $2,695 per person.

Before fishing you'll need a license, available from sport stores, co-ops, and outfitters. A three-day license will cost $15 for Canadians, $30 for nonresidents. An annual license is $20 or $40, respectively. A separate license is required for fishing in national parks. For the *NWT Sport Fishing Guide* write to Fisheries and Oceans, P.O. Box 2310, Yellowknife, NT X1A 2L9.

ACCOMMODATIONS AND FOOD

Indoor Accommodations

Every community has at least one hotel, often run by the local native co-op. Prices in Yellowknife and southern towns begin at around $100 s or d for a basic room. Farther north, and in those communities without road access, prices are generally quoted per person, ranging $90-170. Often, the hotel offers the only restaurant in town and meals will be included in the rate ($50-80 per person per day). In smaller communities you will be asked to share your room if it's busy, and it is standard practice to accept. Bed and breakfasts, starting at $55 s, $65 d, operate in Yellowknife, Inuvik, and Iqaluit.

Campgrounds

Camping is the only way to stay cheaply in the north. Territorial campgrounds are located at regular intervals along the road system. Some are very basic; others—usually those on the outskirts of towns—have showers. Most have bug-proof kitchen shelters. They are $10 per night or $100 for a 14-night pass for one park. Payment is often on an honor system. Many of the more remote communities have an area designated for campers, often a short walk from the airport. Always make a point of asking at the hamlet office before pitching a tent away from a designated area. In national parks and other wilderness areas campers should practice no-trace camping and pack out all rubbish. North of the treeline there is no source of firewood (although driftwood can often be found on beaches). This means that a lightweight campstove is indispensable. White gas, known as naphtha in the north, is not allowed on scheduled flights but is available in most northern stores and co-ops. If it's late in the season, call ahead to check availability—some communities only receive supplies once a year.

Food

Part of the northern experience is tasting local foods. Most restaurants serve these dishes when availability allows. Favorites are musk ox, caribou, and arctic char, all of which can be bought as jerky or, from meat co-ops, as steaks. When meals are part of an accommodations package, they are usually served cafeteria-style and offer little or no choice. For a true northern experience, have a meal at the **Wild Cat Cafe** in Yellowknife or **To Go's** on Inuvik's main drag.

GETTING THERE

Air

The main air route into the NWT is from Edmonton or Calgary, in Alberta, to the capital Yellowknife, from where easy connections can be made throughout the north. Airlines flying this route are: **Canadian North,** tel. (800) 665-1177 or in the U.S. (800) 426-7000, and **NWT Air,** tel. (800) 661-0789. From Edmonton, both charge $426 one-way, $469 for a 14-day APEX roundtrip. Fares from Calgary are only slightly

higher. From Whitehorse (Yukon), **Alkan Air,** tel. (403) 668-2107 or (800) 661-0432, flies four times weekly to Inuvik; $310 one-way, $620 roundtrip.

For destinations in Nunavut, **Canadian North** and **First Air,** tel. (800) 267-1247, fly at least once daily to Iqaluit from Ottawa and Montreal; $715 one-way, $807 for a 14-day APEX roundtrip with taxes being less from Montreal. **NWT Air** flies between Winnipeg and the Nunavut communities of Rankin Inlet ($657 one-way, $643 for a seven-day APEX roundtrip) and Iqaluit ($1,141 one-way, $1,164 for a seven-day APEX roundtrip). From Montreal and Great Whale River **Air Inuit,** tel. (514) 636-9445, flies to Iqaluit via Sanikiluaq (Belcher Islands) and Cape Dorset.

For those keen on circumpolar travel **First Air** flies to Iqaluit from Sondrestrom Fjord (Greenland) twice weekly; $360 one-way, $432 for a 14-day APEX roundtrip. This could, conceivably, be linked with an **SAS** flight from Copenhagen or an **Icelandair** flight from New York or Luxembourg via Reykjavik. The best people to contact for travel in this part of the world are at **Arctic Experience,** 29 Nork Way, Banstead, Surrey SM7 1PB, England, tel. 0737-362321.

Bus

From Edmonton, **Greyhound,** tel. (403) 421-4211, or, in Canada only, (800) 661-8747, goes as far north as Hay River ($128.23 one-way), just over the NWT border.

Car

Driving is the most popular way to come north. The main route is the **Mackenzie Highway,** which begins northwest of Edmonton at Grimshaw. From Grimshaw the road is paved beyond the 60th parallel to Hay River. From there, gravel highways lead east to Fort Smith and Wood Buffalo National Park, northwest to Yellowknife, and west to Fort Simpson. A loop known as the **Deh Cho Connection** can be made by taking the **Liard Highway** from southeast of Fort Simpson, south to Fort Nelson (British Columbia) and back to Edmonton. The other route north is the **Dempster Highway** from Dawson City (Yukon) to Inuvik in the western Arctic. This is the northernmost public road on the continent.

GETTING AROUND

Air

In many cases, the only way to get from place to place is by plane. If you are flying into the NWT make reservations for all onward flights before coming north; this works out much cheaper than buying flight sectors separately. If roundtrip tickets are bought 14 days in advance, and you meet certain requirements, they will be similar in price to one-way tickets bought on the spot. Student standby tickets (anyone under 25) will save 30-60% of regular ticket prices. Officially, stops are not permitted on regular fares, but if you buy the tickets in the north, and have some skill at negotiation, you may be able to work something out.

The major carriers are: **Canadian North,** tel. (800) 665-1177, serving all major centers in the NWT; **NWT Air,** tel. (800) 661-0789, serving Inuvik, Cambridge Bay, and Iqaluit; and **First Air,** tel. (800) 267-1247, serving the Baffin and Arctic coast regions with connections to Yellowknife. Each of the above has affiliated connector airlines serving smaller communities. **Air Nunavut,** tel. (819) 979-2400, operates services around the Baffin region.

Bus

Frontier Coachlines, tel. (403) 873-4892, continues to Fort Smith and Yellowknife from Hay River (the end of the line for Greyhound). A good transportation deal is offered by **Touch the Arctic Adventure Tours,** tel. (800) 661-0894. It includes bus transportation between Edmonton and Yellowknife with a return flight to Edmonton for $355 per person. To include Inuvik in the itinerary (roundtrip flight from Yellowknife) is $679 per person.

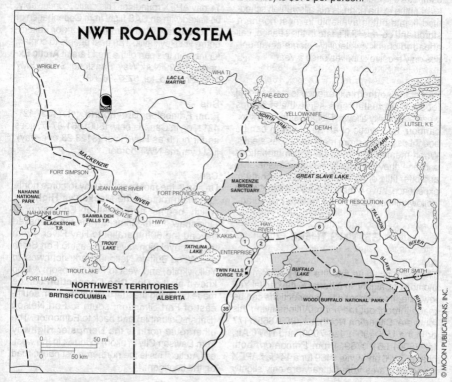

NWT ROAD SYSTEM

© MOON PUBLICATIONS, INC.

Floatplanes are an integral mode of transportation in the north.

Car and RV Rental

Car rental companies with offices in Yellowknife include **Avis,** tel. (403) 873-5648; **Budget,** tel. (403) 873-3366; **Rent-a-Relic,** tel. (403) 873-3400; and **Tilden,** tel. (403) 920-2970. Avis also has offices in Fort Smith, tel. (403) 872-2211, and Inuvik, tel. (403) 979-4751, while Budget has rentals available in Fort Simpson, tel. (403) 874-2808.

Frontier RV Rentals, P.O. Box 1088, Yellowknife, NT X0E 0N0, tel. (403) 873-5413, rents a variety of campers, but the kilometer charge will add up quickly on northern highways.

Tours

The *Northwest Territories Explorers' Guide* provides a full listing of all tour operators and outfitters in the territories. **Touch the Arctic Adventure Tours,** operated by NWT Air, offers a cross section of tours to suit all tastes. The tours include air transportation from Yellowknife or Edmonton, accommodations, and services of local outfitters, and they are also exceptional value, as the included airfares are at a reduced rate. Some of the highlights include day tours to Inuvik or Rankin Inlet, fishing adventures, running the South Nahanni River, and extended tours around Yellowknife. The programs don't stop at the end of summer. Some unique winter options to consider are viewing the northern lights from the barrenlands north of Yellowknife and experiencing the winter lifestyle in Inuvik, shrouded in darkness for two months a year. For details call (800) 661-0894.

INFORMATION

Money

All prices quoted in this book are in the local currency, **Canadian dollars.** As this book went to press, one American dollar would buy you $1.40 Canadian. Banks are located in all major centers, and you should check with hotels and outfitters before expecting them to accept U.S. dollars or credit cards. The NWT is liable to the same taxes as Alberta, including the seven percent Goods and Services Tax (GST), which applies to all goods and services, including hotel accommodations.

Telephone

The NWT has two area codes: **403** is used for all phone numbers except those in Nunavut, where the area code is **819.**

Road Information

For information on highways through the Accessible North section call (800) 661-0750. For information on the Dempster Hwy., call (403) 979-2678. For ferry information call (800) 661-0751. If you plan a trip north during spring or fall, call ahead to confirm dates of river crossing closures at freeze-up and break-up.

Tourism Information

For detailed information on accommodations and outfitters, write to **NWT Economic Devel-**

opment and Tourism, P.O. Box 1320, Yellowknife, NT X1A 2L9, tel. (800) 661-0788. On the Internet, their web site can be found at http://www.edt.gov.nt.ca. Nunavut, Canada's new territory as of 1 April 1999, already has a tourism department. For details on the region—encompassing the Arctic coast, Hudson Bay communities (Keewatin), and Baffin Island—contact **Nunavut Tourism,** P.O. Box 1450, Iqaluit, NT X0A 0H0, tel. (819) 979-6551 or (800) 491-7910. The e-mail address is nunatour@nunanet.com.

Chasmosaurus

BOB RACE

NORTHWEST TERRITORIES
THE ACCESSIBLE NORTH

Whether it's your first time or your 40th, crossing the 60th parallel marks the beginning of a new adventure. And the adventure starts in the most accessible section of the territories, sandwiched between the Alberta/NWT border and Great Slave Lake. It's a vast expanse of spruce, poplar, and aspen forests, stunted in growth by the harsh climate and scarred by wildfires that sweep unforgivingly through the region every few years. Two of North America's largest rivers, the **Slave** and **Mackenzie,** flow through the area en route to the Arctic Ocean. Many of their smaller tributaries are perfect for wilderness canoe trips and offer streamside hiking and some of the world's best fly-fishing. To the north lies **Great Slave Lake,** named for the Slavey Dene who have trapped and fished along its southern shores for thousands of years. This vast inland sea of freshwater is the world's 10th-largest lake. It covers an area of 28,438 square km and is 456 km in length. It is also the world's sixth-deepest lake (615 meters), meaning water

temperatures remain cold year-round and ice is present for at least five months of the year. The lake remains frozen long after the rivers flowing into it have broken up, creating an annual cycle of flooding at rivermouths.

The region's main communities are Hay River, on the south shore of Great Slave Lake, and Fort Smith, gateway to Wood Buffalo National Park, the second-largest national park in the world. Paved and improved gravel roads link the two towns and continue around the west and north sides of Great Slave Lake to the territorial capital, Yellowknife.

60TH PARALLEL TO HAY RIVER

The wood-and-stone structure marking the 60th parallel is a welcome sight after the long drive north through Alberta up the Mackenzie Highway. North of the border, the highway number changes from 35 to 1, and follows the Hay River

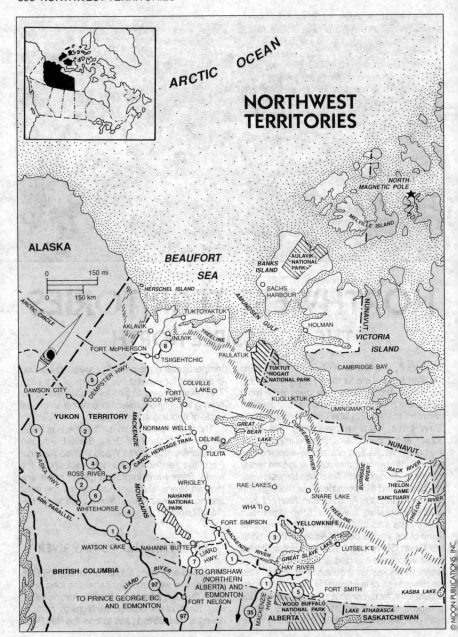

ARCTIC OCEAN

NORTHWEST TERRITORIES

NORTH-MAGNETIC POLE

MELVILLE ISLAND

ALASKA

BEAUFORT SEA

AULAVIK NATIONAL PARK

BANKS ISLAND

SACHS HARBOUR

HERSCHEL ISLAND

AMUNDSEN GULF

HOLMAN

NUNAVUT

VICTORIA ISLAND

0   150 mi
0   150 km

ARCTIC CIRCLE

TUKTOYAKTUK

AKLAVIK

INUVIK

TREELINE

PAULATUK

CAMBRIDGE BAY

FORT McPHERSON

8

TSIIGEHTCHIC

TUKTUT NOGAIT NATIONAL PARK

DEMPSTER HWY.

5

COLVILLE LAKE

KUGLUKTUK

DAWSON CITY

FORT GOOD HOPE

UMINGMAKTOK

YUKON TERRITORY

1   2

NORMAN WELLS

GREAT BEAR LAKE

COPPERMINE RIVER

NUNAVUT

MACKENZIE

CANOL HERITAGE TRAIL

DELINE

TULITA

BACK RIVER

4

ROSS RIVER

6

WRIGLEY

RAE LAKES

BURNSIDE RIVER

THELON GAME SANCTUARY

ALASKA HWY.

2

60th PARALLEL

6

MOUNTAINS

NAHANNI NATIONAL PARK

SNARE LAKE

TREELINE

THELON RIVER

WHITEHORSE

4

WHA TI

FORT SIMPSON

YELLOWKNIFE

1

MACKENZIE RIVER

3

WATSON LAKE

NAHANNI BUTTE

LIARD HWY.

7

LIARD RIVER

1

GREAT SLAVE LAKE

LUTSEL K'E

HAY RIVER

BRITISH COLUMBIA

97

TO GRIMSHAW (NORTHERN ALBERTA) AND EDMONTON

FORT NELSON

1

FORT SMITH

KASBA LAKE

TO PRINCE GEORGE, BC AND EDMONTON

97

35

MACKENZIE HWY.

5

WOOD BUFFALO NATIONAL PARK

ALBERTA

LAKE ATHABASCA

SASKATCHEWAN

© MOON PUBLICATIONS, INC.

118 km to Great Slave Lake. This stretch of road is known as the **Waterfalls Route,** for the impressive falls along the way.

Just beyond the border is the **60th Parallel Visitors Centre,** tel. (403) 920-1021, well worth a stop just to have a chat with the friendly hosts. The center offers maps and brochures, camping permits, fishing licenses, and displays of local arts and crafts. And the coffeepot is always on, accompanied by freshly made scones if you're lucky. Behind the center is **60th Parallel Campground,** a small facility overlooking the Hay River; $10. The Visitors Centre is open May to mid-September daily 9 a.m.-9 p.m.

Twin Falls Gorge Territorial Park

North of the border, the Hay River has carved a deep gorge into the limestone bedrock. Punctuating the river's flow are two dramatic waterfalls that formed a major barrier for early river travelers, forcing a portage along the west bank. Encompassing both falls, and the equally impressive **Escarpment Creek,** is Twin Falls Gorge Territorial Park. From the first day-use area a short trail leads to a viewing platform overlooking **Alexandra Falls,** where the peat-colored Hay River tumbles 34 meters. **Louise Falls,** three km downstream, is not as high, but its intriguing steps make it just as interesting. A walking trail through jack pine, aspen, and white spruce links the two sets of falls. Escarpment Creek (also known as Twin Falls Creek) flows into the Hay River four km downstream and has some smaller falls worthy of the short walk. **Louise Falls Campground** has water, pit toilets, and bug-proof kitchen shelters; $10.

Enterprise

Following the completion of the Mackenzie Hwy. in 1948, two gas stations opened here, marking the beginning of this small community of 55. The community had hoped to become a transportation hub for freight heading north, but nothing materialized. Today, with a gas station, restaurant, a few motel rooms, and a highway-maintenance depot, it just manages to hang on. East of the highway are excellent views of the Hay River Gorge. Located at the junction of Hwys. 1 and 2 is **Ed's Place,** tel. (403) 984-3181, where basic rooms are $54.95 s, $59.95 d. Also at Ed's Place is a popular restaurant. The gas pumps here are open until midnight. A **Tourist Information Centre** is located in the Esso Station; open in summer daily 8 a.m.-9 p.m.

HAY RIVER

This town of 3,100 is a vital transportation link for waterborne freight bound for communities along the Mackenzie River and throughout the western and central Arctic. Within town limits, a number of distinct communities surround the delta, which was formed where the Hay River flows into Great Slave Lake. Most modern development—including motels, restaurants, and government offices—is located in **New Town,** on the west bank of the Hay River. A bridge links New Town to **Vale Island,** where the airport, campground, and excellent beaches are located. Also on the island are the communities of **Old Town,** partially destroyed by flooding in 1963, and **West Channel Village,** which grew around the commercial fishing industry. Across the mouth of Hay River is the **Hay River Dene Reserve,** the only Indian reserve in the NWT. Farther upstream are **Delancey Estates,** a modern subdivision, and **Paradise Gardens,** where at a wide, sweeping curve of the river the particularly rich soil has sprouted the territories' largest truck-farm operation. Follow a gravel road down to this small community, 24 km south of Hay River, to a sign advertising fresh produce. Look around for the Greenfields, who will no doubt be in their extensive gardens, toiling away as they have done for years. Many of their customers come from Hay River, although any self-respecting Yellowknife resident returning from a trip south will stop by for the freshest and best-priced produce north of the 60th parallel.

History

For thousands of years Slavey Dene inhabited the area. Their nomadic lifestyle required no permanent settlements. Rival fur-trading companies had opened posts along the Hay River as early as 1806, but it wasn't until 1868 that the Hudson's Bay Company built a post on the east bank at the river's mouth. It closed after 10 years of poor trade. Soon after, Chief Chatla of the Slavey Dene constructed some log cabins near the defunct post and asked church officials to build a small mission to serve his people. The community grew and by the turn of the century had a school, boatyard, and vegetable gardens. The traditional transportation route north to Slave Lake, along the Athabasca and Slave Rivers and through Fort Smith, was superseded in 1939 by an overland route from Grimshaw, following the west bank of the Hay River to Vale Island at the mouth. Before long, the west side of the island was crisscrossed with streets lined with shops, and the waterfront was alive with tugs and barges being loaded with goods for the long trip north.

In 1945 Great Slave Lake was opened to commercial fishing, and a community known as West Channel Village was established on the west side of the island. Fishing soon became the town's leading employer, with 10 companies and eight processing plants harvesting up to eight million tons of fish annually, including the whitefish for which Great Slave Lake is renowned. Vale Island was once linked to the mainland by a causeway removed each spring to prevent flooding during break-up. But in 1963, the causeway was left in place and the fast-flowing Hay River—which breaks up well be-

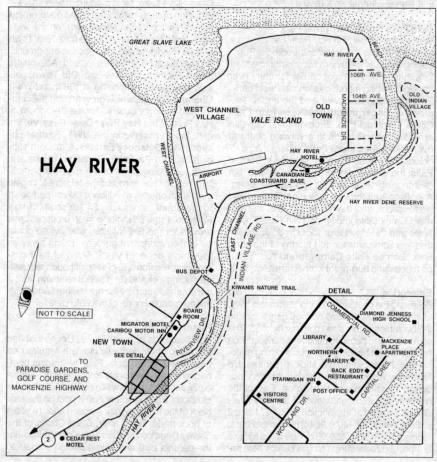

fore the lake—flooded much of the island. As a result, the town was moved to the mainland and a permanent bridge was built over the channel.

New Town Sights

With the opening of the Pine Point Mine and arrival of the railway in the 1960s, and general economic growth of the western Arctic in the '70s, the new townsite grew at a rapid pace. In anticipation of further growth, the 17-story **Mackenzie Place Apartment Building** was constructed in the center of town. Grab a key from the manager's office (second floor) and ride the claustrophobic elevator to the roof, from where panoramic views of the Great Slave Lake, Hay River, and the boreal forest extend to the horizon. The **Diamond Jenness High School,** on Riverview Dr., was named for a famed northern anthropologist and is without a doubt the town's most unique structure. It was designed by Douglas Cardinal, an Albertan architect whose distinctive work is found throughout that province. Its unique curved walls alone would have made it a northern landmark, but the choice of color for the entire exterior was left to the students—and they chose purple! Behind the school, the **Kiwanis Nature Trail** leads along the banks of Hay River (look for fossils) to various signposted points of interest.

Vale Island

The boarded-up shop fronts, dusty streets, and empty houses of Vale Island belie the activity that still takes place along the waterfront. The port facilities are the closest to the western and central Arctic and have been used as a transportation hub for the Canol Project and construction of the Distant Early Warning Line stations. The large **Canadian Coastguard Base** is responsible for all search-and-rescue operations in the western Arctic. And the facilities of **Northern Transportation Co.,** a large shipping concern, include shipyards, a dry dock, freight-storage areas, and a syncrolift—a hydraulic device that removes vessels from the water for easy maintenance (it's one of only four in Canada; it can be seen to the right along 106th Ave.).

From Old Town, Mackenzie Dr.—the island's main thoroughfare—continues past a popular swimming beach and a radio observatory before it dead-ends in **West Channel Village.** This once-prosperous fishing community is a shadow of its former self, since processing is now done at the Freshwater Fish Marketing Board Plant in New Town.

Hay River Dene Reserve

Across East Channel from Vale Island is the site of Hay River's first permanent settlement. To get there, backtrack to the Fort Smith turnoff and head north (turn left) shortly after crossing the Hay River. Indian Village Rd. follows the river to New Indian Village, which, through the work of a dedicated Band Council, has a school, new houses, a grocery store, and scheduled bus service to Hay River. The road continues through the community to the original site of the village. Here you will see early churches and the remains of the Hudson's Bay Company post, sitting in mute testimony to the two major influences on early life in the north.

Recreation

The beaches of Vale Island are very popular during summer, even if the water may be a little cold for most. The best beach is at the end of 106th Ave.; those farther around the island will be quieter. Anglers will find plentiful northern pike and pickerel in the Hay River.

Located 15 km south of town is the territories' finest golf course. It has nine holes with artificial greens, a driving range, and a superbly crafted log clubhouse (well worth a look, even for nongolfers). A round of golf (18 holes) is $26 and club rentals are available. The clubhouse is used as a base for cross-country skiers who set tracks around the course in winter.

Festivals and Events

Winter carnivals are held on the first weekends of March and April, and **Heritage Days,** in early June, celebrates the fishing industry. With the best golf course in the north, it's natural that the town is host to many tournaments throughout the summer. The most important of these is the **NWT Open Championship** on the Labour Day weekend in September. This fully sanctioned event attracts golfers from throughout the north, but everyone is welcome to enter. The entry fee of $60 includes green fees and two evening meals. Book well in advance; tel. (403) 874-2340.

Accommodations

The least expensive rooms in town are at **Hay River Hotel** on Vale Island, tel. (403) 874-6022, and you'll see why before you've taken a step inside. The medium-sized, self-contained rooms are $45 s, $55 d. Common sense dictates that you ask for one in the back—as far away from Vale Island's only bar as is possible. Other motels are located along the highway in New Town. Least expensive of these, but a couple of km from downtown, is **Cedar Rest Motel,** tel. (403) 874-3732, a place the looks half finished, with a massive gravel parking lot out front; $55 s, $62 d. **Caribou Motor Inn,** tel. (403) 874-6706, has rooms for $75 s, $85 d; similar in standard is **Migrator Motel,** tel. (403) 874-6792, $85 s, $96 d; and one step up, with a restaurant and lounge, is the **Ptarmigan Inn,** tel. (403) 874-6781 or (800) 661-0842; in the center of town, with rooms for $100 s, $113 d.

Hay River Campground, on Vale Island, is a short walk from the beach and seven km from downtown. The sites are very private, a few have power, and all have picnic tables and fire rings. It's open mid-May to mid-September; $12. South of town is **Paradise Garden Campground,** which has showers and an enclosed cooking shelter with a woodstove. The camping area is operated by farmers whose delicious vegetables are a welcome and inexpensive addition to any meal; unserviced sites $8.50, powered sites $12.

Food

Worth the effort to find is **Back Eddy Restaurant,** tel. (403) 874-6680. It's above Rings Drug Store on Capital Crescent. Meals are served in the lounge or, for families, in a separate dining area. Expect to pay $6-10 for lunch and a few dollars more for dinner. **The Keys,** tel. (403) 874-6781, in the Ptarmigan Inn, is popular with locals, especially at lunchtime—but it can get very smoky. Beside Northern, **Hay River Bakery,** tel. (403) 874-2322, has a wide variety of cakes and pastries and is a good place for an inexpensive lunch. Meals at **The Board Room,** tel. (403) 874-2111, are also well priced; Chinese combos are $8.95, burgers from $5.95, and main dishes around $11. The restaurant is a pleasant place, with new furniture and a glass-enclosed section that catches the afternoon sun. It's on the road toward Old Town and open daily from 11 a.m.

Transportation

Hay River Airport is located on Vale Island, a $10 cab ride from town. During freeze-up and break-up of the Mackenzie River, road traffic through to Yellowknife is blocked and Hay River Airport becomes the center of frenzied activity; freight and passengers arriving by road from the south transfer to planes for the short hop over Great Slave Lake. **Canadian North,** tel. (403) 874-2434 or (800) 665-1177, has daily flights to Hay River from Edmonton Municipal Airport (via Fort Smith and continuing to Yellowknife). **Buffalo Airways,** tel. (403) 874-3333, a connector airline for NWT Air, flies daily to Yellowknife for $110 one-way, $183 roundtrip. Local flightseeing is done by **Landa Aviation,** tel. (403) 874-3500. A flight over the Hay River Delta and Louise and Alexandra Falls costs $45 per person, three-person minimum; flights to view bison in Wood Buffalo National Park are $100 per person.

The bus depot is located at the south end of Vale Island. **Greyhound** departs daily for Edmonton (16 hours, $116.63 one-way). Connecting with the Greyhound services is **Frontier Coachlines,** using the same depot. Buses run to Yellowknife ($64.50) and Fort Smith ($46.55). For all bus times call (403) 874-6966, or (800) 661-8747 in Canada only.

Services and Information

The **post office** is located on Capital Crescent. Just around the corner, at the base of Mackenzie Place Apartment Building, is a **laundromat;** open daily 8 a.m.-8 p.m. **NWT Centennial Library,** opposite Northern on Woodland Dr., tel. (403) 874-6486, is headquarters for the NWT library system. Books are transported by road, air, and sea to 18 other libraries, including those in the most remote communities. The library has a reasonable selection of books and magazines, including material on the north; open Mon.-Thurs. 11 a.m.-9 p.m., Fri.-Sat. 1-5 p.m. The **hospital** is located along Woodland Dr., tel. (403) 874-6512. The **Visitors Centre,** tel. (403) 874-3180, located at the south entrance to town, has bundles of literature and books to read, and the coffeepot is always on; open mid-May to mid-September daily 9 a.m.-9 p.m.

TO FORT SMITH

The 270-km road linking Hay River to Fort Smith (Hwy. 5) is paved for the first 60 km then turns to improved gravel. No services are available along this route. The road bisects a typical boreal forest of stunted spruce and aspen. Jack pine dominates areas scorched in a disastrous fire that consumed 160,000 hectares in 1981. The fire burned for three months, and pockets continued to smolder under the snow until the following spring. Visible to the north along the paved section of road is a rail bed used by the Great Slave Lake Railway to link the now-abandoned mine at Pine Point to Roma, Alberta, 680 km to the south. A gravel road to the north, 49 km from Hwy. 2, leads two km to **Polar Lake,** a camping and picnic area developed by the community of Pine Lake. The lake is stocked with rainbow trout and has good birdwatching around the shoreline. Camping is $5. Eleven km farther the road divides; the right fork continues to Fort Smith, the left to Pine Point and Fort Resolution.

Pine Point

Early prospectors interested in gold and silver largely ignored the area east of Hay River. But in 1951, Pine Point Mines Limited, owned by Cominco, began extracting lead and zinc from an open-pit mine at a site known as Pine Point. In 1965 the Great Slave Lake Railway was built, linking the mine to outside markets. With production on the increase, a town was built, at one time boasting over 2,000 residents. Low lead and zinc prices, coupled with rising operational costs, forced Cominco to close the mine in 1988. One of the lease conditions was that Cominco was to restore the land to its original condition when it left. As a result, the whole town—a school, hospital, supermarket, and hundreds of houses—had to be moved. After standing empty for a few years, the buildings were moved to various locations throughout the north. Today all that remains are tailing piles from the mine, paved streets, sidewalks, and an overgrown golf course.

Fort Resolution

This historic community of 500 is located in a forested area on the southeastern shore of Great Slave Lake at the end of Hwy. 6, 170 km east of Hay River. The original fort, built by the North West Company in 1786, was to the east, on the Slave River Delta. When the post was moved, a Chipewyan Dene settlement grew around it, and in 1852, Roman Catholic missionaries arrived, building a school and hospital. A road connecting the town to Pine Point was completed in the '60s, and today the mainly Chipewyan and Métis population relies on trapping and a sawmill operation as an economic base.

Walking tours through town can be arranged through the Community Office on the main road. Also ask here about walking along the lakeshore to the site of the original fort. The town is a good jumping-off point for exploring the spectacular East Arm of Great Slave Lake. **Res Delta Tours,** tel. (403) 394-3141, offers a variety of excursions including two-and-a-half-hour tours of the delta ($60 per person) and overnight trips along the East Arm and to Fort Smith.

Fort Resolution has no motel accommodations. The only option is to camp down a gravel road just west of town where there appears to have been a campground at one time. Also in town is a gas station, cafe, and a community hall where evening meals are served for reasonable prices. Scheduled transportation is from Yellowknife on **Ptarmigan Airways,** tel. (403) 873-4461 or (800) 661-0808; $96 each way.

Continuing to Fort Smith on Highway 5

From the Fort Smith/Fort Resolution junction, 60 km east of Hay River, it is 210 km southeast to Fort Smith. For much of the way the highway is paralleled by power lines. A hydroelectric plant was built on the Taltson River, east of Slave River, in the 1960s to provide electricity to Pine Point. Now it runs well below capacity, supplying towns in the Big River region. Many of the power line's towers are capped by masses of sticks and twigs—the nesting sites of ravens. Twenty-seven km from the Fort Resolution junction is a 13-km road to **Sandy Lake,** which has a good beach, swimming, and fishing for northern pike, but no camping.

The road then enters Wood Buffalo National Park, the largest national park in North America. Five km beyond the park entrance sign is the **Angus Fire Tower.** Behind the tower is one of many sinkholes found in the northern reaches of the park. This example of karst topography occurs when underground caves collapse, creating a craterlike depression. This one is 26 meters deep and 40 meters across. The next worthwhile stop is at **Nyarling River,** 14 km farther east. The dried-up riverbed is actually the path of an underground river, hence the name Nyarling, meaning "underground" in the Slavey language.

Little Buffalo Falls Territorial Park

As the highway continues east it enters an area where the Precambrian Shield is exposed, making for a rocky landscape where stunted trees cling to shallow depressions that have filled with soil. After crossing the Sass River, the road passes an area of shallow lakes and marshes where whooping cranes—one of North America's rarest birds—nest. As the road crosses Little Buffalo River it leaves the park. To the north,

an access road leads to a series of small waterfalls in Little Buffalo Falls Territorial Park. This was only a small part of an enormous area affected by fire in 1981. An interpretive trail follows the cycle of regeneration from stands of aspen and spruce to jack pine, whose seeds are released at high temperatures. Near the end of the access road is a campground with pit toilets, a kitchen shelter, and firewood; $10.

FORT SMITH

Until 1967, this town of 2,500 on the west bank of the Slave River was the territorial capital. It still functions as an administrative center for various governmental offices and is the educational center for the western regions of the North-

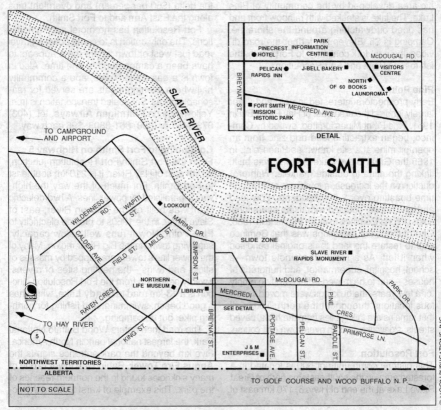

TO CAMPGROUND
AND AIRPORT

SLAVE RIVER

FORT SMITH

PINECREST
HOTEL

PARK INFORMATION
CENTRE

McDOUGAL RD.

PELICAN
RAPIDS INN

J-BELL BAKERY

VISITORS
CENTRE

NORTH
OF 60 BOOKS
LAUNDROMAT

FORT SMITH
MISSION
HISTORIC PARK

MERCREDI AVE.

DETAIL

BREYNAT ST.

LOOKOUT

WILDERNESS RD.

WAPITI ST.

MARINE DR.

CALDER AVE.

FIELD ST.

MILLS ST.

SIMPSON ST.

SLIDE ZONE

SLAVE RIVER
RAPIDS MONUMENT

NORTHERN
LIFE MUSEUM

LIBRARY

RAVEN CRES.

MERCREDI
SEE DETAIL

McDOUGAL RD.

PINE CRES.

PARK DR.

TO HAY RIVER

5

KING ST.

BREYNAT ST.

PORTAGE AVE.

PELICAN ST.

PADDLE ST.

PRIMROSE LN.

J & M
ENTERPRISES

NORTHWEST TERRITORIES
ALBERTA

NOT TO SCALE

TO GOLF COURSE AND WOOD BUFFALO N.P.

MOON PUBLICATIONS INC

PROVINCIAL ARCHIVES OF ALBERTA

Rather than portaging the rapids, some brave souls attempted to run them in scows.

west Territories, with students studying at the Thebacha Campus of Arctic College. But its glory days are over. The transportation routes upon which the town was built have long been abandoned, and the governmental hierarchy that once resided here is long gone. Rapids in the Slave River (the Dene name for the area is Thebacha, meaning "along the rapids") are the nesting grounds of white pelicans—a unique location considering its northern latitude, and considering that the pelicans somehow manage to raise young among the fast-flowing waters of the river.

History
It was because of the formidable rapids that the town was established. The Slave River was a vital link for all travelers heading north, but rapids here and upstream necessitated a 25-km portage around them. In 1872 the Hudson's Bay Company opened a post, later known as Fort Fitzgerald, at the southern end of the rapids. Two years later the company established a fort near the northern end of the portage route, at Fort Smith.

Occasionally the brave attempted to run the rapids. In 1876 five paddlers for the North West Company successfully negotiated the three upstream sets but then misinterpreted instructions and perished on the rapids in front of Fort Smith. Their misfortune won't be forgotten; these rapids are now known as Rapids of the Drowned. Around this time, sternwheelers began replacing the slower and more cumbersome voyageur canoes and larger York boats. Red River carts, drawn by oxen, replaced human portagers, and were in turn replaced by tractors in 1919. By this time Fort Smith had become the administrative center of the NWT. It remained so until an all-weather road was built from Peace River to Hay River and through to Yellowknife, and river transportation slid into oblivion.

Sights
Most people who venture to Fort Smith do so to visit Wood Buffalo National Park, although it is possible, at a stretch, to spend a day sightseeing in town. Back in the 1920s, when Fort Smith was capital of the Northwest Territories, ad-

ministrative duties fell to the local bishop whose house and gardens are now part of **Fort Smith Mission Historic Park,** at the corner of Mercredi Avenue and Breynat Street. It's an ongoing restoration project; at this stage interpretive signs explain the various buildings, and gardens are planted for each summer. **Northern Life Museum,** 110 King St., tel. (403) 872-2859, is shaped like a fort and houses a large collection of artifacts from the days of the fur trade, as well as mushing equipment, Inuit carvings, the first printing press in the north, and displays on bison; open in summer Mon.-Fri. 9 a.m.-5 p.m., Sat.-Sun. 1-5 p.m. At the end of Breynat St., signs indicate the **slide zone,** where many of Fort Smith's riverfront buildings once stood. Continue downstream and onto Marine Dr. to **Slave River Lookout,** a gazebo with a telescope through which you can watch the pelicans. Overlooking the rapids (the view is slightly marred by trees) is the **Slave River Rapids Monument,** dedicated to the explorers and riverboat guides of the 1800s who courageously tackled the river. To get there follow McDougal Rd. east through town and turn left on Park Dr.; the monument is off to the left in the trees.

Fort Fitzgerald, 25 km upstream of Fort Smith, was once a hive of activity at the beginning of the north's most notorious portage. Today, all that remains along with a small population are abandoned houses, a deserted mission, and, down on the river, rotting docks.

Recreation and Tours

Pelican Rapids Golf and Country Club, through town to the southeast, has been carved out of the forest by the town's surprisingly large golfing population; green fees are $10. The clubhouse has rentals, but for all your other golfing needs, you should head to **Northwind Sports,** 182 McDougal Rd., tel. (403) 872-2465. This shop also stocks fishing tackle and camping gear.

Subarctic Wildlife Adventures offers a multitude of one-day and overnight tours throughout the area, including into Wood Buffalo National Park. Day trips include rafting on the Slave River (five hours, $55 per person) and bus tours into the national park (six hours, $90 per person). For details on these and longer excursions write to P.O. Box 685, Fort Smith, NT X0E 0P0, tel. (403) 872-2467.

Accommodations and Food

The least expensive motel is **Pinecrest Hotel,** 163 McDougal Rd., tel. (403) 872-2320; $60 s, $70 d. Much nicer is **Pelican Rapids Inn,** 152 McDougal Rd., tel. (403) 872-2789, with large rooms for $95 s, $105 d, $15 extra for kitchenettes; call in advance, this place fills up fast. Another option is **Thebacha B&B,** 53 Portage Ave., tel. (403) 872-2060, which offers a couple of rooms for $75 s, $90 d.

The only campground close to town is **Queen Elizabeth Campground,** four km west toward the airport; turn north on Teepee Trail Road. Sites cost $10 per night and are spread out and private with pit toilets and cooking shelters. Showers and flush toilets are in the warden's compound. Alternatives are **Thebacha Campground,** 16 km west of Fort Smith on Hwy. 5, or **Pine Lake,** 60 km south in Wood Buffalo National Park.

The **Old Skillet Restaurant** in the Pinecrest Hotel, tel. (403) 872-3161, may look a mess from the outside but inside it's clean and comes highly recommended by locals; open from 7 a.m. **J-Bell Bakery,** corner of McDougal Rd. and Portage Ave., serves hot and cold lunches and great pastries.

Transportation

The **airport** is located five km west of town along McDougal Road. **Canadian North,** tel. (403) 872-2057 or (800) 665-1177, flies daily to Edmonton ($343 one-way, $362 for a seven-day APEX roundtrip), Hay River ($162 one-way, $177 roundtrip), and Yellowknife ($192 one-way, $216 roundtrip). **Northwestern Air,** tel. (403) 872-2216, operates a scheduled air service to and from Fort Chipewyan; $95 one-way, $190 roundtrip. **Loon Air,** tel. (403) 872-3030, is a charter air service operating out of Fort Smith; $355 gets you a one-way flight to Fort Chipewyan in a small Cessna that seats five. **Frontier Coachlines,** tel. (403) 872-2031, runs a passenger service between Fort Smith and Yellowknife. **J & M Enterprises** on Portage Ave., tel. (403) 872-2211, is open daily 8 a.m.-midnight and has a mechanic, car wash, and car rentals. For a taxi, call **Slave River Cabs** at (403) 872-3333.

Information

Mary Kaeser Library is at 170 McDougal Rd., tel. (403) 872-2296, and **North of 60 Books,**

across from the Visitors Centre, tel. (403) 872-2606, offers a great selection of books, maps, and souvenirs. The **Fort Smith Visitors Centre** is on Portage Rd., tel. (403) 872-2515. It's open mid-May to mid-September 10 a.m.-10 p.m.

WOOD BUFFALO NATIONAL PARK

The sheer size of Wood Buffalo National Park, second-largest national park in the world (the largest is in Greenland), can be overwhelming at first. With few conventional "sights," many first-time visitors leave disillusioned. The park really is a place where you must stop, pause, and take it all in. Through this 45,000-square-km chunk of boreal forest, boreal plains, shallow lakes, and bogs flow two major rivers—the Peace and Athabasca. These drain into **Lake Claire,** forming one of the world's largest freshwater deltas. The Peace-Athabasca Delta is a mass of confusing channels, shallow lakes, and sedge meadows, surrounded by a wetland that is prime wintering range for bison, rich in wa-

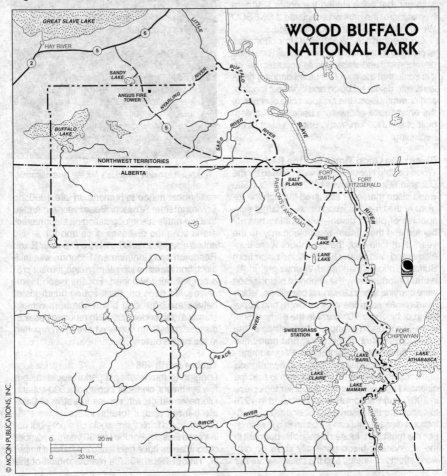

WOOD BUFFALO NATIONAL PARK

terfowl, and home to beavers, muskrats, moose, lynx, wolves, and black bears. From the delta, the Slave River—which forms the park's eastern boundary—flows north into Great Slave Lake.

Probably best known for being the last natural nesting habitat of the rare whooping crane, the park is also home to the world's largest free-roaming herd of bison. It has extensive salt plains and North America's finest example of gypsum karst topography—a phenomenon created by underground water activity. For all these reasons, and as an intact example of the boreal forest that once circled the entire Northern Hemisphere, the park was declared a UNESCO World Heritage Site in December 1983.

On the surface, Wood Buffalo epitomizes everything that a national park should be—little development and stable wildlife populations—so it is ironic that the park has faced ongoing problems with diseased bison and clear-cut logging, and currently faces the prospect of a collapse of the entire delta ecosystem because of a dam built over 1,000 km away. But let's start at the beginning.

Bison: The Good Times and the Bad

Wood Buffalo National Park was created by the Dominion Government in 1922 to protect 1,500 wood bison that were scattered through the region. At the time, the wood bison—a larger subspecies of plains bison—were being heavily hunted and their future was in jeopardy. In the years that followed, their numbers were supplemented with nearly 6,000 plains bison from Buffalo National Park near Wainwright, in Alberta. Unfortunately, the imported plains bison were carrying tuberculosis and brucellosis, which have remained in the park's now hybrid population of bison for 70 years. In the early 1950s, large-scale bison roundups took place in the Sweetgrass area of the delta, and many diseased bison were slaughtered. Park administrators set up a small settlement at Sweetgrass and constructed over 30 km of corrals to hold the diseased animals. The last slaughter took place in 1967, and the corrals were last used in 1976 to vaccinate the bison against anthrax—an infectious disease that can kill bison in a few days. For the most part, these diseases lie dormant in the ecosystem; bison generally show no outward effects of illness, and the diseases are not

The bison is North America's largest land mammal.

easily transmitted to humans. In late 1990, an Environmental Advisory Board recommended that the entire bison population be slaughtered, eradicating the diseases once and for all. No action was taken and in 1995 a five-year Bison Research and Containment Program was initiated, from which a long-term management program will be developed. For the bison themselves, life goes on; each spring hundreds of calves are born and bison numbers remain steady at just under 3,000. No reported cases of disease transfer to humans have been reported in the park's history.

Timber Berth 408

Logging in most national parks would raise a few eyebrows, clear-cut logging of a 500-square-kilometer old-growth spruce forest would create a furor, and, if foreign interests were involved, you'd think there would be a riot—but not in Wood Buffalo. For the last 30 years a number of companies have held leases to harvest timber in "Timber Berth 408," a remote region of the park along the Peace River. Through the years, many infractions were made on the leases, but they were always extended. The final lease was held by Canadian Forest Products Ltd. (Canfor), whose logging operations feed a sawmill in High Level owned by Diashowa Canada Co. Ltd., a Japanese multinational corporation. On 7 March 1991 the operation was shut down after further lease violations . No further logging has taken place within the park and reforestation is being planned for the near future.

Peace-Athabasca Delta

For thousands of years, the silt-laden waters of the Peace and Athabasca Rivers flowed into Lake Claire, forming a delta rich in vegetation that provided diverse habitats for larger mammals and a traditional hunting ground for Chipewyan and Cree natives. Each spring a natural cycle of flooding would take place when the Peace River would break its banks, replenishing sloughs and marshes. This created hundreds of square kilometers of wetland, vital to the millions of birds that use the delta as a stopover on their annual migratory path and to the fur-bearing mammals whose survival is dependent on this annual cycle.

That age-old natural cycle was broken in the 1980s by the construction of the W.A.C. Bennett Dam, on the Peace River over 1,000 km upstream in British Columbia. Since the river has been dammed, the flow has been regulated and the flood-cycle ended. Now the delta is slowly drying up. Protein-rich sedges along the sloughs have been replaced by silverweed and thistle, and large areas of once-rich marshland are now dried-up mudflats, severely affecting the wintering range of bison. In an attempt to return the delta to its natural state, several groups, including the federal government and local native associations, came together for the Peace-Athabasca Delta Technical Studies, a management program that culminated in the artificial flooding of a small section of the delta during the break-up of 1996. Adding to the tarnished image of the park are worries about water contamination from mills upstream on the Peace and Athabasca Rivers and the threat of a dam on the Lower Slave River, which would flood northern sections of the park, including the salt plains.

Whooping Cranes: A Park Success Story

When, in 1954, a flock of 21 whooping cranes was discovered nesting in the park, the species was on the verge of extinction. Today, the population of the highly publicized and heavily studied flock has increased to over 130, more than half the number that remain worldwide (most of those remaining are in captivity). The birds nest in a remote area of marshes and bogs in the northern reaches of Wood Buffalo far from human contact. They stand 1.3 meters, have a wing span of 2.4 meters, and are pure white, with long black legs. They are often confused with the slightly smaller, reddish-brown-colored sandhill crane, which is quite common in the park.

Salt Plains

The expansive salt-encrusted plains located in the northeast of the park are one of Wood Buffalo's dominant natural features. Underground water flows through deposits of salt left behind by an ancient saltwater ocean, emerging in the form of salt springs. Large white mounds form at their source, and where the water has evaporated the ground is covered in a fine layer of salt. The best place to view this phenomenon is from the **Salt Plains Overlook,** 35 km west of Fort Smith, then 10 km south on Parson's Lake Road. The panoramic view of the plains is spectacular from this spot but **Salt Plains Trail** (one km each way), which leads to the bottom of the hill, is well worth the effort. If you decide to go beyond the trail take your shoes and socks off (squishing through the mud is good fun—and you'll appreciate clean shoes back at the car). The salt attracts many mammals including bison, wolves, foxes, and black bears. Their tracks can often be seen in the mud, along with those of various birds that feed on the aquatic vegetation unique to the plains.

Gypsum Karst

A gypsum bedrock underlies many areas of the northeast corner of the park. Gypsum is a soft, white rock that slowly dissolves in water. Underground water here has created large cavities beneath this fragile mantle. This type of terrain is known as karst, and this area is the best example of karst terrain in North America.

As the bedrock continues to dissolve, the underground caves enlarge, eventually collapsing under their own weight, forming large depressions known as **sinkholes.** The thousands of sinkholes here vary in size from a few meters to 100 meters across. The most accessible large sinkhole is behind the Angus Fire Tower, 150 km west of Fort Smith. The short **Karstland Trail,** which begins behind the Salt River Picnic Area, 24 km south of Fort Smith, passes several smaller sinkholes. The **North Loop Trail,** which starts as part of the Karstland Trail but branches right, off the gravel trail, is a longer hike through typical gypsum karst terrain ending on the main road a short walk from the picnic area. The total loop is nine km; allow two and a half hours. **Pine Lake,** 60 km south of Fort Smith, is a sinkhole that formed beneath the water table. This deep, clear lake is excellent for canoeing and fishing. A trail follows the southern shore or you can continue south to **Lane Lake,** a 6.5-km (one-way) hike.

Sweetgrass

The Peace-Athabasca Delta is in a remote part of this remote park and is therefore rarely visited. Getting to the delta requires some planning as no roads access the area. The most popular visitor destination on the delta is **Sweetgrass Station,** located 12 km south of the Peace River. The site is on the edge of a vast meadow that extends around the north and west shore of Lake Claire, providing summer range for most of the park's bison. The corrals at Sweetgrass Station were built in 1954 to help the fight against diseased bison. Although now abandoned, facilities remain to vaccinate the herd if the need ever arises. A cabin with bunks and a woodstove is available for visitors to the area at no charge, although reservations at the park information center are required. The cabin is an excellent base for exploring the meadows around Lake Claire and viewing the abundant wildlife. Drinking water can be obtained from Sweetgrass Creek but should be filtered and boiled.

The easiest access is with **Loon Air,** tel. (403) 872-3030, or **Northwestern Air,** tel. (403) 872-2216, who charge around $340 each way for two people and their gear. The latter company also offers flightseeing over the area for $55 per person. The other, more complicated way to access Sweetgrass is by canoe, paddling down the Peace River to Sweetgrass Landing, from where it's a 12-km hike or a five-km portage and easy float down

Sweetgrass Creek to the station. Getting out requires a pick-up by floatplane from Fort Smith or boat operator from Fort Chipewyan.

Park Practicalities

Park headquarters is in Fort Smith at 126 McDougal Road. There the excellent **Park Information Centre,** tel. (403) 872-2349, offers current park information, a short slide display, and an exhibit room. The center is open in summer Mon.-Fri. 8:30 a.m.-5 p.m. and Sat.-Sun. 10 a.m.-5 p.m., the rest of the year Mon.-Fri. only. Another small park office is located in Fort Chipewyan. It has an interesting exhibit on the Peace River and is open year-round Mon.-Fri. 8:30 a.m.-5 p.m.; tel. (403) 697-3662.

The park's only developed facilities are at **Pine Lake,** 60 km south of Fort Smith. The lake has a campground with pit toilets, covered kitchen shelters, and firewood; sites $7.50. The park staff presents a summer interpretive program at various locations—check the schedule at the park information center or on the campground notice board.

For further information write to: Superintendent, Wood Buffalo National Park, P.O. Box 750, Fort Smith, NT X0E 0P0. Seven 1:250,000 topographic maps are needed to cover the entire park. Order copies through any specialty map shop or at North of 60 Books in Fort Smith, tel. (403) 872-2606.

HAY RIVER TO YELLOWKNIFE

Yellowknife, located on the north shore of the Great Slave Lake, is a long 480-km haul from Hay River, through a monotonous boreal forest of spruce, poplar, and jack pine. The trees diminish in size as the road heads north. The gravel road is slowly being replaced, but it will be many years before the territorial capital is linked to the outside world by a paved road. Twice a year, for three to six weeks in spring and again in late fall (at break-up and freeze-up, respectively, of the Mackenzie River), the road to Yellowknife is not passable.

Lady Evelyn Falls

From Enterprise, south of Hay River, Hwy. 1 heads northwest, coming to Lady Evelyn Falls

Lady Evelyn Falls

after 53 km. These falls, where the wide **Kakisa River** cascades off a 15-meter escarpment, are easily accessible from the highway, seven km down a gravel road. A short trail leads from the day-use area down to a platform overlooking the falls. A path continues upstream past a different view of the falls to a miniature version of the larger falls downstream. The falls are part of a territorial park that has a campground with pit toilets, bug-proof kitchen shelters, and firewood; sites $12.

Kakisa

Kakisa is a small Slavey community on Kakisa Lake at the end of the Lady Evelyn Falls access road. It was established in 1962 when the community, then located farther south on Tathlina Lake, moved to have access to the newly constructed highway. Kakisa has no services, although the lake is known for good pickerel and whitefish fishing.

Fort Providence

Eighty-five km from Enterprise the highway forks. To the left Hwy. 1 continues west to Fort Simpson, while Hwy. 3 heads north toward Yellowknife. Highway 3 crosses the Mackenzie River, via a ferry, 24 km from the junction. Across the river and just up the highway, a spur road leads eight km to the Slavey Dene community of Fort Providence, perched high above the river on its steep northern bank. A Roman Catholic mission was established here in 1861, attracting natives from nearby communities. The mission continued to play an important role in the area, encouraging agriculture and operating a school. Some of the town's older residents can speak French, a legacy of the French-speaking Catholic missionaries who taught at the school. Local artisans are known for moosehair tufting and intricate porcupine-quill weaving. On the riverfront is a **visitors center,** and farther along, historical markers honoring the roles played by Alexander Mackenzie and the church in the region's history. Fishing in the Mackenzie River is excellent, with catches of northern pike up to 12 kilograms—ask a local where the best spots are. You can rent a boat, organize river tours, and book cabin accommodations through **Aurora Sport Fishing,** tel. (403) 699-4321. **Snowshoe Inn,** tel. (403) 699-3511, on the riverfront, has basic rooms; $80 s, $100 d. Out on the highway you'll find a gas station, a cafe with reasonable food, and a few motel rooms in ATCO trailers ($70 per night). The cafe is open till 10 p.m. and the gas station till midnight. A **campground** is located along the Fort Providence access road; sites $10.

Mackenzie Bison Sanctuary

Many years after the wood and plains bison in Wood Buffalo National Park had interbred, a small herd of pure wood bison was found in a remote corner of the park. In 1963, 18 of these animals were moved to the northwest side of Great Slave Lake. The herd has now grown to

2,000, occupying an area of around 10,000 square km. The region between the highway and Great Slave Lake is a bison sanctuary, although their range extends well beyond these boundaries. The animals were thought to be disease-free, but in August 1993, an outbreak of anthrax killed over 100 bison before it was quelled.

Rae-Edzo

Rae-Edzo, 214 km north of Fort Providence, is the largest Dene community in the Northwest Territories with a population of 1,500 Dogrib Dene. Dogrib have hunted and trapped in the area for centuries, but a permanent settlement wasn't established until 1852 when Dr. John Rae—an early explorer who had adopted the Indian way of life—built a Hudson's Bay Company post nearby. Soon after, the post was moved to the present site of Rae on Marian Lake, an extension of the North Arm of Great Slave Lake.

The Dogrib were severely affected by measles, tuberculosis, and influenza—diseases brought by traders and explorers. The spread of disease was exacerbated by the poor drainage at Rae, which caused sanitation problems that continue to affect the community. By the 1940s, the Dogribs' survival was in doubt. In 1965 the government began developing a new townsite, Edzo, closer to the highway. The school at Rae was closed and a new one opened at Edzo. But despite outbreaks of disease, most of the community continued living at Rae where the water access is better for fishing and hunting.

The 10-km side-trip to Rae is worthwhile. The resilient community is perched on a rocky outcrop jutting into **Marian Lake.** The main road through town leads to a small island where the rocky beaches are littered with boats, fishing nets, and dogs tied up waiting for snow. Apart from the snowmobiles, the village looks much as it did 100 years ago. **Rae Industrial Lodge,** tel. (403) 392-6044, is an alternative to the higher prices of Yellowknife, 100 km away. The rate of $95 per person includes three meals in the adjoining cafe.

North of Rae-Edzo are the remote communities of Wha Ti (formerly Lac La Martre), Rae Lakes, and Snare Lake, accessible only by plane from Yellowknife (see "Communities in the Vicinity of Yellowknife" under "Yellowknife and Vicinity," below).

YELLOWKNIFE AND VICINITY

Built on dreams, perseverance, and the ingenuity of a small group of pioneers who came in search of gold, the territorial capital of Yellowknife has grown into a modern urban center of 18,500. Its frontier-town flavor and independent spirit distinguish it from all other Canadian cities. It's the northernmost city in Canada, the *only* city in the NWT, and the only predominantly nonnative community in the territories. Located on the North Arm of the Great Slave Lake, the city clings precariously to the ancient, glacial-scarred rock of the Canadian Shield. Edmonton is 1,524 km south by road, 965 km by air. The Arctic Circle is 442 km north. At first, Yellowknife looks little different from other small Canadian cities, but unique contrasts soon become apparent. While some residents are writing computer programs, others are preparing caribou hides; architect-designed houses are scattered among squatters' log cabins; and the roads are seemingly always under repair, a legacy of permafrost. To the Dene, Yellowknife is known as Som bak'e, meaning "place of money."

History

Samuel Hearne dubbed the local Dene natives the Yellowknife for the copper knives they used. Their numbers were devastated by disease and by warring with the Dogrib who had traditionally hunted in the area. Miners on their way to the Klondike were the first to discover gold in the area, but they didn't rush in to stake claims due to the area's remote location and the difficulty of extracting the mineral from the hard bedrock. But as airplanes began opening up the north, the area became more attractive to gold-seekers. Hundreds of claims were staked between 1934 and 1936, and a boomtown sprang up along the shore of Yellowknife Bay. Very few struck it rich, but the rush continued until WW II, with miners coming north in scows, barges, floatplanes, and a sternwheeler that plied the lake from Fort Smith. After the war,

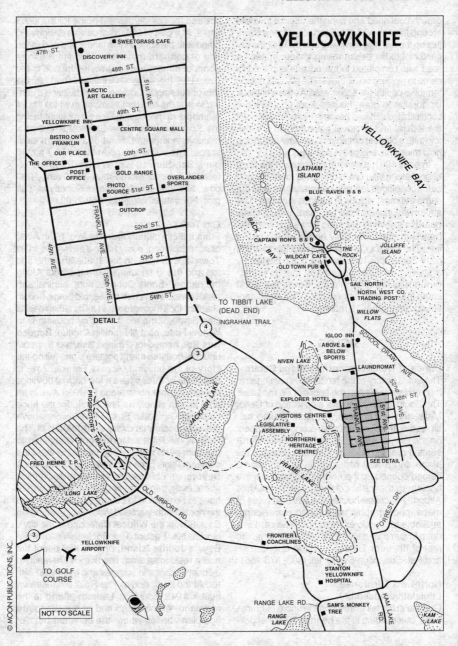

YELLOWKNIFE

DETAIL

SWEETGRASS CAFE
DISCOVERY INN
47th ST.
48th ST.
51st AVE.
ARCTIC ART GALLERY
49th ST.
YELLOWKNIFE INN
CENTRE SQUARE MALL
BISTRO ON FRANKLIN
50th ST.
OUR PLACE
THE OFFICE
POST OFFICE
GOLD RANGE
OVERLANDER SPORTS
PHOTO SOURCE
51st ST.
OUTCROP
52nd ST.
FRANKLIN AVE.
(50th AVE.)
53rd ST.
49th AVE.
54th ST.

TO TIBBIT LAKE (DEAD END)
INGRAHAM TRAIL
4
3

YELLOWKNIFE BAY

LATHAM ISLAND
BLUE RAVEN B & B
OTTO DR.
BACK BAY
JOLLIFFE ISLAND
CAPTAIN RON'S B & B
WILDCAT CAFE
OLD TOWN PUB
THE ROCK
SAIL NORTH
NORTH WEST CO. TRADING POST
WILLOW FLATS
SCHOOL DRAW AVE.
IGLOO INN
ABOVE & BELOW SPORTS
NIVEN LAKE
LAUNDROMAT
52nd ST.
EXPLORER HOTEL
FRANKLIN AVE.
51st AVE.
48th ST.
VISITORS CENTRE
LEGISLATIVE ASSEMBLY
NORTHERN HERITAGE CENTRE
SEE DETAIL
JACKFISH LAKE
PROSPECTORS TRAIL
FRED HENNE T.P.
LONG LAKE
OLD AIRPORT RD.
FRAME LAKE
FORREST DR.
3
YELLOWKNIFE AIRPORT
TO GOLF COURSE
NOT TO SCALE
FRONTIER COACHLINES
STANTON YELLOWKNIFE HOSPITAL
RANGE LAKE RD.
SAM'S MONKEY TREE
RANGE LAKE
KAM LAKE RD.
KAM LAKE

© MOON PUBLICATIONS, INC.

growth continued and soon the original townsite around the bay was at full capacity. A new town, just up the hill, was surveyed, and by 1947 the city center of today began taking shape. In 1967 a road was completed to the outside and the city came to rely less on air travel. The city was named territorial capital the same year. As the white-collar population grew, houses went up and more sophisticated services became available. Although the federal and territorial governments are Yellowknife's biggest employers, several producing gold mines have kept the economy alive.

In early 1991, a general downturn in the price of gold along with union demands for better and safer conditions led to a general strike that became the most vicious in Canada's history. The strike was violent from the start, with security guards protecting the mine and scab workers, brawls in bars, and daily battles at the picket line. The strike's darkest hour was the morning of 18 September 1992, when a bomb planted by a striking miner exploded 150 meters underground, killing nine miners. It was the worst crime in Canadian labor history. The strike continued for another 18 months.

SIGHTS

Prince of Wales Northern Heritage Centre

The entire history of the territories is cataloged at this modern facility on the shore of Frame Lake. The South Gallery displays a collection of Dene, Métis, and Inuit artifacts. The North Gallery catalogs the arrival of Europeans and their impact on the environment. The Aviation Gallery presents a realistic display of a bush pilot and his plane and a wall of fame for the pilots who helped opened up the north. Also here is a live hookup to the traffic controllers at Yellowknife Airport. The center houses the NWT Archives of maps, photographs, books, and manuscripts available for public examination. The center is open in summer daily 10:30 a.m.-5:30 p.m., the rest of the year Tues.-Fri. 10:30 a.m.-5 p.m. and Sat.-Sun. noon-5 p.m.; tel. (403) 873-7551.

Northwest Territories Legislative Assembly

Opened in the fall of 1993 on the shore of Frame Lake, this building is the heart of territorial politics and the first permanent home for the legislature. At a cost of $25 million, it was designed to blend with the surrounding landscape and made use of northern materials. Through the front doors of a massive glass-walled facade is the Great Hall, topped by skylights and lined with the artwork of Angus Cockney. The building's centerpiece is the circular Chamber, in which the 24 members of the legislative assembly sit facing the Speaker. Behind the Speaker stretches a massive zinc-plated mural of a northern landscape. The building is open Mon.-Fri. 7 a.m.-6 p.m., Sat.-Sun. 10 a.m.-6 p.m. Tours are offered in summer Mon.-Fri. at 10:30 a.m., 1:30 p.m., and 3:30 p.m. as well as Sunday at 3:30 p.m. For details, call (403) 669-2200.

Old Town

From the city center, Franklin Ave. (50th Ave.) descends a long, dusty hill to Yellowknife's Old Town. It was here, in the 1930s, that the first log and frame buildings were erected. Along the narrow streets Quonset huts, original settlers' homes, converted buses, old boats, and tin shanties look incongruous in a Canadian capital city. Some of the most unusual housing is in **Willow Flats,** east of Franklin Avenue. **Ragged Ass Rd.,** named for a mine claim, has the most unusual houses, many posting signs telling the story of the building. Across Franklin Ave. is **Peace River Flats** where a few original buildings remain. Farther north along Franklin Ave. is an area known simply as **The Rock,** for the huge chunk of Canadian Shield that towers above the surrounding landscape. At the top of The Rock is the **Pilot's Monument,** dedicated to the bush pilots who opened up the north. At the corner of Pilots Lane and Wiley Rd. is **Weaver & Devore,** an old-time general store selling just about everything. Many of their larger orders have to be flown in to buyers scattered through the north. Farther around Wiley Rd., overlooking Back Bay, is the **Wildcat Cafe,** one of the city's landmarks. East of The Rock, in Yellowknife Bay, is **Jolliffe Island,** once a fuel depot but now a residential area. The homes are reached by boat or canoe in summer and by road in winter. At the north end of The Rock a causeway, built in 1948, connects **Latham Island** to the mainland. At the south end of the island are floatplane bases where the constant buzz of

The eclectic housing of Ragged Ass Road is a reminder of the city's earliest days.

small planes taking off and landing symbolizes the north.

Fred Henne Territorial Park

Forest-encircled **Long Lake,** opposite Yellowknife Airport, is used by visitors mainly for the excellent camping facilities. But it's also a good example of the wilderness surrounding the city. The four-km **Prospector's Trail,** which begins from the campground, is a good way to experience the unique landscape. You can hike to the park from the city center along the trails around **Frame Lake.**

Ingraham Trail

Apart from Hwy. 3 from the south, the Ingraham Trail (Hwy. 4 East) is the only route out of the city. The road passes a string of lakes—great for fishing, boating, and swimming—and the **Royal Oak Mine.** It then crosses the Yellowknife River and passes **Prosperous, Pontoon,** and **Prelude Lakes,** each with day-use areas. Continuing east, the road parallels the **Cameron River.** Trails lead down to the riverbank and waterfalls dot the route. The road ends at **Tibbit Lake,** 71 km from Yellowknife.

Detah

This community, originally a seasonal fish camp for the Dogrib Dene, is located east of Yellowknife across Yellowknife Bay. As Yellowknife grew, the Dogrib people settled here permanently to take advantage of the growing services of the new city, while maintaining a traditional way of life. Today the 150 residents continue a lifestyle of fishing, hunting, and trapping.

RECREATION

Hiking

Hiking trails exist around Frame and Niven Lakes, but the best way to truly appreciate the city's unique surroundings is with **Cygnus Ecotours,** tel. (403) 873-4782. Led by Jamie Bastedo, author of the book *Shield Country,* there are various tour options, the least strenuous being a three-and-a-half-hour stroll around Frame Lake learning about the formation of the Canadian Shield, its plant and bird life, and the area's traditional owners. The cost is $42 per person, which includes a light snack.

Fishing and Boating

The brochures of many fishing-charter operators fill the Northern Frontier Regional Visitors Centre, but **Bluefish Services,** tel. (403) 873-4818, offers the widest range of fishing opportunties. These include fishing for arctic grayling from local river banks, chasing northern pike out on North Arm, and trawling the deepest parts of Great Slave Lake for massive lake trout. Rates are from $65 per person for four hours and $105-160 for a full day. **True North Safaris,** tel. (403) 873-8533, offers two- and four-hour fishing trips on the North Arm of Great Slave Lake ($75 and

$95, respectively). **Vern's Venture,** tel. (403) 873-4650, also leads fishing trips that work out slightly cheaper with four or more people.

Sail North, P.O. Box 2497, Yellowknife, NT X1A 2P8, tel. (403) 873-8019, charters motorboats and sailboats. Motorboats start at $20 per hour for a four-meter boat ($100 per day) and $80 per hour for a 12-meter boat. Per week, the same boats are $500-2,699. Sailboats ranging eight to 14 meters rent for $185-549 per day or $735-2,699 per week and make a great way to explore the hundreds of uncharted bays on the East Arm. You can sail yourself or hire a skipper ($85 extra per day). Booked through Touch the Arctic Adventure Tours, tel. (800) 661-0894, five days yacht charter, a skipper, all meals, and roundtrip flights between either Edmonton or Calgary and Yellowknife is a reasonable $1,461 per person.

Canoeing and Kayaking

Down the hill from the city center, on the way to Old Town, is **Above and Below Sports,** 4100 Franklin Ave., tel. (403) 669-9222, renting canoes for $15 for four hours, the perfect length of time to explore nearby Jolliffe Island and its surrounding waters. For those looking at longer trips, canoes are $30 per day. Opportunities for kayaking around Yellowknife are more limited, although some interesting opportunities exist along the Cameron River, accessed from the Ingraham Trail (see above). Above and Below Sports rents single kayaks ($25 for four hours, $50 per day, and $200 per week) as well as doubles ($40 for four hours, $75 per day, and $260 per week). **Overlander Sports,** 5103 51st St., tel. (403) 873-2474, has the same rental rates but is closed Sunday. Overlander also rents folding kayaks ($150 per week, $500 per month).

Scuba Diving

For diving enthusiasts, the Northwest Territories may not have the appeal of, say, the Carribean, but locals manage to enjoy the sport at various locations within a close proximity to the city. The experts can be found at **Above and Below Sports,** 4100 Franklin Ave., tel. (403) 669-9222. As well as advice on all the best dive sites, this company offers rentals ($49 per day for all the gear, including an air fill), dive instruction through the PADI system, and a boat for charter.

Golf

Yellowknife Golf Course is located west of downtown along Hwy. 3. The greens of this nine-hole course had always been oil-soaked sand but were recently replaced by artificial grass. One thing that won't change is the rock and gravel fairways. Each shot must be hit from a small mat that players carry around the course; green fees are $13. The club has a pro shop with rentals, a restaurant, and some great photos of the course's early days. For details call (403) 873-4326.

Entertainment

Entertainment at the **Gold Range Hotel,** 5010 50th St., tel. (403) 873-4441, best known as the "Strange Range," is like no other in the country. Don't be put off by the unusual characters, hundreds of empty beer glasses, and bouncers with legs like tree trunks; it isn't as rowdy as it seems. There's live entertainment on weekends, including one bloke who, in the winter months, rides 50 km on his snowmobile from his remote trapper's cabin to perform. If you like to mix with the locals this is the place to do it, and you may help them claim the title for highest beer sales per capita in Canada; so far they only run second. On Franklin Ave. **The Gallery,** tel. (403) 873-2651, also has live entertainment but is rougher.

Down in Old Town, overlooking Back Bay, is the **Old Town Pub,** 3502 Wiley Rd., tel. (403) 920-2739. A casual bar here serves beer and light meals. The bar top is the wing of a De-Haviland Beaver that crashed nearby. Beer is $5.50 a pint. Out front is a rusty plane engine that spent three years on the bottom of the bay. The pub is open Mon.-Sat. 11:30 a.m.-midnight.

Shopping

Yellowknife has many arts and crafts shops, but the best place for browsing is the **North West Co. Trading Post,** 5005 Bryson Dr., tel. (403) 873-8064. The store sells native arts, warm clothing, northern literature, and tacky souvenirs. It's a replica of trading posts that once dotted the north; open daily 10 a.m.-9 p.m. For limited-edition prints, paintings and carvings from throughout the north head to the **Arctic Art Gallery,** 4801 Franklin Ave., tel. (403) 873-5666.

Festivals and Events

Not many visitors are around for the **Caribou Carnival,** the last weekend of March. Events include bingo on ice and log-sawing, flour-packing, igloo-building, dog-mushing, and ugliest truck contests. The weekend closest to Summer Solstice (21 June) is **Raven Mad Daze,** featuring street entertainment and a midnight-sun golf tournament (this event is popular with visitors, so make reservations in advance, tel. (403) 920-4999). **Folk on the Rocks,** the third weekend of July, takes place on the shore of Long Lake and attracts northern and southern performers. The **Commissioner's Cup Race,** the last weekend of August, is a yacht race from Yellowknife across Great Slave Lake and back again. Call (403) 873-8019 for entry details.

ACCOMMODATIONS

Hotels and Motels

Yellowknife Inn, P.O. Box 490, Yellowknife, NT X1A 2N4, tel. (403) 873-2601, is right in the center of the city. Each room has a mini-bar and is well decorated. Guests have use of a health club, laundry, and an airport shuttle; $139 s, $159 d. Other hotels are: **Igloo Inn,** 4115 Franklin Ave., P.O. Box 596, NT X1A 2N4, tel. (403) 873-8511, halfway to Old Town, $94 s, $99 d, extra for kitchenettes; **Discovery Inn,** 4701 Franklin Ave., P.O. Box 784, NT X1A 2N6, tel. (403) 873-4151, simply furnished with older-style rooms and a bar downstairs, $105 s, $120 d; and **Explorer Hotel** on 47th St., Postal Service 7000, NT X1A 2R3, tel. (403) 873-3531 or (800) 661-0892, an eight-story luxury hotel with air-conditioned rooms, many with views of Old Town and the rolling tundra beyond, $152 s, $167 d.

Bed and Breakfasts

Ask at the Visitors Centre for a current list of B&Bs. **Captain Ron's,** 8 Lessard Dr., Yellowknife, NT X1A 2G5, tel. (403) 873-3746, overlooking the floatplane base, has four rooms, a sundeck, library, and guest lounge; $75 s, $90 d. **Blue Raven B&B,** 37B Otto Dr., Yellowknife, NT X1A 2T9, tel. (403) 873-6328, on top of a hill on Latham Island, overlooks Great Slave Lake; $60 s, $75 d. For a full listing write to Yellowknife B&Bs, 22 Otto Dr., Yellowknife, NT X1A 2T8, or call (403) 873-6238.

Lodges

Of the many wilderness lodges surrounding the city, the only one accessible by road is **Prelude Lake Lodges,** P.O. Box 447, Yellowknife, NT X1A 2P8, tel. (403) 920-4654. It's 32 km east of town along the Ingraham Trail and offers cabins beginning at $65. Boats are available for rent and fishing is good in the lake. **Enodah Wilderness Travel,** P.O. Box 2382, NT X1A 2P8, tel. (403) 873-4334, has a lodge on Trout Rock, a two-square-km island 30 km west of Yellowknife that was once the site of a Dogrib community. The lodge specializes in fishing; three-day fishing trips start at $675 per person. **Plummer's Great Slave Lake Lodge,** 950 Bradford St., Winnipeg, MB R3H 0N5, tel. (204) 774-5775 or (800) 665-0240, is located at Taltheilei Narrows on the northeast corner of the lake at a point of fish migration. The lodge offers cabins (each with private bathroom), a trading post, restaurant, and fishing from six-meter boats. Access is from Winnipeg—aboard a Boeing 737 each Saturday, or smaller planes from Yellowknife during the week.

Campgrounds

The city's only campground is at **Fred Henne Territorial Park,** tel. (403) 920-2472, across from the airport and a one-hour walk from downtown. Facilities include bug-proof kitchen shelters, woodstoves, showers, and some powered sites; $10 per night. Along the Ingraham Trail, at Reid Lake, is a primitive campground. Both are open late May-September.

FOOD

Cheap Eats

Fortunately, you need not spend a fortune to experience true northern cuisine or hospitality. The **Wildcat Cafe,** 3904 Wiley Rd., tel. (403) 873-8850, has been famous since it was opened by Willy Wiley and Smoky Stout in 1937, becoming the first place in Yellowknife to sell ice cream. The cafe closed its doors in 1959 but reopened with some remodeling in 1979. It only has a few tables and is perpetually full—chances are you'll end up sharing a table. The menu features mostly northern dishes from $12. It's open in summer only, Mon.-Sat. 7 a.m.-10 p.m., Sunday 10 a.m.-9 p.m. Across the road, **Old Town Pub,** tel. (403) 920-2739, has a popular barbecue Fri.-Sat. nights.

Red Apple in the Discovery Inn, tel. (403) 873-2324, opens at 6 a.m. and is a popular spot for breakfast. It also serves a variety of dishes starting at $7.50 the rest of the day. Farther out is **Sam's Monkey Tree,** 483 Range Lake Rd., tel. (403) 920-4914, a good, clean, family-style restaurant. **Latitudes,** in Centre Square Mall below the Yellowknife Inn, tel. (403) 920-7880, is a stylish, dimly lit restaurant open daily for breakfast and lunch and Thurs.-Fri. until 9 p.m. Cooked breakfasts are $6.25 and the rest of the day main meals start at $10.

McDonald's and **KFC** (once voted the national dish of the NWT) have one franchise each in Yellowknife, and here in the north, take-away really means take-away; when people from outlying communities visit the capital they often take a large supply home with them to microwave. KFC has even developed special boxes that will fit under airplane seats.

Other Restaurants

A number of upscale restaurants in Yellowknife serve northern specialties. Small and dimly lit, **The Office,** 4915 50th St., tel. (403) 873-3750, serves delicious arctic char and other seafood dishes from $18. **Bistro on Franklin,** 4910 Franklin Ave., tel. (403) 873-3991, is similarly priced but with a more intimate atmosphere. **Our Place** in the 50/50 Mini Mall Building on Franklin Ave., tel. (403) 920-2265, is a well-decorated cocktail lounge serving meals. Another option is the more-casual **Sweetgrass Cafe,** 5022 47th St., tel. (403) 873-9640, with an outside patio for those warm summer afternoons.

TRANSPORTATION

Air

Yellowknife Airport, five km west of the city along Hwy. 3, is the hub of air travel in the NWT. It is open daily 24 hours, has an inexpensive cafe (5:30 a.m.-10 p.m.), a bar, lockers, and rental cars. Airlines with scheduled flights to Yel-

lowknife from Edmonton and Calgary include: **Canadian North,** tel. (403) 873-4484, (800) 665-1177, or, in the U.S., (800) 426-7000; and **NWT Air,** tel. (403) 920-2500 or (800) 661-0789. Both these airlines provide scheduled services from Yellowknife to points throughout the Arctic. Other scheduled airlines flying to Yellowknife include: **Alkan Air,** from Whitehorse, tel. (403) 668-2107 or (800) 661-0432; **First Air,** from the Baffin region, tel. (403) 873-6884 or (800) 267-1247; **Air Tindi,** from communities around Great Slave Lake, tel. (403) 920-4177; **Buffalo Airways,** from Hay River and Fort Simpson, tel. (403) 873-6112; **Great Bear Aviation,** from communities along the Mackenzie River, tel. (403) 873-3626; **Northwestern,** from Fort Smith, tel. (403) 872-2216; **North-Wright Air,** from communities along the Mackenzie River, tel. (403) 920-4287; and **Ptarmigan Airways,** from communities around Great Slave Lake and the Arctic coast, tel. (403) 873-4461 or (800) 661-0808.

Touch the Arctic Adventure Tours

If you're flying up to Yellowknife from Edmonton or Calgary, the best options are with Touch the Arctic Adventure Tours, tel. (800) 661-0894. Operated by NWT Air, the company offers excellent deals on airfare and accommodation packages to the capital. For example, airfare, three nights accommodation, and a rental car is $734 per person. Off-season tours, which focus on the northern lights as well as dog sledding, ice fishing, and viewing caribou, are $931 per person.

Bus

Frontier Coachlines, 328 Old Airport Rd., tel. (403) 873-4892, offers bus service five times weekly from Hay River to Yellowknife ($64.50 one-way), with connections from there to Greyhound's other Canadian services.

Getting Around

Flag charge for a cab is $2.50, then it's $1.40 for every kilometer. To the campground is $10, to the airport $12; call **City Cab** at (403) 873-4444. Rental-car agencies include: **Rent-A-Relic,** tel. (403) 873-3400; and **Yellowknife Motors,** tel. (403) 873-4414. Rates start at $35 per day and $190 per week for a small car, plus 20 cents per kilometer. Other rental agencies include **Avis,** tel. (403) 920-2491 or (800) 879-2847;

Budget, tel. (403) 873-3366 or (800) 268-8900; and **Tilden,** tel. (403) 920-2970 or (800) 387-4747. **Sports Traders,** 5 Old Airport Rd., tel. (403) 893-9030, rents bikes for $5 per hour and $20 per 24 hours.

City Tours

Raven Tours, tel. (403) 873-4776, runs a three-hour City of Gold Sightseeing Tour that takes in all the sights of New Town, Old Town, Latham Island, and a sled-dog kennel; $20 per person. The tour departs Mon.-Sat. at 1:15 p.m. from the Visitors Centre. The company also offers guided hikes to Cameron River Falls ($38 per person), a two-hour lake cruise ($24 per person), and flightseeing (from $49 per person).

SERVICES AND INFORMATION

Services

The **post office** is located at 4902 50th Street. **Arctic Laundromat,** 4310 Franklin Ave., is open daily 8:30 a.m.-9 p.m. **Photo Works,** in the Centre Square Mall, tel. (403) 873-2389, develops film in one hour and has a limited range of camera supplies. On the main drag, **Yellowknife Foto Source,** 5005 Franklin Ave., tel. (403) 873-2196, has the same services.

    Stanton Yellowknife Hospital is on Old Airport Rd. at Range Lake Rd., tel. (403) 920-4111. For the **RCMP** call (403) 669-1111.

Books and Bookstores

Yellowknife Public Library is on the second floor of Centre Square Mall at 5022 49th St., tel. (403) 873-5980. Although small, it has newspapers from throughout Canada and lots of literature on the north. It's open year-round Mon.-Thurs. 10 a.m.-9 p.m., Fri.-Sat. 10 a.m.-6 p.m. **Yellowknife Book Cellar,** in Panda II Mall, tel. (403) 920-2220, has a wide selection of northern and Canadian literature. The north's biggest publisher, **Outcrop,** at 5022 51st St., tel. (403) 920-4652, has back issues of *Up*

Here for sale and catalogs of all books they publish.

Tourist Information

The **Northern Frontier Regional Visitors Centre** overlooks Frame Lake at 4807 49th St., tel. (403) 873-4262. It is stocked with brochures on everything you'll need to know about Yellowknife, historic photographs, and interesting displays. It's open in summer daily 8 a.m.-8 p.m., the rest of the year weekdays only.

COMMUNITIES IN THE VICINITY OF YELLOWKNIFE

Within a 250-km radius of Yellowknife are five communities accessible only by air, or in the case of Reliance and Lutsel K'e, by boat. Each receives few casual visitors, and if you plan to stay overnight, you should reserve accommodations before arriving. **Air Tindi,** tel. (403) 920-4177, and **Ptarmigan Airways,** tel. (403) 873-4461, fly to each of the communities. Fares range $90-119 each way.

Lutsel K'e

Formerly known as **Snowdrift,** this community of 260 Chipewyan Dene is located on a peninsula extending into the East Arm of Great Slave Lake. The Hudson's Bay Company established a post here in 1925, which quickly attracted Chipewyan families from the surrounding area. Nearby you'll find some excellent fishing and sheer cliffs that drop into the lake. **Snowdrift Co-op Hotel,** General Delivery, Lutsel K'e, NT X0E 1A0, tel. (403) 370-3511, has three rooms, each with shared bath; $115 per person.

Wha Ti

Meaning "Marten Lake" in English, Wha Ti (formerly known as **Lac La Martre**) is a community of 400 Dogrib Dene on the southeast shore of a shallow lake 160 km northwest of Yellowknife. A North West Company trading post was established on the lake in 1793. Today, the community functions much as it did then, relying on the area's abundant fish and mammals to provide a subsistence lifestyle. **Meni Khon Hotel,** General Delivery, Wha Ti, NT X0E 1P0, tel. (403) 573-3161, has 12 rooms for $180 per person per day inclusive of meals, as well as a lodge on the northeast shore of the lake.

Rae Lakes

This community had until recently been used as an outpost for hunting by the Dogrib Dene. It is located on the shore of a lake that is part of a chain between Great Slave and Great Bear Lakes. Permanent facilities and new housing have kept the population around 200.

Gameti Motel, General Delivery, Rae Lakes, NT X0E 1R0, tel. (403) 997-3031, has eight rooms with private bath and the staff can organize fishing trips; rooms are $160 per person inclusive of meals.

Snare Lake

Until recently this community was, like Rae Lakes to the west, an outpost for hunters of the Dogrib Dene. The community of 100 is located east of Rae Lakes. Accommodations are offered in four rooms at **Snare Lake Hotel,** General Delivery, Snare Lake, NT X0E 1W0, tel. (403) 713-2700. Rates are $175 per person per day including meals. The hotel organizes fishing and wildlife viewing trips for guests.

RIVERS OF MYTH, MOUNTAINS OF MYSTERY

Tucked into the southwest corner of the territories—between the Mackenzie River to the north and east and the Yukon Territory and British Columbia to the south and west—is a wild, uninhabited, roadless land of jagged peaks, thundering rivers, a waterfall twice the height of Niagara, and pristine lakes so full of fish that you'll need to bait your hook behind a tree. Not only is it one of North America's most remote mountain regions, it is one of the least understood. Scientists are only recently beginning to unravel the mysteries of the strikingly varied landforms within Nahanni National Park, a UNESCO World Heritage Site. The region's history is equally mysterious. A little-known band of Indians once lived here, high in the mountains, which was feared by the Slavey Dene who lived along the Liard and Mackenzie Rivers. Legends of lost gold mines, tropical valleys, and headless bodies have been luring adventurers to the area for over 100 years. The first white men to travel up the South Nahanni River were fur trappers and missionaries. Those who managed to return brought back stories that helped create the region's mythical allure. Today, visitors from around the world come to paddle down the South Nahanni (Canada's finest wilderness river), climb in the Cirque of the Unclimbables, or just fly into this spectacular part of the world. But with names on the map like Headless Creek, Deadmen Valley, Hell's Gate, Funeral Range, Devils Kitchen, Broken Skull River, and Death Canyon, you'd better tell someone where you're going.

Nahanni National Park is visited by fewer than 1,500 people each year. Roads have replaced rivers as transportation routes through much of the region, but communities built around fur-trading posts still remain. The Mackenzie Hwy., which begins in northern Alberta, ends 427 km west of Hay River in Fort Simpson, the main jumping-off point for wilderness trips into the Nahanni and beyond.

Saamba Deh Falls Territorial Park

From the Yellowknife junction, the Mackenzie Hwy. continues west through a typical northern boreal forest, along the way crossing many small creeks. Approximately 136 km from this junction, the road crosses **Trout River,** which flows alongside Saamba Deh Falls Territorial Park. The falls are directly downstream from the road bridge and are easily accessible from the day-use area. Here, the river is forced through a narrow gorge, exploding into the deep pond below. Worthwhile is the one-km hike upstream from the day-use area to **Coral Falls,** named for the abundant marine fossils found in the surrounding limestone banks. Most common are crinoids and brachiopods that are around 400

ALBERT FAILLE

Each break-up from 1916 to 1961, Albert Faille left Fort Simpson by scow in a feverish, determined quest for the elusive Nahanni gold. Some said it was sheer lunacy, others said a waste of time. But his relentless obsession and exploits against insurmountable odds created the Faille legend, which has become synonymous with the Nahanni.

Of Swiss descent, Faille was born in Minnesota and first ventured into Nahanni Country in 1927. He was one of the earliest men to tackle the river alone, and at the time, the first to winter there in seven years. He built a cabin at the mouth of the Flat River, but it was at Murder Creek, upstream from the cabin, that Faille believed his fortune in gold lay. At times he'd be given up for dead, and rumors and tales would begin to unfold—but then he would turn up at Fort Simpson for supplies. He spent most winters in a small cabin that still stands today, overlooking the Mackenzie River in Fort Simpson. He died there in 1974. His scows still lie out front, ready for break-up and another attempt for the elusive key to finding gold. His final trip is documented by a 1961 National Film Board production that can be seen in the Fort Simpson and Blackstone visitor centers.

million years old (Late Devonian period). The trail is well defined at first, then climbs steeply, making getting down to the river level in one piece rather interesting. The alternative is to scramble down along the river as soon as the trail begins climbing. The **Visitors Centre** has a small fossil display and free coffee. Across the parking lot is a TV room where the friendly staff can put on videos pertaining to the region's natural and human history; it's open mid-May to mid-September daily 8 a.m.-8 p.m. The park also has a small campground with showers, bug-proof kitchen shelters, and well-maintained sites for $10 a night.

From here, the Mackenzie Hwy. continues in a northwesterly direction to a junction with the Liard Hwy. (which heads south to Fort Liard and into British Columbia). Past the junction 46 km, it crosses the Liard River by ferry and, 16 km farther, ends in Fort Simpson. The ferry operates in summer daily 8 a.m.-11:45 p.m.

Trout Lake

This small community was established in the late 1960s as a permanent base for the Slavey Dene who had hunted, trapped, and fished in the area for thousands of years. It's located in a heavily wooded area where the Island River drains into Trout Lake, approximately 100 km east of Fort Liard. The community's only link to the outside world is by charter flight from Fort Liard or Fort Simpson or by a winter road from the Mackenzie Hwy., just east of Saamba Deh Falls Territorial Park. With a name like Trout Lake, it's not surprising that the fishing is excellent, especially for lake trout, pickerel, and whitefish. The best spot is at the lake's northern end, where the Moose River flows into the lake. The main problem with coming here to fish is that you reach your daily limit too quickly. The local Dene band runs a fishing lodge on the lake. The lodge costs $60 per person per day, with use of kitchen facilities, or $160 per person including meals and guided fishing. Boat rentals are also available. For more information call (403) 695-9800. **Deh Cho Air,** tel. (403) 770-

Lake trout inhabit the aptly named Trout Lake.

4103, in Fort Liard, flies to Trout Lake and also offers day trips to the lake for $170 per person.

Jean Marie River

The Slavey Dene of this small community (pop. 70) still hunt, trap, and fish for a living in the old way but are best known for their moose-hair tufting and porcupine-quill work, which can be purchased in Fort Simpson and Yellowknife. Located at the confluence of the Jean Marie and Mackenzie Rivers with no summer road access, the people of the community travel downstream to Fort Simpson to trade and buy supplies. No visitor services are available, but those en route down the Mackenzie are always welcome to drop in. Fort Simpson is 68 km downstream, along a section of river dotted with islands.

FORT SIMPSON

Best known as one of the jumping-off points for Nahanni National Park, the town of Fort Simpson (pop. 1,000) is at the confluence of two major rivers—the Liard and Mackenzie—and at the western terminus of the Mackenzie Highway. Throughout summer the town is a hive of activity, a constant buzz of floatplanes taking off to remote fly-in fishing lakes, groups of Gore-Tex–clad adventurers from around the world checking their equipment before heading off for the adventure of a lifetime down the South Nahanni River, and the occasional canoeload of paddlers stopping in on their way to the Arctic Ocean. The town provides a good base for exploring the region—whether by car, plane, boat, or on foot. Wildlife is abundant, and the lakes and rivers teem with fish.

History

It wasn't until 1815, after Alexander Mackenzie had paddled on his way to the Arctic Ocean, that a permanent settlement was established at this strategic location. Originally known as "Fort of the Forks," it was built by North West Company in 1804 but was renamed Fort Simpson in 1821. As well as being an important fur-

BOB RACE

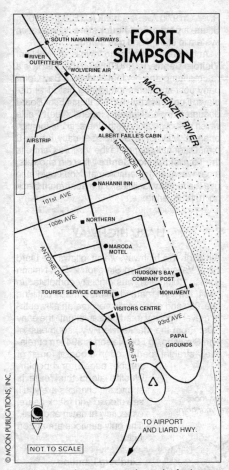

NOT TO SCALE

© MOON PUBLICATIONS, INC.

Around Town

At one time the town's main street was Mackenzie Dr., along the riverfront. But when the highway was completed, many buildings were moved closer to it. Now most town services are along 100th Street. At the south end of Mackenzie Dr. is an area known as "The Flat," where many people lived until severe flooding in 1963 forced relocation of homes. The large tepee and other structures here, known as the **Papal Grounds,** were built for a visit by Pope John Paul II on 20 September 1987. Walking north from here along Mackenzie Dr., a sternwheeler on the riverbank soon comes into view. Built in 1920, this boat was one of many that plied the Mackenzie River. Also here is a small monument noting the importance of the river in the town's history. Across the road is the site of the Hudson's Bay Company post; the only original building remaining is the company's outhouse. Continuing farther along the river you pass the site of an Anglican church, the RCMP, an early hotel, the Power Corporation building, and the cabin of Nahanni legend Albert Faille. Faille wintered here between his gold-seeking trips. Peering through the windows and marveling at the wooden scows laying in the yard will give you some insight into the life of this amazing man, particularly if you've watched the National Film Board documentary about him shown at the Visitors Centre (see "Services and Information," below). Faille is buried behind the post office on 100th Street. North along Mackenzie Dr., at the far end of the airstrip, is the staging area for the four outfitters operating trips down the South Nahanni River.

Recreation

Many local lakes have great fishing. **McGill Lake** and **Mustard Lake** are two of the many fly-in spots with trophy-size northern pike, pickerel, lake trout, and arctic grayling. If you've never gotten hooked on fishing, perhaps golf sounds better. Down by the entrance to town on Antoine Dr. is the local golf course. It can boast only six holes and has no clubhouse or rentals, but the local golfing population is proud of it.

Accommodations and Food

Along the road into town is **Bannockland Resorts B&B,** P.O. Box 656, NT X0E 0N0, tel.

trading post, it was a stopping point for barges plying the Mackenzie River loaded with supplies, fuel, and furs. Missions were established in 1858 and 1894, and the area's potential for agriculture began to be realized. The government operated an experimental farm here for years, but it was closed in 1969 when a highway linking Fort Simpson to the outside was completed and importing food overland became practical. During the 1960s the town became a base for oil exploration along the Mackenzie Valley and an administrative center for the territorial government.

(403) 695-3337. It's the home of long-time north-erners, the Sibbestons, who have opened a few rooms to visitors. Each room has private facilities and rates include a cooked breakfast; $75 s, $100 d. Rooms in both of Fort Simpson's hotels are little more than basic. **Maroda Motel,** P.O. Box 67, Fort Simpson, tel. (403) 695-2602, charges $100 s, $115 d; **Nahanni Inn,** P.O. Box 248, tel. (403) 695-2201, has a coffee shop (open daily at 8 a.m.) and dining room; rooms are $105 s, $115 d. Both are within walking distance of everything. On the road to the Papal Grounds is **Fort Simpson Campground.** The sites—$5 a night—provide ample privacy, and a large supply of firewood is available. On the Yellowknife-side of the ferry is another primitive campground. Anyone heading into the Nahanni with a river outfitter may pitch a tent at the airstrip compound for free; ask permission first.

For breakfast, everyone heads to the coffee shop in the Nahanni Inn, but it's nothing special. Northern has a take-out outlet for Pizza Hut and KFC specialties.

Transportation

The main airport is 12 km south of town ($15 in a cab, tel. 403-695-2777). Two airlines fly to Fort Simpson, both from Yellowknife (all connections from the south are through the territorial capital). **Buffalo Airways,** tel. (403) 874-3333, a connector airline for Air Canada, flies from Yellowknife Monday, Wednesday, and Friday at 10:10 a.m. The fare is $170 each way. **Ptarmigan,** tel. (403) 873-4461, flies the same route, as well as across the Mackenzie Mountains to Whitehorse; $369 each way. The floatplane base is along Mackenzie Dr. at the north end of town.

Services and Information

Groceries and basic camping supplies are available from **Northern,** but you should stock up in Hay

Save a moose, honk your horn.

BOB RACE

River. On 97th Ave. is a **bank** (C.I.B.C.), on 100th St. are a **post office, liquor store** (with a ration system in effect), and **gas station.**

At the south entrance to town is an excellent **Visitors Centre,** tel. (403) 695-3182. Inside is a re-creation of the original Hudson's Bay Company post and some interesting historical displays. Don't miss the 1961 National Film Board documentary on Nahanni legend Albert Faille which is shown, along with others, in the theater; open 15 May to 15 September daily 8 a.m.-8 p.m. Diagonally opposite the Visitors Centre is the **Tourist Service Centre** with coin showers, a car wash, and a laundromat. You could also use the laundry facilities in the apartment block on 101st Avenue.

LIARD HIGHWAY

Although this highway, which follows the Liard River Valley from Fort Simpson to Fort Nelson (British Columbia), was officially completed in 1984, it wasn't marked on most maps until the late '80s and didn't really become an all-weather gravel highway (read passable) until the early '90s. From the Mackenzie Hwy., southeast of Fort Simpson, to Fort Nelson is 394 km of relatively straight road through a boreal forest of spruce, aspen, and poplar. Wildlife along this route is abundant; chances are you'll see moose and black bears, especially at dawn and dusk. The only services are at Fort Liard.

Lindberg Landing

Although the highway parallels the Liard River, access to the water is limited. One of the first landings is 100 km south of the Mackenzie Hwy. at the home of Ed and Sue Lindberg, who provide accommodations and have an amazingly diverse vegetable garden. Ed Lindberg's father, Ole, arrived from Sweden in the mid-1920s and was the first permanent settler along the river. The service offered by the Lindbergs is excellent for those beginning or ending a journey down the South Nahanni River. **Blackstone Aviation** will pick you up at the landing and drop you upriver, allowing you to float back to Lindberg Landing farm and finish your trip with a bed, beer, and shower. Reservations for rooms are essential; no walk-ins. Dinner, bed, and breakfast is $65 per person. A housekeeping room, which sleeps four, is $70. For bookings write to P.O. Box 28, Fort Simpson, NT X0E 0N0. From within the territories dial 0 and ask the operator to connect you to Pointed Mountain Channel Mobile JR3-6644. From the north, Lindberg Landing is marked by a small sign in a tree. If you pass Blackstone Territorial Park you missed it.

Blackstone Territorial Park

Just south of the Lindberg's homestead, where the Blackstone River drains into the Liard River, a small territorial park has been established at a site known as **Blackstone Landing**. A Visitors Centre overlooks the river and from there a short trail leads along the river to a trapper's cabin. The campground has flush toilets, showers, and two bug-proof, woodstove-equipped kitchen shelters hidden among the trees. Sites cost $10 a night. Black bears are common so keep your food securely stored. The Visitors Centre has interesting displays on the area's history, a good selection of videos, and information on Nahanni National Park (although registering for a trip into the park must be done in Fort Simpson); open mid-May to mid-September daily 8 a.m.-8 p.m.

From the park, Fort Liard is 114 km farther south. The highway crosses many small creeks, passes the winter road to Nahanni Butte, and provides views of the Liard Range to the west. Approximately 68 km south of Blackstone Territorial Park is a winter road that was cut through the muskeg to the now-abandoned Paramount Mine, on the opposite side of the Liard River. It is a pleasant one-km hike (15 minutes each way) down to the river.

Nahanni Butte

Named for the steeply sided butte across the South Nahanni River, this small Slavey Dene community of under 100 is located across the Liard River from the highway. Although you can drive to it in winter, the rest of the year it is accessible only by plane or boat. The town is fairly modern. It was established by the government to house a group of once-nomadic natives who, at times, traded with the Tahltan and Tlingit of the Pacific coast. For many years Nahanni National Park headquarters was here, and a small office still operates in summer for "checking-out" after a river trip. Most paddlers stop by anyway as the town is in a picturesque setting and holds an interesting log church and log school. Except for a small general store, no services are available. **Blackstone Aviation,** tel. (403) 695-2111 (or call the operator on 0 and ask for Arrowhead Channel YJ3-9704), flies from Lindberg or Blackstone Landing to Nahanni Butte for $180 roundtrip.

FORT LIARD

Best known as the "Tropics of the North," this town of 400 is set among a lush forest of poplar and birch on the banks of the Liard River. The southern location, warm climate, and rich soil mean that residents are able to grow a variety of vegetables. Log homes and green gardens make the six-km detour from the Liard Hwy. worthwhile.

The North West Company established a post in 1807 where the Petitot River drains into the Liard, but abandoned it after many of the residents were massacred by natives. In 1821, after the company merged with the Hudson's Bay Company, the post reopened, but trade was continually disrupted by warring native tribes. Until the 1960s most of the Dene inhabitants spent winter away from Fort Liard, and it wasn't until the highway opened to Fort Nelson that modern development began. Traditional lifestyles are still important to residents, nearly all of whom spend time trapping, hunting, fishing, and making clothing and crafts.

Birchbark Baskets

The women of Fort Liard are famous for these baskets, made for storing food, collecting berries, carrying supplies, or even boiling water. Birch is abundant in the area and has a remarkably pliable nature, ideal for bending and sewing. The bark contains a natural wax, making it not only rot-resistant but waterproof. Baskets are still made in the long, tedious process handed down from generation to generation. They are sewn together with specially prepared roots and decorated with porcupine quills. If you are unable to afford a soapstone carving from Cape Dorset, these baskets are a good second choice for a northern souvenir. They are available from the small gift store on Fort Liard's main street, or in Fort Simpson and Hay River.

Practicalities
The small but well-maintained **Hay Lake Campground** has pit toilets, firewood, and drinking water. It's located along the Fort Liard access road; sites are $10 a night. The small motel (above the grocery store) sleeps 24 in 12 basic rooms, for $90 s, $120 d; tel. (403) 770-4441. Back out on the highway is a gas station open 7 a.m.-11 p.m.

Deh Cho Air, P.O. Box 78, Fort Liard, NT X0G 0A0, tel. (403) 770-4103, flies from Fort Liard into Nahanni National Park, and to Trout Lake for legendary fishing.

NAHANNI NATIONAL PARK

Through this rugged land of mountains flows one of the most spectacular, wildest, and purest stretches of whitewater in the world—the South Nahanni River. Protecting a 300-km stretch of this remote river is 4,766-square-km Nahanni National Park, which boasts some of the world's most breathtaking, undeveloped mountain scenery. The park holds North America's deepest river canyons and a waterfall twice the height of Niagara. It's home to legends of deadly Indian tribes and hapless prospectors whose bodies turned up headless. The roadless park is a vast wilderness inhabited only by bears, mountain goats, Dall's sheep, caribou, moose, and wolves, and is accessible only by air or water.

The best way to really experience the park is on a one- to three-week canoe or raft trip down the river, offered by four outfitters. However you decide to visit the park, whether with an outfitter, on your own carefully prepared expedition, or even just on a daylong flightseeing trip, it will be an adventure that will remain with you for the rest of your life.

Of Myths and Legends
Slavey Dene, who lived on the lowlands along the Mackenzie and Liard Rivers, feared a mysterious group of Indians living high in the Mackenzie Mountains. The mountain people, who became known as the Nahanni (meaning "the people who live far away"), would travel down the South Nahanni River each spring in boats up to 20 meters long. The boats were constructed of moose hide stretched over a spruce frame. Upon arrival at the trading post, the Indians would dismantle the boats, trading furs and the moose hides before returning on foot to the mountains.

Around 1900 a Nahanni Indian arrived at the trading post with a chunk of quartz bearing gold. That got some people's attention. In 1905 Willie and Frank McLeod began prospecting tributaries of the Flat River in search of an elusive mother lode. Three years later their headless bodies were discovered at the mouth of what is now known as Headless Creek; for many years thereafter, the entire valley was called Deadmen Valley. Very quickly, stories of gold mines, murder, lush tropical valleys, and a tribe of Indians dominated by a white woman became rampant. These stories did nothing but lure other prospecting adventurers to the valley—Jorgenson, Shebbach, Field, Faille, Sibbeston, Kraus, and Patterson. Many died mysteriously: Jorgenson's skeleton was found outside his cabin, his precious rifle gone; Shebbach died of starvation at the mouth of Caribou Creek; the body of Phil Powers was discovered in his burned out cabin; Angus Hall just plain disappeared.

The Land
The **Mackenzie Mountains** rise abruptly from the lowlands west of the Mackenzie River. The headwaters of the **South Nahanni River** are high in these mountains, northwest of the park along the NWT/Yukon border. Flowing in a roughly southeasterly direction for 540 km, it drains into the Liard River, a major tributary of the Mackenzie River. The South Nahanni, cut deeply into the mountains, is known as an "antecedent;" that is, it preceded the mountains. It once meandered through a wide-open plain. As uplift in the earth's surface occurred, the river cut down through the rising rock strata and created the deep, meandering canyons present today.

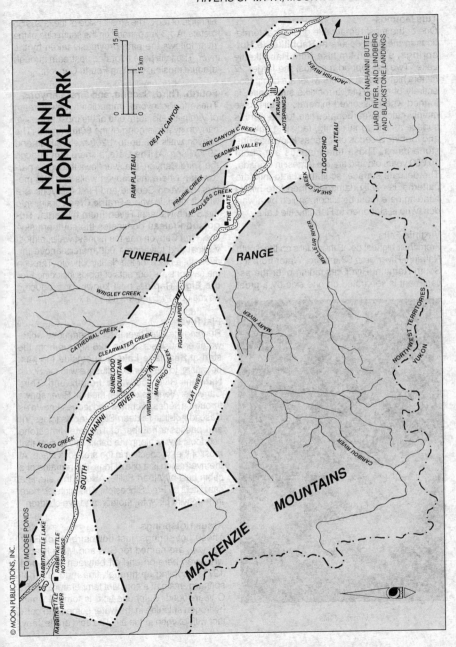

NAHANNI
NATIONAL PARK

© MOON PUBLICATIONS, INC.

Tufa Mounds

One of the most remarkable geological formations in the park occurs at **Rabbitkettle Hotsprings,** a seven-km hike from Rabbitkettle Lake. Two flat-topped mounds, the larger 27 meters high and 60 meters wide, are composed entirely of tufa. Tufa, a rocklike substance, is formed when dissolved minerals, in this case mainly calcium carbonate, rise to the earth's surface as a thermal spring, radiating outward and forming a series of terraces known as rimstone dams. These tufa mounds are about 10,000 years old and are the largest in Canada. The delicate surface, sculptured into intricate patterns, is easily damaged, therefore hikers heading here must be accompanied by a warden, who is stationed at Rabbitkettle Lake.

Virginia Falls

From their highest point, these falls on the South Nahanni River drop 92 meters. Water from the South Nahanni River cascading over the escarpment is separated on one side by a great

Virginia Falls

pinnacle of rock. The smaller side of the falls is 55 meters. A 1.3-km portage on the south side of the river follows the path previously taken by the river. The falls have migrated upstream through gradual erosion, creating Fourth Canyon.

Fourth, Third, Second, and First Canyons

These four canyons, immediately downstream of Virginia Falls, form one of the most extensive canyon systems north of the 60th parallel. The canyon walls are up to 1,200 meters high and 19 km long. At **The Gate,** a sharp turn through the Third Canyon, the river flows through a narrow gap where the canyon walls rise 460 meters. Between Second and First Canyons is a wide floodplain where **Prairie Creek** drains into the South Nahanni River. From this area, **Tlogotsho Plateau** dominates the southern skyline. First Canyon has the highest walls, almost vertical and towering 1,000 meters above the river; not a place for the claustrophobic. Through the canyons are four sets of rapids including **Figure Eight Rapids,** best known for producing waves up to 1.5 meters high.

Flat River

Running the Flat River is for experienced whitewater enthusiasts. It is a 125-km run from the start at **Seaplane Lake,** just outside the park boundary, to the river's confluence with the South Nahanni River between Fourth and Third Canyons. Along its course, the Flat River spews through a series of chutes and ledges known as Cascade-of-the-Thirteen-Steps rapids (class VI) and passes a number of 15-meter limestone hoodoos. It was along the banks of this river that most of the prospecting in the area took place. At the rivermouth is a pile of logs, the remains of a cabin built by Albert Faille. Also at this site is a cabin built by Fred Sibbeston, who wintered here in 1944 with his wife, mother, and five children.

Kraus Hotsprings

These hot springs, just downstream of First Canyon, are named for Gus and Mary Kraus, who lived here on and off between 1940 and 1971. Bubbling up through fine mud, the hot springs remain at a constant temperature of 35° C year-round. Sulphuric acid is formed when hydrogen sulphide in the water comes into contact with oxygen in the air. The acid erodes any tufa that forms, and, more importantly for those planning a relaxing soak, it produces a strong rotten-egg smell. Many exotic plants thrive here, a legacy of the Krauses' garden.

Running the South Nahanni with an Outfitter

For most people, whether experienced canoeists or never-evers, the advantages of a trip down the South Nahanni River with a licensed outfitter far outweigh the disadvantages. Four companies, all based in Fort Simpson, have licenses to operate guided river trips. Each offers trips of varying lengths—three weeks from Moose Ponds, two weeks from Rabbitkettle Lake, or eight to 12 days from Virginia Falls. Itineraries are worked out so that no more than four to seven hours per day are spent on the river, leaving plenty of time for hiking, exploring, and viewing wildlife. Craft used are either rafts, 5.5-meter canoes, or longer voyageur-type canoes. The small canoes hold two people and are generally for those with some previous paddling experience. Inflatable rafts are great if you want to lay back and relax as you float down the river under a guide's supervision. Only Nahanni River Adventures offers trips in the voyageur canoes, which are 10 meters long and seat eight, including a guide. They are an excellent compromise, offering the stability of a raft, but with the feeling of canoeing; you can paddle as much, or as little, as you like.

Prices between operators vary little and are generally $2,000-3,500. Some offer a small discount for those with their own tent, others charge more for those without. Check whether the price includes GST (seven percent). Most importantly, talk to each outfitter (they all love "their" river, so getting them to talk is no problem). Guided trips operate mid-June to early September and many dates fill up fast. The staging area for all commercial outfitters is the north end of the old airstrip in downtown Fort Simpson.

Outfitters include: **Nahanni River Adventures,** P.O. Box 4869, Whitehorse, YT Y1A 4N6, tel. (403) 668-3180; **Nahanni Wilderness Adventures,** Box 4, Site 6, R.R. 1, Didsbury, AB T0M 0W0, tel. (403) 637-3843; **Whitewolf Adventure Expeditions,** 41-1355 Citadel Dr., Port Coquitlam, BC V3C 5X6, tel. (604) 944-5500 or (800) 661-6659; **Black Feather,** 1960 Scott St., Ottawa, ON K1Z 8L8, tel. (613) 722-9717 or (800) 574-8375.

Your Own Whitewater Expedition

Experienced whitewater enthusiasts planning their own trip down the Nahanni have four main components to organize: permits and fees, transportation into the park, transportation down the river, and supplies.

Permits and Fees: Due to the high number of visitors using the river, a reservation and fee system have been implemented. Two nonguided parties are allowed to start out each day, with a maximum of two nights at Virginia Falls. For those beginning their river trip upstream of Virginia Falls, their allotted time starts when they reach the falls. The fee is $100 per person. Outfitters incorporate the cost into their charges. For all the relevant forms and further information, call park headquarters at (403) 695-2310.

Entering the Park: Most expeditions begin from Virginia Falls. Floatplanes land upstream from the falls from where, in readiness for the trip downstream, a steep portage must be made to the base of the falls. To prevent the cost of an air charter at the end of your trip it is best to pull out along the Liard River at Blackstone or Lindberg Landing, a full day's paddle downstream of the park boundary.

Four charter companies take paddlers into the park. They use three different types of planes. These are: Cessna 185s, capable of carrying two passengers, a canoe or kayak, and gear to a total of 500-600 pounds; Beavers, capable of carrying four passengers, two (nesting) canoes, and gear to a total of 1,000-1,200 pounds; and Twin Otters, which can carry six passengers, three (nesting) canoes, and gear to a total of 1,500 pounds. **Blackstone Aviation,** P.O. Box 117, Fort Simpson, NT X0E 0N0 (call the operator at 0 and ask for Arrowhead Channel YJ3-9704), is the only charter operator who is based at the pull-out point, meaning that you can start and finish the trip at the same place. Blackstone flies a Cessna 185. Charter rates are $660 to Virginia Falls, Rabbitkettle Lake $980, and Moose Ponds $1,400. **Deh Cho Air,** P.O. Box 78, Fort Liard, NT X0G 0A0, tel. (403) 770-4103, leaves from Fort Liard, but charter rates include van transportation from Blackstone Landing back to Fort Liard. Charter rates in the Cessna 185 are: to Virginia Falls, $750; Rabbitkettle Lake, $1,050; Moose Ponds, $1,500; and Glacier Lake, $1,100. Air mileage from Fort Simpson is longer and therefore more expensive, but the town has canoe rentals, restaurants, motels, groceries, and an airport with connections to the outside world. **Wolverine Air,** P.O. Box 316, Fort Simpson, NT X0E 0N0, tel. (403) 695-2263, runs a Cessna 185 and a Beaver; rates according to destination are: Virginia Falls, $860 in the Cessna and $1,069 in the Beaver; Rabbitkettle Lake, $1,138 and $1,426; Moose Ponds, $1,662 and $2,054; and Glacier Lake, $1,209 and $1,499. **South Nahanni Airways,** P.O. Box 40, Fort Simpson, NT X0E 0N0, tel. (403) 695-2007, is used by the outfitters for its larger Twin Otter. To Virginia Falls is $2,707; Rabbitkettle Lake, $3,567; Moose Ponds, $5,140; and Glacier Lake, $3,429.

A few years back, I picked up a bloke who'd just come down the river and was hitchhiking back to Watson Lake from Blackstone Landing. He'd started at Moose Ponds, which is closer to Watson Lake (Yukon) than any NWT community, therefore chartering a plane from Watson Lake cost less. But it seemed an inconvienent way to save less than $100.

Down the River: The river can easily be divided into four sections. From Moose Ponds to Rabbitkettle Lake takes three to five days and includes a 60 km stretch of rapids. From Rabbitkettle Lake to Virginia Falls is a two- to three-day float down one of the river's easier stretches. After a short but steep portage around the falls there is a three- to four-day paddle through spectacular canyon scenery with many sets of rapids to an area known as "The Splits." Here the river flows into a broad floodplain, passing the community of Nahanni Butte and draining into the Liard River. Allow two days to get to Blackstone Landing from The Splits. The entire trip from Moose Ponds can be done in under two weeks, but make sure to allow extra days for hiking, exploring, or just relaxing.

Most people choose canoes for the trip, although kayaks and inflatable rafts are also feasible. Whatever craft you decide to use will need a spray deck, and all gear should be securely waterproofed. **Nahanni River Adventures** and **Nahanni Wilderness Adventures** rent canoes ($30-35 per day) and rafts ($150 per day). All rentals should be organized well before the summer season begins.

Supplies: Charter operators have reasonably generous load limits, allowing you to take plenty of food. But no amount of food can substitute for good prior planning; a crate of oranges picked up in British Columbia's Okanagan Valley or vegetables from Paradise Gardens, near Hay River, all help to make the trip more enjoyable—and oranges float if they finish overboard. Fort Simpson has a small grocery store, but don't count on finding your favorite brand of anything, especially at your favorite price. Stock up on plenty of bug repellent, bring lots of film, and if you bring a video camera, don't forget extra batteries—you'll be hundreds of miles from the nearest power source.

Hiking

Renowned for its river running, the park also has some fantastic hiking opportunities. Apart from the portage route around Virginia Falls, the park has no developed trails. **The Cirque of the Unclimbables,** near the Yukon border, is a spectacular arc of sheer-walled rock rising nearly 1,000 meters. It is a mecca for rock climbers from around the world but is in a nearly inaccessible part of the Logan Mountains. Most climbers access the region by helicopter from Watson Lake or hike in from Glacier Lake, on a tributary of the South Nahanni River. **Rabbitkettle Hotsprings** is a seven-km hike from Rabbitkettle Lake, a staging area where floatplanes drop river runners off. Most guided trips allow time for a hike to these amazing tufa mounds. All hikers heading to the hot springs must be accompanied by a park warden based at the lake.

The eight-km hike to the summit of **Sunblood Mountain** from Virginia Falls is one of the park's most popular hikes. Breathtaking views of the surrounding mountainscape and the river below are afforded from the top. **Marengo Falls,** four km from Virginia Falls, is another popular destination. Farther downstream the **Tlogotsho Plateau** is reached by an 18-km trek up Sheaf Creek; the **Ram Plateau** is accessible along Deadmen Valley; and six km up **Dry Canyon Creek** is a much smaller tundra-like plateau.

Flightseeing

Getting into the park for just the day is problematic but well worth the effort and cost. Typically, charter operators fly to Virginia Falls, with two hours on the ground. If you have three or more people in your group, there are no problems; just call each operator for their best quote (or get the staff at Fort Simpson Visitors Centre to do it). Groups of less than three have the choice of chartering an entire plane (from around $600) or waiting around for other interested parties to turn up. Each of the air charter companies can tailor flights to suit your need. By waiting around until the plane is full, or by booking in advance, you have more of a chance of keeping the cost down. **Blackstone Aviation** offers one-hour flights into the southern end of the park for $300 or a half-day trip including time on the ground at Virginia Falls for $640; maximum three people. To contact them call the operator at 0 and ask for Arrowhead Channel YJ3-9704. **Deh Cho Air,** tel. (403) 770-4103, has similar rates but is a little more flexible and gives you a choice of aircraft. At last report **Wolverine Air** in Fort Simpson, tel. (403) 695-2263, was flying a Beaver to Virginia Falls each Saturday. The cost, $195 per person, includes a couple of hours on the ground.

Camping
Campsites along the river should always be chosen on alluvial fans or sandbars occurring at the mouths of tributaries. Primitive campsites are located at Rabbitkettle Lake, Virginia Falls, and Kraus Hotsprings. **Virginia Falls** is a good base if you don't plan on a trip down the river. **Blackstone Aviation,** tel. (403) 695-2111, can carry three passengers and gear (without canoe) to the falls for $640 each way. **Deh Cho Air** offers the same overnight package for $300 per person roundtrip, but you'll need six people to get this rate. All campers should register at park headquarters in Fort Simpson.

More Information
A lot has been written about the Nahanni, both the natural and human history. One well-known book is *The Dangerous River* (1990) written by R.M. Patterson. Patterson is one of the river's legendary figures, and he spent many years in Nahanni Country with Albert Faille. Another storyteller and writer, Dick Turner, homesteaded for many years beside the Lindbergs on the Liard River. He is best known for his book *Nahanni* (1975), describing his life trapping and hunting in the Mackenzie Mountains. *Nahanni: River of Gold, River of Dreams* is a contemporary look at the river through yarns told by one of the river's most experienced guides, "Nahanni" Neil Hartling of Nahanni River Adventures. *National Geographic* published an article about the river in September 1981.

The outfitters on the river are experts in their own right and can answer many of your questions long before you arrive. For specific information on the park write to Superintendent, Nahanni National Park, P.O. Box 348, Fort Simpson, NT X0E 0N0, tel. (403) 695-2310. **Park Headquarters,** once located in Dick Turner's old cabin at Nahanni Butte, is now in Fort Simpson. Head there for further information and to pick up trip permits. Fort Simpson Visitors Centre has park displays as well as relevant videos and books for visitor use. The same service on a smaller scale is offered at Blackstone Territorial Park.

MACKENZIE RIVER VALLEY

Between the treeless barrenlands and the jagged peaks of the Mackenzie Mountains flows one of the world's mightiest rivers—the Mackenzie. The river begins at Great Slave Lake and flows in a northwesterly direction 1,800 km to the Arctic Ocean, draining one-fifth of Canada in the process. In places it is three km across. The lowlands of the wide valley flanking the river are covered in a boreal forest of black spruce, tamarack, and paper birch, with an understory of moss and lichens, high bush, cranberry, and blueberry. East of the river is 31,400-square-km Great Bear Lake, eighth-largest lake in the world.

For thousands of years the North Slavey Dene lived along the Deh Cho (Big River), hunting, fishing, and trapping. In 1789 Alexander Mackenzie became the first European to travel the river, which now bears his name. After his reports of rich fur resources reached the outside, the North West Company established fur-trading posts along the river. The Dene, who were originally nomadic, settled at the trading posts, forming small communities. In addition to these native settlements, communities along the river today include old fur-trading posts and the modern oil and government towns of Norman Wells and Inuvik, respectively. North of Fort Simpson and south of the Arctic Circle are four riverside communities: Wrigley, Tulita (formerly Fort Norman), Norman Wells, and Fort Good Hope. The only community on Great Bear Lake is Déline (formerly Fort Franklin), a base for fishing trips. Just north of the Arctic Circle, east of the Mackenzie River, is Colville Lake, famous for its world-class artists. The only road into the region begins at Fort Simpson and extends north to Wrigley. In winter this road continues to Norman Wells along the frozen river and ends at Fort Good Hope. In summer, the only highway is the Mackenzie River, along which tugs and barges carry freight to and from Hay River. Ambitious hikers in the area can attempt the challenging 372-km Canol Heritage Trail, which begins across the river from Norman Wells and heads deep into the rugged Mackenzie Mountains.

Traveling the Mackenzie River

Paddlers in canoes and kayaks set out along the river every summer with the Arctic Ocean in their sights. The entire trip, from Fort Providence to Tuktoyaktuk, is 1,800 km but can be broken up into shorter sections. Generally the river has no rapids and is more of a paddle than a float, but strong winds and sudden storms can create high waves that are a real danger. Advance planning is required as communities are generally at least 200 km apart. The prime canoeing season on the river is late June-August. This leaves little time for a long trip, but the days are generally sunny with up to 24 hours of daylight. The RCMP should be informed of your plans and approximate arrival times. Boats along the river will generally keep an eye out for paddlers and pull alongside for a chat. Communities along the river all have grocery stores but prices are high. Wherever you decide to end the trip (Inuvik is a popular destination) you must organize with an airline to get the canoe back to civilization or be prepared to sell it in the north. Peter Clarkson, P.O. Box 1554, Inuvik, NT X0E 0T0, tel. (403) 979-2594, buys and sells canoes from his base in Inuvik and can arrange canoe dropoffs along the Mackenzie River.

If you're really adventurous, the **Rat River Route** may be to your liking. This entails pulling out of the Mackenzie River north of Tsiigehtchic, portaging 75 km up the Rat River to MacDougall Pass, paddling the Bell River to the Porcupine River, and then into the Yukon River into Alaska. Good luck.

Once a year the *Norweta,* a small cruise boat, sails from Yellowknife to Inuvik on a 10-day (one-way) journey, staying in Inuvik for a week and then returning to Yellowknife the following week. Cost of the all-inclusive trip is $3,795 per person one-way for a cabin with two berths or $5,195 single occupancy. For more information write to Whitlock Family, 17 England Crescent, Yellowknife, NT X1A 3N5, tel. (403) 873-2489.

Wrigley

In 1994 a summer road was completed to the town of Wrigley, 225 km northwest of Fort Simp-

brave adventurers paddling down the Mackenzie River

son. It is the first section of an all-weather road planned to extend to Inuvik eventually. From **Ndulee Ferry Crossing** (daily 9-11 a.m. and 2-8 p.m.), 84 km out of Fort Simpson, the road passes through thick boreal forest to Wrigley.

Most of the community's 160 residents are Slavey Dene who live a semitraditional lifestyle, having settled in the area since the North West Company's Fort Alexander opened at the mouth of Willow Lake River in 1817. Over the next 150 years, the community moved several times. The present community of Wrigley sits at the site of an airstrip built during WW II. Opposite Wrigley is **Roche qui-Trempe-à-L'eau,** meaning "the rock that plunges into the water." It's an isolated hill that has been eroded away by the river on one side, creating a sheer cliff that drops 400 meters into the water below. Peregrine falcons are occasionally seen swooping down on cliff swallows that nest here.

Petanea Co-op Hotel, General Delivery, Wrigley, NT X0E 1E0, tel. (403) 581-3102, has five rooms with shared bath for $120 per person per day, $170 with three meals. Ask here about boat rentals. The hotel also has a small coffee shop and a dining room that opens in the evening. Camping anywhere along the river is accepted.

NORMAN WELLS

Residents were expecting the news, but on 15 June 1996 the official announcement was made: the oil wells and refinery that had been the lifeblood of Norman Wells were to close. Their closure is only a page in Norman Wells's fascinating history. The town is best known by adventurers for the Canol Heritage Trail, a wilderness trek following a route punched through the Mackenzie and Selwyn Mountains to transport oil to Alaska. It is also a good staging area for trips into the surrounding mountains, along the many rivers, or to world-class fly-in fishing lodges.

History

Unlike other settlements along the Mackenzie River, Norman Wells did not originate as a trading post but owes its existence to oil. Oil seeps along the riverbank were known to the Dene who named the area Le Gohlini, which translates to "where the oil is." And Alexander Mackenzie reported oil in the area in 1789 on his historic voyage to the Arctic Ocean. But it wasn't until 1919 that the first well, "Discovery," was drilled, and it was 1932 before it became productive. Increased mining activity in the western Arctic and a change from woodburning riverboats to those using petroleum-based fuel meant that demand for oil quickly grew. Despite the ill-fated Canol Project (see below), oil production at Norman Wells oil fields continued to increase to a maximum production of 10 million barrels a year from a field tapped by 160 wells. It was a unique field, and the infrastructure will remain for many years. Six manmade islands in the middle of the Mackenzie River, directly offshore from town, allowed oil extraction to continue throughout break-up and freeze-up of the river. Today, Norman Wells (pop. 550) remains as a firefighting base, transportation hub, and regional government center.

Canol Project

The large U.S. military force present in Alaska during WW II needed oil to fuel aircraft and ships, in place for expected Japanese attacks. The strategically located Norman Wells oil fields were chosen as a source of crude oil—with little regard for the engineering feat needed to build a pipeline over the Mackenzie Mountains. To this day, it remains one of the largest projects ever undertaken in northern Canada. Over $300 million was spent between 1942 and 1945, employing 30,000 people who laid 2,650 km of four- and six-inch pipeline and 1,600 km of telephone lines, and built a road over some of North America's most isolated and impenetrable mountain ranges. Conditions were terrible; makeshift camps housed thousands of men, temperatures dipped to 40 below, and the isolation took its toll. Through the impossible terrain thousands of tons of equipment was hauled, pump stations were installed, and camps set up. Then, less than a year after completion, the pipeline was very quietly abandoned for less expensive oil sources elsewhere. In 1947 the pipeline was dismantled and sold. Today, the roadbed remains, strewn with structures, trucks, and equipment used in the project's construction.

Norman Wells Today

The **Norman Wells Historical Centre,** tel. (403) 587-2415, tells the story of the Canol Project through historical displays, photographs, artifacts recovered from along the road, and an excellent propaganda movie, commissioned to help finance the project. The center is officially open in summer daily 10 a.m.-10 p.m. Next door is an interesting church. Actually, the church is fairly normal but the congregation is unique. Roman Catholics meet on one side, Protestants on the other. The center of town, a 20-minute walk from the airport, is a semicircle of semi-permanent buildings around a dusty parking lot. Also in town you'll find a bank, motels, restaurants, Northern, and a post office. Farther down the road is a small refinery and, overlooking the river, a gazebo from where the manmade islands can be seen.

Accommodations and Food

Yamouri Inn, P.O. Box 268, Norman Wells, NT X0E 0V0, tel. (403) 587-2744, is located in the center of town and has a bar and restaurant; $90 s, $110 d. Across the parking lot is **Rayuka Inn,** P.O. Box 308, tel. (403) 587-2354, which is slightly more expensive. Closer to the airport is **Mackenzie Valley Hotel,** Bag Service 1250, tel. (403) 587-2511, $99 s, $129 d. The town has no developed campgrounds; pitching your tent beside the Mackenzie River is an accepted practice (but don't leave valuables in it). The cheapest place to eat is the coffee shop or dimly lit cocktail lounge in the Yamouri Inn.

Transportation

Norman Wells has an impressive three-story airport complete with an observation deck and revolving baggage claim—not bad for a town of 600 people. It is a one-km walk into town. **Canadian North,** tel. (403) 587-2361 or (800) 665-1177, has daily flights from Yellowknife to Norman Wells, continuing north to Inuvik. One-way to Norman Wells is $318, $343 for a seven-day APEX roundtrip. **North-Wright Air,** tel. (403) 587-2333 or (800) 661-0702, flies from Norman Wells to all Mackenzie River communities ($92-172 each way), including Inuvik ($193).

Canol Heritage Trail

Considered by many to be one of the world's great wilderness hikes, the Canol is by no means typical. It follows the Canol Road (see "Canol Project," above) from Mile Zero (Canol Camp) on the west bank of the Mackenzie River across from Norman Wells, to Mile 230 on the Yukon border—a distance of 372 km (distances on the trail are in miles, a legacy of imperial measurement). To hike the entire trail takes three to four weeks. Following the road causes little problem, but the logistics of getting to the beginning of the trail, arranging food drops, crossing rivers, and returning to Norman Wells require much planning. Every year a few hikers attempt the entire length of the trail, while many others opt for a shorter section. The trail has been done on horseback, motorcycle, mountain bike, and all-terrain vehicle, but walking is the most popular and reliable.

The most popular jumping-off point is Norman Wells, from where you can charter a plane or helicopter and be dropped as far along the trail as desired. From the Yukon side you can drive from Ross River to Mile 208. Many hikers organize food drops with charter operators in Norman Wells to help ease the load.

All bridges along the route have been washed out, making many river crossings necessary. The most difficult of these is the **Twitya River** at Mile 131. This fast-flowing, cold (3-4° C) river is approximately 50 meters wide and up to five meters deep. Inner tubes purchased in Norman Wells (ask at Esso Resources) are a popular way of floating gear across, but check that they inflate before hitting the trail. General consensus is that the crossing is easier upstream of the old bridge. With two or more persons a length of rope can be strung across the river for ferrying packs across.

Along the length of the trail are many Quonset huts used during construction of the road. Many are uninhabitable, but others have bunk beds and cookstoves.

OTHER COMMUNITIES

Tulita

Formerly known as Fort Norman, the Slavey Dene of this small community (pop. 300) have known it as Tulita, meaning "where the two rivers meet," for many years. Its strategic location where the **Great Bear River** joins the Mackenzie River has made it a transportation hub since the days of Sir John Franklin. Upstream five km are the **Smoking Hills,** where an exposed seam of coal burns permanently. The first trading post was built here in 1810. An Anglican church, built of squared logs and dating to the 1860s, sits on the riverbank, beside the Hudson's Bay Company post. Many houses have colorful tepees in their yards, which are used for drying and smoking fish. The tepees provide a stark contrast to the modern school and the now defunct Norman Wells–Zama pipeline, which passes through the outskirts of the community. The Great Bear River is navigable for its 128-km distance into Great Bear Lake, with the exception of one set of rapids which can easily be portaged. The river's clear, aqua-colored waters provide excellent fishing for arctic grayling. **Fort Norman Lodge,** General Delivery, Tulita, NT X0E 0K0, tel. (403) 588-4311, has rooms with single and double beds, all with shared bathroom and kitchen. Meals can also be arranged. Rates are $120 s or

d per night. **North-Wright Air,** tel. (403) 587-2333, flies daily between Tulita and Norman Wells; $92 one-way.

Déline

Formerly known as Fort Franklin, Déline, meaning "flowing water," is on Keith Arm of **Great Bear Lake,** at the outlet where the Great Bear River begins flowing west to the Mackenzie River. The population is about 550. A North West Company trading post opened here in 1810 but closed soon after. It was reopened by the Hudson's Bay Company in 1825 as a winter home and supply depot for Sir John Franklin, who led several expeditions to the Arctic in search of the Northwest Passage. Then it was abandoned again. With the discovery of pitch-blende ore at Port Radium in the 1920s, traffic on the lake and river increased and a small community grew. Today the Slavey Dene of Déline live a traditional lifestyle, trapping, fishing, and making crafts, including moccasins for which they are well known. The tepee-shaped church is worth a visit, and the hike along the shore of Great Bear Lake offers rewarding vistas and passes a number of historic sites (ask at the hotel). **Great Bear Lake Hotel,** General Delivery, Déline, NT X0E 0G0, tel. (403) 589-3705, is a modern but basic accommodation in the middle of town. Rooms have private bathrooms and kitchenettes; $120 per person. Also here are a coffee shop and restaurant. Groceries and crafts are available at **Northern. North-Wright Air,** tel. (403) 587-2333, flies daily between Norman Wells and Déline; $138 one-way.

Where the Big One Won't Get Away

Great Bear Lake is one of the world's best fresh-water fishing lakes, and it has the records to prove it. This lake holds world records for *all* line classes of lake trout; the overall world record, caught in 1991, weighed in at a whopping 30 kilograms (66.5 pounds). It also holds world records for most classes of arctic grayling, including the overall record. Around the lake are small fishing lodges offering all-inclusive packages. The best of these are run by **Plummer's,** 950 Bradford St., Winnipeg, MB R3H 0N5, tel. (204) 774-5775 or (800) 665-0240, which operates five lodges around the lake. Accommodations, all meals, guides, professionally equipped boats, and roundtrip air charters from Winnipeg or Yellowknife are included in the package; $3,195 for eight days.

Fort Good Hope

Overlooking the Mackenzie River and flanked by boreal forest, this Slavey Dene community of 550 is located on the east bank of the Mackenzie River, just south of the Arctic Circle and approximately 193 km downstream of Norman Wells. A trading post established here in 1805 by the North West Company attracted not only the Slavey Dene but Inuit, who lived in the Mackenzie Delta. During the 1860s, Father Emile Petitot, a well-known northern missionary, constructed **Our Lady of Good Hope Church,** which has been declared a National Historic Site. The church's interior is decorated in ornate panels and friezes painted by Petitot, depicting aspects of his travels and life in the north.

One of the highlights of a trip to Fort Good Hope is visiting **The Ramparts,** where 200-meter-high cliffs force the Mackenzie River through a 500-meter-wide canyon. Although the cliffs continue for many kilometers, the most spectacular section is upstream of town and can be reached on foot or by boat. Arrange boat rentals and tours through **Ramparts Hotel,** General Delivery, Fort Good Hope, NT X0E 0H0, tel. (403) 598-2500. This hotel overlooks the river and has a restaurant with a simple menu, at northern prices; expect to pay $15-25 for a main meal. Rooms are $110 per person. **Hume River Enterprises,** tel. (403) 598-2416, offers tours of the town and fishing trips on the river. **North-Wright Air,** tel. (403) 587-2333, flies daily from Norman Wells to Fort Good Hope, $113 one-way.

Colville Lake

This community of 50 North Slavey Dene, located just north of the Arctic Circle on the southeast shore of Colville Lake, was established in 1962 when a Roman Catholic mission was built. It is the territories' only community built entirely from logs. The largest building is the church, which supports a bell weighing 454 kilograms. The mission was built by Father Bern Will Brown, who has now left the church and is one of the north's most respected artists. His paintings, which depict the lifestyle of northerners, are in demand across North America. Brown is also the host at **Colville Lake Lodge,** which combines excellent fishing for lake trout, arctic grayling, northern pike, whitefish, and inconnu, with a small museum highlighting life in the north. The lodge also has an art gallery, boat and canoe rentals, and common kitchen facilities. It is located in the town of Colville Lake. For more information write to Bern Will Brown, Colville Lake via Norman Wells, NT X0E 0V0. By phone, contact the mobile operator in Whitehorse (Yukon) and ask to be connected to 2M4486 on the Chick Lake "Y.R." Channel. **North-Wright Air,** tel. (403) 587-2333, flies Saturday between Colville Lake and Norman Wells, $172 one-way.

WESTERN ARCTIC

The far northwestern corner of the territories, where the mighty Mackenzie River drains into the Arctic Ocean, is linked to the outside world by the Dempster Hwy., the continent's northernmost public road. The region, entirely above the Arctic Circle, encompasses the Mackenzie River Valley and the vast barrens flanking the Arctic Ocean.

The **Mackenzie Delta,** a 90-km-long and 60-km-wide twisted maze of channels, is one of the world's greatest waterfowl nesting grounds and is home to muskrats, beavers, and marten, the mainstay of an early fur-trading economy. In the vicinity of the delta live red foxes, lynx, wolves, black bears, and moose. Large numbers of both woodland and barrenground caribou migrate through the region in early spring and fall; the Porcupine herd, named for the Porcupine River, migrates as far as Alaska. Arctic foxes inhabit the Arctic coast, while the king of the land, the grizzly bear, lives on the tundra. Banks Island has the world's largest population of musk oxen, protected by a national park. Beluga whales spend summer in the shallow waters around the delta and can be viewed from the air or in a boat. Hundreds of thousands of birds migrate to the delta each spring; among them are swans, cranes, hawks, bald eagles, and peregrine falcons.

At the end of the Dempster Hwy. is the region's largest community, Inuvik, a planned government town. Aklavik, west of Inuvik on a low area of land in the middle of the delta, was officially moved to Inuvik, but its residents stayed. Tuktoyaktuk is a "must-see" for those who want to dip their toes in the Arctic Ocean. To the east is Paulatuk, a traditional Inuvialuit community known for its excellent arctic char fishing, as well as its proximity to Tuktut Nogait National Park, the home range of the Bluenose caribou herd. The community of **Sachs Harbour,** on Banks Island, is a good base for exploring Aulavik National Park. To the east is massive Victoria Island. Most of the island is part of Nunavut. The exception is the western corner, where the community of Holman lies.

DEMPSTER HIGHWAY

This 741-km highway, which begins east of Dawson City in the Yukon, is the only road leading into the western Arctic. It ends at Inuvik, but from November to late March you can drive on a winter road across the frozen Mackenzie Delta all the way to Tuktoyaktuk on the Arctic Ocean.

Finished in 1978 after nearly 20 years of work, the highway stretches through some of North America's most inhospitable terrain. It was named after RCMP Inspector W.J.D. Dempster, who was sent to look for the "Lost Patrol"— a team of Mounties who disappeared near Fort McPherson during the winter of 1910-11. (He found them—dead.) Driving the Dempster Hwy. should not be taken lightly. Services are few and far between, and the gravel road has a reputation for shredding tires. Always carry spare gas and tires, have plenty of water, and be prepared to drive slowly. Many large mammals are seen from the highway but the most impressive sight is the **Porcupine caribou herd,** which migrates through the area each spring and fall.

The **Northwest Territories Visitors Centre** in Dawson City (in the B.Y.N. building on Front St.), tel. (403) 993-6167, is a good place to head before commencing the long drive north. It's open mid-May to mid-June Mon.-Fri. 8:30 a.m.-5 p.m. and through summer daily 9 a.m.-9 p.m.

The Dempster Hwy. crosses the **Arctic Circle** at Km 403, then climbs into the Richardson Mountains. The Continental Divide, at Km 471, marks the Yukon/NWT border. West of the divide, water flows to the Pacific Ocean; eastside waters end up in the Arctic Ocean. The highway then descends to the **Peel River,** crossed by ferry from mid-June to October and by an ice bridge most of the rest of the year. No crossings are possible during freeze-up and break-up.

Fort McPherson

After crossing the Peel River the highway soon comes to Fort McPherson, a Gwich'in Dene community on the river's east bank. The tribe lives at the eastern edge of their territory and has strong links to the Yukon and Alaska. A Hudson's Bay Company post was established here in 1840, and in 1852 a nearby Dene village was moved to Fort McPherson, away from the annual flooding that occurred at lower elevations. An RCMP post here became an important center for annual patrols throughout the western Arctic. It was from here, on 21 December 1910, that a patrol led by Inspector Fitzgerald left for Dawson City. The four members perished on the return trip, just one day short of Fort McPherson. An account of their journey is found in Dick North's *Lost Patrol*. The patrol is buried on the banks of the Peel River and a monument stands in their memory. Beside the monument, in a log cabin, is a small **Visitors Centre** open through summer daily 9 a.m.-9 p.m. Well worth a visit is **Fort McPherson Tent and Canvas,** a thriving local business producing high-quality backpacks, tote bags, and tents; open Mon.-Fri. 9:30 a.m.-5 p.m.

Tetlit Nitainlaii Co-op, tel. (403) 952-2417, has the only rooms in town; $100 s, $125 d. **Nutuiluie Territorial Campground** is located 10 km south of town, with sites for $10.

Tsiigehtchic

One hour's drive northeast of Fort McPherson is another ferry crossing, this time over the Mackenzie River (mid-June to October, 9 a.m.-midnight). Here, at the confluence of the Mackenzie and Arctic Red Rivers, a small mission was established in 1868, followed soon after by a Hudson's Bay Company post. For hundreds of years it has been a popular fishing spot for Dene and, today, traditional fishing camps still operate on the river; look for fish being prepared and dried by the ferry landings. Until 1996, the community was known as **Arctic Red River.** The traditional name, Tsiigehtchic, means "mouth of the iron-colored river" in the language of the Dene. The most recognizable landmark is a red-roofed mission church built in 1931. It stands on a small rise overlooking the river. The town has few services and may or may not have gas, so top up in Fort McPherson for the 180-km run to Inuvik. To visit the community, which is off the main ferry route, you must tell the ferry operators, who will happily make the detour for you.

South of Tsiigehtchic is the **Peel River Preserve.** High in the Mackenzie Mountains, this habitat is home to Dall's sheep, moose, lynx, woodland caribou, and grizzly bears. It is accessible only by traveling up either the Arctic Red or Peel River.

The last worthwhile stop before Inuvik and the end of the road is **Gwich'in Territorial Park.** This 8,800-hectare park extends from the Dempster Hwy. to the east bank of Campbell Lake, encompassing typical delta landscape.

INUVIK

You must see Inuvik with your own eyes to believe it, and then you may still doubt what you see: brightly painted houses on stilts, a monstrous church shaped like an igloo, metal tunnels snaking through town, and a main street where businesses have names such as Eskimo Inn, 60 Below Construction, and Polar TV. It's obviously a planned community, transformed from some architect's drafting board into full-blown reality high above the Arctic Circle. All aspects have been scientifically planned, right down to the foundations—all structures sit on piles of rock, ensuring stability in the permafrost and preventing heat from turning the ground into sludge.

History

In 1954 the Canadian government decided to build an administrative center for the western Arctic. The traditional center was Aklavik, located in the middle of the Mackenzie Delta. But since Aklavik had continual problems with erosion and flooding, and offered little room for expansion, a new site was decided upon. The location chosen was a large, level area alongside the East Channel of the Mackenzie River, 200 km north of the Arctic Circle and just below the treeline. Inuvik, meaning "place of man" in Invialuktun, was the first planned Canadian town above the Arctic Circle. By the summer of 1961, most of the major construction had been completed.

Today Inuvik serves not only as a government headquarters, but also as a transportation hub and oil-and-gas exploration base. The Canadian Armed Forces Station, which closed in 1986, has been converted to the Aurora Campus of Arctic College. The town's population of

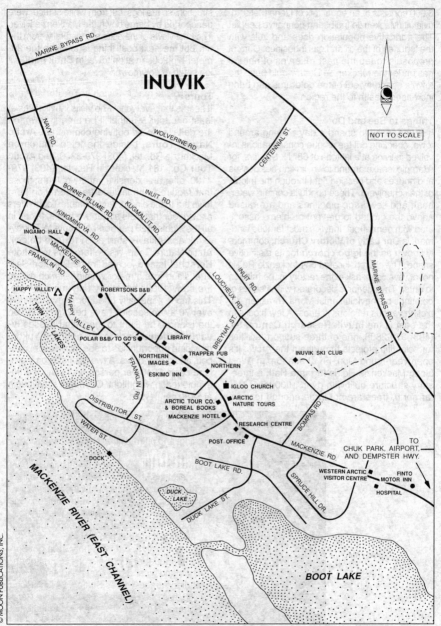

INUVIK

NOT TO SCALE

MARINE BYPASS RD.

WOLVERINE RD.

CENTENNIAL ST.

NAVY RD.

BONNET PLUME RD.

INUIT RD.

KUGMALLIT RD.

KINGMINGYA RD.

MACKENZIE RD.

INGAMO HALL

FRANKLIN RD.

MARINE BYPASS RD.

HAPPY VALLEY

TWIN LAKES

HAPPY VALLEY

ROBERTSONS B&B

LOUCHEUX RD.

INUIT RD.

POLAR B&B/TO GO'S

LIBRARY

BREYNAT ST.

INUVIK SKI CLUB

NORTHERN IMAGES

TRAPPER PUB

ESKIMO INN

NORTHERN

FRANKLIN RD.

IGLOO CHURCH

ARCTIC TOUR CO. & BOREAL BOOKS

ARCTIC NATURE TOURS

DISTRIBUTOR ST.

MACKENZIE HOTEL

RESEARCH CENTRE

BOMPAS RD.

WATER ST.

POST OFFICE

MACKENZIE RD.

TO CHUK PARK, AIRPORT, AND DEMPSTER HWY.

DOCK

BOOT LAKE RD.

SPRUCE HILL DR.

WESTERN ARCTIC VISITOR CENTRE

FINTO MOTOR INN

DUCK LAKE

HOSPITAL

DUCK LAKE ST.

MACKENZIE RIVER (EAST CHANNEL)

BOOT LAKE

© MOON PUBLICATIONS, INC.

3,000 consists of an equal mix of Dene/Métis, Inuvialuit (Mackenzie Inuit), and nonnative people. The nonnative population rises and falls with the fortunes of the oil and gas industries. Current proposals to tap the vast reserves of natural gas under the Mackenzie Delta would push the town's economy out of the doldrums and bring increased wealth to the region.

Things to See and Do

It is very easy to spend a day walking around town, checking out the unique considerations involved in living at a latitude of 68° N. *Utilidors,* for example, snake around town, linking businesses and houses and passing right through the middle of the schoolyard. These conduits contain water, heat, and sewerage pipelines and are raised above the ground to prevent problems associated with permafrost. Inuvik's most famous landmark is **Our Lady of Victory Church,** commonly known as the **igloo church** for its distinctive shape. The church, located on Mackenzie Rd., is not always open; ask at the rectory for permission to enter. The interior is decorated with a series of paintings by Inuvialuit artist Mona Thrasher, depicting various religious scenes. A few blocks to the east is the **Inuvik Research Centre,** tel. (403) 979-3838, one of three support facilities for scientific projects throughout the Arctic. It's open year-round Mon.-Fri. 9 a.m.-5 p.m. West along Mackenzie Rd. is **Ingamo Hall,** a three-story structure built with over 1,000 logs. This far north, trees are not large enough for construction, so the logs, cut from white spruce, were transported by barge down the Mackenzie River. The best views of the delta are, naturally, from the air, but the next best thing is to climb the 20-meter-high observation tower in **Chuk Park,** six km south of downtown.

Tours

It seems that everyone who visits Inuvik takes at least one tour, whether it be around town, on the delta, or to an outlying community. **Arctic Nature Tours,** beside the igloo church on Mackenzie Rd., tel. (403) 979-3300, and **Arctic Tour Co.,** 181 Mackenzie Rd., tel. (403) 979-4100, offer an extensive variety of tours; those that require flying include transportation from town out to the airport. Arctic Nature Tours offers a town tour that lasts about two hours, taking in all the sights; $20 per person. Tours to Tuktoyaktuk and Aklavik start at $110 (see below). Arctic Nature Tours also offers trips to remote **Herschel Island** located in the Beaufort Sea. The island was a major whaling station during the early 1900s but today only ruins remain. This trip is especially good for birdwatchers—over 70 avian species have been recorded on the island. The flight to the island passes **Ivvavik National Park** in the northern Yukon, providing opportunities to see musk oxen, caribou, and grizzly bears. A two-hour stay on the island costs $240 per person, including the 90-minute (each way) flight. Overnight stays begin at $480 per person.

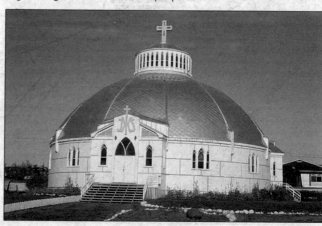

igloo church

Midnight Express Tours, booked through Arctic Nature Tours at (403) 979-3300, are a great way to experience the vastness of the delta. A three-hour cruise to the bush camp of an Inuvialuit elder where tea and bannock is served; $40 per person. Evening tours on the river including a traditional northern meal cost $70. Also offered are fishing trips, naturalist tours, or a boat trip to Aklavik or Tuktoyaktuk returning by plane (from $110).

Recreation

The town has no set hiking trails, but in summer you can hike along the tracks used by cross-country skiers in winter. Two trails—four and six km—begin from the ski club on Loucheux Rd., opposite the elementary school. They may be muddy. The treeline passes invitingly close to town to the east. Look for trails leading in that direction out by Marine Bypass Rd. and Long Lake. Another option is to walk around Boot Lake.

Paddling the length of the Mackenzie River is the stuff legends are made of, but it's also possible to experience the river just for a day. Peter Clarkson, tel. (403) 979-2594, rents canoes for $35 per day and can provide drop-offs up near the airport, the perfect starting point for a leisurely paddle back to Inuvik. If you're planning a longer trip through the Western Arctic, canoes can be rented from $200 per week.

Drinking and Dancing

Inuvik's most famous nightspot is **The Zoo,** in the Mackenzie Hotel, where a colorful mixture of oil field workers, German backpackers, drunken Aussies, fur-coated southerners, pin-striped businessmen, and locals who've been kicked out of every other place in town converge to listen to the best music the 1980s had to offer or some band that lost its way down in Whitehorse and wound up in Inuvik. There's no cover charge and things usually end around 2 a.m. Next door is the more mellow **Brass Rail Lounge,** where the bar is covered in roofing materials—a legacy of the owner's profession before becoming involved in the hotel business. If the bar's quiet, the owner will join you in sampling his specially imported German liqueur, kept behind the bar for when outsiders drop by. **Sly Fox** in the Eskimo Inn is a locals' hangout, as is **Trapper Pub** across the road, where local musicians jam on Saturday afternoons at 4 p.m., hoping one day to play at the Zoo.

Festivals and Events

After a month of darkness, the first day that the sun rises above the horizon is celebrated with the **Inuvik Sunrise Festival** (5-6 January). Although the sun actually rises at about 1:30 p.m. on the 6th there's a parade the day before, as well as ice-skating and an exciting fireworks display at Twin Lakes. **Summer Solstice** in June also provides a cause for celebration, although as the sun doesn't set for a month, the actual date of the festival is of little importance. Celebrations on the weekend closest to the solstice include traditional music and dancing. **The Great Northern Arts Festival,** the third week of July, features demonstrations, displays, and sales of northern art. And on the second weekend of October, street dances, parades, northern games, and traditional foods highlight **Delta Daze.**

Through summer **Inuvik Delta Dinner Theatre,** booked through Arctic Nature Tours, tel. 403-979-3300, features two performances weekly in the Banquet Room of the Finto Motor Inn. The show highlights life in the north and includes a hearty dinner. The cost is $39 per person.

Accommodations

Each of Inuvik's three motels has a coffee shop, restaurant, and basic rooms with private baths starting at $115 s, $125 d. **Mackenzie Hotel,** 185 Mackenzie Rd., P.O. Box 1618, Inuvik, NT X0E 0T0, tel. (403) 979-2861, is the nicest and is in town. Also in town is **Eskimo Inn,** 133 Mackenzie Rd., P.O. Box 1740, tel. (403) 979-2801. On the way to the airport is **Finto Motor Inn,** 288 Mackenzie Rd., P.O. Box 1925, tel. (403) 979-2647, which has a good view of the delta.

A few locals run bed and breakfasts, which are less expensive than the motels and provide a good way to meet the locals. **Robertson's B&B,** 41 Mackenzie Rd., P.O. Box 2356, tel. (403) 979-3111, is close to downtown, and its large outdoor deck offers a great view of the delta; $80 s, $90 d. Another good choice is **Polar B&B,** Mackenzie Rd., tel. (403) 979-2254. Accommodations are comfortable, with shared bathroom, kitchen, laundry, and lounge with television. Rates are $75 s, $85 d, which includes a meal at the adjacent To Go's restaurant.

Happy Valley Campground is located on a bluff overlooking the delta. It has private, unserviced sites and a gravel parking area for RVs and trailers that need power. Facilities include flush toilets, showers, and firewood; unpowered sites $10, powered $15. Outside of town toward the airport is **Chuk Park**; it's quiet but has limited facilities.

Food

If you don't mind your wallet taking a battering, the thing to do this far north is sample the local fare. The least expensive way to do this is at **To Go's,** 71 Mackenzie Rd., tel. (403) 979-3030, which has a few tables and a take-out menu. Caribou burgers and musk ox burgers ($5.50) are the same price as regular hamburgers, but cheaper than mushroom burgers. Pizza starts at $10; extras such as musk ox are $2, and the Northern Pizza—with the works—is $17. It's open daily till 4 a.m. Across the road is **Cafe Gallery Coffee Shop,** a city-style coffeehouse with decent coffee and muffins and a selection of local artwork down the back. The coffee shop in the **Mackenzie Hotel** is the most popular breakfast hangout, but it can get smoky. The **Green Briar Dining Room,** tel. (403) 979-2414, also in the Mackenzie Hotel, serves a good selection of northern cuisine (starting at $13.95 for a caribou burger); open from 5 p.m. The **Peppermill Restaurant,** tel. (403) 979-2999, in the Finto Motor Inn, offers much of the same; try caribou steaks smothered in blueberry sauce (made from locally picked blueberries), $17.50. The town's only supermarket is located at 160 Mackenzie Road. Prices aren't as high as you might expect.

Getting There

Mike Zubko Airport, named for an early Arctic aviator, is small but always busy, thanks to its status as the hub of air transport in the western Arctic. A cab to the airport, 12 km south of town, is $25 for one or two, $30 for three, and $36 for four. **Canadian North,** tel. (403) 979-2951 or (800) 665-1177, and **NWT Air,** tel. (403) 979-2341 or (800) 661-0789, fly into Inuvik daily from Yellowknife; $460 one-way, $501 for a seven-day APEX roundtrip. Sit on the left side of the plane for views of the Mackenzie Mountains. From Edmonton, the least expensive high-

season fare is $721 roundtrip. **North-Wright Air,** tel. (403) 587-2333, flies from Norman Wells to Inuvik; $193 each way. **Alkan Air,** tel. (403) 979-3999 or (800) 661-0432, based in Whitehorse (Yukon), flies to Inuvik via Old Crow. **Arctic Wings,** tel. (403) 979-2220, has scheduled flights to Aklavik and Tuktoyaktuk. **Aklak Air,** tel. (403) 979-3777, flies from Inuvik to all western Arctic communities.

Touch the Arctic Adventure Tours, tel. (800) 661-0894, offers a variety of air tours to Inuvik out of Edmonton starting at $729 for two days, with winter trips from $824.

Getting Around

For a taxi call (403) 979-2525 or 979-2121. The cabs don't have meters; fares are set: $4.50 anywhere around town, $25-36 to the airport, and $280 to Tuktoyaktuk on the winter road. Car rentals are available from **Avis,** tel. (403) 979-4571. **Northern Recreation,** 60 Franklin Rd. behind the laundromat, tel. (403) 979-2098, rents mountain bikes for $25 per day.

Services

The **post office** is at 187 Mackenzie Road. **Northern Images,** upstairs at 115 Mackenzie Rd., has a fantastic collection of paintings and sculptures from throughout the territories. The **hospital** is located at the east end of town, tel. (403) 979-2955. For the **RCMP** call (403) 979-2935. The local newspaper is the *Inuvik Drum,* published each Thursday.

Information

Inuvik Centennial Library, tel. (403) 979-2749, located in the center of town, has a fairly extensive collection of northern books and literature; open Monday and Friday 2-5 p.m. and Tues.-Thurs. 10 a.m.-9 p.m. **Boreal Bookstore,** 181 Mackenzie Rd., tel. (403) 979-3748, has a large selection of northern material, both new and used, as well as relevant topographical maps and marine charts.

The **Western Arctic Visitor Centre** is at the entrance to town, a 10-minute walk from downtown, tel. (403) 979-4321. This new facility has displays on the people of the north, details on each of the western Arctic communities, and all the usual tour information. It's open in summer daily 9 a.m.-8 p.m. Out the back a trail leads through a re-creation of an Inuvialuit whaling camp and Gwich'in fishing camp. For road and ferry information call (403) 979-2678.

AKLAVIK

Theoretically, this community in the middle of the Mackenzie Delta was abandoned over 20 years ago. But don't tell that to the 700 Dene and Inuvialuit who call Aklavik home. The Hudson's Bay Company post, established here in 1918, became the trading and transportation center of the muskrat-rich Mackenzie Delta. River erosion and surface instability seriously threatened the physical existence of the town so the feder-al government decided to relocate it to the East Channel, 58 km west. The planned town of Inuvik serves the purpose of the government well. But for many delta old-timers, living in a town that sprang from the muskeg isn't their cup of tea. In fact, since Inuvik was established, this ramshackle community, cut off from the outside world, has reported steady population increases.

Wooden sidewalks, a legacy of Aklavik's one-time importance, link the Hudson's Bay Company post and a mission church (now a small museum) to newer structures, built before the big move east was announced. Many large houses still stand, testimony to the fortunes made by prosperous traders in days gone by. Trails lead in all directions from town, inviting the curious to explore this small delta island. The most popular attraction is the grave of Albert Johnson, "The Mad Trapper of Rat River" (see the special topic), who sparked the north's most famous manhunt.

Tours and Transportation
Most people arrive in Aklavik as part of a tour from Inuvik, either through **Arctic Nature Tours,** tel. (403) 979-3300, or **Arctic Tours Co.,** tel. (403) 979-4100. On clear days, the 20-minute flight is awe-inspiring. Both companies offer flights to Aklavik with a one-hour town tour ($110), but a better way to experience the delta is by boat. To boat one-way then fly the other is $135. Tours that combine Aklavik and Tuktoyaktuk begin at $189.

If you would like to spend more time in town, scheduled flights leave daily from the airport with **Aklak Air,** tel. (403) 979-3777, and **Arctic Wings,** tel. (403) 979-2220. Usually the tour operators can arrange cheaper flights and advise on accommodation in the small hotel in Aklavik. Between December and March a winter

THE MAD TRAPPER OF RAT RIVER

For seven long weeks, ravaged by brutal winter temperatures, hunger, and exhaustion, a man whose identity remains a mystery to this day led Mounties on an astonishing chase through the Arctic. No one quite knows what instigated the murderous events of the winter of 1932, nor from where the mad, mysterious trapper came. Natives knew him as "the man who steals gold from men's teeth"; they were afraid of him and rumors surfaced that he was a notorious Chicago gangster.

In 1931 a man going by the name Albert Johnson arrived in Fort McPherson. He first raised a few eyebrows by purchasing unusually large amounts of ammunition and supplies with a fistful of notes. Then he left for the Rat River region to build a small cabin that doubled as an impregnable fortress—evidence that from the start he anticipated trouble. Answering complaints of a strange white man interfering with traplines, Constable King went to question Johnson. Instead of answers, King was met by a bullet.

A seven-man posse, carrying 20 pounds of dynamite, came from Aklavik to bring the gunman in. For 15 hours Johnson withstood the mounted siege, finally forcing the posse to retreat. Johnson fled, heading west. In temperatures that dipped below -40° C, and with meager supplies, four Mounties took up the chase. Four times Johnson repelled them with gunfire, killing a Mountie in the process. It became obvious to the Mounties that, against incredible physical hardships, Johnson was attempting to cross the mountains to Alaska. His cunning kept him alive for seven weeks, long enough for "Wop" May, a famed bush pilot, to be summoned. Surrounded by 17 men and with Wop May circling overhead in a plane loaded with bombs, Johnson never had a chance. His death ended the north's most notorious manhunt but was the beginning of the mystery—just who was the Mad Trapper of Rat River?

road is constructed between Inuvik and Aklavik; Arctic Wings operates a winter-only bus service between the two communities for $35 each way.

TUKTOYAKTUK

Most travelers, not satisfied with driving to the end of the road, hop aboard a small plane in Inuvik for the flight along the Mackenzie Delta to Tuktoyaktuk, a small community perched precariously on an exposed gravel strip on the Beaufort Sea. Although it would be a harsh and unforgiving place to live, a visit to "Tuk," as it is sensibly known, is a delightful eye-opener. The community is spread out around **Tuktoyaktuk Harbour** and has spilled over to the gravel beach, where meter-high waves whipped up by cold Arctic winds roll in off the Beaufort Sea and thunder up against the shore. The most dominant natural features of the landscape are **pingos,** massive mounds of ice forced upward by the action of permafrost. The mounds look like mini-volcanoes protruding from the otherwise flat environs. The ice is camouflaged by a natural covering of tundra growth, making the pingos all the more mysterious. Some 1,400 pingos dot the coastal plain around Tuk, one of the world's densest concentrations of these geological wonders peculiar to the north. **Ibyuk,** visible from town, is the world's largest pingo. It's 30 meters tall and has a circumference of 1.5 km.

History
This area was traditionally the home of Karngmalit, or Inuvialuit, who lived along the coast in small family camps hunting beluga whales. Earlier this century, an epidemic of influenza wiped out over half of their people. As Herschel Island lost importance as a base for whaling in the Beaufort Sea, the Hudson's Bay Company opened a post at the safe harbor of Tuk in 1937. Reindeer herding was attempted in the late 1930s, with animals brought over from Scandinavia. Today a large herd of these mammals— the same species as the indigenous caribou but a little smaller—live in the area. A Distant Early Warning Line station was constructed in 1955. Although the residents harvest fish, seals, and whales, most wage earners are land based, involved in government, transportation, and

tourism. The town is also a base for oil and gas exploration in the Beaufort Sea.

Around Town
Most visitors see Tuk from the inside of a transporter van driven by accommodating locals who never tire of the same hackneyed questions about living at the end of the earth. The bus stops at *Our Lady of Lourdes,* once part of a fleet of vessels that plied the Arctic delivering supplies to isolated communities. Here also are two mission churches built in the late 1930s. A stop is also made at the Arctic Ocean, where you are encouraged to dip your toes in the water or go for a swim if you really want to impress the folks back home. (Tuk is actually on the Beaufort Sea, an arm of the Arctic Ocean, but who's telling). For a few extra bucks you are given some time to explore on your own. This will give you a chance to walk along the beach, climb a nearby pingo, and check out the well-equipped ocean port.

Practicalities
Tuk is the most popular flightseeing destination from Inuvik and a variety of trips are offered by the two tour operators in Inuvik. Trips start at $125, which includes the return flight (worth the price alone) and a tour of the town. The flight into Tuk is breathtaking—the pilots fly at low altitudes for the best possible views. For those who wish to spend longer in Tuk (there are enough things to do to hold your interest for at least one day), both companies offer extended tours, with Arctic Nature Tours offering an excellent Cultural Tour that includes a visit to the community's unique cool room, for $169 per person. For tour details contact **Arctic Nature Tours,** tel. (403) 979-3300, or **Arctic Tour Co.,** tel. (403) 979-4100. Overnight trips, airfare and tour only, will cost from $165. Tour operators use the services of **Arctic Wings,** tel. (403) 979-2220, and **Aklak Air,** tel. (403) 979-3777, which also have daily scheduled flights ($200 roundtrip).

Hotel Tuk Inn, P.O. Box 193, Tuktoyaktuk, NT X0E 1C0, tel. (403) 977-2381, and **Pingo Park Lodge,** P.O. Box 290, tel. (403) 977-2155, are of an acceptable northern standard. Prices start at $125 s, $150 d, and both have dining facilities. Arctic Nature Tours offers a package of airfare, one night's accommodation, and a town tour for $285 per person. Camping is acceptable; down on the beach is a favorite place to pitch tents, but check the weather forecast (tel. 403-979-4183) before putting too much faith in your trusty canvas companion. **Northern,** for groceries, and a **post office** are by the public dock. Crafts are available in a small store next to *Our Lady of Lourdes.*

PAULATUK

Meaning "place of the coal" in the local language, Paulatuk is the western Arctic's smallest community, with a population of 110 Inuvialuit who live a traditional lifestyle hunting, trapping, and fishing. A Roman Catholic mission and trading post, established in 1935, attracted Inuvialuit families from camps along the Arctic coast. Their descendants continue living off the abundant natural resources. The community is located on a sandy strip of land between the Beaufort Sea and an inland lake along a rugged stretch of coastline, 400 km east of Inuvik. To the northeast are the **Smoking Hills,** seams of coal, rich with sulphide, that were ignited centuries ago and still burn today, filling the immediate area with distinctively shaped clouds of smoke.

The Hornaday, Horton, and other rivers whose headwaters are north of Great Bear Lake drain into the ocean near Paulatuk, providing unparalleled opportunities for extended whitewater trips (experienced paddlers only).

Sprawling across Parry Peninsula, to the west of Paulatuk, is **Tuktut Nogait National Park,** the major staging area for the **Bluenose caribou herd,** which migrates across the north. The coastal cliffs of **Cape Parry Bird Sanctuary** are a nesting site for rare murres. In spring local outfitters will take you far out onto the pack ice of **Amundsen Gulf** in search of polar bears.

Practicalities
The only accommodation in town is **Paulatuk Hotel,** General Delivery, Paulatuk, NT X0E 1N0, tel. (403) 580-3027, with eight rooms with shared bath and a small restaurant; $110 per person. You can camp along the beach, but ask at the hamlet office before pitching your tent. **Kopatkok Arctic Sightseeing** leads fishing and day tours

around the area. Contact David Ruben at General Delivery or call (403) 580-3222. The only scheduled flights to Paulatuk are on **Aklak Air,** tel. (403) 979-3777, leaving Inuvik on Tuesday and Friday ($280 one-way). Check with Inuvik tour operators for cheaper deals.

BANKS ISLAND

Banks Island is one of the best places in the western Arctic for viewing wildlife, including foxes, polar bears, wolves, and the world's largest concentration of musk oxen. The island is separated from the mainland by **Amundsen Gulf** and from Victoria Island by **Prince of Wales Strait,** and is the most westerly island in the Canadian Arctic archipelago. Through the barren, low rolling hills that characterize this island flow some major rivers including the **Thomsen,** the northernmost navigable river in Canada. **Aulavik National Park** protects the river and 12,000 square km of its watersheds. To get to the park you need to charter a plane in Inuvik.

Sachs Harbour (Ikaahuk)
The only permanent settlement on Banks Island is Sachs Harbour, located at the foot of a low bluff along the southwest coast, 520 km northeast of Inuvik. An abundance of white foxes had attracted Thule people to the island for centuries, and early Arctic explorers such as Beechley and McLure had charted the island. But it wasn't until the late 1920s that three Inuvialuit families settled permanently in what is now known as Sachs Harbour. The island has always been regarded as one of the finest trapping areas in the Canadian Arctic, and the people who lived here were able to afford such luxuries as washing machines and holidays to Aklavik. The town of 200 remains relatively self-sufficient. The first weekend of May is the **White Fox Jamboree,** a three-day festival of traditional northern games, food, and dance.

Practicalities
The least expensive way to visit Sachs Harbour is on a tour organized by **Arctic Nature Tours,** tel. (403) 979-3300. Airfare from Inuvik and a town tour is $399 per person, but this tour only leaves if there are at least four people on it. An-

other tour includes airfare, two nights' accommodations, meals, and tours by boat and ATV to see local wildlife populations, including musk oxen, for $999 per person. This tour departs every Thursday regardless of numbers. Accommodations on this tour are at **Kuptana's Guesthouse,** General Delivery, Sachs Harbour, NT X0E 0Z0, tel. (403) 690-4151. Rates are $175 per person including three meals. Facilities for the five rooms are shared, but each room has a television. The owners offer tundra tours for $50 per person for half a day out on the water or tundra. Camping along the beach should be okay, but check first with the hamlet office. The town has no restaurants, only a small co-op grocery store (closed Sunday). **Aklak Air,** tel. (403) 979-3777, has a twice-weekly scheduled flight to Sachs Harbour from Inuvik; $355.50 one-way. This is the flight used by Arctic Nature Tours, so inquire here about cheaper fares.

HOLMAN (ULUQSAQTUUQ)

Most of Victoria Island, seperated by Prince of Wales Strait from Banks Island, falls within Nunavut. The exception is the island's western corner, including Diamond Jenness Peninsula, where the community of Holman (pop. 300) lies. Holman is on a gravel beach at the end of horseshoe-shaped Queens Bay and is surrounded by steep bluffs that rise as high as 200 meters.

Copper Inuit had traditionally wintered on nearby Banks Island and spent summer hunting caribou on Victoria Island. But when a Hudson's Bay Company post that had been on Prince Albert Sound was moved to what is now Holman in 1939, the Inuit began to settle around it. As they moved to the post, they were taught print-

making by a missionary, Rev. Henri Tardi, who had come to the settlement as an oblate missionary. To this day printmaking is a major source of income for the community, as are trapping and hunting.

The area is renowned for arctic char and trout fishing. **Kanayok Outfitting,** General Delivery, Holman, NT X0E 0S0, tel. (403) 396-3401, is the best way to get among the fish. This outfitter also takes visitors to Holman's original townsite and on wildlife viewing trips out on the tundra. Holman has a golf course, the northernmost in the world. Playing a round of golf here is really something to tell the boys back at the country club about; for the record, the course is at a latitude of 70 degrees 44 minutes North. The first weekend of every August the course hosts the **Billy Joss Open,** attracting sports celebrities from as far away as the United States.

Practicalities

Holman's only hotel is the **Arctic Char Inn,** tel. (403) 396-3501. Rates are $130 per person. The town has no established campgrounds, but many locals camp at Okpilik Lake. If you'd like to be closer to town ask at the hamlet office for the best place to pitch a tent. Meals are available at the Arctic Char Inn and groceries across the road in **Northern.** Local arts and crafts are available in the Arctic Char Inn or at the **Co-op.**

The only scheduled flights into Holman are three times weekly from Yellowknife with **First Air,** tel. (403) 396-3063 or (800) 267-1247; $483 one-way, $677 for a seven-day APEX roundtrip. **Arctic Nature Tours,** based in Inuvik, tel. (403) 979-3300, combine Holman and Sachs Harbour in a day trip for $499 per person if there are enough interested people (at least four) floating around Inuvik.

BOB RACE

NUNAVUT
ARCTIC COAST

Imagine a strip of coastline that stretched from San Diego to Seattle with an offshore island the size of California and a total population that would fit easily into a couple of jumbo jets; without traffic lights, power lines, road systems, or McDonald's, and a complete absence of trees. Such is the Arctic coast. For nine months of the year it is a cold, frozen land where it seems no life-forms could possibly exist. Then, during the short Arctic summer, the land comes alive. Its rivers provide what many regard as the ultimate canoe trips, naturalists and photographers are drawn by the abundant wildlife-viewing opportunities, and anglers from around the world arrive, hoping to catch the most prized of all northern fish, the delicious **arctic char.**

Lowland arctic makes up the bulk of the region, including the Arctic coast mainland and lower Arctic islands such as King William, Prince of Wales, and Victoria (the world's 12th-largest island). It is a land of low rolling hills, scoured by glacial ice during the last ice age, deeply in-

cised by meltwater streams, and scattered with shallow lakes. Boothia Peninsula, in the east part of the region, is a classic example. This, the northernmost point of mainland on the continent, is a bleak, barren land, rarely penetrated, even by the Inuit.

For centuries, Copper and Netsilik Inuit spent summer traveling the length of the Arctic coast, fishing and hunting seals and caribou. They moved as the seasons dictated and had no permanent settlements. As the quest for a northwest passage to the Orient heated up, the Hudson's Bay Company began establishing posts at remote locations throughout the region. These posts attracted the nomadic Inuit, whose lifestyle began to change as a result. The posts formed the basis of today's six Arctic coast communities. In many, the characteristic red-and-white-trimmed Hudson's Bay Company buildings still stand, as do stone churches built by missionaries.

All communities, except Pelly Bay, rely on supplies barged down the Mackenzie River from

Hay River once a year. Otherwise the only links to the outside world are by plane. Scheduled flights from Yellowknife serve all communities except Bathurst Inlet, where charter flights bring guests into one of the world's premier naturalist lodges. For whatever reason you visit this fascinating region it is important to be prepared. Each community has a hotel serving meals, but reservations should be made well in advance.

Groceries and basic camping supplies are available in all communities, but there are no banks.

CAMBRIDGE BAY (IKALUKTUTIAK)

Cambridge Bay is located on the southeast coast of 212,688-square-km **Victoria Island,** Canada's second-largest island. A busy ad-

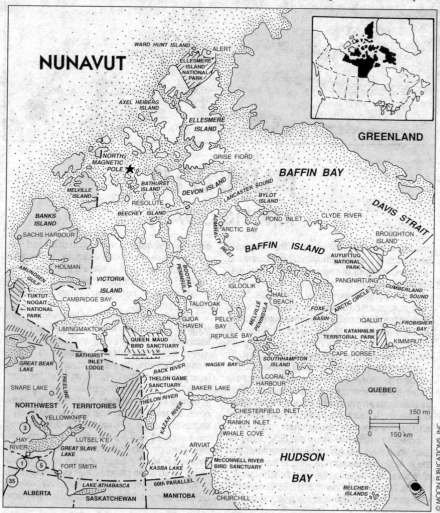

ministrative center for the western section of Nunavut, it lies 1,300 km west of Nunavut's capital, Iqaluit. The Inuit name for the bay is Ikaluktutiak, meaning "good fishing place." For hundreds of years before European arrival, Copper Inuit gathered here in summer to take advantage of the abundant caribou and seals, and to fish for arctic char. These people fashioned tools and implements from copper, hence the name Copper Inuit. Doctor John Rae, who visited the bay in 1851 in search of the Franklin Expedition, was one of many Arctic explorers who stopped to rest in its sheltered waters.

The Hudson's Bay Company established a trading post on the bay in 1921 and bought Roald Amundsen's schooner *Maud* as a supply ship. After being used for many years, the ship fell into disrepair and sank in the bay. It is still visible from the shores of Old Town, resting in the shallow waters of Cambridge Bay. A stone church, built by Anglican missionaries in the 1920s, is a Cambridge Bay landmark.

The landscape surrounding the bay is very barren, but the summit of 220-meter **Mt. Pelly,** a 15-km (each way) hike from town, affords a panoramic view and a chance to spot musk oxen. Another interesting destination is **Greiner Lake,** 10 km northwest of town, where over 50 species of birds have been reported. In town, the **Ikaluktutiak Co-op** operates a fishery that is a major supplier of arctic char to the rest of Canada, and **Kitikmeot Meats** processes caribou and musk ox. Both are open to visitors, selling smoked arctic char and musk ox jerky, respectively.

The **Arctic Coast Visitors Centre,** tel. (403) 983-2224, has interesting displays on all coastal communities; open May-Sept. daily 9 a.m.-5 p.m.

Accommodations and Food
Campers can pitch tents along the shoreline, as long as they're out of sight of the community. For those wanting to stay indoors, choices are: **Ikaluktutiak Inns North Hotel,** P.O. Box 38, Cambridge Bay, NT X0E 0C0, tel. (403) 983-2215 ($110 per person and $50 per person extra for meals); **Enokhok Inn,** P.O. Box 103, tel. (403) 983-2444, with self-contained units, each with a kitchenette ($125 per person); and the newest accommodation, **Arctic Islands Lodge,** P.O. Box 92, tel. (403) 983-2345, where each room has private bath, and a restaurant

and laundry are on the premises ($140 s, $180 d). You may camp at **Freshwater Creek,** five km from town. Meals are available in the hotels, groceries from **Northern.**

Transportation and Tours
Airlines serving Cambridge Bay include **Canadian North,** tel. (403) 983-2434 or (800) 665-1177; **NWT Air,** tel. (403) 983-2591 or (800) 661-0789; and **First Air,** tel. (403) 983-2919 or (800) 267-1247. Each has two to six flights per week from Yellowknife; $390 one-way, $410 for a seven-day APEX roundtrip. If you are planning to visit Arctic coast communities east of Cambridge Bay, First Air provides connections.

For hiking, canoeing, and fishing trips around Cambridge Bay contact **Ahvauch Tours,** P.O. Box 1092, Cambridge Bay, NT X0E 0C0, tel. (403) 983-2024.

KUGLUKTUK

Formerly known as Coppermine, Kugluktuk (pop. 1,000) lies at the mouth of one of North America's finest wilderness rivers. It is located 600 km north of Yellowknife on **Coronation Gulf,** a vital link in the Northwest Passage.

History
Historians believe that Inuit fished at the mouth of the Coppermine River for over 4,000 years before Samuel Hearne arrived there on 14 July 1771. The Hudson's Bay Company had sent Hearne to find the source of the copper that traders were starting to bring in to posts farther east. When Hearne and his Chipewyan Dene guides neared the rivermouth, they encountered a party of Copper Inuit. Relations between the Dene and Copper Inuit had traditionally been tense, and as the result of an argument the Inuit were massacred. Hearne named the site of the tragedy Bloody Falls, now a popular hike from Coppermine (Kugluktuk means "place of rapids"). As the great inland caribou herds began to decline in number, Inuit spent more time near the coast hunting sea mammals. In 1927, a Hudson's Bay Company post was established at the rivermouth, followed by an Anglican mission and RCMP outpost in 1932, and a weather station in 1937. Today fishing and

caribou

J. PETERSON / NWT ECONOMIC DEVELOPMENT & TOURISM

hunting play an important role in the local economy, as does oil-and-gas exploration and tourism.

Coppermine River

The Coppermine River makes for one of North America's classic paddling trips, combining tundra wilderness with unparalleled opportunities for viewing moose, wolves, caribou, grizzly bears, and musk oxen. A sense of history prevails—after all, it's the same route north taken by Hearne, Franklin, and Hood. The headwaters of this remote river are below the treeline at a series of joined lakes, 360 km north of Yellowknife. The 325-km float from the headwaters to Coppermine takes a minimum of 10 days, but most people allow time for tundra hikes, arctic char fishing, and relaxing. The river flows primarily through tundra, but the valley is characteristically lushly vegetated, creating prime habitat for larger mammals. Hawks, falcons, and eagles nest in the cliff faces along the route. The only portage is at Bloody Falls, 16 km from the ocean. **Whitewolf Adventure Expeditions,** 41-1355 Citadel Dr., Port Coquitlam, BC V3C 5X6, tel. (800) 661-6659, offers 12- and 14-day river expeditions in canoes and rafts; from $3,085 out of Yellowknife.

For those planning their own expedition, **Air Tindi,** tel. (403) 920-4177, does charter flights the 360 km from Yellowknife to the river's headwaters.

Things to Do around Town

Although most keen naturalists are drawn to nearby Bathurst Inlet Lodge (see below), the immediate vicinity of Coppermine provides many opportunities for wildlife viewing. The best way to get a feel for the area is by hiking along one of the numerous trails that radiate from town. The trail to **Bloody Falls** is less than 20 km one-way but the going can get rough. Chances are you'll want to make numerous stops, both to search out routes through the many swampy sections of the trail, and to admire the colorful tundra vegetation. Rewards are ample, none more so than the final destination where the Coppermine River plunges into a narrow canyon. Most hikers opt to camp here overnight. Other possible hikes include walking along the beach west of town to **Expeditor Cove** or climbing the rocky ridge above the garbage dump road for a view of town and the ocean. **Aime's Arctic Tours,** P.O. Box 158, Coppermine, NT X0E 0E0, tel. (403) 982-3330, organizes fishing trips to nearby islands and up the Coppermine River for arctic char. Inquire at the **Hunters and Trappers Association Office,** tel. (403) 982-4908, by the recreation center for other outfitters. The year's biggest festival is **Nattik Frolics,** at the end of April, which includes traditional northern sports and other not-so-traditional events such as poker and snowmobile races. A **fishing derby** on the first weekend of September attracts arctic char enthusiasts from throughout the north; call (403) 982-4471 for details.

Practicalities

Coppermine Inn, P.O. Box 282, Coppermine, NT X0E 0E0, tel. (403) 982-3333, is in the center of town. Guests have a choice of motel rooms or self-contained units; $125 per person. Breakfast, lunch, and dinner are $15, $20, and $30, respectively, and should be booked in advance. Nonguests may also eat here but should book meals a day in advance. **Enokhok Inn,** P.O. Box 162, tel. (403) 982-3197, has four rooms for $150 per person, which includes meals. **Northern,** just up from the dock, sells groceries and souvenirs, and usually has white gas (check supplies before flying in, tel. 403-982-4171). The town has a **post office, library,** and **craft shop,** but no bank.

The airport is a short walk from town and is served by **First Air,** tel. (403) 982-3208 or (800) 267-1247, from Yellowknife; $281 one-way, $318 for a seven-day APEX roundtrip.

BATHURST INLET

Bathurst Inlet, 210 km east of Coppermine, is the name of an expansive bay, an abandoned Hudson's Bay Company post, and a popular naturalist lodge. The Hudson's Bay Company established a trading post on the southwest side of the inlet at the mouth of the **Burnside River** in the 1930s. Various Inuit had inhabited the Bathurst Inlet area for thousands of years, but the post, along with others along the rugged coastline, was the first permanent settlement. In 1964 the post moved across the inlet and 120 km north to Bay Chimo. Four years later it closed for good. The small Inuit community here, now known as **Umingmaktok,** meaning "place of many musk oxen," continues to prosper and is one of the north's more traditional communities. Residents are noted for crafts, which can be bought at Bathurst Inlet Lodge.

Bathurst Inlet Lodge

Glenn Warner, a former Mountie, and his wife Trish bought the various Hudson's Bay Company buildings at the mouth of the Burnside River and in 1969 opened what has evolved into the north's most renowned naturalist lodge. Most of the original buildings remain—as a lounge, dining room, and guest rooms for up to 25 visitors at a time. But it is not the quaint red-and-white-trimmed buildings that attract people from around the world. It is the chance to become immersed in the fascinating natural world of the Arctic, with a soft bed and a hot shower at the end of each day. One of the beauties of the lodge, apart from its magnificent setting, is the diversity of things to see and do in the surrounding area. The *Arctic Queen,* a pontoon boat, cruises the inlet in search of ringed seals and musk oxen grazing on the shore. Birdwatchers will be captivated by the sea- and shorebirds that spend summer in the area. Local Inuit families, who have become part owners of the lodge, teach guests their own interpretation of the land's natural history. And there's plenty of time for fishing, photography, hiking, or just soaking up the scenery.

Rates for the lodge include charter flights from Yellowknife, seven nights' accommodations at the lodge, all meals, guided day trips (except flightseeing, $200), and a traditional drum dance on your final night. Essentially, all you have to do is get to Yellowknife. Cost is $3,180 out of Yellowknife; book through Touch the Arctic Adventure Tours, tel. (800) 661-0894, for $3,940, which includes airfare from Edmonton or Calgary and two nights' accommodations in Yellowknife. The floatplane leaves from Back Bay in Old Town Yellowknife at 3618 McAvoy Road. For more information contact Bathurst Inlet Lodge, P.O. Box 820, Yellowknife, NT X1A 2N6, tel. (403) 873-2595, fax (403) 920-4263.

GJOA HAVEN (URSUQTUQ)

Gjoa Haven is the only settlement on **King William Island,** which is separated from the mainland by the narrow Simpson Strait. The island had long been the traditional territory of the Netsilik Inuit, who were expert seal hunters. Early explorers named it King William Land, mistakenly thinking that it was part of the mainland. The island has been the scene of much conjecture ever since the disappearance of Sir John Franklin, one of many explorers sent to find the elusive Northwest Passage. One of the Franklin Expedition's main mistakes was underestimating the Netsilik, whose advice could have prevented the tragedy. Roald Amundsen made no such mistakes on his 1903-06 expedition. After spending two winters on King William Island learning from the Netsilik, at a harbor he named after his ship *Gjoa*, he went on to become the first person to successfully navigate the Northwest Passage. Today the location of what Amundsen called "the finest little harbor in the world" is home to around 700 Inuit who live a traditional lifestyle—hunting, fishing, and making crafts such as wall hangings and soapstone carvings. The well-signposted **Northwest Passage Historic Park** tells the story of the search for the passage and the part Gjoa Haven played in it. The trail is three km long and can be boggy early in the summer. Ask at the hamlet office, tel. (403) 360-7141, just up from Northern, for an interpretive brochure explaining the historical importance of sites along the trail. Apart from the excellent arctic char fishing, Gjoa Haven is a good base for sled dog trips across Rae Strait to Taloyoak. The end of winter is celebrated with the **Qavvarrik Carnival,** which takes place on the still-frozen bay in front of the community in late May. The carnival features events for everyone—an egg toss, blindfolded sled race, harpoon throw—all with small cash prizes. For outsiders, winning the weightlifting competition will cause some problems—first prize is a 44-gallon drum of fuel!

Practicalities
Amundsen Hotel, P.O. Box 120, Gjoa Haven, NT X0E 1J0, tel. (403) 360-6176, sleeps 24 in 12 rooms, so if it's busy, you'll be sharing a room; $140 per person plus $60 per person for meals. The small restaurant is open to nonguests, but reservations should be made in advance. For groceries head to **Northern** and for local crafts to the **Kekertak Co-op,** behind the hotel.

The only scheduled air service to Gjoa Haven is with **First Air,** tel. (403) 360-6612 or (800) 267-1247, via Cambridge Bay from Yellowknife; $579 one-way, $811 for a seven-day APEX roundtrip.

TALOYOAK

Formerly known as Spence Bay, this Inuit community of 550 lies in low, rolling hills and is surrounded by fish-filled lakes. It is located on the west side of an isthmus linking the mainland to

Boothia Peninsula. The tip of this peninsula, 250 km north of Taloyoak at Bellot Strait, is the northernmost point of mainland North America. Spence Bay was named by John Ross, a British explorer who wintered in the area in the early 1830s. Taloyoak, its Inuit name, refers to a caribou blind built by early natives to corral and kill caribou. The Netsilik Inuit traveled great distances through the region—hunting, trapping, and trading. By following Inuit directions, John Ross escaped certain death after becoming icebound. His abandoned vessel, a paddle-steamer, the first such boat to be used for Arctic exploration, was a source of wood and iron to Inuit for many years. It is interesting that Ross was able to accurately pinpoint the magnetic North Pole to a spot along the southwestern coast of Boothia Peninsula. The pole, which annually moves 25 km north and six km west, has since moved many hundreds of kilometers to a point northwest of Resolute.

It was not until 1947 that a permanent settlement was established at Spence Bay, one of the only safe harbors on the west coast of Boothia Peninsula. Local Inuit artisans are known for their stuffed "packing dolls" of animals such as whales and seals. At the mouth of the harbor stand the distinctive red-and-white Hudson's Bay Company buildings. A short hike leads to a stone caribou blind. It is also possible to travel overland to **Fort Ross,** or 80 km north to **Thom Bay,** where the *Victory* was abandoned by Ross in 1929. Inland are lakes where the local Inuit travel each summer to fish.

Practicalities
The **Paleajook Hotel,** General Delivery, Taloyoak, NT X0E 1B0, tel. (403) 561-5803, has rooms with shared facilities for $110 per person. Meals are an extra $50 per person per day. **Boothia Inn,** P.O. Box 18, tel. (403) 561-5300, has rooms for $170 per person including meals. A semi-official camping area is near an old mission church, west of the post office. Meals are available at the Paleajook Hotel and should be booked in advance. Groceries and limited camping supplies are available at **Northern** or **Paleajook Co-op.** Ask at the Hunters and Trappers Association for locally harvested food such as arctic char and caribou; tel. (403) 561-5066. The community also has a **post office** and **medical center** but no bank.

The small airport, within walking distance of town, is served by **First Air,** tel. (403) 561-5400 or (800) 267-1247, from Yellowknife; $648 one-way, $907 for a seven-day APEX roundtrip. First Air also flies between Taloyoak and Iqaluit twice weekly; the Tuesday flight is a real milk run with seven stops. **Lyall's Taxi and Cartage,** tel. (403) 561-6363, operates a cab service.

PELLY BAY (ARVILIQJUAT)

Pelly Bay is a Netsilingmiut Inuit community of 300 located 177 km southeast of Taloyoak. The community is named for Sir Henry Pelly, an early governor of the Hudson's Bay Company. It grew around a Roman Catholic mission established in 1935. The mission's founder, Father Henri, was for many years the only *qallunaaq* (nonnative) to reside here. Today the residents of Pelly Bay continue to fish and hunt as they have for generations. Its location deep in Pelly Bay makes accessibility for barge traffic nearly impossible and gives the town the distinction of having the highest cost of living of any community in the north.

A stone church located on the road to the dock, built by Father Henri, houses a small museum. In the immediate vicinity of the community are some interesting sites. On the top of a nearby hill is a unique cross built out of empty gasoline drums by early missionaries. Also close to town are a number of *inukshuks* and scraps of metal from the fuselage of a U.S. plane. Hikes lead along the rocky shoreline, inland to fishing lakes, and to archaeological remains of Inuit camps. Seals and, occasionally, narwhals are seen in the bay. The Inuit name for Pelly Bay, Arviliqjuat, means "place of the bowhead whale," but these magnificent creatures are long gone.

Practicalities

The lack of tourist facilities here is more than made up for by the friendliness of the locals. **Inukshuk Inn,** General Delivery, Pelly Bay, NT X0E 1K0, tel. (403) 769-7211, has 11 rooms with shared facilities, a TV room, and a small restaurant, and can book tours through local outfitters; $125 per person, meals are $50 per day. Meals in the restaurant are by prior arrangement, whether a guest or not. Groceries are available at **Koomiut Co-op,** next door to the hotel. The town has no bank and alcohol is not allowed. Ask at the Co-op about campsites close to town.

First Air, tel. (403) 769-7302 or (800) 267-1247, flies into Pelly Bay three times weekly from Yellowknife; $713 one-way, $983 for a seven-day APEX roundtrip.

KEEWATIN

The Keewatin stretches along the west coast of Hudson Bay from north of Churchill, Manitoba to the Melville Peninsula and west to the heart of the barrenlands. Each summer vast herds of caribou migrate across the region to their calving grounds. Wolves, foxes, and grizzlies are scattered throughout the region while musk oxen graze in small herds in Thelon Game Sanctuary. Polar bears migrate along the coastal regions and are best viewed at Wager Bay. The thousands of lakes and rivers dotting the region are alive with fish; arctic char is dominant, but huge lake trout and whitefish also inhabit all lakes large enough not to freeze to the bottom. Whaling took place throughout the Arctic, but Hudson Bay was affected more than anywhere. All species were hunted to near extinction during this period and today whales exist in only a small fraction of their former numbers. The most common sea mammal here is the ringed seal, which spends summer basking on the shoreline or ice floes.

Dorset and Thule cultures inhabited the region for thousands of years before European whalers arrived, but it was the latter that had the most dramatic effect on animal populations. Trading posts, built to support the whaling industry, attracted the Inuit, and in time, communities developed around them. Rankin Inlet is the largest of seven communities and the transportation hub of the Keewatin.

The area code for all Keewatin communities is **819.**

RANKIN INLET (KANGIQTINQ)

Rankin Inlet is the communication, administrative, and transportation center of Keewatin region. It is located on rocky terrain, west of where the Meliadine River drains into Rankin Inlet, approximately 25 km from Hudson Bay. It wasn't established until 1955 when the North Rankin Nickel Mine opened. A Hudson's Bay Company store, hospital, homes, three churches, and a school were soon added to the mine structures as many Inuit moved to the area seeking a wage. In 1958, the Department of Indian Affairs, appalled at the living conditions of the nomadic Inuit, set up a relocation program, moving them to **Itivia**, one km southeast of Rankin Inlet. Here the government constructed huts, a school, and a store. Due to a depletion of ore, the mine closed in 1962 and the population dipped to 350. Itivia was deemed a failure soon after. An arts and crafts manufacturing program was the turning point in Rankin Inlet's fortunes. Although recovery has been slow, the population has increased to 1,500, and today the streets are the typical northern clutter of weathered buildings joined by a net of electrical wires. The Keewatin's only paved road links downtown to the airport.

Around Town

The **North Rankin Nickel Mine** is located on a gravel hill overlooking the harbor and town. Although it has been closed since 1962, much of the machinery remains, slowly rusting away and leaving a graphic memory of the eastern Arctic's first mine. Across the road from the mine site is a commercial fish-processing plant where arctic char is prepared for shipment south. From the mine site the road continues down to the harbor where there's a dock and a small fleet of fishing boats. On the opposite side of town, near the Matchbox Gallery, a one-km trail leads to Itivia. Little remains of the settlement but from the site there is a good view of the Barrier Islands. An important archaeological site is located 10 km north of town on the Meliadine River. The area was never particularly good for hunting but had been used for centuries as a seasonal fishing camp. Many stone tent rings, foundations of semi-subterranean houses, and a number of graves can be found in the area. The road to

the site is used by locals going fishing, so if you walk you may be able to hitch a ride along the way. Alternatively, **Hudson Bay Tour Company,** P.O. Box 328, Rankin Inlet, NT X0C 0A0, tel. (819) 645-2618, will make the run out there with an Inuit guide.

Marble Island

Lying 40 km east of Rankin Inlet is an island where many dramas have been played out over the years. The lineaments are simple; it is a barren island dominated by slabs of cream-colored quartzite protruding from an otherwise featureless terrain. European traders and explorers probably landed on the island as early as the 1600s. In 1721 Capt. James Knight and his crew were searching for the Northwest Passage when his two ships were wrecked on a shallow bar at the east end of the island. Everyone made it ashore, and a stone house was built to winter in. One by one they perished, waiting for a rescue that never came. During the late 1800s the island was used as a wintering site for whalers. Today it is regarded as a mystical place; Thule camps can be seen along with the remains of Knight's house and the site of an open-air theater, used by the whalers for entertainment. The least expensive way of visiting the island is with **Hudson Bay Tour Company,** tel. (819) 645-2618.

Accommodations and Food

Rankin Inlet's two accommodations are in the center of town and should be able to organize transportation from the airport if you book a room in advance. **Nanuq Inn,** P.O. Box 175, Rankin Inlet, NT X0C 0A0, tel. (819) 645-2513, has 10 rooms with cable TV in each and shared bathrooms. The inn also has a coffee shop, dining room, and lounge; $115 per person. Larger is **Siniktarvik Hotel,** P.O. Box 190, tel. (819) 645-2807, where each of the 65 rooms has a private bath, and a restaurant and lounge is available for guests. Rates are $136 per person.

Northern has a good range of groceries and a snack bar serving fast food (closes 5 p.m.). Dining in the two hotel restaurants is expensive, but not outrageously so.

Transportation

Rankin Inlet is the transportation hub of the Keewatin. **NWT Air,** tel. (819) 645-2849 or (800)

661-0789, flies in from Yellowknife five times weekly ($516 one-way, $506 for a seven-day APEX roundtrip) and Winnipeg three times weekly ($657 one-way, $643 roundtrip). **First Air,** tel. (819) 645-2961 or (800) 267-1247, flies between Iqaluit and Rankin Inlet via Coral Harbour; $506 one-way, $557 roundtrip. For a cab call (819) 645-2411.

Services and Information

The **post office** is behind the Siniktarvik Hotel; the only bank is a C.I.B.C. in the Kissarvik Co-op. For the **medical center** call (819) 645-2816. A small **visitor center,** tel. (819) 645-5091, in the Siniktarvik Hotel, features Inuit displays and details of the Knight Expedition and has local crafts for sale.

WHALE COVE (TIKIRARJUAQ)

Whale Cove's Inuit name means "where many people arrive," a reference to the whalers, trading ships, and Inuit who stopped here. This small community of 200 is located 80 km south of Rankin Inlet, on a peninsula where the Wilson River drains into Hudson Bay. The area was explored in 1613 by Capt. Thomas Button, and from the early 1700s onward Hudson's Bay Company traders regularly visited the area. It wasn't until 1959 that the community was officially established. At this time, the federal government began moving Caribou Inuit to the coast, where they adapted their hunting and fishing skills to the abundant coastal resources.

The community has little to offer in the way of tourist facilities but provides a unique opportunity to view the traditional Inuit lifestyle, including women scraping caribou skins and fishermen returning with their daily catches. On one side of the town are large tanks, filled each summer with fuel for the winter. On the other side is a small dock and beach. The beach is lined with freighter canoes, engines, and the ubiquitous snowmobile. Behind town is **Whale's Tail Monument,** built in 1967 to celebrate the community's link to the ocean. A rough trail leads to this viewpoint. Other trails lead inland to a number of lakes, the deeper ones supporting lake trout and whitefish.

Practicalities

The **Tavanni Inns North,** Whale Cove, NT X0C 0J0, tel. (819) 896-9252, is in the center of town and has six rooms, each with a private bathroom; $200 per person per day includes three meals. Ask at the hamlet office next door about camping; tel. (819) 896-9961. A **grocery store** and **post office** are located by the fish plant opposite the waterfront. The only scheduled flights to Whale Cove are with **Calm Air,** tel. (819) 645-2746 or (800) 839-2256, from Rankin Inlet; $94 one-way, $103 for a 14-day APEX roundtrip.

ESKIMO ICE CREAM

Recipes vary from region to region depending on the ingredients available. This version is from the eastern Arctic and, once started, must be completed without interruptions.

Pound an amount of seal fat until soft, then melt over low heat until there is a thick layer of grease on the base of the pot. Grind up dried arctic char roe and berries, then stir slowly into the melted fat; make sure the temperature remains low—a guide is to keep the mixture at a temperature that is not too hot to touch. Add salt to taste. If the mixture congeals, water will soften it up. Freeze the mixture, then serve with bread or meat.

ARVIAT

For many centuries Arviat (formerly known as Eskimo Point), 240 km southwest of Rankin Inlet, was a summer camp for Pallirmiut Inuit who came to the coast to hunt seals. They spent the rest of the year inland, but during their time in the area in the late 1600s they made contact with traders from Churchill. A Hudson's Bay Company post was established in 1921, followed by Roman Catholic and Anglican missions. Inuit were attracted to the settlement for food, medicine, and trade goods. During the 1940s and '50s migration patterns of the caribou changed and their numbers declined, causing great hardship for the remaining inland Inuit who were relocated to Arviat by the Canadian government. Today this community of 1,300 is still largely dependent on hunting, trapping, and fishing for its livelihood.

To the south is **McConnell River Bird Sanctuary,** a 330-square-km area of wetlands and tidal flats that is a breeding ground for 250,000 lesser snow geese and a staging area for one million birds each fall. For boat transfers to the sanctuary or to good fishing areas, call the hamlet office, tel. (819) 857-2841.

Practicalities

Padlei Inns North, P.O. Box 90, Arviat, NT X0C 0E0, tel. (819) 857-2919, has 10 rooms, a lounge, and a laundry; $190 per person includes three meals.

Calm Air, tel. (819) 645-2746 or (800) 839-2256, flies daily from Rankin Inlet; $191 one-way, $213 for a 14-day APEX roundtrip.

In town is the **Margaret Aniksak Visitors Centre,** tel. (819) 857-2698, with a tour-booking service and displays of local archaeological sites.

CHESTERFIELD INLET (IGLULIGAARJUK)

This community of 290 north of Rankin Inlet was an important medical and educational center for the eastern Arctic until the government helped other communities develop their own facilities. Although there was much whaling activity in Hudson Bay in the 1700s, it wasn't until 1912 that the Hudson's Bay Company established a post on the Keewatin Coast, at Chesterfield Inlet. The community, situated on a gravel strip of a land overlooking the inlet, has several historic buildings including the impressive three-story **St. Theresa Hospital,** built in 1931.

Kanayuk Sammurtok Outfitting, General Delivery, Chesterfield Inlet, NT X0C 0B0, tel. (819) 645-2618, offers half-day tours of the community, three-day tours up the inlet to archaeological sites, and five-day tours up the coast to Cape Fullerton, the site of the eastern Arctic's first RCMP post (which has been restored to its original condition).

Practicalities

The only tourist services are at **Tangmavik Hotel,** P.O. Box 500, Chesterfield Inlet, NT

Inukshuks *were built by the Inuit as navigational aids on the featureless tundra.*

DAN HERINGA / NWT ECONOMIC DEVELOPMENT & TOURISM

X0C 0B0, tel. (819) 898-9190; $170 per person includes three meals.

Calm Air, tel. (819) 645-2746 or (800) 839-2256, has daily flights from Rankin Inlet; $97 one-way or $111 for a 14-day APEX roundtrip.

BAKER LAKE (QAMANITTUAQ)

Baker Lake (pop. 1,000), located west of Chesterfield Inlet, is the only inland Inuit community (Qamanittuaq means "far inland"). Rankin Inlet is 260 km to the east and, surprisingly, the geographical center of Canada is located a few kilometers to the northeast. The community is a good jumping-off point for sightseeing in Thelon Game Sanctuary or canoeing the various wilderness rivers to the south and west.

The local population is thought to have descended from a group of Inuit of the Thule culture who migrated onto the barrenlands to hunt caribou. Before the Hudson's Bay Company established a post in 1916 on an island in the lake, few whites had ventured into the area. The post moved to the present site in 1936 and the community has been steadily expanding since. Local Inuit are renowned for their art, much of which reflects the importance of the caribou herds. Their artworks can be viewed at the **Jessie Oonark Arts and Crafts Centre.**

Accommodations

The two accommodations are **Baker Lake Lodge,** P.O. Box 239, Baker Lake, NT X0C 0A0, tel. (819) 793-2905, and **Iglu Hotel,** P.O. Box 179, tel. (819) 793-2801. Both charge $160 per person inclusive of meals. Camping is possible along the lakeshore, but check with the hamlet office before pitching a tent.

Services and Information

Calm Air, tel. (819) 645-2746 or (800) 839-2256, has flights daily from Rankin Inlet into Baker Lake; $212 one-way, $238 14-day APEX roundtrip.

Limited groceries and camping supplies are available at **Northern.** The **Akumalik Visitors Centre,** tel. (819) 793-2456, is in the original 1936 Hudson's Bay Company trading post, which has been restored. Bookings can be made at the area's center for tours.

Thelon Game Sanctuary

This 67,340-square-km sanctuary was established in 1927 for the sole purpose of wildlife conservation. Its dominant natural feature, the **Thelon River,** begins from 200 km east of Great Slave Lake and is the largest unaltered watershed emptying into Hudson Bay. The river flows through a wide valley, surrounded in barrenlands yet lined with stands of spruce, protected from the elements by the valley wall. The Beverly caribou herd—numbering 330,000—migrates through the sanctuary. Other mammals present are wolves, musk oxen, moose, wolverines, foxes, lynx, and grizzly bears. Rare raptors, such as the peregrine falcon, nest in the sanctuary along with 10,000 Canada geese.

The Thelon River has been designated as a Canadian Heritage River, not only for its abundant wildlife and natural heritage but for the unique wilderness recreation it offers. Canoeing

is by far the most popular activity. Although it is possible to begin a canoe trip from the Upper Thelon or Hanbury Rivers, strenuous portages are required to do so. The most popular put-in point is the confluence of these two rivers, from where it is 300 km to Beverly Lake or an extra 100 km of open-water paddling to the community of Baker Lake. **Peter Tapatai,** P.O. Box 74, Baker Lake, NT X0C 0A0, tel. (403) 793-2618, organizes pick-ups for canoeists coming off the river as well as day tours from Baker Lake to where the river flows into Chesterfield Inlet.

Great Canadian Ecoventures, P.O. Box 155, 1896 West Broadway, Vancouver, BC V6J 1Y9, tel. (604) 752-1099 or (800) 667-9453, offers a variety of popular Dance with the Wildlife tours, hosted by experts in various fields of study, which search out wolves, caribou, and musk oxen. Costs are from $2,990 for five days and $3,550 for eight days, which includes charter flights from Yellowknife. Also offered are guided canoe trips down the Thelon River.

REPULSE BAY (NAUJAT)

Although Repulse Bay was used as a refuge for whaling ships, a permanent settlement wasn't established until 1962. The community is located right on the Arctic Circle, at the south side of an isthmus between the Gulf of Boothia and Hudson Bay. The community sits on sloping land, overlooking Repulse Bay, and with steep coastline cliffs on either side. The bay is good for whalewatching, especially in August when belugas and narwhals can often be seen from the shoreline. Contact the hamlet office, General Delivery, Repulse Bay, NT X0C 0H0, tel. (819) 462-9952, for details of outfitters offering fishing trips or tours up the coast to either **Harbour Island**—the site of an old whaling camp—or a stone house built in 1846 by explorer John Rae.

Practicalities

Naujat Inns North Hotel, General Delivery, tel. (819) 462-4304, has private bathrooms and a TV room; $180 per person includes three meals. **Calm Air,** tel. (819) 645-2846, flies three times weekly from Rankin Inlet into Repulse Bay; $331 one-way, $359 for a 14-day APEX roundtrip.

Wager Bay

Isolated, rugged terrain and a rich food base contribute to make Wager Bay—which penetrates 150 km into the Arctic tundra south of Repulse Bay—prime habitat for a wide variety of land and sea mammals. This abundance of wildlife has led to proposals that the bay and a wide strip around its perimeter be designated a national park. The south shore is one of the Arctic's major polar bear denning sites. Ice floes, which remain in the bay until midsummer, make hunting ringed seals easy for the bears. Seals, in turn, are attracted by healthy populations of arctic char. On the land, caribou graze on the tundra throughout summer, attracting wolves and wolverines. In contrast to other flatter areas of the barrenlands, the landscape surrounding the bay features 500-meter cliffs, prime nesting sites for the rare gyrfalcon, waterfalls cascading down glacially carved rock, and rocky crests, with sweeping panoramas of the bay.

The closest community to Wager Bay is Repulse Bay, 160 air km northeast and much farther by boat, making it too far for Inuit hunters. **Sila Lodge,** 774 Bronx Ave., Winnipeg, MB R2K 4E9, tel. (204) 949-2050 or (800) 663-9832, located on the shoreline, is the only accommodation in the bay. The cost of staying at the lodge is, as you'd expect, very expensive. Seven nights, including air charter from Baker Lake, boat tours, and all meals, is $3,595.

CORAL HARBOUR (SALLIQ)

Coral Harbour (pop. 500) is the only community on 40,663-square-km **Southampton Island,** a large island of low, rolling hills that rises from the waters of the north end of Hudson Bay. Upon its shores one of the Arctic's most intriguing tragedies occurred in 1902-03 when the last remaining **Sallirmiut Inuit** mysteriously died. The Hudson's Bay Company established a post on **Coats Island** to the south, to serve fleets of whalers. In 1927 it was moved to the head of South Bay on Southampton Island to serve Inuit who had been moved to a newly established Anglican mission. The community today is very traditional, relying heavily on the abundance of sea mammals in the immediate vicinity.

Coral Harbour is the best jumping-off point for trips to the large walrus colonies in the region; the animals gather in the thousands along the coast and on Coats and Depot Islands. Other mammals often seen are polar bears and ringed and bearded seals. Also on Southampton Island is the **Harry Gibbons Bird Sanctuary,** a nesting site for various species of geese, including 200,000 lesser snow geese. And within hiking distance of Coral Harbour are the spectacular **Kirchoffer Falls** and various historic and prehistoric sites.

The Mystery of the Sallirmiut

Arctic historians engage in much speculation as to who the Sallirmiut were and what caused their demise. But it is known that in the winter of 1902-03, after surviving on a bleak and inhospitable spit of land for many hundreds of years, they all died. They may have descended from the Dorset culture, who disappeared elsewhere in the north around 700 years ago, or from the Thule, who had evolved into the Inuit culture found elsewhere in the Canadian Arctic. Whoever their ancestors, this splinter group settled at **Native Point,** 60 km southeast of the community of Coral Harbour, and remained in near-total isolation, culturally distinct from the rest of the world. They lived a Stone Age existence until that fateful winter earlier this century, building homes from stone, sod, and whalebone, and hunting sea mammals with flint-headed weapons. Their demise was probably caused by contact with a whaling fleet that transmitted a disease such as dysentery or smallpox—killing off the entire Sallirmiut population in one long winter. The following year visitors to the settlement found bodies everywhere, with dogs being the only sign of life.

The site, a two-hour boat trip from Coral Harbour, attracts few visitors. But walking around the 100-odd houses with sun-bleached bones scattering the rocky ground provokes feelings of veneration for a now-extinct culture that, after surviving unbelievable natural hardships, was wiped out by fellow humans.

Practicalities

The only accommodations at Coral Harbour is **Leonie's Place,** P.O. Box 29, Coral Harbour, NT X0C 0C0, tel. (819) 925-9751, which has six double rooms; $190 per person includes three meals. Ask at the hamlet office about camping.

Calm Air, tel. (819) 645-2846, flies three times weekly from Rankin Inlet to Coral Harbour; $322 one-way, $354 for a 14-day APEX roundtrip. Once a week **First Air,** tel. (819) 925-8244 or (800) 267-1247, flies from Rankin Inlet to Coral Harbour and across Foxe Channel to Cape Dorset and Iqaluit on Baffin Island. For details of outfitters contact the hamlet office, tel. (819) 925-8867.

BAFFIN AND BEYOND

Baffin Island, the surrounding administrative region, and the islands of the high Arctic sit atop the continent of North America—a vast, rugged, virtually uninhabitable, and relatively unexplored part of the world that has only recently been viewed as a viable travel destination. Within this area are endless opportunities for adventure travel, whether it's hiking in two of the world's most remote national parks, canoeing a Canadian Heritage River, climbing the towering peaks along the spectacular fiords of North Baffin Island, or making the ultimate trip—to the North Pole. If you're looking for something equally satisfying but less challenging, you can visit the many prehistoric Thule sites, chase the legend of the ill-fated Franklin Expedition, view the abundant sea mammals from the safety of a boat, visit islands that are home to millions of seabirds, learn more about the Inuit culture by visiting the 14 communities, and, yes, you too can visit the North Pole, with a champagne lunch thrown in.

Baffin Island is the world's sixth-largest island (after Australia, Greenland, New Guinea, Borneo, and Madagascar) at 507,500 square km. Most of the island is lowland arctic, made up of gently rolling hills, rarely rising more than 700 meters above sea level and broken only occasionally by a rocky headland or bluff. The southern end of the island is made up of three distinct peninsulas, two of which are separated by Frobisher Bay where Iqaluit, capital of Nunavut, lies. In lower-central Baffin Island, northwest of Iqaluit, is the **Great Plain of the Koukdjuak,** which rose so quickly from the surrounding sea that colonies of seals became landlocked in two large lakes and have evolved into freshwater mammals. The northeastern coast of Baffin Island, from Cumberland Peninsula to Bylot Island, is the mountainous Arctic. Here, glaciated peaks rising over 2,000 meters are incised by steep-sided fiords cutting deeply into the land. Auyuittuq National Park, on Cumberland Peninsula, is the most accessible part of this spectacular region and attracts hikers and mountaineers from around the world.

IQALUIT

Iqaluit is the government, transportation, and administrative center for all eastern Arctic communities. In 1999, the town—which was known as Frobisher Bay until 1987—will become capital of Canada's new territory, Nunavut. The terrain on which the community is built is uninspiring, a glacially scoured landscape of rocky ridges and exposed bedrock. The land is dotted with many lakes, the coastline with many islands. It is located on Koojesse Inlet at the northwest head of **Frobisher Bay** on southern Baffin Island. The national capital, Ottawa (2,080 km south), is closer than the territorial capital, Yellowknife (2,260 km west).

The first recorded contact the local Inuit had with Europeans was in 1576 when Sir Martin Frobisher entered the bay that now bears his name. He was searching for the Northwest Passage. Instead he found ore samples that he mistakenly thought were gold. He returned with 15 ships and had established a camp before the mistake was realized. Although whalers frequented the area in the 18th and 19th centuries, it wasn't until after the construction of the north's largest United States Air Force base in 1942 that the community took hold. The Hudson's Bay Company established a post, and in 1959 the federal government moved its regional headquarters to the townsite. Although many of the 3,800 Inuit who live here earn a wage, Iqaluit is still relatively traditional.

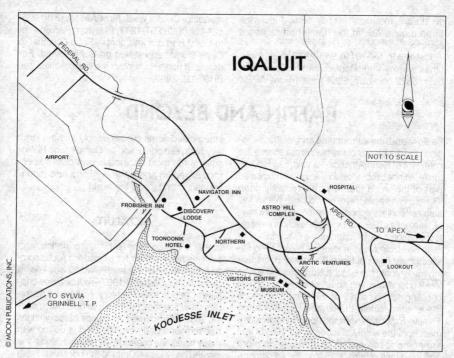

Sights

The best place to begin a visit is **Unikkaarvik Visitors Centre,** tel. (819) 979-4636, located on the beach at the southeast end of town. The staff supplies brochures and maps and can set up trips with local outfitters. (You'll need a map; although there are street signs, no one uses them.) Also here is a life-size marble carving of an Inuit drum dancer and a model of the inside of a Thule sod house. Next door, housed in a restored Hudson's Bay Company post, is **Nunatta Sunakkutaangit Museum,** tel. (819) 979-5537, housing a collection of prehistoric and historic artifacts. Farther along the beach is a sod house. Behind the visitors center is Arctic Ventures gift shop and, farther up the hill, a lookout and another gift shop. From this gift shop a gravel road leads five km east to **Apex,** a residential part of Iqaluit. Before Apex, a road leads to some historic Hudson's Bay Company buildings.

Most businesses, including the airport, are to the west of the Visitors Centre. A 15-minute walk south from the airport is **Sylvia Grinnell Territorial Park,** 148 hectares of rolling Arctic tundra. Over 160 species of plants have been recorded in the park, and the cliffs there provide excellent views across the bay. A trail leads up Sylvia Grinnell River, past a traditional fishing spot, but the going is rough.

Qaummaarviit Historic Park

Twelve km west of Iqaluit near Peale Point, a small island (connected to the mainland only at low tide) has been inhabited intermittently for nearly 1,000 years. Thule, who migrated from Alaska, settled on the island for the abundance of both sea and land mammals in the vicinity. More than 3,000 tools and 20,000 bones have been discovered. Today, a series of boardwalks leads through the sod houses on the south end of the island and through a shallow valley to graves and tent rings.

Outfitters

To get to Qaummaarviit you'll need to use the services of an outfitter. Both **Qairrulik Outfitting,** P.O. Box 863, Iqaluit, NT X0A 0H0, tel. (819) 979-6280, and **North Winds,** P.O. Box 849, tel. (819) 979-0551, offer trips to the island; $90-130 per person includes a bannock meal. You can also charter a boat from either company for fishing, whalewatching, or taking a trip to fossil beds.

Events

Toonik Tyme, a weeklong festival at the end of April, is a celebration of spring with traditional Inuit games, a snowmobile race to Kimmirut, harpoon throwing, igloo building, and a community feast.

Accommodations

Iqaluit has four hotels, a couple of B&Bs, and a campground. **Toonoonik Hotel,** P.O. Box 1859, tel. (819) 979-6733, features good views but has small rooms; $125 s, $145 d. Other choices are: **Frobisher Inn,** P.O. Box 610, tel. (819) 979-2222, which has a good restaurant, $131 s, $140 d; **Discovery Lodge,** P.O. Box 387, tel. (819) 979-4433, the pick of the bunch, $140 s or d; and **Navigator Inn,** P.O. Box 158, tel. (819) 979-6201, across the road from the Discovery, $145 s, $150 d. **By-the-sea Accommodations,** P.O. Box 341, tel. (819) 979-0219, is a bed and breakfast in Apex, five km east of town. Facilities include a kitchen and laundry. Rates include a cooked breakfast and transportation from the airport; $95 s, $120 d.

Camping is available at **Sylvia Grinnell Territorial Park,** a 15-minute walk ($5 taxi ride) from the airport. The park's facilities include tent platforms, foul-weather shelters, pit toilets, and fire rings.

Food

Coffee shops are located in **Northern** and the **Navigator Inn,** while a small bakery is located in the Astro Hill Complex. For something more substantial, the Navigator Inn is a favorite, especially on Friday nights for pizza. The rest of the week, arctic char and caribou are served and there's a good salad bar. For dessert, fresh fruit is flown in and delicious chocolate crepes, made in-house, are served. All other hotels have licensed dining with local specialties such as Cumberland Sound scallops, seal, and shrimp served in season.

Transportation

The distinctive yellow air terminal, a short walk from downtown Iqaluit, is a northern landmark. The airport is always busy and handles 10,000 take-offs and landings per year. **Canadian North,** tel. (819) 979-5331 or (800) 665-1177, and **First Air,** tel. (819) 979-5329 or (800) 267-1247, fly from Yellowknife to Iqaluit ($817 one-way, $801 for a seven-day APEX roundtrip) and to Montreal ($759 one-way, $834 roundtrip). **NWT Air,** tel. (819) 979-6905 or (800) 661-0789, also flies from

WOLFGANG WEBER / NWT ECONOMIC DEVELOPMENT & TOURISM

Travel by dog team is a unique way to visit the sights around Iqaluit.

Yellowknife, but via Rankin Inlet; $875 one-way, $859 roundtrip. First Air also links Iqaluit to communities in the Keewatin, along the Arctic coast, and to Sondrestrom Fjord, in Greenland ($360 one-way, $432 roundtrip).

Air Nunavut, tel. (819) 979-2400, has scheduled flights to all communities on South Baffin Island. It also has flightseeing from $90 per person for a 30-minute tour.

A cab anywhere in town costs $3.50 and out to the campground $5.

Services and Information
Iqaluit has a post office, banks, one-hour photo developing, a hospital, and an indoor pool. The massive **Northern** store sells everything from camping gear to fresh cakes and pastries. **Unikkaarvik Visitors Centre,** tel. (819) 979-4636, has all the information you'll need for touring through the Baffin region; open year-round Mon.-Fri. 10 a.m.-noon and 1-7 p.m., Sat.-Sun. noon-7 p.m. The local newspaper, *Nunatsiaq News,* tel. (819) 979-5357, comes out weekly and is available by subscription; $30 per year, $45 from the United States.

KIMMIRUT

Meaning "looks like a heel" in Inuktitut (for the spit of land on which it lies), this community of 350 was known as **Lake Harbour** until 1996. It's located on the south coast of **Meta Incognita Peninsula** 120 km south of Iqaluit, overlooking a picturesque harbor. The peninsula is separated from the mainland of northern Quebec by Hudson Strait. From the low peaks of this peninsula flows the Soper River, one of the world's great wilderness canoeing rivers. Jutting westward are the low-lying wetlands of **Foxe Peninsula.** In spring the nearby floe edge is a good place for viewing sea mammals.

The anchorage of Lake Harbour was the most important on South Baffin Island for whaling ships. The Hudson's Bay Company opened a post in 1911, and during WW II a radio station was set up. Although most of the population moved to Iqaluit in the 1960s, the local Inuit population of 350 remains steady, hunting, fishing, and carving local soapstone, distinguished by its apple-green color.

A limestone outcrop, immediately to the east, has good views. A variety of geological formations and flora can be found close to town. To the northwest is a chain of lakes including **Shoogle Lake,** which has a 60-meter waterfall at its far end. Many of the lakes offer excellent fishing for landlocked arctic char. **Mayukalik Outfitting,** P.O. Box 99, Kimmirut, NT X0A 0N0, tel. (819) 939-2355, takes boat trips around the harbor, to 3,500-year-old archaeological sites at McKellar Bay and Cape Tanfield, and trips into the open water in search of sea mammals. It also rents canoes and other gear for trips down the Soper River.

Practicalities
Kimik Co-op Hotel, P.O. Box 69, tel. (819) 939-2093, has 12 rooms with private bathrooms; $185 per person includes three meals. Although the community has no established campgrounds, the beach is only a short walk from the airport and, with advance bookings, you can eat at the hotel. White gas and groceries are available at the co-op.

First Air, tel. (819) 939-2250 or (800) 267-1247, serves Kimmirut three times weekly from Iqaluit; $98 one-way, $157 for a seven-day APEX roundtrip.

Katannilik Territorial Park
The watershed of the **Soper River** is protected by this 1,269-square-km park that spans Meta Incognita Peninsula from the waters of Frobisher Bay to the community of Kimmirut (formerly Lake Harbour) near Hudson Strait. The Soper River has carved out a deep valley near **Mt. Joy** (610 meters) and becomes wider and shallower as it flows through low-lying wetlands to the south. To the east the peninsula is nearly devoid of vegetation, but the river valley is carpeted in colorful wildflowers and is lined with willow bushes. The most common mammals are arctic foxes and arctic hares. A herd of 3,000 caribou grazes throughout the area. Ermines and lemmings are also present. Just upstream from **Fleming Hill** is one of the world's few deposits of high-quality lapis lazuli. Four km north of Kimmirut is **Soper Lake.** At the southern outlet are meromictic (reversing) falls where water drains out of the lake at low tide and pours back in again at high tide. At the north end of the lake is **Soper Falls.**

The easiest way to explore the park is on foot from Kimmirut. Two designated landing strips can be accessed by Twin Otter or helicopter from Iqaluit from where you can hike to Kimmirut. The third, and most challenging option, is to charter a boat in Iqaluit and be dropped at the northeast corner of the park. The hike from there to Kimmirut would be 120 km. Park information and trail maps are available at Unikkaarvik Visitors Centre in Iqaluit or from the park at P.O. Box 1000, Iqaluit, NT X0A 0H0, tel. (819) 979-4636.

CAPE DORSET (KINGAIT)

For a community recognized around the world for fine arts and crafts, the cluster of weathered houses on a small island off the southwest coast of Baffin Island bears little resemblance to an art colony. Cape Dorset is named for the remains of an ancient people who flourished in the area between 1000 B.C. and A.D. 1000. The cape is ac-

DAN WALKER / NWT ECONOMIC DEVELOPMENT & TOURISM

Although the Inuit have been strongly influenced by white settlers, many retain a traditional lifestyle.

tually an island, attached to the Foxe Peninsula of southwest Baffin Island only at low tide. The Hudson's Bay Company established a trading post at the cape in 1913, and in 1953 a nursing station was built to help avert diseases that ravaged other communities. Also in this year James Houston, an award-winning writer, and his wife arrived. They spent 10 years working with the local Inuit, encouraging the development of soapstone carving and printmaking. They also initiated the formation of the **West Baffin Eskimo Co-operative,** which has since gained international recognition for the artists it represents. Today the industry is worth $4 million annually with 75% of the local residents earning all or part of their income from the production of art.

Called soapstone, but really a form of serpentine, the soft rock used for carving is generally a mottled dark green. It is found 130 km east of Cape Dorset at **Korak Inlet,** and many artists spend summer at this site. If you walk around the streets of Cape Dorset you'll see artists at work, but to buy work head to the co-op overlooking the bay, tel. (819) 897-8944. Also of interest are numerous Thule sites, including two within walking distance of the airport. **Mallikjuak Island** can be reached on foot at low tide and has some high peaks offering good views and more archaeological sites, including a reconstructed sod house.

Practicalities
Kingnait Inn, General Delivery, Cape Dorset, NT X0A 0C0, tel. (819) 897-8863, has 17 rooms with private bathrooms; $190 per person including three meals. No designated camping areas exist, but anywhere out of sight of the community should be all right. Nonguests may eat at the hotel with advance reservations. The hotel also has take-away service.

The airstrip, within walking distance of the hotel, is served by **First Air,** tel. (819) 897-8938 or (800) 267-1247, and **Air Nunavut,** tel. (819) 879-8075, from Iqaluit; $338 one-way, $327 for a seven-day APEX roundtrip. These flights continue to Rankin Inlet ($243 one-way).

BELCHER ISLANDS

Chances are, these islands will never make the cover of *Islands* magazine, nor will they ever be on the main tourist trail. But for those who seek them out, the enchanting lifestyle of local Ungava Inuit and the absolute isolation the islands afford will be unforgettable.

The islands are spread over 5,000 square km of southern Hudson Bay—low, barren, and windswept, with only one settlement, that of **Sanikiluaq** on Flaherty Island. Although geographically and culturally removed from the rest of the Northwest Territories, the islands are nevertheless politically a part, administered from Iqaluit 1,024 km to the north.

Inuit migrated to the islands from northern Quebec 200 years ago, but with no airstrip, surrounded by shallow and treacherous waters, and a four-day kayak trip from the mainland, they remained almost forgotten.

The lack of land mammals meant that the Inuit had no source of furs for clothing. But living near one of the densest wildfowl nesting areas in Hudson Bay, the Inuit became one of the few peoples in the world to use feathered bird skins for clothing. Their tradition of making such clothing remains, although today they supplement their wardrobe with modern down-filled garb. The islanders are also known for their carvings of bird figures from dark green argillite.

Practicalities

Amaulik Hotel, Mitiq Co-op, Sanikiluaq, NT X0A 0W0, tel. (819) 266-8821, has accommodations for 18 in seven rooms with shared bath; $190 per person includes three meals. The campground, on a gravel beach north of the harbor, can become windy. Access to the islands is by **Air Tindi,** tel. (514) 636-9445, from Kuujjuarapik (Great Whale River) and La Grande in Quebec.

HALL BEACH (SANIRAJAK)

Although part of the mainland, the flat, lowland region of Melville Peninsula, separated from Baffin Island by the narrow Fury and Hecla Strait, is part of the Baffin region. On its northeastern coastline are the communities of Hall Beach and Igloolik, good bases for fishing trips or exploring Thule historic sites.

Thule Inuit have hunted and fished on the peninsula for 7,000 years. A Distant Early Warning Line station, constructed in 1955, attracted Inuit who stayed and became dependent on a wage economy. A few years ago, when news reached the Inuit that the 20-meter radar screens were to be dismantled, they asked that the screens remain—they served as ideal landmarks on the otherwise featureless tundra. Their request was granted.

Hall Beach certainly isn't the place to come for scenery (Sanirajak means "flat land" in Inuktitut) but there is good arctic char fishing and viewing of sea mammals such as walrus and seals. Numerous archaeological sites are located in the area, including the Uglit Islands four km offshore, where you'll find broken-down sod houses and grave sites. Between town and the airstrip are the remains of a whale, estimated to be 500 years old.

Practicalities

Hall Beach Hotel, General Delivery, tel. (819) 928-8952, has five rooms, each with three beds; $170 per person with three meals. Ask here or at the hamlet office about camping.

Canadian North, tel. (800) 665-1177, and **First Air,** tel. (819) 928-8927 or (800) 267-1247, fly four times weekly between Iqaluit and Hall Beach; $436 one-way, $567 for a seven-day APEX roundtrip.

IGLOOLIK (IGLULIK)

North of Hall Beach is Igloolik, large by Arctic standards, with the usual clutter of buildings. It is surrounded by low-lying topography and is a small island, separated from the mainland by Hector Strait. Archaeological sites on the island provide records of nearly unbroken habitation since 2000 B.C. Capt. William Parry spent the winter of 1822-23 on the island; a grave of one of his English sailors who died in the spring is located just outside town. Before the Hudson's Bay Company established a post in 1939, the Inuit had traveled to Pond Inlet and Repulse Bay to trade. Of the various Thule and Dorset sites, those at Ungalujat Point, 18 km from Igloolik, including a ceremonial house, are the most interesting. In town, the **Igloolik Research Centre,** tel. (819) 934-8836, a large, mushroom-shaped building, is a government facility for scientific research and also functions as a weather and seismic station. It also has a general Arctic reference section and small library.

Practicalities

Tujormivik Hotel, P.O. Box 39, Igloolik, NT X0A 0L0, tel. (819) 934-8814, is $185 per person per day including three meals, usually local game or pastas in the evening. There is no set area for camping; ask at the hamlet office, tel. (819) 934-8830. For tours out on the tundra and ocean searching out sea mammals at the floe edge, contact **Igloolik Tourism Association,** General Delivery, tel. (819) 934-8866, which can supply a list of local outfitters.

First Air, tel. (800) 267-1247, flies between Iqaluit and Igloolik four times weekly; $436 one-way, or $567 for a seven-day APEX roundtrip.

PANGNIRTUNG (PANNIQTUUQ)

Meaning "lots of caribou," Pangnirtung sits in a spectacular setting, flanked by sheer cliffs rising nearly 1,000 meters out of Pangnirtung Fiord. Most visitors come here on their way to somewhere even more awesome, Auyuittuq National Park (see below).

The fiord was a base for whalers as early as 1840, but it wasn't until 1921, a decade after the decline of the whaling industry, that the Hudson's Bay Company established a trading post. Through the years a community has grown with Inuit from other areas moving here. Today, with a population of 1,100, "Pang," as it's best known, is Baffin Island's second-largest community.

Although the national park to the north is the main drawcard, the picturesque community itself is worth exploring. The **Ukama Trail** follows a well-worn path from behind the arena along the west bank of Duval River, passing numerous waterfalls; six km (two and a half hours) one-way. Another trail, to the top of **Mt. Duval** (670 meters), begins near the campground and is seven km (three to three and a half hours) each way. The views from the summit are spectacular, but the hike is strenuous.

Kekerten Historic Park

For nearly a century, hundreds of whaling ships plied the waters of the Baffin region. Instead of returning to their European or American ports, many overwintered here at the end of the short summer season. This historic park, on a small island 50 km south of Pangnirtung, was one of two shore-based whaling stations in the eastern Arctic. The site has been partially restored; interpretive signs explain the importance of the artifacts and foundations that remain. The *Easonian,* a ship used to hunt beluga whales, burned in 1922 and is visible at low tide. From May to mid-June, access to the island is by snowmobile, after mid-July by boat. **Alivaktuk Outfitting,** P.O. Box 3, Pangnirtung, NT X0A 0R0, tel. (819) 473-8721, offers a 12-hour trip including lunch for $420 for two people. The price drops to $90 per person for a group of six.

Accommodations and Food

Auyuittuq Lodge, P.O. Box 53, tel. (819) 473-8955, is located on a slight rise overlooking an old whaling station and the fiord. The 50 rooms with shared bath and laundry cost $120 per person; $65 extra for three meals. The rate includes airport transfers. **Pisuktinu Tungavik Territorial Campground** is located east of town over the Duval River, a 20-minute walk from the airport. The campground is free but has only pit toilets (ask at Auyuittuq Lodge for showers). In bad weather the Anglican Church, behind Northern, opens its doors to campers. Groceries and white gas are available at **Northern.**

The dining room in Auyuittuq Lodge was renovated in the mid-'80s. Fixed-price dinners cost $30 per person, with arctic char served in season. Mealtimes are 7-9 a.m., noon-1 p.m., and 6-7 p.m.; reservations required. Near the airport is a snack bar.

Services and Information

The **airport** is located behind the main community and within walking distance of all services. **First Air,** tel. (800) 267-1247, has six flights weekly from Iqaluit; $134 each way. Connections can also be made from Yellowknife ($1,012 roundtrip) and Montreal ($935 roundtrip).

Angmarlik Visitors Centre has information on the community, relics from whaling days, a library, and Inuit elders on hand to interpret the area's natural history. The staff here can also organize outfitters and trips to a char-fishing camp 20 km from Pangnirtung; open in summer daily 9 a.m.-9 p.m., tel. (819) 473-8737.

AUYUITTUQ NATIONAL PARK

Auyuittuq, meaning "the land that never melts," is a 21,000-square-km wilderness of vast icefields, glacial lakes, some of the world's highest cliffs, and one long valley paralleled by peaks nearly 3,000 meters high. The most popular trip within this totally undeveloped park is the hiking over **Akshayak Pass** (also called Pangnirtung Pass).

The Land

The park is part of a spine of mountains along the **Cumberland Peninsula,** which was formed by the same forces of Continental Drift that separated Baffin Island from Greenland. Draped over these mountains is **Penny Ice Cap,** a sheet of ice up to 300 meters thick that covers 6,000 square km. This icefield is drained on all sides by glaciers, slow-moving rivers of ice that have sculpted many of the park's features, including a 97-km-long valley that cuts across Cumberland Peninsula. The highest elevation of the valley occurs midway along its length at Akshayak Pass (500 meters). From the pass, the **Weasel River** flows south to Summit Lake and South Pangnirtung Fiord, and the **Owl River** flows north into Davis Strait. Along the southern half of the valley are Mounts Asgard, Thor, and Overlord, steep granite peaks that attract climbers from around the world.

Flora and Fauna

Plantlife in the pass is best observed around summer solstice when the ground is carpeted by masses of purple **willow herbs, arctic poppies,** and **arctic willow.** This sparse vegetation supports very few species of animals. The **lemming** is the most common mammal, although their numbers differ dramatically from season to season. Also common are the large **arctic hare** and the small **arctic fox.** Although the **polar bear** is essentially a seal hunter, it occasionally wanders inland to feed on berries. **Caribou,** rare in the pass but occasionally seen in the northwest corner of the park, are hunted by **wolves.** Birds most commonly seen are **ptarmi-**

gan, ravens, and **snowy owls.** The **red-throated loon** is also common during the short nesting season. **Cape Searle,** adjacent to the park, is the breeding ground for 10,000 **northern fulmars.**

Practicalities

A trip to Auyuittuq requires advance planning, preparation, and, for those attempting the pass, experience in the wilderness. Hikers must ford swiftly flowing streams and negotiate ankle-wrenching slopes of glacial moraine. No services are available, and the barren land offers no trees to block the wind or provide firewood. Most trips begin with a boat or snowmobile trip (Pangnirtung Fiord is choked with ice until mid-July) from Pangnirtung to **Overlord Warden Station** ($75-85 per person) where a campground is set among huge boulders. Many hikers travel only as far as Summit Lake, returning to Overlord the same way. This section of the trail is the most inspiring and also crosses the **Arctic Circle,** which is flanked by the towering peaks of Mt. Odin to the west and Mt. Thor to the east. The second half of the valley is broader and less impressive, its terrain is more rugged, and it is traveled by fewer people. If you plan to hike the entire pass, you will have to prearrange a pick-up at Broughton Island. Travel is by snowmobile or dogsled in early summer and by boat after mid-August. Although the most popular time of year for hiking is July and August, late June is good for the 24 hours of daylight.

Park Information Centres are located in Pangnirtung, tel. (819) 473-8828, and Broughton Island, tel. (819) 927-8834. For further information on the park write to Auyuittuq National Park, P.O. Box 353, Pangnirtung, NT X0A 0R0. Each center has topographical maps of the park ($9 each) and fishing licenses ($3).

BROUGHTON ISLAND (QIKIQTARJUAQ)

On an island of the same name, this community of 500 Inuit adjoins an area rich with seals, whales, and polar bears. The community is located off the east coast of Baffin Island on a raised beach flanked by glaciated hills. It is a five- to six-hour trip from the terminus of the Akshayak Pass hiking trail in Auyuittuq National

Park, and that is the reason many people spend time here. The community came into being when Inuit families were moved to the site to help construct a Distant Early Warning Line station in 1956. **Pikaluyak Outfitting,** General Delivery, Broughton Island, NT X0A 0B0, tel. (819) 927-8316, has a 10-meter boat for drop-offs and pickups in Auyuittuq ($220 one-way for two), or for viewing the abundant icebergs, sea mammals, and colonies of seabirds along the Baffin Island coast. **Nauyaq Outfitting,** General Delivery, tel. (819) 927-8427, offers the same services.

Practicalities

If you're planning a trip with Pikaluyak Outfitting, ask about their Quonset hut (no running water or electricity) for $35 per night. **Tulugak Hotel,** General Delivery, tel. (819) 927-8874, has rooms with private baths and is close to the airport; $185 per person includes three meals. The campground has running water and tent platforms and is one km from the community. **Northern** sells groceries and white gas.

First Air, tel. (819) 927-8873 or (800) 267-1247, flies six times weekly from Iqaluit to Broughton Island with some flights stopping at Pangnirtung; $291 one-way, $422 for a seven-day APEX roundtrip.

CLYDE RIVER (KANGIQLUGAAPIK)

This remote community is located on a floodplain, surrounded by mountainous scenery. It's near the mouth of Clyde Inlet, a fiord that slices southwest into the mountainous east coast of Baffin Island. Most of the 500 residents of Clyde River live a traditional lifestyle, fishing and hunting. The site has never been a traditional hunting ground but Inuit families moved here in the 1950s when the Hudson's Bay Company opened a post to take advantage of high seal prices.

Sawtooth Mountain, 25 km from the community, is a good vantage point for viewing the surrounding peaks and bays. Unfortunately, to reach most other sights in the area will require the services of an outfitter. **Qullikkut Guides and Outfitters,** P.O. Box 27, Clyde River, NT X0A 0E0, tel. (819) 924-6268, offers fishing and sightseeing trips. Rates are $275 per person per day by dog team and $300 per person by

boat. At Cape Hewitt, 35 km from town, are tent rings from the Thule culture; at Cape Christian is an abandoned U.S. Coast Guard Station; and farther down the coast is **Isabella Bay,** breeding ground for many of the world's remaining bowhead whales. These slow, copepod-eating whales were decimated by whalers in the 1800s and their numbers have never recovered.

Practicalities

Qammaq Hotel, General Delivery, tel. (819) 924-6201, charges $190 per person including three meals. Camping is $100 per week, which includes use of bathroom facilities. Meals are available at the hotel, groceries from **Northern.**

First Air, tel. (819) 924-6365 or (800) 267-1247, flies from Iqaluit; $422 one-way, $613 for a seven-day APEX roundtrip.

POND INLET (MITTIMATALIK)

In late spring and early summer the waterways around Pond Inlet host the highest concentrations of sea mammals in the eastern Arctic. Narwhal, beluga, and bowhead whales, polar bears, seals, and walruses can all be viewed from the floe edge or a boat. Across the channel from the community is **Bylot Island Bird Sanctuary.** In summer 50 species of birds nest here, including tens of thousands of murres and kittiwakes and a major part of the world's snow goose population. Also on the island are hoodoos, archaeological sites, and glaciated peaks rising to 2,000 meters.

The first Europeans in the area, Robert Bylot and William Baffin, came in 1616, but the local Inuit, who have strong links to the Greenland Thule, hunted in the area well before then. The first permanent settlement on the southern shore of Eclipse Sound was an RCMP post established in 1921. The community has grown to 800, mostly Inuit, living in a brightly colored clump of civilization overlooking Bylot Island.

Mt. Herodier (765 meters) is a 15-km (one-way) hike from town with only one difficult stream crossing. If the weather cooperates, kayaking is a great way to explore Eclipse Sound. **Eclipse Sound Outfitting,** P.O. Box 60, Pond Inlet, NT X0A 0S0, tel. (819) 899-8870, rents kayaks for $45 per day. The company can also organize snowmobile trips to the floe edge (best time for wildlife viewing is early July, including the chance to see narwhals), dogsled trips around the sound, and boat trips to historic sites and over to Bylot Island. The rate is $300 per person per day, which includes all meals and overnight accommodations.

Practicalities
Sauniq Hotel, General Delivery, tel. (819) 899-8928, has 15 rooms, each with two single beds and a private bathroom; $180 per person per day includes three meals. The hotel has a gift shop selling carvings and can set up tours onto the sound. Salmon Creek, two km west of town, has a campground with tent platforms. You can also pitch your tent on the beach just west of town. Meals are available with advance reservations at the hotel; groceries are available from **Northern.**

First Air, tel. (819) 899-8882 or (800) 267-1247, flies daily between Iqaluit and Pond Inlet; $551 one-way, $799 for a seven-day APEX roundtrip.

ARCTIC BAY AND VICINITY

The northern reaches of Baffin Island are made up of two peninsulas, Borden and Brodeur. These desolate plateaus of land are divided by **Admiralty Inlet,** the world's longest fiord and also one of the deepest. No one knows just how deep it is, but at one point its depth is so great that, combined with upwellings of water, currents, and tides, an expanse of water remains ice-free year-round. This phenomenon, which has intrigued scientists for decades, is known as a polynya. The only inhabited area is on Borden Peninsula.

Arctic Bay (Ikpiarjuk)
Arctic Bay is surrounded on three sides by hills and on the fourth by Admiralty Inlet. The only road in the Baffin region connects the community of 500 to Nanisivik, to the east. The area has been occupied by nomadic Inuit hunters for nearly 5,000 years. The first permanent settlement was a Hudson's Bay Company post established in 1924. Remains of prehistoric cultures can be found around the area, including **Uluksan Point,** a low-lying area to the west of

the community. To the east is a distinctive cairn, erected by the crew of a government steamer who wintered here in 1910-11.

Lancaster Sound
Between the northern tip of Baffin Island and the rugged southern coast of Devon Island is Lancaster Sound, the eastern entrance to the **Northwest Passage.** Each year tens of thousands of sea mammals migrate through this corridor, in turn attracting seabirds and polar bears. Each spring they must wait at the floe edge that spans the sound, until the ice has broken up and they are free to travel through to the islands of the high Arctic. This spectacle of mammals and birds is the destination of a high Arctic expedition offered by **Niglasuk Co.,** Arctic Bay, NT X0A 0A0, tel. (819) 439-9949. Four seven-night trips are undertaken each June, with a base camp established on the shoreline closest to the floe edge and daily trips made to view the wildlife. The cost is $3,500 per person from Arctic Bay. This tour books up months in advance. The company also offers shorter trips, including dog sledding, sea kayaking, and fishing.

Prince Leopold Island is a flat-topped, barren island of 85 square km rising 300 meters from the waters northeast of Somerset Island. In summer it supports four species of seabirds who nest in the hundreds of thousands on the island's narrow ledges. The island has been designated a migratory bird sanctuary.

Nanisivik
The infrastructure at Nanisivik, 21 km east of Arctic Bay, has been in place since 1974. It serves the 300 workers who mine the silver, lead, and zinc deposits on the shore of Strathcona Sound. To protect against the high winds that howl through camp, all buildings have curved walls. Once extracted, ore is stored on the beach for summer shipment to European markets. No tours of the mine are offered, nor are there any tourist services.

The **Midnight Sun Marathon,** which takes place on the weekend closest to 1 July, is the world's northernmost. The race, which attracts marathoners from around the world, is run between Nanisivik and Arctic Bay; the most grueling event is 84 km. For information call the mine at (819) 436-7502 or (416) 869-0772 in Toronto.

Practicalities

Enokseot Hotel, P.O. Box 69, Arctic Bay, NT X0A 0A0, tel. (819) 439-8811, charges $120 per person per night, with meals an extra $60 per person. The campground is at **Victor Bay,** five km from the community ($10 in a taxi). These accommodations are handy if you'd like to visit Lancaster Sound without forking out for a seven-day trip. If that's the case Niglasuk Co. can arrange travel to the floe edge ($400 per person per day). Food is available, cafeteria-style, at the hotel, and **Northern** has groceries.

The airport is at Nanisivik, 21 km from Arctic Bay. Taxis meet all flights. **First Air,** tel. (819) 436-7481 or (800) 267-1247, flies twice weekly from Iqaluit; $553 one-way, $782 for a seven-day APEX roundtrip. From Yellowknife both airlines fly to Nanisivik via Resolute.

RESOLUTE: GATEWAY TO THE HIGH ARCTIC (QAUSUITTUQ)

Although small, the community of Resolute is an important jumping-off point for expeditions to the high Arctic. It also holds an important scientific research station and a number of excellent outfitters. The community is located on Resolute Bay on the south coast of **Cornwallis Island,** a low-lying island on the north side of the Northwest Passage.

William Parry was the first white man to report seeing the island, and in the 1850s the island was the center of much activity during the search for the lost Franklin Expedition. In fact, the town was named after the HMS *Resolute,* one of the vessels involved in the search. An airfield established in 1947 as a weather station soon became the hub of air transportation in the high Arctic.

Since the late 1950s, Resolute has been operations base for the Polar Continental Shelf Project, a program of Arctic research. The research center and a weather station at the airport are open for tours. Near the dock is a small aquarium stocked with local specimens. The surrounding hills, once under the sea, are full of fossils, and five km west of the airport are Thule tent rings.

A Controversial Move

In 1953 Inuit families from Inukjuak, Quebec and Pond Inlet were relocated to Cornwallis Island and Southern Ellesmere Island; more followed in 1955. At the time, the Dept. of Northern Affairs and National Resources claimed the island was a land of plentiful resources and the move was for the good of the Inuit. More recently it has been revealed that they had been moved to help reinforce Canada's right to sovereignty in the islands of the high Arctic. The full story is only just beginning to be revealed, but apparently, after the families were separated into two groups, they were left in a totally alien environment, with scant regard for their needs and feelings. With only a U.S. Forces garbage dump as a food source they were lucky to survive. For 35 years little was known about their

"Do you think we can tow it to Southern California?"

NWT ECONOMIC DEVELOPMENT & TOURISM

plight, and it wasn't until 1988 that they received their first government support and the promise of repatriation. After a two-year inquiry by the Royal Commission into Aboriginal Peoples, a report released in July 1994 concluded that "the relocation plan was an ill-conceived solution that was inhumane and damaging in its design and effects," and that "there was a significant lack of care and skill in various aspects of the project, including a severe shortage of clothing and bedding during the first winter, causing hardship and suffering." It also recommended that the Canadian government apologize and provide compensation.

Practicalities

The largest accommodation in Resolute is **Narwhal Inn,** P.O. Box 88, Resolute, NT X0A 0V0, tel. (819) 252-3968, near the airport, which sleeps 45 in 30 rooms. Meals are served cafeteria-style and the demands of government workers keep the standard of food high. The other choice is **High Arctic International Explorer Services,** P.O. Box 200, tel. (819) 252-3875. Camping is available at **Resolute Lake,** one km from the airport, and at Mecham River, five km farther. **Northern** and the **post office** are by the airport and the accommodations and other services are in the Inuit village, eight km away. The road has regular traffic, and commuting between the two is relatively easy.

Resolute is a long way from anywhere; in fact London is closer than many U.S. cities. **Canadian North,** tel. (819) 252-3880 or (800) 665-1177, and **First Air,** tel. (819) 252-3981 or (800) 267-1247, have flights from Yellowknife ($536 one-way, $590 for a seven-day APEX roundtrip) and Iqaluit ($607 one-way, $601 for a seven-day APEX roundtrip). From Montreal the fare is $1,013 one-way, $1,067 for a seven-day APEX roundtrip. **Kenn Borek Air,** tel. (819) 252-3845, and **Bradley Air Services,** tel. (819) 252-3981, have aircraft for charter with Kenn Borek Air offering scheduled flights from Resolute to Grise Fiord ($235 one-way), Nanisivik ($241 one-way), and Pond Inlet ($367 one-way).

Devon and Beechey Islands

Devon Island, to the north of Baffin Island across **Lancaster Sound,** is a smaller version of its southerly neighbor. The eastern part of this 350-km long island is lowland arctic, while in the west, cliffs drop 1,000 meters into the ocean below. West of Cape Sparbo are the **Truelove Lowlands,** lake-strewn meadows that have been the scene of much Arctic research and are currently the site of a summer camp of the Arctic Institute of North America, based in Calgary.

Off the island's southwest coast is Beechey Island, where the Franklin Expedition wintered while searching for the Northwest Passage. Beechey is only an island at high tide; at low tide a sandbar joins it to Devon Island. It was here, on one of the many gravel beaches on the north side of the island, that graves and artifacts were found, giving clues to the fate of one of the Arctic's most famous sagas. Access is by snowmobile, boat, or chartered Twin Otter from Resolute, 80 km away.

The Parry Islands

To the west of Resolute are **Little Cornwallis Island** and the uninhabited islands of **Bathurst** and **Melville,** collectively known as the Parry Islands. Little Cornwallis Island is home to the **Polaris Mine,** northernmost metal mine in the world. It is a modern, year-round operation producing lead and zinc for European markets. The self-contained operation employs 200 and even boasts an indoor pool.

Polar Bear Pass, on Bathurst Island, is an ecological reserve with high concentrations of land mammals and birds. Generally it is visited only by Inuit hunting parties and scientific expeditions.

The **magnetic North Pole,** which is continually changing positions in a wobbly, circular motion, currently lies in the general area of **Cameron Island,** to the north of Bathurst Island. It was first located in 1831 when James Ross found his compass dipping downward on King William Island, just off the Arctic coast. The pole moves due to magnetic distortions caused by convection deep below the earth's crust. On the southwest coast of Cameron Island is **Bent Horn A-O2,** an oil well operated by Panarctic Oils, a company that has been at the forefront of high Arctic oil exploration since 1968. Oil produced here is so light that it can be used directly in diesel engines on site; the rest is shipped to Montreal.

TO THE TOP OF THE WORLD

On 6 April 1909, an expedition led by American explorer Robert Peary—including four other men, five sledges, and 38 dogs—became the first to reach the geographic North Pole.

Every year audacious adventurers attempt to reach the pole under their own steam, with dogs, and on snowmobiles. But relative to the South Pole or the summit of Mt. Everest, the North Pole receives few visitors. From the most popular staging area, Ward Hunt Island, it's 772 km to the pole. Most expeditions spend at least two years in preparation, including a few months under Arctic conditions, and budget upward of $1 million. For less adventurous adventurers it's possible to get there on an organized trip in a couple of days, have a champagne lunch, and return to a warm bed at night. The least expensive option, without the trimmings, would be to get a group of six people together and charter a Twin Otter from **Bradley Air Service** in Resolute. The flight, with an overnight stop in Eureka, costs $26,000. **Quark Expeditions,** tel. (800) 356-5699, often charters a Russian icebreaker—complete with all the facilities of a top hotel and an onboard helicopter—for the long trip north; US$17,900 per person.

ELLESMERE ISLAND

Ellesmere Island sits at the top of the North American continent, a wild, rugged landscape of steep-sided fiords and glaciers. At 212,688 square km, it's the 10th-largest island in the world. It extends 800 km from its southern coast and the picturesque community of Grise Fiord to above the 83rd parallel, and east to within 30 km of Greenland. **Axel Heiberg Island,** to the west of Ellesmere and separated by narrow **Eureka Sound,** has peaks over 1,000 meters. On the east coast of Axel Heiberg Island, across from **Eureka** (a high Arctic weather station), are the **Geodetic Hills.** In the hills is a fossilized forest, the remains of thick forests that grew in a lush valley here 40 million years ago.

Grise Fiord (Aujuitittuq)

Overlooking Jones Sound and backed by the spectacular ice-capped peaks of southern Ellesmere Island, this small Inuit community of 130 has reached near-mythical status as North America's northernmost community. Here, at a latitude of 76° N, the sun dips below the horizon for 3.5 months each year and the sound is only ice-free in August.

Otto Sverdrup coined the name Grise—which means "pig" in Norwegian—when he wintered here in 1899-90. The community was born in 1953, when Inuit from Port Harrison and Pond Inlet were brought here as part of a relocation program. Today the Inuit live a traditional lifestyle, hunting, trapping, and fishing. Although Resolute, 383 km southwest, is the major hub of the high Arctic, Grise Fiord is used as a staging point for trips into the interior of Ellesmere Island and to Greenland, accessible by dogsled and snowmobile for six months of the year.

Grise Fiord Inuit Co-op, General Delivery, Grise Fiord, NT X0A 0J0, tel. (819) 980-9913, can organize outfitters for all seasons, has a recently refitted lodge ($185 per person including three meals), and sells groceries.

Kenn Borek Air, tel. (819) 252-3845 in Resolute, flies between Grise Fiord and Resolute twice weekly; $235 each way.

Ellesmere Island National Park

This 37,775-square-km park is literally at the top of the world. It extends from a vast icefield in the central part of Ellesmere Island to the northern coastline where the Grant Land Mountains drop dramatically into the Arctic Ocean. **Mt. Barbeau** (2,629 meters) is the highest peak in North America east of the Rockies. **Lake Hazen,** in the center of the park, is the most popular destination for backpackers. It is 80 km long and the largest lake north of the Arctic Circle. The lake is a thermal oasis, attracting diverse species of birds and mammals during the short summer season. The park receives less than 100 millimeters of precipitation annually, making it one of the driest areas in the world. But where wind has deposited soil, pockets of lush vegetation manage to survive, and brightly colored arctic flowers soak up the sun's rays. The most common mammals here are foxes and hares, although Peary caribou, musk oxen, and wolves are also present. The park also provides suitable nesting habitat for 30 species of birds. The best place for viewing all wildlife is the Lake Hazen area.

The main access point is park headquarters at Tanquary Fiord, a five-hour flight in a chartered Twin Otter from Resolute. Both Resolute charter companies fly to the park but it is very expensive. An alternative is through **Canada North Outfitting,** 87 Mill Ave., Almonte, ON K0A 10A, tel. (613) 256-4057, which coordinates air charters, bringing together travelers to the park. Depending on numbers, the cost from Resolute would be $1,430-3,070 per person roundtrip. You will need to be totally self-sufficient and prepared for all climatic conditions. From Tanquary Fiord the hike to Lake Hazen is 130 km, including one glacier crossing. For more information write to Superintendent, Ellesmere Island National Park, P.O. Box 353, Pangnirtung, NT X0A 0R0; or call (819) 473-8828.

Ward Hunt Island
North of the national park at the mouth of Markham Fiord is four-km long Ward Hunt Island. At 83° 5 minutes N, it's the northernmost point of land in North America. Therefore it is the main staging point for land-based expeditions to the North Pole, 772 km farther north.

Alert
The high Arctic weather station of Alert, 170 km west of Ward Hunt Island, is the continent's northernmost occupied site and has been since 1950. The average high temperature in July is only 6.5° C. Temperatures in winter are not as harsh as you might expect, rarely dropping below -40° C. But the base is in total darkness for four months of the year.

Tyrannosaurus

BOB RACE

BOOKLIST

GEOGRAPHY AND TRAVEL

Kane, Alan. *Scrambles in the Canadian Rockies.* Calgary: Rocky Mountain Books, 1992. Routes detailed in this guide lead to summits, without the use of ropes or mountaineering equipment.

Kariel, Herbert G. *Alpine Huts in the Canadian Rockies, Selkirks, and Purcells.* Canmore: Alpine Club of Canada, 1986. Covers the history of all huts in the Rockies, with current access routes and status and descriptions of nearby peaks to climb.

Kunelius, Rick, and Dave Biederman. *Ski Trails in the Canadian Rockies.* Banff: Summerthought, 1981. Detailed guide to cross-country skiing in all national parks of the Canadian Rockies.

MacDonald, Janice E. *Canoeing Alberta.* Edmonton: Lone Pine Publishing, 1985. Comprehensive guide to all navigable rivers in the province.

Patterson, Bruce. *The Wild West.* Canmore: Altitude Publishing, 1993. From the Calgary Exhibition and Stampede to the working ranches of Alberta's foothills, this book covers all aspects of life in the West.

Patton, Brian, and Bart Robinson. *The Canadian Rockies Trail Guide.* Banff: Summerthought, 1992. This regularly updated guide, first published in 1971, covers all hiking trails in the mountain national parks.

Savage, Brian. *Ski Alberta.* Edmonton: Lone Pine Publishing, 1985. Comprehensive guide to cross-country ski trails across the province. Downhill ski areas are also detailed.

FLORA AND FAUNA

Alberta Forestry, Lands, and Wildlife. *Alberta Wildlife Viewing Guide.* Edmonton: Lone Pine Publishing, 1990. Describes where to see particular species of animals, with color photos, small maps of certain areas, and best viewing seasons.

The Atlas of Breeding Birds of Alberta. Edmonton: Federation of Alberta Naturalists, 1992. Comprehensive study of all birds that breed in the province with easy-to-read distribution maps, details on nesting and other behavioral patterns, and color plates.

Buffalo. Edmonton: University of Alberta Press, 1992. A series of essays by noted historians and experts in the field of the American bison, addressing their disappearance from the prairies, buffalo jumps, and current problems in Wood Buffalo National Park.

Gray, David R. *The Muskoxen of Polar Bear Pass.* Markham: Fitzhenry & Whiteside, 1987. A detailed yet entertaining look at the lives of one of North America's least understood mammals.

Herreo, Stephen. *Bear Attacks: Their Causes and Avoidances.* New York: Nick Lyons Books, 1985. Through a series of gruesome stories, this book catalogs the stormy relationship between people and bruins, provides hints on avoiding attacks, and tells what to do in case you're attacked.

Lauriault, Jean. *Identification Guide to the Trees of Canada.* Markham: Fitzhenry & Whiteside, 1989. Makes tree identification easy through drawings of leaves, and maps detail distribution of species.

Nelson, Joseph S. *The Fishes of Alberta*. Calgary: University of Calgary Press, 1992. Describes 59 species of fish and provides maps of their distribution. Also looks at fish management and fishing in the province.

Scotter, George W. *Birds of the Canadian Rockies*. Saskatoon: Western Producer Prairie Books, 1990. Description of most recorded species including habitat and habits. Color photos.

Scotter, George W. *Wildflowers of the Canadian Rockies*. Edmonton: Hurtig Publishers Ltd., 1986. Color plates of all flowers found in the mountain national parks. Chapters are divided by flower colors, making identification in the field easy.

Smith, Hugh C. *Alberta Mammals: An Atlas and a Guide*. Edmonton: Provincial Museum of Alberta, 1993. Written from a database accumulated by the author over 23 years as curator of mammalogy at the Provincial Museum, this book describes range, identifying characteristics, and habitat of each species, accompanied by full-page maps of their distribution.

Vacher, André. *Summer of the Grizzly*. Saskatoon: Western Producer Prairie Books, 1985. True story of a grizzly bear that went on a terrifying rampage near the town of Banff.

Wetlands of Canada. Ottawa: Polyscience Publications, Environment Canada, 1988. Each chapter deals with a region of Canada and its specific areas of wetland.

HISTORY

Alberta in the 20th Century. Edmonton: United Western Communications Ltd., 1991. Each volume of this series covers a decade in the history of Alberta through a comprehensive essay.

Fryer, Harold. *Ghost Towns of Alberta*. Langley, BC: Stagecoach Publishing, 1976. Alberta's ghost towns are unlike those found in the western states of the United States. Many towns have slipped into oblivion and this guide looks at more of these than you'd ever dreamed existed.

Hamilton, Jacques. *Our Alberta Heritage*. Calgary: Calgary Power Ltd., 1977. Available in one hardbound copy or as five softcover editions, each covering a different aspect of the province's history.

Jones, David. *Empire of Dust*. Edmonton: University of Alberta, 1987. Complete history of Alderston and the surrounding prairie; a sorry story of drought and the destruction it brings.

MacGregor, James. *A History of Alberta*. Edmonton: Hurtig Publishers, 1981. Complete history of Alberta from a wild frontier to world leader.

Marty, Sid. *Men for the Mountains*. New York: Vanguard Press, 1979. Written by a park warden, this book tells the story of those who lived in the Canadian Rockies and the risks and adventures involved.

Newman, Peter C. *Company of Adventurers*. Markham: Penguin Books Canada, 1985. The story of the Hudson's Bay Company and its impact on Canada.

Sandford, R.W. *The Canadian Alps: The History of Mountaineering in Canada*. Canmore: Altitude Publishing, 1990. Complete human history of the Canadian Rockies from the earliest explorers to first ascents of major peaks.

Schäffer, Mary T.S. *A Hunter of Peace*. Banff: Whyte Museum of the Canadian Rockies, 1980. This book was first published in 1911 by G.P. Putnam & Sons, New York, under the name *Old Indian Trails of the Canadian Rockies*. Tales recount the exploration of the Rockies during the turn of the century with many of the author's photographs appearing throughout.

Smith, Cyndi. *Off the Beaten Track*. Jasper: Coyote Books, 1989. Accounts of women adventurers and mountaineers and their impact on the early history of western Canada.

Touche, Rodney. *Brown Cows, Sacred Cows.* Hanna: Gorman, 1990. The story of the development of Lake Louise ski area as told by a former general manager.

Woodman, David C. *Unravelling the Franklin Mystery.* Montreal: McGill-Queen's University Press, 1991. Many volumes have been written on the ill-fated Franklin Expedition. This one, using Inuit recollections, is among the best.

PALEONTOLOGY

Grady, Wayne. *The Dinosaur Project.* Toronto: Macfarlane, Walter, & Ross, 1993. Tells the story of paleontological expeditions to China and the Albertan badlands and how the work has enhanced our knowledge of dinosaurs and their movements between Asia and North America. Accounts of actual field trips are given as well as easy to read backgrounds on each area.

Gross, Renie. *Dinosaur Country.* Saskatoon: Western Producer Prairie Books, 1985. Describes Alberta's earliest inhabitants, their habitat, why they disappeared, and the history of dinosaur hunting in the province.

Russell, D.A. *An Odyssey in Time: The Dinosaurs of North America.* Toronto: University of Toronto Press, 1989. Complete details of all known dinosaurs on the North American continent.

Spalding, David A.E. *Dinosaur Hunters.* Toronto: Key Porter Books, 1993. Tells the story of the men and women who have devoted their lives to the study of dinosaurs.

POLITICS AND GOVERNMENT

Bone, Robert. *The Geography of the Canadian North.* Toronto: Oxford University Press, 1992. An in-depth look at the role Canada's north has played and will play in the management of world resources, and the impact of self-government upon the region.

Watkins, Ernest. *The Golden Province.* Calgary: Sandstone Publishing, 1980. A political history of Alberta from 1905, focusing on the Social Credit Party.

Wood, David G. *The Lougheed Legacy.* Toronto: Key Porter Books, 1985. Tells the story of Peter Lougheed's 14-year reign as premier of Alberta.

PERIODICALS

The Canadian Alpine Journal. Canmore, Alberta. Annual magazine of the Alpine Club of Canada with articles from its members and climbers from around the world.

Canadian Geographic. Ottawa: Royal Canadian Geographical Society. Bimonthly publication pertaining to Canada's natural and human histories and resources.

Equinox. Markham, Ontario. This bimonthly publication looks at Canada's natural world and humanity's relationship with it.

Explore. Calgary. Bimonthly publication of adventure travel throughout Canada.

Up Here. Yellowknife: Outcrop Ltd. Bimonthly magazine of life in Canada's north.

FREE CATALOGS

Alberta Accommodation and Visitors' Guide. Alberta Hotel Association. Lists all hotel, motel, and other lodging in the province. Available at all Tourist Information Centres or by calling (800) 661-8888.

Alberta Campground Guide. Alberta Hotel Association. Lists all campgrounds in the province. Available at all Tourist Information Centres or by calling (800) 661-8888.

Tour Book: Western Canada and Alaska. Booklet available to members of the Canadian or American Automobile Associations.

LITERATURE

Mowat, Farley. *Never Cry Wolf.* Toronto: Mc-Clelland and Stewart, 1990. This story of living with Arctic wolves on the Keewatin barrenlands is an international bestseller and has been made into a feature film.

Turner, Dick. *Nahanni.* Surrey, BC: Hancock House, 1975. One of the north's most celebrated authors recounts stories of early life in the north and particularly on the South Nahanni River.

REFERENCE

The Atlas of Alberta. Edmonton: Interwest Publications Ltd., 1984. Historical, resource, city, and town maps of Alberta.

Daffern, Tony. *Avalanche Safety for Skiers & Climbers.* Calgary: Rocky Mountain Books, 1992. Covers all aspects of avalanches including their causes, practical information on how to avoid them, and a section on rescue techniques and first aid.

Gray, D.M. and D.H. Male. *Handbook of Snow.* Toronto: Pergamon Press, 1991. Comprehensive guide on everything you ever wanted to know about snow but didn't ask because no one else would have known either.

Guide to Manuscripts: The Fonds and Collections of the Archives, Whyte Museum of the Canadian Rockies. Banff: Whyte Museum of the Canadian Rockies, 1988. This book makes finding items in the Whyte Museum easy through alphabetical lists of all parts of the collection.

Hare, F.K. and M.K. Thomas. *Climate Canada.* Toronto: John Wiley & Sons, 1974. One of the most extensive works on Canada's climate ever written. Includes a chapter on how the climate is changing.

Karamitsanis, Aphrodite. *Place Names of Alberta.* Calgary: University of Alberta Press, 1991. An ongoing toponomy project. Volume 1 alphabetically lists all geographic features of the mountains and foothills with explanations of each name's origin. Volume 2 does the same for southern Alberta's geographical features.

Patterson, W.S. *The Physics of Glaciers.* Toronto: Pergamon Press, 1969. A highly technical look at all aspects of glaciation, why glaciers form, how they flow, and their effect on the environment.

INDEX

Page numbers in **boldface** indicate the primary reference. *Italicized* page numbers indicate information in captions, charts, illustrations, maps, or special topics.

A

Abraham Lake: 270
accommodations: 33-35; *see also specific place*
Admiralty Inlet: 466
Aerospace Museum: 51
Aetna: 112
Agnes, Lake: 219-220
agriculture: 22
Airdrie: 272
airfares: 36
airports: Calgary International 73; Edmonton International 317; Hay River 400; Lethbridge 92; Medicine Hat Municipal 104; Mike Zubko 440; Yellowknife 416
air travel: 36, 37-38, 39-40, 391, 392
Akamina Parkway: 120
Aklavik: 441-442
Akshayak Pass: 464
Alberta Aviation Museum: 302
Alberta Ballet: 58, 306
Alberta Bicycle Association: 26
Alberta Birds of Prey Centre: 97
Alberta Book Festival: 308
Alberta Cowboy Poetry Gathering: 31
Alberta Hotel Association: 33
Alberta Legislature Building: 291-294
Alberta Poetry Gathering and Western Art Show: 130
Alberta Prairie Steam Tours: 279
Alberta Railway Museum: 303
Alberta Sled Dog Championship: 32, 176
Alberta Special Crops and Horticultural Research Centre: 154
Alberta Temple: 110
Alberta Theatre Projects: 57
Alberta Tourism Partnership: 42
alcohol: 35
Alder Flats: 271-272
Alert: 470
Alexander Wilderness Park: 89
Alexandra Falls: 397
Alex Taylor Theatre: 298

Alfalfa Dehydrating and Cubing Plant: 98
Allison Creek Brood Trout Station: 139
Allison Lake: 139
Alpine Club of Canada: 26, 34, *177, 178*
alpine zone: 9
Amber Valley: 345
Americans: 24
Amethyst Lakes: 248
Amisk: 283
amphibians: 15
Amundsen Gulf: 443
Amundsen, Roald: 449-450
Andrew: 329
Andrew Wolf Wine Cellars: 302
Angel Glacier: 245
Angus Fire Tower: 401
animals: *see* fauna; *specific animal*
Annette, Lake (Banff): 220-221
Annette, Lake (Jasper): 245
Annual Pow Wow: 85
antelope: *see* pronghorn
antique show: 32
Anzac: 338
Apex: 458
Appaloosa Horse Club of Canada Museum and Archives: 80
Arboretum: 274
Arctic Art Gallery: 414
Arctic Bay: 466-467
arctic char: 385
Arctic Circle: 435
Arctic Ocean: 442
Arctic Red River: *see* Tsiigehtchic
area: 4
area codes: 41-42, 393, 451
Armengol Structures: 48
art centers, festivals, and galleries: Arctic Art Gallery 414; Art of the Wild 196; Banff Arts Festival 204; Banff Centre for the Arts 195; Canada House 196; Cotton & Willow 57; Creative Picture Gallery 57; Crowsnest Pass Art Gallery 135; Edmonton Art Gallery 290-291; Great Northern Arts Festival 439;

Marika Jewellery and Fine Art 196;
Medicine Hat Museum and Art Gallery 102;
Northern Images 306; Oppertshauser
Gallery 302; Prairie Art Gallery 364; Quest
for Handcrafts 196; Southern Alberta Art
Gallery 87; Walter Phillips Gallery 195
Art of the Wild: 196
arts and crafts: 30-31; basketry 423-424;
Jessie Oonark Arts and Crafts Centre 455
Arviat: 453-454
Arviliqjuat: *see* Pelly Bay
Ashmont: 329
Asians: 24
aspen parkland: 9-10
Assiniboine people: 106
Astoria River Trail: 250
astronomy: 50
Athabasca: 343-345
Athabasca Delta Interpretive Tours: 341
Athabasca Falls: 241-242
Athabasca Glacier: 240
Athabasca Landing Church: 343
Athabasca, Mt.: 240
Athabasca Oil Sands: 19-20, **337-338**
Athabasca Pass: 239, 248
Athabasca River: 6-7, 27, 341
Athabasca River Valley: 235
Athabasca Tower: 358
Athabasca University: 344-345
Atlas Coal Mine Museum: 148
Aujuitittuq: *see* Grise Fiord
Aulavik National Park: 382, 443
aurora borealis: *375*
Auyuittuq National Park: 382, 389, **464**
Axel Heiberg Island: 469
Aylmer Lookout Trail: 198

B
Babel Creek: 221
backcountry huts and lodges: 33-34; *see also
specific place*
backpacker lodges: 34; *see also specific
place*
backpacking: *see* hiking
badgers: 14
Badlands Trail: 157
Baffin Island: 457-470
Baker Lake: 454-455
Bald Hills Trail: 251-252
Balfour, Mt.: 227
ballet: 58, 306

ballooning: 32, 55, 304-305, 366
Banff 186-215, *187, 189;* accommodations
204-209; festivals and events 203-204;
food 209-212; hiking 196-200; recreation
196-203; services and information 214-215;
shopping 212; sights and drives 188-196;
transportation 212-214
Banff Arts Festival: 204
Banff Centre for the Arts: 195
Banff Festival of Mountain Films: 32, 204
Banff/Lake Louise Cowboy Jubilee: 203
Banff long-nose dace: 184
Banff Mountain Book Festival: 204
Banff Mt. Norquay: 28, 202
Banff National Park: 25, 26, 180-233, *181;*
Banff 186-215; flora and fauna 182-185;
history 185-186; Icefields Parkway 227-
233; Lake Louise 215-226; land 182
Banff Park Museum: 193
Banff Public Library: 214
Banff Springs Golf Course: 28, 201
Banff Springs Hotel: 195-196, 206-207, 211-
212
Banff Television Festival: 203
Banff Winter Festival: 204
Bankhead: 186, 191
banks: 42
Banks Island: 443-444
Baptiste Lake: 345
Barbeau, Mt.: 469-470
bareback riding: *62*
Barr Colony Heritage Cultural Centre: 328
barrel racing: *63*
Barrhead: 351
Bar U Ranch National Historic Site: 165
baseball: 57, 305
basketry: 423-424
Bassano: 153
Bassano Dam: 153
Bathurst Inlet: 449
Bathurst Island: 468
Battle River: 282-283
Battle River Pioneer Museum: 373
Bauerman Creek: 119
Bay, The: 59
Bear Creek Golf Club: 366
Bear Creek Reservoir: 364
bearded seals: 385
bears: 11-12, *11,* 184, 238, 384
Bear's Hump: 120
Bear's Hump Trail: 118

Beauvais Lake Provincial Park: 130
Beaverhill Bird Observatory: 283
Beaverhill Natural Area: 283
Beaverlodge: 367
beavers: 14
bed and breakfasts: 33; *see also specific place*
Beechey Island: 468
beer: 35
Beerfest: 339
Beiseker: 274
Belcher Islands: 461-462
Bellevue: 132-133
Bellevue Mine: 132, 133
beluga whales: 384
Bent Horn A-O2: 468
Bertha Falls: 118
Bertha Lake Trail: 118
Bicentennial Highway: 348
Bicentennial Museum: 341
bicycling: 26; Calgary 55; Peter Lougheed P.P. 169
Big Bear, Chief: 331
Big Beehive Trail: 220
Big Hill Springs Provincial Park: 162
Bighorn Canyon: 270
bighorn sheep: 13, 184, 238, *249*
Big Knife Provincial Park: 280
Big Rock: 164
Big Rock brewery: 35
Big Valley: 152
Big Valley Jamboree: 30, 281
Bike Trail: 169
Bill Fowler Centre: 281
birchbark baskets: 423-424
birds/birdwatching: 15, 385; Alberta Birds of Prey Centre 97; Banff N.P. 185; Bathurst Inlet 449; Beaverhill Bird Observatory 283; Bradshaw Bird Sanctuary 373; Bylot Island Bird Sanctuary 465; Cape Perry Bird Sanctuary 443; Cypress Hills P.P. 106; Harry Gibbons Bird Sanctuary 456; Inglewood Bird Sanctuary 54; Jasper N.P. 238-239; McConnell River Bird Sanctuary 454; McLennan 350; Okotoks Bird Sanctuary 164; Peregrine Falcon Hatchery 284; Saskatoon Island P.P. 367
bison: 13-14, 84-85, 323-325, 406, 409-410
Bistcho Lake: 376
black bears: 11-12, *11*, 184, 238
Black Diamond: 164

Blackfoot people: 87, 95, 106, 116-117
Blackfoot Recreation Area: 326
Black Prince Cirque Trail: 172
Blackstone Landing: 423
Blackstone Territorial Park: 423
Blairmore: 135-137
Blakiston, Mt.: 120
Bleriot Ferry: 146-147
Bloody Falls: 448
blues: 58
boating: 201, 413-414
bobcats: 12
bobsledding: 53
Bonnyville: 331
Boothia Peninsula: 450
boreal forest: 10
Boreal Forest Interpretive Trail: 349-350
Botterill Bottom Park: 89
Boulder Pass: 222
Boulton Creek Trail: 171
Bourgeau Lake Trail: 198-199
Bow Falls: 190
bowhead whales: 384
Bow Glacier Falls Trail: 231
Bow Island: 98
Bow Lake: 229
Bow Peak: 227
Bow River: 7, 27
Bow River Loop Trail: 218-219
Bow River Trail: 197
Bow Summit: 229
Bow Valley Parkway: 192-193, 207-208
Bow Valley Provincial Park: 166-167
Brûlé Lake: 358
Bradshaw Bird Sanctuary: 373
Bragg Creek: 162-163, *162*
Bragg Creek Provincial Park: 163
Brant: 81
Brant, Paul: 30
Brazeau Collieries: 269
Brazeau Reservoir: 272
Brewery Gardens: 93
Brewster, Jim and Bill: *213*
Bridal Veil Falls: 220
Bridge Valley Golf Course: 90
British people: 24
Brooks: 153-154
Brooks and District Museum: 154
Brooks Aqueduct: 153
Brooks Pheasant Hatchery: 154
Broughton Island: 464-465

Brown, John George "Kootenai": 117
Buckingham House: 330
Bud Cotton Buffalo Paddock: 284
Bud Country Jamboree: 30, 91
Bud Miller Park: 328
buffalo: *see* bison
Buffalo Head Hills: 348
buffalo jumps: 84-85, 274
bull riding: *62*
Bull Trail Park: 89
Burmis: 131
Burnside River: 390, 449
Burstall Pass: 172
bus travel: 37, 38, 391, 392; *see also specific place*
Bylot Island Bird Sanctuary: 465

C
Cadomin: 358
Cadomin Caves: 358
Calaway Park: 55-56
Calderwood Buffalo Jump: 85
calf roping: *62-63*
Calgary: 43-75, *46-47, 49;* accommodations 66-69; Calgary Stampede 60-65; food 69-72; history 43-45; recreation 55-60; services and information 74-75; sights 45-55; transportation 73-74
Calgary Airshow: 59
Calgary Cannons: 57
Calgary Centre for Performing Arts: 48
Calgary Chinese Cultural Centre: 50
Calgary Eaton Centre: 58
Calgary Flames: 56
Calgary Folk Music Festival: 59
Calgary International Airport: 73
Calgary International Children's Festival: 59
Calgary International Jazz Festival: 31, 59
Calgary Opera: 57-58
Calgary Philharmonic Orchestra: 58
Calgary Police Service Interpretive Centre: 50
Calgary Science Centre: 50
Calgary Soccer Centre: 57
Calgary Stampede: 31, **60-65,** *62-63, 64;* events 61, *62-63;* history 60-61; practicalities 63-65; tickets *64,* 65
Calgary Tower: 48
Calgary Winter Festival: 59
Calgary Zoo: 53-54
Calling Lake Provincial Park: 345
Call of the Wild Horn Music Festival: 333-334

Cambridge Bay: 446-447
Cameron Falls: 113
Cameron Island: 468
Cameron Lake: 113, 120
Cameron River: 413
campgrounds: 34-35; Banff 209; Calgary 68-69; Cypress Hills P.P. 107; Edmonton 312; Icefields Parkway 233; Jasper 257; Jasper N.P. 243; Lake Louise 224; Northwest Territories 391; Peter Lougheed P.P. 171; Waterton Lakes N.P. 125; *see also specific place*
camping equipment: 59, 308
Camp Wainwright: 284
Camrose: 281-282, *282*
Camrose & District Museum: 281-282
Canada Act of 1982: 22
Canada Day: 31; Banff 204; Calgary 59; Canmore 176; Fort McMurray 339; Medicine Hat 103; Red Deer 277
Canada goose: *276*
Canada House: 196
Canada Olympic Park: 29, 53, 56, 59
Canada's Aviation Hall of Fame: 280
Canadian Coastguard Base: 399
Canadian Country Music Hall of Honour: 291
Canadian Cowboys Association Rodeo Finals: 328
Canadian Finals Rodeo: 309
Canadian Forces Base Cold Lake: 332
Canadian Pacific Railway: 19, 44, 96-97, 127-128, 175, 298
Canadian Salt Company: 331
Canadian School of Mountaineering: 28
C&E Railway Museum: 298
Canmore: 28, 174-179, *174;* history 174-175; practicalities 176-179; sights and recreation 175-176
Canmore Golf Course: 176
Canmore Hotel: 175
Canmore Nordic Centre: 175
canoeing: 27; Banff 201; Jasper 253; Milk River 94; Nahanni N.P. 427-428; North Saskatchewan River: 268; Northwest Territories 390; Yellowknife 414; *see also* kayaking; rafting
Canol Heritage Trail: 389, **432-433**
Canol Project: 432
Canyon Creek: 359
Canyon Ski Area: 277
Cape Dorset: 461

Cape Perry Bird Sanctuary: 443
Cape Searle: 464
Cardston: 109-112, *109*
caribou: 11, 184, 384, 435, 443
Caribou Carnival: 415
Caroline: 263
Carson-Pegasus Provincial Park: 352
Carter Camp: 369
Carter, Wilf: 30
Carthew-Alderson Trail: 119
Carthew Summit: 119
car travel: 38-39, 391, 393
Cascade Amphitheatre Trail: 198
Cascade Gardens: 190
Cascade Ponds: 191
Cash Casino Place: 58
Casino A.B.S.: 307
casinos: 58, 307
Castle Lookout Trail: 200
Castle Mountain: 193
Castle Mountain Village: 193
Cat Creek Interpretive Trail: 173
Cave and Basin Centennial Centre: 189-190
Cavell Meadows Trail: 250
Centennial Library: 319
Centennial Museum: 351
Centrosaurus Bone Bed Hike: 156-157
Chain Lakes Provincial Park: 165
Challenger Centre: 299
Chateau Lake Louise: 216-217, 223-224, 225
Chephren Lake Trail: 231
Chephren, Mt.: 230
Chesterfield Inlet: 454
Chief Mountain: 112
Chief Mountain International Highway: 121
Chinatown (Calgary): 50
Chinatown (Edmonton): 291
Chinatown (Lethbridge): 87
Chinese people: 24
chinooks: 7, 113, *128*
Chip Lake: 357
chuck wagon races: 61
Chuk Park: 438
Cinema Ride Edmonton: 301
cinemas: Calgary 58; Edmonton 306-307;
    Lethbridge 90
Cirque Lake: 231
Cirque of the Unclimbables: 428
cirques: 6
Cirrus Mountain: 230
Citadel Theatre: 306

City Hall Park: 276
Claresholm: 79-80
Claresholm Museum: 80
Clark, Terri: 30
Classic Jazz Guild of Calgary: 58
Clay Products Interpretive Centre: 102
C Level Cirque Trail: 198
climate: Alberta 7-8; Northwest Territories
    382
climbing: *see* mountaineering
Clyde River: 465
coal: 22, 87, 127-128, 132-133, 148, 357-358
Coalbanks Interpretive Site: 89
Coal Dust Daze: 362
Coats Island: 456
C.O. Card Home: 110
Cochrane: 161-162
Cochrane, Matthew: 19, 161-162
Cold Lake: 332-334, *333*
Cold Lake Fish Hatchery: 332
Cold Lake Oil Sands: 332
Cold Lake Provincial Park: 332-333
Coleman: 137-139
Colonial Days: 328
Columbia Icefield: 239-241, *240*
Colville Lake: 434
Combined Driving Events: 111
comedy clubs: Calgary 58; Edmonton 307
Commissioner's Cup Race: 415
Consolation Lakes Trail: 221
Consort: 280
Continental Divide: 182
Coppermine: *see* Kugluktuk
Coppermine River: 390, 448
Coral Falls: 419-420
Coral Harbour: 456-457
Cornfest: 97
Cornwallis Island: 467
Cory Pass Trail: 198
Cosmopolitan Hotel: 136
costs: 36, 41
Cotillion Park: 369
Cotton & Willow: 57
Cottonwood Flats Trail: 157
cougars: 12, *172*, 184
country music: 30, 291
Courthouse Museum: 110-111
coyotes: 12, 184
crafts: *see* arts and crafts
Crandell Lake: 119
cranes: *386, 407*

Creative Picture Gallery: 57
credit cards: 41, 393
Cree people: 87, 106, 276, 331
Crescent Falls: 270
Crimson Lake Provincial Park: 268
Cronquist House: 276-277
cross-country skiing: 29; Banff 203; Canmore
    175; Edmonton 205; Jasper 254;
    Kananaskis Country 168; Lake Louise 222
Cross Lake Provincial Park: 351
Crowfoot: 17
Crowfoot Glacier: 227-229
Crowsnest: 140
Crowsnest Lake: 140
Crowsnest Mountain: 139
Crowsnest Museum: 138
Crowsnest Pass: 127-140, 132-133
Crowsnest Pass Art Gallery: 135
Crowsnest Pass Golf and Country Club: 136
Crypt Lake Trail: 119
Cumberland Peninsula: 464
currency: **40-41,** 393
Cypress Hills Massacre: 106
Cypress Hills Provincial Park: 25, **105-108,**
    107
Czar: 283

D
dance: 58, 306
Dawson, George M.: 141
Deane House: 52
Deception Pass: 222
Deep Sea Adventure: 300-301
deer: 184
Deh Cho Connection: 373, 391
Dekker Islands: 283
Delancey Estates: 397
Déline: 433
Delta Daze: 439
Dempster Highway: 391, 435-436
Dene people: 386, **389,** 397-398, 399, 410,
    424, 430, 447
Den Wildlife Museum: 245
Detah: 413
Devil's Coulee Dinosaur Egg Site: 93-94
Devonian Botanic Garden: 302
Devonian Gardens: 51
Devon Island: 468
Devonshire Beach: 347
Diamond Jenness High School: 399
diamonds: 388

Diamond Valley Parade: 164
Dillberry Lake Provincial Park: 284
Dinosaur Golf and Country Club: 149
Dinosaur Lake: 141-158, 142
Dinosaur Provincial Park: 25
dinosaurs: 93-94, 141-146, 143, 145, 155-
    158, 155
Dinosaur Trail: 146
Disabled Adult Transportation System: 318
Discovery Centre: 164
District Museum: 351
diving: 28; Waterton Lakes N.P. 121;
    Yellowknife 414
Dixonville: 373
Dog Island: 347
Dogrib Dene people: 410
dogsledding: 203
Dolomite Pass: 231
Dome Glacier: 240
Dominion of Canada: 17
Donnelly: 350
Dorset culture: 386
downhill skiing: 28-29; Banff 202; Calgary 56;
    Cypress Hills P.P. 107; Dummy Downhill
    31; Edmonton 305; Jasper 254;
    Kananaskis Country 167-168; Lake Louise
    222-223; Pincher Creek 130; Slush Cup 31
Drayton Valley: 272
Dreamspeakers Festival: 308-309
Driftwood Ranch and Wildlife Haven: 367
driving: 39, 391
Drumheller: 142-150, 144, 147; practicalities
    149-150; recreation 148-149; scenic drives
    146-148; sights 143-146
Drumheller Dinosaur and Fossil Museum: 146
Drumheller Valley Ski Club: 149
Dry Canyon: 428
Dry Island Buffalo Jump: 274
Dummy Downhill: 31, 203
Dunes Golf Club: 366
Dunvegan: 369
Duval, Mt.: 463

E
eagles: 15
East Arm of Great Slave Lake: 382
East Coulee: 148
Eastern Irrigation District: 153
East Kananaskis Country: 172-173
Eau Claire Market: 50, 58
Echo Dale Park: 102

economy: Alberta 21-22; Northwest Territories 387-388
Edith Cavell, Mt.: 245; hiking 250
Edith Lake: 245
Edmonton: 285-320, *286-287, 292-293, 297, 301;* accommodations 310-312; food 313-317; history 288-290; recreation 304-309; services and information 319-320; sights 290-303; transportation 317-318
Edmonton Art Gallery: 290-291
Edmonton Civic Centre: 290-291
Edmonton Eskimos: 305-306
Edmonton Folk Music Festival: 32, 309
Edmonton Heritage Festival: 32, 309
Edmonton International Airport: 317
Edmonton International Street Performers Festival: 32, 309
Edmonton Oilers: 305
Edmonton Opera: 306
Edmonton Police Museum: 291
Edmonton Public Schools Archives and Museum: 291
Edmonton Ski Club: 29, 305
Edmonton's Klondike Days: 32, 289, 309
Edmonton Skydive Centre: 304-305
Edmonton Space and Science Centre: 299
Edmonton Symphony Orchestra: 306
Edmonton Trappers: 305
Edson: 357
Edson Trail: 364
Eiffel Lake Trail: 221
Eiffel Peak: 221
electrical voltage: 42
Elizabeth Hall Wetlands: 89
elk: 10, 183
Elk Island Golf Course: 325
Elk Island National Park: 25, 323-326
Elk Point: 330
Elkwater: 105
Elkwater Lake: 105
Elkwater Park Golf Club: 107
Ellesmere Island: 382, 469-470
Ellesmere Island National Park: 469-470
emergency services: Calgary 75; Edmonton 319
Emerson Creek Road: 358-359
Emerson Lakes: 359
employment: 39
Empress Theatre: 82, 83
Em-te: 271-272
Endless Range: 241

End of Steel Heritage Park and Museum: 370
Energeum: 50
Enterprise: 397
entertainment: 29-30; *see also specific place*
Entwistle: 357
Environmental Training Centre: 357
equestrian sports: 31, 59-60
Escarpment Creek: 397
E.S. Huestis Demonstration Forest: 353
Eskimo ice cream: *453*
Etzikom: 96
Etzikom Museum: 96-97
Eureka: 469
Eureka Sound: 469
events: *see* festivals
Evergreen Park: 366
Ewart-Duggan Home: 99
exchange rate: 40-41
Expeditor Cove: 448
exploration: 16-17

F
Faille, Albert: *419*
Fair Days: 80
Fairholme Range: 191
Fairview: 369
falcons: 15, 284
Family Leisure Centre: 56
Farmfair: 309
fauna: Alberta 10-15, *11, 13;* Auyuittuq N.P. 464; Banff N.P. 183-185; Cypress Hills P.P. 106; Jasper N.P. 235-236; Northwest Territories 383-385; *see also specific fauna*
Fawcett Lake: 345
Fenland Trail: 196
festivals: 31-32; *see also specific place; specific festival*
Field Naturalists Society: 338-339
Field Station of the Royal Tyrrell Museum: 156
Figure Eight Rapids: 426
film: 204
First Canyon: 426
First Night: 32; Banff 204; Calgary 59; Edmonton 309
fish: 15, 184, 385
Fish Creek Library: 75
Fish Creek Provincial Park: 54-55
fishers: 14
fish hatcheries: 54
fishing: 27-28, 390; Banff 201; Canmore 176;

Cold Lake 332; Fort Simpson 421; Grande Cache 362; Great Bear Lake 433-434; Jasper 253; Lesser Slave Lake 347; Trout Lake 420; Waterton Lakes N.P. 121; Wyndham-Carseland P.P. 153; Yellowknife 413-414; *see also* fish

fishing, commercial: 388, 398

fishing, ice: 29, 203

fishing tournaments: fishing derby 448; Golden Walleye Classic 350

Flat River: 426

Fleming Hill: 460

flightseeing: 428-429

flora: 8-10, 383; Auyuittuq N.P. 464; Banff N.P. 182-183; Cypress Hills P.P. 105-106; Jasper N.P. 235; Waterton Lakes N.P. 113-116

folk music: 59, 309, 415

Folk Music Festival: 32

Folk on the Rocks: 415

food: 35; *see also specific place*

football: 57, 305-306

Footner Lake Forest: 376

Forbes, Mt.: 230

Foremost: 96

forestry: 22, 406-407

Forestry School Trail: 357

Forestry Trunk Road: 138, 266, 269-270

Fort Assiniboine: 351

Fort Calgary: 44

Fort Calgary Historic Park: 52

Fort Chipewyan: 340-341

Fort Edmonton: 288-289

Fort Edmonton Park: 295-296

Fort Fitzgerald: 404

Fort Franklin: *see* Déline

Fort George: 330

Fort Good Hope: 434

Fort Liard: 423-424

Fort Macleod: 81-84, *82*

Fort McKay: 338

Fort McMurray: 335-340, *342*

Fort McMurray Golf Club: 339

Fort McPherson: 435-436

Fort Museum: 82-83

Fort Norman: *see* Tulita

Fort Normandeau: 275-276

Fort Providence: 409

Fort Resolution: 401

Fortress Lake Trail: 242

Fortress Mountain ski area: 28-29, 168

Fort Ross: 450

Fort Saskatchewan Historic Site: 303

Fort Simpson: 420-422, *424*

Fort Smith: 402-405, *402*

Fort Smith Mission Historic Park: 404

Fort Vermilion: 375-376

Fort Whoop-Up: 88-89

Forty Mile Coulee Reservoir: 96

Forum Peak: 120

fossils: *see* dinosaurs; paleontology

Fourth Canyon: 426

Fox Creek: 353

Foxe Peninsula: 460

foxes: 12

Fox, George: 30

Fox Hollow Golf Club: 55

Frame Lake: 413

Frank: 134-135

Franklin, John: 449

Frank Slide Interpretive Centre: 135

Fred Henne Territorial Park: 413

Freighter Lakeshore Trail: 347

French people: 24

Fringe Theatre Event: 32, 309

Frobisher Bay: 457

Frobisher, Martin: 457

Frog Lake: 331

Frog Lake Massacre: 331

frogs: 184

frostbite: 41

Funland Amusement Park: 146

fur trading: 16-17

G

Gaetz Lakes Sanctuary: 277

Galaxyland Amusement Park: 300

Gallery Walk: 306

Galloway Station Museum: 357

Galt, Elliot: 87

Galt Gardens: 87

gardens: Arboretum 274; Brewery Gardens 93; Cascade Gardens 190; Devonian Botanic Garden 302; Devonian Gardens 51; Galt Gardens 87; Kurimoto Japanese Garden 302; Muttart Conservatory 294; Nikka Yuko Japanese Garden 90

Gargoyle Valley: 198

Garner Lake Provincial Park: 329

garter snakes: 15, 184

gasoline: 41

geese: 150, *276*

Genesee Fossil Beds: 272
Geodetic Hills: 469
geography: *see* land
geology: 4-7, 113
Geraldine Lakes Trail: 242
Germans: 24
Ghost Lake: 166
Ghost River Wilderness Area: 25, 166
Giant Steps: 221
giardia: 41
Gibbons: 343
Gibbons Anglican Church: 343
Gilwood Golf Club: 347
Gjoa Haven: 449
Glacier Lake Trail: 231-232
glaciers: 6, 227-230, 240, 241; *see also*
   icefields; *specific glacier*
Glenbow Museum: 29, 51
Glendon: 331
Glenora: 298
Goat Haunt: 118, 121-122
Goat Lake Trail: 119
Goat Lookout: 241
goats: 13, 184, 238
gold: 289, 309, 388
Golden Walleye Classic: 350
golf: 28; Banff 201; Calgary 55; Edmonton
   304; Grande Prairie 366; Hay River 399;
   Jasper 253; Kananaskis Country 167;
   Lethbridge 90; *see also specific course;*
   specific place
Goodfare: 367
Goods and Services Tax: 40, 393
Gooseberry Lake Provincial Park: 280
Goose Hummock Golf Course: 343
Goose Mountain Ecological Reserve: 352
government: Alberta 22-23; Northwest
   Territories 387
Grain Academy: 54
Grand Centre: 332
Grande Cache: 360-363, *361*
Grande Cache Golf Course: 362
Grande Prairie: 364-368, *365, 368*
Grande Mountain Trail: 361
Grande Prairie Golf and Country Club: 366
Grande Prairie Little Theatre: 366
Grande Prairie Museum: 364
Grande Prairie Regional College: 364
Grande Prairie Regional College Theatre: 366
Grandin House: 303
Grand Slam Canada Recreation Centre: 90

Grand Trunk Railway: 19, 243
Grassi Falls: 175
Grassi Lakes Trail: 175
Great Bear Lake: 433
Great Bear River: 433
Great Buffalo-Chip Flip: 325
Great Divide Waterfall: 290-291
great horned owls: 15
Great Northern Arts Festival: 439
Great Plain of the Koukdjuak: 457
Great Slave Lake: 395
Gregoire Lake Provincial Park: 338
Greiner Lake: 447
Grimshaw: 373
Grise Fiord: 469
grizzly bears: *11,* 12, 184, 238, 352, 384
Grizzly Trail: 352
Grouard: 349-350
Grouard Native Cultural Arts Museum: 349
GST: 40, 393
GuZoo Animal Farm: 274
Gwich'in Territorial Park: 436
gypsum karst: 407-408

H
Hall Beach: 462
Hall's Lagoon: 333
Hand Hills: 146
Hanna: 150-151
Hanna Museum: 150
Harbour Island: 455
harbour seals: 385
Hardisty: 283
Hardisty Lake: 283
hares: 14
harp seals: 385
Harry Gibbons Bird Sanctuary: 456
hawks: 15
Hay River: 397-400, *398*
Hay River Airport: 400
Hay River Dene Reserve: 397, 399
Hay-Zama Lakes: 377
Hazen, Lake: 469-470
Head-Smashed-In Buffalo Jump: 84-85
health: 41
Hearne, Samuel: 447
Hector, Mt.: 227
Helen Lake Trail: 231
Helen Schuler Coulee Centre: 89
heli-hiking: 26
heli-skiing: 202-203, 222

Hell's Half Acre Bridge: 163-164
Henday, Anthony: 16
Henderson Lake Park: 90
Henderson Lake Golf Club: 90
Herbert Lake: 227
Heritage Acres: 129
Heritage Day: 339
Heritage Day Festival: 328
Heritage Day Folk Festival: 176
Heritage Days: 399
Heritage Mile: 163
Heritage Park (Calgary): 52-53
Heritage Park (Fort McMurray): 338
Heritage Ranch: 276
Heritage Square: 276
Heritage Trail: 290
Herodier, Mt.: 465
Herschel Island: 438
Hidden Valley ski hill: 107
Highland Games (Canmore): 176
Highland Games (Grande Prairie): 366
Highlands Library: 320
High Level: 376
High Level Bridge (Edmonton): 290
High Level Bridge (Lethbridge): 89-90
High Prairie: 350
High Prairie and District Museum: 350
High River: 165
Highwood/Cataract Creek Area: 173
Highwood Pass: 169
Hi-grade Feed Lot: 283
hiking: 26; Banff 196-200; Canmore 175;
    Canol Heritage Trail 432-433; Cypress Hills
    P.P. 106; Dinosaur P.P. 156-157; Elk
    Island N.P. 325; Fort McMurray 338-339;
    Grande Cache 361-362; Icefields Parkway
    231-232; Jasper 248-252; Jasper N.P. 242-
    243; Lake Louise 218-222; Maligne Lake
    250-252; Mt. Edith Cavell 250; Nahanni
    N.P. 428; Northwest Territories 389-390;
    Peter Lougheed P.P. 171-172; Waterton
    Lakes N.P. 118-120; White Goat
    Wilderness Area 271; *see also specific trail*
Hillcrest: 133-134
Hillcrest Cemetery: 134
Hillcrest Mine: 134
Hilliard's Bay Provincial Park: 349-350
Hines Creek: 370
Hinton: 357-360
history: 16-21, *18,* 386-387; see also specific
    place

hoary marmots: 14
Hobie's Howler: 176
hockey: 30, 56, 205
Hole-in-the-wall: 192
holiday work visas: 39
Holman: 444
Home Oil Ltd.: 283
Homestead Antique Museum: 145-146
Hondo: 345
hooded seals: 385
Hoodoo Interpretive Trail: 95
hoodoos: 94, 197
Horn and Antler Museum: 146
horseback riding: 26-27; Banff 200; Grande
    Cache 362, 363; Jasper 252-253; Lake
    Louise 218; Waterton Lakes N.P. 122
horse racing: 306
Horseshoe Meadow: 221
Horsethief Canyon: 146
hostels: 34; *see also specific place*
hot-air ballooning: *see* ballooning
Hotel Macdonald: 291
hotels: 33; *see also specific place*
hot springs: 190, 203, 248, 426-427
Howse Peak: 230
Hudson's Bay Company: 16-17, 397, 403,
    447
Hunt House: 52
Husky Oil Operations: 377
Hutch Lake: 376
Hutterites: 24, 130
hypothermia: 41

I
Ibyuk: 442
ice ages: 6
icefields: 6, 227-230, 239-241, *240; see also
    specific icefield*
Icefields Parkway: Banff 227-233; bicycling
    26; Jasper 239-243
ice fishing: 29, 203
ice hockey: 30, 56, 205
Ice Palace: 301
ice skating: 203, 222
igloo church: 438
Igloolik: 462
Igloolik Research Centre: 462
Igluligaarjuk: *see* Chesterfield Inlet
Iglulik: *see* Igloolik
Ikaahuk: *see* Sachs Harbour
Ikaluktutiak: *see* Cambridge Bay

Ikpiarjuk: *see* Arctic Bay
Indian Battle Park: 89
Indian Cabins: 377
Indians: 23-24; arts and crafts 30-31; arts
festival 59; early history 16; *see also
specific tribe*
information: 42, 393-394; *see also specific
place*
Ingamo Hall: 438
Inglewood Bird Sanctuary: 54
Inglismaldie, Mt.: 191
Ingraham Trail: 413
Ink Pots: 192
insurance: 39
International Biosphere Reserve: 117-118
International Children's Festival: 31
International Folk Festival: 277
International Native Arts Festival: 32, 59
Interpretive Theatre: 122
Inuit people: 389, 447, 467-468
inukshuks: 454
Inuktitut: 387
Inuvialuit people: 442
Inuvik: 436-441, *437*
Inuvik Centennial Library: 440
Inuvik Research Centre: 438
Inuvik Sunrise Festival: 439
Iosegun Lake: 353
Iqaluit: 387, **457-460,** *458*
Ironwood Lake: 335
Irricana: 274
Isabella Bay: 465
Island Lake: 345
Ivvavik National Park: 438

J
Jack Singer Concert Hall: 48
Jacques Lake Trail: 251
Jasper: 243-261, *244, 246;* accommodations
255-257; festivals 255; food 257-259;
hiking 248-252; recreation 248-255;
services and information 261; sights and
drives 243-248; transportation 259-261
Jasper Heritage Folk Festival: 255
Jasper in January Winter Festival: 255
Jasper Lions Pro Indoor Rodeo: 255
Jasper National Park: 25, 234-261, *236-237;*
flora and fauna 235-239; hiking 26; history
239; Icefields Parkway 239-243; Jasper
243-261; land 234-235
Jasper Park Lodge: 245-247, 259

Jasper Park Lodge Golf Course: 28, 253
Jasper Place Library: 320
Jasper to Banff Relay: 203, 255
Jasper Tramway: 245
Jasper-Yellowhead Museum and Archives:
245
Jaywalkers Jamboree: 372
jazz: 58, 59, 307, 309
Jazz City International Festival: 309
Jean Marie River: 420
Jensen's Trading Post: 112
Jessie Lake: 331
Jessie Oonark Arts and Crafts Centre: 455
John Janzen Nature Centre: 296
Johnson, Albert: 441
Johnson Lake: 191-192
Johnston Canyon: 192
John Walter Museum: 294-295
Jolliffe Island: 412
Joy, Mt.: 460

K
Kakisa: 409
Kakisa River: 409
Kananaskis Country: 166-173; golf 28; hiking
26
Kananaskis Country Golf Course: 28, 167
Kananaskis Guest Ranch: 178
Kananaskis Lakes Trail: 169
Kananaskis Valley: 166
Kananaskis Village: 168-169
kangaroo rats: 14
Kangiqlugaapik: *see* Clyde River
Kangiqtinq: *see* Rankin Inlet
Karstland Trail: 408
Kart Gardens International: 56
Katannilik Territorial Park: 382, 389, **460-461**
kayaking: 27; Grande Cache 362; Northwest
Territories 390; Yellowknife 414; *see also*
canoeing; rafting
Keephills: 355
Keewatin: 451-457
Kekerten Historic Park: 463
Kensington: 59
Kerr-Wallace Home: 99
Kerry Wood Nature Centre: 277
Kicking Horse River: 27, 218
killer whales: 384
Kimiwan Lake: 350
Kimmirut: 460-461
Kinbrook Island Provincial Park: 154

Kingait: *see* Cape Dorset
King William Island: 449
Kinsmen Pitch & Putt: 304
Kinsmen Sports Centre: 304
Kinuso: 349
Kirchoffer Falls: 456
Kitchener, Mt.: 241
Kiwanis Nature Trail: 399
Kleskun Hill Natural Area: 364
Klondike Ferry: 3251
Klondike gold rush: 289, 309
Knob and Kettle Trail System: 283
Kootenai Brown Historic Park: 129
Kootenai Indians: 116
Kootenay Plains Ecological Reserve: 270
Korak Inlet: 461
Krause Lake Recreation Area: 352
Kraus Hotsprings: 426-427
Kugluktuk: 447-449
Kurimoto Japanese Garden: 302

L
Lac La Biche: 334-335
Lac La Biche Mission: 334-335
Lac La Martre: *see* Wha Ti
Lacombe: 279
Lacombe, Albert: *349*
La Crete: 375
Lady Evelyn Falls: 408-409
Laggan: 185
Lake Agnes Trail: 219-220
Lake Annette (Banff): 220-221
Lake Annette (Jasper): 245
Lake Claire: 405
Lake Harbour: *see* Kimmirut
Lake Hazen: 469-470
Lakeland: 323-335, *324*
Lakeland Provincial Park: 335
Lake Louise: 215-226, *217;* history 215-216;
   practicalities 223-226; recreation 218-223;
   sights 216-218
Lake Louise Loppet
Lake Louise Ski Area: 28, 222-223
Lake Minnewanka: 191-192
Lake Newell: 154
Lake Trail: 251
Lakeview Trail: 325
Lancaster Sound: 466, 468
land: 4-8, 381-383; Auyuittuq N.P. 464; Banff
   N.P. 182; Jasper N.P. 234-235; Nahanni
   N.P.: 424; Waterton Lakes N.P. 113-116

lang, k.d.: 30
language: 387
Larch Valley Trail: 221
Latham Island: 412-413
Leavings, The: 79
Lebel Mansion: 129
Lee Foundation Trail: 245
Legislative Assembly Interpretive Centre: 294
Leitch Collieries: 131-132
Lesser Slave Lake: 345-347
Lesser Slave Lake Provincial Park: 347
Lethbridge: 85-93, *86, 88*
Lethbridge Airport: 92
Lethbridge Centre: 87
Lethbridge Nature Reserve: 89
Lethbridge Public Library: 93
Lethbridge Symphony Orchestra: 90
Liard Highway: 391, 422-423
Lille: 137
Lindberg Landing: 422-423
Lions Park: 102
Little Beehive: 220
Little Bow Provincial Park: 81
Little Buffalo Falls Territorial Park: 402
Little Church: 146
Little Cornwallis Island: 468
Little Fish Lake Provincial Park: 146
Little Lake: 367
Little Smoky: 353
Livingstone Falls: 138
Livingstone Gap: 138
Livingstone Range: 138
Lloydminster: 327-329, *327, 328*
logging: *see* forestry
Long Island Lake Municipal Park: 351
Long Lake: 413
Long Lake Provincial Park: 329
Loose Moose Theatre Company: 57
Lougheed, Peter: 20
Louise Creek Trail: 218
Louise Falls: 397
Louise Lakeshore Trail: 219
Lucerne Foods: 97
luge facilities: 53
lumber industry: *see* forestry
Lunchbox Theatre: 57
Lundbreck Falls: 131
Lupin: 388
Lutsel K'e: 417
Luxton Museum: 193-194
lynxes: 12, 184

M

Maccarib Pass Trail: 250
MacDonald Island Recreation Complex: 339
MacDonald, John A.: 185
Mackenzie, Alexander: 420
Mackenzie Bison Sanctuary: 409-410
Mackenzie Delta: 435
Mackenzie Highway: 373-377, *374*, 391
Mackenzie Mountains: 381, 424
Mackenzie River: 6, 381-382, 395, 430
Mackenzie River Valley: 430-434
Macleod, James F.: 17, 44, 81
Macleod Livery: 83
Magnetic Hill: 165
Magrath: 112
mail: 41
Maligne Canyon: 247, 254-255
Maligne Canyon Trail: 250
Maligne Lake: 247; hiking 250-252
Maligne Range: 251
Maligne River: 247, 253
Mallikjak Island: 461
Ma-me-o Provincial Park: 272
Mandelin Eldon Museum: 267
Manning: 373
Manyberries: 97
Manyberries Sandhills: 97
Maple Ridge golf course: 55
maps: 26, 42
Marble Island: 452
Marengo Falls: 428
Margaret Zeidler Star Theatre: 299
Mariana Lake: 337
Mariana Lake Recreation Area: 337
Marian Lake: 410
Marika Jewellery and Fine Art: 196
Marl Lake Trail: 171
Marmot Basin Ski Area: 29, 254
marmots: 14
martens: 14
Mary Kaeser Library: 404
Maskinonge Lake: 116, 121
Massacre Butte: 131
Max Bell Regional Aquatic Centre: 90
McCall Lake golf course: 55
McConnell River Bird Sanctuary: 382, 454
McDonald Creek Trail: 271
McDougall Centre: 50
McGill Lake: 421
McKay Avenue School: 291
McLennan: 350

McMullen Island: 145
Meander River: 376, 377
measurements: 42
Medicine Hat: 99-105, *100, 101*
Medicine Hat City Hall: 101
Medicine Hat Exhibition and Stampede: 32, 103
Medicine Hat Municipal Airport: 104
Medicine Hat Museum and Art Gallery: 102
Medicine Lake: 247
Medley: 332
Melissa's Mini Marathon: 204
Melville Island: 468
Meta Incognita Peninsula: 460
Métis people: 389
metric system: 42
Michener Mountain: 270
Midland Provincial Park: 145
Midnapore: *54*
Midnight Sun Marathon: 466
Miette Hot Springs: 248
Mighty Peace Golf and Country Club: 372
Mike Zubko Airport: 440
Mildred Lake: 338
Milk River: 7, 27, 93-94
Mill Creek Park: 304
Millwoods Library: 320
minerals: 22, 388
mining: 387, 388; see also coal
mink: 14
Minnewanka, Lake: 191-192
Minnewanka Landing: 28
Miquelon Lake Provincial Park: 283
Mirror Lake: 220
Misery Mountain Ski Centre: 372
Mistaya Canyon: 230
Mistaya Lake: 230
Mistaya River: 230
Mist Creek Trail: 173
Misty Ridge Ski Hill: 351
Mitchener House Museum: 279
Mittimatalik: see Pond Inlet
money: 40-41, 393
Monkman Pass: 367
Montana: 118, 121-122
montane forest: 8
Moonshine Lake Provincial Park: 369
moose: 10-11, 184
Moose Lake: 331
Moose Lake Provincial Park: 331-332
Moose Lake Trail: 252

Moose Meadows: 192
Moraine Lake: 217-218
moraines: 6
Morinville: 343
Mormons: 110
Morrin: 152
motels: 33; see also specific place
motor racing: 57
Mount Hamel Trail: 362
mountain biking: 26; Banff 200; Grande
    Cache 362; Jasper 252
mountaineering: 28, 253, 305
mountain goats: 13, 184, 238
mountain lions: 12
Mountain Park: 358
Mounted Police Musical Ride: 83
movie theaters: see cinemas
Mt. Athabasca: 240
Mt. Balfour: 227
Mt. Barbeau: 469
Mt. Blakiston: 120
Mt. Chephren: 230
Mt. Duval: 463
Mt. Edith Cavell: 245; hiking 250
Mt. Forbes: 230
Mt. Hector: 227
Mt. Herodier: 465
Mt. Inglismaldie: 191
Mt. Joy: 460
Mt. Joy Ski Area: 328
Mt. Kitchener: 241
Mt. Murchison: 230
Mt. Outram: 230
Mt. Patterson: 230
Mt. Pelly: 447
Mt. Rundle Trail: 197
Mt. Temple: 221, 227
Mt. Victoria: 217
Mt. Wilson: 230
Mt. Yamnuska: 166
mule deer: 10, 184
Muleshoe: 192
Murchison, Mt.: 230
Muriel Lake: 331
Musée Heritage Museum: 303
Museum of the Highwood: 165
Museum of the Regiments: 51
museums: 29; Aerospace Museum 51;
    Alberta Aviation Museum 302; Alberta
    Railway Museum 303; Appaloosa Horse
    Club of Canada Museum and Archives 80;
Atlas Coal Mine Museum 148; Banff Park
Museum 193; Battle River Pioneer
Museum 373; Bicentennial Museum 341;
Brooks and District Museum 154; C&E
Railway Museum 298; Camrose & District
Museum 281-282; Centennial Museum
351; Claresholm Museum 80; Courthouse
Museum 110-111; Crowsnest Museum
138; Den Wildlife Museum 245; District
Museum 351; Drumheller Dinosaur and
Fossil Museum 146; Edmonton Police
Museum 291; Edmonton Public Schools
Archives and Museum 291; End of Steel
Heritage Park and Museum 370; Etzikom
Museum 96-97; Fort Museum 82-83;
Glenbow Museum 51; Grande Prairie
Museum 364; Grouard Native Cultural Arts
Museum 349; Hanna Museum 150; High
Prairie and District Museum 350;
Homestead Antique Museum 145-146;
Horn and Antler Museum 146; Jasper-
Yellowhead Museum and Archives 245;
John Walter Museum 294-295; Luxton
Museum 193-194; Mandelin Eldon
Museum 267; Medicine Hat Museum and
Art Gallery 102; Mitchener House Museum
279; Musée Heritage Museum 303;
Museum of the Highwood 165; Museum of
the Regiments 51; Naval Museum of
Alberta 51; Nickle Arts Museum 51; Natural
History Museum 195; Northern Life
Museum 404; Nose Creek Valley Museum
272; Nunatta Sunakkutaangit Museum 458;
Old Strathcona Model and Toy Museum
298; Oyen Crossroads Museum 151;
Peace River Centennial Museum 370-372;
Pincher Creek Museum 129; Pioneer Acres
Museum 274; Pioneer Village Museum
263; Prairie Panorama Museum 283;
Provincial Museum of Alberta 298-299;
Redcliff Museum 102; Red Deer and
District Museum 276; Remington-Alberta
Carriage Centre 110; Reynolds-Alberta
Museum 280; Reynolds Antique Machinery
Museum 280; Rocky Mountain House
Museum 267; Royal Tyrrell Museum of
Palaeontology 143-145, 155; Sir Alexander
Galt Museum 87-88; Sodbuster's Museum
283; South Peace Centennial Museum
367; Stettler Town and Country Museum
279; Sturgeon River Historical Museum

343; Telephone Historical Information Centre 298; Three Rivers' Rock and Fossil Museum 129; Tsuu T'ina Culture Museum 52; Ukrainian Canadian Archives and Museum 294; Ukrainian Museum of Canada 294; Vermilion Heritage Museum 326-327

music: 30, 57-58, 78, 291, 306, 309, 333-334, 415

Muskeg Creek Park: 344

Muskeg Falls Trail: 361-362

Muskoseepi Park: 364

musk oxen: 384

muskrats: 14

Mustard Lake: 421

Muttart Conservatory: 294

mutton busting: *63*

N

Nahanni Butte: 423

Nahanni National Park: 382, 424-429

Nahanni River: 390

Nakiska at Mt. Allan: 28, 167-168

Nanisivik: 466-467

Nanton: 77-79

Nanton Lancaster Society Air Museum: 77

Nanton Nite Rodeo: 78

narwhals: 384

national parks: 25, 382; Aulavik 443; Auyuittuq 464; Elk Island 323-326; Ellesmere Island 469-479; Ivvavik 438; Nahanni 424-429; Tuktut Nogait 443; Waterton Lakes 113-127; Wood Buffalo 405-408

National, The: 31, 60

native Canadians: *see* Indians; *specific tribe*

Native Point: 456

Nattik Frolics: 448

natural gas: 22, 163

Natural History Museum: 195

Naujat: *see* Repulse Bay

Naval Museum of Alberta: 51

Ndulee Ferry Crossing: 431

Neerlandia: 351

Neutral Hills: 280

Newell, Lake: 154

New West Theatre Society: 90

nickel: 452

Nickle Arts Museum: 51

Nigel Pass Trail: 232

Nigel Peak: 232

nightlife: 30; Banff 212; Calgary 58; Edmonton 307

Nikka Yuko Japanese Garden: 90

Nordegg: 268-269

Nordegg Heritage Centre: 269

Nordegg Historic Heritage Interest Group: 269

Norman Wells: 388, **431-433**

Norman Wells Historical Centre: 432

North American Chuckwagon Championships: 165

North American tournament: 60

North Baffin Island: 382

Northern Alberta International Children's Festival: 308

northern flying foxes: 14

Northern Images: 306

Northern Life Museum: 404

northern lights: *375*

Northern Light Theatre: 206

Northern Woods and Water Route: 345

North Loop Trail: 408

North Pole: geographic *469;* magnetic 468

North Rankin Nickel Mine: 452

North Saskatchewan River: 7, 230, 323

North Saskatchewan River Valley: 285

North Star: 373

North West Company: 16

North West Co. Trading Post: 414

Northwest Passage: 386, 466

Northwest Passage Historic Park: 450

Northwest Territories: 381-470, *396;* accommodations and food 390-391; flora and fauna 383-385; government and economy 387-388; history 386-387; land 381-383; people 388-389; recreation 389-390; services and information 393-394; transportation 391-393; *see also* Nunavut

Northwest Territories Legislative Assembly: 412

Nose Creek Valley Museum: 272

Nose Hill Library: 75

Notikewin Provincial Park: 373-375

Nunatta Sunakkutaangit Museum: 458

Nunavut: 382-383, 387, 445-470, *446*

Nunavut Tourism: 394

NWT Centennial Library: 400

NWT Economic Development and Tourism: 394

NWT Open Championship: 399

Nyarling River: 402

O

observatories: 50, 299
Ogre Canyon: 358
oil: 4-6, **19-22**, 45, 117, 163, 289-290, 332,
    337-338, 377, 388
Oil City: 117, 120
Oil Sands Interpretive Centre: 337-338
Okotoks: 164-165
Okotoks Bird Sanctuary: 164
Old Fort Point Trail: 249
Oldman Dam: 129
Oldman River: 7
Oldman River Provincial Recreation Area: 83
Old Rectory: 330
Old St. Mary's Ukrainian Catholic Church:
    343
Old Strathcona: 296-298, *297*, 315-316
Old Strathcona Farmer's Market: 296
Old Strathcona Model and Toy Museum: 298
Olympic Hall of Fame: 53
Olympic Plaza: 48
Olympics: 45, 48, 53
Olympic Saddledome: 54
One Yellow Rabbit: 57
Onion Lake: 331
Opal Hills Trail: 251
Oppertshauser Gallery: 302
Orion: 97
Orkney Hill: 147
ospreys: 15
otters: 14
Our Lady of Good Hope Church: 434
Our Lady of Victory Church: 438
Outram, Mt.: 230
Owl River: 464
owls: 15
Oyen: 151
Oyen Crossroads Museum: 151

P

Paddle Prairie: 375
Pakowki: 97
Palace Casino: 307
paleontology: 93-94, 141-146, *143*, *145*, 155-
    158, *155*
Palliser, John: 17, *96*, 175
Palliser Triangle: *96*
Pangnirtung: 463
Pangnirtung Pass: 464
Panniqtuuq: *see* Pangnirtung
Panther Falls: 231

Papal Grounds: 421
Parade of Power and Annual Show: 130
Paradise Canyon golf course: 90
Paradise Creek: 220
Paradise Gardens: 397
Paradise Valley Trail: 220-221
Parker's Ridge Trail: 232
Park Interpretive Program: 204
Park Lake Provincial Park: 90
parks: 25
Parks Day: 204
Parry Islands: 468
Parry, William: 467
passports: 39
Pass Powder Keg Ski Hill: 136
Path of the Glacier Trail: 245
Patricia Lake: 28, 245
Patricia Lake Circle: 248
Patterson, Mt.: 230
Paulatuk: 443
Pavan Park: 89
Peace-Athabasca Delta: 407
Peace Park Pavilion: 117
Peace Regional Pool: 372
Peace River: 6, 370-372, *371*
Peace River Centennial Museum: 370-372
Peace River Valley: 369-377
Peace View Golf & Country Club: 372
Pearce Estate Park: 54
Peary, Robert: *469*
pedway: 290
Peel River: 435
Peel River Preserve: 436
Peenaquim Park: 89
Peerless Lake: 348
Pelican Island: 283
Pelican Rapids Golf and Country Club: 404
Pelly Bay: 451
Pelly, Mt.: 447
Pembina River Provincial Park: 355-357
Penny Ice Cap: 464
people: 23-24, 388-389; *see also specific*
    peoples
Peregrine Falcon Hatchery: 284
performing arts: 29-30, 90
Performing Arts Centre: 90
permafrost: 382
Peter Lougheed Provincial Park: 169
Peyto Glacier: 229-230
Peyto Lake: 229-230
Peyto Lake Trail: 231

Peyto, William "Wild Bill": *194,* 227, 229
Phoenix Theatre: 306
Pierie Grey Lakes: 360
Pigeon Lake Provincial Park: 272
pig races: 372
pikas: 14
Pilot's Monument: 412
Pincher Creek: 128-132, *129*
Pincher Creek Fair and Rodeo: 130
Pincher Creek Museum: 129
Pine Hills Golf Course: 268
Pinehurst Lake: 335
Pine Lake: 408
Pine Point: 401
pingos: 442
Pioneer Acres Museum: 274
Pioneer Day: 367
Pioneer Village Museum: 263
Plain of the Six Glaciers Trail: 219
plains bison: 14, 324
plants: *see* flora
Pleiades Theatre: 50
Pocahontas: 239
Polar Bear Pass: 468
polar bears: 384
Polar Continental Shelf Project: 467
Polaris Mine: 468
Polar Lake: 401
Polar Park: 303
Police Coulee: 95
Police Outpost Provincial Park: 111, **112**
Police Point Park: 102
political parties: 23
politics: *see* government
Pond Inlet: 465-466
Pond, Peter: 16
Pontoon Lake: 413
Porcupine Hills: 80
porcupines: 14
postal services: 41
prairie: 9
Prairie Art Gallery: 364
Prairie Creek: 426
Prairie Panorama Museum: 283
Prairie Sun Grains: 281
Pratt's Landing: 369
Prehistoric Park: 146
prehistory: 16, 155-156, 386
Prelude Lake: 413
prices: 40
Prince Leopold Island: 466

Prince of Wales Hotel: 117, 123
Prince of Wales Northern Heritage Centre:
    412
Prince of Wales Strait: 443
Prince's Island Park: 50
pronghorn: 13, *151*
Prospector's Trail: 413
Prosperous Lake: 413
Provincial Archives: 299
Provincial Courthouse: 99
Provincial Museum of Alberta: 29, 298-299
provincial parks: 25; Beauvais Lake 130; Big
    Hill Springs 162; Big Knife 280; Bow Valley
    166-167; Bragg Creek 163; Calling Lake
    345; Carson-Pegasus 352; Chain Lakes
    165; Cold Lake 332-333; Crimson Lake
    268; Cross Lake 351; Dillberry Lake 284;
    Fish Creek 54-55; Garner Lake 329;
    Gooseberry Lake 280; Gregoire Lake 338;
    Hilliard's Bay 349-350; Kinbrook Island
    154; Lakeland 335; Lesser Slave Lake 347;
    Little Bow 81; Little Fish Lake 146; Long
    Lake 329; Ma-me-o 272; Midland 145;
    Miquelon Lake 283; Moonshine Lake 369;
    Moose Lake 331-332; Notikewin 373-375;
    Pembina River 355-357; Peter Lougheed
    169-172, *170;* Pigeon Park 272; Police
    Outpost 111, 112; Queen Elizabeth 373;
    Rochon Sands 279; Saskatoon Island 367;
    Sir Winston Churchill 335; Taber 98;
    Thunder Lake 351-352; Tillebrook 154;
    Vermilion 326; Wabamun Lake 355;
    Whitney Lakes 330-331; William A. Switzer
    359-360; Williamson 354; Willow Creek 78-
    79; Winagami Lake 350; Woolford 111,
    112; Writing-On-Stone 94-96; Wyndham-
    Carseland 153; Young's Point 354
Provincial Sales Tax: 40
Provost: 283
Ptarmigan Cirque Trail: 171-172
Punchbowl Falls: 248
pygmy shrews: 14
Pyramid Lake: 245
Pyramid Lake Loop: 248
Pyramid Mountain: 245
pysanka: 326

Q
Qamanittuaq: *see* Baker Lake
Qaummaarviit Historic Park: 458
Qausuittuq: *see* Resolute

Qavvarrik Carnival: 450
Qikiqtarjuaq: *see* Broughton Island
Queen Elizabeth Park: 304
Queen Elizabeth Provincial Park: 373
Queen Maud Gulf bird sanctuary: 382
Queens Hotel: 82
Quest for Handcrafts: 196

R
Rabbit Hill Ski Area: 205
Rabbitkettle Hotsprings: 426, 428
Race City Speedway: 57
Rae-Edze: 410
Rae Lakes: 418
rafting: 27; Banff 201; Grande Cache 362;
  Jasper 247, 253; Lake Louise 218; Milk
  River 94; Nahanni N.P. 427-428; *see also*
  canoeing; kayaking
railroads: 19, 44, 96-97, 303
rail travel: 36-37, 38
Rainbow Lake: 377
Ralph Connor Memorial United Church: 175
Ramparts, The: 434
Ram Plateau: 428
Ranchers Rodeo: 130
ranching: 44-45, 159-161
Rangeland Derby: 61
Rankin Inlet: 452-453
raptors: 15, 97, 284
Rat River Route: 430
rattlesnakes: 15
Raven Mad Daze: 415
recreation: 25-32, 389-390; entertainment 29-
  30; shopping 30-31; festivals and events
  31-32; outdoor activities 26-29; parks 25;
  see also specific activity
Redcliff: 102
Redcliff Museum: 102
Red Deer: 274-278, *275*
Red Deer and District Museum: 276
Red Deer International Air Show: 32, 277
Red Deer River: 27
Red Earth Creek: 348
Red Rock Canyon: 120
Red Rock Canyon Parkway: 120
Red Rock Coulee: 98
Reesor Lake: 106
Reil Rebellion: 276
Remington-Alberta Carriage Museum: 29,
  110
rental cars: 38-39; *see also specific place*

reptiles: 15, 146
Reptile World: 146
Repulse Bay: 455-456
Resolute: 467-468
Reynolds Antique Machinery Museum: 280
Reynolds-Alberta`Museum: 29, 280
Ribbon Creek/Spray Lakes Area: 167-169
rib stones: 284
ringed seals: 385
River Bend Golf Course: 277
River Daze: 372
river otters: 14
Riverside Golf Course: 304
River Valley Park System: 304
Robb: 358
Roche qui-Trempe-à-L'eau: 431
Rochester: 343
Rochon Sands Provincial Park: 279
Rockbound Lake Trail: 200
Rock Glacier Trail: 171-172
Rock Isle Lake Trail: 199
Rock Lake: 360
rock rabbit: 14
Rockwall Trail: 171
Rocky Mountain Elk Foundation: 267
Rocky Mountain Forest Reserve: 80, 262
Rocky Mountain House: 266-268, *266*
Rocky Mountain House Museum: 267
Rocky Mountain House National Historic
  Park: 266-267
Rocky Mountains: 4, 6
Rocky Mountains Park: 186
rodents: 14
Rodeo Royal: 31, 59
rodeos: *62-63;* Calgary Stampede 60-65;
  Canadian Cowboys Association Rodeo
  Finals 328; Canadian Finals Rodeo 309;
  Jasper Lions Pro Indoor Rodeo 255;
  Medicine Hat Exhibition and Stampede
  103; Nanton Nite Rodeo 78; Pincher Creek
  Fair and Rodeo 130; Ranchers Rodeo 130;
  Rodeo Royal 59; Silver Buckle Rodeo 277;
  Spring Outdoor Rodeo 103; Sundre Pro
  Rodeo 263; Wildrose Rodeo Association
  Finals 351
Room Tax: 40
Rope Square: 61
Rosedale: 147-148
Ross, John: 450
Rotary Park: 351
Roundup Days: 78

Rowley: 152
Royal Oak Mine: 413
Royal Tyrrell Museum of Palaeontology: 29, 143-145, 155
Rum Runner Days: 136
Rundle, Mt.: 197
Rutherford House: 295
RVs: 38-39
Ryley: 284

S
Saamba Deh Falls Territorial Park: 419-420
Saamis Archeological Site: 99
Saamis Teepee: 101-102
Sachs Harbour: 435, **443**
Saddleback Trail: 220
saddle bronc riding: *62*
salamanders: 184
Salliq: *see* Coral Harbour
Sallirmiut: 456
salt: 331, 407
Salt Plains Trail: 407
Sam Livingston Fish Hatchery: 54
Sandy Lake: 401
Sanikluaq: 462
Sanirajak: *see* Hall Beach
Sarcee people: 52
Saskatchewan Glacier Trail: 232
Saskatchewan River: 7
Saskatoon Island Provincial Park: 367
Sawtooth Mountain: 465
Schäffer, Mary: *251*
scuba diving: *see* diving
seals: 385
Seaplane Lake: 426
Seba Beach: 355
Second Canyon: 426
Seebe: 166
Seibert Lake: 335
Sentinel Pass: 221
settlement: 19
Sexsmith: 367-368
Sexsmith Blacksmith Shop: 368
Shadow Lake Lodge: 34
Shadow Lake Trail: 199-200
Shady Grove Bluegrass and Old Tyme Music Festival: 78
Shaftesbury: 372
Shaftesbury Ferry: 372
Shaganappi Point golf course: 55
sheep: 13, 184, 238, *249*

Sheep River Valley: 164
Shoogie Lake: 460
shopping: 30-31; Banff 212; Calgary 58-59; Edmonton 308
shorebirds: 15
Shoreline Trail: 325
Shoshoni people: 95
show-jumping: 60
shrews: 14
Sibbald Creek Trail: 173
Siding 29: 186
Siffleur Falls: 270
Siffleur Wilderness Area: 25, 271
Silver Buckle Rodeo: 31, **277**
Silver City: 192
Silverhorn Creek: 230
Silver Summit Ski Resort: 357
Sir Alexander Galt Museum: 87-88
Sir Winston Churchill Provincial Park: 335
skiing: *see* cross-country skiing; downhill skiing
ski jumping: 53
Skoki Lodge Trail: 221-222
skydiving: 304-305
Skyline Trail: 248
Slave Lake: 345-348, *346*
Slave River: 395
Slave River Rapids Monument: 404
Slavey Dene people: *see* Dene people
sleigh rides: 29; Banff 203; Lake Louise 222
Slush Cup: 31, 203
Smith-Dorien/Spray Trail: 169
Smoke Lake: 353
Smoking Hill: 433, 443
Smoky Lake: 329
Smoky River Agriculture Society Fair: 350
snakes: 15
Snare Lake: 418
Sneek-a-peek: 61
Snowdrift: *see* Lutsel K'e
Snow Goose Festival: 31, 283
snowshoeing: 29
Snow Valley ski area: 305
soccer: 57
Sodbuster's Museum: 283
Soper Falls: 460
Soper Lake: 460
Soper River: 382, 390, 460
South Boundary Trail: 248
South Country Hootenanny: 80
Southern Alberta Art Gallery: 87

Southland Leisure Centre: 56
South Nahanni River: 424, 427-428
South Peace Centennial Museum: 367
Spectrum Festival: 103
Spence Bay: see Taloyoak
Spirit Island: 247
Spray River Trail: 197
Spring Outdoor Rodeo: 31, **103**
Spruce Coulee: 106
Spruce Coulee Trail: 106
Spruce Meadows: 31, **59-60**
Spruce Meadows Masters: 32, **60**
Spruce Point Park: 349
squirrels: 14, 183
St. Albert: 302-303
St. Albert Place: 303
Stampede Parade: 61
Stampede Park: 54, 60
Stampede Ranch: 151
Stampeders: 57
St. Ann Ranch Trading Co.: 274
St. Jean Baptiste Church: 343
St. Josephat's Ukrainian Catholic Cathedral: 294
St. Mary's Church: 277
St. Norbert's Church: 283
St. Patrick's Church: 99
St. Paul: 330
St. Paul Culture Centre: 330
Steen River: 377
steer wrestling: **63**
Stephen Avenue Mall: 48
Stettler: 279-280
Stettler Town and Country Museum: 279
Stompede: 366
Stoney Squaw Trail: 197-198
Stony Plain Multicultural Heritage Centre: 302
Stony Trail: 163
Storybook Theatre: 57
Strathcona Centre: 102
Strathcona Hotel: 296
Strathcona Island Park: 102
Strathcona Library: 320
Strathmore: 153
Strome: 283
study: 39
Sturgeon Lake: 354
Sturgeon Lake Indian Band Reserve: 354
Sturgeon River Historical Museum: 343
Stutfield Glacier: 241
subalpine forest: 8-9

Sulphur Mountain Gondola: 188-189
Summer Solstice: 439
Summit Lake: 119
Sunblood Mountain: 428
Suncor Inc.: 337, 338
Sundance Canyon Trail: 197
Sundre: 263
Sundre Pro Rodeo: 263
Sunridge Ski Area: 205
Sunshine Village ski area: 28, 202
Sunwapta Falls: 241
Sunwapta Pass: 231, 239
Sunwapta River: 241
Swan Hills: 352
Sweetgrass: 408
Sweetgrass Hills: 112
swimming: 55, 304
Sylvan Lake: 277
Sylvia Grinnell Territorial Park: 458
Symphony under the Sky: 309
Syncrude Canada Ltd.: 337, 338

T
Taber: 97-98
Taber Provincial Park: 98
Taber Sugar Beet Factory: 97
Taloyoak: 450-451
Tangle Ridge: 241
Taste of Banff/Lake Louise: 204
Tawatinaw: 343
Tawatinaw Ski Hill: 351
taxes: 40, 393
TD Square: 58
Telephone Historical Information Centre: 298
telephone services: Alberta 41-42; Northwest Territories 393
temperature: see climate
temperature inversion: 7
Temple, Mt.: 221, 227
tepee rings: 81
territorial parks: 382; Blackstone 423; Fred Henne 413; Gwich'in 436; Katannilik 460-461; Little Buffalo Falls 402; Saamba Deh Falls 419-420; Sylvia Grinnell 458; Twin Falls Gorge 397
Text Garden: 354
theater: Calgary 57; Edmonton 306; Grande Prairie 366; Lethbridge 90
Theatre Calgary: 57
Thelon Game Sanctuary: 382, **455**
Thelon River: 455

The Works: A Visual Arts Celebration: 309
Third Canyon: 426
Thom Bay: 450
Thompson, David: 239, 243, 266, *270*
Thomsen River: 390, 443
Three Hills: 274
Three Rivers' Rock and Fossil Museum: 129
Thule culture: 386
Thunder Lake Provincial Park: 351-352
Tibbit Lake: 413
Tikirarjuaq: *see* Whale Cove
Tillebrook Provincial Park: 154
Timber Berth 408: 406-407
timber industry: *see* forestry
time zone: 42
tipping: 41
Tlogotsho Plateau: 426, 428
Tofield: 283
Tompkin's Landing: 373
Toonik Tyme: 459
topographic maps: 26
Touchwood Lake: 335
tourism: 22, 388
tours: 39, 393
Tower Casino: 58
Tower Lake: 200
trading: *see* fur trading
train travel: *see* rail travel
Tramline: 218
transportation: 36-39, 391-393, *392;* air 36,
    37-38; bus 37, 38; car/RV 38-39; rail 36-37,
    38; tours 39; *see also specific place*
Trapper Lea's Cabin: 352
traveler's checks: 41
Trochu: 274
trout: 15, 184
Trout Lake (Alberta): 348
Trout Lake (Northwest Territories): 420
Trout River: 419
Truelove Lowlands: 468
trumpeter swans: 367
Tsiigehtchic: 436
Tsuu T'ina Culture Museum: 52
tufa mounds: 426
Tuktoyaktuk: 442
Tuktut Nogait National Park: 382, **443**
Tulita: 433
Tunnel Mountain Trail: 196-197
Turner Valley: *20,* 45, 163-164
Turtle Mountain: 134-135
12 Foot Davis: 370

Twin Falls Gorge Territorial Park: 397
Twitya River: 433
Tyrrell, Joseph B.: 141
Tyson, Ian: 30

U
Ukama Trail: 463
Ukrainian Canadian Archives and Museum:
    294
Ukrainian Cultural Heritage Village: 326
Ukrainian Folk Festival: 31, 326
Ukrainian Museum of Canada: 294
Ukrainians: 24, 294, 326
Uluksan Point: 466
Uluqsaqtuuq: *see* Holman
Umingmaktok: 449
Upper Hot Springs: 190, 203
Upper Peace Valley: 369-370
Upper Therien Lake: 330
Uptown 17: 59
Ursuqtuq: *see* Gjoa Haven

V
Vale Island: 397, 399
Valley of the Five Lakes Trail: 249-250
Valleyview: 353-354
Valley Zoo: 296
Van Horne, William C.: 186-187
Vega: 351
vegetation zones: 8-9, *9*
Vegreville: 326
Vermilion: 326-327
Vermilion Heritage Museum: 326-327
Vermilion Lakes: 190
Vermilion Provincial Park: 326
Vertically Inclined Rock Gym: 305
Victoria Golf Course: 304
Victoria Island: 446
Victoria, Mt.: 217
Victoria Settlement: 329
Viking: 284
Village Square Leisure Centre: 56
Village Square Library: 75
Vimy Peak Trail: 119-120
Virginia Falls: 426
visas: 39
Vista Trail: 188
voles: 14
voyageur canoes: 268
Vulcan: 81

W
Wabamun: 355
Wabamun Lake Provincial Park: 355
Wabasca-Desmarais: 345
Wadlin Lake: 348
Wager Bay: 382, 456
Wainwright: 284
Wainwright Museum: 284
walleye: 350
walruses: 384-385
Walterdale Playhouse: 306
Walter Phillips Gallery: 195
Wandering River: 337
wapiti: 10
Wapta Icefield: 229-230
Waputik Range: 227
Ward Hunt Island: 470
Waskasoo Park: 275-276
Waskatenau: 329
Watchtower Basin Trail: 251
Waterfalls Route: 397
waterfowl: 15
Waterfowl Lakes: 230
Waterton-Glacier International Peace Park:
    117-118
Waterton Lakes Golf Course: 122
Waterton Lakeshore Trail: 118, 122
Waterton Lakes National Park: 25, **113-127,**
    114, 124; accommodations 123-125; food
    125-126; hiking 26, 118-120; history 116-
    118; land 113-116; recreation 118-122;
    scenic drives 120-121; services and
    information 126-127
Waterton Lakes Opera House: 122
Waterton Valley: 113
Watt Mountain: 376
Waugh: 343
Wayne: 148
Wayside Chapel: 133
Weadick, Guy: 60-61
Weasel River: 464
weasels: 14
weather: *see* climate
Weeping Wall: 230
Weldwood: 357
Wenkchemna Pass: 221
West Baffin Eskimo Co-operative: 461
Westcastle Park ski area: 130
West Channel Village: 397, 399
West Edmonton Mall: 300-302, *300, 301*
West End: 298

Westerner Days: 277
Western Heritage Center: 162
Western wear: 31, 59, 308
Westlock: 351
Wetaskiwin: 280-281
Wetlands Nature Trail: 331
Whale Cove: 453
whales: 384
Whale's Tail Monument: 453
Wha Ti: 417-418
wheelchair accessibility: 74, 214, 318
Wheeler, A.O.: *177*
Whispering Pines ski hill: 370
Whistlers Campground Outdoor Theatre: 255
Whistlers, The: 248-249
Whitecourt: 353
White Earth Valley Natural Area: 329
White Fox Jamboree: 443
White Goat Wilderness Area: 25, **270-271**
Whitehorse Creek: 358
Whitehorse Falls: 358
Whitehorse Pass: 358
white-tailed deer: 10, 184
whitewater rafting: *see* rafting
white whales: 384
Whitney Lakes Provincial Park: 330-331
Whoop-Up Days: 32, **91**
whooping cranes: *386,* 407
Whyte Museum of the Canadian Rockies:
    194-195
Wilcox Campground Campfire Talk: 255
Wilcox Pass Trail: 242
wild cow milking: *63*
wilderness areas: 25; Ghost River 166;
    Siffleur 271; White Goat 270-271; Willmore
    362-363
wild horse race: *63*
Wild Rapids Waterslides: 277
Wildrose Rodeo Association Finals: 351
Wild Sculpture Trail: 359
William A. Switzer Provincial Park: 359-360
William Hawrelak Park: 304
Williamson Provincial Park: 354
William Watson Lodge: 169-171
Willmore Wilderness Park: 362-363
Willow Creek Provincial Park: 78-79
Wilson, Mt.: 230
Winagami Conservation Area: 350
Winagami Lake Provincial Park: 350
windchill: 41
windsurfing: Waterton Lakes N.P. 121

wine: 302
winter carnivals: 32, 176, 399
Wintergreen Ski and Golf Resort: 163
Winterstart: 32, 204
winter travel: 41
Wolf Creek Golf Course: 28
wolverines: 14
wolves: 12, 184, 238
wood bison: 14, 324-325, 406
Wood Bison Trail: 325
Wood Buffalo National Park: 25, **405-408,** *405*
Woolford Provincial Park: 111, **112**
World Champion Bull Bustin': 308
World Championship Pumpkin Weigh-In: 329
World Cup Downhill: 204
World Waterpark: 300, 304
W.R. Castell Central Library: 75
Wrigley: 430-431

Writing-On-Stone Provincial Park: 25, **94-96**
Wyndham-Carseland Provincial Park: 153

Y
Yamnuska, Mt.: 166
Yellowknife: 410-417, *411;* history 410-412; practicalities 415-417; recreation 413-415; sights 412-413
Yellowknife Airport: 416
Yellowknife Golf Course: 414
Yellowknife Public Library: 417
YMCA/YWCA: 34
Young's Point Provincial Park: 354

Z
Zama City: 377
zoos: Calgary Zoo 53-54; GuZoo Animal Farm 274
zoos: Valley Zoo 296

ABOUT THE AUTHORS

Since beginning work for Moon Publications, Australians Andrew Hempstead and Nadina Purdon have worked on Moon Travel Handbooks to Alaska, British Columbia, and New Zealand. As well as authoring *Alberta and the Northwest Territories Handbook*, they are coauthors of *Australia Handbook*, and Andrew is currently working on the *British Columbia Handbook*.

MOON TRAVEL HANDBOOKS

THE IDEAL TRAVELING COMPANIONS

Moon Travel Handbooks provide focused, comprehensive coverage of distinct destinations all over the world. Our goal is to give travelers all the background and practical information they'll need for an extraordinary travel experience.

Every Handbook begins with an in-depth essay about the land, the people, their history, art, politics, and social concerns—an entire bookcase of cultural insight and introductory information in one portable volume. We also provide accurate, up-to-date coverage of all the practicalities: language, currency, transportation, accommodations, food, and entertainment. And Moon's maps are legendary, covering not only cities and highways, but parks and trails that are often difficult to find in other sources.

Below are highlights of Moon's North America and Hawaii Travel Handbook series. Our complete list of Handbooks, covering North America and Hawaii, Mexico, Central America and the Caribbean, and Asia and the Pacific, is on the order form on the accompanying pages. To purchase Moon Travel Handbooks, please check your local bookstore or order by phone: (800) 345-5473 Monday-Friday 8 a.m.-5 p.m. PST.

MOON OVER NORTH AMERICA
THE NORTH AMERICA AND HAWAII TRAVEL HANDBOOK SERIES

> "Moon's greatest achievements may be the individual state books they offer. . . . Moon not only digs up little-discovered attractions, but also offers thumbnail sketches of the culture and state politics of regions that rarely make national headlines."
>
> —*The Millennium Whole Earth Catalog*

ALASKA-YUKON HANDBOOK
by Deke Castleman and Don Pitcher, 500 pages, **$17.95**
"Exceptionally rich in local culture, history, and reviews of natural attractions. . . . One of the most extensive pocket references. . . . An essential guide!"　　　　　— *The Midwest Book Review*

ALBERTA AND THE NORTHWEST TERRITORIES
by Nadina Purdon and Andrew Hempstead, 466 pages, **$17.95**
"*Alberta and the Northwest Territories Handbook* provides strong coverage of the most rugged territories in Canada."
　　　　　　　　　　　　　　　　　　　—*The Bookwatch*

ARIZONA TRAVELER'S HANDBOOK
by Bill Weir and Robert Blake, 486 pages, **$17.95**
"If you don't own this book already, buy it immediately"
　　　　　　　　　　　　　　　　　—*Arizona Republic*

ATLANTIC CANADA HANDBOOK
by Nan Drosdick and Mark Morris, 436 pages, **$17.95**
New Brunswick, Nova Scotia, Prince Edward Island,
Newfoundland and Labrador.
"The new *Atlantic Canada* is the best I've seen on the region—
superior maps, travel tips, and cultural essays."
—Peter Aiken, *Providence Journal-Bulletin*

BIG ISLAND OF HAWAII HANDBOOK
by J.D. Bisignani, 349 pages, **$13.95**
"The best general guidebooks available."   —*Hawaii Magazine*

BRITISH COLUMBIA HANDBOOK
by Jane King, 375 pages, **$15.95**
"Deftly balances the conventional and the unconventional, for both
city lovers and nature lovers."
—*Reference and Research Book News*

COLORADO HANDBOOK
by Stephen Metzger, 447 pages, **$18.95**
"Hotel rooms in the Aspen area, in the height of winter sports
season, for $20-$30? . . . who but a relentless researcher from
Moon could find it?"   —The New York *Daily News*

GEORGIA HANDBOOK
by Kap Stann, 360 pages, **$17.95**
"[a] gold medal winner . . . Anyone who is interested in the South
should get this book."   —*Eclectic Book Review*

HAWAII HANDBOOK
by J.D. Bisignani, 1004 pages, **$19.95**
Winner: Grand Excellence and Best Guidebook Awards, Hawaii
Visitors' Bureau
"No one since Michener has told us so much about our 50th
state."   —*Playboy*

HONOLULU-WAIKIKI HANDBOOK
by J.D. Bisignani, 365 pages, **$14.95**
"The best general guidebooks available."   —*Hawaii Magazine*

IDAHO HANDBOOK
by Don Root, 600 pages, **$18.95**
"It's doubtful that visitors to the Gem State will find a better, more
detailed explanation anywhere."

—*The Salt Lake Tribune*

KAUAI HANDBOOK
by J.D. Bisignani, 330 pages, **$15.95**
"This slender guide is tightly crammed. . . . The information
provided is staggering." —*Hawaii Magazine*

MAUI HANDBOOK
by J.D. Bisignani, 393 pages, **$14.95**
Winner: Best Guidebook Award, Hawaii Visitors' Bureau
"*Maui Handbook* should be in every couple's suitcase. It
intelligently discusses Maui's history and culture, and you can
trust the author's recommendations for best beaches, restaurants,
and excursions." —*Bride's Magazine*

MONTANA HANDBOOK
by W.C. McRae and Judy Jewell, 454 pages, **$17.95**
"Well-organized, engagingly written, tightly edited, and chock-full
of interesting facts about localities, backcountry destinations,
traveler accommodations, and cultural and natural history."
—*Sierra Magazine*

NEVADA HANDBOOK
by Deke Castleman, 473 pages, **$16.95**
"Veteran travel writer Deke Castleman says he covered more
than 10,000 miles in his research for this book and it shows."
—*Nevada Magazine*

NEW MEXICO HANDBOOK
by Stephen Metzger, 320 pages, **$15.95**
"The best current guide and travel book to all of New Mexico"
—New Mexico Book League

NEW YORK HANDBOOK
by Christiane Bird, 615 pages, **$19.95**
Contains voluminous coverage not only of New York City, but also
of myriad destinations along the Hudson River Valley, in the
Adirondack Mountains, around Leatherstocking Country, and
elsewhere throughout the state.

NORTHERN CALIFORNIA HANDBOOK
by Kim Weir, 779 pages, **$19.95**
"That rarest of travel books—both a practical guide to the region
and a map of its soul." —*San Francisco Chronicle*

OREGON HANDBOOK
by Stuart Warren
and Ted Long Ishikawa, 520 pages, **$16.95**
". . . the most definitive tourist guide to the state ever published."
—*The Oregonian*

TENNESSEE HANDBOOK
by Jeff Bradley, 500 pages, **$17.95**
Features nonpareil coverage of Nashville and Memphis, as well as
the Appalachian Trail, Great Smoky Mountains National Park, Civil
War battlefields, and a wide assortment of unusual amusements
off the beaten path.

TEXAS HANDBOOK
by Joe Cummings, 598 pages, **$17.95**
"Reveals a Texas with a diversity of people and culture that is as
breathtaking as that of the land itself."
—*Planet Newspaper,* Australia

"I've read a bunch of Texas guidebooks, and this is the best one."
—Joe Bob Briggs

UTAH HANDBOOK
by Bill Weir and W.C. McRae, 500 pages, **$17.95**
" . . . a one-volume, easy to digest, up-to-date, practical, factual
guide to all things Utahan. . . . This is the best handbook of its kind
I've yet encountered." —*The Salt Lake Tribune*

WASHINGTON HANDBOOK
by Don Pitcher, 866 pages, **$19.95**
"Departs from the general guidebook format by offering
information on how to cope with the rainy days and where to take
the children. . . . This is a great book, informational, fun to read,
and a good one to keep." —*Travel Publishing News*

WISCONSIN HANDBOOK
by Thomas Huhti, 400 pages, **$16.95**
Lake Michigan, Lake Superior, and Wisconsin's 65 state parks and
national forests offer unrivaled outdoor recreational opportunities,
from hiking, biking, and water sports to the myriad pleasures of
Door County, the "crown jewel of the Midwest."

WYOMING HANDBOOK
by Don Pitcher, 570 pages, **$17.95**
"Wanna know the real dirt on Calamity Jane, white Indians, and
the tacky Cheyenne gunslingers? All here. And all fun."
—The New York *Daily News*

Hit The Road With Moon Travel Handbooks

ROAD TRIP USA
Cross-Country Adventures on America's Two-Lane Highways
by Jamie Jensen, 800 pages, **$22.50**
This Handbook covers the entire United States with 11
intersecting routes, allowing travelers to create their own
cross-country driving adventures

Packed with both practical information and entertaining
sidebars, *Road Trip USA* celebrates the spontaneity and culture of
the American highway without sacrificing the essential comforts of
bed and bread.

The World Wide Web edition of *Road Trip USA* features the
entire text plus links to local Internet sites. WWW explorers are
encouraged to participate in the exhibit by contributing their own
travel tips on small towns, roadside attractions, regional foods,
and interesting places to stay. Visit *Road Trip USA* online at:
http://www.moon.com/rdtrip.html

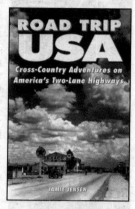

"Essential for travelers who are more interested in finding the real America than the fastest way
from points A to B. Highly recommended."   —*Library Journal*

"For budding myth collectors, I can't think of a better textbook than Moon Publications' cross-
country adventure guide."   —*Los Angeles Times*

MOONBELT

A new concept in moneybelts. Made of
heavy-duty Cordura nylon, the Moonbelt
offers maximum protection for your money and important papers. This pouch, designed for all-
weather comfort, slips under your shirt or waistband, rendering it virtually undetectable and inaccessible to pickpockets. It features a one-inch high-test quick-release buckle so there's no more
fumbling around for the strap or repeated adjustments. This handy plastic buckle opens and closes with a touch but won't come undone until you want it to. Moonbelts accommodate traveler's
checks, passports, cash, photos, etc. Size 5 x 9 inches. Available in black only. **$8.95**

Travel Matters

Smart Reading for the Independent Traveler

Travel Matters is Moon Publications' free newsletter, loaded with specially commissioned travel articles and essays that get at the heart of the travel experience. Every issue includes:

Feature Stories covering a wide array of travel and cultural topics about destinations on and off the beaten path. Past feature stories in *Travel Matters* include Mexican professional wrestling, traveling to the Moon, and why Germans get six weeks vacation and Americans don't.

The Offbeat Path exploring unusual customs and practices from toothfiling ceremonies in Bali to the serving of deep fried bull testicles in a small Colorado bar.

Health Matters, by Dirk Schroeder, author of *Staying Healthy in Asia, Africa, and Latin America,* focusing on the most recent medical findings that affect travelers.

Reviews providing readers with assessments of the latest travel books, videos, multimedia, support materials, and Internet resources.

Travel Q&A, a reader question-and-answer column for travelers written by an international travel agent and world traveler.

To receive a free subscription to *Travel Matters,* call (800) 345-5473, e-mail us at travel@moon.com, or write to us at:

> Moon Publications
> P.O. Box 3040
> Chico, CA 95927-3040

Current and back issues of *Travel Matters* can also be found on our web site at **http://www.moon.com**

Please note: Subscribers who live outside of the United States will be charged $7 per year for shipping and handling.

MOON TRAVEL HANDBOOKS

NORTH AMERICA AND HAWAII

Alaska-Yukon Handbook (0897)	$17.95
Alberta and the Northwest Territories Handbook (0463)	$17.95
Arizona Traveler's Handbook (0714)	$17.95
Atlantic Canada Handbook (0072)	$17.95
Big Island of Hawaii Handbook (0064)	$13.95
British Columbia Handbook (0145)	$15.95
Colorado Handbook (0447)	$18.95
Georgia Handbook (0390)	$17.95
Hawaii Handbook (0005)	$19.95
Honolulu-Waikiki Handbook (0587)	$14.95
Idaho Handbook (0889)	$18.95
Kauai Handbook (0919)	$15.95
Maui Handbook (0579)	$14.95
Montana Handbook (0498)	$17.95
Nevada Handbook (0641)	$16.95
New Mexico Handbook (0862)	$15.95
New York Handbook (0811)	$19.95
Northern California Handbook (3840)	$19.95
Oregon Handbook (0102)	$16.95
Road Trip USA (0366)	$22.50
Tennessee Handbook (0439)	$17.95
Texas Handbook (0633)	$17.95
Utah Handbook (0870)	$17.95
Washington Handbook (0455)	$19.95
Wisconsin Handbook (0927)	$16.95
Wyoming Handbook (0854)	$17.95

ASIA AND THE PACIFIC

Australia Handbook (0722)	$21.95
Bali Handbook (0730)	$19.95
Bangkok Handbook (0595)	$13.95
Fiji Islands Handbook (0382)	$13.95
Hong Kong Handbook (0560)	$15.95
Indonesia Handbook (0625)	$25.00
Japan Handbook (3700)	$22.50
Micronesia Handbook (0773)	$14.95

Nepal Handbook (0412) $18.95
New Zealand Handbook (0331) $19.95
Outback Australia Handbook (0471) $18.95
Pakistan Handbook (0692) $22.50
Philippines Handbook (0048) $17.95
Singapore Handbook (0781) $15.95
Southeast Asia Handbook (0021) $21.95
South Korea Handbook (0749) $18.95
South Pacific Handbook (0404) $22.95
Tahiti-Polynesia Handbook (0374) $13.95
Thailand Handbook (0420) $19.95
Tibet Handbook (3905) $30.00
Vietnam, Cambodia & Laos Handbook (0293) $18.95

MEXICO

Baja Handbook (0528) $15.95
Cabo Handbook (0285) $14.95
Cancún Handbook (0501) $13.95
Central Mexico Handbook (0234) $15.95
Mexico Handbook (0315) $21.95
Northern Mexico Handbook (0226) $16.95
Pacific Mexico Handbook (0323) $16.95
Puerto Vallarta Handbook (0250) $14.95
Yucatán Peninsula Handbook (0242) $15.95

CENTRAL AMERICA AND THE CARIBBEAN

Belize Handbook (0307) $15.95
Caribbean Handbook (0277) $16.95
Costa Rica Handbook (0358) $19.95
Jamaica Handbook (0706) $15.95

INTERNATIONAL

Egypt Handbook (3891) $18.95
Moon Handbook (0668) $10.00
Moscow-St. Petersburg Handbook (3913) $13.95
Staying Healthy in Asia, Africa, and Latin America (0269) . . . $11.95
The Practical Nomad (0765) $14.95

PERIPLUS TRAVEL MAPS

All maps $7.95 each

Bali
Bandung/W. Java
Bangkok/C. Thailand
Batam/Bintan
Cambodia
Chiangmai/N. Thailand
Hong Kong
Indonesia
Jakarta
Java
Ko Samui/S. Thailand
Kuala Lumpur
Lombok
Penang
Phuket/S. Thailand
Sabah
Sarawak
SIngapore
Vietnam
Yogyakarta/C. Java

INTERNATIONAL TRAVEL MAPS

Price as indicated

Alaska.	$6.95
Australia	$7.95
Barbados.	$7.95
Belize	$7.95
British Columbia	$3.95
Central America	$8.95
Costa Rica	$7.95
Jamaica.	$6.95
Mexico	$7.95
Mexico: Baja California	$7.95
Mexico City.	$4.95
Mexico: South Coast	$7.95
San Juan Islands (WA).	$4.95
Vancouver Island	$3.95
Virgin Islands	$7.95
Yucatán Peninsula	$7.95
Yukon.	$4.95

WHERE TO BUY MOON TRAVEL HANDBOOKS

BOOKSTORES AND LIBRARIES: Moon Travel Handbooks are sold worldwide. Please contact our sales manager for a list of wholesalers and distributors in your area.

TRAVELERS: We would like to have Moon Travel Handbooks available throughout the world. Please ask your bookstore to write or call us for ordering information. If your bookstore will not order our guides for you, please contact us for a free catalog.

> **Moon Publications, Inc.**
> **P.O. Box 3040**
> **Chico, CA 95927-3040 U.S.A.**
> **tel.: (800) 345-5473**
> **fax: (916) 345-6751**
> **e-mail: travel@moon.com**

IMPORTANT ORDERING INFORMATION

PRICES: All prices are subject to change. We always ship the most current edition. We will let you know if there is a price increase on the book you order.

SHIPPING AND HANDLING OPTIONS: Domestic UPS or USPS first class (allow 10 working days for delivery): $3.50 for the first item, 50 cents for each additional item.

EXCEPTIONS: *Tibet Handbook, Mexico Handbook,* and *Indonesia Handbook* shipping $4.50; $1.00 for each additional *Tibet Handbook, Mexico Handbook,* or *Indonesia Handbook.*

Moonbelt shipping is $1.50 for one, 50 cents for each additional belt.

Add $2.00 for same-day handling.

UPS 2nd Day Air or Printed Airmail requires a special quote.

International Surface Bookrate 8-12 weeks delivery: $3.00 for the first item, $1.00 for each additional item. Note: Moon Publications cannot guarantee international surface bookrate shipping. Moon recommends sending international orders via air mail, which requires a special quote.

FOREIGN ORDERS: Orders that originate outside the U.S.A. must be paid for with an international money order, a check in U.S. currency drawn on a major U.S. bank based in the U.S.A., or Visa or MasterCard.

TELEPHONE ORDERS: We accept Visa or MasterCard payments. Minimum order is US$15. Call in your order: (800) 345-5473, 8 a.m.-5 p.m. Pacific standard time.

ORDER FORM

Prices are subject to change without notice. Be sure to call (800) 345-5473
8 a.m.–5 p.m. PST for current prices and editions, or for the
name of the bookstore nearest you that carries Moon Travel Handbooks.
(See important ordering information on preceding page.)

Name: _____ Date: _____

Street: _____

City: _____ Daytime Phone: _____

QUANTITY	TITLE	PRICE

Taxable Total_____

Sales Tax (7.25%) for California Residents_____

Shipping & Handling_____

TOTAL_____

Ship: ☐ UPS (no P.O. Boxes) ☐ 1st class ☐ International surface mail

Ship to: ☐ address above ☐ other _____

Make checks payable to: **MOON PUBLICATIONS, INC**., P.O. Box 3040, Chico, CA 95927-3040 U.S.A.
We accept Visa and MasterCard. **To Order**: Call in your Visa or MasterCard number, or send a written order with your Visa or MasterCard number and expiration date clearly written.

Card Number: ☐ **Visa** ☐ **MasterCard**

☐ ☐ ☐ ☐ ☐ ☐ ☐ ☐ ☐ ☐ ☐ ☐ ☐ ☐ ☐ ☐

Exact Name on Card: _____

Expiration date:_____

Signature: _____

THE METRIC SYSTEM

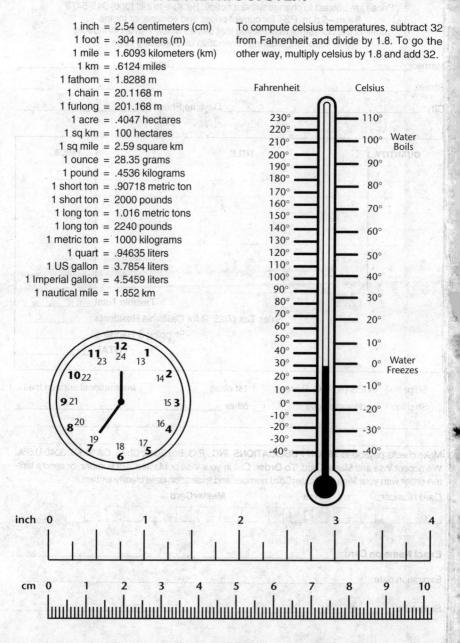

1 inch	=	2.54 centimeters (cm)
1 foot	=	.304 meters (m)
1 mile	=	1.6093 kilometers (km)
1 km	=	.6124 miles
1 fathom	=	1.8288 m
1 chain	=	20.1168 m
1 furlong	=	201.168 m
1 acre	=	.4047 hectares
1 sq km	=	100 hectares
1 sq mile	=	2.59 square km
1 ounce	=	28.35 grams
1 pound	=	.4536 kilograms
1 short ton	=	.90718 metric ton
1 short ton	=	2000 pounds
1 long ton	=	1.016 metric tons
1 long ton	=	2240 pounds
1 metric ton	=	1000 kilograms
1 quart	=	.94635 liters
1 US gallon	=	3.7854 liters
1 Imperial gallon	=	4.5459 liters
1 nautical mile	=	1.852 km

To compute celsius temperatures, subtract 32 from Fahrenheit and divide by 1.8. To go the other way, multiply celsius by 1.8 and add 32.

Fahrenheit   Celsius

230° — 110°
220°
210° — 100° Water Boils
200°
190° — 90°
180°
170° — 80°
160°
150° — 70°
140°
130° — 60°
120° — 50°
110°
100° — 40°
90°
80° — 30°
70°
60° — 20°
50°
40° — 10°
30°
20° — 0° Water Freezes
10°
0° — -10°
-10° — -20°
-20° — -30°
-30°
-40° — -40°

inch 0   1   2   3   4

cm 0 1 2 3 4 5 6 7 8 9 10